Sociology
The Core

ELEVENTH EDITION

Sociology
The Core

Michael Hughes
Virginia Tech

Carolyn J. Kroehler

McGraw Hill

Connect
Learn
Succeed™

SOCIOLOGY: THE CORE, ELEVENTH EDITION

Published by McGraw-Hill, a business unit of The McGraw-Hill Companies, Inc., 1221 Avenue of the Americas, New York, NY, 10020. Copyright © 2013 by The McGraw-Hill Companies, Inc. All rights reserved. Printed in the United States of America. Previous editions © 2011, 2009, and 2008.

Some ancillaries, including electronic and print components, may not be available to customers outside the United States.

This book is printed on acid-free paper.

2 3 4 5 6 7 8 9 0 DOC/DOC 1 0 9 8 7 6 5 4 3

ISBN   978-0-07-8026768
MHID   0-07-8026768

Senior Vice President, Products & Markets: Director, Content Production: *Terri Schiesl*
   Kurt L. Strand   Project Manager: *Erin Melloy*
Vice President & Editor-in-Chief: *Michael Ryan*   Buyer: *Laura Fuller*
Vice President, Content Production & Technology   Cover/Designer: *Studio Montage, St. Louis, MO*
   Services: *Kimberly Meriwether David*   Cover Image: *Courtesy Daniel Allen Schmitt*
Managing Director: *Gina Boedeker*   Media Project Manager: *Sridevi Palani*
Sponsoring Editor: *Patrick Brown*   Typeface: 10/12 TimesNewRomanLTStd
Executive Director of Development: *Lisa Pinto*   Compositor: *Laserwords Private Limited*
Development Editor: *Amy Mittelman*   Printer: *R.R.Donnelley*
Marketing Specialist: *Alex Schultz*

Library of Congress Cataloging-in-Publication Data

Hughes, Michael (Michael D.)
   Sociology: the core / Michael Hughes, Carolyn J. Kroehler.—11th ed.
      p. cm.
   ISBN 978-0-07-802676-8 (alk. paper)
      1. Sociology. I. Kroehler, Carolyn J. II. Title.
HM585.H84 2013
301—dc23

2012027793

www.mhhe.com

To Dave Hughes, who loved life and its many possibilities.

About the Authors

MICHAEL HUGHES is Professor of Sociology at Virginia Tech. He received his Ph.D. in sociology from Vanderbilt University in 1979 and has taught introductory sociology over the past 39 years. He also regularly teaches courses in minority group relations, deviant behavior, the sociology of mental illness, and data analysis. From 2000 to 2004, he served as editor of the *Journal of Health and Social Behavior*. He has held positions as research fellow at the University of Michigan's Institute for Social Research (1992–1994) and research associate at Vanderbilt University (1980–1982). With Walter R. Gove he is the author of the book *Overcrowding in the Household*. His research interests in mental health and mental illness, race and ethnicity, and crowding and living alone have resulted in over 70 professional articles published in a variety of journals, including the *American Sociological Review*, the *American Journal of Sociology, Social Forces,* and *The Archives of General Psychiatry*. In 2004–2005, he served as president of the Southern Sociological Society.

CAROLYN J. KROEHLER is a professional writer and editor who has received her sociological education "on the job." Before her work on *Sociology: The Core,* she contributed to criminology and criminal justice textbooks. She edited and helped with the writing of a guide to academic success for college students, *Straight A's: If I Can Do It, So Can You.* At the Virginia Water Resources Research Center, she wrote public education and technical materials about water quality and other environmental issues, including a book on drinking water standards. Her writing experience also includes several years in a college public relations office and writing and editing for the *Lancaster Independent Press*. She earned her Ph.D. in botany at Virginia Tech and has published in the *Canadian Journal of Botany, Plant and Soil,* and *Oecologia*.

Mike and Carrie live in Blacksburg, Virginia, with their children Edmund and Camilla.

Contents in Brief

Contents

CHAPTER TWELVE

Population and Environment   388

CHAPTER THIRTEEN

Social Change   424

List of Boxes

Preface

The education that students receive should allow them to live fuller, richer, and more fruitful lives. Such a goal is the bedrock upon which we build and justify our careers as educators and sociologists. Students today face the challenges presented by the transformation to an information and global economy, the growth of biotechnology and cloning, the ever-expanding human population, and the environmental problems associated with population growth. To understand and live in this rapidly changing social environment, they need a solid foundation in sociological concepts and perspectives.

Sociology encourages us to examine aspects of our social environment that we might otherwise ignore, neglect, or take for granted, and it allows us to look beneath the surface of everyday life. The introductory course in sociology gives students the opportunity to use this sociological imagination in understanding and mastering their social world, and *Sociology: The Core* provides the information they need to do so.

Providing the Core

A course in sociology should broaden students' horizons, sharpen their observational skills, and strengthen their analytical capabilities. *Sociology: The Core* aims to make the introductory course manageable for instructors and students alike. The eleventh edition retains the core concept with a tight, readable text that provides the essentials. It includes all the major sections of the tenth edition, with streamlined feature boxes, figures that present data critical to an introductory text, and a stick-to-the-basics approach. It provides the core of sociology—the basic foundations of the discipline.

The coverage of many key topics in *Sociology: The Core*—theory, culture, socialization, groups, formal organizations, deviance, social stratification, race, gender, power, the family, religion, and social change—is equal to, and in many cases exceeds, that found in most other introductory textbooks. The **functionalist, conflict,** and **interactionist perspectives** are introduced in the first chapter and applied throughout the book. This helps students to develop a solid understanding of these major sociological perspectives and their contributions to the topics covered here, and it provides something for everyone in departments where all faculty members are required to use the same introductory textbook.

It would be presumptuous for any sociologist to program another sociologist's course. Instead, we hope that *Sociology: The Core* provides a solid resource—a common intellectual platform—that each instructor can use as a sound foundation in developing an introductory course. As a coherent presentation of sociological materials, a core text is an aid to pedagogy. Instructors can supplement the text with papers, readers, or monographs that meet their unique teaching needs. Likewise, students can use *Sociology: The Core as* a succinct source of information.

Bringing Students In

In *Sociology: The Core,* we seek to make sociology come alive as a vital and exciting field, to relate principles to real-world circumstances, and to attune students to the dynamic processes of our rapidly changing contemporary society. The study of a science can captivate student interest and excite student imagination. Our **chapter-end feature** "What Can Sociology Do for You?" stimulates students to begin thinking about what being a sociology major would entail and about what sorts of careers sociology majors select. We capitalize on students' desires to read about issues of interest to them with **feature boxes on Twitter and Google, Facebook, reality TV, blogs, becoming an adult, binge drinking, high school identities, campus rape, and affirmative action in college admissions.** Because students live and will work in an increasingly diverse and global world, we **emphasize global issues** with boxes on exporting toxic trash, family values around the world, and cultural variation in marking time as well as integrating **cross-cultural comparisons** in various chapters. Our box series "Social Inequalities" enhances our **emphasis on issues of race, ethnicity, class, and gender** as a regular part of most topics in sociology.

Pedagogical Aids

In selecting pedagogical aids for the text, we decided to use those that provide the most guidance with the least clutter and to focus on those that students are most likely to use.

Chapter Outline

Each chapter opens with an outline of its major headings; this allows students to preview at a glance the material to be covered.

Cross References

Referrals to material in other chapters are accompanied by specific page references, making it easy for students and instructors to find such material.

Questions for Discussion

Each feature box includes two or three questions geared toward linking the box material to core concepts and toward getting students thinking about the issues raised.

Key Terms

The terms most essential to the core of sociology are set in boldface type and are defined as they are presented in the text. These key terms appear in the chapter summaries, again in boldface type to emphasize their importance and to reinforce the student's memory. At the end of each chapter, a **Glossary** lists the key terms included in the chapter and provides their definitions. All key terms appear in the index, along with an indication of where they are first defined.

Careers Feature

Each chapter includes a feature titled **"What Can Sociology Do for You?"** focused on helping students think about whether they want to major in sociology and, if so, about what sorts of work they might find themselves engaged in when they finish college. In addition, this feature points them toward other courses in which to enroll if they were interested in the subject matter of the chapter.

Chapter Summary

Chapters conclude with a **Chapter in Brief** summary that uses the same outline of major headings used in the chapter outline. The summary recapitulates the central points, allowing students to review in a systematic manner what they already have read. The use of major headings allows students to return to the appropriate section in the chapter for more information. The Chapter in Brief includes all of the glossary terms, boldfaced to remind students that they are key terms.

Review Questions

Each chapter concludes with a list of review questions on the central ideas presented in the chapter.

Internet Exercises

The end-of-chapter feature **Internet Connection** provides students with an opportunity to explore sociological data and information on the Internet and hone their critical thinking abilities.

Boxes

The eleventh edition includes four types of boxes, all of which add to the concepts and theories discussed in the chapter in which they appear, and many of which add insights to other chapters as well.

Social Inequalities boxes explore inequalities of race, ethnicity, class, or gender from a sociological perspective. Topics include race, crime, and punishment; geographical variation in gender inequality; same-sex marriage; affirmative action; disenfranchisement; and unequal childhoods.

Doing Social Research boxes focus on how social scientists approach various research problems; topics discussed have been chosen to illustrate or enhance the topics discussed in the chapter.

Sociology around the World boxes focus on sociological research that extends beyond the United States, on research done with subjects from outside the United States, on cross-cultural sociological research, and on illustrations of sociological concepts in a variety of cultural settings.

Students Doing Sociology boxes summarize the experiences of students who were asked to think like sociologists: to interpret certain events with sociological concepts and principles or to perform sociological research.

Figures and Tables

The data presented in the figures and tables throughout *Sociology: The Core* are as up to date as possible—we update every figure for which new data is available. In many cases, we have generated original analyses from publicly available data sets, and we've done our best to make them user-friendly and accessible. Sources for figures and tables include the U.S. Census Bureau, the National Center for Health Statistics, the General Social Survey, the *Statistical Abstract of the United States,* the Population Reference Bureau, U.S. Department of Labor, the Uniform Crime Reports and National Crime Victimization Survey, and the Federal Reserve Survey of Consumer Finances.

Photographs and Cartoons

Photographs and cartoons serve both to draw the reader in and to illustrate important concepts and principles. Photo captions tie the photographs to the text, and cartoons, in addition to adding a light touch to the text and reinforcing important ideas, make points that can't be made any other way. We include new cartoons and new photos in the eleventh edition.

References

The eleventh edition of *Sociology: The Core* presents new data and references throughout, including updates in family, immigration, religion, education, race and ethnicity, population, gender inequality, the recession and poverty, crimes, global warming, and wealth and income. It includes nearly 200 new references, including articles from the major sociological journals and other scholarly journals, books, government documents and data sets, and findings from research groups, nearly all published in 2010–2012. Full citations appear at the end of the text.

Changes in the Eleventh Edition

Researchers in a variety of disciplines, such as economics, anthropology, medicine, political science, biology, and archaeology, are increasingly doing research on sociological questions, and this is reflected in our reference list. Such research, which does not often appear in sociological journals, adds breadth and depth to our examination of sociology.

As in previous editions, everything that can be updated has been updated. We have incorporated nearly 200 new references. The chapters on crime, stratification, race and ethnicity, gender, family, population and environment, and religion, education, and medicine are full of revised figures and new data, including from the 2010 Census and the March 2011 Current Population Survey. We have also incorporated contemporary examples and new research throughout the book.

While the eleventh edition retains all the core elements of the tenth edition, there are a number of significant additions and enhancements. The eleventh edition:

- Includes in the introductory chapter a new feature box on using Twitter, Google, Wikipedia, cell phones, and crowd sourcing to conduct **social research.**

- Completely updates the feature box on same-sex marriage with a focus on religion, and includes a new feature box on the effects of Facebook and other social networking sites on social isolation and engagement, in the **social change** chapter.

- Discusses the challenges faced by developing nations as they become increasingly urbanized, and some of the strategies used by cities going "green," discusses the generational shift in attitudes about the environment, and presents all new data in the **population and environment** chapter.

- Uses the Bureau of Labor Statistics' American Time Use Survey to update data on the gender division of labor, provides information from a 2011 report on sexual harassment at schools, discusses the FBI's new definition of rape, and presents new research on the stalling of gender role attitudes in the **gender inequality** chapter.

- Revises the discussion of juvenile delinquency, presents data on science fair cheating, adds information about DNA fingerprinting, expands the discussion of the decline in crime, and includes new research on wrongful convictions in the **deviance and crime** chapter.

- Presents all new data in the feature box on family values around the world, updates the section on homosexuality with new data and information on same-sex marriage in the United States, and reorganizes the presentation on lifestyles to reflect the increasing diversity of **family** types.

- Takes a look at the success of Finnish schools, expands the discussion of achievement gaps, and provides new international test score data in the **education** discussion.

- Incorporates data, information, and research related to the Great Recession of 2007–2009, discusses new research on the American dream, and presents Mark Rank's assessment of poverty in America in the **social stratification** chapter.

- Completely updates the data in the **race and ethnicity** chapter, expands the discussion of immigration and non-English language speakers in the United States, and presents information about "minority-majority" areas of the United States.

- Incorporates new information from the Population Reference Bureau in the section on aging in **socialization** across the life course and adds research about foraging societies.

- Adds Suzanne Mettler's "submerged state" research to the **political and economic power** chapter.

Sociology: The Core was originally conceived and written by James W. Vander Zanden, and some of his work is retained in this eleventh edition. However, he did not participate in this revision and is not responsible for any new material, changes, or additions in the eleventh edition. Michael Hughes and Carolyn J. Kroehler are responsible for all of the revisions and changes in the fifth through the eleventh editions.

Ancillary Materials

The eleventh edition of *Sociology: The Core* is accompanied by a number of supplementary learning and teaching aids.

For the Student

Student's Online Learning Center (OLC)

The Online Learning Center website that accompanies this text offers a variety of resources for the student. In addition to various study tools, students will find interactive chapter quizzes, annotated lists of web links, Internet exercises, and flashcards of key terms. Please visit the *Sociology: The Core* OLC at **www.mhhe.com/hughes11e**.

For the Instructor

Instructor's Manual

The Instructor's Manual provides chapter summaries, chapter outlines, learning objectives, teaching suggestions and discussion questions, student exercises and projects, and suggested films/videos. The Instructor's Manual can also be downloaded from the Instructor's Online Learning Center.

Test Bank

The production of the Test Bank has been taken over by the authors. It offers at least 75 multiple-choice, 25 true-false, and 10 essay questions for each chapter in the text. The Test Bank can be downloaded as a Word file from the Instructor's Online Learning Center. **It is also available as a computerized test bank.**

PowerPoint Slides. A collection of tables and figures from the text, augmented by additional graphics, allows instructors to add visual content to their lectures. The PowerPoint files can be downloaded from the Instructor's Online Learning Center.

Instructor's Online Learning Center (OLC)

Password-protected, the Instructor's side of the OLC contains a variety of resources, activities, and classroom tips. The Instructor's Manual, PowerPoint slides, and Test Bank can be accessed electronically on this site, **www.mhhe .com/ hughes11e**.

Acknowledgments

We would like to thank James W. Vander Zanden, who originally conceived of *Sociology: The Core* and who authored the first four editions. We still follow his organization of basic concepts, and many of his other contributions remain. We also would like to thank the McGraw-Hill team that worked to make *Sociology: The Core* a reality, especially our editors Gina Boedeker and Craig Leonard. Many people worked to transform a pile of paper into an attractive and user-friendly textbook: McGraw-Hill project manager Erin Melloy, buyer Laura Fuller, copy editor Wendy Nelson, photo research coordinator Jennifer Blankenship, and project manager Venkat Jayaraman from Laserwords. We would also like to express our appreciation to our marketing specialist, Alex Schultz, for her efforts to promote this book. We would like to thank the many students who have provided feedback on the textbook over the years. Particularly helpful in past revisions was Tarek Turaigi, who provided comments that enlightened us and considerably improved the text. We also thank Virginia Tech student Michael J. Kokes for his contributions to the list of skateboarding terms.

Many thanks also go to Mike's colleagues at Virginia Tech who, through many and varied discussions and suggestions, have directly or indirectly made substantial contributions to this work: Onwubiko Agozino, Carol Bailey, David Brunsma, Toni Calasanti, Sam Cook, Skip Fuhrman, Ted Fuller, Laura Gilman, Ellington Graves, Kwame Harrison, Jim Hawdon, Terry Kershaw, Jill Kiecolt, Minjeong Kim, Neal King, Sarah Ovink, Anthony Peguero, Paulo Polanah, Katrina Powell, Karl Precoda, Wornie Reed, John Ryan, Donna Sedgwick, Paula Seniors, Don Shoemaker, Barbara Ellen Smith, Stacy Vogt-Yuan, Dale Wimberly, and Haiyan Zhu. We would like to particularly thank Keith Durkin, of Ohio Northern University, for comments that have been helpful to us in making revisions over the years. Thanks also go to Inge Terrill, who helped us to check all the references.

We are also very grateful to the following reviewers for their many helpful comments and suggestions: Cynthia Calhoun, Southwest Tennessee Community College; Jeffrey Toussaint, Old Dominion University; Keith F. Durkin, Ohio Northern University; A. J. Jacobs, East Carolina University; Christine Janis, Northern Illinois University; Kara Kleimann, Blinn College; Kathy Miller, Concordia University; David Briscoe, University of Arkansas at Little Rock; Francis Adeola, University of New Orleans; Barbara Johnson, University of South Carolina Aiken; Tara Hefferan, Central Michigan University; Hua-Lun Huang, University of Louisiana, Lafayette; Jolene Sundlie, Saint Paul College; Eric Strayer, Hartnell College.

We would like to extend a special thank you to Daniel Allen Schmitt for allowing us to use his photograph on the book's front cover.

We'd like to thank our children, Edmund and Camilla, for their patience, love, and sociological insights. Finally, we'd like to thank our "families of orientation" for their continued love and support.

Michael Hughes
Carolyn J. Kroehler

CHAPTER 1

Developing a Sociological Consciousness

The Sociological Perspective

The Development of Sociology

Theoretical Perspectives

Conducting Research

Each of us is a social being. We are born into a social environment; we fully develop into human beings in a social environment; and we typically live out our lives in a social environment. What we think, how we feel, and what we say and do all are shaped by our interactions with other people. The scientific study of these social interactions and of social organization is called **sociology.**

Why are some people wealthy and others poor? What causes war? Why do people violate social rules? How do revolutions occur? What causes mass hysteria? We know from ancient folklore, myths, and archaeological remains that humans have long had an interest in understanding themselves and their social arrangements. Yet it has been only in the past two centuries or so that human beings have sought answers to these and related questions through science. This science—sociology—pursues the study of social interaction and group behavior through research governed by the rigorous and disciplined collection of data and analysis of facts.

Many of us are not only interested in understanding society and human behavior. We also would like to improve the human condition so that we might lead fuller, richer, and more fruitful lives. To do this we need knowledge about the basic structures and processes underlying our social lives. Through its emphasis on observation and measurement, sociology allows us to bring rigorous and systematic scientific thinking and information to bear on difficult questions associated with social policies and choices, including those related to poverty, health, immigration, crime, and education.

Sociological research often is applied to practical matters. Businesses use social science research methods in risk analysis, market surveys, employee testing, and cost–benefit assessments, and lobbyists cite sociological studies when they are campaigning for change in Congress (Prewitt, 2011). The U.S. Supreme Court relied on social

Natural disasters directly cause great damage, but social factors such as government policy and the effectiveness of response agencies affect the severity of their impact.

killed more than 200,000 people and left more than a million homeless, injured, hungry, sick, and orphaned, and Japan's 2011 earthquake and tsunami killed more than 16,000 people, eradicated entire towns and villages, and left hundreds of thousands of people homeless (Folger, 2012). The impact of such events is related to where and how people live (Bohannon, 2005), and social organization and social policy are critical factors that can increase or decrease the effect of natural disasters (Stone and Kerr, 2005).

Sociologists may do basic research, seeking to better understand social interaction and group behavior, or they may design studies deliberately to evaluate public policies or to inform us about social conditions, including assessments of criminal justice programs, the social consequences of unemployment, and the effects of family structure on children and their future. The collection of census and other national statistical data, which is the foundation of many federal and state policies on health, education, housing, and welfare, is based on sample survey and statistical techniques developed by sociologists and other social scientists. Sociology, then, is a powerful scientific tool both for acquiring knowledge about ourselves and for intervening in social affairs to realize various goals.

science findings in reaching its historic 1954 decision declaring mandatory school segregation unconstitutional (Jackson, 1990).

Social and behavioral sciences also are central to the world's health and science agenda. Tuberculosis can be cured, but the disease has to be attacked through programs that take into account social factors relevant to its transmission and treatment (Cohen, 2011). Similarly, the usefulness to individuals of medical progress in HIV and AIDS prevention and treatment is dependent on behavioral and population-level structural components, national policies, economic power, and other primarily social factors (Shattock et al., 2011; Mazus, 2011).

And arguably the largest problems facing humankind—climate change and other issues of environmental degradation—are inextricably tied up in social factors (Gardiner, 2011): global and national decision-making, income inequality of individuals and nations, economic and political power struggles, population growth and dynamics, human value systems, and much more.

Sociology can play a role even in natural disasters. The earthquake that struck Haiti in 2010

The Sociological Perspective

The sociological perspective invites us to look beyond what we take for granted about our social lives and examine them in fresh and creative ways. There are many layers of meaning in the human experience. Networks of invisible rules and institutional arrangements guide our behavior. We continually evolve, negotiate, and rework tacit bargains with family members, friends, lovers, and work associates. As we look beyond outer appearances at what lies beneath, we encounter new levels of social reality. This approach to reality is the core of the sociological perspective.

In this section we will see how sociology uncovers new levels of reality, discuss the sociological imagination, and define microsociology and macrosociology.

New Levels of Reality

Tally's Corner, a classic study by social scientist Elliot Liebow (1967/2003), shows us how sociology can reveal new levels of social reality. In the early 1960s, our nation's concern about poverty led Liebow to involve himself in a unique study of low-income urban black men. Of course, most African Americans are not poor; today, for example, more than 70 percent live above the poverty line (DeNavas-Walt, Proctor, and Smith, 2011). Nonetheless, most of the problems of poverty that Liebow observed more than 40 years ago are still with us today, and his findings continue to provide insight into this major U.S. social problem (see Box 1.1). Perhaps more importantly for us, his study provides an excellent example of how sociological research allows us to go beyond outward appearances and simplistic explanations.

Liebow conducted his study by hanging out on a corner in front of the New Deal Carry-out Shop in Washington, D.C., where he won the trust of 20 or so African American men. The men Liebow got to know came to the corner shop, not far from the White House in a blighted section of the city, to eat, to enjoy easy talk, and in general to pass the time. The following excerpt relates what Liebow observed one weekday morning (Liebow, 1967/ 2003:19):

A pickup truck drives slowly down the street. The truck stops as it comes abreast of a man sitting on a cast-iron porch and the white driver calls out, asking if the man wants a day's work. The man shakes his head and the truck moves on up the block, stopping again whenever idling men come within calling distance of the driver. At the Carry-out corner, five men debate the question briefly and shake their heads no to the truck. The truck turns the corner and repeats the same performance up the next street.

The white truck driver viewed the African American streetcorner men as lazy and irresponsible, unwilling "to take a job even if it were handed to them on a platter." Like many middle-class Americans then and today, he believed that inner-city African American men lived only for the moment, with little thought for long-term consequences. The truck driver assumed that all the streetcorner men were able-bodied men with no means of support—and no desire to take the work he offered them. Like many Americans, he assumed that the job problems of inner-city men resulted from the men themselves—from their lack of willingness to work.

Liebow's relationship with the men at the New Deal allowed him to look beyond the stereotyped images of African American men to find another level of reality. Liebow found that most of the men who turned down the truck driver's offer had jobs but, for various reasons, were not at work that particular morning. A few did not have jobs, but with reason; the man on the porch, for example, had severe arthritis. Liebow also discovered that streetcorner men and middle-class men differed not so much in their values and their attitudes toward the future as in the different futures they saw for themselves. Middle-class men have incomes high enough to justify long-term investments, and they hold jobs that offer the promise of career advancement. Like middle-class men, the men on the corner wanted stable jobs and marriages. However, in their world, jobs were only intermittently available, almost always menial, often hard, and invariably low paying. The day jobs offered by such as the driver of the pickup truck usually involved

Tally's Corner in the 21st Century

Are Elliot Liebow's conclusions still valid? The republication in 2003 of his 1967 book *Tally's Corner,* which had sold more than a million copies, is an indication of its value to social scientists, teachers, students, and others. In introducing the new edition, sociologist William Julius Wilson comments, "[Liebow's] arguments concerning the work experience and family life of black streetcorner men in a Washington, D.C., ghetto still ring true today" (Wilson, 2003:xxxiii). Indeed, Wilson says, job market prospects for low-skill black men are worse now than they were when Liebow conducted his research. He explains that structural factors continue to prevent inner-city black men from finding work that allows them to support themselves and their families: "The computer revolution . . . is displacing low-skilled workers and rewarding the more highly trained; and the growing internationalization of economic activity . . . has increasingly pitted low-skilled workers in the United States against low-skilled workers around the world" (Wilson, 2003:xxxiv).

As when Liebow wrote his book, there are those who argue

today that young African American males are without jobs simply because they refuse to accept low-paying jobs. But sociologist Stephen M. Petterson found "no race differences in the wages sought by young jobless men" (1997:605). In fact, black men's reports of the lowest wage they would accept and wages at last employment were *lower* than those of white men. As Liebow found in the 1960s, joblessness is not necessarily related to a lack of willingness to work for low wages, and social programs designed in ignorance of that fact are doomed to failure.

Both Liebow and Wilson acknowledge that urban black men may give up looking for work—*after* experiencing the fruitlessness of searching for decent work at a decent rate of pay. "Liebow was perhaps the first scholar to place appropriate emphasis on the fact that ongoing lack of success in the labor market lowers one's self-confidence and gives rise to feelings of resignation that frequently result in a temporary, or even permanent, abandonment of the job

search," comments Wilson. The fundamental problem of male joblessness contributes to many problems of the inner city: high rates of welfare dependency, teenage pregnancy, drug abuse, and crime. Can anything be done to attack the problem at its roots? Wilson suggests that programs must "address attitudes, norms, and behaviors in combination with local and national attempts to improve job prospects. Only then will fathers have a realistic chance to adequately care for their children and envision a better life for themselves" (Wilson, 2003: xxxix).

Questions for Discussion

1. Think about the life problems faced by your family, friends, or self. Are any of them attributable to structural factors as opposed to individual characteristics?

2. More than 50 years is a long time for poverty to persist. Can you think of other social problems that have been around for a considerable length of time?

back-breaking labor and offered no chance of advancement. Even the jobs held by the men that day offered them little hope for the future.

Social policy based on the truck driver's interpretations would be directed toward changing the motivations of streetcorner men and encouraging them to develop those values and goals that lead to occupational achievement. But such social programs would have no chance of succeeding; the men were already willing to

work and did not need to have their values and goals redirected. What they needed were jobs that provided wages they could live on.

In seeking an explanation for their behavior, Liebow looked beyond the individual men and the outward appearances of streetcorner life. He turned his investigative eye to the social arrangements that are external to individuals but that nonetheless structure their experiences and place constraints on their behavior.

The Sociological Imagination

A basic premise underlying sociology is the notion that only by understanding the society in which we live can we gain a fuller insight into our lives. Sociologist C. Wright Mills (1959) termed this quality of the discipline the **sociological imagination:** the ability to see our private experiences, personal difficulties, and achievements as, in part, a reflection of the structural arrangements of society and the times in which we live. We tend to go about our daily activities thinking only about school, job, family, and neighborhood. The sociological imagination allows us to see the relationship between our personal experiences and broader social and historical events.

Mills, an influential but controversial sociologist, pointed out that our personal troubles and public issues "overlap and interpenetrate to form the larger structure of social and historical life." Job difficulties experienced by many American workers during the recession of 2007–2009 provide an example. During this recession, the unemployment rate went from under 5 percent for most of 2007 to more than 10 percent in October 2009 (Bureau of Labor Statistics, 2010), resulting in an increase of 7.6 million unemployed workers over 2 years. Clearly, the work values and attitudes of 7.6 million Americans did not change so drastically that by the end of 2009 they were unwilling to work. Mills's (1959) point is that in situations of this kind we cannot simply look to the personal character of individuals to explain changes in their employment circumstances. Rather, we need to focus on economic and political institutions for a definition of the problem, for an understanding of its causes, and for a range of possible solutions. The sociological imagination allows us to place the private job frustrations of many Americans into the context of the structural factors operating in the larger society and the workplace.

We see the usefulness of the sociological imagination in other spheres of life as well.

Mills (1959:9) was especially concerned with issues of war and peace:

The personal problems of war, when it occurs, may be how to survive it or how to die in it with honor; how to make money out of it; how to climb into the higher safety of the military apparatus; or how to contribute to the war's termination. . . . But the structural issues of war have to do with its causes; with what types of men it throws up into command; with its effects upon economic and political, family and religious institutions, with the unorganized irresponsibility of a world of nation-states.

In sum, the sociological imagination allows us to identify the links between our personal lives and the larger social forces of life—to see that what is happening to us immediately is a minute point at which our personal lives and society intersect.

Microsociology and Macrosociology

Sociologists seek to extend Mills's insight by distinguishing between the micro, or small-scale, aspects of the social enterprise and the macro, or large-scale, structural components. When we focus on the micro elements, we examine behavior and observe what happens as people interact on a face-to-face basis. Sociologists term this level microsociology—micro meaning "small" as in the word "microscope." **Microsociology** entails the detailed study of what people say, do, and think moment by moment as they go about their daily lives. Liebow's study of the African American men on the Washington street corner provides an illustration of microsociology. Liebow wanted to find out how the men saw themselves, how they dealt with one another in face-to-face encounters, and how they balanced their hopes and aspirations with their real-world experiences. Microsociology, then, deals with everyday life: a woman and a man initiating a conversation on a bus, several youngsters playing basketball on an inner-city playground, guests at a baby shower, a police officer directing traffic at a busy intersection, or students and their teacher interacting after class.

Sociologists also turn an investigative eye upon "the big picture" and study social groups and societies. This approach is termed macrosociology—macro meaning "large." **Macrosociology** focuses upon large-scale and long-term social processes of organizations, institutions, and broad social patterns, including the state, social class, the family, the economy, culture, and society. At this level sociologists may direct their attention to the changes in the structure of a religious sect, the impact of population dynamics and computer technologies on the workforce, shifts in the racial and ethnic composition of a city, or the dynamics of intergroup competition and conflict. When we examine the lives of Liebow's streetcorner men from a macrosociological perspective, we gain a picture of the institutional constraints that minority and economically disadvantaged men face and that limit their job opportunities.

Microsociological and macrosociological levels are not independent of one another (Ritzer, 2011; House, 1995). The circumstances of the streetcorner men Liebow studied testify to this fact. We can most appropriately think of the distinction between "micro" and "macro" as one of degree (Lawler, Ridgeway, and Markovsky, 1993). Macrostructures, such as organizations or the hierarchy of social classes, are composed of routine patterns of interaction at the micro level. Macrostructures provide the social contexts in which people encounter one another at the micro level. Microstructures, such as friendship relations and work groups, form out of these encounters and provide a link from individuals to macrostructures. Microstructures also may cause change and evolution in macrostructures. For example, the macrostructure of education and an organization embedded in it, a high school, may have provided the social context from which a group of friends—a microstructure—emerged. Such a group of students, through letter-writing campaigns, sit-ins,

formation of clubs, and other means, can cause a high school and education in general—macrostructures—to adapt and change. In sum, complex webs of relationship between the micro and macro levels contribute to an ever-changing and diverse social order (Móuzelis, 1992).

The Development of Sociology

Sociology, too, is a product of micro and macro forces. The political revolutions ushered in by the French Revolution in Europe in 1789 and continuing through the 19th century provided a major impetus to sociological work (Ritzer, 2011). At the same time, the Industrial Revolution that swept many Western nations resulted in large numbers of people leaving a predominantly agricultural setting for work in urban factories. New social and economic arrangements arose to meet the many demands of emergent capitalism. These major changes in the way society was organized led some of the thinkers of the day to turn their attention to the study of social organization and social interactions, resulting in the founding of the science we now call sociology (Ritzer, 2011).

In this section we will consider six particularly influential sociologists and their contributions to sociology; the emergence of sociology in the United States; and contemporary sociology.

Auguste Comte: The Founder of Sociology

Auguste Comte (1798–1857) is commonly credited with being the founder of sociology and as having coined the term "sociology" for the new science. He was also an advocate of a philosophical system, positivism, which argues that abstract laws govern the relationships among phenomena in the world, including its social elements, and that these laws can be tested using empirical data (Ritzer, 2011). As a part of this, he emphasized that the study of society must be scientific, and he urged sociologists to use systematic observation, experimentation, and comparative historical analysis as their methods.

Comte divided the study of society into social statics and social dynamics, a conceptual distinction that is still with us. **Social statics** involves those aspects of social life that have to do with order, stability, and social organization that allow societies and groups to hold together and endure. **Social dynamics** refers to those processes of social life that pattern institutional development and have to do with social change. Although his specific ideas no longer direct contemporary sociology, Comte created the intellectual foundation for a science of social life and exerted enormous influence on the thinking of other sociologists, particularly Herbert Spencer, Harriet Martineau, and Émile Durkheim.

Harriet Martineau: Feminist and Methodologist

While Comte was laying the theoretical foundations for sociology in France, the English sociologist Harriet Martineau (1802–1876) was paving the way for the new discipline through her observations of social behavior in the United States and England. Like Comte, she insisted that the study of society represents a separate scientific field. Among her contributions was the first book on the methodology of social research, *How to Observe Manners and Morals,* published in 1838. She also undertook the comparative study of the stratification systems of Europe and the United States. Martineau showed how the basic moral values of the young American nation shaped its key institutional arrangements. Throughout her career Martineau was an ardent defender of women's rights. She showed the similarities between the position of women in Western societies and that of American slaves, and she called for freedom and justice for all in an age in which they were granted only to white males (Deegan, 1991).

Though Harriet Martineau was a popular and influential intellectual and author during her lifetime, her contributions to sociology were marginalized by the men who dominated the discipline during its early years and kept women like Martineau out of powerful academic positions (Ritzer, 2011). Consequently, Martineau's significance in the early development of sociology has only recently been fully recognized (Deegan, 2003; Hoecker-Drysdale, 1994; Lengermann and Niebrugge-Brantley, 2011).

Herbert Spencer: Social Darwinism

Herbert Spencer (1820–1903), an English sociologist, shared Comte's concern with social statics and social dynamics. He compared society to a biological organism and depicted it as a system, a whole made up of interrelated parts. Just as the human body is made up of organs, so society is made up of institutions (e.g., the family, religion, education, the state, and the economy). In his description of society as an organism, Spencer focused on its structures and the functional contributions these structures make to its survival. This image of society is in line with what sociologists now call structural-functional theory.

Spencer viewed static social institutions as the organs of society, but he had an even greater interest in social dynamics. He proposed an evolutionary theory of historical development, one that depicted the world as growing progressively better. Intrigued by the Darwinian view of natural selection, Spencer applied the concept of survival of the fittest to the social world, an approach termed **social Darwinism.** He sought to demonstrate that government should not interfere with the natural processes going on in a society. In this manner, he argued, people and social patterns that were "fit" would survive and those that were "unfit" would die out. If this principle were allowed to operate freely, human beings and their institutions would progressively adapt themselves to their

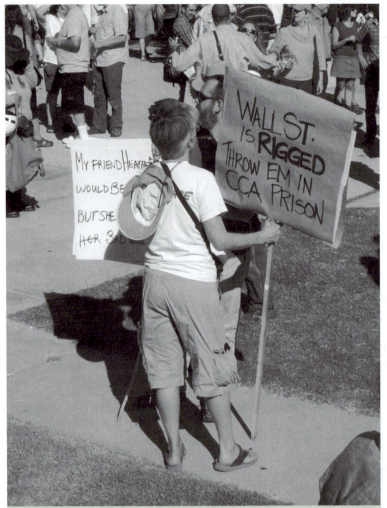

The conflict perspective argues that the structure of our society is powerfully affected by conflicts such as that exemplified by the Occupy Movement of 2011.

fittest. . . . This is not an evil tendency in business. It is merely the working out of a law of nature" (quoted in Lewontin, Rose, and Kamin, 1984:26).

Karl Marx: The Role of Class Conflict

Although Karl Marx (1818–1883) considered himself a political activist and not a sociologist, in truth he was both—and a philosopher, historian, economist, and political scientist as well. He viewed science not only as a vehicle for understanding society but also as a tool for transforming it. Marx was especially eager to change the structure of capitalist institutions and to establish new institutions in the service of humanity. Although he was born in Germany, authorities there viewed him as politically dangerous, and he was compelled to spend much of his adult life as a political exile in London.

Marx tried to discover the basic principles of history. He focused his search on the economic environments in which societies develop, particularly the current state of their technology and their method of organizing production, such as hunting and gathering, agriculture, or industry. At each stage of history, these factors determine the group that will dominate society and the groups that will be subjugated. He believed that society is divided into those who own the means of producing wealth and those who do not, which gives rise to **class conflict.** All history, he said, is

environment and reach higher and higher levels of historical development (Ritzer, 2011).

Spencer's social Darwinist ideas were used extensively within England and the United States to justify unrestrained capitalism. John D. Rockefeller, the American oil tycoon, would echo Spencer and observe: "The growth of a large business is merely a survival of the composed of struggles between classes. In ancient Rome the conflict was between patricians and plebeians and between masters and slaves. In the Middle Ages it was a struggle between guildmasters and journeymen and between lords and serfs. In contemporary Western societies, class antagonisms revolve around the struggle between the oppressing capitalist class or bourgeoisie and the oppressed working class or proletariat. The former derive their income through their ownership of the means of production, primarily factories, which allows them to exploit the labor of workers. The latter own nothing except their labor power and, because they are dependent for a living on the jobs provided by capitalists, must sell that labor power in order to exist.

Marx's perspective is called **dialectical materialism,** the notion that development depends on the clash of opposing social forces and the subsequent creation of new, more advanced structures. The approach depicts the world as made up not of static structures but of dynamic processes, a world of becoming rather than of being. In the Marxian view of history, every economic order grows to a state of maximum efficiency; at the same time, it develops internal contradictions or weaknesses that contribute to its decay. The roots of a new order begin to take hold in the old order. In time the new order displaces the old order while absorbing its most useful features. Marx depicted slavery as being displaced by feudalism, feudalism by capitalism, capitalism by socialism, and ultimately socialism by communism—for Marx, the highest stage of society.

In Marx's theory, political ideologies, religion, family organization, education, and government make up what he called the *superstructure* of society. This superstructure is strongly influenced by the economic base of society—its mode of producing goods and its class structure. When one class controls the critical means whereby people derive their livelihood, its members gain the leverage necessary to fashion other aspects of institutional life—the superstructure—in ways

that favor their class interests. However, the economic structure does not only shape the superstructure; aspects of the superstructure act upon the economic base and modify it in a reciprocal relationship. Marx thought that if a revolutionary ideology emerged to mobilize the working class in pursuit of its class interest, the existing social order would be overturned and replaced by one that would pursue more humane goals. In Marx's view, economic factors—whether one owns and controls the means of production—are primary. For this reason, he is viewed by many as an **economic determinist.**

Though Marx is often identified with the communist revolutions and socialist governments that appeared in many nations in the 20th century, Marx actually had little to say about communism or socialism. Marx was a utopian who centered his attention on capitalism and its internal dynamics, assuming that when socialism replaced capitalism many of the world's problems would disappear.

Marx is now recognized by most sociologists as a major figure in sociological theory (Ritzer, 2011; Pampel, 2006). Today he is better known and understood, and more widely studied, than at any time since he began his career in the 1840s. Much of what is valuable in his work has now been incorporated into mainstream sociology, particularly as it finds expression in the conflict perspective. For most sociologists, Marx's work is too outdated to follow in its particulars, but it remains theoretically important and animates much contemporary research and theory (e.g., Wright, 2000).

Émile Durkheim: Social Integration and Social Facts

While Marx saw society as a stage upon which classes with conflicting interests contested with one another, the French sociologist Émile Durkheim (1858–1916) focused his sociological eye on the question of how societies hold together and endure. The principal objections Durkheim had to Marx's work were that Marx attributed too much importance to economic factors and class struggle and not enough to social solidarity (Turner, 1990) and that Marx did not recognize the capacity of modern society to reform itself (Pampel, 2006).

Central to Durkheim's (1897/1951) sociology is the concept of *social integration.* Social integration refers to the density of social relationships, literally the number of relationships that exist among a collection of people. The more people are connected to one another, the stronger and more meaningful are the sentiments that emerge out of these relationships (Pope, 1976). Durkheim argued that social integration is necessary for the maintenance of the social order and for the happiness of individuals. In particular, he suggested that happiness depends on individuals' finding a sense of meaning outside themselves that occurs within the context of group involvement. Durkheim sought to demonstrate that the destruction of social bonds (e.g., divorce) has negative consequences and under some circumstances can increase the chance that people will commit suicide. Other sociologists picked up on this central idea and showed how the breakdown of group bonds can contribute to deviant behavior (Merton, 1968) and to participation in social movements (Kornhauser, 1959).

In *The Division of Labor in Society* (1893/1964), Durkheim examined *social solidarity,* the tendency of people to maintain social relationships. He distinguished between the types of solidarity found in early and modern societies. In early societies such as hunting and gathering or agrarian societies, the social structure was relatively simple, with little division of labor. People were knit together by their engagement in similar tasks. They derived a sense of oneness from being so much alike, what Durkheim termed *mechanical solidarity.* Modern societies, in contrast, are characterized by complex social structures and a sophisticated division of labor. People perform specialized tasks in factories, offices, and schools. No one person is self-sufficient, and all must depend upon others to survive. Under

these circumstances, society is held together by the interdependence fostered by the differences among people, what Durkheim labeled *organic solidarity.*

In examining social solidarity and other sociological questions, Durkheim believed that we should focus on the group, not the individual. He contended that the distinctive subject matter of sociology should be the study of social facts. **Social facts** are aspects of social life that cannot be explained in terms of the biological or mental characteristics of the individual. People experience social facts as external to themselves in the sense that facts have an independent reality and form a part of people's objective environment. As such, social facts serve to constrain their behavior and include not only legal and moral rules in society but also relationships and behavior patterns of others that affect our day-to-day lives.

Material social facts include society itself, its major institutions (the state, religion, family, education, etc.), and the various forms that underlie society (housing patterns, the crime rate, population distributions, etc.). *Nonmaterial social facts* are the social rules, principles of morality, meanings of symbols, and the shared consciousness that results from these.

Durkheim insisted that the explanation of social life must be sought in society itself. Society, he said, is more than the sum of its parts; it is a system formed by the association of individuals that comes to constitute a reality with its own distinctive characteristics.

Durkheim convincingly demonstrated the critical part social facts play in human behavior in his book *Suicide* (1897/1951), a landmark study in the history of sociology. Whereas earlier sociologists were given to armchair speculation, Durkheim undertook the painstaking collection and analysis of data on suicide. He found that suicide rates were higher among Protestants than Catholics, higher among the unmarried than the married, and higher among soldiers than civilians. Moreover, suicide rates were higher in times of peace than in times of war and revolution, and higher in times of economic prosperity and recession than in times of economic stability. He concluded that different suicide *rates* are the consequence of variations in social solidarity. Individuals enmeshed in a web of social bonds are less inclined to suicide than individuals who are weakly integrated into group life.

Durkheim was the first major sociologist to face up to the complex problems associated with the disciplined and rigorous empirical study of social life. He challenged the idea that suicide was the result of purely individual factors. As an alternative, he proposed that suicide is a social fact: a product of the meanings, expectations, and structural arrangements that evolve as people interact with one another. As such, suicide is explainable by social factors. Like Marx, Durkheim continues to influence modern sociology, stimulating research, tests of his ideas, and theoretical change (Bergesen, 2004; Moody and White, 2003; Stockard and O'Brien, 2002).

Max Weber: Subjectivity and Social Organization

No sociologist other than Marx has had a greater impact on sociology than the German sociologist Max Weber (1864–1920). Over the course of his career, Weber left a legacy of rich insights for a variety of disciplines, including economics, political science, and history. Among sociologists, he is known not only for his theoretical contributions but also for a number of specific ideas that have generated considerable interest and research in their own right. Many common but important ideas that we use to understand social life have their origin in the work of Weber, including *bureaucracy, lifestyle,* the *Protestant ethic,* and *charisma.* His sociological work covered a wide range of topics, including politics, organizations, social stratification, law, religion, capitalism, music, the city, and cross-cultural comparison, and it continues to influence sociological scholarship today (e.g., Swedberg, 2003; Wright, 2002).

Weber contended that a critical focus for sociology is the study of human subjectivity: the intentions, values, beliefs, and attitudes that underlie people's behavior. Weber employed the German word **Verstehen**—meaning "understanding" or "insight"—in describing this approach for learning about the subjective meanings people attach to their actions. In using this method, sociologists attempt to place themselves in the shoes of other people and identify what they think and how they feel.

Another notable sociological contribution Weber made is the concept of the ideal type. An *ideal type* is a concept constructed by sociologists to portray the principal characteristics of something they want to study. It is a tool that allows sociologists to generalize and simplify data by ignoring minor differences in order to accentuate major similarities. For example, a police department and a hospital differ in many obvious respects, but they share many attributes under the heading "bureaucracy." In Chapter 4 (pp. 112–113) we will see how Weber employed the notion of the ideal type to devise his model of bureaucracy. The ideal type serves as a measuring rod against which sociologists can evaluate actual cases. For example, if sociologists determine, on the basis of historical and contemporary evidence, that the ideal type of bureaucracy has a specific set of characteristics, they can compare this ideal type with actual bureaucracies and then develop explanations for why some of the characteristics of actual bureaucracies deviate from the ideal type. In this way we can learn much about causes of variation in how organizations function.

In his writings Weber stressed the importance of a **value-free sociology.** He emphasized that sociologists must not allow their personal biases to affect the conduct of their scientific research. Weber recognized that sociologists, like everyone else, have individual biases and moral convictions regarding behavior. But he insisted that sociologists must cultivate a disciplined approach to the phenomena they study so that they may see facts as they are, not as they might wish them to be. By the same token, Weber recognized that objectivity is not neutrality or moral indifference. *Neutrality* implies that a person does not take sides on an issue, and *moral indifference* that one does not care; *objectivity* has to do with the pursuit of scientifically verifiable knowledge. Though he promoted objectivity as an important goal in social science, he did not take a neutral stance as an intellectual or as a citizen. He was not afraid to express a value judgment or to tackle important issues of the day (Ritzer, 2011).

American Sociology

The sociologists we have considered thus far have been of European origin. Were sociologists to establish a sociological Hall of Fame, Comte, Martineau, Spencer, Marx, Durkheim, and Weber would unquestionably be among its first inductees. Yet, as sociology entered the 20th century, Americans assumed a critical role in its development. In the period preceding World War I, an array of factors provided a favorable climate for sociology in the United States (Calhoun, 2007; Fuhrman, 1980). As in Europe, the Industrial Revolution and urbanization gave a major impetus to sociological study. An added factor was the massive immigration of foreigners to the United States and the problems their absorption and assimilation posed for American society. Further, both sociology and the modern university system arose together. In Europe, by contrast, sociology had a more difficult time becoming established because it had to break into an established system of academic disciplines.

Early American sociology was optimistic, forward-looking, and rooted in a belief in progress, the value of individual freedom and welfare, and a confidence that, though there might be some flaws, American society was basically sound. Some early American sociologists, like Lester Ward (1841–1918), believed that sociologists should identify the basic laws that underlie social life and use this knowledge to reform society. Others, like William Graham Sumner (1840–1910), adapted a survival-of-the-fittest approach derived from Spencer, believing that

society's problems would work themselves out if left alone.

An exception to such optimism is the work of W. E. B. Du Bois (1868–1963), a leading African American intellectual and one of the founders of the National Association for the Advancement of Colored People, who analyzed racial inequality and advocated radical changes to eliminate it (Du Bois, 1903/1990; Blau and Brown, 2001). Du Bois also took sociology out of the ivory tower and did investigative fieldwork, gathering material on the African American community of Philadelphia, which appeared as *The Philadelphia Negro* in 1900. Between 1896 and 1914, Du Bois led the annual Atlanta University Conferences on Negro Problems that produced the first reliable sociological research on the South.

Contributions of considerable significance to sociology also were made by sociologists at the University of Chicago, where the first department of sociology in the United States was established in 1893. Here, in the first 30 years of the 20th century, a number of sociologists carried out work that remains influential in sociology today. The city of Chicago was viewed as a "social laboratory," and it was subjected to intense and systematic study. Included in this research were investigations of juvenile gangs, immigrant ghettos, wealthy Gold Coast and slum life, taxi dance halls, prostitution, and mental disorders.

During this period, Chicago sociologists trained an estimated half of the sociologists in the world. A number of the world's most capable female social scientists were among the university's graduates. But its department of sociology was largely a male world, one that afforded a hostile environment to the political activism espoused by many of the women. The women's world of sociology was centered at Hull House, a Chicago settlement house cofounded in 1889 by Jane Addams and Ellen Gates Starr. Settlement houses were charitable establishments set up in poor neighborhoods to provide services to the urban poor, particularly immigrants. Hull House served as a model for the social reform activities and the civic, recreational, and educational programs that came to be identified with the settlement houses that were established throughout the nation. The juvenile court system and workers' compensation were products of the two women's efforts. Addams and Starr also pioneered campaigns for women's suffrage, better housing, improvements in public welfare, stricter child labor laws, and the protection of working women. The women of Hull House are credited with inventing the research procedures of community case studies and of demographic mapping—showing on city maps the distributions of people with respect to income, age, ethnicity, language, levels of education, and other characteristics—that would later become hallmarks of Chicago sociology (Lengermann and Niebrugge-Brantley, 2011).

Because they were women, Jane Addams and Ellen Gates Starr were not fully recognized and accepted by the male-dominated sociological profession of the time. This was also true of Charlotte Perkins Gilman and two African American intellectuals, Ida Wells-Barnett and Anna Julia Cooper. Each of these women made distinguished contributions to understandings of society, such as a full consideration of the relatively powerless, including women, the poor, and African Americans, and laid the foundation of modern feminist sociology (Lengermann and Niebrugge-Brantley, 2011).

During the 1940s and until the mid-1960s, sociologists at Columbia, Harvard, and the University of California at Berkeley took the lead and established the major directions for sociological research and theory, crafting techniques for surveying public attitudes and refining models that portrayed society as a system made up of parts with interrelated functions. Leading American sociologists believed that sociology should be a science concerned with pursuing knowledge for its own sake, so they insisted that the discipline not be focused directly on solving social problems.

W. E. B. Du Bois conducted path-breaking research on African American life, developed a theoretical understanding of racial inequality, and advocated radical social change to eliminate racism.

However, the social turmoil of the 1960s and early 1970s brought to sociology many students who were activists for civil rights, student power, and peace. These young, "new breed" sociologists contended that the doctrine of sociological neutrality was a cloak concealing moral insensitivity. In their reaction against the neutrality of previous decades, they also broke with established sociological theory and sought new directions in theory and research grounded in the work of Karl Marx and C. Wright Mills (see Lemert, 2002; Ritzer, 2011).

Contemporary Sociology

The evolution of sociology continues. Among the many theoretical developments that have occurred, three influential and related frameworks stand out: critical theory, feminism, and postmodernism.

Critical Theory

Critical theory grew out of a dissatisfaction with 20th-century sociology in general and Marxism in particular (Ritzer, 2011). Early critical theorists were German sociologists who fled the Nazi regime in the 1930s and came to the United States, where some remained. These critical theorists and their followers criticized sociology for having a scientific approach that viewed individuals as passive and helpless entities locked in social structures, and for analyzing societies without detecting social problems or envisioning what societies should be. They also criticized Marxism because they believed it denied the importance of culture by viewing it as part of the "superstructure," largely determined by economic forces.

Critical theorists argue that mass culture (e.g., television, film, and popular music), a product of a capitalist media industry, cannot be a true reflection of people's beliefs, tastes, values, ideas, and lifestyles. Instead, mass culture pacifies, represses, and controls people who might otherwise recognize important contradictions and inequities in their social lives. Critical theorists claim that mass culture makes the political system seem to be a benign entity, supporting the status quo, that benefits all.

Critical theory is both an outgrowth of and a contributor to conflict theory, which we will discuss in the next section. It has also had a major influence on two other contemporary movements in sociology: feminism and postmodern social theory.

Feminism

Feminism is an intellectual movement in the humanities and social sciences that has had a profound impact on the nature and direction of sociology (e.g., Thistle, 2000). Sociological feminism begins with the observation that for most of the history of sociology, women hardly appear in social theory and research. Men's experiences have been viewed as universal, while women's activities and experiences have been ignored. When women have been studied and theorized about, it is in marginal and secondary roles such as housewife or workers in other low-status occupations. Feminism explicitly examines women's roles and experiences in society, working to fully uncover women's contributions to social life and the nature of the structures and processes that maintain gender inequality. At the same time, sociological feminism has worked to develop theories grounded in the experiences and situations of women that can be used to reveal oppressive social relations and produce social transformation for the betterment of all humankind (Lengermann and Niebrugge-Brantley, 2011).

Feminism is not a single theory but an evolving set of theoretical perspectives, including liberal feminism, Marxian feminism, psychoanalytic feminism, radical feminism, and socialist feminism, all of which focus on women's experiences and on gender inequality (England, 1993a) and which have had significant impact on mainstream sociological theory (Chafetz, 1997; Tong, 1998).

Important developments in feminist theory and research grew out of the realization that the social experience of gender is not universal (e.g., Beisel and Kay, 2004; Browne and Misra, 2003). Women's and men's experiences are strongly influenced by their social class, race, ethnicity, nationality, age, and sexual preference and by their social positions in the family, the labor force, and the world economic system. For example, the experience of gender for a young, white, middle-class Episcopalian woman is fundamentally different from that of an elderly woman who is a Cuban immigrant living in poverty. Sociological feminism places much emphasis on different forms of oppression, on how these forms intersect with gender and with each other, on the resulting diversity of experience, and on the implications such an orientation has for the elimination of all

According to postmodernism, we have entered an age in which human society is dominated by images and information disseminated through advertising and mass media.

colonialism, and the ideologies of democracy, individualism, and secularism. According to postmodernists, we have entered an age dominated not by the goods-producing economy of modernity but by the production and dissemination of images and information through mass media and advanced computer technology. If societies are based on ever-changing signs, codes, and models presented in the media, they have no basic structure, and the grand abstract social theories of Marx, Durkheim, Weber, and others we have discussed can be of little use in understanding them. In the world of postmodern theory, culture is an amalgamation of images, symbols, and ideas from television programs, commercials, films, magazines, and other sources and conveys no essential, enduring meanings. Social divisions, where they exist, thus have no legitimacy and should be removed, eliminating barriers between races, ethnic groups, genders, cultures, nations, and academic disciplines.

In its most extreme formulations (e.g., Baudrillard, 1983, 1990), having no confidence that any social and moral principles exist to give meaning to people's lives and no hope that human beings can control the processes that oppress them, postmodernism is a very pessimistic framework (Adam and Allan, 1995; see also Sica, 1996). It argues that there is no foundation for objective, reliable knowledge about social life.

Though postmodernism has no coherent set of theoretical principles, it does point to some of the ways that contemporary societies constrain and control people, particularly through media and advertising (Ritzer, 1995, 1997), and it suggests ways people can liberate themselves. Postmodernism has also broadened sociology

forms of exploitation and oppression (Richardson, Taylor, and Whittier, 1997; Lengermann and Niebrugge-Brantley, 2011).

Postmodernism

Like feminism, postmodernism (Ritzer, 2011; Best and Kellner, 1991; Ritzer, 1997) is an intellectual movement that has influenced scholarship in literature, art, politics, communications, and other disciplines, as well as sociology. Postmodernists are deeply distrustful of science and the principle of objectivity, arguing that scientific knowledge is as much a product of the socially determined interests and biases of investigators as it is of facts, which themselves are products of social processes. In addition, postmodernists point out that scientific knowledge has failed to solve social problems or to prevent war and genocide.

At the core of postmodern social theory is the assumption that the modern period of history is coming to an end. That period, which began with the Enlightenment and the end of the medieval period, included industrialization, urbanization, through its emphasis on the multidisciplinary nature of social inquiry, revitalized sociology's debunking function through the exposure of texts to show hidden assumptions, and encouraged continuous reexamination of basic theoretical assumptions (Ritzer, 2011).

Theoretical Perspectives

As we have seen, sociologists have asked fundamental questions about social life throughout the history of sociology: Why does social inequality exist? How do people learn to interact with each other and be effective participants in society? How and why do societies change? Sociologists have answered these and many more by developing social theories. No one social theory, however, has been so successful that it has been able to eliminate its competitors and dominate the field.

There now exist many different social theories to explain many different facets of our social lives. To reduce complexity, we can combine theories with similar approaches into theoretical perspectives. A *theoretical perspective* provides a set of assumptions, interrelated concepts, and statements about how various social phenomena are related to one another.

Twentieth-century sociology was strongly influenced by three general theoretical perspectives. Each perspective asks somewhat different questions about society and provides different views of social life. Most sociologists would not accept only one model and reject all the others; rather, in contemporary sociology, theoretical perspectives are tools—mental constructs—that provide rules of inference through which new relationships can be discovered and suggestions about how the scope of a theory can be expanded.

The three contemporary theoretical perspectives in sociology are *functionalism,* which emphasizes order and stability; *conflict theory,* which focuses on inequality, exploitation, oppression, social turmoil, and social change; and *symbolic interactionism,* which argues that society emerges from and is changed by the process of human beings interacting with one another using symbols based in shared meanings. Together, these three perspectives form the theoretical background of most current sociological work. We will be returning to them throughout the book. For now, let us briefly examine each in turn.

The Functionalist Perspective

The structural-functional—or, more simply, functionalist—perspective draws substantially upon the ideas of Auguste Comte, Herbert Spencer, and Émile Durkheim, and takes a broad view of society, focusing on the macro aspects of social life. In the 1950s and early 1960s, the functionalist theories of Talcott Parsons (1949, 1951) and his students occupied center stage in American sociology. Indeed, some proponents such as Kingsley Davis (1959) argued that the approach was essentially synonymous with sociology.

Society as a Social System

Functionalists took as their starting point the notion that society is a *system,* a set of elements or components that are related to one another in a more or less stable fashion through a period of time. Functionalists focused on the parts of society, particularly its major institutions, such as the family, religion, the economy, the state, and education. They identified the structural characteristics of each part much as biologists describe the principal features of the body's organs. They then determined what the functions of each part are.

One of the features of a system stressed by functionalists is its tendency toward equilibrium, or balance, among its parts and among the forces operating on it. Change in one part has implications for other parts and for the community or society as a whole, with change and adaptation being a continuous process. Some parts may also change more rapidly than others, contributing to social dislocations. For example, as life expectancy increases and U.S. baby boomers continue to age, our country faces a rapidly expanding group of over-55 workers, an increasing population of frail and vulnerable elderly, and a decreasing pool of potential caregivers for those elderly (Connolly, 2008).

Functions and Dysfunctions

Within system analysis, functionalists paid particular attention to the **functions** performed by a system's parts, especially organizations, groups, institutions, and cultural elements. Functionalists argued that if a system is to survive, certain essential tasks must be performed; otherwise, the system fails to maintain itself and perishes. If society is to exist, its members must make provision for certain functional requirements. Institutions, to be discussed in more detail in Chapter 2 (pp. 59–60), are the principal structures whereby these critical tasks for social living—functions—are organized, directed, and executed. Each institution, such as education, the economy, and the family, is built around a standardized solution to a set of problems. Functions are the observed consequences of the existence of institutions, groups, and other system parts that permit the adaptation or adjustment of a system (Merton, 1968).

Robert K. Merton (1968) pointed out that just as institutions and the other parts of society can contribute to the maintenance of the social system, they can also have negative consequences. Those observed consequences that lessen the adaptation or adjustment of a system he termed **dysfunctions.** Poverty, for example, has both functional and dysfunctional properties (Gans, 1972). It is functional because it ensures that the nation's "dirty work" is done—those jobs that are physically dirty, dangerous, temporary, dead-end, poorly paid, and menial. However, poverty is dysfunctional because it intensifies a variety of social problems, including those associated with health, education, crime, and drug addiction.

Manifest and Latent Functions

Merton (1968) also distinguished between manifest functions and latent functions. **Manifest functions** are those consequences that are intended and recognized by the participants in a system; **latent functions** are those consequences that are neither intended nor recognized. Some ceremonies of the Hopi Indians of the Southwest, for example, are designed to produce rain. Though these rituals do not actually cause it to rain, their latent function is to produce a collective expression by which the Hopi people achieve a sense of social solidarity. What outsiders may see as irrational behavior (performing a rain ceremony) is actually functional for the group itself.

Social Consensus

Functionalists assumed that most members of a society agree on what is desirable, worthwhile, and moral, and what is undesirable, worthless, and evil. Through a social learning process, they come to share a consensus regarding their core values and beliefs. For example, most Americans accept the values and beliefs inherent in democracy, the doctrine of equal opportunity, and the notion of personal achievement. Functionalists say that this high degree of consensus on basic values provides the foundation for social integration and stability in U.S. society.

Evaluation of the Functionalist Perspective

The functionalist perspective is a useful tool for describing society and identifying its structural parts and the functions of these parts at a particular point in time. It provides a "big picture" of the whole of social life, particularly as it finds expression in patterned, recurrent behavior and institutions. For some purposes, it is helpful to have a clear description of what parts make up society and how they fit together.

However, such an approach does not provide us with the entire story of social life. The functionalist approach has difficulty dealing with history and processes of social change. In the real world, societies are constantly changing, but functionalism has done a poor job of accounting for the never-ending flow of interaction among people. Moreover, the functionalist perspective tends to exaggerate consensus, integration, and stability while disregarding conflict, dissent, and instability. The problems that structural-functional theory has in dealing with change, history, and conflict have led critics to charge that it has a conservative bias and that it tends to support existing social arrangements.

The Conflict Perspective

Conflict theorists, like functionalists, focused their attention on society as a whole, studying its institutions and structural arrangements. Yet the two perspectives have been at odds on a good many matters. Where functionalists depicted society in relatively static terms, conflict theorists emphasized the processes of change that continually transform social life. Where functionalists stressed the order and stability to be found in society, conflict theorists emphasized disorder and instability. Where functionalists saw the common interests shared by the members of a society, conflict theorists focused upon the interests that divide. Where functionalists viewed consensus as the basis of social unity, conflict theorists insisted that social unity is an illusion resting on coercion. Finally, while functionalists often viewed existing social arrangements as necessary and justified by the requirements of group life, conflict theorists saw many of the arrangements as neither necessary nor justified.

Diversity of Approaches

Although conflict theory derived much of its inspiration from the work of Karl Marx, it had many other sources as well, including the work of such sociologists as Georg Simmel (1908/1955, 1950), Lewis Coser (1956), Randall Collins (1975), and Eric Olin Wright (1985, 2000). Although class conflict was the core of Marx's theory, many contemporary sociologists view conflict as occurring among many groups and interests—religion versus religion, race versus race, consumers versus producers, taxpayers versus welfare recipients, sunbelt versus snowbelt states, central-city residents versus suburbanites, the young versus the elderly, and so on.

Sources of Conflict

The main source of conflict in human societies is scarcity of social and material resources. Wealth, prestige, and power are always in limited supply, so that gains for one individual or group are usually associated with losses for others. **Power**—the ability to control the behavior of others, even against their will—determines who will gain and who will lose (Lasswell, 1936). Power also determines which group will be able to translate its preferences for behavior (its values) into the operating rules for others. Conflict theorists asked how it is that some groups acquire power, dominate other groups, and effect their will in human affairs. In so doing, they looked at who benefits and who loses from the way society is organized.

How Society Is Possible

If social life is fractured and fragmented by confrontations between individuals or groups, how is a society possible? Functionalists argued that society is held together primarily by a consensus among its members regarding core values and norms, but conflict theorists rejected this view. They maintained that society is often held together in spite of conflicting interests.

When one group enjoys sufficient power, it makes and enforces rules and shapes institutional life so that its interests are served. Many conflict theorists regarded the state—government and the rules it creates and enforces—as an instrument of oppression employed by ruling elites for their own benefit; functionalists tended to view the state as an organ of the total society, functioning to promote social control and stability.

Many divided but overlapping interest groups generate a large number of crosscutting conflicts. People who are opponents in one conflict are allies in another. Society persists because no one conflict can become so great as to tear the society apart (Coser, 1956). For example, an African American woman at odds with her white neighbor over affirmative action policy may agree with her about increasing funding for their neighborhood schools.

Evaluation of the Conflict Perspective

The conflict perspective complements functionalist theory. The functionalist approach has difficulty dealing with history and social change; the conflict approach makes these matters its strength. The conflict approach has difficulty dealing with some aspects of consensus, integration, and stability; the functionalist approach affords penetrating insights.

Some sociologists contend that functionalists and conflict theorists focused on two aspects of the same reality. They note that both consensus and conflict are central features of social life. In addition, both approaches traditionally took a holistic view of social life, portraying societies as systems of interrelated parts (van den Berghe, 1963).

Other sociologists, such as Lewis Coser (1956), drawing upon the seminal work done by Georg Simmel (1908/1955), suggested that under some circumstances conflict is functional for society; it prevents social systems from becoming rigid and fixed by exerting pressure for change and innovation. The civil rights movement, although challenging established interests and racist patterns, may have contributed to the long-term stability of American institutions by bringing African Americans into the "system."

However, it is clear that conflict is often dysfunctional for an existing system. There are many destructive conflicts around the world that are preventing societies and nations from fully developing socially and economically, such as those between the Israelis and Palestinians in the Middle East and between the Sunis and the Shiites in Iraq. The potential for civil war in Iraq among the Shia, Sunni, and Kurdish populations is a serious problem for those who wish to develop a fully functioning, inclusive democracy in Iraq (Packer, 2005).

The Interactionist Perspective

The functionalist and conflict perspectives took a big-picture approach to sociology, focusing on the macro or large-scale structures of society. In contrast, the interactionist perspective has been more concerned with the micro or small-scale aspects of social life. Sociologists like Charles Horton Cooley (1902/1964), George Herbert Mead (1934/1962), Manford Kuhn (1964), and Herbert Blumer (1969) turned their attention to the individuals who make up society and asked how social interaction is possible. Answers to this question focused on individuals' subjective experiences and understandings, and especially on how shared understandings of the world emerge from social interaction and form the basis for social life. As with the functionalist and conflict perspectives, a number of themes recurred in the various formulations of interactionist thought.

Symbols

Interactionists emphasized that we are social beings who live a group existence. However, we possess few, if any, innate behaviors for relating to one another. Whatever inborn capacities we have seem to require exposure to others to fully develop; we will discuss this further in Chapter 3 (pp. 68–70). If we are largely lacking in such inborn mechanisms, how is society possible? Interactionists found the answer in the ability of human beings to communicate by means of symbols. A *symbol* is something that stands for something else. That something else is its *meaning*. Social interaction, and therefore society itself, is possible because people share meanings. The combined emphasis on symbols and interaction gave this perspective its name: *symbolic interactionism.*

Meaning: Constructing Reality

Symbolic interactionism was based on three core assumptions (Mead, 1934/1962; Blumer, 1969; Fine, 1993). First, we respond to things in our environment on the basis of their meanings—that is, the understandings we have of them. Our responses differ if we see people swinging bats as playing a baseball game or as trying to brain us. Second, meanings are not inherent in things, but emerge from social interaction. Turning 16 years of age is no more meaningful than turning 15, except for the social conventions (e.g., obtaining one's driver's license) that make this a particularly meaningful birthday. Third, because we are continually interacting, shared cultural meanings are continually emerging and changing. The world we live in, therefore, is largely a social reality, manufactured by people as they intervene in the world and interpret what is happening there using the symbols and meanings available to them. Accordingly, symbolic interactionists said that we experience the world as a **constructed reality.**

Everyday fashion is a good example. When we encounter a person dressed in a certain way, our reaction is not to the clothes per se, but to the meanings they symbolize. High-topped black tennis shoes, hiking boots, wing-tips, flip-flops, and Birkenstocks each have a different meaning, and the meaning shifts depending on other characteristics of the wearer, including age, gender, and race.

Symbolic interactionists also emphasized how symbols and meanings emerge to provide a more concrete reality to things that are abstract and elusive, such as societies and nations. Though it is difficult to point to a society the way we can point to a chair or a tree, we give our society a name ("the United States," "Canada," or "India"); we draw borders between our society and others; and we come to treat the United States, Canada, and India as objects. By acting and interacting with others as if the United States is real, we make it real. By treating society and its parts as "things," we give them existence and continuity (Hewitt and Shulman, 2011).

All this led symbolic interactionists to argue that if sociologists are to understand social life, they must understand what people actually say and do from the viewpoint of the people themselves. Put another way, sociologists must "get inside people's heads" and view the "world" as it is seen, interpreted, acted upon, and shaped by the people themselves. This orientation is strongly influenced by Max Weber's concept of *Verstehen.*

Fashioning Behavior

Symbolic interactionists portrayed us as creatively constructing our actions in accordance with the meanings we attribute to a situation. In fashioning our behavior, we use symbols to define our perceptual inputs, mentally outline possible responses, imagine the consequences of alternative courses of action, eliminate unlikely possibilities, and finally select the optimal mode of action (Stryker, 1980). We mentally rehearse our actions before we actually act and, upon acting, serve as audiences to our own actions. As a result, our behavior is improvised and unpredictable; we must continually create meanings and devise ways to fit our actions together (Manis and Meltzer, 1994).

Symbolic interactionists argued that we are at least as likely to shape "social structure" as to be shaped by it. Think of the social structure that is your relationship with your roommate(s). It's unlikely that you were handed a list of rules for coexisting; rather, you have negotiated agreements, spoken and unspoken, about how to do so. Your relationship shifts and changes as you encounter problems and solve them. It is a circular process, in which social structure influences individuals and individuals influence social structure.

Evaluation of the Interactionist Perspective

The interactionist perspective provides an image of human beings as active agents who fashion their behavior, as opposed to an image of individuals who simply respond passively in a manner prescribed by social rules and institutional arrangements. This perspective directs our attention to the activities of individuals as they go about their everyday lives. Through interaction they acquire the symbols and the meanings that allow them to interpret situations, assess the advantages and disadvantages of given actions, and then select one of them.

However, the interactionist perspective has its limitations. First, one may be tempted to conclude that because social reality is constructed, there is no reality independent of social constructions. For example, because mental illness is a construction that emerges from a social process of diagnosis based on socially constructed categories of illness, one may wish to argue that mental illness is not "real." However, as philosopher John R. Searle (1995) made clear, we can understand social reality as constructed without rejecting the idea that there is a reality totally independent of us that may affect our social constructions. Second, in their everyday lives, people do not enjoy total flexibility in shaping their actions. Although interactionists have acknowledged that many of our actions are guided by systems of preestablished meanings, including culture and social order, some interactionists have downplayed the parts these larger elements play in our lives. And third, research by symbolic interactionists has often focused on narrow aspects of social life, such as nude beaches, the relationships between prostitutes and truck drivers, and the role of odors in social life.

To rectify some of these problems some sociologists (e.g., Collins, 2000; Fine, 1993) have introduced structural and large-scale components into interactionist thought by linking social structure to the individual and by showing how the intertwined patterns of action and interaction form the foundation for groups and societies.

Using the Three Perspectives

The details of and contrasts among the three sociological perspectives will become clearer as we see how they operate in the chapters to come. As we noted, each theoretical approach has its advantages and its disadvantages. (Table 1.1 summarizes the major theoretical perspectives.) Each portrays a different aspect of reality and directs our attention to some dimension of social life that the other neglects or overlooks.

Let's look at how each perspective might describe poverty. As we discussed earlier, functionalism would highlight the functions and dysfunctions of poverty in terms of the operation of the larger society. Conflict theorists would portray

Table 1.1	Major Theoretical Perspectives in Sociology		
	Functionalist	Conflict	Interactionist
Primary Level of Analysis	Macro	Macro	Micro
Nature of Society	A set of interacting parts	A set of competing interest groups	A social reality that is created and re-created in social interaction
Foundations of Social Interaction	Consensus of shared beliefs and values	Conflict, coercion, and power	Shared meanings
Focus of Study	Social order	Social conflict and social change	The dynamic interplay between the individual and society
Advantages	Gives an understanding of social structure and social stability	Uncovers historical processes that lead to social change	Gives an understanding of human beings as active agents in social life
Disadvantages	Is ineffective in dealing with social change	Gives a weak understanding of social consensus and social stability	Has difficulty dealing with social structure

the inequalities that flow from the way society is organized and show who gains and who loses from these arrangements. Interactionists would suggest that people define certain circumstances as deviating from what they perceive to be an ideal standard of living, assign an unfavorable meaning to these conditions, and apply the label "poverty" to them. Each approach offers a somewhat different insight.

Further, each perspective affords a more effective approach, a better "fit," to some kinds of data—some aspects of social life—than other perspectives do. None of the three perspectives precludes the contribution of another perspective in explaining given data or predicting particular outcomes. Indeed, each approach is useful precisely because it provides us with some piece of information regarding the exceedingly complex puzzle of social life. All three perspectives can be useful sociological tools for describing and analyzing human behavior.

Conducting Research

The sociologists we have considered have provided us with important theories regarding the nature and workings of social life. A *theory* is a general framework or perspective that provides an explanation for a specific social phenomenon. However, as most sociologists would agree, theory unconfirmed by facts has little solid value. We require both theoretical understanding *and* facts; for this reason, both theory and research are essential components of the sociological enterprise. Theory inspires research that can verify or disprove it. Research provides findings that permit us to accept, reject, or modify our theoretical formulations, while simultaneously challenging us to craft new and better theories.

Research also provides the information needed to formulate public policy. Many basic human problems are products of social relations and human behavior. Sociological research can provide citizens, policy makers, and public officials with basic knowledge to fashion solutions

to social problems such as poverty, drug abuse, gender inequality, and racism.

In this section we will discuss the logic of science, define a number of research methods, list the steps in the scientific method, and consider research ethics.

The Logic of Science

Science makes the assumption that every event or action results from an antecedent cause. Indeed, a primary objective of science is to determine what causes what. Sociologists assume that crime, racism, social inequality, and marriages do not simply happen, but that they have causes. Moreover, they assume that under identical conditions, the same cause will always produce the same effect.

Scientists also assume that truth can be empirically tested; data can be gathered and objectively analyzed by means of careful observation and measurement, and the facts discovered by one scientist can be verified by other scientists. For example, if it is true that people behave differently in the presence of others than when alone, then any social scientist who investigates this using careful observation and measurement will obtain the same results.

However, science is not simply a collection of research findings; science is produced through a set of complex social processes. The people who practice science are products of their own societies and of the groups to which they belong. As a result, scientists are subject to a variety of social influences in addition to their core scientific values and principles. These other factors, self-interests, and biases may shape a scientist's research design, collection of data, and interpretation of results. However, the importance of objectivity is not that it is always realized in science, but that it is an important goal toward which all scientists are committed to working.

Methods of Data Collection

Sociologists must collect facts to support or dispute theories and to answer questions about social life. They employ four major techniques of data collection: experiments, surveys, observation, and archival research. Before describing each of these, we need to define some important scientific terms.

Basic Concepts in Research

Scientists look for relationships among variables. A **variable** is a concept that can take on different values. Scientists use this term to refer to something that they think influences (or is influenced by) something else. The variables sociologists typically study have to do with social statuses, conditions, attitudes, and behaviors. In studying political behavior, for example, sociologists might examine variables such as differences in race, gender, age, religion, and socioeconomic standing.

In investigating cause-and-effect relationships, scientists distinguish between independent and dependent variables. An **independent variable** is one that *causes* an effect. The **dependent variable** is the variable that *is affected.* The causal variable (the independent variable) precedes in time the phenomenon it causes (the dependent variable). For example, as the education level of women (independent variable) increases, the mortality rate of their infants (dependent variable) decreases. In their research, scientists attempt to predict the relationship they will find between the independent and dependent variables. Such a statement—or **hypothesis**—is a proposition that can then be tested to determine its validity.

In testing a hypothesis, scientists try to determine the degree of association that exists between an independent and a dependent variable. If the variables are causally related, then they must be correlated with one another. A **correlation** exists if a change in one variable is associated with a change in the other variable. Because the mortality rate of infants decreases as the education level of women increases, for example, the two variables are said to be *correlated.*

Correlation, however, does not establish causation. For example, the death rate is considerably higher among hospitalized individuals than among nonhospitalized individuals. Yet we would be wrong to conclude on the basis of this correlation that hospitals cause death. Likewise, the amount of damage resulting from a fire is closely associated with the number of fire engines on the scene. Again, we would be wrong to conclude that fire engines cause fire damage. The latter two examples are cases of **spurious correlation**—the apparent relationship between the two variables is produced by a third variable that influences the original variables. Severe sickness is associated both with admission to hospitals and with death; similarly, a large, uncontrolled fire is associated with both extensive damage and the mobilization of multiple firefighting units. To reduce the likelihood that their research will be contaminated by third variables, scientists employ *controls,* a matter we will discuss below.

Methods of Research

Experiments The experiment is the ideal design for scientific research because it best provides researchers with data that enable them to evaluate causal hypotheses (Falk and Heckman, 2009). To obtain such data, scientists must try to control all the relevant variables to eliminate other explanations of their findings. Though not perfect, the **experiment** best meets this requirement. In an experiment, researchers work with two groups that are made to be identical in all relevant respects through a process of random assignment. For example, in an experiment on voter preferences, the two groups studied should be of the same size, and their members should reflect a similar socioeconomic, gender, age, and racial mix. Researchers introduce a change in one group—the **experimental group**—but not in the other group—the **control group.** The two groups are identical except for the factor that the researchers introduce in the experimental group. The control group provides a neutral standard against which the changes in the experimental group can be measured.

Experiments allow sociologists to test the effects of an independent variable on a dependent variable. In our voter preference example, one group might be asked to watch a series of television commercials on candidates, while the other would spend the same amount of time watching videos unrelated to voting. The effects of television commercials (independent variable) on voter preference (dependent variable) could then be measured.

We commonly think of experiments as being performed in a laboratory setting, which is the case for much medical research and for a good deal of the research done by psychologists and social psychologists (Falk and Heckman, 2009). However, sociologists also do *field experiments* in which the independent variable is manipulated in a natural setting rather than in a laboratory. This enables researchers to observe various forms of social behavior under conditions in which they normally occur. In a laboratory study, subjects know they are being observed and thus may display the behavior they believe is desirable. This makes studying some social responses difficult in the laboratory.

Although the field experiment combines the strict rules of experimentation with a natural setting, it does have disadvantages (Deaux and

Wrightsman, 1984). In the field, researchers have no control over unexpected intrusions that may reduce or destroy the effectiveness of the changes they make in the independent variable. Further, it is often difficult to use random assignment in field experiments to ensure that the control group and experimental group are identical.

Surveys Some objects of study, such as people's values, beliefs, attitudes, perceptions, motivations, and feelings, are not directly accessible by observation. Others, such as sexual activity, health, religious practices, and drug use, are often sensitive, private matters. Under these circumstances the **survey** is a valuable tool.

Early in 2010, survey results made the news when one survey announced that job satisfaction was at its lowest in two decades while others showed that job satisfaction had been "remarkably stable" for several decades (Morello, 2010). How could such different conclusions be reached?

Survey data are typically gathered in one of two ways: Researchers interview people by reading them questions from a prepared questionnaire, or people receive a questionnaire in the mail, fill it out, and return it by mail. In either case, *self-reports* are the source of data.

In both interview and questionnaire surveys, sampling procedures are critical. If researchers need information about a large population, they do not need to contact every member of that population. Instead, they can draw on a small but *representative sample,* a sample that accurately reflects the composition of the general public. Public opinion pollsters such as the Gallup and Harris organizations often employ a small sample of no more than 1,500 individuals to tap the opinions

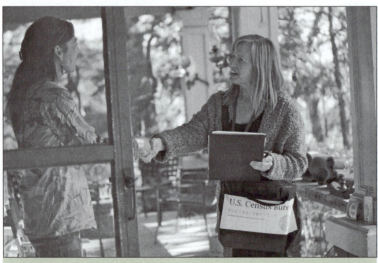

This Census Bureau worker is gathering survey data from respondents by means of an interview.

of more than 311 million Americans. Similarly, physicians need only a small sample of your blood to run tests and draw conclusions about the composition of all your blood and thus about your health.

Sociologists typically employ either a random sample or a stratified random sample in their research. In the **random sample,** researchers select subjects on the basis of chance so that every individual in the population has the same opportunity to be chosen. A **stratified random sample** provides greater precision. Researchers divide the population into relevant categories, such as age, gender, socioeconomic level, and race, and draw a random sample from each of the categories. If African Americans constitute 12 percent of the study population and Hispanics 9 percent, African Americans will comprise 12 percent of the sample and Hispanics 9 percent.

Designing good questionnaires is not easy. The wording of the questions, their number, and the format in which they appear are all critical matters (Fowler, 2001; Schaeffer and Presser, 2003). For example, the wording of a question may systematically bias the answers. When poll respondents are asked, "What do you think is the most important problem facing the country today?" only 1 to 2 percent respond with global warming or the environment (Schuldt, Konrath, and Schwarz, 2011). But when the question is "What do you think will be the most serious problem facing the world in the future if nothing is done to stop it?" the most frequent response is global warming/environment, with the percentage response more than 10 times higher than when the question is asked as first stated. Pretesting should always be done to ensure that questions are understandable, unbiased, and specific enough to elicit the desired information.

A major problem with self-report information is determining its accuracy (Tourangeau, Rips, and Rasinski, 2000). Because individuals are involved in the data they are reporting, they may intentionally or unwittingly supply biased reports.

They may withhold or distort information because, even though many surveys are anonymous, telling the truth can cause people to feel threatened or embarrassed. In addition, many people lack the insight required to provide certain kinds of information. And some people lack the literacy necessary to comprehend even the simplest question.

An increasing problem with survey research is the difficulty in finding respondents (Groves et al., 2002). Of the people who receive a questionnaire in the mail, 20–70 percent fail to complete or return it, distorting the sample's representativeness. More and more Americans are refusing to answer surveys (Dillman, 2009; Dillman and Carley-Baxter, 2001).

Observation As baseball's Yogi Berra once observed, "You can observe a lot just by watching." Observation—watching—is a primary tool of sociological inquiry. Observation becomes a scientific technique when it (1) serves a clear research objective, (2) is undertaken in a systematic rather than haphazard manner, (3) is carefully recorded, (4) is related to a broader body of sociological knowledge and theory, and (5) is subjected to the same checks and controls applied to all types of scientific evidence (Selltiz, Wrightsman, and Cook, 1981).

Sociologists typically observe people in one of two ways. They may observe the activities of people without intruding or participating in the activities, a procedure termed **unobtrusive observation.** Or sociologists may engage in activities with the people that they are studying, a technique called **participant observation.** Elliot Liebow's (1967/2003) study of the African American streetcorner men, which we discussed earlier in the chapter, involved participant observation. Liebow, a white, began his study by striking up a friendship with an African American man, Tally Jackson, at the New Deal Carry-out Shop. Over the next several weeks, Liebow often ate at the Carry-out. The streetcorner men were at first suspicious of Liebow, but Tally eased their distrust by, in effect, sponsoring Liebow as his friend.

Within a few months, Liebow was well enough known and accepted by the streetcorner men to go to their rooms or apartments, needing neither an excuse nor an explanation for doing so. Clearly an outsider, Liebow (1967:164/2003) reflected on his acceptance by the group:

[B]ut I also was a participant in a full sense of the word. The people I was observing knew that I was observing them, yet they allowed me to participate in their activities and take part in their lives to a degree that continues to surprise me.

In many situations observation is the only way to gather data (Anderson, 2001). At times people are unable or unwilling to tell about their behavior: As we have said, they may lack sufficient insight to report on it, or, because their behavior is illicit, taboo, or deviant, they may be reluctant to do so. For instance, we may wish to get answers to such questions as, Why and how are people drawn to crack and heroin? How is the drug market structured? How does drug use affect the social and economic life of the community? What is its role in crime and violence? Some of the most informative answers to these questions have come from researchers who have undertaken unobtrusive observation while living and working in drug-ridden communities (Anderson, 1990, 1999). But observation has limitations similar to those for field experiments: Researchers have no control over unexpected intrusions, and the groups or individuals observed may not be representative of others. Additionally, there is the practical problem of applying observational procedures to phenomena that occur over a long period, such as a certain historical era. For these types of investigation, archival data are particularly useful.

Comparative and Historical Research We may learn a good deal about work, sexual behavior, family life, leisure, and other matters within the United States and other Western societies. But do these insights hold for non-Western peoples? And do they hold for earlier times? To answer these sorts of questions, sociologists need to look to other societies and other historical periods to test their ideas. Comparative and historical research is well suited to the task (Mahoney, 2004).

One approach involves archival research. **Archival research** refers to the use of existing records that have been produced or maintained by persons or organizations other than the researcher. Census data, government statistics, newspaper reports, books, magazines, personal letters, speeches, folklore, court records, works of art, and the research data of other social scientists are all sources for archival research (e.g., Ruef, 2004; Budros, 2004). A new utilization of data already collected for some other purpose may have considerable value and merit.

Comparative and historical materials have provided us with valuable insights on issues relating to the nation-state. A good illustration is sociologist Theda Skocpol's landmark study, *States and Social Revolution* (1979). In this study Skocpol looked for similarities in the societal conditions that existed at the time of the French (1787–1800), Russian (1917–1921), and Chinese (1911–1949) revolutions, comparing them with conditions in nations where revolutions failed or did not take place. Skocpol's comparative historical analysis led her to conclude that successful social revolutions pass through three stages: (1) An old regime's state apparatus collapses; (2) the peasantry mobilizes in class-based uprisings; and (3) a new elite consolidates political power.

Archival research has the advantage of allowing researchers to test hypotheses over a wider range of time and societies than would otherwise be possible. We gain greater confidence in the validity of a hypothesis when we can test it in a number of cultures and historical periods rather than restrict ourselves to a single group in the present time and place. However, the technique also has its disadvantages. The major problem is that missing or inaccurate records often prevent an adequate test. And when material is available, it is frequently difficult to categorize in a way that gives an answer to a research question (Deaux and Wrightsman, 1984).

Feminist Research Methods Feminism has had not only a strong impact on contemporary social theory, as noted earlier in this chapter, but also an important influence on research. Feminist methodology includes a commitment to three goals: (1) to include women's lives in social research and reveal the diversity in the ways women actually live their lives, uncovering what has previously been ignored, censored, and suppressed; (2) to minimize harm by avoiding exploitation of research subjects and by limiting the negative consequences of research; and (3) to focus research efforts so that results will promote social change, reduce inequality, and in general be of value to women (DeVault, 1996).

Though many feminist researchers have done important and influential research using observational methods to examine women's experiential, subjective, and emotional lives, Joey Sprague and Mary K. Zimmerman (1993) stress that the important contributions of feminist methodology are:

1. To create an objective account of social life while being sensitive to the subjective experience of those we study.
2. To develop abstract theories without losing sight of the actual lives of people.
3. To recognize the importance of rationality in social life without ignoring the importance of emotion.
4. To realize that both statistical analysis of quantitative data and qualitative observation can reveal important insights about women's and men's social lives.

In sum, feminist methodology is not a particular method of doing research but an approach that emphasizes inclusion, fairness, and humaneness, as well as the pursuit of all evidence that can be used to transform society and women's lives.

Multiple Methods Many methods are used to gather data in sociology, some radically different from others. Using multiple methods, each with its own strengths and weaknesses, can give us more complete answers to our research questions; different methods provide different windows on reality (Falk and Heckman, 2009). As Peggy Thoits (1995) showed in her study, what we find with one method may be made understandable by examining data collected using another method. For her study of stresses and psychological symptoms, simply examining the average symptom level associated with each stressor was not enough; she needed to know the context in which stresses had occurred. Divorce, for example, might come as a devastating shock to one person and as a welcome relief to another, depending on each person's particular situation, and only Thoits's qualitative analysis of more extended comments from respondents and interviewers allowed her to interpret her data accurately. Box 1.2 provides a more detailed look at how a researcher selects research methods.

Some dimensions of human conduct are hidden, and doing research on them requires nontraditional methods. For example, data on drug seizures, treatment-seeking for drug problems, deaths due to drugs, and self-reported drug use are biased and inconsistent (Bohannon, 2007). In an attempt to estimate cocaine use more accurately, European researchers analyzed paper money to detect cocaine residue left on bills used to snort the drug and river water near cities to detect cocaine that had passed through users and into wastewater. Preliminary findings showed that cocaine use in Ireland and in Germany was substantially greater than had been assumed based on traditional research methods (Bohannon, 2007).

Steps in the Scientific Method: A Close-up Look

The *scientific method,* a series of steps that seeks to ensure maximum objectivity in investigating a problem, allows researchers to pursue answers to their questions by gathering evidence in a systematic manner. Although no single method can eliminate uncertainty, the steps

Twitter, Google, Wikipedia, Mechanical Turk, and Sociology

In this chapter, you've been reading about experiments, interviews, surveys, and archival research. The collection of data for sociological research can be time consuming and expensive, but that is changing—and rapidly. The advent of new digital technology has provided an "onslaught of new social science data . . . huge quantities of digital information about people and their various groupings and connections" (King, 2011:719).

Gary King (2011), at Harvard's Institute for Quantitative Social Science, says that the amount of information suddenly available for social science research is analogous to the advent of the use of microscopes by microbiologists: social media posts, digitized records of previously collected information, real-time geocoded crime incident reports, automated text analysis methods, and the revolution in computer technology all make it possible for sociologists to base their studies on millions of pieces of data instead of on a hundred telephone calls to reluctant survey respondents.

How does this new availability of information translate into research? In 2011 Cornell sociologist Michael Macy and his graduate student Scott Golder published a study that used 509 million public Twitter messages from 2.4 million Twitter users in 84 countries (Golder and Macy, 2011). They showed that across diverse cultures, people wake up in a good mood, and that good mood deteriorates over the course of the day; they also found that people are happier on weekends. This finding is important to other research: If people's Twitter posts change from positive early in the day to negative later on, researchers using Twitter to study attitudes about jobs, families, political candidates, and anything else need to account for differences in response by time of day and day of the week.

In another study, this one on voting behavior, researcher Gabriel Lenz at the University of California, Berkeley, decided to use research subjects ordered through Amazon.com (Bohannon, 2011). People all over the world who are available to do work on computers may be hired to do so through Amazon.com's online marketplace called Mechanical Turk. For $160, Lenz was able to recruit the research subjects he needed. How could he ensure that these subjects-for-hire represented the population he was trying to study? He and others acknowledge that this is a problem, and they are studying "Turkers." They have found that they "are younger and more ideologically liberal" than the general U.S. public but more similar to that group than are university students, who often serve as research subjects. In a replication of two classic experiments, data obtained using Mechanical Turk subjects were consistent with previously published results.

Culture can be studied digitally, too. "'God' is not dead," asserted a research team that published its findings in *Science*, "but needs a new publicist" (Michel et al., 2011:182). The team based its conclusion on an analysis of the appearance of the word "God" in more than 5 million books (about 4 percent of all the books ever published) from between 1800 and 2000. This is an example of culturomics—"the application of high-throughput data collection and analysis to the study of human culture" (Michel et al., 2011:181). The researchers used digitized versions of books to study linguistic and cultural phenomena and found themselves with more than 500 billion words in seven languages from the 1500s to the present, an amount

embodied in the scientific method maximize the chances for obtaining information that is relevant, unbiased, and economical. The scientific method relies on the rigorous and disciplined collection of facts and on the logical explanation of them. Its steps include selecting a researchable problem, reviewing the literature, formulating a hypothesis, choosing a research design, collecting the data, analyzing the data, and stating conclusions.

Ideally, sociological research follows this step-by-step procedure, although in practice it is not always possible. Let's examine each step in Figure 1.1 as we follow a study of adolescents' first experience of sex, their religiosity, and their attitudes about sex (Meier, 2003).

1. Selecting a Researchable Problem.
The range of topics available for social research is as broad as the range of human behavior.

of information impossible for a human to read, or skim, or make sense of in any way—alone. But with computer analyses of the appearance of various words, the team was able to discover changes in grammar over time in various countries, the censorship of ideas and people, the relative fame of public figures, the interest in various food items over the centuries and in various cultures, and even the peaks in various influenza epidemics.

And "God"? That word appeared in books with much greater frequency before 1900 than it has at any time since then. What that means to society is a topic for another study—perhaps one that will be conducted using new digital technology.

Questions for Discussion

1. What factors might influence the data collected by using paid experimental subjects through Mechanical Turk? How might they be accounted for?

2. Is information that researchers obtain from Twitter and Facebook messages reliable? When you post a message on Facebook, do you always tell the truth? Do people exaggerate accomplishments and feelings on social media? How could social scientists work around that?

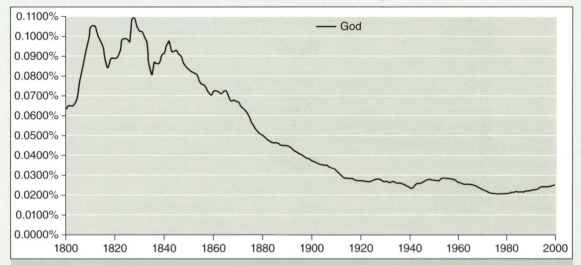

At http:books.google.com/ngrams, you can enter your name or any other word and generate a figure showing the frequency of its occurrence in books over time. This is the graph for "God."

Sociologists focus on problems that merit study and can be investigated by the methods of science. Ann M. Meier was intrigued by the fact that in recent decades more American teenagers have become sexually active at increasingly younger ages. More than 60 percent of all U.S. high school seniors are not virgins (Centers for Disease Control and Prevention, 2010). Meier decided to do a study to uncover social factors that would help explain sexual behavior among contemporary adolescents. She suspected that teenagers' attitudes about sexual behavior and their religiosity might be important determinants of their sexual activity.

2. Reviewing the Literature. Meier surveyed the research literature dealing with religiosity, attitudes, and first sex to find out what had been discovered in previous research. What she found suggested a variety of leads and saved her

Selecting a Researchable Problem
Finding a problem that merits study and can be investigated by the methods of science

Reviewing the Literature
Surveying the existing theory and research on the subject

Formulating a Hypothesis
Arriving at a statement that specifies the relationship between the variables and developing an operational definition that states the variables in a form that permits their measurement

Choosing a Research Design
Determining whether to test the hypothesis by designing an experiment, conducting interviews, observing the ways people behave in particular situations, examining existing records and historical evidence, or combining these procedures

Collecting the Data
Gathering the data and recording them in accordance with the specifications of the research design

Analyzing the Results
Searching for meaningful links among the facts that emerged in the course of the research

Stating Conclusions
Indicating the outcome of the study, extracting the broader meaning of the work for other knowledge and research, and suggesting directions for future research

Figure 1-1   The Steps in the Scientific Method
The chart shows the steps researchers commonly follow in investigating a problem.

from duplicating the work of other researchers. Studies uncovered by her search showed that *having more permissive attitudes* about sexual activity and *being less religious* were each related to a higher likelihood of adolescents having sex. This body of research suggested that adolescents' attitudes about sexual behavior and their religiosity might be important influences on sexual behavior. However, evidence in these studies also supported another possibility—that adolescents might develop more permissive attitudes about sex and become less religious as a consequence of having sex.

When sociologists discover an association, or *correlation,* between variables, they have not established *causation.* Do low religiosity and more permissive attitudes about having sex lead to more sexual behavior among teenagers? Or does having sex lead teenagers to be more permissive about sex and to be less religious?

3. Formulating a Hypothesis. After reviewing the literature, researchers form a hypothesis regarding the relationship they believe exists between variables. A hypothesis can take the form of a predictive statement or a question. Meier hypothesized that there were causal processes going in both directions: that permissive attitudes about having sex and low religiosity would both increase the likelihood of sexual behavior among adolescents, and that having sex would increase permissive attitudes about having sex and would decrease religiosity.

Before undertaking their research, however, researchers must define their variables. In developing **operational definitions,** scientists take abstract concepts and put them in a form that permits their measurement. In this case Meier specified how she would measure adolescents' religiosity, sexual attitudes, and sexual behavior. Religiosity was measured by asking respondents how important religion was to them and how frequently they attended church, prayed, and participated in church youth groups. Responses to these questions were combined into a single index of religiosity. Similarly, the degree of respondents'

permissive attitudes about sexual behavior was measured by seven questions that asked about the perceived benefits and costs of having sex. Sexual behavior was measured by asking respondents whether they had had sexual intercourse. Meier's *operational hypotheses,* stated in terms of measurable variables, were as follows:

- More permissive attitudes toward having sex will increase the probability of having sex.
- Higher levels of religiosity will decrease the probability of having sex.
- Having sex will result in adolescents having more permissive attitudes about having sex.
- Having sex will result in lower levels of religiosity.

4. Choosing a Research Design. Once researchers have formulated their hypotheses, they have to decide how they will collect the data that will provide a test of each hypothesis. The private and sensitive nature of sexual behavior ruled out observation and experimentation as appropriate research methods. Instead, Meier used a survey design in which people were asked questions to measure the concepts in the study. The survey data she used were collected by other researchers as part of a larger project, the National Longitudinal Study of Adolescent Health (Add Health). In this study, measurements were taken through interviews with 15,000 adolescents in 1995 and again in 1996. The longitudinal nature of the study allowed Meier to employ a quasi-experimental design, with some of the subjects being exposed to the "treatment" (first sex) between 1995 and 1996, and others not. Of course, this was not a true experiment; students were not randomly assigned to an experimental group in which having sex was the treatment condition.

5. Collecting the Data. For some researchers, collecting the data is a critical and time-consuming part of the research process. Because Meier's project was a **secondary data analysis**

(analysis of data collected by others), she did not have to worry about conducting this phase of the study herself. As part of the Add Health project, other researchers had already conducted in-home interviews with a sample of adolescents and included all the measures needed in Meier's study. Her subset of this larger sample included 15- to 18-year-old never-married adolescents, all of whom were virgins at the first interview and none of whom had experienced forced sex by the time of the second interview. Some of these adolescents had sex for the first time between the first and second waves of data collection, and others did not.

Respondents are not always honest in face-to-face interviews about private matters such as sexual behavior. For this reason, sexual behavior was measured using a computer-assisted self-interview, in which the respondents answered questions on a computer in a private setting.

6. Analyzing the Data. Once researchers have their data, they must analyze them to find answers to the questions posed by their research project. Analysis involves a search for meaningful links among the facts that have emerged in the course of the research. Meier chose methods of data analysis that would show two things: (1) whether attitudes and religiosity expressed in the first interview (i.e., in 1995) were correlated with having sex between the first interview and the second interview (in 1996), and (2) whether having sex between the first and second interviews was related to a change in religiosity and/or attitudes between the two interviews.

In the first analysis, Meier found that lower religiosity and more positive attitudes about having sex (as measured in the first interview) were both related to having sex between the two interviews. In the second analysis, she found that having sex between the two interviews did not result in lower religiosity in the second interview, but it did result in more positive attitudes about sex among females in the second interview. For males, who on average had more positive attitudes

about sex to begin with, having sex between the interviews did not significantly change their attitudes about sex.

7. Stating Conclusions. After completing their analysis of the data, researchers are ready to state their conclusions. They typically accept, reject, or modify their hypothesis and seek to extract broader meaning from their work by linking it to other knowledge and theory. Typically, findings also suggest questions for future research.

Meier's findings support two of her hypotheses—students who have more positive attitudes about having sex and those who are less religious are more likely to engage in sexual activity. A third hypothesis, that having sexual activity results in more positive attitudes about having sex, is supported only for females. And the findings indicate that we should reject the fourth hypothesis—having sex did not result in lower levels of religiosity. Religious students are apparently less likely to have sex, but students who have sex do not therefore become less religious.

These conclusions signal the end of this particular study, but not the end of the research process. Research is cyclical, and the conclusions of one study are often the starting point for additional studies. In this case, one might ask why initiation of sexual activity among females affects their attitudes about sex and whether there are factors, such as being in a close relationship with a partner, that affect the strength of this association. In addition, one might ask why initiation of sexual activity does not affect males' attitudes about sex. Answers to these questions may suggest additional questions, continuing the cycle of research.

In a broader context, Meier's study provides a method for other researchers to use when there is concern about the direction of causation. By looking at interviews with respondents conducted a year apart, she was able to determine the effects of religiosity and attitudes on first sex *and* the effects of first sex on religiosity and attitudes. Without two sets of data at two separate times, our knowledge about how attitudes and religiosity are related to sexual behavior would be incomplete.

Research Ethics

Though scientific research on human beings is potentially valuable and important, it also can be dangerous and harmful to the people who are studied. Anthropologists have been accused of conducting unethical research among the Yanomami Indians of Venezuela (Mann, 2009). In Guatemala in the 1940s, a U.S. Public Health Service researcher exposed more than 1,300 prisoners, mental health patients, and soldiers to sexually transmitted diseases and took blood and spinal fluid samples from more than 5,000 patients without their consent (Kaiser, 2011). These and other research scandals have caused sociologists to be increasingly sensitive and committed to ethical considerations in their research.

Yet sociologists confront a dilemma in conducting research. On the one hand, they must not distort or manipulate their findings to serve untruthful, personal, or institutional ends. On the other hand, they are obligated to consider people as ends and not means.

Because of the possible conflicts between these various responsibilities, the American Sociological Association (1989), the major professional organization for the discipline in the United States, has provided a code of ethics to govern the behavior of its members. Among these principles are the following:

- *Sociologists should not misuse their positions as professional social scientists for fraudulent purposes or as a pretext for gathering intelligence for any organization or government. Sociologists should not mislead respondents involved in a research project as to the purpose for which that research is being conducted.*

- *The process of conducting sociological research must not expose respondents to substantial risk of personal harm. Informed consent must be obtained when the risks of research are greater than the risks of everyday life. Where modest risk or harm is anticipated, informed consent must be obtained.*

- *Sociologists must not coerce or deceive students into serving as research subjects.*

- *No sociologists should discriminate in hiring, firing, promotions, salary, treatment, or any other conditions of employment or career development on the basis of sex, sexual preference, age, race, religion, national origin, handicap, or political orientation.*

In sum, because sociological knowledge can be a form of economic and political power, sociologists must exercise care to protect their discipline, the people they study and teach, and society from abuses that may stem from their professional work.

What Can Sociology Do for You?

If you are at the end of the first chapter of an introductory sociology textbook, you may be a sociology major, or you may be majoring in another subject and taking sociology as an elective. You may also be a beginning college student without a firm plan for your college career. In any case, now is a good time to think about how sociology might fit into your life.

What does a sociology major prepare you for? The American Sociological Association (ASA) wondered what sociology graduates were doing and sponsored a study to find out. Open the web page for the ASA, **http://www.asanet.org/.** Click on "Trends in Sociology" under "Research on Sociology" on the menu bar across the top of the home page. Then click on "Degrees," and you'll find data on the types of sociology degrees that have been awarded and the gender, race, and ethnicity of those earning sociology degrees. Under "Related Research," find the brief titled "What Are They Doing with a Bachelor's Degree in Sociology?" Read this research brief. How was the study conducted? What sorts of jobs do sociology majors get? Use Table 1 to make a list of the kinds of jobs students who graduate with a bachelor's degree in sociology have taken. Might any of the jobs be of interest to you?

If you enjoyed Chapter 1, you might like to take a course in sociological theory or perhaps a methods class that helps you learn to conduct sociological research yourself.

The Chapter in Brief: *Developing a Sociological Consciousness*

The Sociological Perspective

Sociology is the scientific study of social interaction and social organization.

■ **New Levels of Reality**   The sociological perspective encourages us to examine aspects of our social environment in ways that delve beneath the surface. As we look beyond the outer appearances of our social world, we encounter new levels of reality.

■ **The Sociological Imagination**   The essence of the **sociological imagination** is the ability to see our private experiences and personal difficulties as entwined with the structural arrangements of our society and the times in which we live.

■ **Microsociology and Macrosociology** **Microsociology** is the detailed study of what people say, do, and think moment by moment as they go about their daily lives. **Macrosociology** focuses upon large-scale and long-term social processes of organizations, institutions, and broad social patterns.

The Development of Sociology

■ **Auguste Comte: The Founder of Sociology**   Auguste Comte is commonly credited as being the founder of sociology. He emphasized that the study of society must be scientific, and he urged sociologists to employ systematic observation, experimentation, and comparative historical analysis as their methods. He divided the study of society into **social statics** and **social dynamics.**

■ **Harriet Martineau: Feminist and Methodologist**   Harriet Martineau wrote the first book on social research methods and was among the first to do systematic, scientifically based social research. Her comparative analysis of slavery and the position of women in the Western world paved the way for feminist scholarship and the further pursuit of gender equality.

■ **Herbert Spencer: Social Darwinism** Herbert Spencer depicted society as a system, a whole made up of interrelated parts. He also set forth an evolutionary theory of historical development. **Social Darwinism** is Spencer's application of evolutionary notions and the concept of survival of the fittest to the social world.

■ **Karl Marx: The Role of Class Conflict** Karl Marx focused his search for the basic principles of history on the economic environments in which societies develop. He believed that society is divided into those who own the means of producing wealth and those who do not, giving rise to **class conflict.** **Dialectical materialism** is Marx's theory that development depends on the clash of contradictions and the creation of new, more advanced structures out of these clashes.

■ **Émile Durkheim: Social Integration and Social Facts**   Émile Durkheim was especially concerned with social solidarity, distinguishing between mechanical and organic solidarity. He contended that the distinctive subject matter of sociology should be the study of **social facts.**

■ **Max Weber: Subjectivity and Social Organization**   Max Weber said that a critical aspect of the sociological enterprise is the study of the intentions, values, beliefs, and attitudes that underlie people's behavior. He used the word *Verstehen* in describing his approach and contributed his notions of the ideal type and a **value-free sociology.**

■ **American Sociology**   In the United States, sociology and the modern university system arose together. The first department of sociology was established at the University of Chicago in 1893, and Chicago served as a "social laboratory" at the beginning of the century. Midcentury sociologists crafted survey techniques and refined models of society. "New breed" sociologists in the 1960s and 1970s refined Marxism and established new research approaches and perspectives.

■ **Contemporary Sociology**   Contemporary movements in sociology include critical theory, feminism, and postmodern social theory.

Theoretical Perspectives

Contemporary sociologists acknowledge three general theoretical perspectives, or ways of looking at how various social phenomena are related to one another. These are the functionalist, the conflict, and the symbolic interactionist perspectives.

■ **The Functionalist Perspective**   The structural-functional—or, more simply, functionalist—perspective saw society as a system. Functionalists identified the structural characteristics and **functions** and **dysfunctions** of institutions, and distinguished between **manifest functions** and **latent functions.** Functionalists also typically assumed that most members of a society share a consensus regarding their core beliefs and values.

■ **The Conflict Perspective**   The conflict approach drew much of its inspiration from the work of Karl Marx and argued that the structure of society and the nature of social relationships are the result of past and ongoing conflicts. **Power** determines who will gain and who will lose.

■ **The Interactionist Perspective**   Symbolic interactionists contended that society is possible because human beings have the ability to communicate with one another by means of symbols. They said that we act toward people, objects, and events on the basis of the meanings we impart to them. Consequently, we experience the world as **constructed reality.**

■ **Using the Three Perspectives**   Each theoretical approach has its advantages and disadvantages, portraying a different aspect of reality and directing attention to a dimension of social life that the others neglect or overlook. Together, they serve as useful tools for describing and analyzing human social behavior.

Conducting Research

■ **The Logic of Science**   Sociology is a social science. Science assumes that every event or action results from an antecedent cause—that is, cause-and-effect relationships prevail in the universe. These causes and effects can be observed and measured, and sociologists look for **correlations** among **variables** as a way of doing so.

■ **Methods of Data Collection**   Four major techniques of data collection are available to sociologists: experiments, surveys, observation, and archival research. In the **experiment,** researchers work with an **experimental group** and a **control group** to test the effects of an **independent variable** on a **dependent variable.** Interviewing and questionnaires constitute the primary techniques used in **surveys,** using **random** or **stratified random samples.** Observation can take the form of **participant observation** or **unobtrusive observation.** Other techniques include **archival research** and feminist methodology.

■ **Steps in the Scientific Method: A Close-Up Look** The scientific method includes selecting a researchable problem, reviewing the literature, formulating a **hypothesis,** creating an **operational definition,** choosing a research design, collecting the data, analyzing results, and stating conclusions. In **secondary data analysis**, researchers use data collected by someone else.

■ **Research Ethics** It is important that sociologists observe the ethics of their discipline in carrying out research. They have an obligation not to expose their subjects to substantial risk or personal harm in the research process and to protect the rights and dignity of their subjects.

Glossary

archival research The use of existing records that have been produced or maintained by persons or organizations other than the researcher.

class conflict The view of Karl Marx that society is divided into those who own the means of producing wealth and those who do not, giving rise to struggles between classes.

constructed reality Our experience of the world. Meaning is not something that inheres in things; it is a property that derives from, or arises out of, the interaction that takes place among people in the course of their daily lives.

control group The group that affords a neutral standard against which the changes in an experimental group can be measured.

correlation A change in one variable associated with a change in another variable.

dependent variable The variable that is affected in an experimental setting.

dialectical materialism The notion in Marxist theory that development depends on the clash of contradictions and the creation of new, more advanced structures out of these clashes.

dysfunctions Observed consequences that lessen the adaptation or adjustment of a system.

economic determinist A believer in the doctrine that economic factors are the primary determinants of the structure of societies and social change.

experiment A technique in which researchers work with two groups that are identical in all relevant respects. They introduce a change in one group but not in the other group. The procedure permits researchers to test the effects of an independent variable on a dependent variable.

experimental group The group in which researchers introduce a change in an experimental setting.

functions Observed consequences that permit the adaptation or adjustment of a system.

hypothesis A proposition that can be tested to determine its validity.

independent variable The variable that causes an effect in an experimental setting.

latent functions Consequences that are neither intended nor recognized by the participants in a system.

macrosociology The study of large-scale and long-term social processes.

manifest functions Consequences that are intended and recognized by the participants in a system.

microsociology The detailed study of what individuals say, do, and think moment by moment as they go about their daily lives.

operational definition A definition developed by taking abstract concepts and putting them in a form that permits their measurement.

participant observation A technique in which researchers engage in activities with the people that they are observing.

power The ability to control the behavior of others, even against their will.

random sample A sampling procedure in which researchers select subjects on the basis of chance so that every individual in the population has the same opportunity to be chosen.

secondary data analysis Analysis of data collected by others.

social Darwinism The application of evolutionary notions and the concept of survival of the fittest to the social world.

social dynamics Those aspects of social life that pattern institutional development and have to do with social change.

social facts Those aspects of social life that cannot be explained in terms of the biological or mental characteristics of the individual. People experience the social fact as external to themselves in the sense that it has an independent reality and forms a part of their objective environment.

social statics Those aspects of social life that have to do with order and stability and that allow societies to hold together and endure.

sociological imagination The ability to see our private experiences and personal difficulties as entwined with the structural arrangements of our society and the historical times in which we live.

sociology The scientific study of social interaction and social organization.

spurious correlation The apparent relationship between two variables produced by a third variable that influences the original variables.

stratified random sample A sampling procedure in which researchers divide a population into relevant categories and draw a random sample from each of the categories.

survey A method for gathering data on people's beliefs, values, attitudes, perceptions, motivations, and feelings. The data can be derived from interviews or questionnaires.

unobtrusive observation A technique in which researchers observe the activities of people without intruding or participating in the activities.

value-free sociology The view of Max Weber that sociologists must not allow their personal biases to affect the conduct of their scientific research.

variable A concept that can take on different values; the term scientists apply to something they think influences (or is influenced by) something else.

Verstehen An approach to the study of social life developed by Max Weber in which sociologists mentally attempt to place themselves in the shoes of other people and identify what they think and how they feel; translates roughly as "understanding."

Review Questions

1. What is the sociological imagination?
2. Define microsociology and macrosociology.
3. Name four major figures from the history of sociology, and briefly describe their contributions to the field.
4. What are the three major sociological perspectives? Give a brief description of each.
5. How do sociologists collect data?
6. What is a settlement house? What part did settlement houses play in the development of sociology?
7. List and describe the steps of the scientific method.
8. What are some of the ethical issues involved in social science research?

 ## Internet Connection   www.mhhe.com/hughes11e

In a brief introductory textbook, our ability to cover everything of importance and interest is limited by space. In this "Internet Connection" feature, we will guide your use of the Internet in discovering more about specific topics in sociology.

The Internet is a powerful tool for sociologists. Many of the large data sets that sociologists use to answer various sociological research questions are available to the general public via the Internet. You also can find research papers, archival and current magazine and newspaper articles, encyclopedia entries, links to books, and much more.

Ibn Khaldun, born in the 1300s in North Africa, is widely considered the father of all the social sciences. His most famous work, "Muqaddimah," or "Introduction to History," includes many social and cultural analyses and insights. Since our history of sociology focused on European and American founders, we'd like this first Internet assignment to be for you to learn more about Ibn Khaldun. Type his name in the search field of your choice. How many sites come up? What kind of information is it? Read about Ibn Khaldun and look for parallels to what you have learned about sociology in this chapter.

CHAPTER 2

Culture and Social Structure

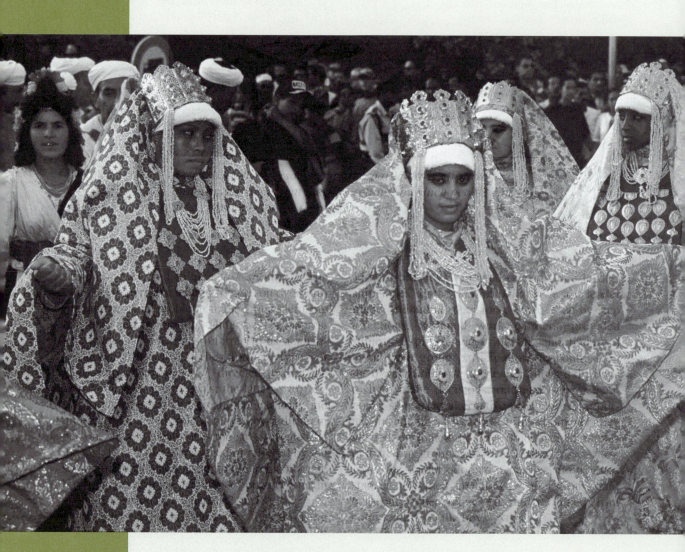

Components of Culture

Cultural Unity and Diversity

Social Structure

In 1789, mutineers led by Fletcher Christian seized control of the ship *Bounty* shortly after it had departed from Tahiti, an island in the South Pacific. They set William Bligh, the ship's captain, and 18 of his men adrift. The mutineers returned to Tahiti, where some of the men decided to remain. Nine men elected to seek another island and induced 6 Tahitian men and 12 Tahitian women to sail with them to Pitcairn Island.

The story of the mutiny on the *Bounty* and the subsequent settlement on Pitcairn Island is a perennial favorite. For sociologists, Pitcairn Island—where descendants of the first settlers still live today—offers a unique social experiment in the founding of a society and the fashioning of a new culture. Imagine the problems that confronted the English and Tahitian colonists when they arrived on this tiny, uninhabited South Pacific island. How would they find food? How would they protect themselves from the elements? How would they maintain order? How would they manage their sexual relationships, a matter of no small concern in a community of 15 men and 12 women? How would they provide for any children born on the island?

In finding solutions to their problems, the English and Tahitian colonists could not fall back on the sorts of genetic adaptations such as those that permit insects to live a group existence. They lacked the built-in behavioral responses and highly specialized appendages that would prepare them for a particular environmental niche. An ability to adapt is found not in humans' genetic heritage, but in culture and society, the topics of this chapter.

Culture refers to the social heritage of a people—those learned patterns for thinking, feeling, and acting that are transmitted from one generation to the next, including the embodiment of these patterns in material items. It includes both *nonmaterial culture*—abstract creations like values, beliefs, symbols, norms, customs, and institutional arrangements—and *material culture*—physical artifacts or objects like stone axes, computers, loincloths, tuxedos, automobiles, paintings, electric guitars, hairstyles, and domed stadiums. **Society** refers to a group of people who live within the same territory and share a common culture. Very simply, culture has to do with the customs of a people, and society has to do with the people who are practicing the customs. Culture provides the meanings that enable human beings to interpret their experiences and guide their actions, whereas society is constituted by the networks of social relations that arise among a people.

In fashioning a new society, the Pitcairn Islanders had the combined heritage of two cultures to draw on, and the cultural patterns they evolved were a blend of their different backgrounds. Because Pitcairn ecologically resembles Tahiti, their food patterns consisted principally of Tahitian items. However, their tools—metal hoes, spades, and mattocks—were of English origin. Because the women took responsibility for the preparation and cooking of food, the nonmaterial aspects of Tahitian culture came to dominate in household arrangements; as in Tahiti, the Pitcairn Islanders ate their meals in the late morning and in the early evening. And Pitcairnese language evolved as a stew of 18th-century English, Polynesian, and seafaring terms.

Serious conflicts over women in the early years were eventually overcome. An 1833 visitor, Captain Freemantle, found the residents to be "a well-disposed, well-behaved, kind, hospitable people." They had developed a culture that promoted deep attachments to their island and strong bonds of social unity. Social rules evolved to discourage close interpersonal relations, even romantic ones, out of concern that such relations weaken commitment to the group. A late-20th-century visitor to the island found a social order where the interests of individuals are second to the interests of the community. Culture and society on Pitcairn today continue to be affected significantly by its isolation from other cultures and societies (Birkett, 1997).

In this chapter we will discuss components of culture, consider cultural unity and diversity, and introduce a number of key concepts related to social structure.

Components of Culture

When some people hear the word *culture,* they think of the opera, the ballet, the art museum, or the symphony. But when social scientists use the term, they have in mind something more comprehensive and consequential (Gusfield, 2006). They mean something that provides individuals with a set of common understandings used to fashion behavior. Culture allows us to "know" in rather broad terms what we can expect of others and what they can expect of us.

Culture also provides a set of guideposts for finding our way through life, a complex of patterned mental stop-and-go signs that tell us about the social landscape: "Notice this," "Ignore that," "Avoid this action," and "Do that" (Kluckhohn, 1960:21). If we know a people's culture—their design for living—we can understand and predict a good deal of their behavior. For example, Pitcairn Islanders visiting other Pitcairn Islanders can expect meals in the late morning and early evening (Birkett, 1997); Pitcairn Islanders visiting the United States might be surprised to be served breakfast, lunch, and dinner.

Culture does not determine behavior. Indeed, as Ann Swidler (1986:277) has pointed out, "people know more culture than they use." Instead, Swidler argues (1986:273), culture is a kind of toolkit that includes "habits, skills, and styles from which people construct strategies of action." At the same time, because these common understandings are widely shared, they bind the separated lives of individuals into a larger whole, making society possible by providing a common framework of meaning. Only by sharing similar perspectives with one another—knowledge of the various cultural tools available—can we weave integrated webs of ongoing interaction. Let us examine more carefully some of the key components of culture that make these shared understandings possible: norms, values, and symbols and language.

Norms

To live with others in a group setting, we must share understandings that tell us which actions are permissible and which are not. For example, unless we have a prior understanding, we cannot take something from a neighbor's yard; the difference between borrowing and stealing is based on shared understandings. These understandings give our daily lives order and allow us to determine which behaviors we can legitimately insist others perform and which they can legitimately insist we perform. When we enter a clothing store, begin a college course, get married, or start a new job, we understand at least some of the expectations that will hold for us and others in these settings. Such expectations are norms. **Norms** are social rules that specify appropriate and inappropriate behavior in given situations. They tell us what we "should," "ought," and "must" do, as well as what we "should not," "ought not," and "must not" do. In all cultures the great body of these social rules deal with matters involving sex, property, and safety.

But norms are not just moral rules. They provide guidance so that we can align our actions with those of others when situations are unclear or ambiguous, and they provide standards by which we judge other people and make decisions about how we will interact with them. Faculty at your college or university provide an example. Inappropriate behaviors for classroom instructors include treating students negatively, failing to plan a course or failing to communicate class requirements to students, and grading

This child, who has been living in the context of one set of norms in the family, is about to confront another set of norms—those of the school.

exams or papers unfairly (Braxton and Bayer, 1999). A professor who makes occasional sarcastic remarks about students may be tolerated (but not appreciated) by students, while one who never hands out a course syllabus may be reported to the dean.

These efforts at social control involve not only individual interests but also group interests. Because you are a member of numerous groups, other people—your family members, friends, neighbors, and co-workers—may also benefit or suffer from your conduct. Group members may be held accountable for one another's actions, as in the case of employees in group incentive plans or military recruits in boot camp barracks. Such spillover effects give group members a stake in regulating one another's behavior. In the case of some groups (e.g., criminal and revolutionary organizations), a person's peers often have a stake in helping the violator avoid detection and punishment (Heckathorn, 1990).

Though norms are subjective human creations, we experience them as objective and independent features of our social environment (Reno, Cialdini, and Kallgren, 1993). People attach a good deal of importance to some norms, called **mores** (singular *mos*), and they mete out harsh punishment to violators. Other norms, called **folkways,** people deem to be of less importance, and they exact less stringent conformity to them (Sumner, 1906). Some norms are formalized and are enforced by special political organizations. These we refer to as **laws.** Folkways, mores, and laws are discussed below.

Folkways

Folkways have to do with the customary ways and ordinary conventions by which we carry out our daily activities. We bathe, brush our teeth, groom our hair, wear shoes or sandals, wave to friends, mow lawns, and sleep in beds. We view people who violate folkways, especially those who violate a good number of them, as somehow "different" and even "strange." Ordinarily, however, we do not attach moral significance to folkways. For example, we may regard people who wear soiled clothing as crude but not as sinful, and people who are late for appointments as thoughtless but not evil. Gossip and ridicule are important mechanisms for enforcing folkways.

Mores

Members of a culture or society are more concerned about violations of mores. Murder, theft, rape, treason, and child molestation bring strong disapproval and severe punishment in the United States. Mores are seen as vital to a society's well-being and survival. People usually attach moral significance to mores, and they define people who violate them as sinful and evil. Consequently, the punishment for violators of a society's mores is severe; they may be put to death, imprisoned, cast out, mutilated, or tortured.

Folkways and mores are distinguished from laws by the fact that they are usually enforced by people acting in a spontaneous and often collective manner. On contemporary Pitcairn Island, islanders are afraid that if they do or say something against someone, that person will get back at them later (Birkett, 1997). When one

Pitcairner cut down another's banana tree, he was greeted the next morning with 3-inch nails planted in the mud path outside his house. Social censure also is achieved through the ancient but formidable weapon of gossip. Sometimes rumors will reach the culprit very rapidly, and once accused, a person is as good as guilty in the eyes of many (Birkett, 1997).

Laws

Some norms are formalized into laws, rules that are enforced by a special political organization composed of individuals who have the right to use force (see Vago, 2012). As anthropologist E. A. Hoebel (1958:470–471) observed: "The essentials of legal coercion are general acceptance of the application of physical power, in threat or in fact, by a privileged party, for a legitimate cause, in a legitimate way, and at a legitimate time." Laws tend to be the result of conscious thought, deliberate planning, and formal declaration. They can be changed more readily than folkways and mores.

Values

Norms are rules for behavior; **values** are broad ideas regarding what is desirable, correct, and good that most members of a society share. Values are so general and abstract that they do not explicitly specify which behaviors are acceptable and which are not (Rohan, 2000; Hitlin and Piliavin, 2004). Instead, values provide us with criteria and conceptions by which we evaluate people, objects, and events as to their relative worth, merit, beauty, or morality. According to Robin Williams's classic study, the major value configurations within the dominant American culture include the assignment of high importance to achievement and success, work and activity, efficiency and practicality, material comfort, individuality, progress, rationality, patriotism, and democracy (Williams, 1970). Values tend to be the ultimate rationales for the choices people make in life.

At times different norms are based on the same values. For instance, two Americans may both place a premium on the same value—social equality. However, one may express this sentiment by supporting affirmative action programs and the other by opposing such legislation as "reverse discrimination," favoring instead "color-blind" civil rights laws. Values also can change over time (Rokeach and Ball-Rokeach, 1989). For example, in many societies around the world, values placing women in a subservient position to men are slowly giving way to egalitarian gender values. The increased presence of women in the workforce, greater educational opportunities for women, and declining fertility have all contributed to this change.

Symbols and Language

Norms and values are intangible aspects of social life, what sociologists term "nonmaterial culture." But if they lack a physical existence, how can we get a handle on them? How in the course of our daily lives can we talk to one another about rules and standards, mull them over in our minds, and appraise people's behavior in terms of them? The answer has to do with symbols. **Symbols** are acts or objects that have come to be socially accepted as standing for something else. They come to represent other things through the shared understandings people have. Consider the word "unfriend." Not many years ago, it had no meaning. Now this word—a symbol—stands for a specific action: taking someone off a networking page. A word becomes a vehicle of communication because a community of users (in this case, people on social networking sites) agree that the symbol and the meaning are linked. Symbols are a powerful code or shorthand for representing and dealing with aspects of the world about us (Hewitt and Shulman, 2011).

Symbols assume many different forms. Gestures are one example. Greeting and leave-taking gestures, for instance, are different in different cultures. Even the gestures used to communicate numbers are not universal. Malawians use their thumbs to indicate 1, four fingers paired to indicate 4, a fist to indicate 5, and two shakes of a fist to indicate 100, a system very different from that used by most Americans (Selin, 2002). Though gestures are easily understood within a society of persons who share their meaning, they are often the basis for misunderstandings between cultures.

Many of the ordinary features of our everyday lives have important symbolic content. Objects, events, and displays—such as flags, musical performances, paintings, religious icons, badges, ways of wearing hats, parades, and athletic contests—may function as expressive symbols, representing the beliefs of a society or group and implying certain values and norms (Peterson, 1979).

Probably the most important symbols of all are found in **language**—a socially structured system of sound patterns (words and sentences) with specific and arbitrary meanings. Language is the cornerstone of every culture; some 6,000 languages are spoken in the world (Forster and Renfrew, 2011). It is the chief vehicle by which people communicate ideas, information, attitudes, and emotions to one another, and it is the principal means by which human beings create culture and transmit it from generation to generation.

The Significance of Symbols

We can gain an appreciation for the part that symbols, particularly words, play in our daily lives by recalling the experiences of Helen Keller, who was stricken with a severe illness at the age of 21 months that left her deaf and blind. In her autobiography *The Story of My Life* (1904), Keller recounted that in her early years she remained imprisoned in her body, having only nebulous and uncertain links to the outside world. Later, she learned the American Sign Language for the deaf, and as she grasped the significance of symbols, particularly words, she acquired an intelligent understanding of her environment.

Is Culture Unique to Humans?

In 1960, Jane Goodall sent a message from Zaire to her mentor, anthropologist Louis Leakey, to let him know that she had observed chimpanzees making tools to "fish" for termites. He telegraphed back, "Now we must redefine *tool,* redefine *Man,* or accept chimpanzees as humans" (Goodall, 1990:19).

At that time scientists believed, and teachers taught, that one of the characteristics distinguishing humans from all other species was the ability to make and use tools. The sight of a chimpanzee trimming a wide blade of grass and using it to extract termites from a termite mound knocked toolmaking off the list of exclusively human behaviors, and since then many more examples of making and using tools have been found in chimpanzees and other species (McGrew, 2010).

Nearly 50 years later, culture may be suffering the same fate. What makes scientists think animals have culture? Researcher Christophe Boesch claims there are three components of culture common to humans and chimpanzees: Culture is learned from group members; culture is a distinctive collective practice; and culture is based on shared meanings between members of the same group (Boesch, 2003:83).

Chimpanzees' tool use and their complex grooming and courtship

Chimpanzee tool-using behaviors appear to be specific to specific groups of chimpanzees, learned from individuals, and passed down to the next generation.

The association between a word and an experience allowed her to use the symbol in the absence of the experience. By virtue of symbolic expression, "reality" becomes internally coded in a condensed and more easily manipulated mental form. Helen Keller was reluctant to apply the term "idea" or "thought" to her mental processes before she learned how to employ words. Of equal significance, she could share her experiences with other people, and they could share their experiences with her. The ability to use symbols, especially language, was the ticket that admitted Helen Keller to social life and hence to full humanness. With language she was able to enter the world of shared understandings provided by culture.

Human beings live their lives primarily within symbolic environments. Other organisms communicate in a variety of generally programmed ways, including the use of gestures, touch, chemical signals, and sounds, but humans stand apart from other species in their use of language. Although great apes can learn sign language, their facility with it is not equivalent to human language use. In fact, the average human fairly effortlessly learns 60,000 words by the time he or she graduates from high school, whereas chimpanzees, given persistent training, can learn only several hundred hand signs (Hauser, Chomsky, and Fitch, 2002). Research on culture in orangutans has shown that, while humans and orangutans share some elements of behaviors are specific to specific groups of chimpanzees, and they seem to be learned from individuals and passed down to the next generation. In one of the groups he studied, Boesch observed young chimpanzees learning to crack nuts using hammers (rocks or branches) and anvils (surface roots) (Boesch, 2003). He found that mother chimps stimulate their offspring's attempts by leaving the supplies needed for nut cracking behind while they search for more nuts. They also help their offspring solve technical problems and facilitate their offspring's attempts by providing better hammers and intact nuts.

What about the "shared meanings" component of culture? Some chimpanzees engage in a behavior called "leaf clipping," in which they bite a leaf into pieces without eating any of it. Leaf clipping, it turns out, has a specific meaning—and the meaning is different in different groups of chimps (Boesch, 2003:86):

All males in the Tai forest regularly leaf-clip before drumming. Among Bossou chimpanzees, leaf clipping is performed in the context of playing, as a means to enlist a playmate, while Mahale chimpanzees leaf-clip as a way to court estrous females. Tai chimpanzees have never been observed to leaf-clip in the context of playing nor in courtship. Similarly, Mahale chimpanzees have never been seen to leaf-clip in the context of playing nor when drumming.

Primate researchers are careful to define exactly what they mean by *culture*. Recent work with orangutans specified that a behavioral variant be considered cultural only if "it is customary (shown by most or all relevant individuals) or habitual (shown by at least several relevant individuals) in at least one site but is absent in at least one other ecologically similar site" (van Schaik et al., 2003:102). The researchers found many such behaviors and concluded that great ape cultures probably have existed for at least 14 million years.

Studies of primate culture indicate that it is much more complex than the cultures of other species.

Likewise, primatologists agree that human cultures are much more complex than those of primates. The use of symbols—language—plays a major role in making human culture more complex, as it introduces a new method for the social transmission of traditions (Boesch, 2003).

Culture has been studied by sociologists and anthropologists for years; now it is of interest to animal behaviorists and evolutionary biologists as well (Perry and Manson, 2003; Krützen et al., 2005; Stiffler, 2011). How genes and culture coevolved, and to what extent our common ancestors had culture, will be topics of research for years to come (Cohen, 2007).

Questions for Discussion

1. What do chimpanzee and orangutan cultures have in common with human culture? Give examples of specific behaviors.

2. Find the article on orca culture by Lisa Stiffler cited above. How do findings about orcas differ from those about chimpanzees?

culture, only human cultures have "unambiguously symbolic elements" (van Schaik et al., 2003). Box 2.1 describes some of the findings on culture in non-human species.

The Linguistic Relativity Hypothesis

The languages found among the world's people are quite diverse. Arabs have some 6,000 words that are connected in some way with the camel, involving camels' colors, camels' breeds, camels for different purposes, states of camel pregnancy, and camel behavior. Inuits and Eskimos make minute distinctions among different kinds of snow. And Americans have a vast number of words pertaining to automobiles and accessories.

According to the *linguistic relativity hypothesis* (also known as the *Whorfian hypothesis*), proposed by Edward Sapir (1949) and his student Benjamin L. Whorf (1956), people conceptualize the world differently depending on the nature of the concepts available in their language. Language serves as a screen, admitting some things while filtering out others. For example, people living in the Florida Keys, with only a single word for snow, actually fail to distinguish the many types of snow identified by the many Inuit words. Experience as it is perceived through one set of linguistically patterned sensory screens is quite different from experience perceived through another set (Hall, 1966).

The linguistic relativity hypothesis has been somewhat controversial in social science, and some of its major claims have been challenged (Martin, 1983). Most sociologists would not agree that language determines thought. Regardless of their culture, people can make the same distinctions made by Arabs with regard to camels, Inuits with regard to snow, and Americans with regard to automobiles. Clearly, however, language has a powerful influence on thought by helping or hindering certain kinds of thought (Bickerton, 1995). For example, the use of terms such as "broad," "babe," and "chick" to refer to women can promote stereotypical thinking.

Expressive Symbolism and the Production of Culture

Expressive symbolism is an important vehicle for communicating the norms, values, and beliefs of a society. Both elite culture and popular culture, including art, music, and literature, are carriers of expressive symbolism. So are public events, displays, fashion, advertisements, and the public presentations produced by the mass media, religion, sports, science, and other institutions. As sociologist Richard Peterson (1979) pointed out, expressive symbolism is intimately connected to society in several important ways.

First, expressive symbolism is a reflection of society. We can understand much about how a society is organized by examining its culture. For example, patterns of change in country music lyrics from the 1930s to the 1990s—from expressing the problems of the rural lower class to bewailing the angst of the suburban middle class—mirrored the change in the situation of southerners in the United States (McLaurin, 1992).

Second, expressive symbolism carries a code that enables people to re-create society from one day—and from one generation—to the next. Through experiencing the expressive symbolism of television, literature, popular and classical music, fashion, parades, religious services, demonstrations, and so on, people internalize values, norms, and beliefs. By choosing to consume certain cultural products and not others, people publicly signal their social status (Peterson, 2002; Bryson, 1996). In addition, as some critical and feminist theorists argue, expressive symbolism can be designed to enhance the power positions of certain groups and categories of people at the expense of others. This can be seen in the advertising, films, music videos, and pornographic materials that encourage the sexual exploitation of women.

Finally, the form and content of culture is heavily affected by economic, organizational, legal, and technological factors involved with its production; in short, social structure affects culture (Peterson and Anand, 2004). Prior to 1940, for example, very little in American popular music was a direct reflection of either African American culture or the culture of rural southerners. The breaking of a monopoly in music licensing resulted in a major explosion in jazz, rhythm and blues, and what we now know as country music (Ryan, 1985). American culture had not changed so much as there had been a change in the constraints affecting what kinds of culture were produced for mass sale (Peterson, 1982). In the past, video culture was largely confined to television. Today people use a variety of digital and interactive technologies—what sociologists refer to as *media streams* (movies, Internet news, iPods, Internet streaming, YouTube, video and Internet games, online networking, and more)—to create culture and make sense of their worlds (Grindstaff and Turow, 2006; Lessig, 2008).

Cultural Unity and Diversity

The great merit of culture is that it permits us to circumvent the slow pace of genetic evolution. Behavior patterns that are wired into organisms by their genes do not allow rapid adaptation to changing conditions. In contrast, cultural change can be rapid. Early human cultural evolution probably affected the evolution of the human brain, creating a greater capacity in humans for culture, leading to more cultural evolution, and so on. Indeed, some scientists contend that cultural evolution is a far more important source of behavioral change for human beings than is biological evolution (Lewontin, Rose, and Kamin, 1984; Wilson, 1988). When cultures change and evolve, cultural unity and cultural diversity are affected, a matter to which we now turn our attention. In this section we will define and discuss cultural universals, cultural integration, ethnocentrism, cultural relativism, and subcultures and countercultures.

Cultural Universals

Although culture provides guideposts for daily living—a blueprint or map for life's activities—these guideposts often differ from one society to another. The "oughts" and "musts" of some societies are the "ought nots" and "must nots" of other societies; the "good" and "desirable" among this people are the "bad" and "undesirable" among that people. Should this fact of cultural variation lead to the conclusion that cultures are different in all respects and hence not comparable? Or, to put the question another way, can we realistically speak of **cultural universals,** the patterned and recurrent aspects of life that appear in all known societies?

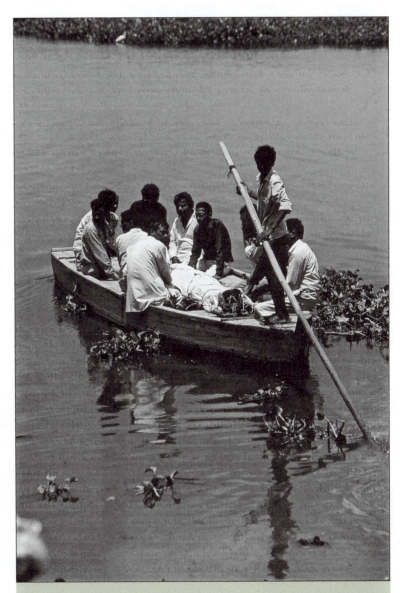

How does this funeral scene differ from a typical funeral in the United States? The funeral rite is a cultural universal, but its specific form is dictated by the culture in which it occurs.

There are indeed such common denominators or cultural constants, because all people confront many of the same problems. They must secure a livelihood, socialize children, handle grief, and deal with deviants. Culture represents an accumulation of solutions to the problems posed by human biology and the generalities of the human situation.

George Peter Murdock and his associates at Yale University (1950) developed a classification of cultural components that has universal application. They listed some 88 general categories of behavior that are found among all cultures, including food quest, clothing, settlements, property, travel and transport, fine arts, social stratification, kinship, political behavior, death, religious practices, and infancy and childhood. However, these universal components do not include the specific details of actual behavior. The universals relate to broad, overall categories and not to the content of culture, the specific "cultural toolkits" made available in different cultural systems. For example, although marriage is found in all cultures, some societies favor monogamy (one spouse), others polyandry (plural husbands), and still others polygyny (plural wives).

Cultural Integration

The items that form a culture tend to constitute a consistent and integrated whole. Though human equality and dignity were important values in American culture from the beginning, for the first 86 years of U.S. history, slavery was a legal institution, and for another 100 years, there were no effective legal guarantees of civil rights for African Americans. Thus the value—human equality—was inconsistent with the common belief that African Americans need not be accorded the same rights as whites. This was, as Gunnar Myrdal (1944) pointed out in the title of his landmark study *An American Dilemma,* a contradiction in American culture. The strain of this contradiction was, and is, pushing American society toward a resolution, one that took the form of Supreme Court decisions and civil rights laws in the 1950s and 1960s and continues today in debates about racial equality and affirmative action.

This strain toward consistency means that there are powerful forces linking the various elements of culture. The parts of a culture comprise a closely interwoven fabric, so that the meaning of one part depends on its connections to other parts. However, if we think of culture as a toolkit, and assume that people assemble strategies of action by combining different elements in different situations and different times, we can expect that perfect integration of culture will never be achieved.

Ethnocentrism

Once we acquire the cultural ways peculiar to our own society, they become so deeply ingrained that they seem second nature to us. Additionally, we have difficulty conceiving of alternative ways of life. Just as a fish never "notices" water unless it is out of it, so we tend not to notice our own culture until we are in someone else's. We judge the behavior of other groups by the standards of our own culture, a phenomenon sociologists call **ethnocentrism.** Sumner (1906:13) described this point of view as one "in which one's own group is the center of everything, and all others are scaled and rated with reference to it." Thus, in 1495, when French soldiers fighting in Italy were afflicted with what we today know as syphilis, they called it the Italian disease. As they spread it across Europe, new victims called it the French disease. When it traveled yet farther, Arabs called it the Christian disease (Zimmer, 2008). In fact, its true origin was the New World (Harper et al., 2008).

All groups are ethnocentric: families, tribes, nations, cliques, colleges, fraternities, businesses, churches, and political parties. The notion that one belongs to the "best people" can be functional for groups because it provides a

Is Today Tuesday? That Depends on Culture

Tuesday is Tuesday is Tuesday, right? Or, in some countries, Mardi, or Dienstag, or Martes? Actually, no. In some parts of our world, Tuesday is not Tuesday. In fact, in some parts of our world, people do not use a seven-day week, or a 12-month year, or anything even close to our naming system for markers of time.

As mathematician Marcia Ascher explains in her book *Mathematics Elsewhere,* "[Calendars] are cultural products often involving religion and/or politics combined with observations of the physical universe" (Ascher, 2002:39). Calendars are very diverse, primarily because "one of the main functions [of calendars] is to set the schedule of the culture and, thereby, coordinate the activities of individuals in the culture" (Ascher, 2002:39). Cultural differences, then, are linked to diversity in ways of marking time. Let's look at just one example.

In the Trobriand Islands, where agriculture is a major focus of people's lives, the calendar is based on lunar cycles. The important days, when the moon provides enough light for outdoor activities to take place at night, have specific names, while the days with dark nights are unnamed. Each lunar cycle has 29 or 30 days, and each Trobriand year has 12 or 13 months, but the names and number of months vary within a year—and even in different locations within the Trobriands. How can that be? The Trobriands have four different districts, in each of which a different major crop is grown, and each crop has its own particular harvest time. Ascher explains how this affects the Trobriand calendar (2002:43):

The month of Kuluwasasa . . . is *always* the harvest time, and so it occurs first on the outlying island of Kitava, next on the southern end of the main island of Kiriwina, then on the northern end of Kiriwina, and finally on the island of Vakuta.

In other words, wherever and whenever a major crop is being harvested, it is Kuluwasasa.

Because the people of the Trobriands are farmers, the sun-related seasons are extremely important. During the earth's trip around the sun, there are 12.368 lunar cycles, meaning that the number of lunar cycles in a year has to shift from 12 to 13 every few years to resynchronize the calendar. Rather than rely on record keeping, mathematical calculations, or astronomical knowledge, Ascher explains, the Trobrianders use the internal clock of a marine worm. This worm spawns only once a year, at the time of the full moon. If the worm does not appear in the sea at the expected time in the Trobriand calendar, they repeat the month they are in to recalibrate the calendar, and that Trobriand year will have 13 months.

The Trobriand Islanders' calendar system highlights the importance of the principle of *cultural relativism:* From a sociological point of view, we should evaluate a cultural trait from the perspective of the culture in which it occurs. With regard to organizing time, we should consider two points. First, the way calendars are constructed allows people to function efficiently in their own societies. We would be lost if we had to get to a job interview during the "unripe moon" in the

month of Milamala, which would occur at different times on different islands. Similarly, a Trobriand Islander would find it meaningless to be instructed to begin planting on the first Tuesday of October. Second, the methods for constructing calendars are linked to other elements of culture, an example of *cultural integration.* In the Trobriand Islands, getting soil prepared, seeds planted, fencing constructed, and harvesting done are key to the calendar, as are religious rites and festivals that must be accounted for in the organization of time.

Ascher found that in some cultures calendars focus on organizing ritual and agricultural activities, such as that used in the Trobriands, while others are more concerned with "structuring the flow of historical events" (2002:52) or with incorporating environmental, social structure, or psychological components. Each focus is connected with specific elements of culture.

Because of our *ethnocentrism,* much of what we do every day we assume to be universal human activity. In fact, most of what we do each day is culturally determined—including how we think about what day, what month, and what time of the year it is.

Questions for Discussion

1. How does the culture of the Trobiand Islanders affect their way of creating a calendar?

2. What is another example of a calendar system that is not the same as that used by the majority of people in the United States? With what culture is it associated?

kind of social glue cementing people together. But it can also be dysfunctional when it generates intergroup conflict. Combined with competition for scarce resources and a power imbalance between groups, ethnocentrism is particularly destructive (Noel, 1968). It plays a part in group conflicts ranging from small skirmishes to world wars (see, e.g., Lim, Metzler, and Bar-Yam, 2007).

Cultural Relativism

Ethnocentrism can get in the way of the scientific study of culture. We cannot grasp the behavior of other peoples if we interpret it in the context of our values, beliefs, and motives. Rather, we must examine their behavior in the light of their values, beliefs, and motives. This approach, termed **cultural relativism,** views the behavior of a people from the perspective of their own culture. In Box 2.2 we see how the calendar systems of various cultures can be understood only in the context of each culture. In sharp contrast to ethnocentrism, cultural relativism employs the kind of value-free or neutral approach advocated by Max Weber (see Chapter 1, p. 13).

A perspective characterized by cultural relativism asks not whether a particular trait is moral or immoral, but what part it plays in the life of a people. For example, early anthropological research found that among some Inuit peoples, the elderly were left behind to perish in the cold. Instead of simply condemning the practice, social scientists examined the behavior in the context of Inuit culture, where it was defined as a humane measure (Murdock, 1934). The Inuits believed that individuals experience in the next world a standard of health similar to that which they enjoyed in the period preceding death. Consequently, the Inuits saw the practice as minimizing the disabilities and infirmities their loved ones would encounter in the hereafter. Social scientists have pointed out that the practice can be adaptive for a people

whose subsistence is precarious and who must strictly limit their dependent population. For Americans who are appalled at this traditional Inuit custom, it is worth noting that many Japanese find quite abhorrent our practice of placing the elderly in nursing homes rather than caring for them at home.

Subcultures and Countercultures

Cultural diversity may also be found within a society. In many modern nations, the members of some groups participate in the main culture of the society while simultaneously sharing with one another a number of unique values, norms, traditions, and lifestyles. These distinctive cultural patterns are termed a **subculture.** Subcultures abound in American life and find expression in various religious, racial, ethnic, occupational, and age groups.

The Old Order Amish are a case in point. The Amish are a religious sect that originated in Germany and Switzerland during the 16th-century conflicts of the Reformation. Because of religious persecution, many Amish migrated to Pennsylvania in the early 1700s. Most Amish families live on farms, although some work in skilled crafts like carpentry, furniture making, and blacksmithing. They believe in a literal interpretation of the Bible and turn their backs on modern standards of dress, "progressive" morality, "worldly" amusement, automobiles, and higher education. Above all, the Amish value hard physical work and believe that those who do not find joy in work are somehow abnormal. Far from being ashamed of their nonconformity to "worldly standards," the Amish pride themselves on being a "peculiar people" who separate themselves from the world (Hostetler, 1980).

Youth culture is another example of a subculture. Western nations have postponed the entrance of their adolescents into adulthood for economic and educational reasons, segregating them in schools and colleges and effectively

Through clever use of media, advertisers draw upon youth subcultural processes, including identity formation, in order to sell products. This affects youth behavior, but it also affects the content of youth subculture itself.

relieving them from competing with adults for wealth, power, and status in society's mainstream until they are 21 or older. This has created conditions favorable to the development of a unique culture among youths. Instead of competing with adults along the value dimensions of mainstream culture, adolescents compete with each other along dimensions of youth culture.

Youth culture patterns find expression in fads having to do with popular music, entertainment idols, dance steps, personal adornment and hairstyles, and distinctive jargons. Such patterns change over time, keeping youths always distinctive from generations that have come before. In the early 2000s, FBI agents posing online as teenage girls to catch pedophiles discovered that to be effective, they needed knowledge of youth culture. Pedophiles question chatters about trends and pop culture to determine whether they're talking to a teenage girl or a law enforcement officer. For help, the agency turned to eighth-grade girls, three of whom taught a series of classes for the FBI. The classes included tips on instant messaging, celebrity gossip, clothing trends, and popular magazines. Among the lessons: "Never begin a chat with 'hello'; never use proper grammar in instant messages; and 'pos' stands for 'parent over shoulder'" (Ly, 2003). Distinctive language patterns exist in many subcultures. Table 2.1 provides an example of some of the different patterns of slang used in activity subcultures.

Large organizations and corporations such as Microsoft, General Motors, and Exxon also have distinctive subcultures that make working in one organization a very different experience from working in another, even when both are involved in the same activities. If you have transferred from one university to another, you have probably experienced this; the subculture of one college is not the same as that of another. Working at Apple is not the same as working at IBM.

At times the norms, values, and lifestyles of a subculture are substantially at odds with those of the larger society and constitute a **counterculture.** A counterculture rejects many of the behavioral standards and guideposts that hold in the dominant culture.

Table 2.1	"I Really Ate It!" Subcultural Behavior: A Sampler of Slang

The following terms have specific meanings for skateboarders:

Gap: A space or area jumped over on a skateboard; also a verb (to perform the jump)

Hubba: The ledge bordering a stair

Mongo: Kicking/pushing with front foot; only acceptable if skating switch

Ollie: A particular skateboarding jump; also a verb (to perform an ollie)

Razortail: The tail end of a skateboard, sharpened by repeated use as a braking system

Sketchy: Landing a trick wobbly or off balance

Stall: A momentary pause at the top of a halfpipe or vertical ramp with some part of the skateboard above the lip of the pipe; also a verb

Stease: Style with ease

Stomped: Landed a trick really well; this is also called "solid"

Switch: Riding on a skateboard opposite to the way one normally rides; a skater who usually rides left foot forward is "riding switch" when he or she rides right foot forward

Source: Skateboarders Edmund Hughes and Michael J. Kokes.

In many societies, countercultures involve primarily adolescents and young adults (Spates, 1983). In the late 1960s and early 1970s, the dominant youth subculture in the United States included the hippie movement and the anti–Vietnam War movement. It was a counterculture that emphasized political beliefs, sexual standards, and attitudes about drug use that challenged mainstream U.S. culture. In recent years the Internet and cell phones have helped to facilitate countercultural activity. The importance of the role they play was highlighted in 2011 when the Egyptian government blocked both cell phone service and access to the Internet in an attempt to disable antigovernment protesters (Richtel, 2011).

Social Structure

Earlier in the chapter, we noted that culture has to do with the customs of a people, and society with the people who are practicing the customs. Culture supplies the framework that allows people to interpret events and guide their actions; society consists of the actual web of relationships that people enter into as they go about their daily activities. For the most part, people do not interact in a haphazard or random manner. Rather, their relationships are characterized by social ordering. Sociologists apply the term **social structure** to this social ordering—the interweaving of people's interactions and relationships in more or less recurrent and stable patterns. It finds expression in a matrix of social positions and the distribution of people in them.

Social structure provides an organized and focused quality to our group experiences, and it allows us to achieve our collective purposes. By virtue of social structure, we link certain experiences, terming them, for example, "the family," "the church," "the neighborhood," and "General Motors." A clique, a family, a rock band, an army, a business organization, a religious group, and a nation are all social structures. Social structure consists of the recurrent and orderly relationships that prevail among the members of a group or society. It gives us the feeling that life is characterized by organization and stability.

Consider the social structure of your college. Each term you enter new classes, yet you have little difficulty attuning yourself to unfamiliar classmates and professors. Courses in sociology, calculus, American history, English composition, and physical education are offered year after year. A new class enters college each fall, and another class graduates each spring. New students, professors, coaches, players, and deans pass through the system and in due course make their exits, but the college endures.

Sociologists view social structure as a social fact of the sort described by Émile Durkheim (see Chapter 1, p. 12). We experience a social fact as external to ourselves—as an independent reality that forms a part of our objective environment. Consequently, social structures constrain our behavior and channel our actions in certain directions. When you entered college for the first time, you felt somewhat awkward because you did not yet fit into your college's way of doing things. The college's way is a social structure, the shape or form that a particular organization has taken through the years as students, professors, and administrators have interacted on a regular basis.

As sociologist William H. Sewell, Jr. (1992:27), observed, "Structure is dynamic, not static; it is the continually evolving outcome and matrix of a process of social interaction." Thus, a college is not a fixed entity that, once created, continues to operate perpetually in the same manner. All social ordering must be continually created and re-created through the interweaving and stabilizing of social relationships. For this reason, organized social life is always undergoing modification and change. In the next sections we will discuss the concepts that help us to understand social structure and to describe our social environment: statuses, roles, groups, institutions, and societies.

Statuses

In our daily conversations, we use the word *status* to refer to a person's ranking as determined by wealth, influence, and prestige. However, sociologists employ status somewhat differently: **Status** means a position within a group or society. By means of statuses, we locate one another in various social structures. Mother, mayor, management trainer, friend, supervisor, female, elementary school principal, child, Cuban American, shopper, professor, convict, and fortune teller are all statuses.

As Theodore Newcomb observed in his classic social psychology textbook (1950), a status is like a ready-made suit of clothes. Within certain limits, the prospective buyer can choose regarding matters of style and fabric. Our choice is limited to a size that will fit, as well as by our pocketbooks. Having made our choice within these limits, we can have certain alterations made. But apart from minor modifications, we tend to be limited to what retailers already have on their racks. Statuses, too, come ready-made, and the range of choice among them is limited. Societies commonly limit competition for statuses with reference to gender, age, and social affiliations. For instance, realistically, not every American can be elected president. Until 2008, only white males had served as U.S. presidents; racial, ethnic, and religious minorities, members of the lower class, and women suffer severe handicaps in reaching the presidency. This observation brings us to a consideration of ascribed and achieved statuses.

Ascribed and Achieved Statuses

Some statuses are assigned to us by our group or society and termed **ascribed statuses.** Age and gender are common ascribed statuses. For example, age is assigned to us according to the passage of time. Besides staying alive, there is nothing one can do to change one's age. Race, ethnicity, and family background are also common bases for assigning statuses to individuals.

We secure other statuses on the basis of individual choice and competition. We call these **achieved statuses.** All societies recognize some kinds of individual accomplishment and failure, which results in the allocation of some statuses on the basis of individual achievement. Quarterback, choir director, physician, ballet dancer, college student, pastor, nurse practitioner, pickpocket, prostitute, president of Exxon, hair stylist, and teacher are illustrations of achieved statuses.

Master Statuses

Some of our statuses overshadow our other statuses both in our own minds and in those of other people. A **master status** is a key or core status that carries primary weight in a person's interactions and relationships with others. For children, age is a master status; similarly, gender is a master status in most societies, and race and occupation are particularly critical statuses in American life. As shown in Adler and Adler's (1989) study of college basketball players, celebrity status is a powerful master status. Aided by media attention and fan reactions, status as a college athlete becomes a master status through a process of "self-glorification." As such, it limits athletes' lines of action and future orientations by subordinating other statuses, such as student, to a position of secondary importance in their lives.

Race, Class, and Gender

For many sociologists, categories of race, class, and gender are more than master statuses; they are basic categories for social analysis (Andersen and Collins, 2007; Richardson, Taylor, and Whittier, 1997). From this perspective, race, class, and gender are forms of inequality that profoundly affect human experience and operate as interlocking systems of privilege and oppression (Collins, 2000; Browne and Misra, 2003). One's gender combines with one's class position and one's race to produce a life experience that is substantively different from the life experienced at a different combination of these statuses.

Gender inequality may disadvantage women, but the experience of this depends on whether one is, for example, Asian, black, or white; and wealthy, middle class, or poor (e.g., Beisel and Kay, 2004).

Roles

A status carries with it a set of culturally defined rights and duties, what sociologists term a **role.** These expectations define the behavior people view as appropriate and inappropriate for the occupant of a status. Quite simply, the difference between a status and a role is that we occupy a status and play a role.

Sociologists have taken the notion of role from the theater. Actors perform their roles in accordance with a script (analogous to culture), the words and actions of other actors, and the reactions of the audience. But the theater analogy has its weaknesses. Unlike actors, we are seldom conscious of "acting" according to a script as we go about our daily activities. And in life we must do a good deal of improvising, continually testing and changing our actions in accordance with the behavior of other people.

Roles allow us to formulate our behavior mentally so that we can shape our actions in appropriate ways. They permit us to assume that in some respects we can ignore personal differences and say that people are interchangeable. For example, every American knows the difference between a physician and a carpenter. Hospitalized for emergency surgery, we probably won't ask many questions about who is handling the emergency, as long as it is a physician and not a carpenter.

Role Performance

In real life a gap often exists between what people should do and what they actually do. A role is the *expected* behavior we associate with a status. **Role performance** is the *actual* behavior of the person who occupies a status. People vary in how they implement the rights and duties associated with their roles. You frequently take differences in role performance into account when you select one professor over another for a given course. One professor may have a reputation for coming late to class, lecturing in an informal manner, and assigning difficult term papers. Another professor may be a distinguished authority in the field, monitor class attendance, and assign take-home examinations. Regardless of which professor you select, you will still occupy the status of student and play its associated role. However, you will have to modify your behavior somewhat depending upon your selection.

Role Set

A single status may have multiple roles attached to it, constituting a **role set.** The status of student may involve one role as pupil, one role as peer of other students, one role as loyal supporter of your school's teams, one role as user of the library, and one role as "good citizen" of the college community.

A role does not exist in isolation. Instead, it is a bundle of activities that are meshed with the activities of other people. Indeed, the definition of one role depends upon the existence of another: There can be no professors without students, no wives without husbands, no police officers without criminals, and no psychiatrists without the mentally ill. Every role has at least one reciprocal role attached to it.

Role relationships tie us to one another because the rights of one end of the relationship are the duties of the other. **Duties** are the actions others can legitimately insist that we perform, and **rights** are the actions we can legitimately insist that others perform (Goffman, 1961a). The rights of one role are the duties of the other role. For example, your rights as a student—to receive authoritative material in lectures, to be administered fair

exams, and to be graded objectively—are the duties of your professor.

Individuals are linked together in groups through networks of reciprocal roles. Groups consist of intricate complexes of interlocking roles, which their members sustain in the course of interacting with one another. People experience these stable relationships as social structure—a school, a hospital, a family, a gang, an army, and so on.

Role Conflict

Role conflict results when individuals are confronted with conflicting expectations stemming from their simultaneous occupancy of two or more statuses. A football coach whose son is a member of the team may experience role conflict when deciding whether to make his own son or another, more talented player the starting quarterback. One way to handle role conflict is to subdivide or compartmentalize one's life and assume only one of the incompatible roles at a time. For example, college students may attempt to segregate their school and home experiences so they do not have to appear before their families and peers simultaneously.

Role Strain

Role strain occurs when individuals find the expectations of a single role incompatible, so that they have difficulty performing the role. The relationship physicians have with their patients provides an example (Klass, 1987). Doctors are expected to be gentle healers, humanitarians, and self-sacrificing saviors of the sick. They also are expected to be small-business retailers of knowledge that they have obtained at considerable cost and sacrifice. While aggressive bill collecting is consistent with the small-business-retailer aspects of the role, it is inconsistent with that of the gentle healer. Supervisors often confront similar difficulties. They are asked to be both commanding parent figures and reassuring, comforting big brothers or sisters. For the most part there are few well-defined or accepted answers to the dilemmas posed by these contradictory expectations.

Role Exit

Role exit is another dynamic process that sometimes leads to stressful outcomes. Role exit occurs when people stop playing roles that have been central to their lives and to their social identities (Ebaugh, 1988). When people exit roles, they also exit the statuses connected to those roles. As a result, the nature of people's patterned social relationships, the way they are viewed and treated by other people, and the way they think about themselves change (see Stepp, 2006). This may be a welcome change, as when someone is released from prison, or it may be unwelcome, as when a romantic partner breaks off a valued relationship. People also may experience ambivalence about role exits, as when one graduates from college and is no longer a student: Old relationships and an old identity are lost, but new opportunities and identities open up. Specific outcomes of role exit vary depending on the centrality, voluntariness, degree of control, and institutionalization of former roles. For example, one of the new identities that a person who exits a role takes on may be that of one who has exited a particular role, such as ex-mental patient, ex-husband, ex-nun, or ex-drug abuser. In some circumstances these new identities may be the source of social difficulties and stress, while in other situations they may be the foundation of a new life and may lead a person

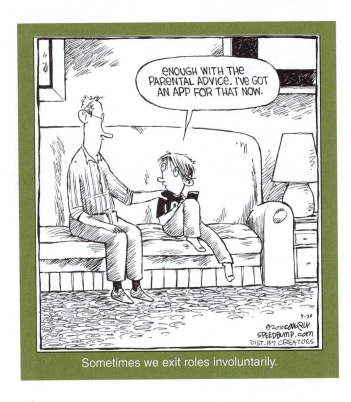

Sometimes we exit roles involuntarily.

to important new social connections and to support from similar others.

Groups

Statuses and roles are building blocks for more comprehensive social structures, such as groups. Sociologists define a **group** as two or more people who are bound together in relatively stable patterns of social interaction and who share a feeling of unity.

As previously pointed out, roles link us within social relationships. When these relationships are sustained across time, four things can happen: First, we come to think of the relationships as encompassed by boundaries, so that people are either inside or outside a group. Second, we attribute an "objective" existence to groups and treat them as if they are real and exact things. Third, we view a group as having a distinct subculture or counterculture—a set of unique norms and values. Fourth, we develop a sense of allegiance to a group that leads us to feel we are a unit with a distinct identity.

Sociologists mean something quite specific when they use the word *group,* and we will discuss this in Chapter 4. Here it is important to distinguish a group from two related entities: *aggregate* and *category*. An **aggregate** is simply a collection of anonymous individuals who are in one place at the same time, such as shoppers in a mall or individuals waiting in line for football tickets. Individuals shift in and out of an aggregate rather easily and frequently. Because the people in aggregates interact with one another only transiently and temporarily, patterns of social ordering in them are short-lived. However, this quality should not lead us to dismiss aggregates as inconsequential. They provide the foundation for many forms of collective behavior (see Chapter 13, pp. 441–446).

A **category** is a collection of people who share a characteristic—such as a status, a physical feature, or a behavior pattern—that is deemed to be of social significance. Common categories include the subdivisions of age, gender, race, occupation, and educational attainment, but being tall, living alone, and having indoor plumbing also qualify one for being in a particular category. Categories differ from groups in that they are so broad that social relations and group dynamics linking all members may not occur. However, common experiences of persons in categories, particularly those who share a status, may be the basis for social movements or political activity. For example, some women have banded together in the League of Women Voters and the National Organization for Women (NOW) because they recognize they are a social category that shares certain problems.

Information regarding categories can have important uses. For example, if we know the proportions of people in each age category in a population, we can make projections that anticipate the demand for various social services, such as public education and Medicare benefits.

Institutions

Sociologists use the term **institution** for the principal social structures that organize, direct, and execute the essential tasks of living. Each institution is built around a standardized solution to a set of problems. For example, all human societies face the problem of how to protect and nurture children in their early years. This is one of many problems that the institution of the family deals with. How do societies transfer raw materials into products and distribute those products to people? This problem is dealt with by the institution called the economy. All societies face the problem of helping people to understand the inexplicable events in their lives; religion is the institution that deals with the death of loved ones, fatal events, and the like.

Admittedly, this classification oversimplifies matters. An institution may perform more than one function, and several institutions may contribute to the performance of the same function. Further, there is a wide variety of interconnected institutions that serve diverse human needs and desires, including the institutions of sports, entertainment, organized crime, prostitution, medicine, and journalism.

As sociologists typically define an institution, it encompasses both cultural patterns and social structure. Institutions constitute (1) the more or less standardized solutions (cultural patterns) that serve to direct people in meeting the problems of social living and (2) the relatively stable relationships that characterize people in actually implementing these solutions. Neither the institutional structure of societies nor institutions themselves are static and unchanging. Institutions change, and new institutions emerge as societies face ever-changing challenges. For example, the rapid increase of the world's human population over the past 200 years has resulted in serious threats to the resources and ecosystems that make human life possible (see Chapter 12). As a result, it is increasingly clear to environmental scientists that "we need greater interaction among existing institutions, as well as new institutions" (Walker et al., 2009:1346) to enable nation states to cooperate in adapting to these threats.

Societies

Societies represent the most comprehensive and complex type of social structure in today's world. As we noted earlier in the chapter, society refers to a group of people who live within the same territory and share a common culture. By virtue of this common culture, the members of a society typically possess similar values and norms and a common language. The members perpetuate themselves primarily through reproduction and compose a more or less self-sufficient social unit. A society can be as small as a tribal community of several dozen people or as large as modern nations with hundreds of millions of people.

Although we often use the term *nation-state* interchangeably with *society,* the two are not necessarily the same. A state is a political entity centering on a government. Among many peoples of the world, the state binds together nationality and tribal groups that in their own right constitute societies. For example, Great Britain is made up of Scots, Welsh, and English. Belgium is composed of Flemings and Walloons. Similarly, many African nation-states contain multiple tribal groups—for instance, 250 in Nigeria, 200 in Zaire, and 130 in Tanzania.

Sociologists have classified societies in many ways. One popular approach is based on the principal way in which the members of a society derive their livelihood (Nolan and Lenski, 2010). All peoples must provide for such vital needs as food, clothing, and shelter; the manner in which they do so has vast consequences for other aspects of their lives. Each of these types of societies has different institutions and different numbers of institutions, depending on the complexity of the societies and of the problems to be solved in each.

Hunting and gathering societies represent the earliest and longest-lived form of organized social life; we have lived as foragers for 95 percent of human history (Hill et al., 2011). In this type of society, individuals in groups of about 50 survive by hunting animals and gathering edible foods. Kinship—ties by blood and marriage—has long been thought to be the foundation for most relationships, but analysis of 32 contemporary foraging societies showed that, while primary kin associations are important, most adult band members are not close kin (Hill et al., 2011). It appears that these networks of cooperating adults emerged as a mechanism of adaptation, rather than being grounded in kinship. Hunter-gatherer societies lack the institutions of contemporary industrial and postindustrial societies.

Some 10,000 years ago, human beings learned how to cultivate a number of the plants on which they depended for food. The more efficient economies of these *horticultural societies* allowed for the production of a social surplus—goods and services over and above those necessary for human survival. This surplus became the foundation for social stratification; the specialization of some economic, political, and religious roles; a growth in the importance of warfare; and more complex forms of culture and social structure (Lenski, 1966; Kerbo, 2011). Even so, the upper limit for most horticultural communities was about 3,000 persons.

Around 5,000 or 6,000 years ago the plow heralded an agricultural revolution and the emergence of *agrarian societies* (Childe, 1941), with larger crops, more food, expanding populations, and even more complex forms of social organization. Continuing advances in productive and military technologies contributed to a substantial growth in the power of the state, the size of the territory it controlled, and the emergence of large capital cities. The massive pyramids of Egypt, the roads and aqueducts of Rome, the great cathedrals of medieval Europe, and the far-flung irrigation systems of the Middle East and China are products of agrarian societies.

About 250 years ago the Industrial Revolution gave birth to *industrial societies* whose productive and economic systems are based on machine technologies. Economic self-sufficiency and local market systems were displaced by complex divisions of labor, exchange relationships, and national and international market systems. The ability to read and write became essential in advanced industrial societies and led to the growth of educational institutions. Many activities that were once the responsibility of families were relinquished to other institutions. Populations grew and people increasingly congregated in cities. Large-scale bureaucracies and formal organizations came to predominate in both the private and public spheres, finding expression in big business, big unions, big universities, big hospitals, and big government.

As we discuss in more detail in Chapter 13 (pp. 435–439), some social analysts contend that the United States is currently moving in the direction of a *postindustrial society,* often referred to by journalists as the "information age" or "service society." In a postindustrial society more workers find employment in the provision of services than in the extraction of raw materials and the manufacture of goods. Computers and robots have replaced people in many processes. These changes are accompanied by the knowledge explosion based on the creating, processing, distribution, storage, and retrieval of information (Bell and Gemmell, 2009), and where they will lead us is hard to predict because the changes are so rapid. For example, in 1990 less than half a million computers in the United States had access to the Internet. This number grew to 30 million by 1998 (Brown and Flavin, 1999), and by 2009, 82 million U.S. households had computers with Internet connections (U.S. Census Bureau, 2010).

What Can Sociology Do for You?

At the end of Chapter 1, you had an opportunity to find out about the types of jobs sociology majors might get. Now let's turn to the college career of a sociology major. What sorts of classes does a sociology major take? Again, the website for the American Sociological Association, **http://www.asanet.org/,** has some answers. Find the home page and click on "Undergraduate Students: Resources" under "Teaching and Learning" on the menu bar across the top. Then find "Navigating the Sociology Major," by Stephen Sweet and James Rothenberg, and go to the section titled "What Courses Should I Take?" Do sociology majors take only sociology courses? Do sociology majors learn how to do research? What are some of the topics sociology classes address?

If Chapter 2 was of interest to you, you might enjoy taking a sociology of culture class or an anthropology course.

The Chapter in Brief: *Culture and Social Structure*

Components of Culture

Culture provides individuals with a set of common understandings that they employ in fashioning their actions and makes society possible by providing a common framework of meaning.

■ **Norms**   **Norms** are social rules that specify appropriate and inappropriate behavior in given situations. They afford a means by which we orient ourselves to other people. **Folkways, mores,** and **laws** are types of norms.

■ **Values**   **Values** are broad ideas regarding what is desirable, correct, and good that most members of a society share. Values are so general and abstract that they do not explicitly specify which behaviors are acceptable and which are not.

■ **Symbols and Language**   **Symbols** are acts or objects that have come to be socially accepted as standing for something else. Symbols assume many different forms, but **language** is the most important of these. Language is the chief vehicle by which people communicate ideas, information, attitudes, and emotions, and it serves as the principal means by which human beings create culture and transmit it from generation to generation.

Cultural Unity and Diversity

■ **Cultural Universals**   **Cultural universals** are patterned and recurrent aspects of life that appear in all known societies. All people confront many of the same problems; culture represents an accumulation of solutions to the problems posed by human biology and the human situation.

■ **Cultural Integration**   The items that form a culture tend to constitute a consistent and integrated whole. For example, societies that value universal education also usually have norms and laws about schools, organize education into a collective activity, and create symbols and share meanings about the value of education and educational organizations.

■ **Ethnocentrism**   The cultural ways of our own society become so deeply ingrained that we have difficulty conceiving of alternative ways of life. We judge the behavior of other groups by the standards of our own culture, a phenomenon sociologists term **ethnocentrism.**

■ **Cultural Relativism**   In studying other cultures, we must examine behavior in the light of the values, beliefs, and motives of each culture, an approach termed **cultural relativism.**

■ **Subcultures and Countercultures**   Cultural diversity can be found within a society in the form of **subcultures.** When the norms, values, and lifestyles of a subculture are at odds with those of the larger society, it is a **counterculture.**

Social Structure

People's relationships are characterized by social ordering. Sociologists apply the term **social structure** to this social ordering—the interweaving of people's interactions and relationships in recurrent and stable patterns.

■ **Statuses**   **Status** represents a position within a group or society. It is by means of statuses that we locate one another in various social structures. Some are assigned to us— **ascribed statuses;** others we secure on the basis of individual choice and competition— **achieved statuses.** A status carrying primary weight in a person's interactions with others is a **master status.**

■ **Roles**   A status carries with it a set of culturally defined **rights** and **duties,** what sociologists term a **role.** A role is the expected behavior we associate with a status. **Role performance** is the actual behavior of the person who occupies a status. **Role conflict** arises when individuals are confronted with conflicting expectations stemming from their occupancy of two or more statuses. **Role strain** arises when individuals find the expectations of a single role incompatible. **Role exit** occurs when people stop playing roles that have been central to their social identities.

■ **Groups**   Statuses and roles are building blocks for more comprehensive social

structures, including **groups** of two or more people. Roles link us within social relationships. When these relationships are sustained across time, we frequently attribute group properties to them. Sociologists distinguish groups from **aggregates** and **categories.**

■ **Institutions**   **Institutions** are the principal social structures used to organize, direct, and execute the essential tasks of social living. Each institution is built around a standardized solution to a set of problems and encompasses the notions of both cultural patterns and social structure.

■ **Societies**   **Societies** represent the most comprehensive and complex type of social structure in today's world. By virtue of their common culture, the members of a society typically possess similar values and norms and a common language. One particular approach for classifying societies is based on the way people derive their livelihood: hunting and gathering societies, horticultural societies, agrarian societies, industrial societies, and postindustrial societies. Another approach rests on the distinction between traditional and modern types.

Glossary

achieved status   A status that individuals secure on the basis of choice and competition.

aggregate   A collection of anonymous individuals who are in one place at the same time.

ascribed status   A status assigned to an individual by a group or society.

category   A collection of people who share a characteristic that is deemed to be of social significance.

counterculture   A subculture whose norms and values are substantially at odds with those of the larger society.

cultural relativism   A value-free or neutral approach that views the behavior of a people from the perspective of their own culture.

cultural universals   Patterned and recurrent aspects of life that appear in all known societies.

culture   The social heritage of a people; those learned patterns for thinking, feeling, and acting that are transmitted from one generation to the next, including the embodiment of these patterns in material items.

duties   The actions that others can legitimately insist that we perform.

ethnocentrism   The tendency to judge the behavior of other groups by the standards of one's own culture.

folkways Norms people do not deem to be of great importance and to which they exact less stringent conformity.

group Two or more people who share a feeling of unity and who are bound together in relatively stable patterns of social interaction.

institutions The principal instruments whereby the essential tasks of living are organized, directed, and executed.

language A socially structured system of sound patterns (words and sentences) with specific and arbitrary meanings.

laws Rules that are enforced by a special political organization composed of individuals who enjoy the right to use force.

master status A key or core status that carries primary weight in a person's interactions and relationships with others.

mores Norms to which people attach a good deal of importance and exact strict conformity.

norms Social rules that specify appropriate and inappropriate behavior in given situations.

rights Actions that we can legitimately insist that others perform.

role A set of expectations (rights and duties) that define the behavior people view as appropriate and inappropriate for the occupant of a status.

role conflict The situation in which individuals are confronted with conflicting expectations stemming from their simultaneous occupancy of two or more statuses.

role exit Occurs when people stop playing roles that have been central to their social identities.

role performance The actual behavior of the person who occupies a status.

role set The multiple roles associated with a single status.

role strain The situation in which individuals find the expectations of a single role

incompatible, so that they have difficulty performing the role.

social structure The interweaving of people's interactions and relationships in more or less recurrent and stable patterns.

society A group of people who live within the same territory and share a common culture.

status A position within a group or society; a location in a social structure.

subculture A group whose members participate in the main culture of a society while simultaneously sharing a number of unique values, norms, traditions, and lifestyles.

symbols Acts or objects that have come to be socially accepted as standing for something else.

values Broad ideas regarding what is desirable, correct, and good that most members of a society share.

Review Questions

1. What is the difference between norms and values, and what part does each play in society?

2. How do symbols and, more particularly, language shape the way we see our world?

3. Name six cultural universals.

4. What is cultural integration?

5. Define ethnocentrism and describe at least one phenomenon in which it plays a part.

6. What is a subculture? Describe the characteristics of a specific subculture.

7. How do sociologists define status? What is the difference between ascribed and achieved statuses?

8. Give one example of role conflict.

9. Define group, institution, and society.

Internet Connection   www.mhhe.com/hughes11e

Use an Internet search engine such as Yahoo! or Google to search on the word *slang*. Explore two or more of the slang sites that appear and write a short report on subcultural slang. What subcultural groups use the slang vocabularies you uncovered? What are some examples of slang terms? Speculate on some of the reasons that these groups use special vocabularies to communicate among themselves.

CHAPTER 3

Socialization

Foundations for Socialization

The Self and Socialization

Socialization across the Life Course

*S*he came from a low, sand-coloured house on Golden West Avenue, Temple City. . . . The house was just like every other on that street—a strip of lawn, the suburban trees—but she had been left in there, day after day, year after year, for nearly twelve years, ... tied to a potty chair, sewn into a harness to attach her to the seat, only able to move her hands and feet, naked. All day, every day, she was left like that (Newton, 2004:209).

At age 13 this abused and socially isolated child was discovered by workers in a California family aid center. She was the size of an 8-year-old, malnourished, and incontinent. The years spent tied in a sitting position had left her physically deformed: "Stooped and frail, her gait pigeon-toed, her body was bent at the waist, her shoulders hunched forward, her hands held up before her like a rabbit" (Newton, 2004:214). Her behavior was equally shocking: "She spat continually, wiping the spit and mucus on to herself. . . . Her eating habits were revolting. . . . She took people's things willfully, pulling on their clothes, invading their space. She would go up to them, getting very close, making eye contact and pointing at the thing of theirs that she wanted, demanding possession. . . . Most difficult of all, she masturbated continually" (Newton, 2004:215).

This child, named Genie by those who worked to rehabilitate her, had essentially no language. On attainment and maturity tests, she scored in the range of a 1-year-old. She could understand no more than a few words. Specialists designed a program to rehabilitate and educate her, and her vocabulary increased dramatically, but her ability to form sentences and communicate normally never caught up to her age; her speech remained slow, awkward, and unclear. Born in 1957, Genie is still alive today, living in an adult care home.

Genie's case is not unique. In the 1940s two girls named Anna and Isabelle were born to single mothers who kept them hidden in secluded rooms, giving them just enough care to be kept alive. When local authorities discovered them, they were about 6 years old. They were extremely retarded and displayed few human capabilities or responses. Sociologist Kingsley Davis reported on these two cases in a classic 1949 study.

How much of your behavior can you trace to your upbringing? How different do you think you would be if you had had minimum contact with other human beings during your childhood? Neuro-cognition research increasingly supports "the critical importance of the social world for the surviving and thriving of humans" (Lieberman and Eisenberger, 2009). The cases of Genie, Anna, and Isabelle testify that much of the behavior we regard as somehow given in the human species does not occur unless it is put there through communicative and social contact with others.

In comparison with other species, we enter the world as amazingly "unfinished" creatures. We are not born as social beings, able to participate in society, but become so only in the course of **socialization**—a process of social interaction by which people acquire the knowledge, attitudes, values, and behaviors essential for effective participation in society. Socialization is the process of becoming a social being, a process that continues throughout one's life. The cases of children reared under conditions of extreme isolation illustrate the importance of socialization.

In Chapter 2 we focused our attention on culture. Were it not for socialization, the renewal of culture could not occur from one generation to the next. We humans are uniquely dependent upon a social heritage—the rich store of adaptations and innovations that countless generations of ancestors have developed over thousands of years. Through culture each new generation can move on from the achievements of the preceding one. Without socialization society could not perpetuate itself beyond a single generation. Individuals would lack those common understandings necessary to align their actions and to bind their separated lives into a larger whole. Both the individual and society are mutually

dependent on socialization. It blends the sentiments and ideas of culture with the capacities and needs of the organism (Davis, 1949:195).

In this chapter we will examine the process of socialization. We will consider its foundations, its relationship to the development of the self, and its changing nature over the life course.

Foundations for Socialization

As the cases of Genie, Anna, and Isabelle clearly demonstrate, our biological endowments are not sufficient to produce a normal human personality in the absence of social interaction. A normal human, then, is a product of both hereditary and environmental factors. In this section we will look more closely at how those factors interact. We also will discuss theories and agents of socialization, examine social communication, and consider how socialization provides a socially constructed reality, what sociologists refer to as the "definition of the situation."

Nature and Nurture

Children from severely deprived backgrounds offer a moving illustration of the nurturing that human nature needs to develop, but the relative contributions of nature and nurture are difficult to determine. The question used to be, "nature or nurture?" Today the primary issue is understanding how nature and nurture interact to produce behavior (Stiles, 2008).

Scientists have frequently asked which factor, heredity or environment, is more important in fashioning a particular trait, such as obesity, extroversion, or intelligence. They have attempted to determine which of the differences among people can be attributed to heredity and which to environment. As genetic research continues, evidence accrues that depression (Levinson, 2006), schizophrenia (McClellan, Susser, and King, 2007), alcoholism (Beylotte, 2003), antisocial behavior

(Caspi et al., 2002), and voting (Fowler, Baker, and Dawes, 2008) all have genetic components. Some studies suggest that heredity is the primary factor in personality and development. For example, in her 1998 book *The Nurture Assumption,* Judith Rich Harris argued that biological parents' genetic influence on their children is far more important than their social influence. Other studies indicate that once we account for siblings' genetic similarity, they are no more alike in personality, abilities, and adjustment than are people selected at random from the population (Turkheimer and Waldron, 2000). However, research also shows that, however important heritable traits are, the expression of those traits depends on a broad range of environmental factors (Collins et al., 2000).

Studies of identical twins (who have exactly the same genes) have provided a unique opportunity for drawing out genetic versus environmental effects (Johnson et al., 2007; Guo, 2005). This research shows that twins raised apart are as similar as twins raised together on many measures of personality, temperament, interests, and social and political attitudes (Bouchard et al., 1990; Bouchard, 1994; Pinker, 2002), indicating that those characteristics are influenced by genetic factors. At the same time, such studies also suggest that culture and environment may actually play the larger role, accounting for more than half of the variation in personality and behavioral traits (Feldman, Otto, and Christiansen, 2000).

Sometimes the difference between hereditary and environmental causes is only a matter of shifting one's focus. In a society in which everyone smokes but not everyone is genetically predisposed to lung cancer, we would see lung cancer as a genetic problem—only those with the "gene for lung cancer" die. If we imagine a population of people all of whom are genetically predisposed to lung cancer, we would see lung cancer as caused by smoking—only those who smoke die (Sommer, 2009).

It is clearly an oversimplification to think of organisms as passive objects either programmed

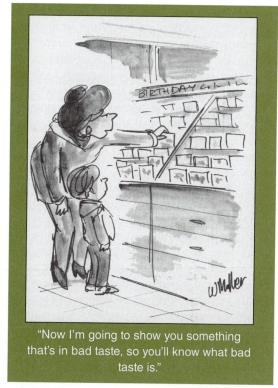

"Now I'm going to show you something that's in bad taste, so you'll know what bad taste is."

by internal genetic forces or shaped by the external environment. Substantial evidence indicates that hereditary and environmental factors interact with and affect one another (Stiles, 2008; Moffitt, 2005; Feldman, Otto, and Christiansen, 2000). Recent studies have found a relationship between human brain anatomy and social network size, but which causes the other has not been demonstrated (Miller, 2011a).

As children develop, their behavior becomes less directly dependent on nature. Instead, learning becomes more important, and the brain is affected by interaction with the environment. For example, the physiological development of the brains of small children is affected by early traumatic events (Perry et al., 1995) with adversity in the first two years of life causing potentially lifelong effects (Vanderwert et al., 2010). Likewise, the neural connections within the brain are enhanced by a rich, stimulating, and secure early environment. Not only do nature, nurture, and their interaction affect behavior, but behavior and individual experiences affect neurological development that in turn affects subsequent experience and behavior. An investigation of genetics and the environment that will track 90,000 children from their 25th week after conception until age 21 is under way in the United Kingdom ("New Long-Term Study," 2011).

We humans are not locked into an unchangeable physical body or an unchangeable social system; both can change and each exerts an influence on the other. In learning we modify ourselves by responding; we literally change ourselves by acting. We thus are active agents, shaping both ourselves and our environments. As we act on and modify the world in which we live, we in turn are shaped and transformed by our own actions. This dynamic interplay of socialization processes involving the individual and the social and natural environment in which we live is the foundation of human intelligence, knowledge, and culture.

Theories of Socialization

While social scientists acknowledge that we are biological organisms, biological factors have not been fully integrated into social psychological theory, though there is movement in that direction ("New Long-Term Study," 2011; Behrens, Hunt, and Rushworth, 2009; Bergesen, 2004; Cacioppo et al., 2000; Gove, 1994). The theories of socialization that are central to sociology today continue to emphasize social structure, learning, and social interaction, and they include insights from both sociologists and psychologists.

The two macrolevel theoretical perspectives in sociology—functionalism and conflict theory—view socialization as a process that has important consequences for society as a whole (Corsaro and Eder, 1995). For functionalists society would not be possible if people did not internalize the values, norms, and beliefs that ensure that they can and will occupy the statuses

and play the roles that make up social structures (Inkeles, 1968). Conflict theorists also recognize that socialization prepares people to play various roles in society, but they view socialization critically, emphasizing the ways socialization controls people and ensures that social inequities will be reproduced from one generation to the next (Bowles and Gintis, 1976, 2000). Proponents of these macrolevel approaches to socialization view it as a deterministic process, focusing mostly on the outcomes of socialization and tending to ignore both the active individuals and the actual social processes involved.

Three microlevel theories—social learning theory, cognitive developmental theory, and symbolic interactionism—examine how socialization occurs. We will describe each.

Social Learning Theory

One view of how socialization occurs is that we are socialized through positive and negative reinforcement by our parents, friends, and society and that we observe and imitate socialized behavior around us. The two processes emphasized in social learning theory are conditioning and observational learning (Wiggins, Wiggins, and Vander Zanden, 1994). **Conditioning** is a form of learning in which the consequences of behavior determine the probability of its future occurrence (Skinner, 1953). Consequences of behavior that increase the chance that a behavior will occur are *reinforcements;* consequences that reduce that probability are *punishments*. Socialization occurs when a person's behavior is shaped by the reinforcing and punishing activities of other people and groups.

Psychologist Albert Bandura drew attention to the fact that conditioning, which occurs subsequent to behavior, cannot explain the initial learning of a behavior. Through observation people may learn both a certain mode of behavior and that the behavior may elicit certain rewards or punishments (Bandura, 1965). **Observational learning** (also referred to as modeling or imitation) occurs when people reproduce the responses they observe in other people, either real or fictional.

Cognitive Developmental Theory

Another view emphasizes that a child's socialization occurs in step with his or her cognitive development. Though learning is a fundamental part of socialization, what and how a person learns depends on his or her ability to understand and interpret the world, something that progresses through several stages. The Swiss psychologist Jean Piaget (1926/1955) hypothesized that every normal child goes through four such stages of cognitive development, each of which is dominated by a different scheme for handling information and understanding how the world works.

In the *sensorimotor stage,* from birth to about 18 months, children learn directly through their senses and their movements. Their initial inability to distinguish between themselves and their environment limits the kind of socialization that can occur. Gradually, they realize that they exist independently of the people and things around them. The scheme developed in this stage is essential for moving on to more complex understandings of self, others, and the wider world that develop in subsequent stages.

The *preoperational stage* usually lasts from about 18 months to 6 or 7 years old. A major accomplishment of this stage is *representational thought,* made possible by learning symbols and language. However, children at this stage identify symbols very closely with the objects they represent, making thinking rigid and inflexible and making it difficult to distinguish the real from the make-believe. A critical factor inhibiting socialization at this stage is children's extreme egocentricity—their inability to see things, including themselves, from other people's perspectives. Until this happens, children's moral sensibility and self-concept remain undeveloped.

From age 6 or 7 until about 11 or 12, children go through the *concrete operational stage,* in which they learn to think more abstractly, to do simple arithmetic in their heads, to be able to separate a symbol from the thing it represents, to think less rigidly, and to be able to see things the way others do. Thinking at this stage remains focused on concrete, tangible objects, limiting the abstractions and complexity that can be reached.

Piaget's last stage, from age 11 or 12 to adulthood, is the *formal operations stage,* marked by the further development of abstract and logical abilities, such as the ability to do more complex mathematics and to understand formulas and proofs. Children now begin to be able to develop abstract arguments and to conceive of a variety of ways of looking at a problem. Identity and moral sensibility become deeper and more complex, influenced by the ability to internalize and critically evaluate the points of view of others.

Psychologist Lawrence Kohlberg (1969, 1981) extended Piaget's framework by arguing that beginning with the preoperational stage, children have a very strong motivation to be competent. Children learn not only through the rather passive conditioning and observational learning processes discussed above but also through the active process of trying to learn what they need to know about themselves and their environment to be competent, a critical component of socialization.

Symbolic Interactionism

Social learning theory and cognitive developmental theory are rooted in psychology. A third, more sociological view of socialization comes from the symbolic interactionist perspective. Symbolic interactionism is more than just a theory of socialization. As we pointed out in Chapter 1 (pp. 21–23), it is a broad sociological perspective that helps us understand social processes in many settings. Some symbolic interactionist reasoning is particularly relevant to understanding socialization.

Actions through which people observe, interpret, evaluate, communicate with, and attempt to control themselves—what symbolic interactionists call **reflexive behavior**—are important to socialization (Wiggins, Wiggins, and Vander Zanden, 1994). As we will see, a particularly important kind of reflexive behavior involves people observing their own behavior from the perspective of others. For example, in many cases in which you feel yourself becoming angry, you probably reflect on how your expression of anger will be interpreted by others and then use this reflection to guide your actual expression of anger.

Reflexive behavior is critical in the development of the self—a central part of the socialization process—because it is through reflexive behavior that people learn who they are. This is the process emphasized by both Charles Horton Cooley and George Herbert Mead in their theories of self-concept development that we discuss later in this chapter. Although learning who one is may be influenced by both conditioning and by observational learning, according to the symbolic interactionist view the individual takes an important and active role in this learning process. Individuals monitor their own behavior, monitor others' responses, make interpretations, try out new ways of behaving, and come to new understandings about themselves.

Agents of Socialization

The family, peers, schools, and the mass media are important agents of socialization. Traditionally the main social environment for young children, the family has provided the earliest and closest models to guide learning. With more than 12.3 million U.S. children under school age being cared for by someone other than their parents (NCCIC, 2008), day care providers and peers also are important early agents of socialization. Sociological research investigates how family structure and parenting styles influence socialization outcomes (Amato and Sobolewski, 2001; Nelson, Clark, and Acs, 2001; Stacey and Biblarz, 2001), and studies of the cognitive development, language, and social behaviors of children show that parent and family characteristics are more important than any aspect of child care (NICHD, 2006).

As the child's world expands beyond the family, whether the child is of school age or earlier, the *peer group* becomes an important influence on emotional, cognitive, and social

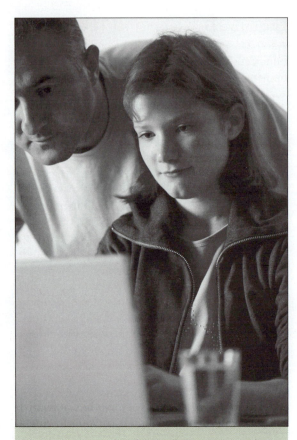

An important role of parents, as agents of socialization, is to control the influence of other agents of socialization such as the Internet.

development. In the United States, an increasingly large part of a child's early social life is spent in the peer group, where the reactions of same-age peers serve as powerful reinforcements and punishments that shape behavior. As a child increasingly identifies with his or her peers and uses them as role models, the child's self-definition becomes strongly influenced by the characteristics and standards of his or her peer group—standards that often vary significantly from those of parents and other adults. The high rates of what parents and others define as "deviant" behavior among youths (see Chapter 5) may stem from this difference in standards of behavior. For youths, such behavior currently includes tattooing, body piercing, underage drinking, experimenting with drugs, and more serious criminal behavior. For this and other reasons, parents often attempt to control a child's choice of peer associates.

Formal socialization occurs in schools through instruction in mathematics, English, and other subjects. But the role of the *school* as agent of socialization goes far beyond teaching the standard subjects. Praise and reprimands in schools are structured to teach and enforce school rules, thus socializing children to adapt to impersonal bureaucratic requirements. Emphasis on grades teaches individualistic values of competition and achievement. The gender, racial, and ethnic composition of teaching staffs teaches lessons about what kinds of people are regarded as knowledgeable and competent to wield authority, and may thus reinforce societal inequalities. Extracurricular activities from athletics to helping the teacher are differentially distributed across the student body, leading to differences in socialization experiences and thus outcomes (see Box 3.1).

Although school dominates the lives of most children, television and other visual media also play a huge role (Grindstaff and Turow, 2006). The average American child between the ages of 4 and 11 spends more than three hours a day engaged in "screen time," watching television or using a computer to play video games (Anderson, Economos, and Must, 2008). One-third of children ages 2–7 and two-thirds of those ages 8–18 have a television in their bedrooms. Such exposure begins very early in children's lives, with 40 percent of 3-month-olds and 90 percent of 2-year-olds being regular watchers of television (Zimmerman, Christakis, and Meltzoff, 2007). Television and other media such as radio, the Internet, music, movies, comic books, video games, books, magazines, and newspapers are important in socialization because they provide models for behavior. For example, with 20–25 violent acts per hour shown on children's television, media model violent behavior. Laboratory studies, field experiments, survey samples, and longitudinal studies all link television violence to aggression (Anderson and Bushman, 2002), and a long-term study showed that television watching during adolescence and early adulthood was connected to subsequent aggressive acts including assaults, robbery, and criminal weapon use (Johnson et al., 2002). A 15-year longitudinal study showed that exposure to television violence between ages 6 and 9 was significantly correlated with adult aggressive behavior (Huesmann et al., 2003).

Media also provide images that can affect our understandings of the world. For example, Hollywood films once reflected overt racism in our society, portraying African Americans as slaves, servants, or criminals. Sociologist Matthew W. Hughey (2009) argues that recent popular films overtly celebrate racial cooperation and egalitarianism but contain underlying messages of antiblack stereotypes with portrayals of black characters as powerful but racially subservient.

Which agents of socialization are most important? The direct impact of mass media on the socialization process can be overestimated (Sternheimer, 2003, 2007). The symbolic interactionist perspective suggests that images from television and other media must be defined and interpreted by viewers before they can influence behavior. If the family, peers, and schools create the meanings people use in interpreting media images, then they are the critical agents in socialization. Media-related aggression, for example, can be lessened by reducing exposure to violent media, but it also can be reduced by changing children's attitudes toward the violence they see on television and in video games (Anderson and Bushman, 2002). The effect of television and other media also may be through the displacement of other activities that might socialize children differently; children who watch television are not reading, visiting interesting places, exercising, or playing (American Academy of Pediatrics, 2001).

Does High School Identity Affect Your Adult Life?

Emo, bandie, bro, gangsta, nerd, geek, Goth, druggie, prep, popular, indie—how would you describe your high school self? Author Alexandra Robbins (2011) has spent years visiting schools, talking to students, and recording the labels teens apply to one another. Such labels reflect social identities, with students both inside and outside of each group using the terms. Do these identities drop away as students leave high school, or do they have an impact on later life?

In a long-term study of 900 young people who were in high school in the 1980s, researchers Bonnie Barber, Jacquelynne Eccles, and Margaret Stone (2001) investigated the impact of social (or "crowd") identity in adolescence on adult outcomes. As an indicator of identity, they used categories borrowed from the well-known 1985 film about adolescents, *The Breakfast Club.* In 1987 the researchers asked the 10th-grade study participants to ignore gender and select which of the five *Breakfast Club* characters was most like them: the Brain, the Princess, the Jock, the Criminal, or the Basket Case. Forty percent selected Princess, 28 percent chose Jock, 12 percent selected Brain, 11 percent picked Basket Case, and 9 percent chose Criminal. Participants also indicated which athletic and other sorts of extracurricular activities they were involved in, which the researchers grouped as follows:

- Team sports
- Performing arts (school band, drama, dance)
- School involvement (student government, pep club, cheerleading)
- Prosocial activities (church attendance, community service)

In the first part of their analysis, Barber and her colleagues discovered that the social identity categories were linked to 10th-grade activity participation, with Jocks and Criminals most strongly represented in sports, Basket Cases and Princesses in performing arts, and Brains in prosocial activities. Princesses also were well represented in school involvement activities. But did their high school social identities predict what sorts of young adults they would become?

It turns out that for a number of measurements taken in 1996, when the respondents were around 24 years old, the answer was yes. High school identities predicted adult substance use, education, psychological adjustment, and work outcomes. For example, alcohol consumption in early adulthood was significantly correlated with 10th-grade social identity: Jocks and Criminals drank the most, and Basket Cases and Brains the least. Brains were the most likely to have graduated from college by age 24, followed by Princesses, Jocks, Basket Cases, and finally Criminals. The lowest levels of worry were reported by Jocks and Brains, while the highest levels were reported by Criminals and Basket Cases. Similarly, Jocks and Brains had the highest self-esteem, and Criminals and Basket Cases reported the lowest. Jocks were the least likely to report social isolation, and Basket Cases the most.

Not many people want to think that their adult lives depend on their identities as high school sophomores. Why do the crowd identities and activities of 10th graders predict adult outcomes? Barber and her colleagues have some guesses (2001:450–451):

Perhaps adolescents make use of the formal activities and the informal social organizations of the high school to negotiate and formalize their identities. The patterns of behavior expressed, solidified, and formalized first in high school organizations may carry forward, providing continuity in connection to others with similar values and backgrounds as well as ongoing validation of the social identity established in adolescence.

These processes may cause individuals to emphasize and build on some of their personal characteristics and deemphasize others, and may have unexpected consequences. Alienation and exclusion in high school, for example, may prove beneficial in adulthood. Based on her work with teens, Alexandra Robbins has developed what she calls "quirk theory" (2011:8):

Many of the differences that cause a student to be excluded in school are the same traits or real-world skills that others will value, love, respect, or find compelling about that person in adulthood and outside of the school setting.

Questions for Discussion

1. Identities of adolescents today may be different from those in 1987. If you were designing a replication of this study and were using contemporary adolescents as subjects, which movie(s) or television program(s) would you use? What characters and what identity models would you pick for your study? What hypotheses would you have? What would you expect to find when you interviewed your subjects again nine years from now?

2. How could you test Robbins's "quirk theory"?

Social Communication

Communication is a fundamental process in socialization. It is also essential in human adaptation. If we are to adapt to the environment, we must be able to communicate with one another. Indeed, all social interaction involves communication. **Communication** refers to the process by which people transmit information, ideas, attitudes, and mental states to one another and is made possible by the human ability to create complex symbol systems including language, as discussed in Chapter 2 (pp. 45–48). It includes all those verbal and nonverbal processes by which we send and receive messages. Communication allows us to establish "commonness" with one another; senders and receivers can come together through a given message. It is this commonness that makes socialization possible. Although we probably think first of talking when we hear the word "communication," in *A History of Communications* Marshall Poe (2011) assesses each of five major human communication media: speaking, writing, printing, audiovisual media, and the Internet. Communication of whatever form is an indispensable mechanism by which human beings attain social goals. It permits them to coordinate complex group activities, and as such it is the foundation for institutional life.

Verbal Communication

For years many social scientists asserted that infants come into the world essentially unprogrammed for language use. Then linguists began noticing similarities in languages throughout the world: All languages have nouns and verbs and allow individuals to ask questions, give commands, and deny statements. Moreover, children acquire language with little difficulty, despite the need to master an incredibly complex, abstract set of rules for transforming strings of sounds into meanings. Even deaf children have a strong bias to communicate in language-like ways (Goldin-Meadow and Mylander, 1984). And speakers can understand and produce an infinite

set of sentences, even sentences they have never before heard or uttered.

In 1957 the eminent linguist Noam Chomsky put these observations together to suggest that human beings possess an inborn language-generating mechanism, which he termed the **language acquisition device.** As viewed by Chomsky (1957, 1980), the basic structure of language is biologically channeled, forming a sort of prefabricated filing system to order the words and phrases that make up human languages. All a child needs to do is learn the peculiarities of his or her society's language.

Chomsky's hypothesis attracted interest, generated controversy, and remains influential (Jackendoff, 2002). Social scientists have pointed out that because a biological predisposition for the development of language exists does not mean that environmental factors play no part in language development. The example of a boy with normal hearing but with deaf parents highlights this point. Although he was exposed to television daily, the boy's social interactions were limited to people who communicated in sign language. At age 3, he was fluent in sign language but neither understood nor spoke English (Moskowitz, 1978). This case suggests that to learn a language, children must be able to interact with people in that language.

In sum, the acquiring of language cannot be understood by examining genetic factors and learning processes in isolation from one another. Instead, complex and dynamic interactions between nature and nurture occur, involving biochemical processes, maturational factors, learning strategies, and the social environment (Pinker, 2007, 1994). No one aspect by itself can produce a language-using human being. Although infants possess a genetic capacity for language, that ability can be acquired only in a social context.

Nonverbal Communication

Verbal symbols are only the tip of the communication iceberg. Nonverbal messages abound, and we "read" a good deal into them without

Unanticipated consequences of the use of communication technologies are common.

DILBERT reprinted by permission of United Feature Syndicate, Inc.

necessarily being aware of doing so. On the basis of his experiments, psychologist Albert Mehrabian (1968) concluded that the total impact of a message is 7 percent verbal, 38 percent vocal, and 55 percent facial. Another specialist has suggested that "no more than 30 to 35 percent of the social meaning of a conversation or an interaction is carried by its words" (Birdwhistell, 1970:197). This suggests that 65 percent to 93 percent of the potential impact of a communication is lost via e-mail, text messages, and social media postings.

Differences in the environment in which nonverbal communication is used affect its meaning. For example, if a man and woman at a singles bar spot each other and become interested, they signal with eye contact. The man might hold the woman's gaze, look away, and then look back quickly once or twice. If the woman responds in kind, the two may maneuver within speaking distance and strike up a conversation. On the other hand, if you establish and hold eye contact with a stranger on an elevator, it is perceived to be a threatening communication. Similarly, in American culture you generally do not look directly at another person unless you are talking (Mazur, 1985).

Cultural diversity in the workplace has created a need for greater sensitivity among managers and employees regarding people's use of nonverbal communication. For example, white

Americans define eye contact in the course of a conversation as showing respect. But many Latinos do not, and many Americans of Asian ancestry deem eye contact with an employer to be an exceedingly disrespectful behavior. Potential conflicts may arise when white supervisors consider Hispanic or Asian employees furtive or rude for casting their eyes about the room. Multicultural training programs can teach employers and employees to look beyond their culture-bound notions about what constitutes "proper" and "improper" behavior.

There are many nonverbal communication systems, including the following:

- **Body language:** Physical motions and gestures provide signals. The way a person stands or sits, for example, can communicate aggression, receptivity, boredom, or hostility.

- **Paralanguage:** Nonverbal vocal cues surrounding speech—voice pitch, volume, pacing of speech, silent pauses, and sighs—provide a rich source of information. Paralanguage has to do with how something is said rather than with what is said.

- **Proxemics:** The way we employ social and personal space also contains messages. Students who sit in the front rows of a classroom communicate that they are interested, while those in the rear communicate that they are alienated and prone to mischievous activities (Sommer, 1969).

- **Touch:** Through physical contact such as touching, stroking, hitting, holding, and greeting (handshakes), we convey our feelings toward one another. However, touch can also constitute an invasion of privacy, and it can become a symbol of power when people want to make power differences visible.

- **Artifacts:** We commonly employ objects, including certain types of clothing, makeup, hairpieces, eyeglasses, beauty aids, perfume, and jewelry, that tell other people our gender, rank, status, and attitude.

Some aspects of nonverbal communication, such as many gestures, are especially susceptible to cultural influence (Ekman, Friesen, and Bear, 1984; see Figure 3.1). The American "OK" gesture made by joining the thumb and forefinger in a circle has quite different meanings, depending on the culture. It has an insulting connotation in France and Belgium: "You're worth zero!" In southern Italy it means "You're a jerk," in Greece and Turkey it conveys an insulting or vulgar sexual invitation, and in Germany it is an obscene anatomical reference. However, facial expressions seem to have universal meanings. Surprise, disgust, fear, anger, sadness, and happiness were identified from photos by people from five different cultures (Ekman, Friesen, and O'Sullivan, 2005). The ways of displaying and interpreting certain feelings may be universal, but each culture provides its own "display rules" regulating how and when given emotions may be exhibited and with what consequences.

Definition of the Situation

An important part of socialization is learning social definitions of reality—the basic schemes we use to make sense of and to understand the social and physical world. William I. Thomas introduced this through his concept of **definition of the situation:** the interpretation or meaning we give to our immediate circumstances (Thomas and Thomas, 1928; Merton, 1995).

People vary in their perceptions of and reactions to different situations. For example, a gun means one thing to a soldier and something else to an armed robber; it has still other meanings for a holdup victim, a hunter, or a gun control advocate. A man mowing a lawn may be seen as beautifying his yard, avoiding his wife, getting exercise, supporting neighborhood property values, annoying a neighbor who is attempting to sleep, earning a living by mowing lawns, and so on.

Our symbolic environment mediates the physical environment so that we experience not simply stimuli, but a definition of the situation. Although our definitions of the situation may differ, it is only as we arrive at common understandings that we are able to fit our action to the actions of other people. Whatever we do—play football, chat with a friend on the telephone, rob a store, make love, give a lecture, cross a busy intersection, or purchase a book—we must attribute similar meanings to the situation if we are to achieve joint action with others. Moreover, a definition of the situation arrived at on one occasion may not hold for future occasions. Viewed in this manner, culture may be thought of as the agreed-upon meanings—the shared definitions of situations—that individuals acquire as members of a society. Socialization is the process by which these shared definitions are learned and transmitted from one generation to the next.

Sociologists point out that our definitions influence our construction of reality. William I. Thomas and Dorothy S. Thomas (1928:572; Merton, 1995) captured this insight in what has become known as the **Thomas theorem:** "If [people] define situations as real, they are real in their consequences." The Thomas theorem draws our attention to the fact that people respond not only to the objective features of a situation but also to the meaning the situation has for them. Once the meaning has been assigned, it serves to shape not only what people do or fail to do but also some of the consequences of their behavior.

Kiss on the cheek: How many are appropriate? Zero to one in Britain, two in most of Europe, three in Belgium and French-speaking Switzerland—and in Paris, four.

The V sign: What Churchill meant was "victory"— but the same signal with the knuckles turned out is England's and Australia's equivalent of the American middle finger.

Tapping the nose: In England, Scotland, and, strangely, Sardinia, this means, "You and I are in on the secret." But if a Welsh person does it, he means, "You're really nosy."

Twisting the nose: The French gesture of putting one's fist around the top of the nose and twisting it signifies that a person is drunk, but it is not a gesture used in other cultures.

Tapping the temple: Do this almost anywhere in Europe if you want to say someone or something is crazy—except in Holland, where the gesture means, "How clever!"

Thumbs up: This gesture was employed by Roman emperors to spare the lives of gladiators in the Colosseum. It is now favored by American and Western European airline pilots, truck drivers, and others to mean "All right." But in Sardinia and northern Greece, it is an insulting message paralleling the middle-finger gesture of American society.

Thumb-and-index circle: America's "OK" sign means different things in different countries, including Germany, where it is an obscene anatomical reference.

The chin rub: That's what people in France, French-speaking Switzerland, and Belgium do when they're bored. Don't try it elsewhere: no one will get it.

The wave: Careful with this friendly greeting while in Greece. It could be misinterpreted as "Go to hell." When Greeks wave goodbye, they show the backs of their hands.

Figure 3.1   **Symbolic Gestures: Barriers to Cross-Cultural Communication**

Source: Figure generated by the authors based on text "In Athens, It's Palms In," *Newsweek* (November 12, 1990).

In this way, a definition of the situation can become a self-fulfilling prophecy.

For example, one of the reasons that racial prejudices are so damaging is that they are definitions of the situation that can become self-fulfilling prophecies. For many generations whites defined African Americans as racially inferior. Whites controlled the centers of institutional power, and they allocated to African Americans fewer of the privileges and opportunities of society. By acting upon their racial definitions, whites fashioned social structures—institutional arrangements—in which African Americans have enjoyed fewer advantages than whites. And while most African Americans live well above the poverty line (DeNavas-Walt, Proctor, and Smith, 2011), compared to whites, African Americans are less likely to be well educated and have high incomes and more likely to hold menial jobs, live in poor housing, and have poor health. Thus, by creating and applying definitions of the situation, whites have created a social order characterized by institutional discrimination.

The Self and Socialization

The formation of the **self**—the set of concepts we use in defining who we are—is a central part of the socialization process. It is not a biological given but emerges in the course of interaction with other people and is affected by the social structures in which these interactions occur (Burke, 2004).

The self represents the ideas we have regarding our attributes, capacities, and behavior. In everyday speech, we note the existence of the self in phrases such as proud of myself, talking to myself, losing control of myself, ashamed of myself, testing myself, hating myself, and loving myself. These conceptions represent the heart of our humanness, our awareness that each of us is a unique being apart from other beings

and is the same person across time (Zussman, 2005). The image that each of us has that we are a distinct, bounded, coherent being gives us a feeling of psychic wholeness.

The development of the self begins at birth as the process of socialization begins. Sociologist J. Milton Yinger (1965:149) observed:

Retrospectively, one can ask "Who am I?" But in practice, the answer has come before the question. The answer has come from all the definitions of one's roles, values, and goals that others begin to furnish at the moment of birth.

We typically place ourselves at the center of events, a tendency sociologists call an **egocentric bias** (Zuckerman et al., 1983; Schlenker, Weigold, and Hallam, 1990). By virtue of the egocentric bias, we overperceive ourselves as the victim or target of an action or event that in reality is not directed at us. For example, if we are lottery players, we sense that our ticket has a far greater probability of being selected a winner than it has (Greenwald and Pratkanis, 1984). This self-centered view of reality affects the socialization process by shaping first our perception of events and later our recall of the events.

As noted earlier in this chapter, symbolic interactionists argue that through the process of reflexive behavior we become objects of our own action. We mentally take a place on the outside and, from this vantage point, become an audience to our own actions and an active agent in our own self-development and change (Granberg, 2006; Kiecolt, 1994). Viewed in this dynamic manner, the self is a process by which we devise our actions in order to fit them to the ongoing actions of other people—a process central to socialization (Burke, 2006). Sociologists such as Charles Horton Cooley, George Herbert Mead, and Erving Goffman have contributed a good deal to our understanding of these matters. We will consider their insights, and those of researchers who followed them, in this section.

Charles Horton Cooley: The Looking-Glass Self

At the beginning of the 20th century, the notion was prevalent in both scientific and lay circles that human nature is biologically determined. Charles Horton Cooley (1864–1929) vigorously challenged this assertion. He maintained that people transform themselves and their worlds as they engage in social interaction. In particular, Cooley (1902/1964) contended that our consciousness arises in a social context. This notion is best exemplified by his concept of the **looking-glass self**—a process by which we imaginatively assume the stance of other people and view ourselves as we believe they see us. Our ability to take the perspective of another person is a basic requirement of all social behavior.

Self-Awareness

Cooley suggested that the looking-glass self is an ongoing mental process characterized by three phases. First, we imagine how we appear to others. For example, we may think of ourselves as putting on weight and becoming "fat." Second, we imagine how others judge our appearance. We are aware, for instance, that people typically think of obese people as unattractive. Third, we have an emotional reaction, such as pride or shame, based on what we perceive others' judgments to be. In this case we are likely to experience anxiety or embarrassment regarding our "obese" state. The looking-glass self entails a subjective process and need not accord with objective reality. For example, victims of anorexia nervosa willfully starve themselves, denying that they are actually thin or ill, in the belief that they are too fat.

The notion of the looking-glass self does not imply that our self-conception changes radically every time we encounter a new person or a new situation. Accordingly, it is useful to distinguish between self-images and self-conceptions (Turner, 1968; Marsh, 1986). A **self-image** is a mental conception or picture that we have of ourselves that is relatively temporary; it changes as we move from one context to another. Our **self-conception** is a more overriding view of ourselves, a sense of self through time—"the real me" or "I myself as I really am." Layers of self-images typically build up over time and contribute to a relatively stable self-conception. Embarrassment affects self-image but not self-conception.

Self-Evaluation

Self-conception is not only a description of who we are. It also includes our evaluation of ourselves. Two important dimensions of this evaluation are self-esteem and personal efficacy (Cast and Burke, 2002).

Self-esteem is the belief that one is a good and valuable person. Why do some people have high self-esteem and others low? Self-esteem is governed by three principles (Rosenberg, 1981). First, as we interact with others, we monitor their behavior for pieces of information about how they are appraising us. These are **reflected appraisals,** appraisals of ourselves that we see reflected in the behavior of others. If we conclude from our observations that others respect and look up to us, we will probably have good self-esteem, but if we think that they look down upon and disparage us, our self-esteem will probably be low. In a complex world we cannot be highly concerned with everyone's views of us, so the most important reflected appraisals tend to be those of people who are most important to us, those we love and care about, and those we most respect—family, close friends, and people we admire (Murray et al., 2003; Rosenberg, 1973).

People also arrive at evaluations of themselves through **social comparisons,** comparing their performance, ability, or characteristics with those of others and rating themselves as superior, equal, or inferior (Pettigrew, 1967). We cannot compare ourselves with everyone else along all dimensions, so we use dimensions that we learn are important through the various agents of socialization (family, peer group, school, and the mass media), and we compare ourselves with relevant others. That is, instead of comparing themselves with middle-aged people with respect to personal income, adolescents compare themselves with others of their own age and in a similar situation. An adolescent's income may be low in comparison with that of a middle-aged woman at the height of her career, but it may still be a source of high self-esteem if it compares favorably with that of other working adolescents.

Even if we feel that others respect us and we are able to compare ourselves favorably with them, we still may not experience high self-esteem if we do not believe that we can take credit for what produces the respect and the favorable comparisons. By the same token, if we do not blame ourselves for how others are evaluating us or for our negative comparisons, we will probably not suffer low self-esteem. This is because of the principle of *self-attribution:* For a characteristic to affect our self-esteem, we must believe we are responsible for it and therefore deserve the credit or blame that results. For example, a man who gets an A in a difficult college course by cheating is not likely to conclude that he is a great scholar, but he may take credit for successful cheating and conclude that he is a very good cheater.

Personal efficacy is another aspect of self-evaluation that is influenced by socialization processes. It is the belief that one can overcome obstacles and achieve goals. The primary determinant of personal efficacy is personal experience. When we experience ourselves as effective actors and then attribute to ourselves the characteristic of being effective, our personal efficacy is increased (Gecas and Schwalbe, 1983). For example, doing well in school or holding a job that gives one authority and relative autonomy increases personal efficacy (Kohn and Schooler, 1983). However, this means that the development of personal efficacy can be a problem. To develop personal efficacy, one needs to achieve things; lacking personal efficacy, such achievement may be difficult. Structured social inequality is an important factor in personal efficacy (Hughes and Demo, 1989). People with higher education, more autonomous jobs, and higher incomes are all in situations that facilitate experiencing oneself as efficacious. People with little education, routine jobs, and low incomes may be locked into situations in which the sense of efficacy necessary for changing one's situation has little chance of developing.

George Herbert Mead: The Generalized Other

George Herbert Mead (1863–1931), one of the major figures in the symbolic interactionist perspective, elaborated on Cooley's concept of the looking-glass self and contributed many insights of his own to the processes of development of the self and socialization. Mead (1934/1962) contended that we gain a sense of selfhood by acting toward ourselves in much the same fashion that we act toward others. In so doing we "take the role of the other toward ourselves." We mentally assume a dual perspective: We are simultaneously the subject doing the viewing and the object being viewed. In our imagination we take the position of another person and look back on ourselves from this standpoint.

Mead designated the subject aspect of the self-process as "I" and the object aspect as "me." Consider what sometimes happens when you contemplate whether to ask your professor a question. You think, "If I ask a question, he'll consider me stupid. I'd better keep quiet." In this example you imagine the attitude of the professor toward students. In so doing you mentally take the role of the professor and view yourself as an object or "me." It is you as the subject or "I" who decides that it would be unwise to ask the question. The use of personal pronouns in the statement illustrates the object–subject dimensions.

According to Mead, the key to children's development of the self—a central part of the socialization process—resides in their acquisition of language. By virtue of language, we arouse the same tendencies in ourselves that we do in others. We mentally say to ourselves, "If I want to get this person to respond this way, what will it take to do so? What would it take to get me to act in this fashion?" Language allows us to carry on an internal conversation. We talk and reply to ourselves in much the same manner that we carry on a conversation with others. In this fashion we judge how other people will respond to us.

Mead saw children as passing through three stages in developing a full sense of selfhood: the "play" stage, the "game" stage, and the "generalized other" stage. In play, children take the role of only one other person at a time and "try on" the person's behavior. The model, usually an important person in the life of the child, such as a parent, is called a **significant other.** Whereas children in the play stage take the role of only one other person at a time, in the game stage they assume many roles. Individuals must take into account the roles of many people, and children must become familiar with the expectations that hold for a variety of roles if they are to play their own roles successfully.

In Mead's third stage, children recognize that they are immersed within a larger community of people and that this community has very definite attitudes regarding what constitutes appropriate and inappropriate behavior. The social unit that gives individuals their unity of self is called the **generalized other.** The attitude of the generalized other is the attitude of the larger community. Although we gain our conceptions of given rules from particular people (e.g., our mother, a teacher, or a peer), these notions are generalized or extended to embrace all people within similar situations. To think about our behavior, then, is to interact mentally with ourselves from the perspective of an abstract community of people. According to Mead, the generalized other is the vehicle by which we are linked to society. By means of the generalized other, we incorporate, or internalize, the organized attitudes of our community within our own personalities so that social control becomes self-control. According to Mead, our ability to participate effectively in society is the end result of passing through the play, game, and generalized other stages.

Erving Goffman: Impression Management

Erving Goffman (1922–1982) has provided an additional dimension to our understanding of the self and socialization. Cooley and Mead examined how our self-conceptions arise in the course of social interaction and how we fashion our actions based on the feedback we derive about ourselves and our behavior from other people. Goffman (1959) directed our attention to another matter. He pointed out that only by influencing other people's ideas of us can we hope to predict or control who we become. We have a stake in presenting ourselves to others in ways that will lead them to view us in a favorable

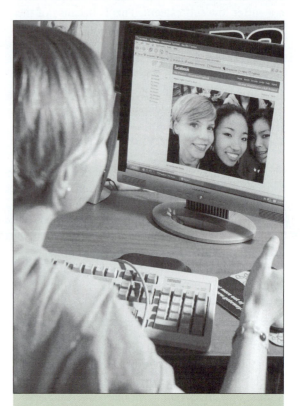

Social networking sites such as Facebook and MySpace allow for significant impression management, as users can describe and present themselves in a variety of ways.

light, a process Goffman called **impression management.** In doing so we use both concealment and strategic revelation. For example, a young professor fresh out of graduate school may spend several hours preparing and rehearsing a lecture in hopes of appearing "knowledgeable" to her students. You are probably aware of engaging in impression management when deciding what to wear for a particular occasion, such as a party, a physician's appointment, a job interview, or a date (Leary and Kowalski, 1990).

Goffman saw the performances staged in a theater as an analytical analogy and tool for depicting and understanding socialization and the shaping of the self, a perspective called the **dramaturgical approach.** He depicted social life as a stage on which people interact; all human beings are both actors and members of the audience, and the parts are the roles people play in the course of their daily activities. According to Goffman, the self is a product of the ongoing performances that characterize a person's everyday interaction with others and of how these performances are interpreted by others. In this view the self is not so much something that people possess and then carry unchanged from situation to situation as it is a "dramatic effect" (Goffman, 1959:253) that emerges from social situations in which people attempt to manage others' impressions of them.

Goffman illustrated his approach by describing the changes that occur in waiters' behavior as they move from the kitchen to the dining room. As the nature of the audience changes, so does their behavior. "Frontstage" in the dining room, the waiters display a polite demeanor to the guests. "Backstage" in the kitchen, they openly flaunt and otherwise ridicule the servility they must portray frontstage. Further, they seal off the dirty work of food preparation—the gristle, grease, and foul smells of spoiled food—from the appetizing and enticing frontstage atmosphere. As people move from situation to situation, they drastically alter their self-expression. They undertake to define the situation for others by generating cues that will lead others to act in ways they wish.

Socialization across the Life Course

Socialization is a continuing, lifelong process. The world about us changes and requires that we also change. The self is not carved in granite, somehow finalized for all time during childhood. Life is adaptation—a process of constant renewing and remaking. Three-year-olds are socialized within the patterns of a nursery school, engineering students within their chosen profession, new employees within an office or plant, a husband and wife within a new family, and elderly patients within a nursing home.

In one way or another, all societies have to deal with the **life course** that begins with conception and continues through old age and ultimately death. Societies weave varying social arrangements around chronological age (Nanda and Warms, 2011; Mayer, 2009). A 14-year-old girl may be expected to be a middle school student in one culture and a mother of two in another; a 45-year-old man may be at the peak of a business career, still moving up in a political career, retired from a career as a professional football player, or dead and worshipped as an ancestor in some other society. All cultures divide biological time into socially relevant units. While birth, puberty, maturity, aging, and death are biological facts of life, it is society that gives each its distinctive meaning.

In making their way through life, individuals are strongly influenced by **age norms**—rules that define what is appropriate for people to be and to do at various ages. In a sense, people set their personal watches by a **social clock,** and most people can readily report whether they themselves are early, late, or on time with regard to major life events.

Some psychologists have undertaken the search for what they view as the regular, sequential periods and transitions in the life cycle (e.g., Erikson, 1963). They depict life as a succession of stages. Interactions that occur between an individual and society—socialization processes—at each stage can change the course of personality, or development of the self, in a positive or negative direction. Erikson's chief concern was with psychological development, which he divided into the eight major stages of development described in Table 3.1. Each stage poses a unique task that revolves about a crisis—a turning point of increased vulnerability and heightened potential. According to Erikson, the crises posed by each stage must be successfully resolved if healthy development is to take place.

People are significantly affected during the life course by **life events**—turning points at which people change some direction in the course of their lives. Some of these events are related to social clocks, but many are not, such as suffering severe injury in an accident, being

raped, winning a lottery, undergoing a born-again conversion, being in a war, living through a disaster, or suffering financial ruin. Not surprisingly, gender affects a person's experience of life events. For example, men are more likely than women to report being distressed by work and financial events; women are more strongly influenced by exposure to negative events within the family (Conger et al., 1993).

Sociologists emphasize that modern societies are ordered in ways that formally structure people's preparation for new roles through education, rehabilitation, and resocialization. This *role socialization* commonly involves three phases (Mortimer and Simmons, 1978). First, people think about, experiment with, and try on the behaviors associated with a new role, what

Table 3.1	Erikson's Eight Stages of Development		
Development Stage	Psychosocial Crisis	Predominant Social Setting	Favorable Outcome
1. Infancy	Basic trust vs. mistrust	Family	The child develops trust in him- or herself, his or her parents, and the world.
2. Early childhood	Autonomy vs. shame, doubt	Family	The child develops a sense of self-control without loss of self-esteem.
3. Fourth to fifth year	Initiative vs. guilt	Family	The child learns to acquire direction and purpose in activities.
4. Sixth year to onset of puberty	Industry vs. inferiority	Neighborhood; school	The child acquires a sense of mastery and competence.
5. Adolescence	Identity vs. role confusion	Peer groups and out-groups	The individual develops an *ego identity*—a coherent sense of self.
6. Young adulthood	Intimacy vs. isolation	Partners in friendship and sex	The individual develops the capacity to work toward a specific career and to involve himself or herself in an extended intimate relationship.
7. Adulthood	Generativity vs. stagnation	New family; work	The individual becomes concerned with others beyond the immediate family, with future generations, and with society.
8. Old age	Integrity vs. despair	Retirement and impending death	The individual acquires a sense of satisfaction in looking back upon his or her life.

sociologists term **anticipatory socialization.** Children informally acquaint themselves with such adult roles as spouse and parent by "playing house." Most college-bound high school students go through such a process by learning about and then adopting clothing styles and recreational habits that are common among college students. Second, once individuals assume a new status, they find that they must not only learn the expectations of the associated role but may need to shape the role itself in response to new situations and to their individual needs. For example, a couple entering marriage must evolve new interpersonal skills because as children they learned little about the marital role. Third, as individuals move through their lives, they not only enter roles but must disengage or exit from many of them. Such rituals as graduation exercises, marriage ceremonies, retirement banquets, funerals, and other rites of passage are socially established mechanisms for easing some role transitions. Because socialization across the life course is increasingly important to sociological research, we will take a closer look in this section at some of the transitions that center on life course roles.

Childhood

Humans differ from other primates in having childhoods beyond weaning (Gibbons, 2008). Anthropologists have found that there is no human society in which offspring can provide food for themselves before age 6 or 7. By contrast, chimpanzees are independent soon after they stop getting milk from their mothers. Beyond this biological constraint, our expectation of what childhood is and how long it lasts is an aspect of our culture and affects socialization. Whatever definitions they hold of children, societies begin socializing them as soon as possible. But those definitions affect the socialization that occurs. In the Middle Ages, for example, the concept of childhood as we know it was unheard of. Children were regarded as small adults (Ariès, 1962). No special word existed for a young male between the ages of 7 and 16.

The word *child* expressed kinship, not an age period (Plumb, 1972). Not until about 1600 did a new concept of childhood begin to emerge.

The notion that children should be attending school rather than working in factories, mines, and fields is also of relatively recent origin. In the 1820s half of the cotton mill workers in New England were children who worked 12- to 15-hour days. Even as late as 1924, the National Child Labor Committee estimated that 2 million American children under age 15 were at work, the majority as farm laborers.

Research shows that "the foundations of educational achievement, lifelong health, economic productivity, and responsible citizenship are formed early in life" (Shonkoff, 2011:982), and early childhood adversity can result in long-term problems. Humans are social beings from the start; children display people-oriented responses at very early ages. Even before their first birthday, children are contributors to social life (Rheingold, Hay, and West, 1976; Lewis et al., 1989). Before they are 7, most children have developed the ability to recognize and act out social roles and to combine these roles in complicated ways. The greatest development occurs between 7 and 8 years of age; then the rate of change in conceptualization slows. Indeed, the differences between children who are 7 years old and those who are 8 are frequently greater than the differences between 8-year-olds and 15-year-olds (Barenboim, 1981).

Of course, these patterns are not the same for all children. Not only is there considerable individual variability in child development, but patterns are affected by the social capital of a child's family: their financial resources, cognitive skill of parents, and the connections between family and community (Shonkoff, 2011; Coleman, 1988, 1990; see Box 10.2).

Adolescence

During adolescence, individuals undergo revolutionary changes in growth and development. After years of inferiority, they suddenly catch up with adults in physical size, strength, and

What Makes You an Adult?

The hard thing is, while the ceremony is going on you're not allowed to move your body an inch. You can't twitch your finger or move your mouth. Even your eyelashes have to stay absolutely still. . . . It's believed that if you survive the first three cuts, it will change your life. And there were my brothers, already circumcised, saying, "Don't blink. Don't move. Don't bring embarrassment to our family." (Lekuton, 2003)

This is how Joseph Lemasolai Lekuton, who went on to get a master's degree at Harvard, recalls his circumcision at age 13 in a Maasai village in Kenya. "The most important event of my whole life was my circumcision," he says. "In Maa culture, the circumcision ceremony is the initiation that makes a boy a man."

In many cultures *rites of passage* and *initiation rituals* precisely mark the transition from childhood to adulthood and occur when a child reaches puberty; sexual maturity marks an individual's readiness for marriage and child rearing, both hallmarks of adulthood. While there is great cultural variability, coming-of-age rituals may include tests of strength, endurance of pain, circumcision, scarification, or seclusion. One researcher concluded that such rituals, and the solemnity with which they were practiced, were essential to communicating "the seriousness of life and its duties" to young people (Nanda and Warms, 2011). In other societies the point of transition is less clear. For example, Margaret Mead's classic work *Coming of Age in Samoa* showed that children's participation in society increased gradually, and they reached adulthood with little adolescent trauma (Nanda and Warms, 2011). Similarly, the Inuit people think of maturity as "the exercise of reason, judgment, and emotional control"; these characteristics are believed to develop naturally as children grow (Nanda and Warms, 2011).

What determines when one becomes an adult in modern U.S. society? Some see religious and educational milestones as American rites of passage: confirmation, bar and bat mitzvahs, high school and college graduations, and the like. In 1989 anthropologist Michael Moffatt published *Coming of Age in New Jersey*, in which he describes how becoming an adult can take place in college for the American middle class. He saw college as an environment in which students acquire social skills through interacting with other students, take increasing responsibility for their own lives, and learn to survive within a bureaucratic structure.

In 2002 the National Opinion Research Center at the University of Chicago asked U.S. adult survey respondents how important various life transitions and events were as indicators of adulthood. Is it reaching sexual maturity and starting a family, as in some cultures? It turns out that is not important in the United States.

physiological sexual maturation. Humans are biologically distinct from other animals in having this late-childhood growth spurt and in delaying reproduction for about six years after the onset of puberty (Gibbons, 2008). In much of the world, adolescence is not a socially distinct period in the human life course (Burbank, 1988). Although young people everywhere undergo the physiological changes associated with puberty, children in many countries are socialized to assume adult responsibilities by age 13 and even younger.

Many non-Western societies use **puberty rites**—initiation ceremonies—to symbolize the transition from childhood to adulthood. Mild versions of puberty rites in Western societies include the Jewish bar mitzvah and bat mitzvah, confirmation in some Christian denominations, the securing of a driver's license, and graduation from high school and college. Box 3.2 discusses becoming an adult in America.

In the United States adolescence appears to be an "invention" of the past 100 years (Kett, 1977; Raphael, 1988). As the nation changed from an agricultural to an industrial society, children no longer had a significant economic function in the family. In time, mandatory school attendance, child labor laws, and special legal procedures for "juveniles" established adolescence as a well-defined social reality.

In the view of neo-Freudians like Erik Erikson (1963, 1968), the main task of adolescents in Western societies is to build and confirm a reasonably stable identity, that development of self so important to socialization. For adolescents, Erikson said, the search for identity is particularly acute. Erikson's view of adolescence is in keeping

A substantial majority of Americans say to be an adult is to be financially independent, finished with school, employed full time, and *able* to support a family—in other words, to be fully integrated into the economy. Eighty percent of survey respondents indicated that financial independence was quite or extremely important to being an adult, 90 percent said that formal schooling should be completed, 84 percent said that full-time employment was a marker of adulthood, and 82 percent indicated that one should be able to support a family. Leaving one's family of origin—the family one grows up in—and starting a new family was much less important in people's minds. Just over half of survey respondents thought that it was quite or extremely important to being an adult that one not live with one's parents, a third believed that getting married conferred adulthood, and only 28 percent indicated that having children was an important marker of adulthood.

Using this research as a guide, when *do* Americans "come of age"?

If we use full-time employment as the indicator of becoming adult, a quarter of 18-year-olds, half of 21-year-olds, and three-quarters of 24- to 49-year-olds qualify for adult status. In other words, the youngest age group for which most people are employed full-time is 24. When do Americans finish their formal education? Nearly half of all 20-year-olds are still in school, but by age 22 or 23, about 70 percent are finished with school. Between the ages of 26 and 29, only 13 percent are still in school, and the number keeps dropping. What about moving away from home? More than half of all 18- to 24-year-old males and 46 percent of females live at home (these percentages include unmarried college students living in dorms during the academic year). For 25- to 34-year-olds, those percentages drop to 13.6 (male) and 8.3 (female).

Some cultures mark the transition of their youths from childhood to adulthood at age 12 or 13. It appears that in the United States most people make the transition to adulthood by about the age of 26.

Questions for Discussion

1. Why does it take about twice as long to become an adult in the United States as it does in societies based on hunting and gathering or simple agriculture?

2. How and, more importantly, why do the results of this research differ from legal and other institutional criteria for adulthood (e.g., voting, being drafted into the military, standing trial as an adult, buying alcoholic beverages, paying adult ticket prices, and serving in government positions such as Congress)?

Original data analysis for this box was done by the authors using the General Social Survey data for 2002 (Smith et al., 2010). Data on ages by which people have accomplished tasks associated with adulthood come from Current Population Survey (CPS) data published by the U.S. Census Bureau at http://www.census.gov.

with a long Western psychological tradition that has portrayed adolescence as a period of "storm and stress" caused by the difficult transition from childhood to adulthood (Raphael, 1988; Hamburg and Takanishi, 1989). By the mid-1980s, however, research had accumulated challenging the view that adolescence among American youth is inherently a turbulent period (Rosenberg, 1986, 1989; Nottelmann, 1987; Savin-Williams and Demo, 1984). Although the self-images and self-conceptions of young people change, the changes are not invariably "stormy." Rather than experiencing dramatic change and disruption, adolescents gradually fashion their identities based on their sexual circumstances and their evolving competencies and skills (Corsaro and Eder, 1995), resulting in improvement in self-esteem across the adolescent years for most youth.

Although the media make a good deal out of generational differences between adolescents and their parents, the notion of a "generation gap" vastly oversimplifies matters. Research shows that the peer group has the greater influence on musical tastes, personal adornment, and entertainment idols and, in some cases, with substance use. But the family has the greater influence on future life goals, fundamental behavior codes, and core values (Gecas and Seff, 1990) and can reduce the risk of substance abuse (Mann, 2003).

Young Adulthood

The socialization process continues as we grow out of adolescence. Recent developments in the Western world—the growth of service industries, the prolongation of education, and the enormously high educational demands of post-industrial society—have lengthened the transition to adulthood (Buchmann, 1989). In some respects our society appears to be evolving a new status between adolescence and adulthood: youth—men and women of college and graduate school age (Neugarten and Neugarten, 1987a, 1987b). In leaving home, youths in their late teens or early twenties may choose a transitional institution, such as the military or college, to start them on their way. Or young people may work (provided they can find a job) while continuing to live at home. During this time a roughly equal balance exists between being in the family and moving out. Individuals become less financially dependent, enter new roles and living arrangements, and achieve greater autonomy and responsibility. With the passage of time, the center of gravity in young people's lives gradually shifts away from the family of origin, and they face two core developmental tasks: learning to build and manage trusting and supporting love relationships (Erikson, 1963) and learning how to adapt to the world of work by managing a career and job changes (Freud, 1938).

Recent research on young people's aspirations and their attainment of goals relating to these core tasks shows that the type of aspirations they have affects their well-being. College graduates who placed greater importance on what the researchers defined as intrinsic aspirations (personal growth, close relationships, community involvement, and physical health) and who achieved those aspirations had better psychological health than graduates whose aspirations focused on extrinsic factors including money, fame, and an appealing physical image (Niemiec, Ryan, and Deci, 2009).

Middle Adulthood

Middle adulthood lacks the concrete boundaries of infancy, childhood, and adolescence. It is a catchall category that includes people from 30 to 65 years. The core tasks of middle adulthood remain much the same as they were for men and women in young adulthood and revolve around love (which we will discuss in Chapter 10) and work (which we will discuss in Chapter 4).

The central portion of the adult life span of both men and women is spent in work; thus, much of their socialization revolves around work. Levinson (1986) found that men in their early thirties tend to establish their niche in the world, dig in, build a nest, and make and pursue long-range plans and goals. In their mid- to late thirties, men seek to break out from under the authority of others and assert their independence. In their early forties, men begin assessing where they stand in relation to the goals they set for themselves earlier. Around 45 some men may experience a "midlife crisis." In contrast to the popular media image of midlife crisis, however, researchers find that middle-aged men and women report less psychological distress than other age groups (Wethington, Cooper, and Holmes, 1997; Kessler et al., 1992).

Evidence suggests that women progress through the same developmental periods as the men in Levinson's study and at roughly the same ages, but there are important differences. Although the timing of the periods and the nature of the developmental tasks are similar, the ways women approach these tasks and the outcomes they achieve are different. To a considerable extent, these differences derive from the greater complexity of women's visions for their future and the difficulties they encounter in living them out. Whereas men see autonomy and competition as central to life, women view life as a means for integrating themselves into human relationships. Psychologist Carol Gilligan (1982; Gilligan, Ward, and Taylor, 1989) argues that the development of women involves the recovery in adulthood of confidence, assertiveness, and a positive sense of self that are lost during adolescence. But studies dealing with phases in adult female development have lagged behind those of men, and there is much to be learned about gender differences in socialization and the effects those differences have.

Later Adulthood

Socialization is as important in old age as in other stages of adult development. Indeed, for many people the last years of one's life may be filled with more dramatic changes than any previous stages. Retiring, losing one's spouse, becoming disabled, moving to a nursing home or other care facility, and preparing for death all require individuals to change and adapt. However, the way "old age" proceeds varies considerably across cultures and for people in different gender, racial, ethnic, and class categories within societies (Jacobsen et al., 2011).

Like other periods of the life course, the time at which later adulthood begins is a matter of social definition. In a country such as Zimbabwe, where the life expectancy at birth is 46 years (Haub and Kaneda, 2011), issues of "later adulthood" and death and dying are very different from those in postindustrial nations with life expectancies in the 70s and 80s. In U.S. society, race, class, and gender affect life expectancy and the onset of old age, with the poor and minorities becoming "old before their time" (Newman, 2003:114). As population growth slows, societies experience population aging; by 2050 more than a fifth of the U.S. population will be over the age of 65, and this population aging is increasingly a global phenomenon (Jacobsen et al., 2011).

Societies differ in the prestige and dignity they accord the aged. In many traditional rural societies, elders enjoyed a prominent, esteemed, and honored position (Lang, 1946). In contrast, youth is the favored age in the United States. As the U.S. population ages and people stay in the workforce longer, the prestige and respect accorded to older adults may change.

The "elderly" in the United States are a widely varied group. In 2007, 93 percent of Americans aged 65 and older were living in traditional housing, with only 4 percent in long-term care facilities and 2 percent in housing with services such as laundry, meals, housekeeping, and help with medications. Even among those 85 and older, only 7 percent were living in retirement facilities with services and only 15 percent in long-term care facilities. Many older Americans remain healthy, with more than a third of those who are 65 and over reporting excellent or very good health in 2009, and they are working longer, with more than a fifth of men and about a sixth of women of that age in the labor force in 2009 (Jacobsen et al., 2011).

Although disability among Americans who are 80 and older has been decreasing for several decades, the levels of depression and diabetes among the "young old" (60–69) and middle-aged (50–64) suggests that disability may increase among the elderly as these groups age (Jacobsen et al., 2011). More than 35 percent of U.S. adults aged 65 and older were obese or overweight in 2009, and although studies have not found a direct relationship between obesity and disability among the elderly, arthritis,

Many elderly people continue to lead productive working lives far beyond retirement age.

diabetes, rheumatism, and musculoskeletal conditions all contribute to disability.

Race, ethnicity, and gender all play a role in aging in the United States. For example, the poverty rate for non-Hispanic whites aged 65 or older is 7 percent, while 17 percent of Hispanic and 23 percent of black older Americans live in poverty (Jacobsen et al., 2011). Of older people who live alone, more than 33 percent of blacks and Hispanics and just under 33 percent of Asian Americans live in poverty, compared to 14 percent for whites. And in every racial and ethnic group, women are more likely than men to be poor, with poverty rates in 2009 reaching 40 percent for older black and Hispanic women living alone. Health, life satisfaction, and the experience of being old also thus vary according to gender, race, and ethnicity.

Recent research indicates that many skills improve with age, especially verbal abilities and social skills (Helmuth, 2003). Adult brains lose fewer neurons than previously thought and grow new neurons. The elderly have better mental health, fewer negative emotions, and better social relationships than younger people, and they maintain and improve the skills that are important to them. While openness to new experiences decreases a little in old age, in this time of life, people become more agreeable and conscientious, and, for the most part, they retain their emotional stability as they age further (Roberts, Walton, and Viechtbauer, 2006). Dependency in old age is not inevitable, but a by-product of social definitions and social policies and procedures that vary across cultures, governments, and economic systems (Calasanti and Zajicek, 1997).

Old age entails exiting from some social roles. One of the most obvious of these exits in Western society is retirement from a job. Retirement often has been portrayed as having negative consequences for the elderly because occupational status is a master status—an anchoring point for adult identity. But the importance of retirement has been challenged (Calasanti and Slevin, 2001). For one thing, many Americans do not have an uninterrupted work life, and the "unemployment" of retirement may be just one more in a series.

Even white men, for whom the idea of a 40-year career may hold true, increasingly report that withdrawal from full-time work is followed by part-time or temporary employment; a clearly defined retirement is less common. Gender plays a role, too; when women "retire," they withdraw only from paid labor. Their roles in cooking, cleaning, shopping, doing laundry, and caring for family members continue. Race also affects the retirement picture. For example, African American men spend a greater proportion of their lives in the labor market and suffer higher rates of disability than whites (Calasanti and Slevin, 2001).

Many elderly individuals also experience another role loss, that of being married. Although 75 percent of American men 65 and over are married, the same holds true for only 44 percent of women; typically, women outlive men, marry men older than themselves, and are less likely than men to remarry when widowed (Jacobsen et al., 2011). In 2010, among those 65 and older, 40 percent of women were widowed and 11 percent were divorced, compared to 13 percent of men widowed and 9 percent divorced. The importance of the marital relationship and the stress of losing one's spouse are highlighted by the fact that widowed men and women in industrialized countries have higher mortality rates than currently married persons even after adjustments are made for age (Hu and Goldman, 1990).

Death

A diagnosis of impending death requires that an individual adjust to a new definition of self. To be defined as dying implies more than the presence of a series of biochemical processes (De Vries, 1981). It entails the assumption of a social status, one in which social structuring not only attends but shapes the dying experience. For example, hospital personnel give different care to patients based on their perceived social worth. In a now classic study of a hospital emergency room, sociologist David Sudnow (1967) found that different social evaluations led the staff to work frantically to revive a young child but to acquiesce in the death of an elderly woman. And although death is a biological event, it is made a social reality through such culturally fashioned events as wakes and funerals.

Changes in medical technology and social conditions have made death a different experience than in earlier times. A century ago, the major causes of death were pneumonia and other acute illnesses. Today 65 percent of U.S. citizens die of long-term illnesses including heart disease, Alzheimer's, and cancer (U.S. Census Bureau, 2011a). Dying in the modern world is often drawn out by invasive medical procedures and enmeshed in formal bureaucratic processes (Blank and Merrick, 2005; Nuland, 1994). Only a few generations ago, most people died at home, and the family assumed responsibility for laying out the deceased and preparing for the funeral. Today, only 25 percent of Americans die at home, though most survey respondents say they would prefer to die at home surrounded by the people who love them (Baker, 2003; see also Blank and Merrick, 2005). Nursing homes or hospitals care for the terminally ill and manage the dying experience. A mortuary—euphemistically called a "home"—prepares the body and makes the funeral arrangements or arranges for the cremation of the remains. As a result, the average American's exposure to the death of others is minimized. The dying and the dead are segregated from others and placed with specialists for whom contact with death has become a routine and impersonal matter.

Because so much can be done to keep people alive, Americans are increasingly grappling with end-of-life issues. One such issue is **euthanasia**—the painless putting to death of an individual who suffers from an incurable and painful disease. Debates over whether to legalize euthanasia must distinguish between voluntary and involuntary euthanasia as well as between active and passive euthanasia. Passive euthanasia, the withholding or withdrawing of life supports, requires permission from the dying person in the form of an advance directive that details his or her end-of-life preferences or permission from someone legally authorized by the dying person to make such decisions.

People in the United States seem to be supportive of euthanasia in some extreme cases. For example, in 2006, 68 percent of survey respondents said that if a patient had an incurable disease, "doctors should be allowed by law to end the patient's life by some painless means if the patient and his family request it" (Davis, Smith, and Marsden, 2006).

An approach that returns death to individuals and families is the hospice movement, which seeks more humane care of the terminally ill. A **hospice** is a program or mode of care that attempts to make the dying experience less painful and emotionally traumatic for patients and their families. Elisabeth Kübler-Ross (1969, 1981) contributed a good deal to the movement to restore dignity and humanity to death. Kübler-Ross argued that it is best if impending death is not hidden and if everyone is allowed to express his or her emotions.

In a cross-national study of end-of-life decision making, Robert Blank and Janna Merrick (2005) point out that end-of-life issues will continue to grow and to involve more than just those who are dying and their families, all over the world. Developed countries have ever-expanding populations of the very old, and in developing countries, AIDS and other chronic diseases cut lives short, while malnutrition and acute infectious diseases continue to result in the deaths of the very young. Death and dying increasingly are not private matters only but matters of great importance to societies, with lifesaving technologies, allocation of health care resources, costs of caring for the terminally ill, the ethics of euthanasia, demographic changes, and more the topics of public debate and public policy (Blank and Merrick, 2005).

What Can Sociology Do for You?

At the end of the first two chapters, we considered jobs sociology graduates might get and courses sociology majors might take. Now let's go a step further—to graduate school. More and more college students are going on to get master's degrees or Ph.D.s in their chosen fields of study. What advanced-degree work might a sociology major pursue? Let's turn once again to the

American Sociological Association (ASA). Open the web page for the ASA, **http://www.asanet.org/**. Type "Graduate Training in Sociology" in the search window on the home page. Look for "American Sociological Association: Graduate Training in Sociology" and open the file. How would graduate school differ from your undergraduate experience? How is a master's degree program different from a Ph.D. program? What would some of the differences be in what you would be qualified to do with the degrees?

If you found the content of Chapter 3 to be interesting, see if your college or university's sociology department offers courses in social psychology and in small groups.

The Chapter in Brief: *Socialization*

Foundations for Socialization

Socialization is the process of social interaction by which people acquire those behaviors essential for effective participation in society, the process of becoming a social being. It is essential for the renewal of culture and the perpetuation of society. The individual and society are mutually dependent on socialization.

■ **Nature and Nurture**   Human socialization presupposes that an adequate genetic endowment and an adequate environment are available. Hereditary and environmental factors interact with and affect each other.

■ **Theories of Socialization**   Theories of socialization include functionalist and conflict perspectives as well as three microlevel approaches. Social learning theory emphasizes **conditioning** and **observational learning.** Cognitive developmental theory argues that socialization proceeds differently in the sensorimotor, preoperational, concrete operational, and formal operations stages. Symbolic interactionists say that **reflexive behavior** facilitates the development of the self.

■ **Agents of Socialization**   One of the most important early agents of socialization is the family. As children grow, peers and schools become important agents of socialization. The mass media, especially television, also serve as agents of socialization.

■ **Social Communication**   If they are to adapt to their social environment, human beings must be able to communicate. Noam Chomsky proposed that humans are born with a **language acquisition device.**

Communication refers to the process by which people transmit information, ideas, attitudes, and mental states to one another. It includes the verbal and nonverbal processes (**body language, paralanguage, proxemics,** touch, and artifacts) by which we send and receive messages.

■ **Definition of the Situation**   An important part of socialization is learning what constitutes reality—the basic schemes we use to make sense of and understand the social and physical world. **Definition of the situation** is the interpretation or meaning we give to our immediate circumstances. Our definitions influence our construction of reality, an insight captured by the **Thomas theorem.**

The Self and Socialization

The formation of the **self**—the set of concepts we use in defining who we are—is a central part of the socialization process. The self emerges in the course of interaction with other people and represents the ideas we have regarding our attributes, capacities, and behavior. It typically includes an **egocentric bias.**

■ **Charles Horton Cooley: The Looking-Glass Self**   Charles Horton Cooley's notion that our consciousness arises in a social context is exemplified by his concept of the **looking-glass self**—a process by which we imaginatively assume the stance of other people and view ourselves as we believe they see us. **Self-image** is differentiated from **self-conception. Self-esteem** is governed by **reflected appraisals, social comparisons,** and self-attribution. **Personal efficacy** is another aspect of self-evaluation.

■ **George Herbert Mead: The Generalized Other** George Herbert Mead contended that we gain a sense of selfhood by acting toward ourselves in much the same fashion that we act toward others. According to Mead, children typically pass through three stages in developing a full sense of selfhood: the play stage, in which the child plays roles modeled on a **significant other;** the game stage; and the **generalized other** stage.

■ **Erving Goffman: Impression Management** Erving Goffman pointed out that only by influencing other people's ideas of us can we hope to predict or control what happens to us. Consequently, we have a stake in presenting ourselves to others in ways that will lead them to view us in a favorable light, a process Goffman called **impression management.** Goffman introduced the **dramaturgical approach.**

Socialization Across the Life Course

Socialization is a continuing, lifelong process. All societies have to deal with the **life course** that begins with conception and continues through old age and ultimately death. Role socialization involves **anticipatory socialization,** altering roles, and exiting from roles. Individuals are strongly influenced by **age norms** and tend to set their personal watches by a **social clock.** Some social scientists have looked for stages through which young adults typically pass. Others believe that unexpected events play a more important role in development. People locate themselves during the life course not only in terms of social timetables but also in terms of **life events.**

■ **Childhood** Though societies differ in their definitions of childhood, they all begin the socialization process as soon as possible. Children display people-oriented responses at very early ages and develop very quickly in other ways. The "social capital" contained within a family's environment is of vital consequence in channeling and shaping children's futures.

■ **Adolescence** In much of the world, adolescence is not a socially distinct period in the human life span. Children in many countries are socialized to assume adult responsibilities by age 13 and even younger, sometimes by way of **puberty rites.** Adolescence is not necessarily a turbulent period, nor does a sharp generation gap separate American adolescents from their parents.

■ **Young Adulthood** The developmental and socialization tasks confronting young adults revolve about the core tasks of work and love.

■ **Middle Adulthood** Middle adulthood is a somewhat nebulous period. The core tasks remain much the same as they were in young adulthood. Increasingly, work is coming to be defined for both men and women as a badge of membership in the larger society. Although economic considerations predominate, people also work as a means to structure their time, interact with other people, escape from boredom, and sustain a positive self-image.

■ **Later Adulthood** The last years of one's life may be filled with more dramatic changes than any previous stage. Retiring, losing one's spouse, becoming disabled, moving to a nursing home or other care facility, and preparing for death all require individuals to change and adapt. Societies differ in the prestige and dignity they accord the aged.

■ **Death**   A diagnosis of impending death requires that an individual adjust to a new definition of self. Changes in medical technology and social conditions have made death a different experience from that of earlier times.

Americans are grappling with the issue of **euthanasia,** and the **hospice** movement has arisen to provide a more humane approach to the dying experience.

Glossary

age norms   Rules that define what is appropriate for people to be and to do at various ages.

anticipatory socialization   The process in which people think about, experiment with, and try on the behaviors associated with a new role.

body language   Physical motions and gestures that provide social signals.

communication   The process by which people transmit information, ideas, attitudes, and mental states to one another.

conditioning   A form of learning in which the consequences of behavior determine the probability of its future occurrence.

definition of the situation   A concept formulated by William I. Thomas, which refers to the interpretation or meaning people give to their immediate circumstances.

dramaturgical approach   The sociological perspective associated with Erving Goffman that views the performances staged in a theater as an analytical analogy and tool for depicting social life.

egocentric bias   The tendency to place ourselves at the center of events so that we overperceive ourselves as the victim or target of an action or event that in reality is not directed at us.

euthanasia   The painless putting to death of an individual who suffers from an incurable and painful disease.

generalized other   The term George Herbert Mead applied to the social unit that gives individuals their unity of self. The attitude of the generalized other is the attitude of the larger community.

hospice   A program or mode of care that attempts to make the dying experience less painful and emotionally traumatic for patients and their families.

impression management   The term Erving Goffman applied to the process whereby we present ourselves to others in ways that will lead them to view us in a favorable light.

language acquisition device   An inborn language-generating mechanism postulated by Noam Chomsky to exist in humans. Chomsky sees the basic structure of language as biologically channeled, forming a sort of prefabricated filing system to order the words and phrases that make up human languages.

life course   The interweave of age-graded trajectories with the vicissitudes of changing social conditions and future options that characterize the life span from conception through old age and death.

life events   Turning points at which people change some direction in the course of their lives.

looking-glass self   The term that Charles Horton Cooley applied to the process by which we imaginatively assume the stance of other people and view ourselves as we believe they see us.

observational learning   Learning that occurs when people reproduce the responses they observe in other people, either real or fictional; also referred to as modeling or imitation.

paralanguage   Nonverbal cues surrounding speech—voice, pitch, volume, pacing of speech, silent pauses, and sighs—that provide a rich source of communicative information.

personal efficacy   The belief that one can overcome obstacles and achieve goals.

proxemics   The way we employ social and personal space to transmit messages.

puberty rites   Initiation ceremonies that symbolize the transition from childhood to adulthood.

reflected appraisals   Appraisals of ourselves that we see reflected in the behavior of others.

reflexive behavior   Actions through which people observe, interpret, evaluate, communicate with, and attempt to control themselves.

self   The set of concepts we use in defining who we are.

self-conception   An overriding view of ourselves; a sense of self through time.

self-esteem   The belief that one is a good and valuable person.

self-image   A mental conception or picture we have of ourselves that is relatively temporary; it

changes as we move from one context to another.

significant other   The term George Herbert Mead applied to a social model, usually an important person in an individual's life.

social clock   A cultural timetable based on age norms and used by individuals to pace the major events of their lives.

social comparisons   Comparing one's performance, ability, or characteristics with those of others and rating oneself as positive, neutral, or negative.

socialization   A process of social interaction by which people acquire the knowledge, attitudes, values, and behaviors essential for effective participation in society.

Thomas theorem   The notion that our definitions influence our construction of reality; as stated by William I. Thomas and Dorothy S. Thomas: "If [people] define situations as real, they are real in their consequences."

Review Questions

1. Describe the interplay of nature and nurture as understood today.

2. Name two macrolevel and three microlevel theories of socialization.

3. What are some of the important agents of socialization in today's society? How might they differ from the past?

4. What are some forms of nonverbal communication?

5. What is the looking-glass self?

6. What is the generalized other?

7. Describe impression management.

8. What are some of the important characteristics of each of the major stages of the life course?

 ## Internet Connection   www.mhhe.com/hughes11e

Several agents of socialization were discussed in this chapter, including the family, the school, peers, and the mass media. To what degree does the Internet serve as an agent of socialization?

The Internet may socialize people directly, or its impact may be that it magnifies or diminishes the effects of other agents of socialization. At the same time, other agents of socialization may buffer or enhance the effects of the Internet.

To complete this exercise, use your browser to log onto at least three of your favorite websites.

(If you have no favorite sites, use any search engine and type your three favorite leisure time activities—one at a time—into the search window, click "search," and follow any links you choose.) Think about how these sites may influence you and others your age. Do the messages you receive from the sites complement or conflict with messages you receive from other agents of socialization: parents, peers, school, and other media? Speculate about how and why some agents of socialization are more important than others.

Social Groups and Formal Organizations

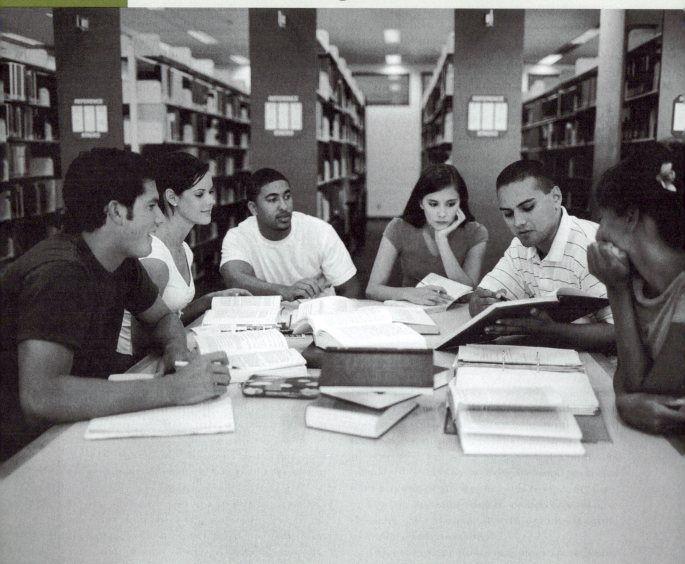

Anyone who has paid for car insurance as a teenaged driver—or begged their parents to do so for them—knows that the rates are high. And with reason: Insurance companies know that accident rates are high for teen drivers. In fact, the leading cause of death for U.S. teenagers is car crashes; more than a third of all deaths of 15- to 19-year-olds result from crashes (Chen et al., 2000).

This death rate is higher when teens travel in groups. In fact, the more teenage passengers per car, the higher the fatal crash rate for teen drivers. The highest death rate is for drivers with three or more passengers, but simply adding a single male teen passenger nearly doubles the probability that the driver will be killed in a wreck. It is just the opposite for older drivers—for 30- to 59-year-olds, fatal crash rates go *down* significantly for drivers with passengers (Chen et al., 2000).

Groups and group interactions are of great interest to sociologists. What is going on with this driving phenomenon? It turns out that dangerous driving behaviors—driving while drunk or high, speeding, skidding, swerving, running red lights, and the like—are "strongly associated with the presence of peers" (Chen et al., 2000:1581). In other words, teen drivers are much more likely to show off, goof off, and in general take more risks when they are driving around in a group of teenagers who are cheering them on or distracting them. Older drivers, on the other hand, are probably motivated to be more careful than usual when driving with passengers, especially when those passengers are children.

As we discussed in Chapter 2, a **group** consists of two or more people who are bound together in relatively stable patterns of social interaction and who share a feeling of unity. Groups are not tangible things; rather, they are products of social definitions—sets of shared ideas. As such they constitute constructed realities. In other words, we make groups real by treating them as if they are real, a clear application of the *Thomas theorem* (see Chapter 3, p. 77). We fabricate groups in the course of our social interaction as we cluster people together in social units: families, teams, cliques, nationalities, races, labor unions, fraternities, clubs, corporations, and the like. In turn we act on the basis of these shared mental fabrications, creating an existence beyond the individuals who are involved. As we discussed in Chapter 2, groups are social structures that have an existence apart from the particular relationships individual people have with one another. For this reason many groups, like the high school you graduated from, have an existence that extends beyond the life spans of specific people.

With groups the whole is greater than the sum of its parts. Groups have distinctive properties in their own right, apart from the particular individuals who belong to them. In Durkheim's terminology (1895/1938), they are *social facts* (see Chapter 1, p. 12). Accordingly, we can speak of families, cliques, clubs, and organizations without having to break them down into the separate interactions that compose them.

Groups provide the structure by which we involve ourselves in the daily affairs of life, yet we may not appreciate the part they play until we are separated from them. How many groups can you think of that form a part of your life? Your answer may include your family; your apartment or dorm mates; the people with whom you work; and friends or acquaintances with whom you skateboard, bowl, knit, go to movies, or study. If you aren't involved with others at college, you might want to be: Researchers have found that undergraduates are more likely to succeed when they have formed alliances with other students, faculty members, and advisers (DePalma, 1991) and when they perceive social adversity during freshman year as both common and transient (Walton and Cohen, 2011). Even physical health is associated with relationships with others. Accidents, suicides, alcoholism, tuberculosis, and heart attacks are more common among socially isolated and lonely individuals (Hawkley and Cacioppo,

2010; Berkman et al., 2000; House, Landis, and Umberson, 1988) and cancer patients with strong emotional support from others live longer than those who lack such support (Goleman, 1991).

In this chapter we will consider group relationships, group dynamics, and a particular type of group, formal organizations. We also will provide a brief introduction to the sociology of work.

Group Relationships

Life places us in a complex web of relationships with other people. As we noted in Chapter 3, our humanness arises out of these relationships in the course of social interaction. Moreover, our humanness must be sustained through social interaction, and fairly constantly so. When an association continues long enough for two people to become linked together by a relatively stable set of expectations, it is called a **relationship.**

People are bound within relationships by two types of bonds: expressive ties and instrumental ties. **Expressive ties** are social links formed when we emotionally invest ourselves in and commit ourselves to other people. Through association with people who are meaningful to us, we achieve a sense of security, love, acceptance, companionship, and personal worth. **Instrumental ties** are social links formed when we cooperate with other people to achieve some goal. Occasionally, this may mean working with our enemies. More often, we simply cooperate with others to reach some end without endowing the relationship with any larger significance.

In this section we will discuss several types of groups: primary groups and secondary groups, in-groups and out-groups, and reference groups.

Primary Groups and Secondary Groups

Sociologists have built on the distinction between expressive and instrumental ties to distinguish between two types of groups: primary and secondary. A **primary group** is a small group characterized by intimate, informal interaction. Expressive ties predominate in primary groups; we view the people—friends, family members, and lovers—as ends in themselves and valuable in their own right. Primary group relationships are more likely to emerge if the number of people is small enough that each person can establish rapport with each other person, if there is enough face-to-face contact that people can exchange ideas and feelings in subtle and personal ways, and if people interact frequently and continuously enough to deepen their ties and develop interlocking habits and interests.

A primary group involves two or more people who enjoy a direct, intimate, cohesive relationship with one another.

Primary groups are critical to the socialization process. Within them infants and children are introduced to the ways of their society. Such groups are the breeding grounds in which we acquire the norms and values that equip us for social life. Sociologists view primary groups as bridges between individuals and the larger society because they transmit, mediate, and interpret a society's cultural patterns and provide the sense of oneness so critical for social solidarity.

Primary groups also are fundamental because they provide the settings in which we meet most of our personal needs. Within them we experience companionship, love, security, and an overall sense of well-being. Not surprisingly, sociologists find that the strength of a group's primary ties has implications for its functioning. For example, the stronger the primary group ties of troops fighting together, the better their combat record (Elder and Clipp, 1988; Copp and McAndrew, 1990). During World War II the success of German military units derived not from Nazi ideology, but from the ability of the German army to reproduce in the infantry company the intimacy and bonds found in

civilian primary groups (Shils and Janowitz, 1948). What made the *Wehrmacht* so formidable was that, unlike the U.S. Army, German soldiers who trained together went into battle together. Additionally, U.S. fighting units were kept up to strength through individual replacement, whereas German units remained on line until there were so many casualties that they had to be pulled back and reconstituted as a new group (Van Creveld, 1982).

Primary groups serve as powerful instruments for social control. Their members command and dispense many of the rewards that are so vital to us and that make our lives seem worthwhile. Should the use of rewards fail, members can frequently win compliance by rejecting or threatening to ostracize those who deviate from the group's norms. For instance, some religious cults employ "shunning" (i.e., a person can remain in the community, but others are forbidden to interact with him or her) as a device to bring into line individuals whose behavior goes beyond that allowed by the group's teachings. Even more importantly, primary groups define social reality for us by structuring our experiences. By providing us with definitions of situations, they elicit from us behavior that conforms to group-devised meanings. Primary groups, then, serve both as carriers of social norms and as enforcers of them.

A **secondary group** entails two or more people who are involved in an impersonal relationship and have come together for a specific, practical purpose. Instrumental ties predominate in secondary groups; we perceive people as means to ends rather than as ends in their own right. Illustrations include our relationships with a clerk in a clothing store and a cashier at a service station. Sometimes primary group relationships evolve out of secondary group relationships. This happens in many work settings. People on the job often develop close relationships with co-workers as they come to share gripes, jokes, gossip, and satisfactions.

In-Groups and Out-Groups

It is not only the groups to which we immediately belong that have a powerful influence upon us. Often the same holds true for groups to which we do not belong. Accordingly, sociologists find it useful to distinguish between in-groups and out-groups. An **in-group** is a group with which we identify and to which we belong. An **out-group** is a group with which we do not identify and to which we do not belong. In daily conversation we recognize the distinction between in-groups and out-groups in our use of the personal pronouns "we" and "they." We can think of in-groups as "we-groups" and out-groups as "they-groups." In-groups typically provide us with our *social identities*—those aspects of our self-concept that we derive from a sense of belonging to groups and the feelings and emotional significance we attach to this belonging (Crocker and Luhtanen, 1990). Our feelings about members of out-groups include pity, scorn, disgust, and envy (Fiske, 2011).

The concepts of in-group and out-group highlight the importance of *boundaries*—social demarcation lines that tell us where interaction begins and ends. Group boundaries are not physical barriers but discontinuities in the flow of social interaction. Some boundaries are based on territorial location, such as neighborhoods, communities, and nation-states. Others rest on social distinctions, such as ethnic group or religious, political, occupational, language, kin, and socioeconomic class memberships. Whatever their source, social boundaries face in two directions. They prevent outsiders from entering a group's sphere, and they keep insiders within that sphere.

An experiment undertaken by Muzafer Sherif and his associates (1961) showed how our awareness of in-group boundaries is heightened and antagonism toward out-groups is generated by competitive situations. The subjects were 11- and 12-year-old healthy, socially well-adjusted boys from stable middle-class homes. The setting was a summer camp where the boys were divided into two groups.

During the first week at the camp, the boys in each group got acquainted, evolved group norms, and arrived at an internal division of labor and leadership roles. During the second week, the experimenters brought the two groups into competitive contact through a tournament of baseball, touch football, tug-of-war, and treasure hunt games. Although the contest opened in a spirit of good sportsmanship, positive feelings quickly evaporated. During the third week, the "integration phase," Sherif brought the two groups of boys together for various events, including eating in the same mess hall, viewing movies, and shooting off firecrackers. But far from reducing conflict, these settings merely provided new opportunities for the two groups to challenge, berate, and harass one another. The experimenters then created a series of urgent and natural situations in which the two groups would have to work together to achieve their ends, such as the emergency repair of the conduit that delivered the camp's water supply. The pursuit of common goals led to a lessening of out-group hostilities and the lowering of intergroup barriers to cooperation.

This study demonstrates how competition with out-groups can create in-group solidarity and out-group hostility. However, other research shows that feelings of in-group favoritism do not require competition with out-groups, but seem to emerge spontaneously from the belief that one is connected to some category of people (see Box 4.1). In one experiment subjects were found to be more likely to trust faces resembling their own (DeBruine, 2002), suggesting a biological basis for some in-group behavior.

Reference Groups

We evaluate ourselves and guide our behavior by group standards. But since Americans are dispersed among many different groups—each with a somewhat unique subculture or counterculture—the frames of reference we use in assessing and fashioning our behavior differ. That is, we have different **reference groups**—social units we use for appraising and shaping attitudes, feelings, and actions (Singer, 1981). Positive reference groups are those having characteristics that we have or wish we had, and negative reference groups are those that represent to us what we are not or do not wish to be. For a high school student who aspires to achieve academically, a positive reference group might be the students who get high grades and belong to the National Honor Society, whereas a negative reference group could be students who attend erratically and fail their classes.

A reference group may or may not be our membership group. We may think of a reference group as a base we use for viewing the world, a source of psychological identification. It helps account for seemingly contradictory behavior: the upper-class person who supports a revolution, the Catholic who speaks against the pope, the union member who supports management, and the civilian who collaborates with the enemy in wartime. These individuals have simply taken as their reference group people other than those from their membership group (Hyman and Singer, 1968). The concept thus helps to illuminate such central sociological concerns as social networks, socialization, and social conformity.

Reference groups provide both *normative* and *comparative* functions (Felson and Reed, 1986). Because we would like to view ourselves as members in good standing within a certain group—or we aspire to such membership—we take on the group's norms and values through the process of anticipatory socialization mentioned in Chapter 3 (p. 85). We cultivate its lifestyles, political attitudes, musical tastes, food preferences, sexual practices, and drug-using behaviors. We also use the standards of our reference group to appraise ourselves—a comparison point against which we judge and evaluate our physical attractiveness, intelligence, health, ranking, and standard of living. When our membership group does not match our reference group, we may experience feelings of **relative deprivation**—discontent associated with the gap between what we have (the circumstances of our membership group) and what we believe we should have (the circumstances of our reference group). Feelings of relative deprivation often contribute to social alienation and provide fertile conditions for collective behavior and revolutionary social movements, which we discuss in Chapter 13 (p. 443). The reference group concept, then, contains clues to processes of social change.

Group Dynamics

To understand groups is to understand much about human behavior. Groups are the wellsprings of our humanness. Although we think of groups as things—distinct and bound entities—it is not their static but their dynamic qualities that make them such a significant force. We need to examine what happens within groups. In this section we will consider group size, leadership, social loafing, social dilemmas, groupthink, and conformity.

4.1 Social Inequalities

What Does Bias Come From? Sometimes, Almost Nothing

When you crack an egg, do you crack it at the small end or at the large end? Who cares, right? Well, if you have a preference, it would place you in one or the other warring nation in Jonathan Swift's *Gulliver's Travels*. Swift was poking fun at the Catholic–Protestant conflict, but social psychologists Myron Rothbart and Oliver P. John (1993:35) saw more: "This example offers a profound insight into the nature of intergroup conflict. . . . In effect, Swift says that differences regarded as profound and intractable may, with a change in perspective, be thought of as trivial." Such an insight applies to conflicts between nations, between groups, and even between individuals today

as well as in Swift's day. But is it well founded?

Rothbart and John described a set of experiments done with English schoolboys that suggest that bias against the out-group can develop among people who have almost no differences at all. Here's the evidence: Social psychologist Henri Tajfel asked schoolboys to estimate the number of dots they saw projected on a screen. Then the boys were told that they would be placed into one of two categories— underestimators or overestimators of the number of dots. The boys were then told which category they were in, but they were placed into categories randomly—they were not

necessarily overestimators if placed in that category, and vice versa.

Once the boys knew which category they were in, each subject was asked to allocate rewards to two other boys, about whom he knew only their category (over- or under-estimator). When both boys receiving rewards were in the same category, the subject divided the rewards for them equally. When one boy was an in-group member (the same category as the subject giving the rewards) and one an out-group member (the other category), the rewards were given preferentially to the in-group member.

Others have replicated this study and affirmed the findings that

Group Size

The size of a group is important because it influences the nature of interaction. The smaller the group, the more opportunities we have to get to know other people well and to establish close ties with them. Two-person groups—**dyads**— are the setting for many of our most intense and influential relationships, including that between parent and child and between husband and wife. Indeed, most of our social interactions take place on a one-to-one basis. Emotions tend to play a greater part in dyads than they do in larger groups (Hare, 1976). But this factor also contributes to their relatively fragile nature: A delicate balance exists between the parties, so if one of them becomes disenchanted, the relationship collapses. Contrary to what you might expect, two-person relationships tend to be more emotionally strained and less overtly

aggressive than other relationships (Bales and Borgatta, 1955; O'Dell, 1968).

The popular adage "two's company, three's a crowd" captures an important difference between two-person and three-person groups. As the German sociologist Georg Simmel (1950) pointed out, forming a **triad** by adding one person to a dyad is far more consequential than adding one person to any other size group. This change fundamentally alters the social situation. Coalitions become possible, with two members joining forces against a third member. With this arrangement one person may be placed in the role of an "intruder" or "outsider." Under some circumstances, however, the third person may assume the role of a "mediator" and function as a peacemaker.

One recurring question that has attracted the interest of social psychologists is what the optimum group size for problem solving and subjects favor in-group over out-group members. Rothbart and John commented on the results (1993:36):

> The two groups were not competing for a limited resource. There was no . . . competition or cooperation between the two groups. There was no historical enmity. There was no aroused frustration in the subjects. There was no objectively determined difference between the two groups; the groups did not differ in terms of language, culture, or physiognomy. . . . As a result of . . . categorization, subjects favored ingroup members with greater resources.

The Tajfel experiments are now referred to as the *minimal group paradigm*. This research showed that bias against an out-group does not depend on a history of enmity between the groups, competition, aggression due to frustration, physical differences, religious differences, or any important value differences at all.

How does the minimal group paradigm relate to group conflict in the real world? Some research suggests that simply the act of categorizing people into groups can lead to significant bias against out-groups: "Categorization generated by the minimal group paradigm implicitly activates the expectation of ingroup superiority ('we' are better than 'they'), and . . . subjects will then selectively remember ingroup and outgroup behaviors in accordance with their perceived superiority" (1993:37).

Other recent research shows that it also activates people's assumption that members of their in-groups are more likely than out-group members to reciprocate favoritism. Gaertner and Insko's 2000 study of the minimal group paradigm found that category members favored the in-group only in situations in which they thought other in-group members could, and would, reciprocate.

So what is bias based on? Well, not much. According to these experiments, merely being told that one belongs to some category is enough to generate group feeling—*for* one's own group and *against* another. "Even in the absence of real differences, competition, and aggression," wrote Rothbart and John, "bias against an outgroup can develop."

Questions for Discussion

1. Do the results of the minimal group experiments indicate that intergroup conflict is inevitable?

2. In view of minimal groups effects, what should we do in our society to reduce intergroup conflict?

decision making is (Laughlin et al., 2006). For instance, if you want to appoint a committee to make a recommendation, what would be the ideal size for the group? Small-group research suggests that five is usually the best size (Hare, 1976). A strict deadlock is not possible because there is an odd number of members. Further, because groups tend to split into a majority of three and a minority of two, being a minority does not result in the isolation of one person, as it does in the triad. The group is sufficiently large for the members to shift roles easily. Finally, five-person groups are large enough that people feel they can express their emotions freely, yet they are small enough that the members show regard for one another's feelings and needs. As groups become larger, they become less manageable. People no longer carry on a conversation with the other members, but address them with formal vocabulary and grammar. As a result they may come to share progressively less knowledge with one another, undermining group stability (Carley, 1991).

Leadership

Imagine a football team without a quarterback, a class of students without a teacher, or youth gangs without chiefs. Without overall direction people typically have difficulty coordinating their activities. Consequently, in group settings some members usually exert more influence than others. We call these individuals *leaders.* Small groups may be able to get along without a leader, but in larger groups a lack of leadership leads to chaos.

Two types of leadership roles tend to evolve in small groups (Bales, 1970). One, an **instrumental leader,** is devoted to appraising the problem at hand and organizing people's activity to deal with it. The instrumental leader is

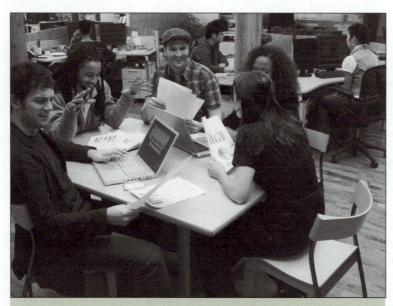

One reason five-person groups are particularly effective for problem solving is that they are settings in which people can take risks and express themselves freely.

sometimes referred to as a *task specialist.* The other, an **expressive leader,** focuses on overcoming interpersonal problems in the group, defusing tensions, and promoting solidarity. The expressive leader is sometimes referred to as a *socioemotional specialist.* The former type of leadership is *instrumental,* directed toward the achievement of group goals; the latter is *expressive,* oriented toward the creation of harmony and unity. Usually, each role is played by a different person, since typically it is the stress created by the task leader that is managed or relieved by the socioemotional leader. Attempting to incorporate both functions in the activities of one person can create role strain (see Chapter 2, p. 58).

Leaders differ in their styles for exercising influence. In classic experiments in leadership by Kurt Lewin and his associates (Lewin, Lippitt, and White, 1939; White and Lippitt, 1960), adult leaders working with groups of 11-year-old boys followed one of three leadership styles. In the *authoritarian style,* the leader made unilateral decisions, gave step-by-step directions, assigned work partners, provided subjective praise and criticism, and remained aloof from group participation. In contrast, in the *democratic style,* the leader allowed the boys to help make decisions, outlined only general goals, suggested alternative procedures, permitted the members to work with whomever they wished, evaluated the boys objectively, and participated in group activities. In the *laissez-faire style,* the leader adopted a passive, uninvolved stance; provided materials, suggestions, and help only when requested; and refrained from commenting on the boys' work.

The researchers found that authoritarian leadership produced high levels of frustration and hostile feelings toward the leader. Productivity remained high as long as the leader was present, but it slackened appreciably in the leader's absence. Under democratic leadership, members were as productive as under authoritarian leadership but were happier, felt more group-minded and friendlier, displayed independence (especially in the leader's absence), and exhibited low levels of interpersonal aggression. Laissez-faire leadership resulted in low group productivity and high levels of interpersonal aggression. While these classic studies suggest that democratic leadership is clearly superior, subsequent research failed to confirm that it always yields better results than authoritarian leadership (Bartol and Martin, 1998; Bass, 1981).

Probably no one leadership style works best in all situations. Different styles may be appropriate in different situations, and elements of both democratic and authoritarian leadership are important factors in effective leadership. Other important contingencies include the leader's personality; the ability, skill, and willingness of followers; and whether the task is clearly defined or involves considerable uncertainty (Fiedler and Garcia, 1987; Vroom and Jago, 1988; Hersey and Blanchard, 1988). Although gender differences in leadership are small, and both women and men can be effective leaders, recent research indicates that female leaders exhibit more characteristics of effective leadership than male leaders (Eagly, Johannesen-Smith, and van Engen, 2003).

Social Loafing

The old saying that "many hands make light the work" turns out to be true: Each "hand" in a group does lighter work than he or she would alone, and the group as a whole does less work than the sum of each of its members working alone. For example, we might expect that three individuals can pull three times as much as one person can and that eight can pull eight times as much. But research reveals that whereas persons individually average 130 pounds of pressure when tugging on a rope, in groups of three

they average 117 pounds each, and in groups of eight only 60 pounds each. One explanation is that faulty coordination produces group inefficiency. However, when subjects are blindfolded and believe they are pulling with others, they also slacken their effort (Ingham, 1974). Apparently, when individuals work in groups, they work less hard than they do when working individually—a process called **social loafing** (Williams, Harkins, and Latané, 1981; Karau and Williams, 1993).

Presumably, people slack off in groups because they think that they can get away with more or because they believe they are not receiving their fair share of credit. For example, recent research (Caruso, Epley, and Bazerman, 2006) shows that people working in groups often believe that they have made disproportionately large contributions to the work of the group, and those who actually have contributed more than others are less satisfied with their work in the group. Fortunately, research suggests that the loafing effect can be minimized by providing a standard against which members are asked to evaluate the group's performance (Harkins and Szymanski, 1989).

Social Dilemmas

A **social dilemma** is a situation in which members of a group are faced with a conflict between maximizing their personal interests and maximizing the collective welfare (Kollock, 1998). Box 4.2 presents one type of social dilemma: the prisoner's dilemma game. Garrett J. Hardin's (1968) "tragedy of the commons" is the classic illustration of a social dilemma. Hardin explored the situation in which a number of herders share a common pasture. Each person may reason that he or she will benefit by adding another cow to the herd, and then another, and so on. But if each person follows this course, the commons will be destroyed through overgrazing, and each will ultimately lose. The idea can be applied to any social-ecological system, including water,

Compete or Cooperate? The Prisoner's Dilemma

Imagine that you are a criminal and that you and your partner in crime have been taken to the police station on suspicion of having committed a crime. The police believe both of you are guilty, but they lack sufficient evidence to turn the case over to the district attorney for prosecution. The police officers place you and your partner in separate rooms, where each of you may confess or maintain your innocence. The police inform you that if both you and your partner remain silent, each of you will get off with 3-year sentences. If both of you confess, you both will serve 7 years. However, should you confess and implicate your partner while your co-conspirator maintains his innocence, you will be released, but your partner will receive a 15-year prison term. The situation will be reversed should you maintain your innocence and your partner confesses. The figure summarizes your alternatives and their consequences.

What you face is a *social dilemma*. A social dilemma exists

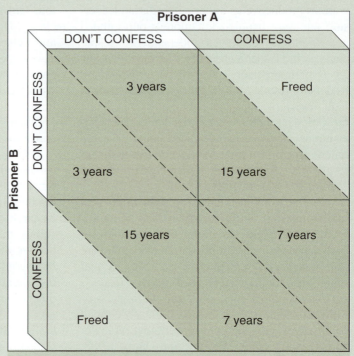

The Prisoner's Dilemma The number in each of the cells shows the number of years each individual would spend in prison.

pasture, forest, cropland, and fisheries resources (Janssen et al., 2010).

Social dilemmas are encountered in many other spheres of life as well. Consider the choice confronting a soldier in a foxhole at the outset of a battle. If every soldier remains in the foxhole, the battle will probably be lost and all will be killed (Kerr, 1983).

In many social dilemmas there is a possibility that some other member of the group can and will provide the public good, making one's own contribution unnecessary. This is termed the "free-rider mechanism" (Petersen, 1992; Yamigishi, 1995). In these situations people can get the benefits of, for example, a social movement with whose goals they agree by contributing nothing and riding free on the efforts of others who are willing to contribute. Many social dilemmas appear to be insoluble without the imposition of government or structured market mechanisms. However, the work of the 2009 Nobel laureate in economics, Elinor Ostrom (Ostrom, 1990; Poteete, Janssen, and Ostrom, 2010), suggests otherwise. She has shown that individuals can solve these problems themselves through systems of self-governance that involve monitoring one another's compliance with policies that benefit the community and punishing violators.

when behavior that is advantageous for one party leads to disadvantageous outcomes for others. One way social scientists have examined cooperative and competitive behaviors is by means of the prisoner's dilemma game. As you can gather, the prisoner's dilemma provides a mixed-motive situation in which players must choose between strategies of cooperation and competition.

What would you do under these circumstances? The "don't confess" option is the cooperative one. You show that you trust your partner not to take advantage of the situation by turning state's evidence. But you run the risk that your partner will confess and you will pay a heavy price. The "confess" option is the competitive one. You attempt to improve your situation by betraying your partner. But you also run the risk that your partner will take the same route, ensuring that you both will receive 7-year terms. The best strategy for you individually results in a particularly punishing outcome if you both select it.

Robert Axelrod (1984) found that the simplest and most effective strategy for playing the prisoner's dilemma game is one he called "tit for tat." You cooperate on the first move. Thereafter, you respond immediately and in kind to your partner's behavior, following a policy of strict reciprocity: a stringent eye-for-an-eye justice. The strategy seems to work because it combines four properties: It is nice, retaliatory, forgiving, and clear. It is *nice* because it avoids unnecessary conflict as long as the other party reciprocates. Tit for tat is *retaliatory* because it responds to provocation. The strategy is *forgiving* because it allows the other party to retreat following retaliation. Finally, tit for tat is *clear* and predictable. Clarity is essential so that the other party can grasp the consequences of his or her actions and thereby adapt new strategies that will promote long-term cooperation. Yet tit for tat does not always work. It is particularly vulnerable to cycles of recrimination that end up hurting both parties through relentless feuding (Kollock, 1993).

Research indicates that rational calculation and strategy are not the only determinants of outcomes in prisoner's dilemma situations. Brent Simpson (2004) found that people who have a prosocial orientation are more likely to cooperate in the first round of a prisoner's dilemma game than are people who have a more individualistic orientation. If the initial exchange involves cooperation, those with a prosocial orientation are more likely to cooperate in subsequent rounds. Other studies have found substantial numbers of subjects trying cooperation when real money is at stake in the game (Putterman, 2010), and a prisoner's dilemma tournament helped kick-start the study of the evolution of cooperation in humans (Pennisi, 2010).

Questions for Discussion

1. University life is filled with opportunities for competitive or cooperative behaviors. Do you have a generalized strategy of cooperation or competition, or do you use different strategies in different situations?

2. No one gets through life without facing situations that fit the definition of social dilemma. Think of at least two examples from your own life.

Groupthink

In 1961 the Kennedy administration undertook an ill-fated invasion of Cuba. More than 1,400 Cuban exiles were trained for the attack by the Central Intelligence Agency and then transported to Cuba's Bay of Pigs, where Fidel Castro's forces killed or captured most of them. The failed invasion solidified Castro's leadership, consolidated the Cuban-Soviet alliance, and contributed to a later attempt to place Soviet nuclear missiles in Cuba, none desirable outcomes for the United States. Later analysis showed that President Kennedy and his advisers had overlooked the size and strength of Castro's army and had failed to gather relevant information that might have led them to act differently.

Social psychologist Irving Janis (1982, 1989) suggested that the president and his advisers were victims of **groupthink**—a decision-making process found in highly cohesive groups in which the members become so preoccupied with maintaining consensus that their critical faculties are impaired. In groupthink, members share an illusion of invulnerability that leads to overconfidence, a greater willingness to take risks, and a tendency to ignore contradictory evidence. Members of the group demand conformity and apply pressure to those who express doubts about a proposed course of action; they withhold dissent and exercise self-censorship. As a result, decisions are made without the benefit of critical analysis. Although most of the examples of groupthink cited by scholars are from decision-making groups in business and government, the framework can also help us to understand decision making in other groups, such as cohesive friendship groups in high school and college.

Research done since Janis's original formulation has changed the way social scientists think about groupthink. For example, we know now that groupthink can occur when decision-making groups are not particularly cohesive; it can result primarily from a strong leader indicating a preference that dominates the thinking of other group members (Bartol and Martin, 1998; Tetlock et al., 1992; see also Granström and Stiwne, 1998; Paulus, 1998). And although groupthink often leads to poor decisions, there is evidence that it sometimes produces a good outcome, just as high-quality decision-making procedures can occasionally result in a poor outcome (McCauley, 1989).

Conformity

Groupthink research testifies to the powerful social pressures that operate in group settings and produce conformity. Although such pressures influence our behavior, we often are unaware of them. We tend to attribute our own choices to rational deliberation and those of others to conformity (Pronin, Berger, and Molouki, 2007). In a pioneering study Muzafer Sherif (1936) demonstrated the power of conformist messages with an optical illusion. If people view a small, fixed spot of light in a darkened room, they perceive it as moving erratically in all directions. However, individuals differ in how far they think the light "moves." Sherif tested subjects alone and found the reference point for each individual. He then brought together in group settings people with quite different perceptions and asked them again to view the light and report aloud on their observations.

Under these circumstances their perceptions converged toward a group standard. Later, in solitary sessions, they did not return to the standard they had at first evolved but adhered to the standard of the group. Significantly, most subjects reported that they arrived at their assessment independently and that the group had had no influence on them.

Sherif presented subjects with an ambiguous situation; Solomon Asch (1952) asked subjects to match lines of the same length from two sets of cards displayed at the front of the room. He instructed the members of nine-person groups to give their answers aloud. However, only one of the individuals was a subject in the experiment; the others were graduate students working with Asch, and they unanimously provided incorrect answers on certain trials. Despite the obviousness of the correct answer, nearly one-third of all the subjects' judgments contained errors identical with or in the direction of the rigged errors of the majority. Some three-fourths of the subjects conformed on at least one of the trials. Thus, Asch demonstrated that some individuals conform to the false consensus of a group even though the consensus is contradicted by the evidence of their own eyes. Asch's findings have been replicated many times and in many nations and cultures, and although people in some countries conform more than in others, the differences are not very great (Sunstein, 2003).

The Sherif (1936) and Asch (1952) studies illustrate two of the main reasons that people conform: the desire to be correct and the desire to be accepted by the group (Aronson, 2008). It is possible that the conforming subjects in Asch's experiment could see that the task had little significance and thus conformed because it was easy and had no serious consequences. But other experiments have shown that humans are likely to obey orders and to go along with the group even when the stakes are considerably higher (see Box 4.3). The tendency of people to conform and their desire to be accepted by a group is being used by colleges and universities to prevent substance abuse (Sunstein, 2003). The campaigns are based on the idea that most college students overestimate how much drinking and drug use there is on campus and misperceive the tolerance of their peers for substance abuse, leading them to conform with behavior that isn't all that widespread. When students are informed of actual levels of drinking and smoking, they appear to be less likely to become smokers or heavy drinkers.

Formal Organizations

As modern societies have become increasingly complex, so have the requirements of group life. Contemporary societies composed of millions of people cannot rely entirely on primary group arrangements to accomplish the tasks of social life. Food has to be produced, preserved, and transported over considerable distances to support large urban populations. The residents of large, anonymous communities cannot count only on family members and neighbors to enforce group norms and standards. For these and many other tasks, people require groups they can deliberately create for the achievement of specific objectives. Such groups are **formal organizations.**

In recent decades the United States has increasingly become a society of large, semiautonomous, and tightly knit formal organizations. Not only is there big government—in municipal organizations as well as the federal government—but also there are big multinational corporations, big universities, big hospitals, big unions, and big farm organizations. Modern society is emerging as a web of formal organizations that appear, disappear, change, merge, and enter into countless relationships with one another.

In this section we will introduce types of formal organization, define bureaucracy and list its characteristics, discuss problems of bureaucracy, and consider various theoretical approaches.

Types of Formal Organization

People enter formal organizations for a variety of reasons. Sociologist Amitai Etzioni (1975) classified organizations on the basis of these reasons and identified three major types: voluntary, coercive, and utilitarian. **Voluntary organizations** are associations that members enter and leave freely. College campuses abound with examples: hiking and biking groups, service organizations, and intramural sports teams are just a few. Members are not paid for participation; they join voluntary organizations to fill their leisure time, to enjoy the company of like-minded people, to perform some social service, to advance some cause, or to change themselves through self-help groups (Woodard, 1987).

When voluntary organizations complete their goals, Americans often refashion them, finding new purposes to validate an enterprise. For example, once vaccines eliminated infantile paralysis, the March of Dimes organization reformulated its goals to embrace new health missions (Sills, 1957). In some cases program failure is essential because the effective solution of the problems the organizations address would eliminate the need for their existence. Skid-row rescue missions provide a good illustration of this principle (Rooney, 1980).

People also become members of some organizations—**coercive organizations**—against their will. They may be committed to a mental hospital, sentenced to prison, or drafted into the armed forces. Sociologist Erving Goffman (1961b) studied life in what he called **total institutions**—places of residence where individuals are isolated from the rest of society for an appreciable period of time and where behavior is tightly regimented. In these environments the "inmates" or "recruits" are exposed to **resocialization** experiences that systematically seek to strip away their old roles and identities and fashion new ones. The induction process often includes **mortification.** Individuals are separated from families and friends who provide networks of support for old

Reality TV and Conformity: *The Experiment*

In 2002 the British Broadcasting Corporation (BBC) televised a social science research project. Called *The Experiment,* the show used 15 volunteer subjects who were assigned to be either prisoners or guards in a studio "prison" for 10 days (Haslam and Reicher, 2002; Ritch, 2002). The volunteers for the show/experiment did not know what was going to happen to them, but they were told that "the environment would be challenging, might involve hunger, hardship, and anger, and would resemble a barracks, a prison, or a bootcamp" (Briggs, 2002; Reicher and Haslam, 2003a).

The Experiment was modeled after a 1970s Stanford University study (Zimbardo, 2007; Haney, Banks, and Zimbardo, 1973). In the original study, conducted by psychologist Philip Zimbardo, 21 male students played the prisoner and guard roles in a mock prison. As the experiment progressed, the prisoners became more passive and withdrawn and the guards conformed more fully with their guard roles, displaying *institutional aggression.* They forced prisoners to perform useless tasks, sing songs, laugh, or refrain from laughing according to their orders. Although they were instructed not to use physical violence, student guards forced student prisoners to clean toilets with their bare hands, call each other names, and curse at one another.

Why did the guards' behavior become so nasty? According to Zimbardo and his colleagues, they were simply acting the way they thought prison guards should act. In the 1960s researcher Stanley Milgram discovered that ordinary people readily behave in morally questionable ways in the name of conformity and obedience. In a now-classic experiment, Milgram used a phony but realistic looking electric chair and instructed a "teacher" to give the "learner" in the electric chair a shock every time the learner made a mistake (Milgram, 1963). Teachers also were told to increase the voltage with each succeeding mistake. The learners were not actually shocked, but the teachers believed that the fake shocks they gave were real. Nevertheless, 65 percent of them obeyed completely and went all the way to the highest voltage. Even when the learners called out for help, asked for the experiment to end, shrieked, and fell silent, the teachers continued to administer "shocks" when instructed to do so by those administering the study.

Milgram then set up an experiment using three teachers—one experimental subject and two "teachers" who were working with him (Milgram, 1964). Each of the three was to recommend a shock level, and the lowest recommendation would be administered. In this

ways. They are made vulnerable to institutional control and discipline by being deprived of personal items, clothing, and accessories and are provided haircuts, uniforms, and standardized articles that establish an institutional identity. Often the new members are humiliated by being forced to assume demeaning postures, to engage in self-effacing tasks, and to endure insulting epithets (what sociologists term a *degradation ceremony*). These procedures leave individuals psychologically and emotionally receptive to the roles and identities demanded of them by the total institution.

Individuals also enter formal organizations formed for practical reasons—**utilitarian organizations.** Universities, corporations, farm organizations, labor unions, and government bureaus and agencies are among the organizations people form to accomplish vital everyday tasks. Utilitarian organizations fall between voluntary and coercive organizations: Membership in them is neither entirely voluntary nor entirely compulsory. For example, we may not be compelled to secure employment with a corporation, but if we wish to support ourselves, doing so is an essential element of life.

Bureaucracy: A Functional Approach to Organizations

As we saw in Chapter 1 (pp. 18–19), the functionalist perspective attempts to understand the existence and structure of social patterns by examining the contributions those patterns make to the larger system of which they are a part. In modern societies, large, complex organizations perform many tasks that are required way the subject could ensure a low level of shock by recommending a voltage lower than that recommended by the others. But Milgram found that the subjects in these groups of three suggested giving learners shocks at *higher* voltages than would a subject acting alone; the subject went along with the higher voltage suggestions of the other two in the group.

Milgram conducted his shock experiment, with slight variations, with nearly 1,000 subjects—all "typical" people. Clearly, the pressure to conform to role expectations and to obey authority caused ordinary people to become nasty "prison guards" and shock-administering "teachers" in these experiments. But the researchers involved in the BBC's *The Experiment* showed that there are important qualifications to these now well-accepted generalizations.

In the BBC study, TV viewers did not get to see the prisoners scrub toilets by hand. In fact, these guards did *not* strongly identify with one another as guards, conform to the stereotypical role of guard, or become abusive to the prisoners (Haslam and Reicher, 2007). Why were these subjects so different from those in Zimbardo's study? One of the primary differences was that the BBC participants knew their behavior would be observed by millions of viewers (Reicher and Haslam, 2003b). Although some have drawn upon the Zimbardo study to explain why the powerful often abuse the powerless, the researchers involved in *The Experiment* maintain that Zimbardo's results cannot be seen as a reasonable excuse for such abusive behavior. People can "resist the roles thrust upon them . . . people *do* have responsibility and choice over the conditions that lead to tyranny" (Reicher and Haslam, 2002). Zimbardo, now near 80, wants to use the lessons of the prison experiment as a force for good (Miller, 2011). In 2010 he founded the Heroic Imagination Project, the goal of which is to increase acts of everyday heroism in the world. The first step? Zimbardo says that it is critical to teach people to recognize the social pressures that work to prevent us from helping those in need or to encourage us to treat others badly.

Questions for Discussion

1. In institutional aggression, people act aggressively or violently because they see it as part of their jobs. Besides guarding prisoners, what examples of work can you think of in which violence is condoned?

2. Think back over the past week. What have you done that you might label *conformity*?

3. What examples of horror and atrocity from history or from recent news events can you think of that may have resulted at least in part from people's desire to conform and to obey instructions?

for those societies to survive and grow. Organizations that manage sewers, the water supply, electricity, phones, public safety, the administration of government, and the manufacturing and distribution of goods are some of the most important examples of these. The functionalist perspective developed the concept of *bureaucracy* to explain the existence and structure of this organizational type.

As long as organizations are relatively small, they can often function reasonably well on the basis of informal, face-to-face interaction. But if larger organizations are to attain their goals, they must establish formal operating and administrative procedures. Only as they standardize and routinize many of their operations can they function effectively. This requirement is met by a **bureaucracy,** a social structure made up of a hierarchy of statuses and roles that is prescribed by explicit rules and procedures and based on a division of function and authority. Sociologists use the concept in a way that differs sharply from the negative connotation "bureaucracy" has when we use it in everyday conversation to refer to organizational inefficiency.

The bureaucratic form of organization has developed over many centuries in the Western world (Bendix, 1977). Early bureaucracies, like bureaucracies in traditional societies today, were based on patrimonialism, a traditional system of authority in which people are committed to serve traditional leaders, rather than a set of codified rules and procedures. The result is an organization that is the personal instrument of a master (Ritzer, 2011).

Only in the 20th century did the modern bureaucracy fully flower in response to the dictates of industrial society. As contemporary

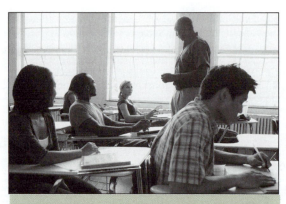

These students are participating in a utilitarian organization, a university, for a particular reason: to get a degree.

organizations increased in size and complexity, more structural units and divisions were required. In turn, some mechanism was needed for synchronizing and integrating various activities. By providing for the performance of tasks on a regular and orderly basis, bureaucracies permit the planning and coordination of these activities in an efficient manner. Additionally, they aim to eliminate all unrelated influences on the behavior of their members so that people act primarily in the organization's interests. Although most complex organizations in the United States are organized as bureaucracies, the degree and forms of bureaucratization vary (Perrow, 1986). In addition, globalization, rapid social change, and the introduction of new technologies have produced much innovation in real-world organizations, and this has changed how social scientists think about organizations (Liker, Haddad, and Karlin, 1999; Jaffee, 2001).

Characteristics of Bureaucracies

The German sociologist Max Weber (1946, 1947) was impressed by the ability of bureaucracies to rationalize and control the process by which people collectively pursue their goals. He developed the concept of bureaucracy as an *ideal type.* By using the term *ideal* in this context, Weber did not mean that the bureaucracy represented a standard of perfection. In fact, Weber was quite critical of bureaucracy as an organizational form. Instead, Weber used the term *ideal type* (Chapter 1, p. 13) to refer to a concept constructed by sociologists to portray the principal characteristics of a phenomenon. The ideal type of the bureaucracy is a model that describes and analyzes organizational arrangements and is based on the common elements of diverse organizations such as government agencies, major religious denominations, labor unions, large corporations, and universities. Perhaps no actual organization is exactly like the model in all respects, but the model isolates the important elements of organizational structure in contemporary society. These elements are presented in Table 4.1.

At first glance, the abstract description presented in Table 4.1 seems fairly irrelevant to our daily lives. But it does outline the kind of organizational structure most of us would like to be able to take for granted. Though we dislike "bureaucracy" and can feel alienated by it, most of us expect that the organizations we encounter will work the way Weber described, and we feel mistreated if they do not.

For example, we wish those holding positions in our schools, government, and corporations to gain these offices and exercise power because of their ability and competence, not because of their race, gender, personal connections, or physical attractiveness (characteristic 4). We would not like courthouse clerks, police officers, or the mayor of our town to sell services to the highest bidder; we define this kind of behavior as the crime of bribery (characteristic 5). We expect that rules will be followed and that exceptions will not be made at the whim of officeholders. For example, we expect that government contracts will be awarded to bidders who follow the correct procedures and submit the lowest bids, not simply to family members of the responsible government official; when we

Table 4.1	Characteristics of Weber's Ideal Bureaucracy

How Does Weber's Ideal Bureaucracy Work?

1. Each office or position has clearly defined duties and responsibilities. In this manner the regular activities of the organization are arranged within a clear-cut division of labor.

2. All offices are organized in a hierarchy of authority that takes the shape of a pyramid. Officials are held accountable to their superiors for subordinates' actions and decisions in addition to their own.

3. All activities are governed by a consistent system of abstract rules and regulations that define the responsibilities of the various offices and the relationships among them. They ensure the coordination of essential tasks and uniformity in performance regardless of changes in personnel.

4. All offices carry with them qualifications and are filled on the basis of technical competence, not personal considerations. Presumably, trained individuals do better work than those who gain an office on the basis of family ties, personal friendship, or political favor. Competence is established by certification (e.g., college degrees) or examination (e.g., civil service tests).

5. Incumbents do not "own" their offices and cannot use offices for personal ends. Positions remain the property of the organization, and officeholders are supplied with the items they require to perform their work.

6. Employment by the organization is defined as a career. Promotion is based on seniority or merit, or both. After a probationary period, individuals gain the security of tenure and are protected against arbitrary dismissal. In principle, this feature makes officials less susceptible to outside pressures.

7. Administrative decisions, rules, procedures, and activities are recorded in written documents preserved in permanent files.

suspect that such a thing has taken place, we complain of nepotism (characteristic 3). When things go wrong with what an organization does, we expect some responsible official to react, track down and correct the problem, and discipline those in the organization who may have fallen short (characteristics 2 and 7). If we are employed in a bureaucracy, we expect there to be clear expectations of what we and others are to do and how we are to coordinate our activities. For example, we expect that other officeholders cannot usurp our authority simply because they want to and can get away with it (characteristic 1). And if we obey the rules and perform competently, we expect that we should be able to make a career within the organization and should not be let go without a very good reason (characteristic 6).

Thus, as much as we sometimes complain about the "red tape" of bureaucracies, and although we all might like to be treated as special cases, bureaucracy is with us because we expect it to be there and to function as Weber said that it should. To live otherwise in modern U.S. society is almost unthinkable.

Bureaucracy is a fixture of our lives not only because it represents how we expect our public lives to be governed but also because, as Weber argued, it is an inherent feature of modern economic organization, whether capitalist or socialist. While some argue that bureaucracy is a fixture only of capitalism, Weber argued that under socialism governments and enterprises would be completely dominated by bureaucrats and bureaucracies. Under capitalism bureaucratic domination is mitigated at least partly; business owners are not bureaucrats and are free to do as they wish, unconstrained by the rules that apply to bureaucrats. For this reason, Weber thought that capitalism would be more likely than socialism to preserve individual freedom and creative leadership in a world dominated by formal organizations (Ritzer, 2011).

But not even Weber was truly optimistic about bureaucracy. He (Weber 1921/1968) and many sociologists who came after him (e.g., Blau and Scott, 1962) have expressed concern that bureaucracies may pose an inherent challenge to human liberty by turning free people into "cogs" in organizational machines. Let us take a closer look at this issue and other problems of bureaucracy as a feature of our social life.

Problems of Bureaucracy

Oligarchy

Organizations, like all other groups, enjoy a formidable capacity for eliciting conformity. As we noted earlier, groups do not simply control and dispense rewards and punishments. They also define social reality by structuring our experiences. Given the predominant role organizations play in contemporary life, some social scientists have expressed concern for the future of democratic institutions. They point out that all too often the needs of organizations take priority over those of individuals (Glassman, Swatos, and Rosen, 1987; Dandeker, 1990). Robert Michels (1911/1966), a sociologist and friend of Weber, argued that bureaucracies contain a fundamental flaw that makes them undemocratic social arrangements: They invariably lead to *oligarchy*— the concentration of power in the hands of a few individuals who use their offices to advance their own fortunes and self-interests. He called this tendency the **iron law of oligarchy:** "Whoever says organization, says oligarchy" (p. 365).

Michels cited a variety of reasons for the oligarchical tendencies found in formal organizations, even those that are presumably democratic. First, because they have hierarchical leadership structures involved in everyday administration, most voting by the membership becomes a ritualistic confirmation of leaders' decisions. Second, officials have special advantages: access to information unavailable to others, superior political skills and experience, and control of a variety of administrative resources, including communication networks, offices, and a treasury, that can be used to ward off challengers and co-opt dissidents and rivals. Third, ordinary members tend to be uninterested in assuming leadership responsibilities and are apathetic toward the problems of the organization.

Michels pointed to the history of European socialist parties and labor unions as evidence in support of his thesis. However, not all organizations are oligarchic (Breines, 1980). For example, in their classic study, Lipset, Trow, and Coleman (1956) showed that the International Typographical Union (ITU), composed of typesetters, maintained a democratic tradition by institutionalizing a "two-party system." Union elections were held on a regular basis, with the two parties putting up a complete slate of candidates. Lipset and his colleagues reasoned that where competing groups are active and legitimate, the rank-and-file have the potential for replacing leaders and introducing new policies.

Dysfunctions of Bureaucracy

Bureaucracies may produce harmful consequences. For example, political scientist Richard Rosecrance (1990) argued that Americans in the post–World War II period came to embrace Weber's bureaucratic society so completely that our corporations became overstaffed, making the nation uncompetitive in world markets. In many organizations, management specialization—not production or meeting consumer needs—became the way to the top. Such outcomes are the typical by-product of a bureaucratic dysfunction that C. Northcote Parkinson (1962) termed **Parkinson's law:** "Work expands so as to fill the time available for its completion." Despite the tongue-in-cheek tone of his writing, Parkinson showed that "the number of the officials and the quantity of the work are not related to each other." He contended that bureaucracy expands not because of an increasing workload but because officials seek to have additional subordinates hired in order to multiply the number of people under them in the

The relentless growth of bureaucracy is reflected in the federal government. When George Washington was inaugurated as president in 1790, there were nine executive units, and 1 in 4,000 Americans was employed by the executive branch. Over the next hundred years, the government bureaucracy grew 10 times as fast as the population, and by 1891, 1 in 463 Americans was a U.S. government employee. This growth continued through most of the 20th century, and by 1970 the figure stood at 1 in 69. While the size of government was stable under President Reagan and the first President Bush, it declined under President Clinton and the second President Bush, and at the beginning of the Obama administration the U.S. government employed approximately 1 in 103 Americans (http://www.census.gov/govs/apes/).

The situation has been no better in the business world. In the mid-1980s more than half of the typical U.S. corporation consisted of workers uninvolved in operations or production (Rosecrance, 1990). Many U.S. firms undertook massive restructuring and downsizing in the 1990s—in everyday language, many people lost their jobs. Some corporations have attempted to

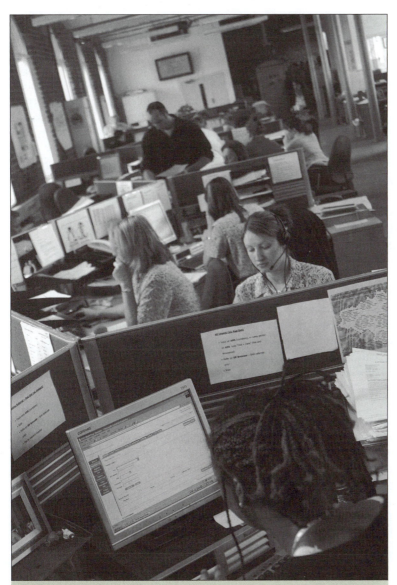

Bureaucracies perform many of the tasks that are required for society to survive and grow. At the same time, as Max Weber and other sociologists have pointed out, they turn people into cogs in organizational machines.

hierarchy. These subordinates, in turn, create work for one another, while the coordination of their work requires still more officials.

undermine Parkinson's law by developing new structural arrangements made possible by the computer and telecommunications revolution

(Wilke, 1993; Huey, 1994). We have yet to see if such attempts to redefine bureaucracies can truly repeal Parkinson's law.

Another dysfunction of bureaucracy was first noted by social critic Thorstein Veblen (1921), who pointed out that bureaucracies encourage their members to rely on established rules and regulations and to apply them in an unimaginative and mechanical fashion, a pattern he called **trained incapacity.** As a result of the socialization provided by organizations, individuals often develop a tunnel vision that limits their ability to respond in new ways when circumstances change. Government bureaucracies are especially risk-averse because they are caught up in such complex webs of constraint that any change is likely to rouse the ire of important constituencies (Wilson, 1990, 1993). This problem may be particularly significant in very successful organizations, which often resist change because of the fear that to do so will prevent repetition of past successes. Such inflexibility can result in self-perpetuating organizational mediocrity.

Bureaucracy as an Idealized Model

The bureaucratic model is difficult, if not impossible, to realize in practice. A number of forces undermine its operation (Perrow, 1986; Jaffee, 2001). First, human beings do not exist only for organizations. People track all sorts of mud from the rest of their lives, including their prejudicial attitudes, with them into bureaucratic arrangements, and they have numerous interests independent of the organization. Second, bureaucracies are not immune to social change. When such changes are frequent and rapid, the pat answers supplied by bureaucratic regulations and rules interfere with rational operation. Third, bureaucracies are designed for the "average" person. In real life, however, people differ in intelligence, energy, zeal, and dedication, so they are not interchangeable in the day-to-day functioning of organizations. Fourth, forms of informal organization emerge within real bureaucracies in response to the

tensions and contradictions of organizational life and thus, as a model of what happens within an organization, the bureaucratic model is incomplete.

Informal organization consists of interpersonal networks and ties that arise in a formal organization but are not defined or prescribed by it. Many people are distressed by the impersonality of bureaucratic arrangements, and therefore they search for warmth, rapport, and companionship in the work setting through informal relationships. Based on their common interests and relationships, individuals form primary groups. These informal structures provide means by which people bend and break rules, share "common knowledge," engage in secret behaviors, handle problems, and "cut corners." Work relationships, then, are much more than the lifeless abstractions contained on an organizational chart that outlines the official lines of communication and authority.

The roots of informal organization are embedded within formal organization and are nurtured by the formality of its arrangements. Official rules and regulations must be sufficiently general to cover a great many situations. In applying general rules to a particular situation, people must use their judgment, so they evolve informal guidelines that provide them with workable solutions. Additionally, to avoid bureaucratic red tape, employees often arrive at informal understandings with one another as a way of keeping the formal organization operating smoothly. Thus, people are tied to the larger group by their membership in primary groups that mediate between them and the formal organization. Informal organizations compete with the formal organization for members' loyalties and challenge bureaucratic rules and authority. This has been the focus of much attention by sociologists.

Factory workers typically evolve their own norms regarding what constitutes a "reasonable" amount of work, and these norms often do not conform with those of management (Roethlisberger and Dickson, 1939; Hamper, 1991). Sociologist Michael Burawoy (1979) studied informal organization among shop workers while working for a year as a machine operator at a large Chicago-area plant. He found that relations on the shop floor were dominated by "making out"—a competitive game the machine operators played by manipulating the rules and regulations governing their work to their benefit.

Conflict and Interactionist Perspectives

Until about 20 years ago, the functionalist approach to bureaucracy identified with Weber dominated American sociology. Sociologists focused their attention on organizations as abstract social structures while often neglecting the behavior of the individuals who compose them. Many sociologists studied formal organizations without noticing the processes by which social structures are produced and reproduced in the course of people's daily interactions. But much has changed, as it has become increasingly clear that organizations in the real world do not operate as the functionalist perspective suggests (Scott, 2004). Sociologists from differing perspectives have looked beyond the bureaucratic model to understand how organizational reality is generated through the actions of people and groups of people (Benson, 1977; Romanelli, 1991). We will consider two of these approaches: the conflict perspective and the symbolic interactionist perspective.

The Conflict Perspective

Conflict theorists contend that organizational goals reflect the priorities of those who occupy the top positions. Viewed in this manner, organizations are not neutral social structures pursuing clear goals but arenas for conflicting interests in which the social issues and power relations of society are played out (Morrill, Zald, and Rao, 2003; Jaffee, 2001). Marxist social scientists have followed in the tradition of Karl Marx

(1970), who saw bureaucracy as a manifestation of the centralizing tendencies of capitalism and an instrument of class domination. They analyze organizations within the context of the broader inequalities that operate within society and find that the distribution of power and the allocation of rewards within them mirror the larger society's class structure (Edwards, 1979; Jaffee, 2001).

In *Capital* (1867/1906), Marx claimed that the modern factory is a despotic regime made necessary by the competitive pressures of the market. These pressures compel technological innovation and work intensification, all of which rest on the availability of workers, who in order to survive must sell their labor power to capitalist employers.

More recent studies by Marxist social scientists suggest that bureaucratic mechanisms arose as much from the desire of capitalists to control workers as from abstract notions of efficiency and rationality (Friedman, 1977; Edwards, 1978).

Marx thought that if a socialist revolution overturned capitalism, the bureaucratic structures inherited from capitalism would have to be altered or eliminated by a revolutionary working class and replaced by a fully democratic structure. However, when a socialist government was finally established following the Russian Revolution of 1917, the result was not the establishment and perpetuation of democratic organizational forms. The primary elements of their policy in what became the Soviet Union centered on the expansion of bureaucratic offices and the dominance of the state apparatus by a "new class" of Communist Party officials (Djilas, 1957), quite the opposite of what Marx had in mind.

Another development has been the emergence of the collectivist-democratic organization (Rothschild and Russell, 1986). Such organizations are formed at the grassroots level in response to the needs of the people who form them, operate on the basis of consensus rather than on bureaucratic authority, and focus on producing products of immediate social value, not products to be sold in the marketplace in pursuit of profit. Examples of collectivist-democratic organizations are food cooperatives, legal collectives, communes, and other low-capitalization enterprises that operate as cooperative businesses (Rothschild and Russell, 1986; Case and Taylor, 1979).

Collectivist-democratic organizations have a tendency to degenerate and disappear or to evolve into a standard bureaucracy (Rothschild and Russell, 1986). State sponsorship, creative tax incentive plans, and financing conditional on the maintenance of democratic cooperative structures are among the mechanisms that help perpetuate collectivist-democratic organizations.

The Symbolic Interactionist Perspective

Symbolic interactionists contend that human beings in organizations are not spongelike, malleable organisms who passively conform to the bureaucratic requirements. Instead, they portray people as active agents who shape and mold their destinies and continually fashion new joint actions based on their definitions of the situation (Blumer, 1969). Organizational constraints only provide the framework with which people appraise and then decide among alternative courses of organizational behavior on the basis of meanings they share with others in the organization. The model of organizations that results is one that emphasizes dynamism and malleability of organizational forms rather than fixed structures and procedures.

A good example of the application of symbolic interactionism to organizations is the classic study by Anselm Strauss and his colleagues (1964) of organizational behavior in two Chicago-area psychiatric hospitals. They treated a formal organization as a **negotiated order**—the fluid, ongoing understandings and agreements people reach as they go about their daily activities. To outsiders the hospitals appeared to be tightly structured organizations that functioned in

accordance with strict bureaucratic rules and regulations. However, the researchers found that in practice the hospitals operated quite differently. The organizations were simply too complex for a single set of rules to hold or for any one person to know all the rules, much less in exactly what situations they applied, to whom, in what degree, and for how long. Given these circumstances, most house rules served more as general understandings than as commands, and they were stretched, argued, reinterpreted, ignored, or applied as situations dictated. Individuals reached agreements with one another that provided a consensus for a time, but the understandings were subject to periodic modification and revision.

Chaos did not reign in the hospitals because the negotiations followed patterns that permitted some degree of predictability. Even so, Strauss and his colleagues concluded:

Practically, we maintain, no one knows what the hospital "is" on any given day unless [he or she] has a comprehensive grasp of the combinations of rules, policies, agreements, understandings, pacts, contracts, and other working arrangements that currently obtain. In a pragmatic sense, that combination "is" the hospital at the moment, its social order. (1964:312)

Research on organizations from the perspective of **ethnomethodology** strongly supports the symbolic interactionist view that organizations are shifting, malleable, dynamic entities. *Ethno,* borrowed from the Greek, means "people" or "folk," while *methodology* refers to procedures by which something is done or analyzed. Thus, "ethnomethodology" refers to procedures—the rules and activities—that people employ in making social life and society intelligible (Garfinkel, 1974). While the focus in symbolic interactionism emphasizes a broader range of shared meanings, the two perspectives are very similar. Both view people as agents who do not simply conform to organizational constraints but actively shape their social lives within organizational contexts.

Ethnomethodologists argue that organizations are not products of their rules, but that people use the rules to explain and justify what they do in organizational contexts.

Sociologist Don H. Zimmerman (1971) applied the ethnomethodological perspective in examining the day-to-day operations of a large-scale organization, a public welfare agency. He studied how the receptionists went about processing applicants for public assistance and apportioning them among caseworkers. The receptionists seemed to follow the "first-come, first-served" rule. But a deeper inspection revealed that receptionists would switch the order of applicants when clients said they had to attend to some urgent matter. Likewise, they would allow some applicants to request a particular social worker. And they routinely assigned "difficult" and "troublesome" applicants to a caseworker known to be good at handling "special problems." In fact, they were skilled at giving the appearance that applicants moved through the system in a sequential and orderly manner, while in fact they followed their own ad hoc procedures for processing applicants.

Zimmerman concluded that as we go about our activities, we continually develop and interpret what a rule means. Bureaucratic rules and regulations serve as a commonsense method by which we account for our behavior. In deciding how to behave in organizations, people ask not "What is the rule?" but "What has to be done?" In practice, a rule may be employed or ignored depending on the context. Its main purpose is not to guide action but to provide an account, explanation, and justification of action.

A Synthesis of Alternative Perspectives

Sociologist Charles Perrow (1982) joined threads from the conflict, symbolic interactionist, and ethnomethodological perspectives to argue that the notion of bureaucratic rationality masks the true nature of organizational life. He claimed that our world is more "loosely coupled"—characterized by a substantial measure of redundancy, slack, and waste—than structural theories admit. Perrow said that organizations do not have goals, only constraints. Take the Sanitation Department of New York City:

To say its goal is to pick up the garbage—even to pick it up frequently, pick it all up, and do it cheaply—does not tell us much. These are not goals of that department but merely loose constraints under which those who use the organization must operate, and these are not really any more important than the following constraints: The cushy top jobs in the department can be used to pay off political debts; some groups can use the Sanitation Department as an assured source of employment and keep others out; upper management can use its positions as political jumping off places or training spots; equipment manufacturers use it as an easy mark for shoddy goods; and, finally, the workers are entitled to use it as a source of job security and pensions and an easy way of making a living. (p. 687)

Perrow contended that private profit-making organizations are not much different. Aerospace companies can be seen as pension plans that make missiles and planes on the side so that their pension plans can be funded. Steel plants are closed even though they make a respectable profit because they are worth more as tax write-offs. Countless other organizations continue to exist even though they fail to provide decent mail service, prepare students for careers, or offer acceptable medical care. But should the organizations fail to satisfy some special-interest group that lives off them, then the consequences are defined as a major social problem. In short, organizations pursue a variety of courses of action, some of them with more enthusiasm than they pursue their publicly stated goals. Perrow concluded, therefore, that organizations do not have goals in the rational sense suggested by organizational theory. Instead, actions are determined by the interests of executives, employees, and other stakeholders, and formally stated goals are determined after the fact, on the basis of what executives observe themselves doing.

Perrow next linked the conflict perspective to his analysis by arguing that social efforts at stating goals, giving accounts, and attributing rationality to organizations serve elites much more than they serve other people. These efforts create a world in which organizational hierarchy, technological requirements, and profit-making motives become legitimized.

The Sociology of Work

Organizations, groups, and group processes provide the social context for most persons employed in the United States and other industrialized countries. Nearly 9 out of 10 U.S. workers are employed by someone else, and about half of these are employed in organizations having 100 or more workers (U.S. Census Bureau, 2011a). Thus, the structures and processes we have been considering in this chapter are key features of life for working people in modern societies. The work that people engage in influences their social class position, income, prestige, health, life satisfaction, life expectancy, and more. Work also is embedded in or linked to major social institutions including the economy, education, medicine, the family, and others. We will touch on issues related to work in upcoming chapters on social stratification, race and ethnicity, gender, power, education, and medicine. Here we will introduce some basic issues explored by sociologists who study work.

The Significance of Work

People work for many reasons. "Self-interest" in its broadest sense, including the interests of family and friends, is a basic motivation for working in all societies. But self-interest need not involve only providing for subsistence or accumulating wealth. Among the Maori, a Polynesian people

of the South Pacific, a desire for approval, a sense of duty, a wish to conform to custom and tradition, a feeling of emulation, and a pleasure in craftsmanship are additional reasons for working (Hsu, 1943). Within the United States, too, work is not simply a response to economic necessity. For example, open source has been called "the most powerful new business model of the twenty-first century" (Pink, 2009:21); it is work that is rewarded by something other than money. Wikipedia, Firefox, Linux, and Apache, examples of open-source products, all are free to users and were created by unpaid writers and programmers. A survey of nearly 700 such open-source developers showed that their motivation is intrinsic and that their drive to perform unpaid work is based on how much they enjoy it and on how creative they feel when working on a project (Pink, 2009). Surveys over the past 30 years reveal that 65–77 percent of Americans would continue to work even if they had enough money to live comfortably for the rest of their lives (Smith et al., 2010).

Work has many social meanings (Levinson, 1964). When individuals work, they gain a contributing place in society. That they receive pay for their work indicates that what they do is valued by other people and that they are a necessary part of the social fabric. Work is a major social mechanism for placing people in the larger social structure and giving them identities. Much of who individuals are, to themselves and others, is interwoven with work.

Work affects an individual's personal and family life in many ways (Small and Riley, 1990). Jobs that permit occupational self-direction—initiative, thought, and independent judgment in work—foster people's intellectual flexibility. Individuals with such jobs become more open in approaching and weighing evidence on current political, social, and economic issues. The effects of occupational self-direction also generalize to other nonwork settings. Individuals who enjoy opportunities for self-direction in their work are more likely to become more self-confident, less authoritarian, less conformist in their ideas, and less fatalistic in their nonwork lives than other individuals. In turn, these traits lead in time to more responsible jobs that allow even greater latitude for occupational self-direction (Kohn and Schooler, 1983). Such work autonomy may increase with the Internet revolution, as most enterprises using new technologies also move to decentralized decision making and task-oriented teamwork (International Labor Organization, 2001; Pink, 2009).

A variety of workplace conditions—the restriction of opportunity to exercise self-direction, work overload, poor quality of interpersonal relations on the job, few opportunities for cooperative problem solving, job insecurities, job loss, and low earnings—have emotional repercussions that can lead to negative family interactions (Menaghan, 1991). So the job affects the person and the person affects the job in a reciprocal relationship across the life course (Kohn and Schooler, 1983; Kohn et al., 1990). In sum, work is an important socializing experience that influences who and what we are.

Changes in the Work Experience

The work experience of Americans has undergone significant change over the past two centuries and continues to undergo change (see Figure 4.1). In 1820, more than 70 percent of the labor force worked on farms. By 1910, only 31 percent of Americans were engaged in agriculture. Today the number of individuals employed in professional, management, technology, administrative, and service jobs has exceeded the 70 percent of people who were involved in farming in 1820, with only 1.5 percent of the labor force today in agriculture and about 25 percent in blue-collar and manufacturing jobs.

These changes have been accompanied by a shift from a nonindustrial to an industrial society and now to a service and information society. In traditional nonindustrial societies, working (earning a living) is not readily distinguishable from other social activities. With the advent of industrial society, this situation changed (Dubin, 1976). In industrial societies, the workplace is physically segregated from the home, working time is temporally separated from leisure time, and specialized organizational structures—complex authority hierarchies—take over the management of work activities (Stinchcombe, 1983). The economic institution increasingly becomes the focus of other institutions, and the family, government, religion, and education are reshaped to accommodate its requirements.

Life and work in an economy dominated by information and communication technologies is affected by values, agreements, and institutions different from those of an industrial era (International Labor Organization, 2001). One difference is that the worker–boss model is changing. There are 18 million "non-employer businesses" in the United States, businesses with a single, necessarily self-directed worker (Pink, 2009). An additional 14.7 million U.S. employees telecommute every day, and 33.7 million do so at least once a week, all of whom are working primarily under their own direction. An "Internet economy" also offers the potential for a better balance between work and leisure or work and family life by reducing or eliminating commuting time and by giving workers more control over how they spend their time. On the other hand, with significant changes caused by globalization, technological advances, and shifts in our national and world economies, even white-collar jobs are being outsourced, and white-collar workers are increasingly being replaced by cheaper overseas laborers and by computer programs (Pink, 2009).

Satisfaction and Alienation in Work

Sociologists find that individuals in occupations that combine high economic, occupational, and educational prestige typically show the greatest satisfaction with their work and the strongest job

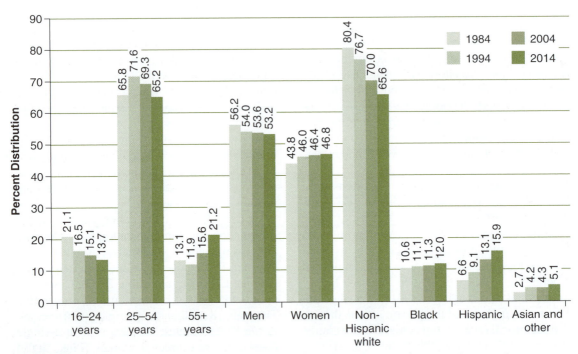

Figure 4.1 Percent Distribution of the Labor Force by Age, Gender, and Race/Ethnicity by Decade, 1984–2014

These analyses by the Bureau of Labor Statistics use data from the U.S. Census Department Current Population Surveys from 1984, 1994, and 2004 and projections to the year 2014. Percentages for each category are within year. For example, in 1984, men were 56.2 percent of the labor force and women were 43.8 percent. These analyses show that the labor force is becoming older, is increasingly diverse racially and ethnically, and is nearly evenly divided by gender. Nonetheless, in the foreseeable future, the labor force will remain dominated by persons of middle age and by non-Hispanic whites. (Percentages do not always add up to 100 within year due to rounding, because Hispanics may be of any race, and because those of "other" race/ethnicity are not included.)

Source: Figure generated by the authors using data adapted from Mitra Toossi, "Labor force projections to 2014: Retiring boomers" from Monthly Labor Review (November 2005) p. 26. (Available at www.cse.sc.edu/~buell/References/BureauLaborStatistics/art3full2014.pdf).

attachment (Kohn and Schooler, 1973, 1982; Hartman and Pearlstein, 1987), and surveys show that the happiest workers are those in helping professions or doing creative work (Smith et al., 2010). The opportunity to exercise discretion, accept challenges, and make decisions has an important bearing on how people feel about their work (Keita and Sauter, 1992; Lawler, 1992; Neil and Snizek, 1988). The most potent factors in job satisfaction are those that relate to workers' self-respect, their chance to perform well, their opportunities for achievement and growth, and their chance to contribute something personal and unique. Surveys show that the vast majority of Americans (87 percent) are very or moderately satisfied with the work they are doing (Smith et al., 2010). Even so, nearly one-third of workers say they would be happier in a different job (Bowman, 2009), perhaps indicating that changing responsibilities is an important factor in job satisfaction.

Alienation and a Lack of Power

When individuals fail to find their work ful-filling and satisfying, they may experience **alienation**—a pervasive sense of powerless-ness, meaninglessness, normlessness, isola-tion, and self-estrangement (Seeman, 1959). Alienation may be structured into the nature of the work itself. For example, in a classic study, Robert Blauner (1964) showed that when work is simple and repetitive and engages workers in only a small part of the overall work process, workers feel disconnected and alienated from it. One expression of alienation is *job burn-out*—a sense of boredom, apathy, reduced effi-ciency, fatigue, frustration, and despondency.

While the "information economy" has the potential to benefit workers, it may result in iso-lation and dead-end careers in data processing for some workers (International Labor Organiza-tion, 2001), and its benefits may be unequally distributed. Although Internet use is increasingly prevalent and widespread in U.S. society, gaps remain. Older people, racial minorities, and those with less education have less experience and background in computer use (U.S. Census Bureau, 2010). For example, African American men are being disproportionately disadvantaged by the outsourcing of unskilled jobs and the increase in skilled and technologically advanced jobs. Even previously unskilled jobs, such as at fast-food restaurants, now require employees to use computers, a problem for those with the least access to education and computer training (Wilson, 2009).

Marx and Durkheim on Alienation

Two very different perspectives on alienation are provided by Karl Marx and Émile Durkheim (Lukes, 1977). Marx saw alienation as rooted in capitalist social arrangements and work as our most important activity as human beings. Through work we create our world and ourselves. The products of our labor reflect our nature and form the basis for our self-evaluations. Further, through work we experience ourselves as active beings who shape the world about us. But according to Marx (1844/1960), individuals in capitalist soci-eties lose control of their labor and become com-modities, objects used by capitalists to make a profit. They are alienated from productive activ-ity, the products of their labor, their co-workers, and their own human potential. Rather than being a process that is inherently satisfying, work becomes an unfulfilling activity that simply pro-duces a subsistence wage.

In Marx's view, alienation is a structural condition. Regardless of how they feel about it, workers are alienated; having no control over the conditions of their work, they can control neither their well-being nor their survival. If workers say they are satisfied, Marx would say they experience false consciousness.

In contrast, Durkheim did not use the term alienation; instead, he focused on *anomie* (as we will discuss in Chapter 5), a condition that mod-ern sociologists often argue leads to feelings of alienation. Durkheim depicted anomie as arising from the breakdown of the cohesive ties that bind individuals to society. For Durkheim the central question was whether people are immersed in a structure of group experiences and memberships that provide a meaningful and valued context for their behavior. A group either coheres and makes life comprehensible and viable for individuals or fails to do so, and this leads to pathological out-comes. Whereas Marx emphasized freedom from social constraint as the source of human happiness, Durkheim stressed that human happi-ness depends on a society that provides people with rules. Rules, said Durkheim, integrate indi-viduals into cohesive social groups and give direction and meaning to their activity.

Humanizing Bureaucracies

Both Marx and Durkheim identified forces that can result in alienation. Clearly, since so much of life is spent at work, both the nature of work and the quality of group bonds at work can profoundly affect human happiness, satisfaction, and how people come to think about themselves. In this section we will take a look at some of the efforts being made that may allow individuals greater range for developing their full capacities and potential in the context of organizational life.

Employee Participation

About the same time that Japanese manufacturers vigorously entered U.S. markets, American business leaders began trying to breathe new life and competitive fire into their companies. Many tried an approach known as "participative management," in which a group of up to a dozen workers and one or two managers from the same department meet together on a regular basis to figure out ways of getting along better with each other, making work easier, raising output, and improving the quality of their products. This approach should result in reduced absenteeism, tardiness, grievances, strikes, and labor costs and improved product quality.

Although some 6,000 American companies, including General Motors, IBM, and AT&T, adopted employee participation programs, most of these programs failed (Saporito, 1986). A Gallup survey found that few corporate employees in such programs thought their companies gave them a chance to participate in the important decisions (Bennett, 1990). Conflict theorists argue that because the relationship between management and labor is inherently adversarial, worker participation programs are simply cosmetic efforts that mask corporate attempts to control workers and to avoid collective-bargaining obligations.

A more radical example of an employee-participation program is that of Semco, a Brazilian manufacturing firm. The head of the company got rid of most of the executives and all of the job titles. The 3,000 employees set their own hours and each has a vote in every major decision affecting the company (Semler, 1993). Giving all workers total autonomy allowed the company to cut its corporate staff by 75 percent and its quality control unit completely—each worker vouches for his or her work, so there is no need for quality control. According to Semler, 12 layers of bureaucracy were reduced to 3 and were reconfigured to meet the needs of the workers.

A small groups or team approach appears highly adaptable within the computer industry, where many tasks are not easily routinized and where small groups can react quickly to abrupt technological change. Beyond the small-workgroups approach is the "no-collar" approach, in which informally dressed employees manage

Conflict theorists argue that employee-participation programs are designed to function as sophisticated control strategies.

DILBERT reprinted by permission of United Feature Syndicate, Inc.

themselves, use the office as a "funhouse" (because play promotes creativity), and are expected to work 70-hour weeks (Ross, 2003).

Overall, new management strategies over the past 30 years have emphasized a lessening of hierarchy and authoritarianism and an increase in worker participation in workplace decision making. But the changes should not be overestimated. When managers must make a tough decision, they often revert to the direct, authoritarian mode.

Alternative Work Schedules

Some companies have attempted to boost job satisfaction and motivation by allowing flexibility in how work time is scheduled. Flextime is one example; workers are allowed to decide how to organize their 8-hour workday. Some may wish to come in early and get off early; others may wish to have their early mornings free and work into the evening. These plans can benefit working parents who often need to schedule their work hours so that adequate child care can be arranged. They also benefit companies since they result in lower absentee and turnover rates (Bartol and Martin, 1998).

Another example is the compressed workweek. This plan involves scheduling workers to put in four 10-hour days per week with three days off. Such a plan can work well for construction, for example, where more can be accomplished on-site during each 10-hour day, and workers can enjoy long weekends. For some types of jobs, such as nursing, 12-hour shifts with appropriate time off work well.

Another innovation in work schedules involves allowing employees more flexibility in what they work on. Google is a good example of a company that has given its employees more autonomy; engineers are allowed 20 percent of their work time for side projects of their choice (Pink, 2009). This "free time" has given birth to Google News, Google Talk, Google Translate, Gmail, Orkut, and more. Post-it notes were invented during employee free-choice project time at 3M. Atlassian, an Australian software company, also allows its engineers a free work day, at an investment of $1 million, and says the result is highly motivated engineers with a high level of job satisfaction (Pink, 2009). A more radical approach to schedules is an innovation termed the Results-Only Work Environment, or ROWE (Pink, 2009). Best Buy's corporate offices have adopted the practice, with employees doing their work when, how, and with whom they can most effectively get it done; only the results count.

Virtual Offices

Some companies find that workers do not need to report to a central office but can work from anywhere and communicate with managers, workers, customers, and others via the Internet (Davidow and Malone, 1993; Jaffee, 2001). These "virtual corporations" with their "virtual offices" provide employees with the ultimate in autonomy and flexibility in organizing their work. Verifone, Inc., a company that designs, manufactures, sells, and services the machines that read credit cards in retail establishments, is an example of a successful virtual corporation (Jaffee, 2001). It has 3,000 employees worldwide but no corporate office and no identification with a nation-state. Corporate operations never cease, with employees communicating and accessing company information through the Internet.

Though workers may find that working in a virtual office enables them to manage the conflicts between their personal lives and their work lives more effectively, it is unclear what the ultimate impact will be on the structure of organizations. The unintended consequences of such arrangements may include increased alienation, the loss of a sense of community, and a weakening of organizational integration (Snizek, 1995).

Specialized Benefits

In an attempt to reduce employee turnover, some companies offer a variety of new benefits to workers. A number offer child care either on-site or nearby in company-owned buildings, providing parents with opportunities to visit their children during the day and cutting day care costs. Some make contributions to college education funds for employees' offspring. Company-provided transportation to jobs has resulted in reductions in tardiness and absenteeism for some employers. Workers in some states can attend classes on company time to earn their high school graduate equivalency diplomas (GEDs). At least one company offers 24-hour on-call social workers to help employees with their personal problems. These specialized benefits programs reflect both a change in attitudes toward workers and the inability of most companies to offer increased wages (Grimsley, 1997).

Employee Stock Ownership Plans
In 2002 nearly 10,000 companies in the United States shared some measure of ownership with more than 8 million employees. Workers owned the majority of the stock in some 2,500 companies. Although employee stock ownership plans (ESOPs) grew rapidly from their inception in 1974 until 1990, there has been little overall growth since then. Nonetheless, the number of majority employee- and 100 percent employee-owned companies continues to increase (ESOP Association, 2003).

In many cases large-scale employee ownership has changed the way companies operate, including their labor–management relationships (Klein, 1987; Blasi, 1988). Greater employee initiative in the workplace has been found to cut costs, but much depends on a firm's profitability. When a company becomes profitable, differences tend to get smoothed over quickly, but a firm that continues to lose money will see dissatisfaction

rise and difficulties deepen. For instance, in the early 1990s, the men and women at Weirton Steel found that ownership did not always translate into power. These employee-owners took pay cuts, accepted layoffs, and acquiesced as management spent $550 million to revamp the company's mill. After years of butting heads with management, the workers launched a battle in 1993 to gain actual control of the firm (Baker, 1993). Thus, employee ownership does not guarantee labor peace.

What Can Sociology Do for You?

This chapter makes us think about how groups and organizations work. Many sociology majors embark on careers in businesses, corporations, or local, state, or federal government in which their knowledge about groups and organizations can be directly or indirectly useful. Let's use the American Sociological Association (ASA) web page, **http://www.asanet.org/,** to find out more about jobs relating to groups and organizations. Type "Sociological Roles Relating to Business, Industry, and Work" in the search window on the home page, and find the report of that title. Read the section titled "Practitioner Roles." What do sociology practitioners do in applied settings? List some of the kinds of jobs and careers identified, and think about the sorts of skills and interests required.

If you enjoyed Chapter 4, you might like to take courses in complex organizations and the sociology of work or investigate the business program at your college to find classes relating to personnel, management, and administration.

The Chapter in Brief: *Social Groups and Formal Organizations*

Group Relationships

Groups—two or more people who share a feeling of unity and who are bound together in relatively stable patterns of social interaction—are products of social definitions. As such they constitute constructed realities. A **relationship** is an association characterized by a stable set of expectations.

■ **Primary Groups and Secondary Groups** **Primary groups** involve two or more people who enjoy direct, intimate, cohesive relationships and are fundamental to both us and society. **Expressive ties** predominate in primary groups. **Secondary groups** entail two or more people who are involved in impersonal, touch-and-go relationships. **Instrumental ties** predominate in secondary groups.

■ **In-Groups and Out-Groups** The concepts of **in-group** and **out-group** highlight the importance of boundaries—social demarcation lines that tell us where interaction begins and ends. Boundaries prevent outsiders from entering a group's sphere, and they keep insiders within the group's sphere.

■ **Reference Groups** **Reference groups** provide the models we use for appraising and shaping our attitudes, feelings, and actions. A reference group may or may not be our membership group. Differences between membership and reference groups may result in feelings of **relative deprivation.**

Group Dynamics

The dynamic qualities of groups make them a significant force in human life and important to sociologists.

■ **Group Size** The size of a group influences the nature of our interaction. Emotions and feelings tend to assume a larger role in **dyads** than in larger groups. The addition of a third member to a group—forming a **triad**—fundamentally alters a social situation. In this arrangement one person may be placed in the role of an outsider.

■ **Leadership** In group settings some members usually exert more influence than others. We call these individuals leaders. Two types of leadership roles tend to evolve in small groups: an **instrumental leader** and an **expressive leader.** Leaders may follow an authoritarian style, a democratic style, or a laissez-faire style.

■ **Social Loafing** When individuals work in groups, they work less hard than they do when working individually, a process termed **social loafing.**

■ **Social Dilemmas** A **social dilemma** is a situation in which members of a group are faced with a conflict between maximizing their personal interests and maximizing the collective welfare.

■ **Groupthink** In group settings individuals may become victims of **groupthink.** Group members may share an illusion of invulnerability that leads to overconfidence and a greater willingness to take risks.

■ **Conformity** Groups bring powerful pressures to bear that produce conformity among their members. Although such pressures influence our behavior, we often are unaware of them.

Formal Organizations

For many tasks within modern societies, people require groups they can deliberately create for the achievement of specific goals. These groups are **formal organizations.**

■ **Types of Formal Organization** Amitai Etzioni classified organizations on the basis of people's reasons for entering them: **voluntary, coercive,** and **utilitarian.** In **total institutions,** individuals undergo **resocialization,** often including **mortification.**

■ **Bureaucracy: A Functional Approach to Organizations** Small organizations can often function reasonably well on the basis of face-to-face interaction. Larger organizations must establish formal operating and administrative procedures. This requirement is met by a **bureaucracy.**

■ **Characteristics of Bureaucracies**   Max Weber approached bureaucracy as an ideal type with these characteristics: Each office has clearly defined duties; all offices are organized in a hierarchy of authority; all activities are governed by a system of rules; all offices have qualifications; incumbents do not own their positions; employment by the organization is defined as a career; and administrative decisions are recorded in written documents.

■ **Problems of Bureaucracy**   Bureaucracies have disadvantages and limitations. These include the principle of **trained incapacity, Parkinson's law,** and the **iron law of oligarchy.** If formal organization is to operate smoothly, it requires **informal organization** for interpreting, translating, and supporting its goals and practices.

■ **Conflict and Interactionist Perspectives** Sociologists from differing perspectives— particularly the conflict, symbolic interactionist, and **ethnomethodological** approaches—have looked at the ways by which organizational reality is generated through the actions of people and groups of people. Formal organizations can be seen as **negotiated orders.**

The Sociology of Work

Organizations, groups, and group processes provide the social context for most U.S. workers. Work influences many aspects of our lives.

■ **The Significance of Work**   People work for many reasons in addition to "self-interest," and work has many social meanings, especially those that define a person's position in the social structure.

■ **Changes in the Work Experience**   The work experience of Americans has undergone significant change over the past two centuries; the proportion working on farms has declined, while the proportion employed in service industries has risen. Work in nonindustrialized societies is very different from work in industrialized societies.

■ **Satisfaction and Alienation in Work** Individuals in occupations that combine high economic, occupational, and educational prestige typically show the greatest satisfaction with their work and the strongest job attachment. When individuals fail to find their work satisfying and fulfilling, they may experience **alienation.** Marx and Durkheim had differing conceptions of alienation.

■ **Humanizing Bureaucracies**   Among programs that make large organizations more humane are those that allow employee participation, flextime, small work groups, and employee ownership.

Glossary

alienation   A pervasive sense of powerlessness, meaninglessness, normlessness, isolation, and self-estrangement.

bureaucracy   A social structure made up of a hierarchy of statuses and roles that is prescribed by explicit rules and procedures and based on a division of function and authority.

coercive organization   A formal organization that people become members of against their will.

dyad   A two-member group.

ethnomethodology Procedures—the rules and activities—that people employ in making social life and society intelligible to themselves and others.

expressive leader A leader who focuses on overcoming interpersonal problems in a group, defusing tension, and promoting solidarity.

expressive ties Social links formed when we emotionally invest ourselves in and commit ourselves to other people.

formal organization A group formed deliberately for the achievement of specific objectives.

group Two or more people who share a feeling of unity and who are bound together in relatively stable patterns of social interaction.

groupthink A decision-making process found in highly cohesive groups in which the members become so preoccupied with maintaining group consensus that their critical faculties are impaired.

informal organization Interpersonal networks and ties that arise in a formal organization but that are not defined or prescribed by it.

in-group A group with which we identify and to which we belong.

instrumental leader A leader who focuses on appraising the problem at hand and organizing people's activity to deal with it.

instrumental ties Social links formed when we cooperate with other people to achieve some goal.

iron law of oligarchy The principle stating that bureaucracies invariably lead to the concentration of power in the hands of a few individuals who use their offices to advance their own fortunes and self-interests.

mortification A procedure in which rituals employed by coercive organizations render individuals vulnerable to institutional control, discipline, and resocialization.

negotiated order The fluid, ongoing understandings and agreements people reach as they go about their daily activities.

out-group A group with which we do not identify and to which we do not belong.

Parkinson's law The principle that states that work expands so as to fill the time available for its completion.

primary group Two or more people who enjoy a direct, intimate, cohesive relationship with one another.

reference group A social unit we use for appraising and shaping our attitudes, feelings, and actions.

relationship An association that lasts long enough for two people to become linked together by a relatively stable set of expectations.

relative deprivation Discontent associated with the gap between what we have and what we believe we should have.

resocialization A process by which a person's old roles and identities are stripped away and new ones are created.

secondary group Two or more people who are involved in an impersonal relationship and have come together for a specific, practical purpose.

social dilemma A situation in which members of a group are faced with a conflict between maximizing their personal interests and maximizing the collective welfare.

social loafing The process in which individuals work less hard when working in groups than they do when working individually.

total institutions Places of residence where individuals are isolated from the rest of society.

trained incapacity The term Thorstein Veblen applied to the tendency within bureaucracies for members to rely on established rules and regulations and to apply them in an unimaginative and mechanical fashion.

triad A three-member group.

utilitarian organization A formal organization set up to achieve practical ends.

voluntary organization A formal organization that people enter and leave freely.

Review Questions

1. How do primary groups differ from secondary groups? List three of each from your own life.

2. What are in-groups and out-groups?

3. Define reference group, and give at least two examples from your own life.

4. What are two major styles of leadership?

5. Describe a social dilemma from your own life.

6. What is groupthink? Have you ever experienced this phenomenon as a member of a decision-making group?

7. Joining a sorority or fraternity is voluntary. Do such organizations have any characteristics of a coercive organization?

8. Define bureaucracy, and list the characteristics of Weber's ideal bureaucracy.

9. What are some of the problems of bureaucracy?

10. What do conflict theorists have to say about bureaucracy? How does it differ from the view of symbolic interactionists?

11. How has work changed in the United States in the last 100 years? What is alienation? What is the significance of work to most people?

Internet Connection   www.mhhe.com/hughes11e

Open this Web page: **http://www.loc.gov//rr/news/fedgov.html.** This site, maintained by the Library of Congress, provides a set of links to the executive branch of the U.S. government. Explore these sites looking for evidence that the executive branch of the U.S. government conforms to Weber's model of bureaucracy. Write a short report on the evidence you have found. Which aspects of Weber's model are revealed here? Which aspects are not? Thinking about the information in these sites and information from other sources, including news reports over the past several years, does the executive branch conform to Weber's ideal type of bureaucracy? Why or why not?

Deviance and Crime

More than a hundred years ago, many students at the best U.S. colleges cheated most of the time. "Whole classes cheated on examinations," says historian Helen Lefkowitz Horowitz (1987:33). "At Yale in the 1860s, perhaps less than half of the compositions were actually written by the supposed author for the occasion."

Today many schools have honor systems run by the students themselves, yet cheating remains a common form of behavior among students. In a 2011 study of high school science fair participants, 60 percent admitted to some form of cheating (Cunningham, 2011), and another study shows that this is not a new phenomenon (Syer and Shore, 2001). Research suggests that the overall percentage of college students who cheat in some way is at least 90 percent and may be as high as 99 percent (Sperber, 2000). And about half of all graduate students report having cheated (McCabe, Butterfield, and Trevino, 2006).

Students are not alone. Despite rigorous review procedures, research institutions and scholarly journals are sometimes "taken for a ride" by dishonest academicians. In a major 2011 scandal, a social psychologist from the Netherlands was found to have fabricated or manipulated data in dozens of papers (Vogel, 2011), just one of a number of cases of scientific misconduct around the world. Such fraud is now recognized by scientists as a more serious and damaging problem than it was in the past (Couzin, 2006), and researchers are studying plagiarism and scientific misconduct (Long et al., 2009; Redman and Merz, 2008).

The term *deviance* suggests unusual and strange behavior of people with twisted minds pursuing twisted activities. However, what we think of as deviant is also an ordinary part of everyday life. Let's look at cheating. Is it deviant or is it normal? If so many people cheat, what purpose do the rules against it serve? These questions introduce two important ideas that form the backdrop for our analysis of deviance.

First, whether something is deviant depends on who is evaluating it. In 19th-century colleges, for example, faculty believed that cheating was deviant. Students, for the most part, believed it was deviant *not* to cheat, and being proud of having achieved good grades through "honest" means was clearly deviant (Horowitz, 1987).

Second, when important *norms,* or rules, are violated, norms and social control function to maintain social organization, social relationships, and the meanings that underlie them. When universities react to cheating, they protect the idea that people earn grades honestly and that grades are at least a rough measure of merit. Establishing norms and defending them in the face of violation are necessary for social order to exist and to be perpetuated. Without norms against cheating and mechanisms for their enforcement, the nature of the university and its place in society would be very different.

In this chapter we will consider the nature and significance of deviance. We will discuss sociological definitions of deviance and see what various sociological perspectives contribute to our understanding of deviance. In addition, we will examine a form of deviance that is particularly prevalent in modern society: crime.

The Nature of Deviance

Deviant behavior is not an anomaly in social life. It is a part of ongoing social processes in all societies and groups and is both cause and consequence of other social processes and outcomes that we discuss in this section.

Social Properties of Deviance

Deviance is any behavior that violates a norm. In every society there is a range of societal reactions to deviance. Some norm violations are viewed as reprehensible and beyond the limits of tolerance, while others seem trivial and generate little reaction. Murderers may be sent to prison for life or executed, while people who wear unfashionable clothes and professors with odd lecture styles are generally tolerated, even if people do talk about them behind their backs.

Deviance cannot exist independently of norms. That is, deviance is not a property inherent in certain forms of behavior (Erikson, 1962; Becker, 1963; Lemert, 1972); it is a property conferred upon particular behaviors by social definitions. In the course of their daily lives, people use the normative schemes available to them and make judgments regarding the desirability or undesirability of various behaviors. They then translate their judgments into favorable or unfavorable consequences for those who engage in the behavior. In this sense, then, deviance is what people say it is. This idea is clarified in Box 5.1.

The Relativity of Deviance

Which acts are defined as deviant varies greatly from time to time, place to place, and group to group. For example, in many cultures homosexual behavior is considered to be deviant, and any sexual behavior involving juveniles is criminal. For the Etoro of New Guinea, however, homosexual acts between adult males and young boys are not just a part of everyday life; they are an essential part of the culture.

As reported by anthropologist Raymond Kelly in 1976, the Etoro believe that humans have a special life force they call the *hame*. According to Etoro culture, this vital energy in men can be diminished through witchcraft and also through sexual relations, because it is especially concentrated in semen. Depletion of the life force is accompanied by weakness and illness, referred to as *hame hah hah*. Each act of sexual intercourse a man engages in depletes his *hame* further, and heterosexual relations among the Etoro, even for the married, are completely prohibited for as many as 260 days per year. The Etoro believe that breaking these prohibitions has serious repercussions, including crop failure, and it is thus severely punished.

Why, then, are homosexual relations essential in this culture? Boys lack semen—the most critical attribute of manhood to the Etoro—and the Etoro believe that semen must be "planted" in them. Although the male who loses semen loses some of his vital life force, for the boy receiving semen, it is an essential gain. All the physical and emotional changes that occur as boys grow up are regarded as the direct results of the oral insemination practiced by the Etoro. Because the *hame* of a youth is strengthened by insemination, there are no prohibitions about when or where such insemination can take place.

As norms vary from one society to the next, so too does deviance. A social audience, through the application of norms, decides whether behavior is deviant. To the Etoro of New Guinea, sexual activity involving children is a normal part of everyday life. In the United States it is an extreme norm violation and can result in criminal charges and severe penalties.

The concepts that the Etoro use to think about sexuality and the moral system that governs sexual behavior are fundamentally different from the cultural principles that shape sexuality and behavior in many other societies—so different, in fact, that some readers may find the example to be difficult to think about. Such reactions illustrate the point of the example: that deviance is relative, and such relativity often involves fundamental, even extreme, differences in how deviance is defined in different cultural systems. Cultures differ not only in what norms they have but in the degree of importance they attach to their norms and the tolerance they have for deviation from those norms (Gelfand et al., 2011).

Saying that deviance is relative and is a matter of social definition does not mean that "anything goes" or that morality has no importance. On the contrary, the relativity of deviance means simply that there are many moralities across societies and over time and that we cannot understand deviant behavior and the reactions to it without knowing the normative context in which they occur. Using a traditional Western antihomosexual moral scheme

to define deviance among the Etoro would reveal nothing about the processes of deviance and reaction that occur there.

By the same token, because deviance is relative, when sociologists study behavior that they refer to as deviant, they are not implying that the behavior is, in fact, immoral or wrong. The issue of morality is a philosophical, ethical, or religious one. Deviance, however, is a matter of whether shared norms have been violated and/or there has been a social reaction to some presumed violation. For example, white southerners who supported the civil rights movement in the South in the 1960s were deviant in that setting (Durr, 1985), though many people now view their behavior as a moral response to an immoral racist social order.

The Power to Make Definitions Stick

In 1776 the British labeled George Washington a traitor; 20 years later he was the first president of the United States, and today he is beloved as the father of his country. This example illustrates the fact that who is defined as deviant and what is defined as deviance depend on who is doing the defining and who has the power to make the definitions stick. Individuals stigmatized and victimized by prevailing social definitions see their circumstances quite differently from those who enjoy power and enforce norms that embody their moral codes. In recent years, some groups, such as gays, lesbians, the disabled, and welfare mothers, have entered the political arena and have had some success in challenging official definitions that portray them as "social problems."

Variability over Time in Definitions of Deviance

In every society and at every time, people define and react to some behaviors as deviant. For that reason deviance appears to be a constant. However, the particular behaviors that people define as deviant change over time. For example, compulsive

Spit, Saliva, and the Social Construction of Deviance

To set the stage on the first day of class for their courses in introductory sociology and in the sociology of deviance, Professors John R. Brouillette and Ronny E. Turner of Colorado State University (1992) undertake an exercise that demonstrates the social construction of deviance. After outlining course procedures and content, one of the professors calls on a student to provide a small amount of saliva in a sterilized spoon. Somewhat embarrassed, the student provides the saliva. The professor thanks her and then he gives a brief lecture on the benefits and functions of saliva for the human body; for instance, saliva moistens the linings of the mouth and throat, aids in the prevention of infection, and facilitates digestion.

After discussing the benefits of saliva, the professor offers the student who initially provided the valuable body fluid an opportunity to take the spoon and return the saliva to her mouth. Invariably the student declines. The instructor comments that he has difficulty comprehending why someone would reject such a valued substance in the age of recycling. He then offers the contents of the spoon to a classmate. Some students respond by making gagging sounds. The professor expresses "surprise" and reminds the students that they often share a can of soda, which also involves the sharing of saliva. The instructor then comments:

Not only that, but some students engage in a formerly criminal

action, French kissing, which most couples consider intimate, loving, and appropriate. Actually, two people place their lips together, intermingle their tongues, and exchange or mix their saliva. Is this deviant? Certainly not! It's sexy . . . cool . . . and a "turn on." Well, if you believe that's cool, picture this. A couple are parked at the top of Lookout Mountain, passionately embracing each other. The woman pulls a spoon from her purse, which she uses to scrape some saliva from her mouth. To soothe her lover's raging hormones and to show her love for him, she offers him the spoon. Do you think it will turn him on to a point of no return?

gambling, alcoholism, drug addiction, shoplifting, and even many forms of mental illness were once defined as evil and sinful—as deviant behaviors. Today they may be defined as medical problems (Conrad, 2007; Grant, Kim, and Odlaug, 2009), illnesses analogous to diabetes and high blood pressure.

Fifty years ago, pregnancy seriously and permanently damaged an unmarried woman's respectability and reputation in the United States because it was a sign that the woman had engaged in sexual behavior without marriage (Bumpass and McLanahan, 1989). However, norms governing premarital sexuality have shifted considerably over time, and this behavior is generally no longer stigmatizing (Risman and Schwartz, 2009). Over the same period, the birth rate among unmarried women has increased dramatically, so that now 41 percent of all American infants are born to unmarried mothers (Martin et al., 2011). In the context of changing norms about sexual

behavior and changes in patterns of births, the status of unmarried childbearing as deviance has significantly shifted. While unmarried mothers may face a multitude of practical problems, loss of social respectability is no longer a serious issue for many of them.

At the same time, many areas of behavior that were once ignored or tolerated are now more likely to be defined as seriously deviant. Old concerns such as child abuse and family violence have become amplified in recent years, receiving much media attention. Simultaneously, new areas of deviancy, including date rape and politically incorrect speech, have been created. And cigarette smoking is increasingly regulated or prohibited.

The Functions and Dysfunctions of Deviance

Most of us think of deviance as "bad"—as behavior that poses a "social problem." Such a view is not surprising given the negative or disruptive

The professor next engages class members in a discussion of the difference between "saliva" and "spit." In the course of the discussion he introduces the students to the sociological concept of the social construction of reality:

There is a difference between spit and saliva. But no chemist will ever find it because the difference is not chemical. It's social. If people believe that spit and saliva are different, they are different. You had better know the difference or suffer the consequences. Spit is saliva in the wrong place or under the wrong circumstances. Nothing inherent in the mouth moisture itself necessitates a particular distinction between spit and saliva; no inherent change occurs. The difference is socially constructed. We social beings have drawn lines around behavior to demarcate deviant from normal, acceptable behavior.

The sociology professor then points out that "spit" and "saliva" are defined differently, depending on who is engaging in a given behavior and on the social context in which the behavior occurs. Mothers are seen wiping dirt from an infant's face with moisture from the mouth. Jesus and other religious leaders reportedly used their "sputum" to cure the blind and the infirm. And, males spit incessantly during athletic contests, a behavior typically deemed "inappropriate" for female athletes. In sum, deviance is socially defined behavior.

Questions for Discussion

1. In 2006, professional football player Sean Taylor of the Washington Redskins was fined $17,000 by the National Football League for spitting in the face of another player during a game. As noted in a *Washington Post* story (Weeks, 2006) about the incident, this reaction would not surprise British sociologist Ross Coomber, who claims that spitting at someone is a form of violence more offensive than hitting them. Do you agree? Why or why not?

2. Have you ever redefined a behavior in order to label yourself or another deviant or nondeviant? Explain.

Source: Excerpt from "Creating the sociological imagination on the first day of class: The social construction of deviance," by John R. Brouillette and Ronny E. Turner. Teaching Sociology, *vol. 21, 1992. Reprinted by permission of the American Sociological Association.*

consequences of much deviance, or what sociologists call *dysfunctions* (see Chapter 1, p. 19). But deviance also has positive or integrative consequences for social life, what sociologists call *functions*.

The Dysfunctions of Deviance Social organization derives from the coordinated actions of numerous people. Should some individuals fail to perform their actions at the proper time in accordance with accepted expectations, institutional life may be jeopardized. For instance, the desertion of a family by a parent commonly complicates the task of child care and rearing. When a squad of soldiers fails to obey orders and runs away in the midst of battle, an entire army may be overwhelmed and defeated. Most societies can absorb a good deal of deviance without serious consequences, but persistent and widespread deviance can impair and undermine organized social life.

Deviance also undermines our willingness to play our roles and contribute to the larger social enterprise. If some individuals get rewards, even disproportionate rewards, without playing by the rules, we develop resentment and bitterness. Morale, self-discipline, and loyalty suffer.

Moreover, our social life requires that we trust social institutions and one another. Trust makes conventional social life, from communities to economic exchange to families, possible. The most mundane, but essential, aspects of life would be impossible without trust. The use of checks and credit cards, for example, requires that we trust our banks to keep our money safe, to honor the checks we write, and to charge our credit cards only as we have authorized. Normal community life is impossible where people cannot trust that those passing them on the street will not try to harm them. The maintenance of families and family life requires that people can trust others to live up

Smoking, once deemed an innocent vice, is now increasingly regulated, forcing smokers out of office buildings, restaurants, hospitals, and other public facilities.

to their obligations. Deviant behavior is dysfunctional because it can undermine this trust, threatening our most important social relationships and institutions.

The Functions of Deviance Although deviance may undermine social organization, it may also facilitate social functioning in a number of ways. First, as sociologist Edward Sagarin (1975) has pointed out, reacting publicly to deviance can promote conformity. Such reactions create a community of the "good," those who know the cost of deviating and who can now define themselves as an *in-group* in contrast to the *out-group* of deviants.

Second, because norms are not always clear, each time the members of a group censure some act as deviance, they highlight and sharpen the contours of a norm (Stevenson, 1991; Durkheim, 1893/1964). Their negative reactions clarify precisely what behavior is disallowed by the "collective conscience." Sociologist Kai T. Erikson (1962) noted that one of the interesting features of agencies of control is the amount of publicity they usually attract. In earlier times the punishment of offenders took place in the public market in full view of a crowd. Today we achieve much the same result through heavy media coverage of criminal trials and executions.

Third, by directing attention to the deviant, a group may strengthen itself. A shared enemy arouses common sentiments and cements feelings of solidarity. The emotions surrounding "ain't it awful" deeds quicken passions and solidify "our kind of people" ties. As we saw in Chapter 4 (pp. 100–101), frictions and antagonisms between in-groups and out-groups highlight group boundaries and memberships. In the same way, campaigns against witches, traitors, perverts, and criminals reinforce social cohesion among "the good people." Erikson (1966) showed that when the Puritan colonists thought their way of life was threatened, they created "crime waves" and "witchcraft hysterias" to define and redefine the boundaries of their community.

Fourth, deviance is a catalyst for change. Every time a rule is violated, it is being contested. Such challenges serve as a warning that the social system is not functioning properly. For example, high robbery rates indicate that there are large numbers of disaffected people, that institutions for socializing youths are faltering, that power relations are being questioned, and that the moral structures of the society require reexamination. Thus, deviance is often a vehicle for placing on a society's agenda the need for social repair and remedies. Deviant activity can simultaneously be a call for an examination of old norms and a new model (Sagarin, 1975). For example, the Reverend Martin Luther King, Jr., and his supporters called the nation's attention to the inhumanity of southern segregation laws through civil disobedience. In due course the civil rights movement led to these laws being changed.

Social Control and Deviance

If the work of the world is to get done, people must follow rules. Social order dictates that people have to be kept in line, at least most people, and that the line must be adhered to within allow-able limits (Sagarin, 1975; Gibbs, 1989; Liska, 1986). Without social order, interaction would be a real problem and expectations would be mean-ingless. Societies seek to ensure that their mem-bers conform to basic norms by means of **social control,** the methods and strategies that regulate behavior within society (Robinson, 2007).

Functionalists and conflict theorists differ in how they view social control. As we will see in Chapter 9 (p. 282), functionalists see social control, particularly as it finds expression in the activities of the state, as an indispensable requirement for survival. If large numbers of people were to defy their society's standards for behavior, massive institutional breakdown, mal-functioning of society, and chaos would result. In contrast, conflict theorists contend that social control operates to favor powerful groups and to disadvantage others. No social arrangements are neutral, they argue. Existing institutional structures distribute the benefits and burdens of social life unevenly while maintaining these structures through the techniques and instruments of social control.

There are three main types of social control processes operating in social life: (1) those that lead us to internalize our society's normative expectations, (2) those that structure our world of social experience, and (3) those that employ various formal and informal social sanctions. Let us briefly consider each of these processes.

Internalization of Norms

As we saw in Chapter 3, the members of a soci-ety undergo continuous *socialization,* a process by which individuals acquire those ways of thinking, feeling, and acting characteristic of their society's culture. For infants and young children, conformity to the expectations of oth-ers is primarily a product of external controls. As they grow older, an increasing proportion of their behavior becomes governed by internal monitors. These internal monitors carry on many of the functions earlier performed by external controls. **Internalization** is the pro-cess by which individuals incorporate within their personalities the standards of behavior prevalent within the larger society.

A good example is the set of norms in U.S. society regarding ownership of property. As all parents eventually learn, young children will pick up, play with, and sometimes destroy any item they find attractive. Only through interac-tion over a long period with parents, caregivers, and peers do children finally learn to respect other people's property even when they are not being watched by others.

Critical steps to social control through internalization are (1) learning what the norms are and (2) learning to believe that the norms are legitimate. In addition, through the process of internalization, norms become part of peo-ple's personalities, as discussed in Chapter 3 (pp. 81–82), with the internalization of the "generalized other." Such standards are often accepted without thought or questioning—indeed, we commonly experience them as "sec-ond nature." The group is our group, and its norms are our norms. Social control thus becomes self-control.

The Structure of Social Experience

Our society's institutions also shape our expe-riences. In large part we unconsciously build up our sense of reality by the way our society orders its social agendas and structures social alternatives. If we are locked within the social environment provided by our culture, we inhabit a somewhat restricted world, and it may not occur to us that alternative standards exist. A simple example is young children raised without sweets. If they have never had a cookie or even heard of one, they will never ask for one. Without experiences that take us out of the patterned routines dictated by the institutions that make up our society, we are *culture-bound.* Many nonconformist patterns do not occur to us because they are not known to our society.

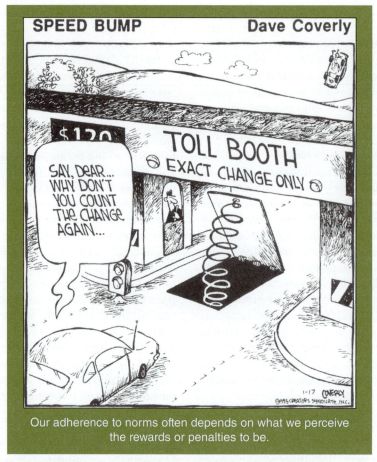

Our adherence to norms often depends on what we perceive the rewards or penalties to be.

Reprinted with the permission of Dave Coverly and Creators Syndicate, Inc.

Formal and Informal Sanctions

Finally, we conform to the norms of our society because we realize that to do otherwise is to incur punishment. Those who break rules are met with dislike, hostility, gossip, ridicule, and ostracism—even imprisonment and death—while the conformist wins praise, popularity, prestige, and other socially defined good things. Clearly, there are disadvantages to nonconformity and advantages to conformity.

Formal sanctions are reactions of official agents of social control, such as the courts, the honor systems that control cheating, and the principal's office in the high school. Students who are caught cheating, for example, may be formally sanctioned by being expelled from school. *Informal sanctions* are reactions to deviance that occur in small communities, in groups of friends, and in the family. Students who report cheating by their friends may be deviant from the point of view of their friendship group and may be informally sanctioned by being ostracized. Informal sanctions generally are more effective than formal sanctions, particularly if they are part of the interaction in the primary groups to which people are strongly committed. That both shame and honor serve to modify behavior has been shown experimentally (Jacquet et al., 2011).

Theories of Deviance

Deviance may have both positive and negative consequences for the functioning and survival of groups and societies. But why, we may ask, do people violate social rules? Why are some acts defined as deviance? Why are some individuals labeled deviants when they engage in essentially the same behaviors as other individuals who escape retribution? And why does the incidence of deviance vary from group to group and society to society? It is these types of questions that interest sociologists.

We should keep in mind that a complete understanding of human behavior, including deviant behavior, requires the inclusion of biological and psychological factors along with social factors (Gove, 1994). For example, both biology and psychology have contributed a good deal to our understanding of *schizophrenia*—a severely debilitating form of mental illness that affects about 1 percent of the population. Biologists and psychologists have shown that hereditary factors predispose individuals to some forms of schizophrenia (e.g., Sawa and Snyder, 2005; Cockerham, 2011).

Yet an understanding of the biological and psychological factors involved in schizophrenia does not provide us with the full story. Consider the following example. A man living in the Ozark Mountains has a vision in which God speaks to him, and he begins preaching. People say he has a "calling." His reputation as a prophet and healer spreads, but when he ventures into St. Louis and attempts to hold a prayer meeting—blocking traffic at a downtown thoroughfare during rush hour—he is arrested. When the man tells the police officers about his conversations with God, they take him to a mental hospital where attending psychiatrists say he is schizophrenic and

hospitalize him (Slotkin, 1955). The man is seen as a prophet, a criminal, and a mental patient, depending on his social environment, because deviance is not a property inherent in behavior but a property conferred upon it by social definitions.

In this section we discuss five specific theories of deviance: the anomie, cultural transmission, conflict, labeling, and control theories. As you will see, each theory of deviance has a connection to the basic reasoning in the three theoretical perspectives we use in this book. Anomie and control grew out of *functionalism;* cultural transmission and labeling emerged from *symbolic interactionism;* and conflict theory is the application of the *conflict perspective* to deviance.

Anomie Theory

As we noted earlier in the chapter, Émile Durkheim (1893/1964, 1897/1951) contended that deviance can be functional for a society. But he also realized that deviance is simultaneously dysfunctional and made another contribution to our understanding of deviance with his idea of **anomie**—a social condition in which people find it difficult to guide their behavior by norms that they experience as weak, unclear, or conflicting. As Durkheim pointed out, anomie is a common occurrence when people's expectations about rewards and gratifications are not closely matched by what they actually receive. In a gold rush many people believe that they can become wealthy overnight. As a result some people abandon their families and jobs, travel long distances in search of riches, and set up nontraditional communities that promote crime, violence, prostitution, and general disorder. When an economy collapses and few jobs are available, the rewards that people are used to receiving are no longer available, and deviance, including crime and delinquency, increases. In both of these examples, norms that previously governed work and family life become weak and ineffectual because conformity to these norms no longer allows people to realize their expectations.

Merton's Theory of Structural Strain

Robert K. Merton's theory of structural strain is an adaptation of Durkheim's anomie theory that emerged from the *functionalist* perspective (Liska and Messner, 1999). Merton (1968) built on Durkheim's ideas and linked them to American life. He said that for large numbers of Americans, worldly success—especially as it finds expression in material *wealth*—has become a cultural goal. However, only certain *means*—most commonly, securing a good education and acquiring high-paying jobs—are the institutionalized and approved ways to achieve success. There might not be a problem if all Americans had equal access to these institutionalized means for realizing monetary success, but this is not the case. The poor and minorities often find themselves handicapped by little formal education and few economic resources (Wilson, 2009).

Americans who internalize the goal of material success but who do not have access to the institutionalized means are pushed by strong social structural strains toward the use of unconventional means. They cannot achieve the culturally approved goals by using the institutionalized means for attaining them. One solution to this dilemma is to obtain the prestige-laden ends by any means whatsoever, including vice and crime.

Merton emphasized that a "lack of opportunity" and an exaggerated material emphasis are not enough to produce strains toward deviance. A society with a comparatively rigid class or caste structure may lack opportunity and simultaneously extol wealth—the medieval feudal system serves as a case in point. When a society extols common symbols of success for the entire population, while structurally restricting the access of large numbers of people to the approved means for acquiring these symbols, antisocial behavior is generated.

Merton identified five responses to the ends–means dilemma, four of them deviant adaptations to conditions of anomie (see Figure 5.1).

Conformity Conformity will be common in a society in which people accept the cultural goal of material success and the institutionalized means to achieve this goal are available. Such behavior is the bedrock of a stable and properly functioning society.

Innovation In innovation individuals hold fast to the culturally emphasized goals of success, but because the institutionalized means to achieve the goals are not available, they pursue their goals in innovative ways. Such people may engage in prostitution, peddle drugs, forge checks, swindle, embezzle, steal, burglarize, rob, or extort to secure money and purchase the symbols of success.

Modes of Adaptation	Cultural Goals	Institutionalized Means
I Conformity	+	+
II Innovation	+	−
III Ritualism	−	+
IV Retreatism	−	−
V Rebellion	±	±

+ = Acceptance

− = Rejection

± = Rejection of prevailing values and substitution of new values

Figure 5.1 **Merton's Typology of Modes of Individual Adaptation to Anomie**

Source: Adapted with the permission of Free Press, a division of Simon & Schuster, Inc. from *Social Theory and Social Structure* by Robert K. Merton. Copyright 1949, © 1957 by The Free Press. Copyright renewed © 1977, 1985 by Robert K. Merton. All rights reserved.

Ritualism Ritualism involves losing touch with success goals while abiding compulsively by the institutionalized means. For instance, the ends of the organization become irrelevant for many zealous bureaucrats. Instead, they cultivate the means for their own sake, making a fetish of regulations and red tape (see Chapter 4, pp. 114–117).

Retreatism In retreatism individuals reject both the cultural goals and the institutionalized means without substituting new norms. Skid row alcoholics, drug addicts, vagabonds, and derelicts are examples of people who have dropped out of society.

Rebellion Rebels reject both the cultural goals and the institutionalized means and substitute new norms for them. Such individuals withdraw their allegiance to existing social arrangements and transfer their loyalties to new groups with new ideologies. Radical social movements on the right and left, such as the militia movement and radical socialism, are good illustrations of this type of adaptation.

Applying Structural Strain Theory

Sociologists have applied structural strain theory to a variety of problems. In a classic study Albert Cohen (1955) found that lower-class boys often find themselves failing in middle-class school environments that reward verbal skills, neatness, and an ability to defer gratification. The boys respond by banding together in juvenile gangs where they evolve "macho" standards that reward "toughness," "street smarts," and "troublemaking"—standards that allow them to succeed. Sociologists Steven Messner and Richard Rosenfeld (1997a, 1997b) extended Merton's structural strain theory. They argue that the strain toward deviance, particularly crime, is stronger when the economy is the dominant institution in society and when social status is primarily dependent on performance in economic roles. Crime rates are particularly high

in societies where people are completely dependent on the labor market for resources necessary for survival; on the other hand, societies that guarantee an acceptable level of income regardless of participation in the labor market have less crime.

Evaluating Structural Strain Theory

Merton's theory of structural strain tells us a good deal about monetary crime and particularly about how individual adaptations to variation and change in the structure of opportunities (i.e., means) in society can influence rates of deviance and crime (Shoemaker, 2010). However, critics have pointed out that not all deviance stems from gaps between goals and means (Cohen, 1965). As we will see, people sometimes learn to deviate. If subcultural values and norms are different from those in the mainstream, when people conform to their subculture, they may be in violation of some important societal norms. Violations of fish and game laws among Native Americans, common-law marriage among some ethnic minorities, cockfighting among some groups with southern rural backgrounds, and the production of moonshine liquor among some Appalachian groups are all examples of such subcultural deviance. In sum, the problem may not be anomie or structural strain but a conflict of values.

Cultural Transmission Theory

Structural strain theory provides us with insight into how society may unwittingly contribute to deviance by the way it structures its goals and opportunities. A number of other sociologists have emphasized the similarities between the way deviant behavior is acquired and the way other behavior is acquired. One of the first was French sociologist Gabriel Tarde (1843–1904), who argued that criminals, like "good" people, imitate the ways of individuals they have met, known, or heard about. In contrast to law-abiding people, however, they imitate other criminals.

During the 1920s and 1930s, sociologists at the University of Chicago were struck by the concentration of high delinquency rates in some areas of Chicago (Thrasher, 1927; Shaw, 1930; Shaw and McKay, 1942; Sampson and Groves, 1989). In a series of investigations, they found that neighborhood delinquency rates remained much the same over time despite the changing composition of the neighborhoods (Shoemaker, 2010). They concluded that delinquent and criminal behaviors are in part a product of economic conditions, but are also culturally transmitted from one generation of juveniles to the next. As new ethnic groups enter a neighborhood, their children learn the delinquent patterns from the youths already there. Hence, the Chicago sociologists contended that youths become delinquent because they associate and make friends with other juveniles who are already delinquent.

Sutherland's Theory of Differential Association

A classic statement of the cultural transmission of deviance is Edwin H. Sutherland's **differential association** theory. Sutherland (1939) was a sociologist associated with the Chicago tradition of sociology. His theory builds on the *interactionist perspective* and emphasizes the part social interaction plays in molding people's attitudes and behavior. Sutherland said that individuals learn deviance primarily in intimate groups of deviant others, such as small groups of friends (Shoemaker, 2010). People not only learn how to be deviant—for example, how to mug people, how to smoke marijuana, and how to apply graffiti—but also learn attitudes favorable to deviance. Of course, people who are involved in deviant groups are also usually involved in more conventional relationships in their families, at school, at work, in church, and in other settings. Sutherland argued that if the definitions favorable to deviance outweigh the definitions unfavorable to deviance learned in other situations, deviance is likely to occur.

When parents move to a new neighborhood to get their children away from gang influences, they are applying the principle of differential association. So are parole officers who try to restrict the associations of the paroled prisoners they supervise. By the same token, the theory suggests that imprisonment may be counterproductive when juveniles are incarcerated with experienced criminals.

Applying Cultural Transmission Theory

Recent studies of differential association have provided strong support for the theory (Matsueda, 1988; Shoemaker, 2010). Sociologist James Orcutt (1987), for example, found that having marijuana-smoking friends and favorable attitudes about marijuana are strong predictors of marijuana smoking. However, just as Sutherland's theory suggests, favorable attitudes lead to marijuana smoking only when they are stronger than unfavorable attitudes. Haynie's (2001) study showed that the impact of friends' delinquency on one's own delinquency is much greater when one is popular and central to the group and where the density of ties among friends is high. Box 5.2 shows how differential association helps explain college binge drinking.

Evaluating Cultural Transmission Theory

Cultural transmission theory shows that socially disapproved behaviors can arise through the same processes of socialization as socially approved ones (Kaplan, Johnson, and Bailey, 1987). It is a particularly useful tool for understanding why deviance varies from group to group and from society to society (Matsueda and Heimer, 1987; Crane, 1991). However, the theory is not applicable to some forms of deviance, particularly those in which neither the techniques nor the appropriate definitions and attitudes are acquired from other deviants. Illustrations include naive check forgers; occasional, incidental, and situational

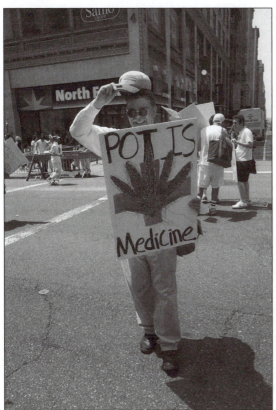

Both conflict theory and labeling theory argue that certain activities are defined as deviant by powerful societal agents. This demonstrator is trying to influence legislators and policy makers to change the dominant societal definition of marijuana use.

offenders; nonprofessional shoplifters; non-career-type criminals; and people who commit "crimes of passion." Further, not everyone who has deviant associates is deviant. Different individuals may interpret the same social relationships differently, producing different outcomes.

Although most of the emphasis in cultural transmission theory has been on how criminal behavior is learned from friends, relatives are probably also important. Most incarcerated juvenile delinquents, and about a third of such adult

offenders, have immediate family members who also have been in jail or prison. The more severe and chronic the criminal behavior, the more likely that an offender has relatives who have been imprisoned (Butterfield, 1992). More research is needed to determine if this association is due to learning (as cultural transmission theory suggests), to shared environment, to shared genetic inheritance, or to some combination of these factors.

Conflict Theory

Cultural transmission theorists emphasize that individuals who are immersed in different subcultures will exhibit somewhat different behaviors because they are socialized in different traditions. Conflict theorists argue that the most important question is, "Which group will be able to translate its values into the rules of a society and make these rules stick?"

Although in the 1980s and 1990s conflict theory took many new directions (e.g., Hagan, 1989; Messner and Krohn, 1990; Grant and Martinez, 1997), its early roots can be traced to the Marxist tradition and the conflict perspective that grew out of it (see Chapter 1, pp. 20–21). According to orthodox Marxism, a ruling class exploits and robs the masses, yet avoids punishment for its crimes. Individuals victimized by capitalist oppression are driven by their struggle to survive to commit acts that the ruling class brands as criminal (Bonger, 1936; Liska and Messner, 1999). Marxists regard other types of deviance—alcoholism, drug abuse, mental illness, family violence, sexual immorality, and prostitution—as products of the moral degeneration and estrangement fostered by the oppression and exploitation of the poor, women, and African Americans or other minorities.

Richard Quinney's Theory of Class, State, and Crime

Because Marx wrote little about crime, it fell to a 20th-century U.S. sociologist, Richard Quinney (1974, 1980), to write a now-classic statement of

Drink 'Til You're Sick: What Explains College Binge Drinking?

Binge drinking—five drinks at a sitting for males, four for females—is on the rise in the United States (Naimi et al., 2003; Substance Abuse and Mental Health Services Administration, 2005). Although 69 percent of binge-drinking episodes occur among adults ages 26 and older, binge-drinking rates—the number of binges in a given time period—are highest for 18-to 25-year-olds. Indeed, close to half of the college students who drink say that they usually binge when they drink and that getting drunk is a good reason for drinking (Wechsler, Lee, et al., 2000). Why is binge drinking so common among college students? No carefully designed studies have been done to answer this question, but available evidence supports both control theory and differential association theory.

Let's look at differential association first. In spite of some recent attempts at change, many campus fraternal organizations seem to encourage excessive drinking (Sperber, 2000). As we can see from the figure, students who are members of fraternities and sororities are much more likely to binge drink than are students in general. And for those who live in fraternity or sorority houses, the percentage of binge drinking is even higher (Wechsler, Lee, et al., 2000). Differential association is even more important for underage drinkers, who are six times more likely to binge drink if they live in a fraternity or sorority house than if they live in a traditional single-sex dormitory (Wechsler, Kuo, et al., 2000). Fraternal organizations are not the only social contexts that facilitate excessive drinking in college. Despite being exposed to more alcohol education programs than other students are, student athletes—both male and female—are significantly more likely to binge drink than are non-athletes (Nelson and Wechsler, 2001). A primary reason for this, consistent with differential association theory, is that college athletes are more likely than other students to have friends who are binge drinkers, who value partying and sports, and who spend a great deal of time socializing.

What about control theory? Students who are married are far less likely to binge drink, and control theory explains this by pointing to the process of commitment. People who are married have strongly invested in social relationships that could be threatened, damaged, or destroyed by deviant behavior such as binge drinking.

No one theory provides a complete explanation for deviance, and survey data such as those presented here leave us with many unanswered questions. Do students drink excessively because they live in fraternities and sororities, or do they choose to live in fraternities and sororities because they like to drink? Do married students drink less because they are married, or are those who drink little or no alcohol more likely to marry? Carefully designed experiments or surveys that collect data from high school

---

the conflict theory of crime. Quinney said that the U.S. legal system reflects the interests and ideologies of the ruling capitalist class. Law makes illegal certain behavior that is offensive to the morality of the powerful and that threatens their privileges and property.

Quinney (1980:39) contended that if we are "to understand crime we have to understand the development of the political economy of capitalist society." Since the state serves the interests of the capitalist class, crime is ultimately a class-based political act embedded in capitalist social arrangements.

In striving to maintain itself against the internal contradictions eating away at its foundations, capitalism commits *crimes of domination* (Quinney, 1980:57). Indeed, "one of the contradictions of capitalism is that some of its laws must be violated in order to secure the existing system." These crimes include those committed by corporations and range from antitrust violations to pollution of the environment. But there are also *crimes of government* committed by the officials of the capitalist state, Watergate being a well-publicized instance. In contrast, much of the criminal behavior of ordinary people, or *predatory crime*—burglary, and college students at several points in time might help us sort out these questions with more certainty.

Questions for Discussion

1. Do these studies support your experiences or the experiences of other students on your campus?

2. How could labeling theory be used to challenge the implicit claim made in this box that binge drinking is deviant?

3. Which theory or theories of deviant behavior offer an understanding of binge drinking that could be used to develop strategies to control it? How and why?

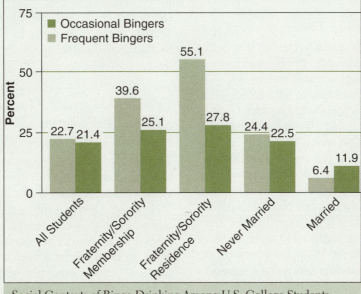

Social Contexts of Binge Drinking Among U.S. College Students
Source: Figure generated by the authors using data from Wechsler, Lee, et al., 2000.

robbery, drug dealing, and hustling of various sorts—is "pursued out of the need to survive" in a capitalist social order. *Personal crime*—murder, assault, and rape—is "pursued by those who are already brutalized by the conditions of capitalism." And then there are *crimes of resistance* in which workers engage in sloppy work and clandestine acts of sabotage against employers.

Applying Conflict Theory

Conflict theory has led social scientists to investigate the ways in which the making and administration of law are biased by powerful interests (Jacobs and Helms, 1996, 1997). Numerous sociologists have noted that crime is defined primarily in terms of offenses against property (burglary, robbery, auto theft, and vandalism), whereas corporate crime is deemphasized (Sutherland, 1949; Coleman, 1987). Moreover, the penalty for crimes against property is imprisonment, whereas the most common form of penalty for business-related offenses is a monetary fine. Clinard and Yeager (1980) found that over a 2-year period, the federal government charged nearly two-thirds of the Fortune 500 corporations (the 500 largest U.S. corporations) with violations of the law. Estimates of the yearly cost of such crimes run as high as $200 billion, compared with $3–4 billion a year for conventional street crimes (Clinard and Meier, 2011). And while the Federal Bureau of Investigation (FBI) keeps track of every murder, rape, assault, and auto theft reported in the United States, no agency keeps a record of crimes committed by corporations.

Evaluating Conflict Theory

Though there may be much in conflict theory that is true (Liska and Messner, 1999), statements of the theory are not always clear (Hawkins, 1987). In addition, it is sometimes hard to tell which specific individuals or groups are covered by such terms as "ruling elites," "governing classes," and "powerful interests." In addition, research results are not always consistent with the theory. For example, the theory predicts that "When sanctions are imposed, the most severe sanctions will be imposed on persons in the lowest social class" (Chambliss and Seidman, 1971:475). Some studies have found few (Bernstein, Kelly, and Doyle, 1977) or no (Chiricos and Waldo, 1975) links between the class level of criminal offenders and the sentences received or between unemployment and incarceration (D'Alessio and Stolzenberg, 1995); other studies have found the relationship to be substantial (Lizotte, 1978; Bridges, Crutchfield, and Simpson, 1987); and still others have found that the relationship depends on specific circumstances (Hagan, Bernstein, and Albonetti, 1980; Humphrey and Fogarty, 1987). Although corporations often seek to influence legislation and public policy about deviance, they do not necessarily predominate over other interest groups (Hagan, 1980, 1989). Clearly, additional research is needed. Conflict propositions cannot be accepted as articles of faith but should be more clearly articulated and more carefully investigated.

Labeling Theory

Conflict theorists contend that people often find themselves at odds with one another because their interests diverge and their values clash. Some people gain the power and ascendancy to translate their values and normative preferences into the rules governing institutional life. They then successfully place negative labels on violators of these rules. A number of sociologists took this core notion, expanded on it using ideas from the *interactionist perspective,* and developed labeling theory. Labeling theorists are interested in the process by which some individuals come to be tagged as "deviants," begin to think of themselves as deviants, and enter deviant careers.

Edwin M. Lemert, Howard S. Becker, and Kai T. Erikson: The Social Reaction to Deviance Approach

The three sociologists responsible for the classic statements of labeling theory—Edwin M. Lemert (1951, 1972), Howard S. Becker (1963), and Kai T. Erikson (1962, 1966)—make a number of points. First, they contend that no act by itself is inherently deviant or not deviant. The "badness" of an act does not stem from its intrinsic content but from the way other people define and react to it. Deviance is always a matter of social definition. Similarly, according to labeling theory, a person who engages in deviant behavior is deviant only if he or she has been so labeled.

Second, labeling theorists point out that we all engage in deviant behavior by violating some norms. They reject the popular idea that human beings can be divided into those who are normal and those who are pathological. For example, some of us exceed the speed limit, experiment with cocaine, shoplift, cheat on a homework assignment, sample homosexual publications, underreport our income to income tax authorities, swim in the nude, become intoxicated, commit vandalism in celebration of a football victory, or trespass on private property. These actions often are what labeling theorists call **primary deviance**—behavior that violates social norms but usually goes unnoticed by the agents of social control.

Third, labeling theorists say that whether people's acts will be seen as deviant depends on which rules society chooses to enforce, in which situations, and with respect to which people. Not all individuals are arrested for speeding, shoplifting, underreporting income on their tax returns, trespassing, or the like. African Americans may be censured for doing what whites are "allowed" to do, women censured for doing what men are "allowed" to do, and certain individuals censured for doing what their friends are also doing; and some may be labeled as deviants even though they have not violated a norm but simply because they are so accused (e.g., they appear "effeminate" and are tagged as "gay"). Of critical importance is the social audience and whether it labels the person a deviant.

Fourth, labeling people as deviants has consequences for them. It tends to set up conditions conducive to **secondary deviance**—deviance individuals adopt in response to the reactions of other individuals. In brief, labeling theorists contend that new deviance is manufactured by the hostile reactions of rule makers and rule abiders. An individual is publicly identified, stereotyped, and denounced as a "delinquent," "mental fruitcake," "forger," "rapist," "drug addict," "bum," "pervert," or "criminal." The label serves to lock the individual into an outsider status. Such a master status overrides other statuses in shaping a person's social experiences and results in a self-fulfilling prophecy. Rule breakers come to accept their status as a particular kind of deviant and organize their lives around this master status.

Fifth, people labeled "deviant" typically find themselves rejected and isolated by "law-abiding" people. Friends and relatives may withdraw from them. In some cases they may even be institutionalized in prisons or mental hospitals. Rejection and isolation push stigmatized individuals toward a deviant group with other individuals who share a common fate. Participation in a deviant subculture becomes a way of coping with frustrating situations and for finding emotional support and personal acceptance.

In turn, joining a deviant group solidifies a deviant self-image, fosters a deviant lifestyle, and weakens ties to the law-abiding community.

In sum, labeling theorists say that the societal response to an act, not the behavior itself, determines deviance. When the behavior of people is seen as departing from prevailing norms, it sets off a chain of social reactions. Other individuals define, evaluate, and label the behavior. Norm violators then take these labels into account as they shape their actions. In many cases they evolve an identity consistent with a label and embark upon a career of deviance.

Applying Labeling Theory

Unlike structural strain and cultural transmission theory, labeling theory does not focus on why some individuals engage in deviant behavior. Rather, labeling theory helps us to understand why the same act may or may not be considered deviant, depending on the situation and on the characteristics of the individuals involved.

Sociologist William J. Chambliss (1973) employed labeling theory to explain the differing perceptions and definitions that community members had of the behavior of two teenage gangs. At Hanibal High School, Chambliss observed the activities of the Saints, a gang of eight white upper-class boys, and the Roughnecks, a gang of six lower-class white boys. Although the Saints engaged in as many delinquent acts as the Roughnecks, it was the Roughnecks who were in "constant trouble" and universally considered to be "delinquent." The community, the school, and the police related to the Saints as though they were good, upstanding youths with bright futures, but they treated the Roughnecks as young punks headed for trouble.

A number of factors contributed to the differential treatment given the two groups. For one thing, the Saints had access to automobiles and engaged in out-of-town escapades that were less visible to Hanibal citizens than those undertaken by the Roughnecks in the center of town. For another, when the Saints were confronted

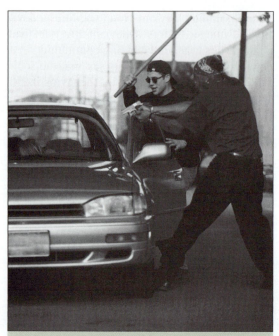

According to control theory, deviant behavior such as gang violence is more likely among people whose bond to conventional society is weak.

by an accusing police officer, they were apologetic and penitent, whereas the Roughnecks were hostile and belligerent. Finally, police officers knew that irate and influential upper-middle-class parents would come to the aid of their youngsters, whereas powerless lower-class parents would have to acquiesce in the law's definition of their sons' behavior.

Chambliss (1973) concluded that when the community responded to the Roughnecks as boys in trouble, the boys' pattern of deviancy was reinforced. As their self-conception as deviants became more firmly entrenched, they began to try new and more extreme acts of deviance. Their growing alienation led to greater disrespect and hostility, which increased the community's negative attitude toward them.

Evaluating Labeling Theory

Evidence on the operations of social control organizations often supports labeling theory. From 1880 to 1920, unprecedented numbers of Americans were confined to mental hospitals. But the labeling perspective showed that this was not due to Americans suddenly going crazy, but rather was caused by a boom in state mental hospital construction and increased funding of state departments of mental hygiene (i.e., health) (Grob, 1983; Sutton, 1991). The capacity to confine people had increased.

Research also shows that once people are hospitalized for mental illness, some feel stigmatized by the label "mental patient," and this may make reintegration into the outside world more difficult (Link et al., 1989, 1991).

Labeling theory also has its critics. While it may help us understand how individuals are labeled as deviants and how labels can promote secondary deviance, labeling theory tells us nothing about causes of primary deviance. Indeed, in many forms of deviance, it is the behavior or condition of the people themselves that is primarily responsible for their being labeled deviant. For example, many people who are hospitalized for mental illness suffer acute disturbance associated with internal psychological or neurological malfunctioning (Gove, 1970) that cannot be explained solely in terms of the reactions of other people.

Another criticism of labeling theory is its almost exclusive focus on societal reactions in the definition of deviant behavior. If behavior is not deviance unless it is labeled, we cannot classify secret and undetected deviance, such as the embezzlement of funds, the failure to pay income taxes, and the clandestine sexual molestation of children. Clearly, deviance cannot be understood without reference to norms.

Control Theory

The theories discussed above are all attempts to explain why people deviate. Control theory turns the question around and asks why people *do not* deviate (Reckless, 1961, 1967; Hirschi, 1969; Shoemaker, 2010). Though we are frequently concerned that there is too much deviance in our society, what is truly remarkable is how much conformity there is. As you walk to and attend class each day, your behavior and that of others around you almost always fits within a narrow and predictable pattern. Most of us conform most of the time; even "deviants" conform most of the time. Such rigid control is particularly remarkable given that the possibilities for human behavior are virtually infinite, limited only by physical laws and people's imaginations.

Control theory's answer to why people conform is an outgrowth of *functionalist* ideas. People conform because they are integrated into mainstream institutions. Societies that have properly functioning institutions will have low deviance.

Travis Hirschi and the Elements of the Social Bond

Travis Hirschi's study (1969) of juvenile delinquency in Richmond, California, provided a classic statement of control theory. Hirschi's argument is that young people are more likely to conform if their bond to society is strong. This bond has four parts: attachment, involvement, commitment, and belief.

Attachment is the process of being involved in social relationships with others. All social relationships entail some degree of control for all participants. Control is more likely where the psychological and emotional connections among group members are high and members care about one another's opinions (Shoemaker, 2010). Being involved in a family, having friends in the community, and being a member of a club are all examples of attachments that reduce the chance that deviance will occur.

By *involvement,* Hirschi meant involvement in conventional activities. One way to keep people from being deviant is to get them to spend their time conforming. Boy Scouts, Girl Scouts, youth fellowship, band, and athletics are only a few of the myriad activities that parents, schools, religious organizations, and neighborhood associations

create to take up the leisure time of children and adolescents. A main purpose of these activities is to provide an alternative to drug and alcohol use, sexual activity, vandalism, and crime.

Commitment refers to the strength of the investment people have made in conventional social ties and relationships. People who have strong commitments in their social lives are not likely to deviate because of the losses they may incur if they are identified as deviant. A student who aspires to become a police officer and who has earned the trust and respect of teachers, school administrators, and local law enforcement officials is unlikely to become a drug dealer; she or he would risk losing the benefits of the investments made in pursuit of this career.

Finally, the bond to society is cemented by *belief* in conventional values and ideas about morality. The less people believe in the conventional values of society, the more likely it is that deviance will occur. If young people do not believe in the conventional idea that having a job or running a legitimate business is the acceptable way to make money, they are more likely to attempt to get money in criminal ways.

Applying Control Theory

Because the essence of control theory is that people will be less likely to deviate if they are integrated into mainstream institutions, much research on control theory has focused on the controlling power of three primary social institutions: religion, the family, and education (Shoemaker, 2010).

Somewhat surprisingly, a number of studies have found that religion seems to have little or no impact on deviant behavior (Jensen and Rojek, 1992; Hirschi and Stark, 1969). The reason is not that religion is ineffective in social control, but that religion is only one of a number of social institutions involved in controlling behavior, and so it is hard to see its impact. It is easier to see the controlling effect of religion where there is low consensus about the deviant nature of acts; nearly everyone agrees that murder is wrong, but fewer people strongly agree that smoking marijuana is wrong. Religion does control deviant behavior, and its effect is clearly seen where competing secular controls are weak (Tittle and Welch, 1983; Burkett and White, 1974).

Most studies of the family and deviant behavior have been concerned with young people. These studies have shown that intact families and good family relations decrease the chances of delinquent behavior among youths (Shoemaker, 2010). However, the effect of intact families is relatively weak and has not been found in all studies. The more important factor is not family structure (broken versus intact), but the way parents communicate and interact with their children (Yablonsky and Haskell, 1988; Cernkovich and Giordano, 1987).

Involvement in schooling controls deviant behavior not only because it takes up people's time in conventional pursuits but also because it promotes conventional attachments, commitment, and beliefs. Hirschi (1969) found that having attachment to school and positive relationships with teachers reduced the chance of delinquency. Cernkovich and Giordano (1992) also found that attachment and commitment to school reduced delinquency, although this effect was somewhat less among black males. Zingraff's 1994 study showed that schooling is an important deterrent to delinquency even when family relations are poor or abusive. And Crutchfield and Pitchford (1997) showed that among people 18 years and over, being a student reduces the likelihood of criminal involvement.

Evaluating Control Theory

Though much of the research on deviance and delinquency is in accord with control theory (Shoemaker, 2010), some problems remain. First, the social bond does not control deviance equally well across social groups (Cernkovich and Giordano, 1992; Gardner and Shoemaker, 1989) or as well in other societies as in the United States (Rahav, 1976; Tanioka and Glaser, 1991; Hartjen and Kethineini, 1993). Second, factors other than the bond to society are clearly important; even the best studies show that no more than 50 percent

of delinquent behavior is explained by factors emphasized in control theory (Shoemaker, 2010). Third, in some circumstances elements of the social bond are not associated with reduced deviance. For example, as differential association theory indicates, when attachment is to delinquent peers, we observe more deviance. Involvement in conventional activities likewise is not related to less deviance if it allows unstructured time with no authority present (Osgood et al., 1996), as members of traveling high school marching bands and athletic teams often attest. Indeed, the National Longitudinal Study of Adolescent Health, the largest-ever national study of adolescents, showed that spending unsupervised time with friends is much more closely linked to drinking, smoking, using weapons, attempting suicide, and having sex than are race, income, or family structure (Stepp, 2000; see also Blum et al., 2000). Finally, control theory cannot explain deviance that occurs among those who are fully integrated into mainstream society. Those implicated in the deviant acts of white-collar, corporate, and government crime are often the employed, married, churchgoing, respectable middle class.

None of the theories of deviance we have examined provides a complete explanation of deviant behavior. Each one highlights for us an important source of deviance (e.g., see Hoffmann, 2003). Deviant behavior takes many forms, so we must approach each form in its own right to determine the specific factors involved. We turn next to a consideration of crime, a form of deviance that is particularly prevalent in modern societies.

Crime and the Criminal Justice System

Within modern societies law is a crucial element in social control. Unlike informal norms such as folkways and mores, laws are rules enforced by the state. As we defined it at the beginning of the chapter, *deviance* is behavior that a considerable number of people view as reprehensible and beyond the limits of tolerance. **Crime** is an act of deviance that is prohibited by law. As we have seen, not all deviant acts are crimes; they may break rules defined only by folkways and mores. As with other forms of deviance, there is nothing inherent in an act that makes it criminal. For an act to be considered criminal, the state must undertake a political process of illegalizing—or *criminalizing*—it (Jenness, 2004). For example, the Cyber-Security Enhancement Act of 2008 made it a crime to remove personal information from a computer without permission (Menn, 2010). Because anything can be a crime if a law is established making it illegal, an infinite variety of acts can be crimes.

What crimes have in common is not that they are necessarily acts we regard as immoral or wicked. For example, many Americans consider it no more "evil" to cheat on their income taxes than did their parents or grandparents to purchase and consume alcoholic beverages during Prohibition. Rather, the distinguishing property of crime is that people who violate the law are liable to be arrested, tried, pronounced guilty, and deprived of their lives, liberty, or property. In brief, they are likely to become caught up in the elaborate social machinery of the **criminal justice system**—the reactive agencies of the state that include the police, the courts, and prisons. So common are "scrapes with the law" that U.S. men have nearly a 50 percent chance of being arrested at least once in their lives (Uggen, 2000).

In this section we will discuss measurement of crime and describe various forms of crime. We will examine the relationship between drugs and crime as well as race and crime and consider the criminal behavior of women. Finally, we will describe the components of the criminal justice system and take a look at the purposes of imprisonment.

Forms of Crime

In this section we consider a number of forms of crime within the United States: violent crime, juvenile crime, organized crime, white-collar and corporate crime, crime committed by government, and victimless crime.

How do we know how many crimes are committed in the United States? Statistics on crime are among the most unsatisfactory of all social data (Biderman and Lynch, 1991). Official crime records suffer from numerous limitations (Tittle and Paternoster, 2000) because many crimes are undetected, unreported, or unrecorded.

Two main data sources are used by researchers who study violent crime trends in the United States. The Uniform Crime Reports (UCR) are collated by the FBI and based on reports to the police. Although Justice Department studies reveal that less than half of all crimes are reported to the police, research also shows that whether citizens report crimes depends primarily on how serious they perceive the crimes to be; thus the Uniform Crime Reports are valid indicators of serious crimes as defined by the citizenry (Gove, Hughes, and Geerken, 1985). The other main data source for crime researchers is the National Crime Victimization Survey (NCVS). The U.S. Census Bureau uses the NCVS to collect crime victimization data twice a year from a nationally representative sample of about 49,000 households. Data are compiled, analyzed, and reported by the Bureau of Justice Statistics. The rates of various crimes according to the NCVS are substantially higher than rates according to the UCR. Self-report-based measures of crime, involving anonymous questionnaires that ask people which offenses they have committed, also reveal much higher rates of crime than those found in official crime statistics.

Another limitation of the UCR and the NCVS is that they focus on crimes that are most likely to be committed by young people and individuals from lower socioeconomic backgrounds. Statistics on many categories of crime, such as white-collar, government, and organized crime, are not routinely compiled. Additionally, some cases of criminal offenses, such as income tax evasion and fraud, are unlikely to be reported in victimization studies.

Violent and Property Crime

The Federal Bureau of Investigation annually reports on eight types of crime in its Uniform Crime Reports. These offenses are called **index crimes** and consist of four categories of violent crime against people—murder, rape, robbery, and assault—and four categories of crimes against property—burglary, theft, motor vehicle theft, and arson. Between 1991 and 2010, rates of violent crime as reported by the FBI decreased by 47 percent and property crime by 43 percent (Federal Bureau of Investigation, 2011). These trends continued through 2011. In 2009, the overall rates of violent crime and property crime were also the lowest ever recorded by the National Crime Victimization Survey (NCVS), which was initiated in 1973 (see Figure 5.2). Survey respondents' attitudes reflect this drop: In 1994, 37 percent of a random sample named crime and violence as the most important problem facing the country, compared to only 1 percent in 2011 (Maguire, 2012).

In spite of this reduction, there is still a large amount of crime in the United States. In 2010, there were 14,748 murders in the United States (Federal Bureau of Investigation, 2011). The total number of criminal victimizations in 2010 was 18.7 million, with 14.9 violent crimes per 1,000 people and 120.2 property crimes per 1,000 households (Truman, 2011).

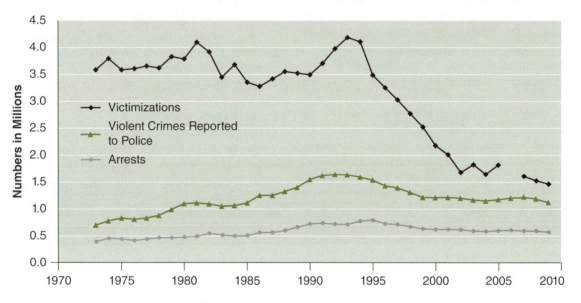

| Figure 5.2 | **Numbers of Violent Crimes, Violent Crimes Reported to Police, and Arrests for Violent Crimes in the United States, 1973–2009, in Millions** |

The amount of violent crime (rape, robbery, aggravated assault, and homicide) in the United States has been declining since the early 1990s, and in 2009 it was the lowest recorded since 1973. The victimization estimate for 2006 is excluded from this graph because methodological changes that occurred in data collection for that year introduced errors into the estimate. For details on this issue, see the technical note published by the Bureau of Justice Statistics (http://bjs.ojp.usdoj.gov/content/pub/pdf/cv06tn.pdf).

Source: Bureau of Justice Statistics, U.S. Department of Justice.

Crime data provide information about how crimes occur. For example, 43 percent of murder victims in 2010 knew their assailants, and more than three-quarters of all murder victims were male (Federal Bureau of Investigation, 2011). Twenty-six percent of all murders were precipitated by arguments, and firearms were the weapons used in 67 percent of all murders in 2010. In rapes and sexual assaults, 63 percent of victims know their assailant (Rand, 2009). Sixty-nine percent of female aggravated assault victims know their assailant, 17 percent of them intimately; in other words, women's assailants are likely to be husbands, boyfriends, and acquaintances. Among male aggravated assault victims, 51 percent know their assailants, but only 8 percent are intimately involved with their assailants. Crime victimization rates also show that victims of violent crime are likely to be male, young, and black (see Figure 5.3).

The decreases in violent crime during the 1990s and into the 2000s represent a greater decline than at any time since World War II and resulted in many headlines and discussions on television

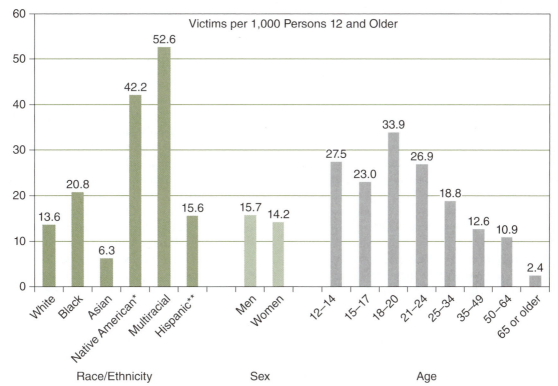

Victims per 1,000 Persons 12 and Older

Race/Ethnicity: White 13.6, Black 20.8, Asian 6.3, Native American* 42.2, Multiracial 52.6, Hispanic** 15.6

Sex: Men 15.7, Women 14.2

Age: 12–14 27.5, 15–17 23.0, 18–20 33.9, 21–24 26.9, 25–34 18.8, 35–49 12.6, 50–64 10.9, 65 or older 2.4

*American Indian or Alaskan Native. ** Hispanics may be of any race.

Figure 5.3 **Rates of Violent Crime in the United States, 2010**
These crime victimization rates for rape, sexual assault, robbery, aggravated assault, and simple assault (taken as a whole) show that victims of violent crime are more likely to be male, young, and black, Native American, or multiracial.

Source: Figure generated by the authors using data from Truman, Jennifer L. 2011. *Criminal victimization, 2010.* Bureau of Justice Statistics, NCJ 235508, September 2011. Available at http://www.bjs.gov/content/pub/pdf/cv10.pdf

talk shows. What accounts for the drop in violent and property crime over recent decades? In his book *The Great American Crime Decline*, social scientist Franklin Zimring (2007) argues that increases in incarceration rates, a decline in the young male population, and improved police procedures in some jurisdictions probably played some role. However, a significant proportion of the decline in crime rates remains unexplained. Economic growth in the 1990s may have had some effect, but since 2008, declining crime rates have coincided with a worsening economy. Although politicians often claim that immigration, particularly illegal immigration, has led to increased crime, recent research indicates that immigrants have lower rates of crime than others, and recent immigration to the United States probably has contributed to the recent crime decline (Wright and Benson, 2010; Stowell et al., 2009; Hickman and Suttorp, 2008; Sampson, 2008).

Despite its declining crime rate, the United States has a reputation for violent crime. Although its property crime rate is similar to or lower than the rate of property crime in other industrialized nations, the U.S. violent crime rate is higher than that of Western Europe or Australia. Why? Zimring and his colleague Gordon Hawkins (1997) explored the question in their book *Crime Is Not the Problem: Lethal Violence in America.* One answer they suggested is that Americans are more heavily armed than citizens of other nations, so that property crimes are more likely to lead to death. Guns do not answer the question entirely, however. Even in robberies in which no guns are used, the death rate is three times higher in New York City than in London. Further, 30 percent of U.S. homicides do not involve a gun. Another explanation for the higher violent crime rate in the United States is that people are more likely to have more frequent and more violent personal conflicts than in other countries.

The influence of American television and other media is often invoked as a possible explanation for high rates of violent crime. But James

Q. Wilson cites historical evidence showing that "the homicide rate in New York City has exceeded that of London by a factor of at least five *for the last two hundred years*" (Wilson, 1997:41)—during which, of course, America's youth were not watching crime shows on TV. The assessment by Zimring and Hawkins that lots of conflict and lots of guns are responsible for a high U.S. violent crime rate fits with those of analysts who see a stable economy, family stability, and effective gun control as accounting for the recent drop in the crime rate.

Juvenile Crime

We have seen that young people are more likely to be victims of crime. They also are more likely than older people to commit crime. Though persons 15–19 years of age represent only 7.1 percent of the population, they constitute 21.3 percent of those arrested for committing crimes (Maguire, 2012). The peak age for property crime arrests is 13–14, and for violent crime it is 18–19 (Maguire, 2012). Among 17-year-olds, 8 percent report having belonged to a gang, 16 percent have sold drugs, and 16 percent have carried a handgun (Snyder and Sickmund, 2006). Juvenile involvement in violent crime has increased over the past several decades (Bartollas, 2003).

The percentage of people arrested for committing crimes drops steadily with increasing age; only a quarter of those who committed offenses when they were 16 or 17 did so again as adults at ages 18–19 (Snyder and Sickmund, 2006). After a peak in violent crime by juveniles in the early 1990s, the juvenile violent crime rate has declined steadily.

If we could prevent all crimes committed by persons under 25 years of age, much of conventional crime would be eliminated from society, though we would still have many white-collar, corporate, and government crimes and about half the homicides. With an ever-increasing number of young people in the country, however, many of whom are at high risk for delinquent behavior, some analysts predict a violent juvenile crime wave (Bartollas, 2003; Siegel and Welch, 2005). Studies of juvenile crimes show that many youngsters of all social classes break some criminal laws and that the amount of unreported crime is enormous (Regoli and Hewitt, 2000; Tittle and Paternoster, 2000).

Although school crime and school violence grab big headlines, school crime has declined just as societywide levels of crime have (Dinkes, Cataldi, and Lin-Kelly, 2007). Students in or away from school are about equally likely to be victims of violent crime, but school is safer with regard to serious violent crime. In 2005, middle and high school students were victims of 5 serious violent crimes per 1,000 students at school but victims of 10 serious violent crimes per 1,000 away from school (Dinkes, Cataldi, and Lin-Kelly, 2007). School shootings are extensively covered by the news media, but they remain relatively rare. During the 2005–2006 school year, for example, there were 14 homicides and 3 suicides that occurred at schools among all school-aged children (5–18), a rate of 1 homicide or suicide per 3.2 million students. Despite the decrease in school-based delinquency, schools are becoming more punitive, disproportionately so where the percentage of black students is high (Welch and Payne, 2010).

The treatment of young people who commit crimes has changed over the past 40 years. In 1972 half of all juveniles taken into police custody were referred to juvenile court, and nearly half were handled within the arresting police department and released. Only 1.3 percent were referred to criminal or adult court (Pastore and Maguire, 2010). By 2002 the proportion handled within a police department and released had dropped to 18 percent, and nearly three-quarters were referred to juvenile court. Referrals to criminal or adult court rose to 7 percent.

During the 1990s nearly every U.S. state changed laws related to juvenile offending, making it easier to transfer juvenile offenders from the juvenile justice system to the criminal justice system, expanding sentencing options for both criminal and juvenile courts, modifying or removing confidentiality provisions, increasing victims' rights, and developing new programs in corrections (Snyder and Sickmund, 2006). The Juvenile Justice and Delinquency Prevention Act of 2002 specifies that juvenile and adult inmates be prevented from having contact, that juveniles not be detained or confined in adult jails or lockups, and that juveniles not charged with acts that would be crimes for adults not be held in detention or correctional facilities (Snyder and Sickmund, 2006).

Although juveniles may end up in juvenile detention centers, they are not exempt from more serious punishment. Comparisons show that juvenile offenders who have been transferred to adult court are punished more severely than are young adults (Kurlychek and Johnson, 2010). More than 100 people are serving life sentences without parole in U.S. prisons for crimes that did not result in deaths and that were committed when the prisoners were not adults (Barnes, 2009). In 2005, the Supreme Court ruled that it is unconstitutional to execute anyone for a crime committed when the person was younger than 18 (Lane, 2005), and a 2012 Supreme Court ruling held that the Eighth Amendment prohibits life sentences without parole for juveniles.

Organized Crime

Organized crime refers to large-scale bureaucratic organizations that provide illegal goods and services in public demand. Such crime is likely to arise where the state criminalizes certain activities—prostitution, drugs, pornography, gambling, and loan-sharking—that large numbers of citizens desire and for which they are willing to pay. Drug and arms trafficking by major crime organizations is the largest business in the world, bringing in between $700 billion and $1 trillion a year (Adler, Mueller, and Laufer, 2004).

The most publicized crime organization has been an Italian-American syndicate, variously termed the Mafia or Cosa Nostra, which gained a substantial impetus from Prohibition. The

Mafia seems to be a loose network or confederation of regional syndicates coordinated by a "commission" composed of the heads of the most powerful crime "families" (Adler, Mueller, and Laufer, 2004; Tittle and Paternoster, 2000). Organized crime is hardly an Italian monopoly, however. Chinese gangs, Colombian and Cuban drug rings, and groups of southern white moonshiners also fall under the category of organized crime. Although we may associate organized crime with various immigrant groups, it is not the case that immigration is tied to higher crime. For example, Hispanic immigrants are less involved in crime than are U.S. citizens (Hagan and Palloni, 1999).

Hate Crimes

Hate crimes, also called bias crimes, are crimes of hatred and prejudice. According to Congress, a hate crime is a "criminal offense against a person or property motivated in whole or in part by an offender's bias against a race, religion, disability, ethnic origin or sexual orientation" (Federal Bureau of Investigation, 2011a). According to the FBI's website (Federal Bureau of Investigation, 2011a), a total of 6,624 hate crime incidents were recorded in 2010, with 8,208 victims. Just under half of all bias incidents were racially motivated, and about 20 percent are related to religious bias, 19 percent to sexual orientation, 13 percent to ethnicity, and fewer than 1 percent are crimes against disabled persons.

In some ways hate has declined significantly in the United States since World War II, but some negative feelings about specific groups have persisted or even increased, and the FBI data cited above vastly underrepresents the actual number of hate crime incidents (Levin and Nolan, 2011). Although we think of the Ku Klux Klan as something from history, the number of U.S. hate groups has increased 48 percent since 2000 (Potok, 2008). The states with the greatest number of such groups are Texas, Tennessee, and Mississippi, with California, Georgia, Louisiana, Missouri, Indiana, Ohio, and Kentucky not far behind. The

groups include the Ku Klux Klan, neo-Nazis, white nationalists, racist skinheads, neo-Confederates, and black separatists (Potok, 2008).

Sociologists are interested in hate crime from a number of angles. Some see it as illegal behavior that is used to control an entire group by intimidating and victimizing individual members of that group—an illegal form of social control (King, Baller, and Messner, 2009). With wide variability in the areas of the country that hate crimes are most likely to occur, researchers also study the factors related to hate crime location (Grattet, 2009; King, Baller, and Messner, 2009). Social scientists also look at the role communication technologies play and at how hate groups gain members. The Internet has vastly expanded and globalized the reach of hate groups, some of which use "cloaked" sites that hide the authorship of the site. For example, one white supremacist site is called MartinLutherKing.org and looks at first like a tribute to Dr. King (Daniels, 2009).

White-Collar and Corporate Crime

One type of crime that has been of particular interest to sociologists is **white-collar crime**—crime most commonly committed by relatively affluent persons, often in the course of business activities (Sutherland, 1949). Bernard Madoff, for example, spent decades taking money from thousands of people who thought they were working with a "financial wizard and investment messiah." He never invested the money and was sentenced to 150 years in prison in 2009 (Oppenheimer, 2009). Included in white-collar crime are corporate crime, fraud, embezzlement, corruption, bribery, tax fraud or evasion, stock manipulation, insider trading, misrepresentation of advertising, restraint of trade, and infringement of patents. More recent research has focused on workplace misconduct at a different level, including such things as drinking or doing drugs on the job, short-changing customers, damaging or stealing employers' property, and falsifying time records (Wright

Environmental degradation can be a personal crime, a corporate crime, or a government crime, when regulatory agencies choose not to notice or prosecute violators.

Corporations have been implicated in a variety of crimes, including overcharging the government on contracts, polluting the environment, shortchanging consumers, violating employee privacy, price-rigging school milk contracts, disposing of hazardous waste in violation of the law, adulterating fruit juice, and engaging in accounting irregularities (Clinard, 1990; Rothchild, 1993). In 2010, the FBI was investigating more than 189 major corporate frauds, 18 of which involve losses of more than $1 billion (Federal Bureau of Investigation, 2010).

The small number of white-collar criminals who are prosecuted and convicted are rarely given sentences comparable to those of other criminals. Street criminals who steal $100 may find their way to prison, while an executive who embezzles $1 million may receive a suspended sentence and a relatively small fine.

and Cullen, 2000). According to the Federal Bureau of Investigation (FBI), many large-scale mortgage fraud and identity theft operations are now the province of organized crime (Federal Bureau of Investigation, 2010). Included on the FBI's web page on white-collar crime are frauds involving health care, Medicare, insurance, mass marketing, bankruptcy, and hedge funds and scams related to adoption, jury duty, and securities.

White-collar crime costs society just as other crimes do, and we are more likely to be victims of corporate crime than of street crime (Simon and Eitzen, 1993). Tax evasion is the most costly white-collar crime in the United States. Fraud, the second-most costly white-collar crime, costs citizens $300 per household in higher insurance premiums (Soupiset, 2003). *Shrinkage,* a term used by retailers to encompass theft by employees, shoplifting, and clerical errors, has been measured at $33.2 billion for a single year (Pressler, 2003). Losses due to health care fraud exceed $50 billion annually (Federal Bureau of Investigation, 2010).

Crime Committed by Government

Conflict theorists have drawn our attention to crime committed by governments (Barak, 1991). Nazi Germany provides an extreme example: More than 6 million Jews were murdered during the Holocaust of the Hitler years (Dawidowicz, 1975). More recently, other governments have participated in "ethnic cleansing" and murdered citizens who were the "wrong" religion or ethnicity. The U.S. government massacred countless Native Americans during the colonization of the country; even as late as 1890, U.S. Army forces armed with machine guns mowed down nearly 300 Sioux at Wounded Knee, South Dakota (Brown, 1971).

But there are other sorts of government crimes. At the federal level, in the Iran–contra scandal during President Reagan's term, operatives of the nation's security organizations engaged in secret arms shipments to the Nicaraguan contra rebels even though Congress had barred aid to them. The Oval Office tapes of the Richard Nixon White House revealed a president bent on victimizing his enemies by using his presidential powers illegally.

Bribery and corruption have been documented at all levels of government. The illegal dumping of toxic materials, prostitution, gambling, drug running, entrance of illegal aliens, smuggling of valuable goods from other countries, and a variety of other crimes often occur because officials at various levels find it worth their while to "look the other way." While fraud and embezzlement are significant costs to society, when they occur in government bureaucracies the money comes directly out of taxpayers' pockets. As with white-collar and corporate crime, those involved in government crime are less likely than "street criminals" to be caught and punished despite the fact that their crimes may cost us more.

Victimless Crime

Usually, a crime has an identifiable victim who suffers as a result of another person's criminal behavior. A **victimless crime** is an offense in which no one involved is considered a victim (Schur, 1965). These crimes include gambling, the sale and use of illicit drugs, and prohibited sexual activities between consenting adults (e.g., prostitution and, in some states, fornication and homosexuality). In victimless crime, if there is any suffering, it is by the offenders themselves, by "innocent bystanders" (as in the case of experiencing the odors associated with public urination), or by the tax-paying public at large.

The behaviors in question in victimless crime are criminalized because society, or powerful groups within a society, defines them as immoral or in some other way a threat to society.

As we have pointed out, crime is an act of deviance that is prohibited by law. Laws prohibiting victimless offenses thereby create crime and cost society money by way of the efforts to arrest and process suspects. When such laws are struck down, the act is decriminalized, as in the 2003 Supreme Court decision overturning Texas's ban on private consensual sex between same-sex adults (Lane, 2003).

Technology and Crime

The information revolution has generated new crimes and made old crimes easier to commit. These **high-tech crimes** are defined as attempts to commit crime through the use of advanced electronic media (Adler, Mueller, and Laufer, 2004). High-tech crimes include child pornography, credit card fraud, mail bombings, software piracy, industrial espionage, and computer network break-ins.

Approximately 30 percent of Americans had become victims of identity theft by 2009, and the annual worldwide loss to Internet crime is estimated at $1 trillion (Menn, 2010). People ages 18 to 24 are at greatest risk of identity theft, a 2010 study showed, because it takes them longer to detect irregular charges and withdrawals (Klein, 2010).

In his recent book *Fatal System Error,* writer Joseph Menn (2010) describes some of the havoc being wreaked by high-tech criminals. As the name "worldwide web" suggests, Internet criminals can operate from anywhere, as in the case of a group of Russian cyber-criminals who extorted money from companies in other countries, threatening to shut down company websites by overwhelming them with requests for information. Hackers in any country can use networks of personal computers owned by others as robots to flood websites with requests, causing the sites to operate sluggishly or to shut down completely. These "botnets" are associated with organized crime as well as with individuals.

Menn explains that computer experts know that the Internet was not designed for security and say that to achieve a secure system will require starting over; common programming errors in software contribute to the vulnerability of personal computers and to breeches of websites. And the potential for crime goes beyond personal and corporate. In 2009, the U.S. director of national intelligence Admiral Dennis Blair warned that both China and Russia could collect intelligence from the U.S. government via computer break-ins and could threaten the country in other ways as well, testifying before the U.S. Senate that he expects "disruptive cyber activities to be the norm in future political or military conflicts" (Menn, 2010:229).

Drugs and Crime

Drugs have been part of American life since the Jamestown colonists first harvested tobacco in 1611; cocaine and heroin use took root as long ago as the 1890s (Musto, 1987). The connection between drugs and crime can be seen clearly in the ongoing Mexican drug wars, with illegal production, transport, sale, and purchase of drugs the obvious drug-related criminal violations and corruption, violence, Wild West–style shootouts, and murder some of the related crimes (Perkins and Placido, 2010). In 2012, the Mexican government reported that 47,515 drug-related murders had occurred since 2006, and other estimates are higher (Cave, 2012).

The link between drugs and crime is complicated by the fact that society defines which drugs are legal and normative and which are illegal and deviant. Nearly half the adults in the United States have used illegal drugs, and a fifth have used prescription drugs for nonmedical purposes (Maguire, 2012). But significantly less than half the population is involved in serious drug-related crime. Alcohol is the fifth leading cause of death and disability worldwide (Grimm, 2008), but its production, sale, and use are entirely legal. And 3–4 million American children take prescribed psychiatric drugs, despite the fact that most of these drugs have never been tested for use in children (Brown, 2003).

Despite our ambivalence about drug use, the relationship between drugs and crime is of interest to criminal justice officials, criminologists, and sociologists. In 2010, the largest category of all arrests was drug abuse violations (Federal Bureau of Investigation, 2011). America's "War on Drugs," which costs $50 billion a year, seems to focus primarily on arrests rather than treatment or prevention; as the United States leads the world in illegal drug use, we don't seem to be winning the war (Moskos, 2009). Many argue that continuing to arrest people for drug violations is not the answer. One problem is that the country lacks the facilities to imprison all violators. Perhaps more importantly, research shows that brain abnormalities are linked to drug abuse (Ersche et al., 2012; Nestler, 2001), adding to strong evidence that drug addiction is not something that can be "cured" by a term of imprisonment. Further, the demand for drugs is at the base of the country's drug problem. When an accused "drug lord" was arrested, he stated that violent drug-trafficking gangs would thrive "as long as Americans keep buying marijuana, cocaine and heroin" (Sullivan and Jordan, 2002).

There are many proposals for dealing with drug abuse, including continued prohibition, removing penalties for possession of drugs (depenalization), and legalizing distribution of drugs (legalization). Some argue that depenalization and legalization would decrease crime rates. Criminal justice professor and former police officer Peter Moskos (2009) has studied the Dutch system of regulating marijuana through controlled distribution. The percent of adults who have tried marijuana is nearly twice as high in the United States as in the Netherlands, heroin usage rates are three times higher in the United States, and crystal meth use is almost nonexistent in the Netherlands. Increasing numbers of U.S. citizens support legalizing marijuana, with 44 percent of respondents to a 2009 Gallup poll supporting legalization, and at least 14 U.S. states now allow medical marijuana use (Hendrix, 2009).

Little consensus exists among either the lay public or professionals on the most effective strategies to fight crime through fighting drug use

(MacCoun, 1993). Many countries have laws similar to those of the United States, yet the United States has higher rates of drug abuse than other countries (Wilson, 1997); clearly, more than government policy plays a part in drug abuse.

Race and Crime

In 2009–2010, African Americans accounted for 13 percent of the U.S. population, 28 percent of all those arrested for index crimes, and 43 percent of the prison population nationwide (Maguire, 2012; Humes, Jones, and Ramirez, 2011; West, 2010). The imprisonment rate for blacks is six times higher than for whites (Stuntz, 2011). Race also plays a part in capital punishment, with offenders being more likely to be sentenced to death when the victim is white, and some research shows that the race of the offender also affects outcomes (Radelet and Borg, 2000). The death penalty also is more likely to be imposed when the victim is high-status (Phillips, 2009). Blacks and Latinos also are more likely than whites to be the victims of urban criminal violence (Krivo, Peterson, and Kuhl, 2009).

Why are African Americans disproportionately involved in crime and in the criminal justice system? Part of the reason, particularly in regard to violent crime, is that African Americans experience more of what sociologists call "structural disadvantage" (Peterson and Krivo, 2005)—the concentration of poverty, low income, family disruption, joblessness, and unemployment at the neighborhood level. When blacks and whites experience the same degree of structural disadvantage, their rates of violent crime are similar (Krivo and Peterson, 1996, 2000). In general, whites are very unlikely to live in structurally disadvantaged neighborhoods. As Peterson and Krivo (2005:335) report, "the most disadvantaged white neighborhoods have less deprivation than the typical black community."

How much of the disproportionate representation of African Americans in the criminal justice system is due to racial discrimination? Criminologist William Stuntz (2011) blamed it on the collapse of the rule of law, contending that as legal doctrine and jury trials have been displaced by "official discretion" and plea bargains, opportunities for discrimination have increased. Studies of traffic stops show that black men are a third more likely than white men to be stopped by the police and twice as likely to have their cars searched once they are stopped (Lundman and Kaufman, 2003). Stuntz (2011) also points to budgetary constraints: arrests and convictions are the cheapest for low-end drug crimes, and as a result poor black neighborhoods in which such crimes take place are targeted for arrests. Whites who favor the death penalty are more likely to be racially prejudiced and to prefer convicting the innocent over letting a murderer go free (Young, 2004), making death penalty juries more likely to be both racially prejudiced and in favor of conviction.

But other studies on arrests, processing, and sentencing do not provide consistent evidence of racial bias. Some studies show that black offenders receive harsher sentences, some find that there are no significant racial differences, and some find that race influences sentencing in certain circumstances (Spohn, 2000). A review by the National Institute of Justice of 40 recent studies of race and sentencing severity showed that race plays a role in sentencing but that the primary determinants of sentencing decisions are the seriousness of the offence and the offender's prior criminal record (Spohn, 2000).

Regardless of the causes of the disproportionate representation of African Americans in the criminal justice system, it has serious consequences (Stuntz, 2011; Harris, Evans, and Beckett, 2010). The losses to African Americans are not limited to disproportionate imprisonment and execution. Those imprisoned—approximately 12 percent of all young black men—are unable to support their families or contribute to their communities, and the economic cost of serving time continues beyond one's sentence. Once a

5.3 Social Inequalities

Being Black Brings Extra Punishment for Crime

The basic design of this study involves the use of four male auditors (also called testers), two blacks and two whites. The testers were paired by race. . . . The testers were 23-year-old college students from Milwaukee who were matched on the basis of physical appearance and general style of self-presentation. . . . Within each team, one auditor was randomly assigned a "criminal record" for the first week; the pair then rotated which member presented himself as the ex-offender for each successive week . . . these testers were bright articulate college students with effective styles of self-presentation. (Pager, 2003:946–47, 959)

Randomly assigned a "criminal record"? What were these "testers" testing? They were part of sociologist Devah Pager's study of the consequences of a criminal record (Pager, 2003). The pairs of young men applied for a total of 350 jobs during the study, with both members of each same-race team applying for the same jobs. What Pager wanted to know was whether reporting a criminal record on job applications affects the probability of being called back for a job interview. The

criminal record the testers reported was having served 18 months in prison for possession of, with intent to distribute, cocaine.

What did Pager find? The "employment penalty" for a criminal record is severe—and it is much worse for blacks than for whites. The white "clean" tester applications (those with no criminal record indicated) resulted in a 34 percent callback rate, while applications made by a white ex-offender tester generated only half as many callbacks. The black ex-offender tester applications, however, resulted in only a *third* as many callbacks as the black "clean" applications.

Pager's study revealed another significant and surprising finding: The black "clean" testers got fewer callbacks than the white "criminal" testers—14 percent for the clean-record blacks compared to 17 percent for the white ex-offenders. In other words, the callback rate for African American applicants with no criminal record is *less than half* that for the white "clean" applicants, *and* the effect of having been incarcerated is greater for blacks than for whites.

Each year more than half a million prisoners are released from incarceration back into society, where they need to find employment if they are to

support themselves honestly. Pager's research shows that finding that employment may be quite challenging, especially for African Americans:

Employers, already reluctant to hire blacks, appear even more wary of blacks with proven criminal involvement . . . the employment barriers of minority status and criminal record are compounded, intensifying the stigma toward this group. (Pager, 2003:959)

Questions for Discussion

1. Pager's study focused on entry-level (high school diploma) jobs. Would you expect to find more or less discrimination against applicants with criminal records for jobs requiring more than a high school education? Explain your answer.

2. The state in which Pager conducted her research has laws aimed at protecting "ex-cons" from discrimination by employers. How would the results of her study have differed had she conducted it in a state without such laws? Do you think other states should pass such legislation? Why or why not?

person is out of prison, a criminal record is a major barrier to employment, and this problem is substantially greater for blacks than for whites (Pager, 2003; see Box 5.3). Ex-inmates who find employment earn an average of 10–20 percent less than those who have not been in prison, and incarceration reduces the rate of wage growth for workers by 30 percent (Western, 2002). Participation in our political system also is taken away,

and this appears to have affected election outcomes; 48 of 50 states bar felons, including those on probation or parole, from voting, and 10 states bar exfelons (Uggen and Manza, 2002). As the prison population has grown, the percentage of the population that is disenfranchised also has grown, and that disenfranchised population is made up primarily of young, poor, black males. The imprisonment of so many young black men reduces their life chances, damages the economic life of the black community, dampens civic involvement, and promotes alienation.

Women and Crime

Women accounted for 25.5 percent of all arrests in 2010, with 19.5 percent of violent crime arrests and 37.6 percent of property crime arrests being women (Maguire, 2012). More women than men (68.7 percent) are arrested for prostitution, and just over half of all embezzlement arrests are female, but for the most part men greatly outnumber women as perpetrators of crime.

Sociological research on women's criminal behavior has included investigations of trends in women's violence (Schwartz, Steffensmeier, and Feldmeyer, 2009), women in prison (Krutt-schnitt, Gartner, and Miller, 2000), prostitutes and drug selling and use (Maxwell and Maxwell, 2000), and juvenile offending (Haynie, 2003; Uggen, 2000).

The participation of females in juvenile delinquency is somewhat higher than the proportion of adult female criminals; 29 percent of the youths arrested in the United States are females. While arrests of male juvenile offenders dropped nearly a quarter between 1998 and 2007, arrests of female juveniles dropped by only 13.5 percent (Federal Bureau of Investigation, 2008). Girls are typically arrested for less serious offenses than boys, with larceny-theft (often shoplifting); liquor law, loitering, and curfew violations; disorderly conduct; and running away the leading female offenses. The National Survey of Youth in Custody found that 91 percent of the youth being held in juvenile facilities in 2009 were male and 9 percent were female (Beck, Harrison, and Guerino, 2010). Research shows that females seem to perceive legal sanctions as more threatening than males do (Blackwell, 2000). Several studies have shown that increases in juvenile female arrest rates can be attributed more to changes in the criminal justice system than to changes in the number of girls engaging in criminal behavior (Shoemaker, 2010). Research suggests that girls' delinquency is related to many of the same factors as that of boys.

Gender also plays a part in crime victimization. Whereas males are more likely to be victims of robbery, total assault, and aggravated assault, females are more likely to be victims of rape and sexual assault (Rennison, 2002). Female victims account for 89 percent of sexual assaults, 76 percent of attempted rapes, and 96 percent of completed rapes (Maguire, 2012).

The Criminal Justice System

On television the evildoer nearly always gets caught and punished. In real life, however, the picture is quite different. According to statistics from the Justice Department, of every 100 criminal victimizations committed in the United States, only 36 are reported to the police. Of these 36 cases, only 7 or 8 result in an arrest. Of these 7 persons arrested, 5 are prosecuted and convicted and 1 is sent to prison; the other cases are rejected or dismissed because of problems with the evidence or witnesses, or the perpetrators are diverted into treatment programs. Of those convicted in state courts, more than half receive a sentence of at least 3.5 years, but the average inmate is released in about 1.5 years (see Figure 5.4 for data on the processing of serious criminals).

Even with so few sentencings for each 100 victimizations, those who are serving time may be innocent. According to a recent study, the investigation of crimes and suspicious deaths in the United States is "plagued by fractionated and inconsistent practices" (Holden, 2009). In an analysis of the first 250 prisoners exonerated through the use of DNA evidence, law professor Brandon Garrett found that 76 percent of the cases had involved eyewitness testimony and 74 percent, forensic evidence (Garrett, 2011). Some of the sources of wrongful conviction

(a) Sentences versus Time Served, 2009

Average years *sentenced* to prison and average years *actually served* by state prison inmates for various convictions

(b) Time from Arrest to Sentencing in State Courts, 2006

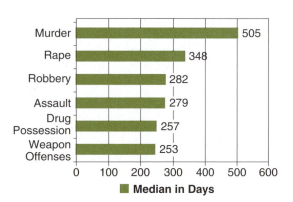

(c) Percentage of Crimes That Resulted in Arrests, 2010

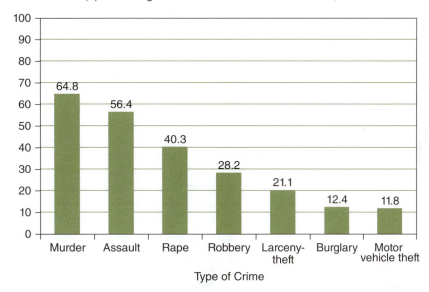

Type of Crime

Figure 5.4   **The Operation of the Criminal Justice System in the United States**

Sources: (a) and (c) Maguire, Kathleen, ed. 2012. *Sourcebook of criminal justice statistics* [Online], Bureau of Justice Statistics. (Available at http://www.albany.edu/sourcebook/) (b) Bureau of Justice Statistics, U.S. Department of Justice. (Available at http://bjs.ojp.usdoj.gov/index.cfm?ty=pbdetail&iid=2152)

listed by Garrett include the use of psychological pressure to obtain confessions, stacked lineups for suspect identification, flawed forensic tests, out-and-out lying by witnesses and informants, and pressuring eyewitnesses, who then misidentify suspects.

In this section we will briefly consider the components of the criminal justice system: the police, the courts, and the prisons. Each of these components operates at local, state, and federal levels.

The Police

The police are a citizen's first link with the criminal justice system and in many ways the most important one. When a crime occurs, the police are usually the first agents of the state to become involved. Yet police officers spend only about 15 percent of their time dealing with crime. Competing demands on their time range from filling out reports and directing traffic to handling complaints about uncollected trash and responding to medical emergency calls.

Many U.S. communities have implemented "community-based policing" or "problem-oriented policing," in which officers establish positive relationships with residents of specific areas and focus on crime prevention as well as reacting to crime. Surveys show that between 61 percent and 73 percent of respondents say police are excellent or pretty good at solving crime, preventing crime, treating people fairly, not using excessive force, responding quickly, and being helpful (Maguire, 2012).

The Courts

In the United States the criminal justice system is an adversary system. The person accused of a crime—the *defendant*—is presumed to be innocent until proved guilty in a court of law by the representative of the state—the *prosecutor*. In many nations the questioning of witnesses is handled by judges, and guilt and innocence are decided by a judge or panel of judges. But the U.S. system assumes that justice is best served by pitting opposing lawyers against each other before a neutral judge and jury.

In practice the fate of most of those accused of crime is determined by prosecutors. Prosecutors typically reject or reduce the severity of 50–80 percent of the criminal charges filed by police. The reasons prosecutors cite range from case overload to police inefficiency in producing evidence. Jury trials have become rare; more than 95 percent of criminal convictions are now by guilty plea, and most of those are the result of plea bargaining (Stuntz, 2011).

Prisons

We have said that the crime rate has been declining over the past decades. The prison population, on the other hand, has been steadily increasing. According to the Bureau of Justice Statistics, in 2009, 7.2 million people in the United States were in jail, in prison, on probation, or on parole—a total of 3.1 percent of the adult population (bjs.ojp.usdoj.gov/index.cfm?ty=tp&tid=11; U.S. Census Bureau, 2011a). There were nearly 1.5 million inmates in state and federal prisons and more than 0.5 million in local jails, more than four times as many as 30 years ago. The United States has the highest incarceration rate in the world (see Figure 5.5).

Why do we incarcerate more prisoners during a period of declining crime? Some analysts point to a "culture of control," with crime management resources devoted to protecting potential victims by locking away offenders rather than working to eradicate any of the causes of criminal behavior (Garland, 2003). In *The Challenge of Crime,* authors Henry Ruth and Kevin Reitz explain the expanding prison population this way:

From the early 1970s to the mid-1980s, the U.S. prisons expanded because the courts were sending more "marginal" felons to prison than they had in the past. Many burglars or auto thieves

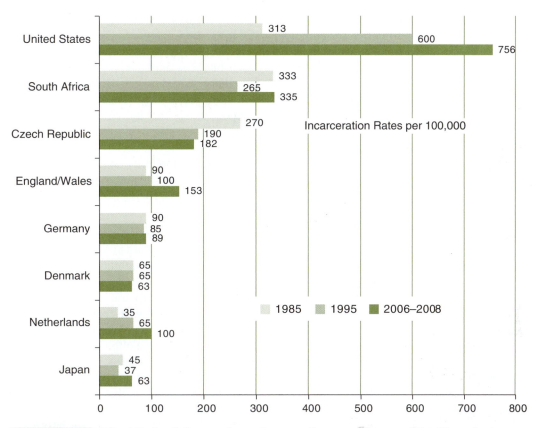

Figure 5.5 **The United States Imprisons a Larger Share of Its Population Than Does Any Other Nation**

According to the most recent World Prison Population List issued by the International Centre for Prison Studies at Kings College, London, the United States has the highest incarceration rate among 211 independent countries and dependent territories around the world. As this figure shows, it also has increasingly high incarceration rates compared to other countries. High incarceration rates in the United States are the result of the high crime rate and increasingly harsh criminal justice policies.

Sources: Figure generated by the authors using data from Walmsley, Roy. 2009. *World prison population list*, 8th ed.. London, UK: International Centre for Prison Studies, King's College, London.

who might have been put on probation in the 1950s or 1960s were instead sentenced to incarceration. . . . Then, from the mid-1980s to the early 1990s, prison growth was driven most forcefully by the war on drugs. . . . In the 1990s, the primary cause of prison growth changed again. For the first time in the expansionist era,

the chief engine of the prison build-up became longer sentences rather than more prison admissions. (2003:95–96)

Other researchers suggest different causes of prison growth. Sociologist John Sutton (2000) has documented connections between the labor market and prison populations and concluded that when opportunities for employment increase, prison growth decreases. Further, he found that declines in welfare spending result in increases in incarceration rates.

What purpose is served by locking offenders away? Let's take a look at traditional purposes of imprisonment.

Punishment Prior to 1800 it was widely assumed that the punishment of deviants was required if the injured community was to feel morally satisfied. In recent years there has been a renewed interest in punishment. The "moral order" argument runs like this: Certain acts are basically antisocial and heinous (e.g., murder, rape, genocide, and the sexual abuse of children). When grossly immoral behavior goes unpunished, people's commitment to social order and to basic values and norms is weakened; punishment is essential to maintain moral order. This approach draws on the functionalist perspective for support.

Rehabilitation In the later 18th and early 19th centuries, the idea that prisons might rehabilitate criminals came to the forefront. The word *penitentiary* was coined to describe a place where a criminal might repent and then resolve to lead a law-abiding life. Rehabilitation may include educational, vocational, and psychological programs geared at helping inmates overcome drug and alcohol addiction, earn their general equivalency diplomas, and gain job skills.

Critics of rehabilitation cite statistics on the high rate of **recidivism** (relapse into criminal behavior). In one study it was found that 67.5 percent of those released from prisons were re-arrested within 3 years. The prisoners had been charged with an average of 5 offenses each before their release, and another 2.7 in the 3 years after their release (Langan and Levin, 2002). Rates of recidivism are particularly high for those charged with robbery and property crimes. Complicating matters is the fact that the likelihood of rehabilitation is affected not only by what happens during imprisonment but also by whether released prisoners are able to reintegrate into the community. This process is strongly influenced by the individual's social circumstances both prior to incarceration and after release, including the social environment of peers, family and community, and state-level policies, particularly those related to postrelease supervision (Visher and Travis, 2003).

Deterrence The notion of deterrence rests on assumptions about human nature that are difficult to prove. Even so, a significant body of research indicates that crime is the result of active decision making by perpetrators (McCarthy, 2002) and that the certainty of apprehension and punishment does tend to lower crime rates (Waldo and Chiricos, 1972; Wolfgang, Figlio, and Sellin, 1972; Paternoster, 1989). But allegiance to a group and its norms typically operates as an even stronger force than the threat of societal punishment in bringing about conformity (Heckathorn, 1988, 1990). By the same token, informal standards and pressures within delinquent subcultures may counteract the deterrent effects of legal penalties (Tittle and Rowe, 1974; Heckathorn, 1988, 1990). Recent research has shown that longer sentences and harsher prison conditions are associated with more postrelease crime, not less (Chen and Shapiro, 2007).

Incapacitation There are those who argue that neither rehabilitation nor deterrence really works, but that imprisonment can be used to reduce crime rates because it keeps criminals off the streets. Peter W. Greenwood (1982) asserted that incarcerating one robber who is among the top 10 percent in offense rates prevents more robberies than incarcerating 18 offenders who are at or below the median. On the other hand, long prison sentences may represent a waste of prison capacity; most crimes are committed by young people, and most "career criminals" retire fairly early from these careers.

Capital Punishment

Capital punishment is the imposition of the death sentence for a capital offense. Since 1622, 18,000–20,000 people have lost their lives in America through capital punishment (Adler, Mueller, and Laufer, 2004). Capital offenses vary by state and have included murder, kidnapping, rape, drug trafficking, and treason (Bonczar and Snell, 2004). Legal execution methods also vary by state and include lethal injection, electrocution, lethal gas, hanging, and firing squad.

Is capital punishment widely used in the United States? In 2011, 43 inmates were executed in 13 states (Snell, 2011). Fourteen states and the District of Columbia do not have a death penalty, and it is under study in a number of other states.

What purpose does capital punishment serve? One argument in favor of applying the death penalty is *deterrence,* the idea that punishing offenders deters others from committing similar crimes. Research has shown, however, that capital punishment is not superior to long prison sentences in deterring crime (Radelet and Borg, 2000). Another use of capital punishment is *incapacitation;* an executed offender cannot be a repeat offender. Supporters of capital punishment also have argued that it is less costly than long-term imprisonment, although recent analyses show that the cost of trials and lengthy appeals far outruns the cost of imprisonment, changing cost to an argument against capital punishment in contemporary times.

In surveys, 64 percent of Americans have said they were in favor of the death penalty for a person convicted of murder (Maguire, 2012). When asked why they favor the death penalty for murderers, nearly two-fifths of those favoring the death penalty responded with retribution—supporters of capital punishment say the punishment fits the crime; 13 percent say that murderers "deserve" the death penalty (Maguire, 2012).

In 2010, 53 people were removed from death row because their sentences or conviction were overturned (Snell, 2011); 140 people have been released from death row since 1973 because they were found to be innocent (Death Penalty Information Center, 2012). Those exonerated spent an average of about 10 years in prison before being shown to be innocent and being released. DNA fingerprinting has played a major role in 17 death row exonerations. Americans know there are problems with the system; although 64 percent of respondents support capital punishment, only 55 percent say they think the death penalty is applied fairly, and that number drops to 32 percent for black respondents (Maguire, 2012).

Other Penalties and Approaches

For all of those who are incarcerated, many more criminal offenders do not serve time in jails and prisons. Probably the most widely used response to criminal behavior is *probation,* the integration of offenders into law-abiding society under the supervision of a trustworthy person (Adler, Mueller, and Laufer, 2004). Probationers are bound by specific conditions but are able to work, care for their families, and pay taxes. Currently, nearly 4 million people are on probation in the United States. *Parole* is somewhat similar to probation, but it involves releasing a prisoner, again under supervision, before the end of his or her sentence. In *home confinement programs,* offenders serve time at home, usually monitored by electronic devices. Offenders may also pay fines, be required to perform community service, or pay restitution to victims. A large percentage of convicted felons are required to serve time in prison or jail or on probation *and* comply with other penalties, including paying fines (38 percent), paying victim restitution (18 percent), receiving treatment (11 percent), or performing community service (11 percent) (Rosenmerkel, Durose, and Farole, 2009).

What Can Sociology Do for You?

In this chapter you have learned about deviant behavior and crime. With an advanced degree, you could go on to do research in deviance. Many sociology majors choose law enforcement (police and security officers and detectives), the courts (lawyers, paralegals, judges, and bailiffs), or corrections (correctional, probation, and parole officers and caseworkers).

For more information about criminology (the study of crime), go to **http:www.asc41.com** and select "Divisions" from the menu bar on the top of the page. Follow links that interest you. What does a criminologist do? What sort of education does a criminologist need?

If you enjoyed Chapter 5, you may want to look for upper-level classes in deviance, criminology, and the sociology of law.

The Chapter in Brief: *Deviance and Crime*

The Nature of Deviance

In all societies the behavior of some people at times goes beyond that permitted by the norms. Social life is characterized not only by conformity but by **deviance,** any behavior that violates a norm.

■ **Social Properties of Deviance**   Deviance is not a property inherent in certain forms of behavior; it is a property conferred upon particular behaviors by social definitions. Definitions as to which acts are deviant vary greatly from time to time, place to place, and group to group. We typically find that norms are not so much a point or a line as a zone. Deviant acts also can be redefined, as has happened in recent years in the United States. Most societies can absorb a good deal of deviance without serious consequences, but persistent and widespread deviance can be dysfunctional. But deviance may also be functional by promoting social solidarity, clarifying norms, strengthening group allegiances, and providing a catalyst for change.

■ **Social Control and Deviance**   Societies seek to ensure that their members conform with basic norms by means of **social control.** Three main types of social control processes operate within social life: (1) those that lead us to internalize our society's normative expectations **(internalization),** (2) those that structure our world of social experience, and (3) those that employ various formal and informal social sanctions.

Theories of Deviance

Other disciplines are concerned with deviance, particularly biology and psychology. Sociologists focus on five main theories.

■ **Anomie Theory**   Émile Durkheim contributed to our understanding of deviance with his idea of **anomie.** Robert K. Merton built on Durkheim's ideas of anomie and social cohesion. According to his theory of structural strain, deviance derives from societal stresses.

■ **Cultural Transmission Theory**   A number of sociologists have emphasized the similarities between the way deviant behavior is acquired and the way in which other behavior is acquired—the cultural transmission theory. Edwin H. Sutherland elaborated on this notion in his theory of **differential association.** He said that individuals become deviant to the extent to which they participate in settings where deviant ideas, motivations, and techniques are viewed favorably.

■ **Conflict Theory** Conflict theorists ask, "Which group will be able to translate its values into the rules of a society and make these rules stick?" and "Who reaps the lion's share of benefits from particular social arrangements?" Marxist sociologists see crime as a product of capitalist laws.

■ **Labeling Theory** Labeling theorists study the processes whereby some individuals come to be tagged as deviants, begin to think of themselves as deviants, and enter deviant careers. Labeling theorists differentiate between **primary deviance** and **secondary deviance.**

■ **Control Theory** Control theory attempts to explain not why people deviate but why people do *not* deviate. Travis Hirschi argued that young people are more likely to conform if their bond to society is strong. This bond has four parts: attachment, involvement, commitment, and belief.

Crime and the Criminal Justice System

Crime is an act of deviance that is prohibited by law. The distinguishing property of crime is that people who violate the law are liable to be arrested, tried, pronounced guilty, and deprived of their lives, liberty, or property. It is the state that defines crime by the laws it promulgates, administers, and enforces.

■ **Forms of Crime** An infinite variety of acts can be crimes. Federal agencies keep records on **index crimes**—violent crimes against people and crimes against property. Juvenile crime is crime committed by youth under the age of 18. **Organized crime** is

carried out by large-scale bureaucratic organizations that provide illegal goods and services in public demand. **Hate crime** is a crime motivated by bias against a race, ethnic origin, religion, disability, or sexual orientation. **White-collar crime** is crime committed by relatively affluent persons, often in the course of business activities. Crime can be committed by corporations and by governments. In **victimless crime** no one involved is considered a victim.

■ **Drugs and Crime** Drugs and crime are related both directly—selling, using, and possessing illegal drugs all are crimes—and indirectly—drug involvement often leads to other sorts of crimes. Drug problems can be dealt with by recognizing that addiction is a brain disease. Other approaches include continued prohibition, depenalization, or legalization.

■ **Race and Crime** African Americans make up 13 percent of the U.S. population, 28 percent of all those arrested for index crimes, and 43 percent of the U.S. prison population. Their disproportionate representation in the criminal justice system has serious social consequences, with imprisonment preventing young black males from supporting their families, criminal records decreasing employment opportunities, and voting rights being withheld from felons in most states and from ex-felons in some.

■ **Women and Crime** A growing percentage of youths and adults in the criminal population is female. One-quarter of the youths arrested in the United States are girls; overall, one in five arrests are female. Girls are more likely than boys to be arrested for such offenses as running away from home.

■ **The Criminal Justice System** The **criminal justice system** is made up of the reactive agencies of the state that include the police, the courts, and prisons. Despite the declining crime rate in the United States, the prison population has been steadily climbing.

There have been four traditional purposes of imprisonment: punishment, rehabilitation, deterrence, and selective confinement. **Capital** **punishment** is the application of the death penalty for a capital offense. Criminal offenders also may be subjected to probation, parole, fines, victim restitution, community service, or in-house arrest.

Glossary

anomie   A social condition in which people find it difficult to guide their behavior by norms they experience as weak, unclear, or conflicting.

capital punishment   The application of the death penalty for a capital crime.

crime   An act prohibited by law.

criminal justice system   The reactive agencies of the state that include the police, courts, and prisons.

deviance   Any behavior that violates a norm.

differential association   The notion that the earlier, the more frequent, the more intense, and the longer the duration of the contacts people have in deviant settings, the greater the probability that they, too, will become deviant.

hate crime   A crime motivated by bias against a race, ethnic origin, religion, disability, or sexual orientation.

high-tech crime   Crime committed through the use of advanced electronic media.

index crimes   Crimes reported by the Federal Bureau of Investigation in its Uniform Crime Reports. These offenses consist of four categories of violent crime against people—murder, rape, robbery, and assault—and four categories of crime against property—burglary, theft, motor vehicle theft, and arson.

internalization   The process by which individuals incorporate within their personalities the standards of behavior prevalent within the larger society.

organized crime   Large-scale bureaucratic organizations that provide illegal goods and services in public demand.

primary deviance   Behavior that violates social norms but usually goes unnoticed by the agents of social control.

recidivism   Relapse into criminal behavior.

secondary deviance   Deviance that individuals adopt in response to the reactions of other individuals.

social control   Methods and strategies that regulate behavior within society.

victimless crime   An offense in which no one involved is considered a victim.

white-collar crime   Crime committed by relatively affluent persons, often in the course of business activities.

Review Questions

1. Define deviant behavior and give two examples.

2. What functions does deviant behavior have?

3. What are the three main types of social control?

4. List and briefly describe the five main theories of deviance.

5. Define crime and list at least six types of crime.

6. Why are so many crimes not reported to the police?

7. Why is the prison population increasing in the United States?

8. Do you think capital punishment should be legal in the United States? Support your answer.

Internet Connection   www.mhhe.com/hughes11e

How safe is your campus? Do you think there is more crime on college campuses than elsewhere, or less? Use the Internet to find a site that provides campus crime statistics. Try typing "security on campus" into a search field. You should find a site hosted by the Office of Postsecondary Education (OPE) and another by an organization called Security on Campus. Use these sites to find crime data for your college or university and to find nationwide data on a particular crime. Also, use these or other sites to find out about the Jeanne Clery Act. What is it? How does it affect you?

Social Stratification

For many centuries, embalmers in ancient Egypt mummified the dead. According to historians, Egyptians believed that the process preserved bodies, rid them of disease, and prepared them for the pleasures of the afterlife. Now research shows that the type of mummification a client received was tied to one's position in Egyptian society (Pringle, 2011). During a period now called the Old Kingdom (4,600 to 4,100 years ago), more powerful and wealthy males got the "full treatment," which included removal of lungs, liver, stomach, and intestines and the preservation of these organs in special containers, while commoners were simply wrapped up with their organs in their bodies.

This archaeological finding fits well within contemporary sociology: social stratification is a phenomenon that pervades all aspects of social life—and death as well. **Social stratification** is the term sociologists apply to the ranking or grading of individuals and groups into hierarchical layers. It represents structured inequality in the allocation of rewards, privileges, and resources. Some individuals, by virtue of their roles or group memberships, are advantaged, while others are disadvantaged.

If social stratification affected only whether or not one's organs were removed before mummification, we might not devote an entire chapter to its discussion. But social stratification does much more: It results in some members of society benefitting greatly and others suffering. Most societies of the world are organized so that their institutions systematically distribute benefits and burdens unequally among different categories of people. Social arrangements are not neutral, but serve and promote the goals and interests of some people more than those of other people.

In this chapter we will examine patterns of social stratification. We will attempt to answer the questions of who gets what and why. We will use a country with which we are familiar, the United States, to discuss class systems. We will see how social inequality has serious consequences for individuals' lives: It affects income, lifestyle, health, and even the number of years one can expect to live. We will define and discuss social mobility, and we will see what the conflict and functionalist perspectives have to offer to our understanding of social stratification.

Patterns of Social Stratification

Social stratification depends upon but is not the same as **social differentiation**—the process by which a society becomes increasingly specialized over time. Very early in their history, human beings discovered that a division of functions and labor contributed to greater social efficiency. Consequently, in all societies we find that different people perform different tasks and, as a result, occupy different statuses.

Although the statuses that make up a social structure may be *differentiated,* they need not be *ranked* with respect to one another. For instance, the statuses of farmer and shop owner in a rural community are differentiated, but one is not obviously of higher rank than the other. They are merely different. Social differentiation creates a necessary condition for social ranking, but it does not create the ranking itself. Whenever we find social stratification, we find social differentiation, but not the other way around.

We begin our consideration of social stratification by examining open and closed stratification systems and some of the important dimensions of stratification: economic standing, prestige, and power.

Open and Closed Systems

Stratification systems differ in the ease with which they permit people to move into or out of particular strata (Kerbo, 2011). As we will see later in the discussion of social mobility, people often move vertically up or down in rank or

horizontally to another status of roughly similar rank. Where people can change their status with relative ease, we refer to the arrangement as an **open system.** In contrast, where people have great difficulty in changing their status, we call the arrangement a **closed system.** A somewhat similar distinction is conveyed by the concepts *achieved status* and *ascribed status* that we considered in Chapter 2 (p. 55). Achieved statuses are open to people on the basis of individual choice and competition and are common in open stratification systems. Ascribed statuses are assigned to people by their group or society and are typical of closed systems.

Although no societies are entirely open or entirely closed, the United States provides a good example of a relatively open system. The American folk hero is Abe Lincoln, the poor boy who made good, the rail-splitter who through hard work managed to move from log cabin to the White House. The American dream portrays a society in which all people can alter and improve their lives.

The United States is founded neither on the idea that all people should enjoy equal status nor on the notion of a classless society. Rather, the democratic creed holds that all people should have an equal *opportunity* to ascend to the heights of the class system. According to U.S. cultural beliefs, the rewards of social life flow to people in accordance with their merit and competence and in proportion to the contribution they make to their community and society. These beliefs generate much optimism about people's chances of enjoying society's rewards. Most Americans believe that they have a good chance of getting ahead, that they have a better standard of living than their parents, and that their children will have a better standard of living than they have now (Smith et al., 2011; Scott and Leonhardt, 2005). In practice, however, the ideal is not fully realized, and the optimism is not fully justified. Though the American system was founded on the ideal of achievement, ascribed statuses based on race, gender, age, and other social dimensions still have an important influence on people's chances of success.

The Hindu caste arrangement, particularly as it operated in India prior to 1900, serves as an example of a closed system. Under the traditional Hindu system, life was ordered in terms of castes in which people inherited their social status at birth from their parents and could not change it in the course of their lives. Members of the lower castes in India were considered inferior and were scorned, snubbed, and oppressed by higher-caste members regardless of personal merit and behavior. Even today, caste still shapes behavior in some localities, especially in rural areas, setting the rules of courtship, diet, housing, and employment (Nanda and Warms, 2011).

Although the distinction between open and closed systems of stratification is clear in theory, in practice systems of one type typically have some of the characteristics of the other type. As Box 6.1 shows, the U.S. system of racial inequality has many characteristics of a caste system.

Dimensions of Stratification

Karl Marx and Max Weber have helped us to unravel the nature of social stratification. Marx believed that the key to social stratification in capitalist societies is the division between those who own and control the crucial means of production—the oppressing capitalist class or bourgeoisie—and those who have only their labor to sell—the oppressed working class or proletariat. In Marx's view, these two groups and their conflicting interests provide the foundation for stratification in capitalist nations. For Marx, social stratification consisted of a single economic dimension.

Weber (1946) felt that Marx provided an overly simplistic image of stratification. He contended that other divisions exist within society that are at times independent of class. Consequently, he took a multidimensional view of stratification and identified three components: *class* (economic standing), *status* (prestige), and *party*

(power). Each of these dimensions constitutes a distinct aspect of social ranking. Some statuses rank high in wealth, prestige, and power, such as that of most physicians. Yet the rankings of some statuses may be dissimilar. Some prostitutes and professional criminals enjoy economic privilege, although they possess little prestige or power. Members of university faculties and the clergy, while enjoying a good deal of prestige, typically rank comparatively low in wealth and power. And some public officials may wield considerable power but receive low salaries and little prestige. For the most part, however, these three dimensions hang together, feeding into and supporting one another (Kerbo, 2011). Let us examine each of them in turn.

Economic Standing

The economic dimension of stratification consists of wealth and income. **Wealth** has to do with what people own at a particular point in time. **Income** refers to the amount of new money people receive within a given time interval. Thus, wealth is based on what people have, whereas income consists of what people get. For example, one individual may have a good deal of property—wealth—in the form of rare coins, precious gems, or works of art, but receive little income from it because it does not grow in value or generate any regular income. Another individual may receive a high salary—income—but have little wealth. A salary of $2 million a year does not generate much wealth if the person receiving it spends $2 million a year on travel, food, entertainment, and personal services.

Prestige

Prestige involves the social respect, admiration, and recognition associated with a particular social status. It entails a feeling that we are admired and thought well of by others. Prestige is intangible, something that we carry about in our heads. However, in our daily lives we commonly seek to give prestige a tangible existence through titles, special seats of honor,

Is Race the Basis for an American Caste System?

Americans often are fascinated by India's traditional caste system. The idea of groups of people having special status and performing only certain jobs seems very undemocratic. The Brahmins, the most pure caste, serve as priests and have special privileges. The Kshatriyas protect society, holding top military and political positions. The Vaisyas fill farming, livestock production, and commerce jobs, and the last caste, the Sudras, serves those above it. The untouchables, not strictly a part of the caste system, do those jobs Hindus consider to be the most polluting: working with excrement and dead bodies.

Does the United States have a caste system? We have said that in some ways the United States provides a good example of an open system of stratification. But we will see in Chapter 7 that the United States also has an entrenched system of racial inequality. Is it a racial caste system?

Let's see if the basic characteristics of a caste system apply to American society. In a caste system, caste membership is hereditary, marriage within one's caste is mandatory, moving out of one's caste is nearly impossible, and occupation is strongly related to caste (Hurst, 1998).

Hereditary caste membership obviously applies to race. In India people are sometimes able to move up in the caste system by "marrying up." In the United States, in contrast, the racial status of biracial children born of black and white parents has traditionally been governed by what is often referred to as the "one drop rule" (Davis, 1991): In the South during the eras of slavery and Jim Crow laws, a person with "one drop of black blood" was black. This idea translated into the practice of classifying a person as black if he or she

had any known black ancestors (Davis, 1991).

Does the "one drop" rule still hold today? Professional U.S. golfer Tiger Woods has a mother from Thailand and a father with African, European, and Native American ancestors (Page, 1997), and he has described himself as "Cablinasian" (for Caucasian, black, Indian, and Asian), yet he is widely regarded as African American in the United States (Nolan, 1997; Foster, 1997; Brand-Williams, 1997).

The second basic characteristic, that marriage within one's caste is mandatory, is not true in the legal sense; there are no longer any laws in the United States that forbid interracial marriages. While it is also true that the rate of interracial marriage in the United States has been steadily increasing since 1970, it remains rare. According to data reported by the U.S. Census Bureau in 2010 (http://www.census.gov/compendia/statab/2011/tables/11s0060.xls), the percentage of all married couples in the United States that include an African American person married to a white person increased from about one-third of one percent in 1980 to nine-tenths of one percent in 2009.

The third characteristic of caste, that mobility is virtually impossible, is clearly true of the black–white distinction. There is little mobility from black to white or from white to black for typical white and black people in the United States. Of course, the phenomenon of "passing" can occur; persons with a small amount of African background and substantial, obvious "white" characteristics have been known to "pass for white" (Johnson, 1927/1989; Scales-Trent, 1995). But passing is something that occurs only in a closed system; were there no racial

caste system, passing would have no meaning.

The fourth characteristic, that occupation is strongly related to caste, also describes American society to a substantial degree. Occupations that can be held by blacks or whites are not dictated by law. But in the 19th and 20th centuries, African American physicians, dentists, engineers, and corporate executives were nearly nonexistent, and nearly all agricultural field workers in the South were black. By now there has been substantial occupational mobility for African Americans, just as there has been for lower-caste persons in India in recent decades. But the occupational distribution in the United States retains significant castelike properties. African Americans are substantially overrepresented in low-status service and manufacturing jobs and underrepresented in highly paid, high-status professional jobs—just as the caste model predicts.

The southern United States before the civil rights movement clearly operated under a castelike system based on race. African Americans rode in the back of the bus, drank from "colored" water fountains, and used "colored" restrooms. The racial caste system in the United States today may be less rigid than this, but nonetheless it has yet to completely disappear.

Questions for Discussion

1. We have argued that the four characteristics of a caste system apply to American society with regard to race. Do you agree? Support your position.

2. Is being gay another factor on which an American caste system is based? Why or why not?

deference rituals, honorary degrees, emblems, and conspicuous displays of leisure and consumption. These activities and objects serve as symbols of prestige to which we attribute social significance and meaning. Much of our interaction with others consists of subtle negotiation over just how much deference, honor, respect, and awe we are to extend and receive.

We show deference—behavior dramatizing and confirming a person's superior ranking—in many ways. In *presentation rituals* we engage in symbolic acts, such as revealing regard and awe by bowing, scraping, and displaying a humble demeanor. In *avoidance rituals* we achieve the same end by maintaining a "proper distance" from prestigious figures.

More than a century ago, Thorstein Veblen (1899) highlighted the part that *conspicuous leisure* and *conspicuous consumption* play in revealing social ranking. He noted that it is not enough merely to possess wealth and power to gain and hold prestige. The wealth and power must be put on public view, for prestige is awarded only on evidence. One way we undertake to advertise high status is to lavish expenditure on clothing, because we can size up one another's apparel at a glance. The automobile serves a similar purpose, particularly a very expensive one. Veblen documented how relative success, tested by comparing one's own economic situation with that of others, becomes an established end. Thus, comparisons find symbolic expression, since displaying one's bankbook or stock certificates would be impractical and considered in poor taste.

As our social positions change throughout the life cycle, the sorts of things that serve as symbols of status change. For young people, having the right clothes is often very important. Tattoos and piercing various parts of the body with jewelry can serve as status symbols for youth. Knowing a great deal about sports, movies, or popular music all serve as status symbols, as does being on the cutting edge of any kind of fashion, be it in clothes, music, cars, computers,

"Actually, son, whether the glass is half full or empty isn't important—it's who owns the glass!"

Copyright © Chris Wildt. From *The Wall Street Journal* April 5, 1994. Reprinted by permission of Cartoon Features Syndicate.

literature, or another cultural product. These also may be important to adult status, but the core of adult status has to do with income, occupation, and lifestyle (Coleman and Rainwater, 1978) and with the status of the people in one's social networks (Chan and Goldthorpe, 2007). Adult status is symbolized primarily by the place where one lives, the nature of one's occupation, and the roles one plays as well as by the status of those with whom one associates in the community, in voluntary organizations, and in informal social relations. Although people still think that money is the most important thing, the lifestyle individuals project and the values they reflect are a critical part in determining their prestige (Jackman and Jackman, 1983).

Power

Prestige typically leads others to conform to our wishes through voluntary compliance, deference, and acceptance; power, in contrast, entails conduct by which we compel others to do what they do not wish to do. As we will see in Chapter 9, power determines which individuals and groups will be able to translate their preferences into the reality of social life. **Power** refers to the ability of individuals and groups to realize their will in human affairs even if it involves the resistance of others. It provides answers to the question of whose interests will be served and whose values will reign. Wherever we look, from families to juvenile gangs to nation-states, we find that some parties disproportionately achieve their way. Even in such a simple matter as eye contact, we find the operation of power. Low-power people typically look less at an individual when they are speaking to a high-power person than when they are listening. In contrast, high-power people display nearly equivalent rates of looking while speaking and listening (Ellyson et al., 1980).

Power affects the ability of people to make the world work on their behalf. To gain mastery of critical resources creates dependency and thus allows one to gain mastery of people. To control key resources is to interpose oneself (or one's group) between people and the means whereby people meet their biological, psychological, and social needs. To the extent that some groups command rewards, punishments, and persuasive communications, they are able to dictate the terms by which the game of life is played, making its outcome a foregone conclusion.

Social Stratification among Societies

Social stratification is not confined to people and groups within societies. Social scientists are increasingly interested in understanding patterns of inequality among societies around the globe (Wade, 2004; Firebaugh, 2003; Chase-Dunn, 1989). Before about 1800, living standards all over the world were low and varied within a narrow range (Spence, 2011). Now differences in income across societies are quite stark. For example, if we measure national income by the value of all goods and services produced by a country (gross national product,

or GNP), in 2009, the per capita national income of the United States was more than 289 times that of Congo, a developing nation in Africa, and about 60 times that of Vietnam in Southeast Asia (U.S. Census Bureau, 2011a). This means that for every one dollar of goods and services produced by the Congolese and Vietnamese economies, the U.S. economy produces $325 and $60, respectively. In general, Japan and the societies of North America and Western Europe are much wealthier than developing nations in Africa, Asia, and Latin America. Important consequences of this are that economic growth and development are slower and poverty is more extreme and more widespread in many poor developing societies around the globe than they are in the United States and other industrialized nations.

Historian Kevin Cahill argues that land ownership is a key component of global inequality, stating that "the main cause of most remaining poverty in the world is an excess of landownership in too few hands" (Cahill, 2010:9). Only about 15 percent of the world's total population owns land or a domicile. According to the World Bank, this landlessness keeps people in poverty; for example, 60 million of India's rural households that are totally dependent on agriculture own no land (Cahill, 2010).

Some sociologists argue that wealthier nations are the core societies of a world system and have benefited much more from globalization, while the poor nations exist on the periphery, are exploited for their raw materials and cheap labor, and have benefited very little (Chase-Dunn, 1989). However, a major shift in world economic power is under way, with China, India, Russia, and Brazil moving into dominant positions (Mahbubani, 2008; Wilson and Purushothaman, 2003). Economist Michael Spence (2011) argues that current economic growth may lead to a convergence of the economies of rich and poor countries. We will consider political and economic power in Chapter 9 and social change in Chapter 13. In the present chapter we primarily examine patterns of inequality within societies, and we continue this focus by looking in depth at the vast amount of inequality that exists in the United States, one of the world's wealthiest societies.

The American Class System

We have discussed open and closed systems of stratification and economic standing, prestige, and power. How is stratification actually manifested in society? In this section we will look first at the question of how much inequality there is in the United States. We will then describe how social classes are identified, discuss the significance of social class, and look at poverty in the United States.

Is There Inequality in American Society?

Traditionally, Americans have thought of theirs as an egalitarian society. As the Declaration of Independence puts it, the United States is a country in which all persons are "created equal." If so, there would be little for a student of stratification to study in the United States. What do the data show on this issue? It is sometimes difficult to reliably measure inequality in power and prestige, so let's look at inequality in terms of something we can easily measure: economic standing in terms of income and wealth.

Figure 6.1 shows the percent of aggregate income received by each fifth (or 20 percent) of households in the United States. Over the past 45 years, the lowest 20 percent of households in income in the United States never received more than 5.2 percent of aggregate income, while the highest 20 percent has always received 40 percent or more. Since the mid-1960s, income inequality in the United States has been increasing, most rapidly between 1980 and 1992, and in the 2005–2010 period was higher

than it has been since 1950. Not only do we have inequality, it has been increasing dramatically over the past decades (Moller, Alderson, and Nielsen, 2009). The United States does not have the highest level of income inequality in the world, but it is clearly not among those with the lowest (see Box 6.2 on page 184). In 2010 the top 5 percent of families received 21.3 percent of the income, more than four times what it would receive if incomes were equal across families (DeNavas-Walt, Proctor, and Smith, 2011).

Inequality in wealth is even greater. We define income as money people receive within a given time interval, such as wages and salaries, while wealth is what they own at a particular time. Figure 6.2 on page 183 presents an analysis of data from the Federal Reserve Board's 2007 Survey of Consumer Finances (Bucks et al., 2009). Wealth can be measured by the net worth of a household, the value of all assets minus debts. The top 20 percent of households in wealth own more than 83 percent of all wealth. If we combine this highest fifth with the next highest category (the "fourth fifth"), we find that nearly 95 percent of wealth is owned by the top 40 percent of households, leaving just over 5 percent of all wealth distributed among the remaining 60 percent of households.

White households are far wealthier than African American and Hispanic households. For every dollar in wealth owned by a white household, the average African American household owns 10 cents and the average Hispanic household owns 12 cents. The recession of 2008–2009 increased these racial and ethnic differences in wealth. A recent analysis showed that by 2009, African American households owned only 5 cents for every dollar owned by a white family, and Hispanics owned about 5.5 cents (Pew Research Center, 2011).

The very rich in the United States increased their share of the nation's total pool of privately held wealth during the economic boom of the 1980s and 1990s, and this trend continued into the

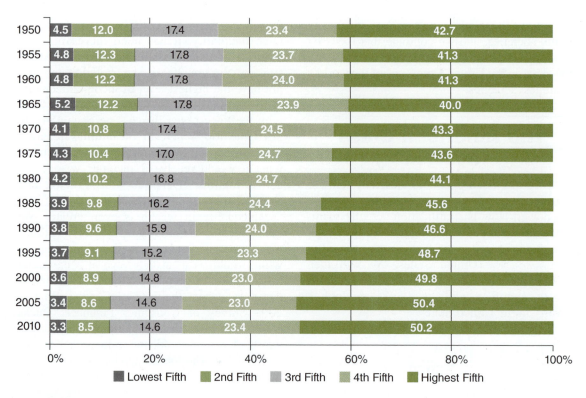

Year	Lowest Fifth	2nd Fifth	3rd Fifth	4th Fifth	Highest Fifth
1950	4.5	12.0	17.4	23.4	42.7
1955	4.8	12.3	17.8	23.7	41.3
1960	4.8	12.2	17.8	24.0	41.3
1965	5.2	12.2	17.8	23.9	40.0
1970	4.1	10.8	17.4	24.5	43.3
1975	4.3	10.4	17.0	24.7	43.6
1980	4.2	10.2	16.8	24.7	44.1
1985	3.9	9.8	16.2	24.4	45.6
1990	3.8	9.6	15.9	24.0	46.6
1995	3.7	9.1	15.2	23.3	48.7
2000	3.6	8.9	14.8	23.0	49.8
2005	3.4	8.6	14.6	23.0	50.4
2010	3.3	8.5	14.6	23.4	50.2

■ Lowest Fifth ■ 2nd Fifth ■ 3rd Fifth ■ 4th Fifth ■ Highest Fifth

Figure 6.1 **The Rich Get Richer and the Poor Get Poorer: Share of Income Received by Households in the United States, 1950–2010**

Income data show that the United States is moving away from income equality, not toward it. Within each bar, the numbers represent the percentage of the total income in the United States that is received by each fifth of households, from the lowest (i.e., poorest) fifth to the highest (i.e., wealthiest) fifth. Looking at 1950, for example, we see that the poorest fifth of households received only 4.5 percent of the income for the whole country, while the wealthiest fifth received 42.7 percent. Since 1950, percentages have fluctuated a bit, but in general, the percentages received by each of the poorer three-fifths of U.S. households have decreased and the percentage received by the wealthiest fifth has increased.

Sources: Figure generated by the authors using data from the U.S. Census Bureau, *Current Population Survey*, Annual Demographic Supplement, and DeNavas-Walt, Proctor, and Smith, 2011.

2000s (Keister and Moller, 2000; Kennickell, 2003; Johnston, 2003). In 1980, the United States had 13 billionaires; now the number is over 500 (Anderson, 2009). According to the Federal Reserve Board Survey of Consumer Finances, wealth is distributed so unequally in the United States that in 2007 the wealthiest 1 percent of U.S. households owned 34.3 percent of all private wealth, more than the bottom 90 percent of households combined (28.5 percent of total wealth).

Clearly, there is much inequality in the United States to explain. Sociologists agree that

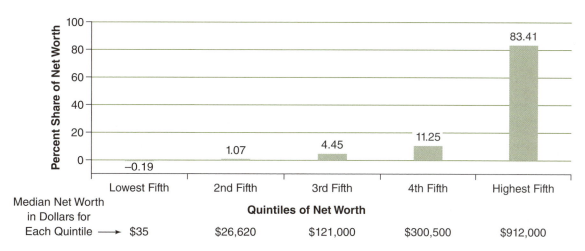

a. If we measure wealth by net worth (assets minus debts), inequality in wealth is extremely high in the United States. More than 83 percent of the wealth is owned by the wealthiest 20 percent of families. The poorest 20 percent of families owe more than they own. The bottom three-fifths of families (60 percent) own less than 6 percent of all wealth.

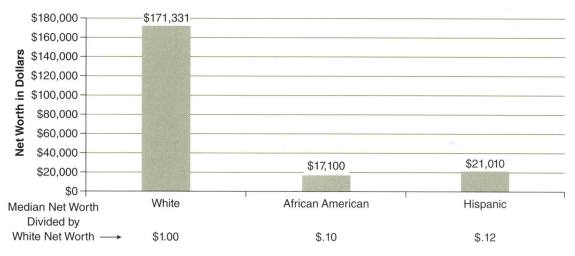

b. White families are, on average, much wealthier than African American and Hispanic families. Differences in median net worth across the three categories show that for every dollar of net worth owned by a typical white family, the typical African American family owns 10 cents, and the typical Hispanic family owns 12 cents.

| Figure 6.2 | **The Concentration of Wealth in the United States, 2007** |

Source: Analysis by the authors of data from the 2007 Survey of Consumer Finances, Board of Governors of the Federal Reserve System (Bucks et al., 2009).

Income Inequality within Societies: A Look around the World

We have shown that wealth and income are distributed unevenly in U.S. society. How do we compare with other countries? How much does income inequality within countries vary around the world and over time? Is income inequality a persistent feature of societies throughout the world? And finally—but perhaps most importantly—how would we answer such questions?

Until the 1990s, it wasn't possible to answer the questions we have posed. A data set put together by World Bank economists Klaus Deininger and Lyn Squire (1996) allowed us to offer at least some tentative answers to these questions. Deininger and Squire calculated the percentage of aggregate income received by each fifth (or 20 percent) of the population from low income to high for 108 countries from the late 1940s to the 1990s. They set quality standards for the data they would accept so that

they could make cross-country comparisons.

What did the data show? As the accompanying figure for the 1990s shows, there was substantial inequality in every region of the world, with the income share of the poorest fifth never rising to 10 percent and that of the wealthiest fifth of the population never falling below 37 percent. Deininger and Squire's (1996) analysis of inequality over time showed no change in the basic overall structure of income inequality. Inequality was highest in sub-Saharan Africa and in Latin America and the Caribbean. Inequality was lowest in the formerly socialist countries of Eastern Europe.

What about the United States? It clearly was *not* one of the most egalitarian societies in the world. While it once had relatively moderate inequality compared to other countries, Deininger and Squire's analysis showed that income inequality in the

United States had been increasing since the early 1980s even while it was decreasing in some other parts of the world (Deininger and Squire, 1996). What has happened to income inequality within societies since the mid-1990s? Unfortunately, there has been no recent comprehensive study comparable to Deininger and Squire (1996) (Pavcnik, 2011). Examination of a more limited list of nations showed that during the 1990s and 2000s, income inequality increased within most societies and held steady or decreased in only a few (Atkinson, Piketty, and Saez, 2011). Data presented in the *World Factbook 2009* shows that income inequality is higher in many developing countries than it is in the United States, but that the United States has higher income inequality than any other high-income industrialized country (Central Intelligence Agency, 2009). Studies of wealth inequality showed similar findings.

---

social inequality is a structured aspect of contemporary life. In saying this, they mean more than that individuals and groups differ in the privileges they enjoy, the prestige they receive, and the power they wield. Structuring means that inequality is hardened or institutionalized, so that there is a system for determining who gets what. Inequality does not occur in a random fashion but follows relatively consistent and stable patterns that persist. One reason for this persistence is that inequalities are typically passed on from one generation to the next. Individuals and groups that are advantaged commonly find ways to ensure that their offspring will also be advantaged; for those that are disadvantaged, the disadvantage may persist for generations.

Identifying Social Classes

Sociologists have borrowed the term *stratification* from geology. Geologists usually find it rather easy to determine where one stratum of rock ends and another begins. But social strata often shade off into one another so that their boundaries are indistinct. How do we go about identifying social strata, or classes, in the United States?

In the course of our everyday conversations, we talk about the "upper class," "middle class," and "lower class," referring to these social classes as distinct groups. Do such groups actually exist? Two views are found among sociologists concerning the accuracy of this popular conception (Lucal, 1994; see also Sørensen, 2000).

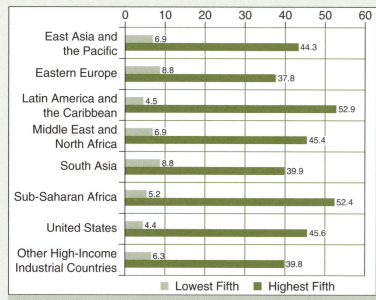

	Lowest Fifth	Highest Fifth
East Asia and the Pacific	6.9	44.3
Eastern Europe	8.8	37.8
Latin America and the Caribbean	4.5	52.9
Middle East and North Africa	6.9	45.4
South Asia	8.8	39.9
Sub-Saharan Africa	5.2	52.4
United States	4.4	45.6
Other High-Income Industrial Countries	6.3	39.8

Percentage of Total Income Received by Those in the Lowest and Highest Fifths of the Population in Income in the 1990s

Sources: Figure generated by the authors using data from Deininger and Squire,1996, and U.S. Census Bureau, 1997.

Since the early 1990s, wealth inequality in the United States has exceeded that of all industrialized countries (Keister and Moller, 2000; Wolff, 1995, 1996). Of the 9.5 million millionaires worldwide, a third can be found in North America, where they make up 0.62 percent of the population (Cahill, 2010).

A primary goal of studying social stratification is to understand the powerful social and economic forces at work that create and perpetuate income inequality. If such inequality varied randomly or could be easily changed, we would expect much more variation than these worldwide data show. Deininger and Squire's study illustrates the fact that income inequality is a persistent feature of life in every region of the world.

Questions for Discussion

1. How would you explain the coexistence of the principle of equality and increasing income inequality in the United States?

2. Some of the poorest regions of the world have the highest income inequality. What social, political, and economic factors do you think are behind this pattern?

The first view holds that classes are real, bounded strata that exist in conflicting relations with one another (the *relational model*). Although this position has been a central element in Marxist formulations (Marx and Engels, 1848/1955; Wright, 1985), it also emerges in the work of other sociologists who have identified a blue-collar/white-collar division in American life (Blau and Duncan, 1972; Sobel, 1989). The second view portrays U.S. society as essentially classless, one in which class divisions are blurred by virtue of their continuous and uninterrupted nature (the *distributional model*). Seen in this manner, social classes are culturally quite alike and simply reflect gradations in rank rather than hard-and-fast social groups (Hodge and Treiman, 1968; Eichar, 1989).

The differing conceptions derive in large measure from different approaches to identifying social classes: (1) the objective method, (2) the self-placement method, and (3) the reputational method. Although all the approaches produce some overlap in classes, there are appreciable differences in the results afforded by each (Kerbo, 2011). Moreover, each approach has certain advantages and disadvantages. Let's consider each method more carefully.

The Objective Method

The **objective method** views social class as a statistical category. The categories are formed by sociologists and/or statisticians. Most commonly, people are assigned to social classes on the basis

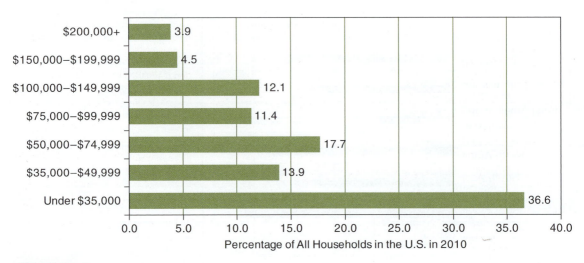

Figure 6.3 | **Distribution of Households by Income, 2010**

Source: Figure generated by the authors using data from Table A-23 in DeNavas-Walt, Proctor, and Smith. 2011. *Income, poverty, and health insurance coverage in the United States: 2010.* U.S. Census Bureau, Current Population Reports, P60-239. Washington D.C: U.S. Government Printing Office (available online at http://www.census.gov/prod/2011pubs/p60-239.pdf).

of income, occupation, or education (or some combination of these characteristics). The label *objective* can be misleading, for it is not meant to imply that the approach is more "specific" or "unbiased" than either of the others. Rather, it is objective in that it uses numerically measurable criteria to categorize individuals. Figure 6.3 shows one way of depicting the distribution of Americans by family income.

The objective method provides a statistical measure for investigating various correlates of class, such as life expectancy, mental illness, divorce, political attitudes, crime rates, and leisure activities. It is usually the simplest and least expensive approach to research social classes because statistical data can be obtained from government agencies like the Census Bureau. However, there is more to class than simply raw statistical data. In the course of their daily lives, people size up one another on many standards of excellence. It is not only the actual income, education, or occupational categories

that matter but also the meanings and definitions others assign to these qualities.

For example, one part of the cultural definition of an occupation is its prestige, the respect and admiration people accord it. Sociologists wishing to assign an "objective" ranking to occupations that reflects the subjective meanings people attach to occupations use occupational prestige scores. To determine the prestige of occupations, researchers do large surveys and ask respondents to estimate the social standing of each of a large number of occupations. The results can be used to assign prestige scores to the occupations of respondents in other studies (see Table 6.1). Many electricians, funeral directors, and farm owners run very successful businesses and have high incomes. But because of the meanings people attach to these occupations, their prestige rankings fall in the middle of the range, as can be seen in Table 6.1.

Prestige, however, is not the only dimension underlying differences among occupations.

Table 6.1	Prestige Rankings of Occupations

Occupation	Score
Physician	86
Lawyer	75
College teacher	74
Chemical engineer	73
Dentist	72
Clergy	69
Pharmacist	68
Secondary school teacher	66
Registered nurse	66
Accountant	65
Athlete	65
Elementary school teacher	64
Police officer, detective	60
Editor, reporter	60
Financial manager	59
Actor	58
Librarian	54
Social worker	52
Electrician	51
Funeral director	49
Mail carrier	47
Secretary	46
Insurance agent	45
Bank teller	43
Farm owner	40
Automobile mechanic	40
Restaurant manager	39
Sales counter clerk	34
Cook	31
Waiter and waitress	28
Garbage collector	28
Janitor	22
Parking lot attendant	21
Vehicle washer	19
News vendor	19

Sources: Figure generated by the authors using data from Keiko Nakao, Robert W. Hodge, and Judith Treas, 1990. "On revising prestige scores for all occupations," GSS Methodological Report No. 69, Chicago: National Opinion Research Center; General Social Surveys, Smith et al., 2005.

Note: Americans ranked a number of occupations in terms of prestige in national surveys. The highest possible score an occupation could receive was 90, and the lowest 10. The table shows the ranking of a number of the occupations.

According to Weeden and Grusky (2005), if we wish to have more complete accounts of how class is associated with various outcomes, such as those discussed in the next section on the significance of social classes, we should measure class by using detailed occupational categories. Using occupational prestige to measure class puts funeral directors and mail carriers, which actually differ on a variety of underlying dimensions, in the same class. Using detailed occupational categories allows us to explore whether the outcomes of being in those different categories may be different.

The Self-Placement Method

The **self-placement method** (also known as the subjective method) has people identify the social class to which they think they belong. Class is viewed as a social category, one in which people group themselves with others they perceive as sharing certain attributes in common. The class lines may or may not conform to what social scientists think are logical lines of cleavage in the objective sense. Researchers typically ask respondents to identify their social class.

An American family's class position historically derived from the husband's position in the labor market. But long-term social and economic changes, particularly the movement of women into the workplace and declining family size, have altered the way women assess their class identity (Baxter, 1994). Most employed women used to appraise their class position primarily in terms of the class position of their husbands. Now both men and women look at husband's and wife's combined income in identifying class but only at the husband's occupational prestige (Yamaguchi and Wang, 2002).

The major advantage of the self-placement approach is that it can be applied to a large population. However, the approach has its limitations. It is likely that people's identification with a particular class category is influenced by their aspirations rather than their current situation, and by processes of impression management (see Chapter 3). When survey respondents are asked to identify themselves as lower class, working class, middle class, upper middle class, or upper class, more than 90 percent identify as something other than lower class or upper class. Few of the poorest respondents identify as lower class, and the wealthiest tend not to label themselves as upper class (Scott and Leonhardt, 2005; Smith et al., 2009).

The Reputational Method

In the self-placement method, people are asked to rank themselves. In the **reputational method,** they are asked how they classify other individuals. This approach views class as a social group, one in which people share a feeling of oneness and are bound together in relatively stable patterns of interaction. Therefore, class rests on the knowledge of who associates with whom. The approach gained prominence in the 1930s when W. Lloyd Warner and his associates studied the class structure of three communities, including "Yankee City" (Newburyport, Massachusetts), a New England town of some 17,000 people (Warner and Lunt, 1941, 1942). In Yankee City, Warner identified six classes: the upper upper, the lower upper, the upper middle, the lower middle, the upper lower, and the lower lower. This formulation was popularized in the media in the 1940s, and it continues to influence how the American public understands social class in American life today.

The reputational method is a valuable tool for investigating social distinctions in small groups and small communities. It is particularly useful in predicting associational patterns among people, but it is difficult to use in large samples where people have little or no knowledge of one another.

One Status Dimension or Many?

Sociologist Talcott Parsons (1940, 1953) pointed out some 60 years ago that social position is determined by one's location on some dimension or dimensions of value. As subcultures based on ethnicity, lifestyle, religious commitment, patterns of consumption, occupation, age, and other dimensions become increasingly important in American cultural life, they have formed the basis of what we might call "status spheres" (Berger and Berger, 1972; Wolfe, 1968). People are increasingly likely to compete with one another within these spheres rather than along a single dimension of status. High status in one sphere may count for little in another; a high-ranking member of the outlaw motorcycle subculture (bikers) may appear to be "just another bum" to someone whose life is dominated by miniature furniture collecting. Likewise, the best fiddle player in Nashville may find it impossible to distinguish between a principal investigator (high status) and a research associate (middle status) on a research team in a large university. As a consequence, status distinctions in the United States that were once clear have become harder to discern.

The Significance of Social Class

Few aspects of social life affect so strongly the way people behave and think as does social class. For one thing, it largely determines their **life chances**—the likelihood that individuals and groups will enjoy desired goods and services, fulfilling experiences, and opportunities for living healthy and long lives. Broadly considered, life chances have to do with people's level of living and their options for choice. For example, social class affects education. The higher the social class of parents, the further their children go in school and the better they perform (Wagmiller et al., 2006). Children from families of low socioeconomic status understand fewer words at age 3, have less ability to use complex syntax as they approach kindergarten, develop gaps in vocabulary that classroom experience does not narrow, and lag in reading comprehension in elementary school (Dickinson, 2011), all of which contribute to achievement gaps throughout school and life. Research shows that many of the effects of serious adversity, including poverty, during early childhood cannot be reversed after the age of 2 (Vanderwert et al., 2010).

Class also affects health and life expectancy (Scott, 2005). Lower socioeconomic status has been called "the most powerful single contributor" to premature morbidity and mortality both in the United States and worldwide (Williams, 1998), and the leading cause of death around the globe, childhood and maternal malnutrition, is directly related to poverty (Holdren, 2008). Health is affected by income, education, and social class in all industrialized societies (Sommer, 2009; Dunn and Hayes, 2000). Together, lifestyle (smoking, obesity, lack of exercise) and exposure to environmental health hazards help to explain why those in the lower classes have worse health (Lantz et al., 1998).

Research shows, however, that more than lifestyle and exposure to health hazards is responsible for the correlation of social class and health. While sociologists Mirowsky and Ross (2003) argue that the primary factor is education, the effect of social class may be through a variety of pathways (Link and Phelan, 1995). Whatever the specific causes, the importance of social class is clearly illustrated by research showing that social class is associated with mortality due to preventable causes (e.g., appendicitis), but not with mortality due to non-preventable causes (e.g., gallbladder cancer) (Phelan et al., 2004).

Social class affects life chances in other ways. During the Vietnam War, some 80 percent of the 2.5 million men who served in Southeast Asia—of 27 million men who reached draft age during the war—came from working-class and impoverished backgrounds (Appy, 1993). When the *Titanic* sank in 1912, passengers traveling in first class were more than twice as likely to survive as those traveling third class (Dawson, 1995). The rate of swine flu deaths in Mexico City in 2009 also was linked to poverty (Partlow and Booth, 2009).

Social class also affects people's **style of life**—the magnitude and manner of their consumption of goods and services. People at different class levels tend to dress differently, eat different foods, buy different styles of furniture, and watch different programs on television. These patterns are due to differences in both income and education.

Social class is also associated with other patterns of behavior. For instance, voting increases with socioeconomic status in most Western nations (Holder, 2006; Gaither and Newberger, 2000). And people in the lower classes begin sexual activities at a younger age, but people in the upper classes are more tolerant of sexual variations and engage in a wider variety of sexual activities (Laumann et al., 1994). In sum, one's social class leaves few areas of life untouched.

Poverty in the United States

More than 50 years after President Lyndon Johnson announced that his Great Society program would end poverty in the United States, poverty remains a significant feature of American life. Census Bureau statistics reveal that the percentage of Americans below the poverty line dropped from 22.4 percent in 1959 to a low of 11.1 percent in 1973. The poverty rate has fluctuated since then, with an upturn in the new century (see Figure 6.4). In 2011, the official poverty rate was 15.1 percent, with nearly 46.2 million

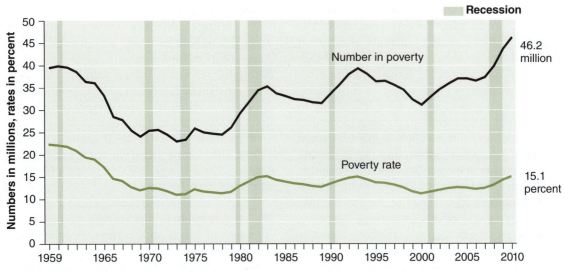

Note: The data points are placed at the midpoints of the respective years.

Figure 6.4 **People in Poverty in the United States, 1959–2010**
In 2010 the government classified a family of four as poor if it had cash income of less than $22,050.

Sources: Figure 4 in DeNavas-Walt, Proctor, and Smith, 2011. *Income, poverty, and health insurance coverage in the United States: 2010.* U.S. Census Bureau, Current Population Reports, P60-236. Washington, D.C.: U.S. Government Printing Office (available online at http://www.census.gov/prod/2011pubs/p60-239.pdf).

people living in poverty (DeNavas-Walt, Proctor, and Smith, 2011).

What exactly is poverty? Who are the poor in the United States? Does the United States have an "underclass"? What causes poverty? And how does the United States approach the problems of poverty? We will discuss these issues in this section.

Defining Poverty

The definition of poverty is a matter of debate. In 1795 a group of English magistrates decided that a minimum income should be "the cost of a gallon loaf of bread, multiplied by three, plus an allowance for each dependent" (Schorr, 1984). Today the Census Bureau defines the threshold of poverty in the United States as the minimum amount of money families need to purchase a nutritionally adequate diet, assuming they use one-third of their income for food. Liberals have contended the line is too low because it fails to take into account changes in the standard of living (Ruggles, 1992). Conservatives have said it is too high because the poor receive in-kind income in the form of public assistance, including food stamps, public housing subsidies, and health care (Rector, 1990). In 2010, the poverty threshold for a family of four (including two children) was $22,050 (DeNavas-Walt, Proctor, and Smith, 2011).

Who Are the Poor?

The recession that began at the end of 2007 provides an example of one of the characteristics of poverty in the United States: "the poor" is an ever-changing category, depending on macrosociological factors such as the economy, politics, education, and employment regulations and practices, and microsociological factors including divorce, illness, death, and individual work ethic. The recession affected many people who had never experienced poverty before. By 2009, 17.4 percent of the U.S. workforce was either unemployed or underemployed (employed part-time instead of full-time or working at jobs below the worker's skill or expertise), leaving many families and individuals struggling financially (Bhargava et al., 2009).

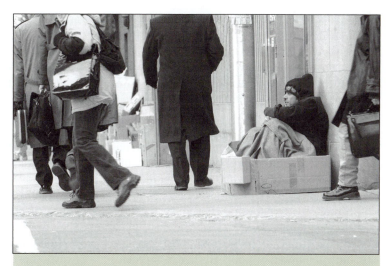

Almost 32 million white people were living in poverty in 2010. Although African Americans are more likely than whites to be poor, 69 percent of the poor in the United States in 2010 were white (DeNavas-Walt, Proctor, and Smith, 2011).

Poverty has become increasingly the lot of single and divorced parents and their children. For example, in 2010 the poverty rate for married-couple families was 6.2 percent, while that for families headed by a female with no spouse present was five times higher (DeNavas-Walt, Proctor, and Smith, 2011). Children are 35.5 percent of those in poverty in the United States but only 24.4 percent of the total population. In 2010, 22 percent of all American children—16.4 million children—were living in poverty (DeNavas-Walt, Proctor, and Smith, 2011).

Poverty rates vary greatly by race, with non-Hispanic whites (9.9 percent) and Asians (12.1 percent) having the lowest rates and Hispanics (26.6 percent) and African Americans (27.4 percent) the highest rates of poverty (DeNavas-Walt, Proctor, and Smith, 2011). The 2008–2009 recession widened the wealth gap between whites and blacks and between whites and Hispanics (Kochhar, Fry, and Taylor, 2011).

The poverty rate for the elderly dropped from 35.2 percent in 1959 to 9.0 percent in 2010. Even so, 20 percent of widowed and 24 percent of divorced older women remain impoverished.

Not everyone who is poor receives welfare. Contrary to popular stereotype, whites use government safety-net programs more than African Americans and Hispanics. Although the poverty *rate* is lower for whites, there were 19.6 million non-Hispanic whites living in poverty in 2010, compared to 10.7 million African Americans and 13.2 million Hispanics (DeNavas-Walt, Proctor, and Smith, 2011).

An "Underclass"?

The term *underclass* has been applied by some social scientists to a population of people, concentrated in an inner city, who are *persistently* poor, unemployed, and dependent on welfare (Coughlin, 1988). Initially, sociologist William Julius Wilson (1987) championed the concept to describe the plight of "the truly disadvantaged." Some argue that the term *underclass* has come to reflect the stereotype that the poor have created their own plight and that the inhabitants of inner-city neighborhoods are both fundamentally different from other Americans and violently dangerous. However, the term "underclass" is used by sociologists not as a stereotype, but to describe the phenomenon of persistent poverty. As historian Jacqueline Jones (1992) showed, the kind of poverty associated with contemporary urban ghettos has a long history dating back at least to the Civil War and has included white sharecroppers, Appalachian white migrants, and marginal white factory workers of the North.

Simply being poor does not make a person a part of the underclass. Indeed, the underclass constitutes a minority of the poor, most of whom are only temporarily poor. Research indicates that over a four-year period in the 1990s, about 34 percent of the population lived in poverty for at least two months, but only 2 percent were continuously in poverty over the entire period (Iceland, 2003). The underclass is a core of inner-city poor, those individuals and families who are trapped in an unending cycle of joblessness and dependence on welfare or criminal earnings. Their communities are often plagued by drug abuse, lawlessness, crime, violence, and poor schools (Wilson, 1996). Many women in the underclass were teenage mothers and high school dropouts who subsequently found themselves sidetracked without the resources or skills to escape a life of poverty. The rise of female-headed families is associated with the inability of men in the underclass to find steady jobs (Wilson, 1987, 1991; Massey, 1990; Jencks, 1992).

In the next section we consider the three major theories of poverty.

Theories of Poverty

Various theories have been advanced through the years to explain poverty.

One approach looks to the characteristics of the poor to explain their difficulties. According to the **culture of poverty** thesis, the poor in class-stratified capitalist societies lack effective participation and integration within the larger society (Lewis, 1966). According to this theory, the poor develop feelings of marginality, helplessness, dependence, and inferiority, which breed weak ego structures, lack of impulse control, a present-time orientation characterized by little ability to defer gratification, and a sense of resignation and fatalism. The resulting lifeways are both an adaptation and a reaction of the poor to their disadvantaged positions. The theory further argues that these patterns become self-perpetuating as the ethos associated with the culture of poverty is transmitted to successive generations (Murray, 1994).

Many sociologists argue that the culture of poverty thesis has serious shortcomings (Valentine, 1968; Duncan, Hill, and Hoffman, 1988; Jaynes and Williams, 1989; Demos, 1990), in part because it blames the poor for their own predicament. For instance, as we pointed out in Chapter 1, Elliot Liebow depicted the economically poor streetcorner men of Washington, D.C., as very much immersed in American life and not as carriers of an independent culture of poverty. They, too, want what other American men want, but they are blocked from achieving their goals by structural barriers.

Another view sees poverty as largely *situational*. This view is supported by a study showing that a majority of the U.S. population uses the welfare system at some point (Rank, 2003, 2004; Rank and Hirschl, 2001). Two-thirds of Americans between the ages of 20 and 65 will use a welfare program, and 90 percent of those who do will use it more than once. Similarly, a long-term study done in the 1970s, 1980s, and 1990s found that between 2 and 3 percent of U.S. families could be classed as persistently poor over multiple years, and about 25 percent of families received welfare at some time, averaging about 8 months' duration (Iceland, 2003; Duncan, Hill, and Hoffman, 1988). Many people who slip into poverty do so for a limited time after major adverse events, such as divorce or illness. For many families, welfare serves as a type of insurance protection, something they use for a brief period but dispose of as quickly as they can. The study, undertaken by the University of Michigan's Institute for Social Research (Duncan, 1984, 1987; Duncan, Hill, and Hoffman, 1988), casts doubt on the culture of poverty thesis. Instead, it portrays the poverty population as a pool, with people flowing in and out. The researchers found "little evidence that individual attitudes and behavior patterns affect individual economic progress." To a far greater extent, individuals "are the victims of their past, their environment, luck, and chance."

Still another view portrays poverty as a *structural feature* of capitalist societies. The cyclical movements between economic expansion and contraction—boom and bust—contribute to sharp fluctuations in employment. More than a century ago, Marx contended that an industrial reserve army is essential for capitalist economies. The industrial reserve army consists of individuals at the bottom of the class structure who are laid off in the interests of corporate profits during times of economic stagnation and then rehired when needed to generate profits during times of economic prosperity. It is disproportionately composed of minorities, who traditionally have been the last hired and the first fired. Contemporary structuralists say that a "new industrial order," characterized by a significant shift from manufacturing to service sector employment, has produced massive vulnerability among all blue-collar workers. This structuralist view sees poverty as deriving from a lack of income-producing employment (Moller et al., 2003) and increasing inequality an inherent feature of capitalist development (Moller, Alderson, and Nielsen, 2009).

Poverty Programs

For much of Western history, assistance to the poor has taken the form of private charity sometimes augmented with public relief. But government intervention has not always been truly charitable. For instance, in 18th-century England, poor laws provided workhouses for the able-bodied indigent to discourage people from adding themselves to the ranks of paupers. Much of the 18th- and 19th-century debate surrounding definitions of poverty and its remedies is similar to that of today.

The first large national poverty programs in the United States were established as part of President Franklin D. Roosevelt's New Deal in the 1930s. Two of these programs had a significant impact on poverty: Social Security and Aid to Families with Dependent Children (AFDC). The Social Security program, designed to aid the disabled and prevent poverty in old age, has sharply reduced poverty among the elderly, so that in 2010, persons over age 65 were less likely than persons ages 18–64 to be in poverty (DeNavas-Walt, Proctor, and Smith, 2011). The AFDC program provided aid to poor families with children. Though it did not end poverty, it did offer humanitarian relief, and the increased aid included in President Lyndon Johnson's Great Society program of the 1960s reduced the percent of persons in poverty (Kerbo, 2011), the results of which can be seen in Figure 6.4.

How does the United States compare with other countries? Despite a persistent perception that the U.S. government spends enormous amounts of money to support the poor, in fact the United States is the only industrialized nation that has no guaranteed-income program for families in poverty and no national health program to meet the medical needs of all its citizens (Kerbo, 2011).

The AFDC program was replaced in 1996 by the Temporary Assistance for Needy Families (TANF) program as part of former President Bill Clinton's welfare reform. The welfare reform program focuses primarily on encouraging work, eliminating long-term use of welfare, and handing welfare over to the states. Its key elements are:

• Welfare recipients must work after two years of assistance.

- Recipients are limited to five years' total assistance, including cycling on and off.

- The guarantee of assistance that was built into AFDC has been replaced with a system of block grants to the states, money that can be used largely as each state wishes. Under this new system, states may limit assistance to less than five years and may use the money from the federal government for things other than welfare assistance (Bane, 1997; Super et al., 1996).

The promotion of marriage also is a key element of TANF, with "encouraging the formation and maintenance of two-parent families" a stated means to ending dependence on government benefits (Lichter, Graefe, and Brown, 2003). The welfare reform program was reauthorized under President George Bush's administration in 2006 and has continued to operate since then through extensions passed by Congress.

What are the consequences of welfare reform? Judging its success is a matter of perspective. Between 1996 and 2004, the number of people receiving government handouts dropped by 7.5 million, and in 2006 the welfare caseload was lower than it had been since the 1960s (U.S. Department of Health and Human Services, 2009). But the number of TANF recipients has been climbing again as a result of the recession and associated joblessness, and in 2011 there were 4.5 million Americans receiving assistance through TANF, 3.4 million of them children (U.S. Department of Health and Human Services, 2012).

The initial decline in welfare recipients did not translate into a decrease in the poverty rate (Lichter and Jayakody, 2002). In 2005, only 40 percent of the families eligible to receive benefits were being helped by TANF, and only 22 percent of poor children were receiving assistance from TANF when the recession was in full swing in 2008 (Bhargava et al., 2009). The amount of assistance provided by TANF

is thought by many to be inadequate; in 2008 benefit amounts were significantly less than poverty thresholds in every state. According to some analysts, welfare reform served primarily to transform welfare recipients into the working poor (O'Connor, 2000). Although people found jobs, they were not earning enough money to rise above the official poverty line—and that line does not take into account the work-related expenditures that welfare leavers incur, such as child care and transportation. One result of this is that the number of children living without their parents has increased; for black children living in cities, the percentage of children left with friends, relatives, or foster families doubled (Bernstein, 2002).

Why are people who work full-time unable to rise above the poverty line? One reason is that the cost of living—and especially the cost of housing—has increased much more quickly than have wages. A report released in 2010 indicated that the average household needed an income of $18.44 per hour in a full-time job to be able to afford a two-bedroom rental, close to three times the federal minimum wage of $7.25 (National Low Income Housing Coalition, 2010). That number was based on a national average; in some areas, the income required is much higher. Despite the variability in housing costs, there is no state in which a family living off the minimum wage can afford to rent a decent two-bedroom house at market value (National Low Income Housing Coalition, 2010). And surveys show that one result of pushing people off welfare has been to *decrease* wages for low-skilled workers (Kerbo, 2011). The TANF program has both critics and supporters. But TANF has not changed this fact: The United States, which is the wealthiest country in the world, also has the highest rates of poverty among developed nations (Rank, 2011).

How might poverty be handled differently? Sociologist Mark Rank (2011) argues that we need to change the way we think about poverty. He says our failure to solve the problem of poverty in the midst of great wealth is because as a society we think of poverty as an individual pathology and that this attitude "seriously misconstrues the true nature of poverty and fosters a lack of political and social will to address the problem" (Rank, 2011:17).

Rank argues that if Americans wish to address the problem of poverty they should recognize three things:

1. Poverty affects us all. It affects us personally because three-quarters of Americans will spend a year either in or near poverty sometime during their adult lives, and two-thirds will use a social welfare program such as the Supplemental Nutritional Assistance Program (SNAP) or Medicaid. And it affects us as a society because poverty is associated with other societal problems. The annual cost of childhood poverty, for example, in terms of crime, loss of productive workers, and other problems, is $500 billion.

2. Poverty is not a personal failing or pathology; it is the result of a shortage of viable opportunities for all Americans. For example, over the past 30 years, more and more of the jobs that are available—and there aren't enough to go around—are low-paying, part-time, and without benefits. They are not jobs that would allow a worker to support him- or herself or a family.

3. Poverty is a moral problem, a serious injustice. As Rank puts it, "Something is seriously wrong when we find that, in a country with the most abundant resources in the world, there are children without enough to eat, families who cannot afford health care, and people sleeping on the streets for lack of shelter" (2011:20). Defining the problem of poverty in moral terms will make it more difficult for people to comfortably accept it.

Rank contends that changing our thinking about poverty will increase the chances that we will change our policies and programs. A 2009 report on eradicating poverty recommended providing affordable, quality health care, child care assistance, increased access to affordable housing, and assistance for college education (Bhargava et al., 2009). More fundamental changes include a minimum wage that would keep full-time workers out of poverty; improved enforcement of child support laws so that families do not have to rely on the income of a single parent; and the provision of jobs to everyone who is willing to work, with the government as the employer of last resort (Bane and Ellwood, 1994). And historian Kevin Cahill asserts that granting ownership of a small portion of land to every person on earth would be a first step to ending poverty worldwide (Cahill, 2010).

Social Mobility

In many societies individuals or groups can move from one level (stratum) to another in the stratification system, a process called **social mobility.** Social inequality has to do with differences in the distribution of benefits and burdens; social stratification is a structured system of inequality; and social mobility refers to the shift of individuals or groups from one social status to another.

Social mobility can occur in at least two ways. First, societies change, altering the division of labor, introducing new positions, undermining old ones, and shifting the allocation of resources. Sometimes such social change occurs because members of the lower strata resent their exclusion from higher ranks and work to change the established social order. Second, social mobility can take place when shifts occur in the availability of different types of talent. Although those in the higher strata may monopolize the opportunities for training and education, they do not control the natural distribution of talent and ability. People often must be recruited from the lower ranks to perform roles in society that increase their status.

J. K. Rowling with a group of children at a One Parent Family festival. J. K. Rowling was a struggling single mother before her Harry Potter books made her wealthy. Such mobility is rare.

In this section we will describe the forms social mobility can take, discuss social mobility and status attainment processes, and take a look at the "American Dream."

Forms of Social Mobility

Social mobility can take a number of forms. For example, mobility may be vertical or horizontal. **Vertical mobility** involves movement from one social status to another of higher or lower rank. As we saw in Table 6.1, Americans differ in the prestige ratings they give to various occupations. If an auto mechanic (prestige score 40) becomes a lawyer (score 75), this shift constitutes upward mobility. On the other hand, if the auto mechanic becomes a garbage collector (score 28), this change involves downward mobility. If the auto mechanic takes a job as a restaurant manager (score 39), this shift represents horizontal mobility. **Horizontal mobility** entails movement from one social status to another of approximately equivalent rank.

Mobility also may be intergenerational or intragenerational. **Intergenerational mobility** involves a comparison of the social status of parents and their children at some point in their respective careers (e.g., as assessed by the rankings of their occupations at roughly the same age). Research shows that a large minority, perhaps even a majority, of the U.S. population moves up or down at least a little in the class hierarchy in every generation. **Intragenerational mobility** entails a comparison of the social status of a person over an extended time. There are limits to the variety of most people's mobility experience. Small moves tend to be the rule, and large moves the exception.

Social Mobility and Status Attainment

When sociologists talk about social mobility, they usually have intergenerational occupational mobility in mind. Over the history of the United States, social mobility has occurred as a result of changes in occupational structure and the economy (Beeghley, 2000). Many Americans assume that the chances of moving up the social ladder are greater in the United States than in other countries. In fact, chances for upward mobility in the United States are no better, and in some cases worse, than they are in other industrialized countries (Scott and Leonhardt, 2005; Breen and Jonsson, 2004). In general, more Americans are upwardly mobile than downwardly mobile across generations.

What accounts for the higher rate of upward than downward intergenerational mobility in the United States? First, changes in occupational structure over time: With technological advances, more jobs are created toward the top of the occupational structure than toward the bottom. Second, fertility differences associated with social class: White-collar fathers generate fewer children than blue-collar fathers, making more room toward the top of the class hierarchy.

The Classic Studies

We can learn more about social mobility by looking at status attainment studies, which identify the processes by which individuals enter occupations and attain status in society. Two classic sociological studies of status transmission and attainment have pinpointed some key factors. The first involved the development of a technique for studying the course of an individual's occupational status over the life cycle (Blau and Duncan, 1972). Called the **socioeconomic life cycle,** it involves a sequence of stages that begins with birth into a family with a specific social status and proceeds through childhood, socialization, schooling, job seeking, occupational achievement, marriage, and the formation and functioning of a new family unit. The second study, conducted by William Sewell and his associates (Sewell et al., 1970; Sewell and Hauser, 1975), was based on a survey of high school seniors and follow-up work over the decade following their graduation from high school.

Both these studies found that education—the years of schooling completed—has the greatest influence on occupational attainment. Blau and Duncan concluded that the social status of one's parents has little *direct* impact on occupational attainment; rather, it plays an *indirect* role in status attainment through its effect on schooling. Sewell and his associates also found that achievement aspirations learned in the family are important factors. A study that followed the participants of Sewell and colleagues' original study from the 1950s to the 1990s found that the impact of family background on occupational attainment operates entirely through educational achievement and cognitive ability (Warren, Hauser, and Sheridan, 2002). In another recent study, Elman and O'Rand (2004) showed that advantaged social origins lead to completion of college before one's first job, and this combination produces a sharp boost to adult wages.

The Critics

Critics of status attainment research contend that it has a functionalist bias (Knottnerus, 1991). They argue that it is not the case that the job market is fully open to individuals who acquire positions based on education and ability. Although some of the most important factors affecting status attainment among white males have been identified, it turns out that for women and African Americans the processes of status attainment are different.

Race

Let's look first at African Americans. A nationwide sample of boys revealed a number of differences between blacks and whites in terms of educational attainment (Portes and Wilson, 1976). Using a model similar to that developed by Sewell and others, based on parents' education, offspring's education and aspirations, and other factors, these researchers found that the model predicted attainment for whites better than it did for blacks. This suggested that the factors that are most important for educational attainment among blacks were not included in the model. Socioeconomic background, mental ability, and academic performance were found to be more important for white attainment, while self-esteem and educational aspirations were significant variables for blacks. Similarly, while Elman and O'Rand (2004) found that education increased adult wages for both whites

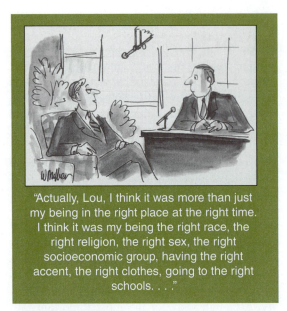

"Actually, Lou, I think it was more than just my being in the right place at the right time. I think it was my being the right race, the right religion, the right sex, the right socioeconomic group, having the right accent, the right clothes, going to the right schools. . . ."

and blacks, the effects of education on wages are greater for whites.

Gender

Research in Great Britain has shown that social mobility findings for white men cannot also be generalized to women (Abbott and Wallace, 1997). While the proportion of jobs done by women and the proportion of women working for pay both have increased, women typically come in as routine workers and at the bottom of job categories. Similarly, in the United States, women are more likely than men to be and remain at the bottom of any scale of salaries and wages and less likely than men to be or remain at the top (Gittleman and Joyce, 1995). Daughters are less likely than sons to "inherit" their fathers' occupations and are more likely to be influenced by their mothers' occupations (Hurst, 1998). For males, education is one of a number of variables affecting status attainment; for females, education is clearly *the most significant* factor related

to status attainment (Hurst, 1998; see also Elman and O'Rand, 2004). Women also are more likely than men to be affected by family and home-life factors; Waddoups and Assane (1993) found that having a child dampens the upward mobility of women but not of men.

Race and Gender

Race also interacts with gender in status attainment. In a study of women in Memphis, researchers found that white women raised in working-class families received less support and encouragement for educational and career attainment than did white women raised in middle-class families and black women raised in either working- or middle-class families (Higginbotham and Weber, 1992). For example, 86 percent of the black middle-class women said their families supported their going to college, compared to 70 percent of the white middle-class women, 64 percent of the black working-class women, and only 56 percent of the white working-class women.

Dual Labor Market

Higginbotham and Weber's study looked at only one aspect of educational and occupational attainment in the United States, but it makes clear the point that the structural model of Blau and Duncan and the social/psychological model of Sewell and his colleagues do not explain all that we need to know about status attainment for a diverse population in the United States. Another factor operating to channel individuals into various occupations is the **dual labor market,** with the primary, or *core,* sector of the economy offering "good jobs" and the secondary, or *periphery,* sector offering "bad jobs" that provide poor pay, poor working conditions, and little room for advancement. Recruitment to these two sectors varies, with African Americans, Hispanics, Native Americans, and women found more often in the periphery sector (Beck, Horan, and Tolbert,

1980; Sakamoto and Chen, 1991). If we want to gain a better understanding of how status attainment functions not just for white men but for both women and men of a variety of races and ethnicities, we need to look beyond education and fathers' occupations and look instead at how race, class, and gender affect the status attainment process.

What Is Happening to the American Dream?

America has long been viewed as the land of opportunity. The American Dream is the belief that an average person, through hard work and perseverance, can achieve as much as he or she wishes. A central part of this belief is that even people born in poverty can live a decent life—that is, have a nice home, own a car, and send their children to college. In short, if they work hard and play by the rules, they can join the middle class.

Is this true? A recent study shows that the American Dream may be just that—a dream. The study assessed the economic status of 39- to 44-year-olds and compared it to the economic status of the subjects' families when they were teenagers (Acs, 2011). A third of Americans who were raised in the middle class in the 1980s "fell out" as adults, and this downward mobility is affected by race, gender, and marital status. Women were more likely to have fallen out of the middle class if they were divorced, widowed, or separated; marital status affects men, too, but not as strongly. Among whites, 30 percent of women fell out of the middle class, compared to only 21 percent of men. Among blacks, women (30 percent) were less likely than men (38 percent) to experience downward mobility. The Great Recession of 2007–2009 increased the economic disparities between racial and ethnic groups: In 2009 the median wealth of whites was 20 times that of blacks and 18 times that of Hispanics (Kochhar, Fry, and Taylor, 2011).

Researchers also have found an increasing age gap in economic well-being (Fry et al., 2011). Households headed by younger adults in 2009 were found to have 68 percent *less* wealth than similar households in 1984, while households headed by adults 65 and over in 2009 were worth 42 percent *more* than similar "older" households in 1984. In other words, over the past 30 years, the economic situation of older adults has improved, while that of younger adults has gotten worse, making it less likely that younger Americans will achieve their economic goals. It also has become more difficult for poor Americans to move out of poverty and for immigrants to achieve economic stability and success (Bernstein, 2003).

Part of the reason for these changes is the transformation that has occurred in the occupational structure. Industrial change is eliminating high-paying working-class jobs and replacing them with low-paying ones. Smokestack industries, such as machine tools, autos, and steel, provide many middle-income jobs; when deindustrialization causes their share of total employment to fall sharply, the middle class shrinks. As jobs in manufacturing decline, most new jobs are created in the service and trade sectors of the economy. But service industries display a two-hump distribution in income—highly paid administrative and professional workers, such as physicians and professional workers, at the top, and low-paid workers, such as hamburger flippers and telemarketers, at the bottom. The study of people "falling out" of the middle class found a significant education effect; both women and men who were raised in middle-class families but never went beyond high school were more likely to have fallen out of the middle class (Acs, 2011). Drug use (heroin or crack cocaine) also correlated with downward mobility. The subjects in this study all had taken a standardized exam as teens, which provided a measure of reading comprehension, math and word knowledge, and arithmetic reasoning. Differences in test scores almost entirely accounted for the large race differences in downward mobility, but the researchers found nothing that explained why white women were more likely than white men to fall out of the middle class.

Despite the fact that inequality has increased and that "equal opportunity" may not be so equal, in real dollars most Americans are well off compared to household incomes from the 1970s and early 1980s (see Figure 6.5). That may account for the optimism noted earlier in this chapter: Most Americans believe that they have a good chance of getting ahead, that they have done better than their parents, and that their children will have more opportunities than they had (Smith et al., 2010).

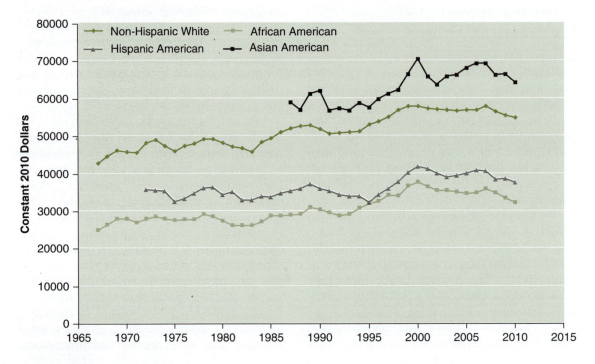

Figure 6.5 **Median Income of Households by Race/Ethnicity, in Constant 2010 Dollars, 1972–2010**

The American Dream: coming true, but not for everyone. The median income figures used to make this graph have been adjusted for inflation (i.e., they are in "real" or "constant" dollars) so that we can compare them over time to see if incomes have been rising or falling. These data show that real household income fluctuates over time with the economy but has been on a generally upward trend since the early 1970s. Regardless of fluctuations, the higher incomes that people expect as part of the American Dream do not flow equally to all groups.

Sources: Figure generated by the authors using data from the U.S. Census Bureau Current Population Survey, Annual Social and Economic Supplements, Table H-5. (Available at http://www.census.gov/hhes/www/income/data/historical/household/) Data for non-Hispanic whites from 1967 to 1971 are estimated using data for all whites (in those years, data were not collected on non-Hispanic whites). For 2001 and earlier, Asian data are for Asians and Pacific Islanders. Data for blacks and Asians are for blacks alone and Asian alone, where possible.

Explanations of Social Stratification

As sociology developed, the question of why social inequality and division should characterize the human condition provided a central focus of the new science. Through the years, two strikingly divergent answers have emerged. The first—the *conservative* thesis that is rooted in functionalism—has supported existing social arrangements, contending that an unequal distribution of social rewards is a necessary instrument for getting the essential tasks of society performed. In sharp contrast, the second view—the *radical* thesis that is rooted in conflict theory—has been highly critical of existing social arrangements, viewing social inequality as an exploitative mechanism arising out of a struggle for valued goods and services in short supply.

The Functionalist Theory of Stratification

The functionalist theory of social inequality holds that stratification exists because it is beneficial for society. All societies require a system of stratification if they are to fill all the statuses composing the social structure and to motivate individuals to perform the duties associated with these positions. Consequently, society must motivate people at two different levels: (1) It must instill in certain individuals the desire to fill various positions, and (2) once the individuals are in these positions it must instill in them the desire to carry out the appropriate roles. This theory was most clearly set forth in 1945 by Kingsley Davis and Wilbert Moore, although it has been subsequently modified and refined by other sociologists. Davis and Moore argued that social stratification is both universal and necessary, and hence no society is ever totally unstratified or classless.

Society must concern itself with human motivation because the duties associated with the various statuses are not all equally pleasant to the human organism, are not all equally important to social survival, and are not all equally in need of the same abilities and talents. Moreover, the duties associated with many positions are viewed by their occupants as onerous. Hence, in the absence of motivation, many individuals would fail to act out their roles.

For example, imagine being a dentist. How likely is it that talented and intelligent people would train to become dentists—pulling teeth; working to correct extensive (and bad-smelling) decay; bending near to people's faces even when they have runny noses, coughs, and bad breath; causing people pain, anxiety, and distress—if the pay and status were not fairly high? Maintaining the dental health of our population is important to society, and so we need to motivate people to become dentists.

On the basis of these social realities, functionalists contend that a society must have (1) some kind of rewards that it can use as inducements for its members and (2) some way of distributing these rewards among the various statuses. Inequality is the motivational incentive that society has evolved to meet the problems of filling all the statuses and getting the occupants to enact the associated roles to the best of their abilities. Since these rewards are built into the social system, social stratification is a structural feature of all societies.

Employing the economists' model of supply and demand, functionalists say that the positions most highly rewarded are those (1) that are occupied by the most talented or qualified incumbents (supply) and (2) that are functionally most important (demand). For example, to ensure sufficient physicians, a society needs to offer them high salaries and great prestige. If it did not offer these rewards, functionalists suggest that we could not expect people to undertake the "burdensome" and "expensive" process of medical education. People at the top must receive the rewards they do; if they do not, the positions will remain unfilled and society will disintegrate.

6.3 Social Inequalities

Why Do Doctors Deliver Babies?

In today's society, having a baby is nearly always associated with doctors and hospitals. But before and after the early days of America's independence, babies were born at home, and mother and baby were cared for by a midwife. Midwives not only delivered babies more competently than doctors, but they were the only source of health care in most communities. Why, then, did doctors begin delivering babies? And what does this change tell us about theories of social inequality?

Martha Ballard was a midwife from 1785 to 1812, a time when women, serving as midwives, provided most of the health care for most of the people in the United States. As Ballard's 27 years of record keeping show, she delivered 816 babies, treated a wide variety of illnesses, manufactured her own medicinal syrups and ointments, and prepared bodies for burial. According to historian Laurel Thatcher Ulrich, who used Ballard's diary to write her Pulitzer Prize–winning *A Midwife's Tale,* the midwife's extensive knowledge was gained not through attendance at a medical school but on the job, working with other women and by herself to care for others in her community.

Ballard observed and participated in a major change in health care in the United States, a change from reliance on midwives to employment of professionally trained—but not necessarily more competent—physicians. Her personal competitor was a young physician named Benjamin Page, who charged $6 to deliver a baby while she charged $2. Page was clearly less experienced and less capable than Ballard at delivering babies, and Ulrich cites many examples of his incompetence.

Ulrich's description of the involvement of physicians in childbirth suggests that Martha Ballard's experience was the rule and not the exception. Records show that deaths of mothers and babies *increased* rather than decreased when physicians began routinely attending births in the 19th century. Ulrich noted that births attended by physicians also involved a much higher rate of complications than those attended by midwives and suggested that birth was being made more complicated by physicians' use of forceps and drugs such as ergot and opiates in deliveries that a midwife would have considered routine.

Why would people employ a young, inexperienced physician? Ulrich explains his appeal: "Ben Page had certain advantages: a gentlemanly bearing, a successfully completed apprenticeship, and

Evaluation of the Functionalist Perspective

This structure–function approach to stratification has been the subject of much criticism. For one thing, the labor market does not operate freely, rewarding only those of high ability. Often jobs and positions are allocated on the basis of social connections and power (see Box 6.3). In addition, many people are born into family positions of privilege or lack of privilege, and as we saw in our discussion of social mobility, this may have a strong influence on where people end up in the stratification system (Kim, 1987).

A 1980s study showed that nearly two-thirds of the chief executives in 243 large U.S. corporations grew up in upper-middle or upper-class families. Such findings lead conflict theorists to contend that society is structured so that individuals *maintain* a ranking that is determined by birth and that is *irrespective* of their abilities, and thus that stratification is *dysfunctional* rather than functional. Melvin Tumin (1953), in his classic critique of the functional theory of stratification, argued that because access to important, highly paid occupations is not entirely determined by ability, many talented people are discouraged from moving into such positions, and as a result our society functions credit with certain younger members of the Kennebec elite" (Ulrich, 1990:178–179). His list of patients included a judge's daughter and the wives of an attorney, a merchant, and a printer, all of whom were new to the town and, like Page, educated and ambitious. Medical sociologist Paul Starr pointed out in his history of U.S. medicine (1982) that the more educated people were, the more likely they were to accept physicians' claims of superior skill; physicians were similar to the elite in education, often shared a similar position of respect in the community, and were involved in the same social networks.

At this critical time, from the late 1700s to the 1840s, women like Martha Ballard and young women who wished to start a career in midwifery did not have the option of going to medical school and making the kind of social connections with the elite that male physicians could. In spite of women's extensive experience in medical matters during this period, male physicians were adamantly opposed to the admission of women into medical school, into the profession (Starr, 1982; Ulrich, 1990), or even into medical training specifically for midwives. The first women's medical school in the United States was not founded until 1848 (Starr, 1982). By that time men were firmly in control of the medical practice of obstetrics, and the up-and-coming ambitious American citizenry had developed a strong preference for them.

The case of Martha Ballard and Benjamin Page provides a clear example of the constraints that operate in the labor market. The change from a reliance on midwifery to employment of physicians occurred not because physicians were better than midwives at what they did, but because they were men and as such were already connected to other powerful institutions, including law, education, business, and politics. Young physicians such as Benjamin Page were employed—and paid at higher rates—to do something they weren't very good at. Though midwives were as competent as or more competent than any physician at prenatal care and delivering babies, men had more power and better social connections and were able to drive the women out of their traditional role.

The functionalist theory of stratification argues that higher rewards go to those who perform the most functionally important tasks in society. The story of midwife Martha Ballard shows that this is not always true; sometimes high rewards flow to those who perform functionally important tasks badly.

Questions for Discussion

1. What were the primary determinants of the change from midwifery to physician-provided health care in the United States?

2. Are most U.S. births now attended by midwives or physicians? Which are safer in today's society, midwife- or physician-attended births? Which profession has higher prestige today, midwife or physician? Explain your answers.

less effectively and is less productive than it could be. Research by Kim A. Weeden (2002) shows that social and legal barriers such as licensing restrictions, educational requirements, associational representation, and unionization limit the labor supply, increase demand, and thus increase salaries and wages in higher-status occupations. These income-enhancing processes are independent of functional occupational characteristics such as the complexity of an occupation's knowledge base.

Critics also point out that many of the positions of highest responsibility in the United States—in government, science, technology, and education—are not financially well rewarded (Bok, 1993). The officers of the largest U.S. corporations, for example, earn about 100 times more than the president of the United States and about 200 times more than Supreme Court justices. Critics also ask whether garbage collectors, with their lower pay and prestige, are more important to the survival of the United States than top athletes who receive incomes in seven and even eight figures. Entertainers also receive disproportionately high incomes. According to *Forbes,* a business magazine that annually reports on the salaries of wealthy people, "Judge Judy," a TV judge, earns $45 million a year (http://www.forbes.com/wealth/celebrities#p_10_s_arank_), while the 2010 salary for a Supreme Court justice was $213,900 (http://www.uscourts.gov/Viewer.aspx?doc=/uscourts/JudgesJudgeships/docs/JudicialSalari-eschart.pdf). In sum, the notion that many low-paying positions are functionally less important to society than high-paying positions is often difficult to support.

The Conflict Theory of Stratification

The conflict theory of social equality holds that stratification exists because it benefits individuals and groups who have the power to dominate and exploit others. Whereas functionalists stress the common interests that members of society share, conflict theorists focus on the interests that divide people. Viewed from the conflict perspective, society is an arena in which people struggle for privilege, prestige, and power, and advantaged groups enforce their advantage through coercion (Grimes, 1991).

The conflict theory draws heavily on the ideas of Karl Marx. As discussed in Chapter 1, Marx believed that a historical perspective is essential for understanding any society. To grasp how a particular economic system works, he said that we must keep in mind the structures and processes from which it evolved. For example, under feudalism, the medieval lords were in control of the economy and dominated the serfs. Under the capitalist system, the manor lord has been replaced by the modern capitalist and the serf by the "free" laborer—in reality a propertyless worker who "has nothing to sell but his hands."

Marx contended that the capitalist drive to realize surplus value is the foundation of modern class struggle—an irreconcilable clash of interests between workers and capitalists. *Surplus value* is the difference between the value that workers create (as determined by the labor time embodied in a commodity that they produce) and the value that they receive (as determined by the subsistence level of their wages).

Although surplus value is due to workers' efforts, capitalists retain it, and it is the primary source of their wealth. This process of capital accumulation is the key incentive for the development of capitalism. Marx believed that the class struggle will eventually be resolved when the working class overthrows the capitalist class and establishes a new and equitable social order.

Workers may remain exploited and oppressed for a long time, blinded by a *false consciousness*—an incorrect assessment of how the system works and of their subjugation and exploitation by capitalists. But through a struggle with capitalists, the workers' objective class interests become translated into a subjective recognition of their true circumstances, and they formulate goals for organized action—in brief, they acquire *class consciousness*. Hence, according to Marxists, if the working class is to take on its historical role of overturning capitalism, it must recognize that it is oppressed and exploited, and it must have the conscious goal of gaining the power to change this situation.

Although conflict theory grew out of Marx's analysis of 19th-century economic relations, some sociologists find that conflict theory is relevant to understanding inequality today. For example, Eric Olin Wright (Wright, 1985, 1993; Steinmetz and Wright, 1989) used four class categories derived from Marxist theory to explain differences in income in the United States. He found that these categories—capitalists (owners of large businesses), managers (those who manage large businesses), workers, and the petit bourgeoisie (small business owners)—explained differences in income about as well as the standard variables of education and occupation do. In addition, he found that capitalists have higher income than others do, even after adjusting for the effects of education, age, and job tenure.

Understanding modern class conflict helps to explain the pattern of increasing income inequality documented earlier in the chapter. In 2010, sociologist Tali Kristal showed that since the early 1980s, the share of income in industrialized countries going to workers (i.e., labor) has decreased and the share going to capitalists has increased. These changes occurred because of a decline in the relative bargaining power of laborers versus capitalists in economic, political, and global spheres, decreasing the ability of labor unions to promote workers' interests through contract negotiations and promotion of beneficial legislation and trade policy.

Evaluation of the Conflict Perspective

The emphasis on economic relations in Marx's conflict theory results in a limited view of both conflict and power. Conflict is a pervasive feature of human life and is not restricted to economic relations. Ralf Dahrendorf (1959) held that group conflict is an inevitable aspect of society that would not be eliminated by revolution as Marx had argued. The Marxist dichotomy between the capitalist class and the working class directs our attention away from other important conflicts that animate social life in modern societies. Debtor and creditor have stood against each other throughout history, as have consumers and sellers. And divisions between racial and ethnic groups, skilled workers and unskilled laborers, and union organizations have been recurrent features of the American landscape.

Ownership of the means of production constitutes only one source of power. Control over human beings—the possession of the means of administration—provides another (Giddens, 1985). Power also flows from knowledge. More than 50 years ago, the Austrian economist Joseph A. Schumpeter (1883–1950) emphasized that knowledge, technology, and innovation are the cornerstones (more than price competition) for energizing economic life (Swedberg, 1991). For example, within contemporary American

For her work as a "desperate housewife" on TV, Teri Hatcher earns approximately $9 million a year. A real housewife engages in a significant amount of household labor and earns nothing for these efforts.

life, engineers, systems analysts, and software design specialists derive organizational and social power by virtue of their expertise. But in all these examples, influence lasts only as long as officeholders stay in their positions. Their hold on power is often tenuous, and they are easily replaceable. Much the same picture emerges from government. The people who actually hold and exercise power are not the owners of the means of production, and they are powerful only as long as they hold office. Marx's response to this point would be his contention that in a capitalist society the government is an administrative unit that runs the society in the service of those who own the means of production. As we will see in Chapter 9, there are a variety of positions in social science about this issue.

A Synthesis of Perspectives

Many sociologists have noted that both the functionalist and conflict theories have merit, but that each is better than the other in answering different questions (Sorokin, 1959; van den Berghe, 1963; Milner, 1987). For example, as the functionalists have proposed, some of the distribution of rewards within the occupational structure is explained by the supply and demand factors in the labor and job markets (Kerbo, 2011). But, as conflict theorists have pointed out, the markets for labor and jobs are not free and unrestricted, and some of the inequality in outcomes can be explained by differences in power and influence across social classes.

Some sociologists have tried to synthesize the functionalist and conflict perspectives. Harold R. Kerbo (2011), for example, has argued that stratification systems are institutions that have evolved in order to reduce conflict. Without systems of stratification, there would be continuing conflict and aggression over the distribution of scarce resources. Institutionalized inequality provides at least a temporary answer to the question "Who gets what, and why?" Kerbo bases much of his reasoning on the work of sociologist Gerhard Lenski (1966), who tried to formally integrate the functionalist and conflict perspectives. Lenski agreed with functionalists that the chief resources of society

are allocated as rewards to people who occupy vital positions and that stratification fosters a rough match between scarce talents and rewards. But as a society advances in technology, it becomes capable of producing a considerable surplus of goods and services. This surplus gives rise to conflicts over who should control it. Power provides the answer to the question of control and determines the distribution of the surplus. Consequently, with technological advances, an increasing proportion of the goods and services available to a society are distributed on the basis of power. In the end, Lenski was not able to resolve the debate. However, many sociologists now agree with one of his main conclusions, that the functionalist and conflict positions each provide part of the answer, but that neither contains the whole truth.

 What Can Sociology Do for You?

In this chapter you have learned about social stratification, with a particular emphasis on the American class system and on inequality and poverty in the United States. If you are concerned about those who live in poverty, you may choose to use your sociology degree to go into social work. How does one become a social worker? You can find information about social work at **www.bls.gov/oco/ocos060.htm.** Those who work on public programs and fiscal policy for low- and moderate-income families also are dealing with issues related to stratification. An example of this kind of work is the Center on Budget and Policy Priorities (**http://www.cbpp.org/info.html**).

If you found the issues and discussions in Chapter 6 to be interesting, you may want to take classes in stratification, inequality, and social problems.

The Chapter in Brief: *Social Stratification*

Most societies are organized so that their institutions systematically distribute benefits and burdens unequally among different categories of people. Sociologists call the structured ranking of individuals and groups—their grading into horizontal layers or strata—**social stratification.**

Patterns of Social Stratification

Social stratification depends upon, but is not the same thing as, **social differentiation**—the process by which a society becomes increasingly specialized over time.

- **Open and Closed Systems** Where people can change their status with relative ease, sociologists refer to the arrangement as an **open system.** A **closed system** is one in which people have great difficulty in changing their status.

- **Dimensions of Stratification** Sociologists typically take a multidimensional view of stratification, identifying three components: economic standing (**wealth** and **income**), **prestige,** and **power.**

- **Social Stratification Among Societies** Social stratification is not confined to people and groups within societies, and social scientists are increasingly interested in understanding patterns of inequality among societies around the globe. Differences in income across societies are quite stark.

The American Class System

Inequality follows relatively consistent and stable patterns that persist through time. We often refer to advantaged and disadvantaged groups in the United States as the upper class, middle class, and lower class.

- **Is There Inequality in American Society?** Since the early 1970s income inequality in the United States has been increasing and is now at its highest level in 50 years. In 2010, the top 20 percent of the population received half of the income. Inequality in wealth is even greater.

- **Identifying Social Classes** Three primary methods are employed by sociologists for identifying social classes: the **objective method,** the **self-placement method,** and the **reputational method.**

- **The Significance of Social Classes** Social class largely determines people's **life chances** and **style of life** and influences patterns of behavior, including voting and sexual behavior.

- **Poverty in the United States** Children and the elderly account for nearly half of all Americans living in poverty. Three theories predominate regarding poverty: the **culture of poverty** theory, poverty as *situational,* and poverty as a *structural* feature of capitalist societies.

Social Mobility

In many societies individuals or groups can move from one level (stratum) to another in the stratification system, a process called **social mobility.**

■ **Forms of Social Mobility**   Social mobility takes a number of forms. It may be **vertical** or **horizontal** and **intergenerational** or **intra-generational.** When sociologists talk about social mobility, they usually mean intergenerational occupational mobility.

■ **Social Mobility and Status Attainment** More Americans are upwardly mobile than downwardly mobile across generations. Sociologists study the course of an individual's occupational status over the life cycle by looking at the **socioeconomic life cycle.** Education has the greatest influence on occupational attainment for white men. The processes of status attainment are different for women and blacks than for white males. Critics of status attainment research contend that it has a functionalist bias and that the **dual labor market** operates to sort people into *core* or *periphery* sector jobs.

■ **What Is Happening to the American Dream?**   Controversy surrounds the issue of whether the American middle class is an endangered species. Although "equal opportunity" does not apply to all Americans, depending on race, gender, and ethnicity, in real dollars most Americans are better off than their parents were.

Explanations of Social Stratification

The question of why social inequality and division should characterize the human condition has provided a central focus of sociology.

■ **The Functionalist Theory of Stratification**   The functionalist theory of social inequality holds that stratification exists because it is beneficial for society. Society must concern itself with human motivation because the duties associated with the various statuses are not all equally pleasant to the human organism, important to social survival, and in need of the same abilities and talents.

■ **The Conflict Theory of Stratification** The conflict theory of social inequality holds that stratification exists because it benefits individuals and groups who have the power to dominate and exploit others. Marx contended that the capitalist drive to realize surplus value is the foundation of modern class struggle.

■ **A Synthesis of Perspectives**   Both functionalist and conflict theories have merit, but each is better than the other in answering different questions. A number of sociologists, including Gerhard E. Lenski, have looked for ways of integrating the two perspectives.

Glossary

closed system   A stratification system in which people have great difficulty changing their status.

culture of poverty   The view that the poor possess self-perpetuating lifeways characterized by weak ego structures, lack of impulse control, a present-time orientation, and a sense of resignation and fatalism.

dual labor market   An economy characterized by two sectors. The primary, or core, sector offers "good jobs," and the secondary, or periphery, sector offers "bad jobs."

horizontal mobility   Movement from one social status to another that is approximately equivalent in rank.

income   The amount of money people receive.

intergenerational mobility   A comparison of the social status of parents and their children at some point in their respective careers.

intragenerational mobility   A comparison of the social status of a person over an extended time.

life chances   The likelihood that individuals and groups will enjoy desired goods and services, fulfilling experiences, and opportunities for living healthy and long lives.

objective method   An approach to the identification of social classes that employs such yardsticks as income, occupation, and education.

open system   A stratification system in which people can change their status with relative ease.

power   The ability of individuals and groups to realize their will in human affairs even if it involves the resistance of others.

prestige   The social respect, admiration, and recognition associated with a particular social status.

reputational method   An approach to identifying social classes that involves asking people how they classify others.

self-placement method   An approach to identifying social classes that involves self-classification.

social differentiation   The process by which a society becomes increasingly specialized over time.

social mobility   The process in which individuals or groups move from one level (stratum) to another in the stratification system.

social stratification   The structured ranking of individuals and

groups; their grading into hierarchical layers or strata.

socioeconomic life cycle   A sequence of stages that begins with birth into a family with a specific social status and proceeds through childhood, socialization, schooling, job seeking, occupational achievement, marriage, and the formation and functioning of a new family unit.

style of life   The magnitude and manner of people's consumption of goods and services.

vertical mobility   Movement of individuals from one social status to another of higher or lower rank.

wealth   What people own.

Review Questions

1.   What is social stratification? What are three components of it?

2.   Describe the differences between open and closed systems.

3.   Discuss inequality in U.S. society with regard to wealth and income.

4.   How do sociologists identify social classes?

5.   How many people in the United States are living in poverty? How do sociologists account for the existence of poverty?

6.   What is social mobility and how does it occur?

7.   How do the processes of status attainment differ for different groups of people?

8.   How do the functionalist and conflict theories of stratification differ?

 ## Internet Connection   www.mhhe.com/hughes11e

Income inequality is a persistent feature of American life. Go to the area of the U.S. Census Bureau's website that presents historical data on income inequality in U.S. society, **http://www .census.gov/hhes/www/income/data/historical/ index.html.** Explore this area for information on how income inequality has changed over time in the United States. Some of this information will be

more detailed than you need. Check through the tables until you come to something that clearly presents some aspect of income inequality over time. Using the data presented to inform your argument, write a short report about income inequality in the United States. Does inequality exist? How do you know? How has it changed over time?

Inequalities of Race and Ethnicity

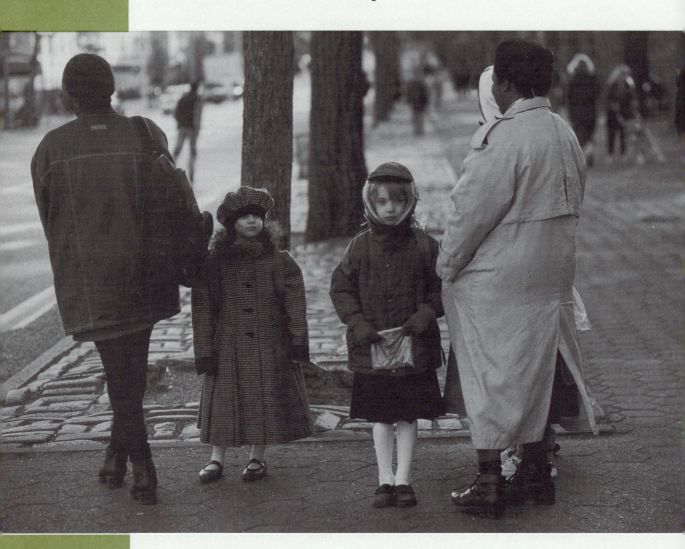

On January 20, 2009, Barack Obama became the 44th president of the United States. Nearly 150 years after the end of slavery in the United States, and more than 50 years after the Supreme Court ruled that schools could not bar children from attendance based on race, President Obama made history as the first African American president in U.S. history.

President Obama's election, a major milestone for a country that once enslaved millions of Africans, raises many questions (Kennedy, 2011). Why had only white males served as president before his election? Does the fact that the United States has a black president mean that the country has entered a postracial era? And why do Americans refer to a man whose mother was white and whose father was from Kenya, who was raised in both Hawaii and Indonesia, whose white grandparents and Indonesian stepfather played major roles in his upbringing, as "black"?

Sociologists are interested in race and ethnicity and the stratification that results from them, and research shows that ethnicity and race remain significant factors of life in the United States—factors that affect health, employment, income, residence, and happiness. Where do race and ethnicity come from? Why and how are they associated with the distribution of society's rewards? How and why do racial and ethnic stratification change? This chapter tries to answer these questions by examining the process of racial and ethnic stratification. We will discuss prejudice and discrimination and various patterns of relationships among groups. We will describe a number of the racial and ethnic groups in the United States. Last, we will look at the insights the functionalist, conflict, and interactionist perspectives provide into matters of racial and ethnic inequality.

Racial and Ethnic Stratification

Societies throughout the world contain peoples with different skin colors, languages, religions, and customs. These physical and cultural traits, by providing high social visibility, serve as identifying symbols of group membership. In turn, individuals are assigned statuses in the social structure—through a process of ascription—based on the group to which they belong (see Chapter 2, pp. 55–56). Many of the same principles we will consider in this chapter also apply to other *socially marginalized groups*—vulnerable and frequently victimized populations who typically have little economic, political, and social power, including cancer and AIDS patients, the elderly, children, and lower-level employees. In this section we will discuss races, ethnic groups, and minority groups, and the potential these groupings create for conflict and separation.

Races

How do you define your racial category? When the U.S. Census Bureau collected data in 2010, every U.S. resident was asked to indicate his or her race. Choices were as follows:

- White
- Black, African American, or Negro
- American Indian or Alaska Native
- Asian Indian
- Chinese
- Filipino
- Japanese
- Korean
- Vietnamese
- Other Asian (print race)
- Native Hawaiian
- Guamanian or Chamorro
- Samoan
- Other Pacific Islander
- Some other race (print race)

Respondents could choose as many races as they wished—both "Black" and "White," for example, for a respondent with parents of different races, or "Chinese," "Black," and "American Indian," if they thought that was appropriate.

The many different racial classification schemes employed by the U.S. Census Bureau over the past 200 years were shaped by a variety of social, political, and cultural factors (Snipp, 2003). The Census 2010 questions on racial identity reflect an increasingly diverse U.S. population and an increase in the number of multiracial citizens. But what is race? How do sociologists define it?

The concept of race typically is used to refer to differences among groups in their physical characteristics. For example, we readily recognize that groups of Europeans, Asians, and Africans look different; people in various parts of the world differ in certain hereditary features, including the color of their skin, the texture of their hair, their facial features, their stature, and the shape of their heads.

Everyday racial categories used in the United States today came originally from popular ways of classifying people that emerged in Europe in the 15th and 16th centuries (Jordan, 1969) following Columbus's voyages to the New World. Scientists, however, have considerable difficulty identifying races and categorizing people in terms of them (Molnar, 1997; Begley, 2003) and are far from agreement in dividing human populations into "races" (Koenig, Lee, and Richardson, 2008). The Human Genome Project found that neither races nor ethnicities can be distinguished by a consistent pattern of genes (GMIS, 2007). For the most part, races are characterized not by fixed, clear-cut differences, but by fluid, continuous differences, and these differences also change considerably with time (Saperstein and Penner, 2010; Lee and Bean, 2004; American Anthropological Association, 1997). Research shows that the characteristics typically used to classify people into racial categories (skin color, hair texture, and facial features) vary more across races than do genes in general (Feldman, Lewontin, and King, 2003). When researchers examine the full range of genetic data, there are fewer differences, overall, between races than within races; about 94 percent of genetic variation is within races, and less than 5 percent is between them (Rosenberg et al., 2002).

Race as a Social Construct

How, then, is the concept "race" useful? For sociologists race is a social construct (Davis, 1991). A **race** is a group of people who see themselves, and are seen by others, as having hereditary traits that set them apart. What interests sociologists is the social significance people attach to various traits. By virtue of individuals' social definitions, skin color or some other racialized trait becomes a sign or mark of a social status (Denton and Massey, 1989).

How do symbols of race become markers of social status that define some people as deserving and privileged and others as undeserving outsiders? According to sociologists Michael Omi and Howard Winant (1994), this happens through *racial formation,* a process by which social, economic, and political forces create and perpetuate racial categories and meanings; and racial categories, in turn, affect social, political, and economic processes and structures.

Racial formation is a process that occurs at both the micro and macro levels. At the micro level, people internalize racial identities in accord with how their society defines them. In the United States, white people develop a white identity, African Americans have a black or African American identity, and so on. These identities are a major factor in structuring people's everyday lives in their communities, at

work, in school, in church, in the family, in encounters with strangers, and in other social situations. At the macro level, race is an organizing principle that affects the nature and content of political, economic, and cultural activities, organizations, and institutions. This occurs in part because of the internalized racial identities of the people who make up these institutions, identities that affect the processes and outcomes of these institutions and are reinforced by such processes and outcomes.

In Omi and Winant's theory, race is socially and culturally defined and is thus not a significant biological reality. But that does not mean that race is a mere illusion. Consistent with the Thomas theorem (Chapter 3), because race is defined as real, it is real in its consequences. These consequences significantly affect how people define themselves, how they interact with others, how they form political and economic alliances, and how they organize their everyday lives and communities. And because racialized social statuses are typically unequal, people experience unequal outcomes in society because of their race.

Race, Ability, and Culture

It has been common throughout history for people to believe that race is associated with personality, moral character, competency, intelligence, and other characteristics. Prominent among claims of this kind is the widely publicized study *The Bell Curve* (Herrnstein and Murray, 1994) that included the argument that racial groups differ in intelligence. The consensus in the scientific community today, however, is that the biological factors that presumably underlie race do not cause race differences in intelligence (Fischer et al., 1996; Jencks and Phillips, 1998; Arrow, Bowles, and Durlauf, 2000) and that claims such as those of Herrnstein and Murray ignore the important impact that environmental conditions have on the measurement of intelligence.

For sociologists, race is a social construct, not a set of biological traits. Gregory Howard Williams, whose father was half black, grew up thinking he was white and being treated by others as if he were white. In his book Life on the Color Line *(1995), he describes what happened when he, his schoolmates, and others in the community learned of his father's background; overnight, he became black.*

For example, research shows that among African Americans, European ancestry, as measured by skin color or by blood type, has no association with measures of intelligence. This is not the finding we would expect if biological factors linked to race were causally linked to intelligence (Nisbett, 1998). In addition, research in Western societies over the past 50 years shows substantial increases in scores on intelligence tests that are much larger than can be explained by genetic change. This finding indicates that environmental factors, particularly culture, can exercise a strong influence on group differences in measured intelligence (Flynn, 2000).

Racism

An important concept based on race is **racism.** Racism exists at two levels—individual and institutional. At the *individual level,* racism is the belief that some racial groups are naturally superior and others are inferior. Individual racism depends on two ideas that have been discredited in contemporary scholarship: (1) that people may be reliably classified into biologically meaningful racial groups (Rosenberg et al., 2002; Feldman, Lewontin, and King, 2003) and (2) that these groups are inherently different in regard to ability, character, intelligence, social behavior, and culture (Block and Dworkin, 1976; Fischer et al., 1996; Nisbett, 1998). Generally, this form of racism gives rise to attitudes of aversion and hostility toward others based on their race. We discuss this later in the chapter in the section on prejudice.

At the *institutional level,* racism involves discriminatory policies and practices that result in unequal outcomes for members of different racial groups. We discuss this in the section on discrimination. While individual racism exists in people's beliefs and attitudes, institutional racism is embedded in the social structure and may operate independently of individual racism.

Ethnic Groups

Groups that we identify chiefly on cultural grounds—language, folk practices, dress, gestures, mannerisms, or religion—are called **ethnic groups.** Within the United States, Jewish Americans, Italian Americans, and Hispanics are examples of ethnic groups. The ethnicity choices for the Census 2010 were "Hispanic, Latino, or Spanish origin" along with Mexican, Mexican American, Chicano; Puerto Rican; Cuban; and other, which respondents were to select in addition to their race(s) selections.

Ethnic groups often have a sense of peoplehood, and to some degree many of them deem themselves to be a nation (Marger, 2012; Stack, 1986). In addition, ethnic groups have a sense of shared history and shared fate that can draw people together into a powerful social unit.

Ethnic identities often are "constructed" by their bearers. For instance, an Asian American consciousness has arisen among many disparate Asian nationality groups in the United States (Espiritu, 1992). The new identity arose in part as a response to political expediency. Political mobilization also has contributed to a supra-tribal identity among many Native Americans (Nagel, 1994).

Minority Groups

Within the United States, African Americans, Hispanics, American Indians and Native Alaskans, Asian Americans, and Jews have been the victims of prejudice and discrimination. They are said to be members of minority groups.

Sociologists commonly distinguish five properties as characteristic of minority groups (Wagley and Harris, 1964; Vander Zanden, 1983):

1. A minority is a social group whose members experience discrimination, segregation, oppression, or persecution at the hands of another social group, the *dominant group,* and lack access to the power necessary to change their situation.

2. A minority is characterized by physical or cultural traits that distinguish it from the dominant group.

3. A minority is a self-conscious social group characterized by a consciousness of oneness. Its members possess a social and psychological affinity with others like themselves, providing a sense of *identity.*

4. Membership in a minority group is generally not voluntary. It is often an ascribed position because an individual is commonly born into the status.

5. The members of a minority, by choice or necessity, often marry within their own group (endogamy).

We may define a **minority group** as a racially or culturally self-conscious population, with hereditary membership and a high degree of in-group marriage, that suffers oppression at the hands of a dominant group (Williams, 1964). The critical characteristic that distinguishes minority groups from other groups is that they lack power.

Although some sociologists have limited the concept of minority group to groups that have hereditary membership, such as ethnic groups, the concept has wide applicability to the situation of any social category that is singled out by a dominant group for unequal treatment by virtue of presumed physical or cultural differences. In a now-classic article, Helen Mayer Hacker (1951, 1974) argued that women were a minority group and had many of the same minority characteristics as African Americans (see Chapter 8, p. 249). Gay men and lesbians similarly share a minority status in contemporary society, as do others whose sexual orientations differ from what is conventional and traditional in American society.

Prejudice and Discrimination

Prejudice and discrimination are so prevalent in contemporary life, so much a part of the racial and ethnic stratification that exists in the United States, that we often assume they are merely part of human nature. Yet this view ignores the enormous variation among individuals and societies in levels of prejudice and discrimination. Even in Hitler's Germany, where large numbers of Germans supported and participated in the Nazi Holocaust (Goldhagen, 1996), some "Aryans" opposed anti-Semitism and helped Jews escape. And whereas Asians have found acceptance in Hawaii and have prospered there, they have had a long history of persecution on the West Coast and in British Columbia (Glick, 1980). In the ancient world, whites held a positive image of blacks, a situation very different from recent history (Snowden, 1983). Even during the civil rights movement in the United States, individuals varied in levels of prejudice. Some southern whites had progressive racial attitudes and supported the African American struggle for equality (e.g., Durr, 1985).

In this section we will define and discuss prejudice and discrimination and consider institutional discrimination.

Prejudice

Prejudice refers to attitudes of aversion and hostility toward the members of a group simply because they belong to it and hence are presumed to have the objectionable qualities ascribed to it (Allport, 1954; Devine, 1989; Bakanic, 2009). As such, prejudice is a subjective phenomenon—a state of mind. Racial prejudices generally have three components: (1) a cognitive component that provides a description of members of the target group, often including negative stereotypes such as "lazy," "thoughtless," "criminal," or "unfeeling"; (2) an affective component that involves negative reactions and emotional feelings about the group; and (3) a behavioral component that may include the tendency to discriminate or behave negatively toward members of the group.

Why are people prejudiced toward members of other groups? Research suggests that a critical factor in the development of out-group stereotypes is social anxiety. In people who lack social anxiety, the tendency to racially stereotype others also is absent (Santos, Meyer-Lindenberg, and Deruelle, 2010). But what triggers such social fears and other factors that promote stereotypes and prejudice? Social scientists in the United States have been studying this issue

for more than 75 years and have come up with two kinds of explanations, one emphasizing social psychological processes and the other emphasizing social structure.

Social Psychology

Social psychological theories argue that social interaction can produce prejudices in individuals. In frustration-aggression theory, prejudice is a form of scapegoating that results from displaced aggression. For example, members of the dominant group may blame immigrants or minority groups when the economy is in decline. Authoritarian personality theory argues that the tendency to be prejudiced emerges out of overly strict child-rearing practices that result in people valuing obedience to authority and desiring to dominate others. There is some value in these theories, but neither provides a satisfactory explanation of prejudice. Frustration-aggression theory cannot explain why ethnic minority groups are chosen as targets of prejudice (Marger, 2012). And prejudice is often so widespread and pervasive that it could not be entirely due to the existence of persons who have authoritarian personalities.

Socialization theories of prejudice argue that prejudiced attitudes are part of the culture people internalize during socialization by parents, friends, and community members, whose messages are reinforced by educational experiences and stereotypes presented in media. Socialization theory can explain widespread prejudice that is learned and supported by the cultural environment. But it cannot explain how and why prejudice can change form and continue to exist when important agents of socialization such as major media outlets and the education system produce messages that oppose prejudice and bigotry.

Social Structure

Social structural theories, in contrast, argue that prejudice is a cultural mechanism emerging out of competition and conflict between groups, and that it can be an important factor enabling a single group to achieve and maintain dominance.

In the view of realistic group conflict theory (Campbell, 1965; Bobo, 1983; Sears et al., 2000), when the interests of groups coincide, intergroup attitudes will be relatively positive. However, if the interests of groups diverge, as is the case when groups compete for scarce resources such as land, jobs, or power, negative prejudicial attitudes will result.

In his now classic "sense of group position" theory, Blumer (1958) argued that prejudice flows from people's perceptions of the position of their group relative to other groups. Actual competition for scarce resources is not essential. Prejudice by a dominant group is the result of (1) a sense that they are superior to members of the minority group, (2) a feeling that minority members are different and alien, (3) a sense that dominant group members have a proprietary claim to privilege, power, and prestige, and (4) a fear and suspicion that members of the minority have designs on dominant group benefits.

Social structural theories of prejudice predict that as the positions of groups change in society, the content of prejudices will change as well, reflecting the new structural reality. Prejudice researchers have observed such a pattern in recent years. Though white prejudice against African Americans was strong throughout most of U.S. history, traditional forms of prejudice declined dramatically following the social changes brought about by the 1960s civil rights movement. Whites now are much less likely to believe that blacks are biologically inferior (but see Box 7.1), are less likely to support racial segregation, and are more likely to support the principle of racial equality than in the past (Schuman et al., 1997; Firebaugh and Davis, 1988).

Symbolic Racism

As traditional racial prejudice declined, new forms of prejudice emerged. This new complex of attitudes is termed **symbolic racism** (Kinder and Sears, 1981), modern racism (McConahay, 1986), or racial resentment (Kinder and Sanders, 1996) by various researchers. Unlike traditional

prejudice, which has decreased over time, symbolic racism increased modestly from the 1970s to 2008 (Valentino and Sears, 2005; Tuch and Hughes, 2011). It stereotypes African Americans as people who do not share the American work ethic, who would rather be on welfare than work, who would be as well off as whites if they would "try harder," and who have recently been "getting more than they deserve." According to group conflict and group position theories, symbolic racism is a reflection of whites' concern that further reductions in racial inequality will result in loss of the special status that whites in the United States have enjoyed over the years (Bobo, 1983; Bobo and Kluegel, 1993; Hughes, 1997). Evidence in support of this comes from research showing that even as whites' support for the *principle* of racial equality has increased, support for policies that would effectively reduce racial inequality has not changed appreciably (Schuman et al., 1997). Symbolic racism and similar attitudes are now the prime determinants of whites' racial policy attitudes (Tuch and Hughes, 2011; Kinder and Sanders, 1996; Tuch and Hughes, 1996; Hughes, 1997).

Discrimination

We have said that prejudice is an attitude or a state of mind. **Discrimination** is action. Discrimination is a process in which members of one or more groups or categories in society are denied the privileges, prestige, power, legal rights, equal protection of the law, and other societal benefits that are available to members of other groups. Discrimination is a form of racism when those discriminated against are a racial minority. As traditional prejudice toward blacks has shifted to symbolic racism, so has discrimination changed in its nature. Since the end of World War II in 1945, whites have shifted from more blatant forms of discrimination to more subtle forms (Kinder and Sanders, 1996; Sears, Sidanius, and Bobo, 2000; Quillian, 2006). In the 1960s, the U.S. Congress passed

Teasing Out Prejudiced Beliefs

In 1957, white people in Little Rock, Arkansas, had to be restrained by soldiers to keep them from attacking the first nine black children to attend a white high school in accordance with the Supreme Court's desegregation ruling. Two years before that, Emmett Till, a 14-year-old African American boy, was murdered—beaten, shot, and thrown into a river in Mississippi—by white men who were angry that he had whistled at a white woman.

We have come a long way in only 55 years. African American students are as likely as white students to finish high school and go on to college—often at integrated schools—and close to a fifth of all blacks over the age of 25 have a college degree (see Figure 7.3). Most whites now agree with the principles of racial equality, and only 1 in 10 whites admits to disapproving of interracial marriage (Smith et al., 2010).

Yet prejudice and discrimination continue; African Americans are still underrepresented in the professional workforce and as graduates of colleges and universities. And some of what we might call "old-fashioned racism" still exists. Over the years survey researchers have asked respondents if they thought blacks were as intelligent as white people, or whether the black–white gap in income and high-status jobs was due to a lack of in-born learning ability among blacks. Since the 1940s the percentage of whites reporting a belief in black intellectual deficiency has dropped from more than half (and more than 70 percent in the South) to 13 percent in 1994 (17 percent in the South) (Schuman et al., 1997). But when whites were given a chance to separately *rate* the intelligence of blacks and of whites, an interesting finding emerges: 46.6 percent of whites rate their own group as more intelligent than blacks (analysis by authors using data in Smith et al., 2010).

What accounts for these findings? First, it is possible that when whites respond to surveys they engage in what Erving Goffman called "impression management" (see Chapter 3)—when asked whether whites are more intelligent than blacks, they respond no because they think it is the socially acceptable answer. A more accurate reflection of their beliefs—that whites are more intelligent—emerges when they are asked the two questions separately. This interpretation of the findings indicates that whites are more prejudiced than many thought, but it also reflects significant cultural change; 55 years ago, the whites jeering at the nine young blacks entering Central High School didn't care whether the whole world knew that they believed in black inferiority. We now live in a culture in which it is socially unacceptable to voice such opinions (Schuman et al., 1997).

Second, whites may not realize that they are prejudiced. They may actually believe, when asked specifically, that whites are not more intelligent than blacks. Asking the two questions separately may bring unconsciously held prejudices to light.

Whatever the explanation, it is important to remember that a simple shift in questioning procedure and wording can result in a very different pattern of response.

Questions for Discussion

1. Do you think people who respond to surveys on racial attitudes tell the truth? What motivates people to respond the way they do?

2. Do people in minority groups have prejudices about whites? If so, what are they? How would you structure survey items to answer this question?

---

civil rights legislation outlawing discrimination. But passing such laws has not translated into equal treatment for all.

Prejudice does not necessarily coincide with discrimination—a one-to-one relationship does not inevitably hold between attitudes and overt actions. While we expect prejudiced people to discriminate, and unprejudiced persons not to, sociologist Robert K. Merton (1968) pointed out that two other outcomes are possible and exist because of different social pressures: unprejudiced people who discriminate and prejudiced people who do not.

A recent study looks at this issue somewhat differently. Kerry Kawakami and colleagues (2009) showed that although white research subjects predict that they would be upset if they observed an overtly racist act on the part of someone else, when whites are actually confronted by such an act they report little emotional distress. In addition, even though subjects said they would be very unlikely to choose to work with a person who acted in a racist manner, in fact, subjects were just as likely to choose to work with a person who had made racist comments as they were to choose a person who had made no such comments. This study suggests that many people who believe themselves to be nonracist may react with indifference to racism, thus allowing racism and discrimination to persist. Even when people are made aware of their prejudices, discrimination can continue. A study of diversity training programs for managers in corporations showed that such programs fail to eliminate bias; increases in the number of minorities in management positions occur only when senior managers are held accountable for hiring more minorities (Kalev, Dobbin, and Kelly, 2006).

Merton points out that organizational policy and climate and the law strongly influence people to behave in ways that are inconsistent with their attitudes. Discrimination, therefore, is not entirely dependent on individual attitudes. In the United States individual attitudes have been liberalized over the past few decades, but social pressures and individual tendencies remain that perpetuate discrimination. A structural process through which this can have a major impact is institutional discrimination.

Institutional Discrimination

The institutions of society may function in such a way that they produce unequal outcomes for different groups. This is called **institutional discrimination,** or **institutional racism** if the disadvantaged group is a racial minority. Businesses, schools, hospitals, and other key institutions need not be staffed by prejudiced individuals in order for discrimination to occur (Carmichael and Hamilton, 1967). For example, employers often specify the qualifications candidates must have to be considered for particular jobs. Usually, the qualifications have to do with prior job-related experience and some measure of formal education. The standards

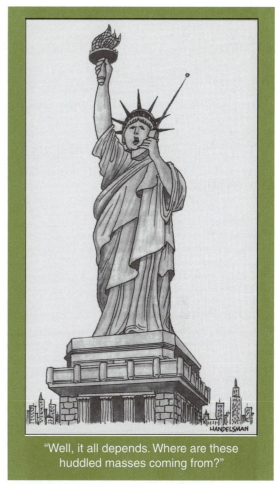

"Well, it all depends. Where are these huddled masses coming from?"

appear nondiscriminatory because they apply to all individuals regardless of race, creed, or color. But the result of applying such "color-blind" employment standards often is to bar entry into the work world for particular racial or ethnic groups whose members have lacked opportunities for education and work experience.

African Americans have been particularly victimized by institutional racism. Research on résumés and callbacks on job applications (presented in Box 5.3) and on other steps to employment provide evidence: At each point along the

7.2 Social Inequalities

Affirmative Action Affirmed by High Court

Davin Fischer sensed he had been given a special break when Georgetown University admitted him two years ago. His high school record was strong but perhaps not as stellar as those of some of his future classmates, a fact that sat uneasily with him in the months before he came to campus. (Argetsinger, 2003:A6)

Why was Fischer admitted if his grades weren't as good as some of the other applicants? Because colleges and universities do not consider only grades and test scores in making admissions decisions. Fischer's admission could have been affected by any of a number of factors colleges and universities review—his athletic skills, his musical ability, his hometown, his admissions essay, or his parents' race, ethnicity, or income. The factor that gave Davin Fischer an edge over students with better high school grades and standardized test scores was that his father had graduated from Georgetown.

"Legacy" applicants, as they are called, have a significantly higher probability of gaining admission at many schools. Children of graduates are about twice as likely as the average applicant to be admitted to Georgetown and to the University of Virginia and three times more likely to get into Harvard (Argetsinger, 2003). If you had better grades than Davin Fischer and didn't get into Georgetown, would you feel cheated?

Although it receives less weight than legacy in the admissions procedures at many schools, the factor that gets the most press attention and is the most controversial is race. Should colleges and universities be allowed to consider the race of applicants in making admissions decisions? If schools give preference to African American or other minority students simply because they are not white, are white students being discriminated against? Those are the affirmative action questions U.S. Supreme Court justices were asked to consider in 2003, when suits against the

University of Michigan law school and its undergraduate program were brought to the country's highest court.

Before we discuss the case, let's review the basics. What is "affirmative action"? Affirmative action is not a term for one specific action or policy; rather, it is a family of policies aimed at resolving racial, ethnic, and gender inequalities in the United States. The term stems from a speech made by President Lyndon Johnson in the 1960s in which he declared that it was not enough to remove barriers from minority groups; the nation also needed to take *affirmative action* to promote the inclusion of all races and ethnicities in society (Harper and Peskin, 2005).

The original affirmative actions planned by federal and state governments included four general categories. The first of these was opportunity enhancement, which included programs aimed at encouraging people of a diversity of backgrounds to apply for jobs or admission to schools. The second category included goals and timetables; federal contractors and

road toward building a satisfying career, African Americans must overcome greater obstacles than those encountered by whites (Ginther et al., 2011; Mervis, 2011; Wingfield, 2010; Pager and Quillian, 2005; Bertrand and Mullainathan, 2003). Moreover, the handicaps associated with poverty—an absence of skills, inadequate education, and low job seniority—tend to perpetuate the low-status position that produces them (Wilson, 2009, 1996, 1987).

In brief, equality of opportunity, even if realized in American life, does not necessarily produce equality of outcome. Consequently,

African Americans and many other minorities have concerned themselves not merely with removing the barriers to full opportunity but with achieving the fact of *equality of outcome*—parity in family income, housing, and the other necessities for keeping families strong and healthy. It has been this sentiment that has propelled proponents of affirmative action, still a controversial issue (see Box 7.2).

One mechanism by which institutional discrimination is maintained is **gatekeeping**—the decision-making process whereby people are admitted to offices and positions of privilege, recipients of federal aid were required to lay out their plans for including people from underrepresented categories, such as minorities and women. Third were plans for giving preferences to minorities in licenses and contracts, and lastly were quota and preferences programs for admissions and employment.

Do we need affirmative action? Why not just ban practices and policies that discriminate against job and school applicants on the basis of race, ethnicity, or gender? Physician Jordan Cohen sums it up well in a discussion about the importance of affirmative action for medical school admissions:

> Although the civil rights movement of the late 1960s and early 1970s succeeded in outlawing the overt barriers that restricted minority enrollment in medical schools, the legacy of centuries of racial discrimination persisted. High rates of poverty, lack of access to educational opportunities, lower educational achievement among family members, as well as other factors conspired to limit significantly the number of underrepresented minority students who chose to apply to medical school. (2003:1145)

Until students from all racial and ethnic backgrounds have an "equivalent range" of academic credentials, he says, it will not be possible to create medical school classes that reflect society's diversity without considering race and ethnicity in admissions decisions.

Let's get back to the Supreme Court case. Although the justices voted against the use of a racial point system by the University of Michigan's undergraduate program and thus confirmed the illegality of quota programs, they preserved the concept of affirmative action and upheld the consideration of race in admissions. Justice Sandra Day O'Connor wrote the majority opinion, stating, "In order to cultivate a set of leaders with legitimacy in the eyes of the citizenry, it is necessary that the path to leadership be visibly open to talented and qualified individuals of every race and ethnicity" (Greenhouse, 2003). As in the last affirmative action case heard by the Supreme Court, in 1978, it was ruled that race can be one of a number of important factors—but not the only determining factor—in admissions policies.

Despite the Supreme Court's ruling, in 2006, Michigan citizens voted to ban affirmative action, and

in 2007 the University of Michigan announced that it would comply with the ban and stop considering both race and gender in admissions decisions (CBS News, 2007). As an alternative, the university indicated that it would use geographic diversity, parents' education, and type of school as admissions factors to achieve diversity in its student population.

Remember Davin Fischer, whose chances of being admitted were doubled by virtue of being the offspring of a Georgetown alum? Being black would have improved his chances only by seven percentage points.

Questions for Discussion

1. Visit the admissions office of your college or university and ask for information on the factors that are used to make admissions decisions. What are the factors? How important is each factor in admissions decisions? What goals do these policies serve at your institution? Are the policies fair and effective? Explain.

2. Why might a medical school want its student body to "reflect society's diversity"?

prestige, and power within a society. Generally, gatekeepers are professionals with experience and credentials in the fields they monitor—for example, individuals in personnel, school admission, and counseling offices. Although in theory gatekeepers assess candidates on the basis of merit, skills, and talents—and not in terms of race, ethnicity, class, family, or religion—their decisions have been biased (Pettigrew and Martin, 1987; Chase and Bell, 1990; Farkas et al., 1990; Karen, 1990).

For example, just having a "black" name is a disadvantage in applying for a job. A study in which 5,000 fake résumés were sent to 1,300 employers found that stereotypically black names (e.g., Tanisha, Jamal, Lakisa) on résumés averaged 1 callback for every 15 résumés sent out, while stereotypically white names (e.g., Brad, Emily, Kristen) averaged 1 callback for every 10 résumés sent out (Bertrand and Mullainathan, 2003). A white name was the equivalent of an additional eight years of job experience in terms of producing callbacks.

Another aspect of institutional discrimination is that merit, skills, and talent are relative matters. Which group's *values* will be used for judging who is "capable," "bright," "conscientious," and "resourceful"? Historically, gatekeepers have been white and male, and they have selected candidates who have resembled themselves in family patterns, dress, hairstyle, behavior, and the ownership and use of property.

Another mechanism of institutional discrimination is called **environmental racism**—the practice of locating incinerators and other types of hazardous waste facilities in or next to minority communities (Grant et al., 2010; Mohai and Saha, 2007). One researcher found that 21 of Houston's 25 legally operating incinerators, mini-incinerators, and landfills were in predominantly African American neighborhoods (Horowitz, 1994).

Patterns of Intergroup Relations: Assimilation and Pluralism

In multiethnic societies, ethnic groups may either lose their distinctiveness through a process of assimilation or retain their identity and integrity through pluralism. In this section we will examine these two patterns of intergroup relations.

Assimilation

In the early 1800s two major ethnic groups in the United States were the Germans and the Dutch. Today neither group is important in ethnic group dynamics in this country. Why? These groups and others from northwestern Europe assimilated, along with the British, into what we now think of as the white population. **Assimilation** refers to those processes whereby groups with distinctive identities become culturally and socially fused. Within the United States two views toward assimilation have dominated. One—the "melting pot" tradition—has seen assimilation as a process whereby peoples and cultures would produce a new people and a new civilization. The

other—the Anglo-conformity view—has viewed American culture as an essentially finished product on the Anglo-Saxon pattern and has insisted that immigrants promptly give up their cultural traits for those of the dominant American group. Governments in the United States have often favored the latter view through policies that provide English-only government services and education that promotes dominant group values and language (Marger, 2012).

Assimilation is a complex process in which cultural changes precede widespread structural change. Members of different groups within a single society must share some cultural elements in order to communicate and carry on ordinary interaction. When cultural elements of one group change in the direction of another group, we call this cultural assimilation, or **acculturation.**

Most cultural assimilation involves cultural traits of the dominant group being taken on by less powerful groups. For example, Africans brought to the American South as slaves learned the language and religion of the slave masters. But acculturation is to some degree always a two-way street. American popular music forms such as blues, jazz, gospel, and rock have strong roots in African music. American English reflects a German influence through words such as "gesundheit" and "kindergarten" and a Dutch influence through sailing terms such as "skipper" and in the use of "cookie" instead of the English "biscuit."

Cultural assimilation makes more extensive social relations among groups possible. When members of different ethnic groups participate with one another in the major institutional structures of society, this is structural assimilation, commonly referred to as **integration.** Typically, structural assimilation occurs first in secondary groups—at work and at school, for example. Research shows that integration is an important factor in promoting cooperation and altruism across ethnic group boundaries (Alexander and Christia, 2011).

Only after there has been a considerable breakdown of ethnic group barriers does structural assimilation routinely occur at the primary group level—clubs, cliques, neighborhood relations, and close friendships. According to Milton Gordon's (1964) theory, once structural assimilation occurs, routine marriage across ethnic group boundaries (marital assimilation) and the sharing of a single ethnic identity (identificational assimilation) are natural consequences. Eventually, social participation, cultural sharing, and intermarriage may occur to such an extent that it is impossible to distinguish the ethnic groups that were formerly distinct within a society. This is the final stage of assimilation, **amalgamation.**

Pluralism

Recent immigrants to the United States appear to be largely assimilating into American society in terms of socioeconomic status, residence, language, and intermarriage (Waters and Jimenez, 2005). However, ethnic groups do not always assimilate into a dominant society or into one another. In fact, racial and ethnic groups have the *potential* for carving out their own independent nation from the existing state. Political separatism may offer racial and ethnic groups a solution that is not available to other disadvantaged categories. Examples abound in the contemporary world of separatist movements, including the French Canadians in Canada, the Palestinians in Israel, the Basques in Spain, the various Muslim and Christian factions in Lebanon, and the Sikhs in India's Punjab.

However, this is not the path taken by mainstream ethnic movements in the United States. American Jews, African Americans, Chinese Americans, and numerous other groups have assimilated in some important ways but also have retained their identities and significant degrees of distinctiveness for many years. This is an example of **pluralism,** a situation in which diverse groups coexist and boundaries between them are maintained.

Pluralism may be perpetuated because minority groups do not wish to be assimilated, valuing their separate identities and customs. Such groups generally favor what Marger (2009) called *equalitarian pluralism;* cultural identity and group boundaries are maintained, but ethnic group members participate freely and equally in political and economic institutions. Equalitarian pluralism is the goal of many American minority groups that are now culturally distinctive but economically and politically disadvantaged. Switzerland provides a good example of cultural pluralism. It comprises several ethnic groups, including French, Germans, and Italians, each maintaining its own language, and the government operates with several official languages.

Pluralism also may be promoted by dominant groups that wish to maintain their power and privilege by controlling the participation of minority groups in society. This is *inequalitarian pluralism;* ethnic group distinctiveness is maintained, but economic and political participation of minority groups is severely limited by the dominant group. The caste system of racial segregation in the southern United States before the 1960s is a good example of inequalitarian pluralism.

Multicultural programs, which promote pluralism, have proliferated on campuses across the United States in response to the increasing diversity of the college student population.

Government policy may heavily influence the course that pluralism takes. Equalitarian pluralism is fostered and encouraged through the legal protection of minorities. For example, Canada's bilingual policies, in allowing the Province of Quebec to declare French the official language in government, commerce, and education, help to prevent total assimilation of French Canadians into a Canada that is dominated by the English-speaking population.

Because minority groups invariably disfavor inequalitarian pluralism, government policy is generally required to maintain it. This may be done by preventing minority populations from contact with the majority. The U.S. government's Indian Removal Act of 1830, which resulted in the forcible removal of virtually all Native Americans from the southeastern states to land west of the Mississippi in the 1830s and 1840s, serves as an example. Governments also may promote the continued subjugation of minority groups through "internal colonialism." For example, before the fall of white power in South Africa, whites maintained *apartheid* arrangements that allowed for the political and economic subjugation of blacks and other non-Europeans. Inequalitarian policies are at their most extreme when they entail the expulsion or extermination of minorities. History abounds with examples of **genocide**—the deliberate and systematic extermination of a racial or ethnic group.

Racial and Ethnic Groups in the United States

We have defined races and ethnic groups and considered the nature of minority groups and the potential for conflict and separation. We have discussed prejudice, discrimination, and institutional discrimination. Here we will take a closer look at the circumstances of a number of groups within the United States to see the effects of racial and ethnic stratification.

The United States is in transition from a predominately white society rooted in western European culture to a global society composed of diverse racial and ethnic groups. While 64 percent of the U.S. population was non-Hispanic white in 2010 (Humes, Jones, and Ramirez, 2011), by the year 2050, according to Census Bureau projections, today's minorities will compose about half of the U.S. population (Figure 7.1). In Hawaii, California, New Mexico, Texas, and the District of Columbia the minority population already exceeds the white population (Humes, Jones, and Ramirez, 2011), and by 2030 fewer than half of the under-20 population of the United States will be non-Hispanic whites (Jacobsen et al., 2011). The Asian population is currently the fastest-growing in the United States (Humes, Jones, and Ramirez, 2011).

A country of immigrants since its founding, the United States is still a country of immigrants. At least a third of recent U.S. population growth is due to immigration, with about a million foreigners coming to the United States every year (Walters and Trevelyan, 2011), and more than 10 percent of the current population is foreign born. The United States attracts immigrants from all over the world, but various periods of history have been marked by influxes from particular areas (Arnold, 2011), including northern European immigrants in the mid-1800s, southern and eastern Europeans in the early 1900s, Latin American immigrants and Asians beginning in the 1960s, and now a shift to 40 percent of recent immigrants being Asian and a quarter Central American (Walters and Trevelyan, 2011). About 20 percent of the U.S. population report speaking a language other than English at home (Shin and Kominski, 2010).

In this section we will look more closely at the circumstances of Hispanics/Latinos, African Americans, Native Americans, Asian Americans, and white ethnics in the United States.

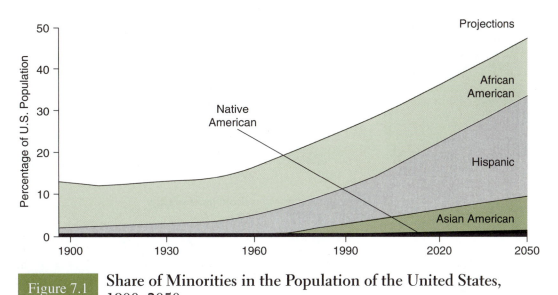

Figure 7.1   **Share of Minorities in the Population of the United States, 1900–2050**

The figures for future years represent population projections by the U.S. Census Bureau.

Sources: O'Hare, William P. 1992. America's minorities—the demographics of diversity. *Population Bulletin* 47 (4): 9 (Figure 1). Data added from U.S. Census Bureau, 2004.

Hispanics/Latinos

Those who were born in or whose ancestors were born in Latin American nations or in Spain became the largest ethnic minority group in the United States in 2002; about one-sixth of the U.S. population is now Hispanic or, as some prefer, Latino (Humes, Jones, and Ramirez, 2011).

How to refer to this group is controversial. Some claim that the term *Hispanic* is offensive because it was applied by a dominant group to a minority group (Granados, 2000). People descended from Spanish-speaking ancestors may prefer to identify themselves as "Latino" (or "Latina," for females). But a poll of 1,200 Hispanic/Latino registered voters showed that 65 percent preferred the term *Hispanic* (Granados, 2000). The Census Bureau is now using the terms *Hispanic* and *Latino* interchangeably (Ramirez and de la Cruz, 2002), as we will in this section.

While there has been some blurring of differences among some Hispanic-origin groups, making many Hispanic Americans more conscious of themselves as a homogeneous group, the Census Bureau provides data on six distinct categories: Mexicans, Puerto Ricans, Cubans, Central Americans, South Americans, and other (see Figure 7.2).

The 50.5 million Hispanics living in the United States in 2010 represent a substantial increase from the 14.6 million recorded in 1980 and 22.4 million in 1990 (U.S. Census Bureau, 1996, 1999; Humes, Jones, and Ramirez, 2011).

Latinos now account for just over half of the foreign-born population in the United States, up from only 9 percent in 1960; Mexico alone accounts for nearly one-third of the foreign-born population (Grieco, 2010). The populations of foreign-born Hispanics are concentrated in just a few areas of the country, including Los Angeles,

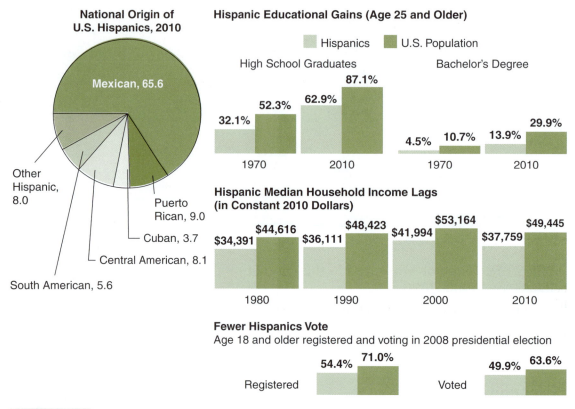

National Origin of U.S. Hispanics, 2010

Mexican, 65.6
Other Hispanic, 8.0
Puerto Rican, 9.0
Cuban, 3.7
Central American, 8.1
South American, 5.6

Hispanic Educational Gains (Age 25 and Older)

Hispanics   U.S. Population

High School Graduates

1970: 32.1% / 52.3%
2010: 62.9% / 87.1%

Bachelor's Degree

1970: 4.5% / 10.7%
2010: 13.9% / 29.9%

Hispanic Median Household Income Lags (in Constant 2010 Dollars)

1980: $34,391 / $44,616
1990: $36,111 / $48,423
2000: $41,994 / $53,164
2010: $37,759 / $49,445

Fewer Hispanics Vote
Age 18 and older registered and voting in 2008 presidential election

Registered: 54.4% / 71.0%
Voted: 49.9% / 63.6%

Figure 7.2

Hispanics/Latinos in the United States

Mexican Americans constitute by far the largest Hispanic group in the United States. Hispanics lag behind the general population in education, income, and voting behavior.

Sources: Hispanic origin data from U.S. Census Bureau, Current Population Survey, Annual Social and Economic Supplement, 2010 (available at http://www.census.gov/population/www/socdemo/hispanic/cps2010.html). Education data from U.S. Census Bureau, Current Population Survey, 2010 Annual Social and Economic Supplement (available at http://www.census.gov/population/www/socdemo/education/cps2010.html) Income data from DeNavas-Walt, Proctor, and Smith, 2011. Election data from U.S. Census Bureau, Current Population Survey, November 2008 (available at http://www.census.gov/hhes/www/socdemo/voting/publications/p20/2008/tables.html).

Chicago, New York, and Miami. But rapid Hispanic population growth has been recorded in rural areas in recent decades (Kandel et al., 2011), and suburbs also are increasingly diverse (Hall and Lee, 2010). About 42 percent of the Latino foreign-born population have become naturalized citizens, although the proportion is different for different groups; 60 percent of the Cuban-born and 24 percent of the Mexico-born

population are naturalized citizens (U.S. Census Bureau, 2011).

Education and Employment

As might be expected for recent immigrants in any country, Latinos lag behind the rest of the country in terms of education, employment, and income. Among Hispanics age 25 and older, only 14 percent had completed college in 2010, compared with 33 percent of non-Hispanic whites and 20 percent of African Americans (see Figures 7.2 and 7.3) (U.S. Census Bureau, 2011). Educational credentials vary greatly among ethnic groups, with 84 percent of the South America–origin population and only 57.4 percent of the Mexico-origin population having at least a high school education.

An assessment of the education gap between Hispanic and white Americans showed that having foreign-born parents or parents with lower education only partly explains the gap (Alon, Domina, and Tienda, 2010).

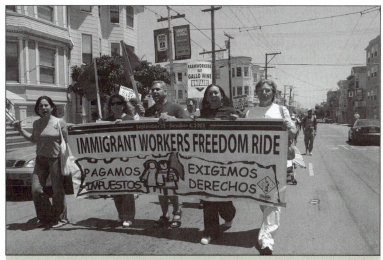

An important concern for many Hispanics in America is the set of laws and policies regarding immigration in the United States.

Although the percentage of Hispanics earning bachelor's degrees doubled between 1970 and 2000, the researchers found that college-educated Hispanic parents are less able than college-educated white parents to pass that education advantage on to their children. The education disadvantage extends to employment and income as well. The unemployment rate for Hispanics in 2010 was 13.2 percent (U.S. Census Bureau, 2011b), and 26.6 percent of Hispanic families were living in poverty, compared with a 9.9 percent rate of poverty for non-Hispanic whites (DeNavas-Walt, Proctor, and Smith, 2011).

Mexicans

With a population of 32 million, Mexican Americans make up two-thirds of the Hispanic population in the United States. Many of them trace their ancestry to the merging of the Native American population with Spanish settlers. Like African Americans and Native Americans, people of Mexican ancestry did not originally become a part of American society through

voluntary immigration. With the exception of the American Indians, they are the only American minority to enter the society through the conquest of their homeland. Though Mexican Americans have been in the United States longer than other Hispanic-origin groups, their median income ranks below and their unemployment rate above that of Cubans and Central and South Americans. Though they are now primarily an urban-based group, they also still are disproportionately found in agricultural occupations as seasonal or permanent workers.

Puerto Ricans

Although Puerto Ricans have lived in the continental United States for more than 100 years, the major emergence of Puerto Rican communities in the United States began after World War II when large numbers of people began migrating to escape unemployment in Puerto Rico. Puerto Rico is a Commonwealth of the United States (it was designated a U.S. territory in 1898), and its citizens migrate from the island to the "mainland" and back again fairly easily and inexpensively, a flow that probably contributes to the strong ethnic communities and low intermarriage rates among Puerto Ricans. Among the 4.4 million Puerto Ricans in the United States (9 percent of the Hispanic population), three-quarters of adults have graduated from high school and 17.5 percent have bachelor's degrees (U.S. Census Bureau, 2011b). Puerto Ricans have been victims of intense prejudice and discrimination and extreme occupational segregation (Bean and Tienda, 1987).

Cubans

In 1950, the Census Bureau counted only 34,000 Cubans; during the late 1950s and throughout the 1960s, the United States welcomed Cubans seeking asylum from the Castro regime, and the population now stands at 1.8 million (U.S. Census Bureau, 2011b). Cuban Americans have been the most socioeconomically successful of the Hispanic-origin groups. Early immigrants were political rather than economic refugees. Many professional, highly educated, and urban people were among the first immigrants who laid the foundation for a vibrant ethnic enclave economy, primarily in Miami (Portes, 1987; Portes and Jensen, 1989). More than four-fifths of the Cuban American population age 25 or over has at least a high school education, a higher proportion than is true for Mexican, Puerto Rican, and Central American Latinos, and 26.2 percent have a bachelor's degree or higher (U.S. Census Bureau, 2011b). Three-quarters of Cuban Americans live in the South, with a very large population in the Miami area (Ramirez and de la Cruz, 2002).

Central and South Americans

As recently as 1970, there were only a few hundred thousand people from Central and South America living in the United States (Bean and Tienda, 1987). By 2010 that number had risen to 7 million (U.S. Census Bureau, 2011b). The greatly increased immigration from Latin America in recent decades is one of the major factors contributing to the overall dramatic increase in the U.S. Hispanic population. The major increases have come primarily from Colombia, Ecuador, El Salvador, and the Dominican Republic. Other countries fairly well represented in the United States include Guatemala, Nicaragua, Peru, and Argentina (Bean and Tienda, 1987).

African Americans

In spite of serious obstacles caused by past and present racism and discrimination, the African American population in the United States has been remarkably successful. In 2010, African Americans composed 13 percent of the U.S. population (Rastogi et al., 2011). The South is home to 55 percent of the nation's blacks, and large concentrations of African Americans live in New York City, Los Angeles, Chicago, Philadelphia, Detroit, Houston, and other large U.S. cities.

In 2000 the poverty rate for African Americans reached its lowest point (22.5 percent) since poverty data have been collected in the United States, and since then it has increased to 27.4 percent (DeNavas-Walt, Proctor, and Smith, 2011; see Figure 7.3 for more on income). Similar proportions of whites and blacks are employed in sales and office support jobs, but black men and women are disproportionately represented in service jobs and as production and transport workers. African Americans have made significant advances in education in recent years. Similar percentages of blacks and whites finish high school and go on to college (McKinnon, 2003). But fewer blacks (20 percent) than whites (33 percent) finish college (U.S. Census Bureau, 2011) (see Figure 7.3). The unemployment rate was nearly twice as high for blacks as for whites during the recession in 2009. Although 76 percent of African American families do not live in poverty, the percentage that does still far exceeds the percentage of poor white families. The poverty associated with single-parent households also takes its toll: In 2009, 67 percent of black children lived in single-parent families (Kids Count, 2011).

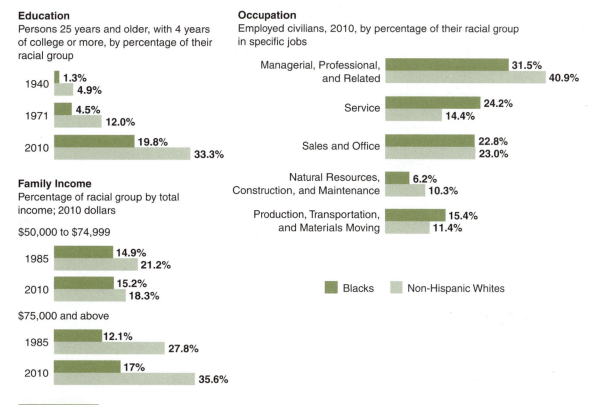

Education
Persons 25 years and older, with 4 years of college or more, by percentage of their racial group

- 1940: 1.3% / 4.9%
- 1971: 4.5% / 12.0%
- 2010: 19.8% / 33.3%

Family Income
Percentage of racial group by total income; 2010 dollars

$50,000 to $74,999
- 1985: 14.9% / 21.2%
- 2010: 15.2% / 18.3%

$75,000 and above
- 1985: 12.1% / 27.8%
- 2010: 17% / 35.6%

Occupation
Employed civilians, 2010, by percentage of their racial group in specific jobs

- Managerial, Professional, and Related: 31.5% / 40.9%
- Service: 24.2% / 14.4%
- Sales and Office: 22.8% / 23.0%
- Natural Resources, Construction, and Maintenance: 6.2% / 10.3%
- Production, Transportation, and Materials Moving: 15.4% / 11.4%

■ Blacks   ■ Non-Hispanic Whites

Figure 7.3 **African American Progress in the United States: A Mixed Message**
Although African Americans have made gains in American life, race problems endure. The United States has not become an integrated society despite the expansion of the African American middle class.

Sources: Education data from the U.S. Census Bureau, Current Population Survey, 2010 Annual Social and Economic Supplement (available at http://www.census.gov/population/www/socdemo/education/cps2010.html). Income data from DeNavas-Walt, Proctor, and Smith, 2011. Occupation data from the U.S. Bureau of Labor Statistics, Current Population Survey (as reported in the U.S. Census Bureau, 2011b).

Young African American males face particularly difficult problems. More than half of all black men living in inner cities do not finish college (Eckholm, 2006; Orfield et al., 2004). In 2004, among black men in their 20s, half of high school graduates and 72 percent of high school dropouts were jobless (i.e., unemployed or incarcerated); 21 percent of those who were not in college were in jail or prison (Eckholm, 2006). By their mid-30s, about 60 percent of black male high school dropouts had been in prison or jail. Research indicates that more black high school dropouts in their late 20s are in prison on any given day than are employed (Eckholm, 2006). The leading cause of death among African American males is homicide (accidents are second, and suicide is third [Anderson and Smith, 2005]). Although black suicide rates have been historically low compared to those for whites, the suicide rate for young black men has increased dramatically over the past 20 years, due in part to the concentrated disadvantage experienced by young black men in urban areas (Kubrin, Wadsworth, and DiPietro, 2006).

Slavery and Segregation

The subjugation of African Americans as slaves began in the 17th century and was well rooted in the British colonies by the time of the American Revolution, with 360,000 Africans part of the U.S. population in 1790 (Cahill, 2010). Slavery was carried on by the new American nation when it achieved independence, and democracy was extended only to the white male population. The Thirteenth Amendment to the Constitution, which outlawed slavery, was ratified following the end of the Civil War in 1865. But 1865 and 1866 also saw the passage of "black codes" discriminating against African Americans in every southern state, as well as the formation of the Ku Klux Klan and outbreaks of violence against blacks. The 1866 Civil Rights Act was passed by Congress to nullify the black codes, and during Reconstruction, African American males were granted the right to vote. Many freed slaves learned to read and write, and the first black senators and state legislators were elected. But by the 1890s, the situation for African Americans in the United States had deteriorated again. In most southern states blacks were barred from voting, and during the 1890s and early 1900s, lynching attained its most staggering proportions. Jim Crow laws mandating segregation were passed throughout the South. As recently as the early 1960s, blacks and whites used separate drinking fountains and restrooms, and children attended segregated schools.

The Civil Rights Movement

The stage was set for drastic change in the South when the Supreme Court ruled on May 17, 1954, that mandatory school segregation was unconstitutional. In the years that followed, the Supreme Court moved toward outlawing legalized segregation in all areas of American life. Simultaneously, the civil rights movement of the 1960s galvanized popular support for the enactment of new civil rights legislation, particularly the Civil Rights Acts of 1964, 1965, and 1968. As the United States entered the 1970s, resistance mounted among segments of the white community, particularly against affirmative action measures and against busing children to promote school integration, and many public schools today are segregated by virtue of the races and ethnicities of neighborhood residents. But the Supreme Court decision in 2003 to preserve the use of affirmative action programs at universities endorsed "the role of racial diversity on campus in achieving a more equal society" (Greenhouse, 2003) (see Box 7.2).

Race or Class?

In Chapter 6 we saw that social class was an important determinant of life chances. How important is class in explaining the continuing disadvantages faced by African Americans? Sociologist William Julius Wilson (1978, 1987; Wilson and Aponte, 1985) argued some years ago that race had become less important than social class because civil rights legislation and affirmative action programs have resulted in greater educational, income, and occupational differentiation. African Americans with good educations and job skills rapidly moved into the American middle class, while African Americans with limited educations and job skills became the victims of soaring joblessness and welfare dependency. In a recent reassessment of the research on poverty and unequal opportunity, Wilson pins much of the blame for the perpetuation of a large African American lower class on structural features of U.S. society:

From a historical perspective, it is hard to overstate the importance of racialist structural factors. Aside from the enduring effects of slavery, Jim Crow segregation, public school segregation, legalized discrimination, residential segregation, the FHA's redlining of black neighborhoods in the 1940s and '50s, the construction of public housing projects in poor black neighborhoods, employer discrimination, and other racial acts and processes, there is the impact of political, economic, and policy decisions that were at least partly influenced by race. (2009:152–3)

Wilson explains a variety of specific structural forces that have contributed to racial inequality, including transportation and highway policies that shifted jobs from the cities to the suburbs, mortgage policies that helped working- and middle-class families get out of the inner city but left poor black families isolated there, the construction of urban freeways and highways that disrupted many stable low-income black neighborhoods, a drastic reduction in federal aid to big cities, shifts in employment opportunities caused by the computer revolution and globalization, and a minimum wage so low that workers with full-time employment are unable to support families (Wilson, 2009).

Wilson also cites two major cultural contributions to the problems experienced by African Americans: the racist beliefs and prejudiced attitudes that persist in U.S. society and the cultural traits that emerge among poor blacks in the inner-city ghettos created by racial segregation and discrimination, including the behaviors, language patterns, clothing styles, manners, and traditions that set ghetto residents apart from other Americans (Wilson, 2009).

Research shows that whites vastly underestimate the costs of being black in American society (Vedantam, 2008), which may contribute to their willingness to ban affirmative action (see Box 7.2) and to fail to recognize institutional racism. White survey respondents are more than twice as likely as blacks to say that the position of African Americans has improved a great deal (Eibach and Keegan, 2006). Whites tend to compare the position of blacks today to their position in the past, while blacks measure progress based on an idealized future in which they suffer no discrimination. In addition, many

whites may hold what Wilson calls "laissez faire racism," the view that government action is not required to help minorities because minorities are responsible for their own economic predicament (Wilson, 2009).

Despite the apparent inability of many whites to see it, the gap between African Americans and whites remains substantial; class interacts with race and gender to produce the social cleavages that remain a continuing feature of American life (Wilson, 2009; Clayton, 1996; Massey and Denton, 1993; Colasanto and Williams, 1987).

American Indians and Alaskan Natives

In 2010, 2.9 million persons who reported to the Census Bureau that they were American Indian or Alaskan Native lived within the United States (Norris, Vines, and Hoeffel, 2012). Although there are some 500 tribes, ranging in size from under 100 to more than 250,000 tribal members (Ogunwole, 2006), American Indians and Alaskan Natives make up only 0.9 percent of the total U.S. population (Norris, Vines, and Hoeffel, 2012). Adding in the people who reported being American Indian or Alaskan Native in addition to other races or ethnicities brings the total to 5.2 million (1.7 percent).

American Indians and Alaskan Natives vary substantially in their history, lifestyles, kin systems, language, political arrangements, religion, economy, current circumstances, and identities. They are perhaps the most unusual American ethnic group, in that each tribe is a nation with special political rights dealing with another nation, the United States. In addition, for many tribes, their ethnicity is "rooted in particular plots of ground" (Page, 2003:2). As with Hispanics/Latinos, this group has many names, including Indian, indigenous peoples, First People, and Native American as well as all the tribal names. American Indians and Alaskan Natives are the most severely disadvantaged of

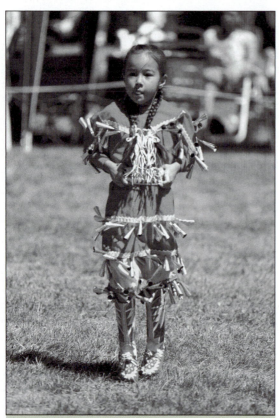

Although Native Americans have survived, increased in population, and maintained a cultural presence, they remain the most severely disadvantaged of any population within the United States on a number of dimensions.

any population within the United States (Snipp, 1989; Visgaitis, 1994).

Estimates of how many American Indians and Alaskan Natives were living in what is now the United States before the arrival of Europeans vary widely, ranging from about 1 million to 18 million and more (Page, 2003). Less open to debate is the effect of colonization. Recent genetic research provides evidence of a 50 percent decrease in the population of indigenous Americans about 500 years ago, just when Europeans were arriving with their foreign diseases (O'Fallon and Fehren-Schmitz, 2011). Most Indian nations originally were farming and fishing peoples with relatively stable communities. Initially, the European powers treated the native groups with respect, as nations that could be either enemies or allies. But as whites increasingly wanted land, tribal territories were appropriated and their inhabitants killed or driven inland. By the beginning of the 20th century, the U.S. population of Indians had dropped to 250,000—a 75–95 percent population reduction, depending on what estimate of pre-European-contact population is used (Page, 2003). Entire tribes have vanished through massacres by whites, disease, destruction of their economic base, or absorption by other groups, and some linguists predict that as few as 30 American Indian languages will be spoken by 2050. Just over 5 percent of people living in American Indian or Alaskan Native areas (reservations, trust lands, and the like) report that they speak a Native American language at home (Siebens and Julian, 2011).

The Removal Act of 1830 provided for the relocation of all eastern tribes to lands west of the Mississippi River. This "Trail of Tears" is widely regarded as one of the most dishonorable chapters in U.S. history. At least 70,000 people were removed; more than 20,000 died en route. West of the Mississippi, the tragedies of defeat and expropriation were repeated. When native groups resisted, they were systematically slaughtered (Josephy, 1991).

Inconsistencies and vacillations in U.S. government policy are to blame for the plight of American Indians and Alaskan Natives. Today about one-third live on reservations (Ogunwole, 2006), which cover 52.4 million acres in 27 states. Forty-one percent of those on reservations live below the poverty level; almost 70 percent of Navajos, the largest nation, are still without electricity. Overall, unemployment among American Indians and Alaskan Natives is high—49 percent in 2003 (U.S. Department of the Interior, 2003). Life expectancy in some tribes is 45 years. Other problems include alcoholism, suicide, obesity, adult-onset diabetes, and other health problems. Tribes across the United States also are grappling with some of the nation's worst pollution problems—uranium tailings, land and water contamination, chemical lagoons, and illegal dumps (Satchell, 1993).

Despite the myriad problems faced by Native Americans, they have both survived and increased in population since the low of 100 years ago. The three-quarters of Indian people who live off reservations live primarily in cities; the largest Indian populations are in New York City, Los Angeles, Phoenix, Oklahoma City, and Anchorage (Norris, Vines, and Hoeffel, 2012). Native American crafts are much sought after, and American Indian religious practices have been adopted by whites as part of "New Age" spiritualism. Powwows are a popular form of entertainment for Indians and non-Indians alike, Native American cultural artifacts and sacred lands have won federal protection, and Indian novelists are nationally recognized. As Page puts it, "An Indian presence, and one that is set forth by the Indians themselves, is now to be felt in the overall culture of America to an extent unseen before" (2003:406).

Asian Americans

There is a great diversity of Asian Americans in the United States, including Chinese, Filipinos, Asian Indians, Koreans, Vietnamese, Japanese, Laotians, Cambodians, Thais, Hmong, and Pakistanis (Reeves and Bennett, 2003). All told, 14.7 million persons of Asian origins live in the United States, and they are currently the fastest-growing group (Humes, Jones, and Ramirez, 2011). More than half of all Asian Americans live in California, New York, and Hawaii (Barnes and Bennett, 2002). Asian Americans are twice as likely as non-Hispanic whites to live in central cities, and the populations of some cities in California are between a quarter and a half Asian American (Barnes and Bennett, 2002).

Asian Americans enjoy the highest median family income of the nation's ethnic groups: $64,308 in 2010 (DeNavas-Walt, Proctor, and Smith, 2011). They are known for their educational and occupational successes; of those 25 years or older, half have a bachelor's degree or higher, and about 64 percent of 18- to 24-year-old Asian Americans are in college or graduate school (Jacobsen and Mather, 2010). (See Box 7.3 for more on the "model minority.") But Asian American leaders also point out that Asian American groups have problems such as crime, high suicide rates, mental disorders, and disintegrating families, especially among poor refugees and immigrants who have difficulty coping with a strange, new society (Lee, 1990).

Although many Asian American youths enjoy remarkable academic success, on the job Asian American workers face discrimination and can be the victims of racially motivated harassment and violence (Dugger, 1992; Mura, 1992). By the same token, Asian Americans find that they soon "top out," reaching positions beyond which their employers fail to promote them.

Chinese

During the early days of the gold rush, the Chinese were welcomed as a source of cheap labor, but when the speculative gold bubble burst, whites faced competition with Chinese workers, and attitudes changed. California led the nation in the passage of anti-Chinese laws, many of which remained in effect until the 1950s; for instance, the California state constitution provided that corporations could neither directly nor indirectly employ Chinese, and it empowered cities and towns to remove Chinese from within city limits.

The Chinatowns of New York City, San Francisco, and a few other large cities expanded as a result of sharp increases in immigration from Hong Kong and Taiwan made possible by the passage of immigration legislation in 1965 that did away with the old quota system, under which only 105 Chinese were allowed entry

The internment of 120,000 Japanese during World War II was based more on racism than on national security: None of the nation's other "enemies in residence" (German and Italian Americans) were subjected to internment, and not one Japanese American was ever convicted of spying.

each year. Above the gaudy storefronts of the nation's Chinatowns, Chinese families are jammed into tiny apartments. More than 71 percent of Chinese in the United States were born overseas (Reeves and Bennett, 2004).

Japanese

The Japanese also have been victims of prejudice and discrimination. On two occasions the government launched an effort to exclude them from American life. In 1907, President Theodore Roosevelt reached an agreement with Japan to limit the immigration of Japanese to the United States. Later, during World War II, the government placed some 120,000 Japanese (two-thirds of whom were U.S. citizens) in 10 internment camps.

A large number of the original immigrants made a place for themselves in California's economy through farming. Wives and families were allowed to join the Japanese men already in the United States; by 1940 nearly two-thirds of Japanese Americans were native born (Marger, 2012). The income of Japanese Americans is higher than that of any other Asian American group (Reeves and Bennett, 2004). Box 7.3 discusses some of the reasons for the economic success of this and other ethnic groups.

Other Asian Groups

Asian Americans are a varied group, with considerable contrasts and diversity. In 1970 the largest proportion of Asian Americans comprised Chinese and Japanese, but they now represent about a third of the total Asian American population. While the Chinese are still the largest component, there are nearly as many Filipinos. The number of Koreans and Asian

Indians in the United States is increasing steadily. The Japanese component of America's Asian population is becoming smaller because of low immigration and birth rates (Marger, 2012).

Some of these many groups have achieved reasonable success in U.S. society: Chinese, Filipino, Japanese, and Asian Indian Americans all have median family incomes higher than the median for the United States as a whole. However, Korean, Vietnamese, Cambodian, Hmong, and Laotian Americans have family incomes lower than the U.S. median (Marger, 2012). The earnings of Laotians, Cambodians, and Vietnamese who came from rural areas and who possess few marketable skills are particularly low (Dunn, 1994).

White Ethnics

Most of the original white settlers of what became the United States were British. Although there were large numbers of people of other nationalities, particularly Germans and Dutch, the British dominated the society with their language, their Protestant religion, and their legal system. Immigration, mostly from northwestern European countries, continued throughout the 19th century, bringing considerable numbers of Irish, Scandinavians, and Germans. But the largest influx came between 1885 and 1920 when about 25 million immigrants entered the United States. Many of these largely Catholic and Jewish immigrants, who are the ancestors of those we now speak of as "white ethnics," came not from northwestern Europe as earlier immigrants had but from eastern and southern European countries such as Italy, Greece, Poland, Russia, and Serbia. Differing from the English-speaking Protestant population in culture, language, and religion, these immigrants appeared alien to most Americans and were considered by some to be "not white." Their apparent challenge to the cultural dominance of the old Protestant middle class stimulated the

growth of prejudicial nativist sentiments that fueled a social and political backlash, resulting in significant discrimination, particularly against the Irish and Italians.

In spite of these problems and the associated prejudice and discrimination, the ethnic groups established in the United States as a result of immigration from the 1880s to the 1920s are now largely integrated into U.S. society and have generally prospered. None are currently considered to be anything but white. The typical pattern for these groups was that the first generation would gain a solid foothold in the working class, the second generation would go to work early in life to help support their families, and the third and subsequent generations would take advantage of educational opportunities to move into higher-status occupations (Marger, 2012; Greeley, 1977; Yans-McLaughlin, 1982). Jewish mobility was an exception to this pattern, with very large numbers entering the middle class in the second generation (see Box 7.3). The success of these groups has been a consequence of much structural assimilation; marital assimilation also has occurred (Lieberson and Waters, 1988), as Gordon (1964) predicted.

The success of these immigrant groups, great as it has been, is not complete. Though they have achieved much in state and local politics, U.S. national political leadership, including the Congress and the executive branch, is heavily dominated by white Protestant males of northwestern European heritage (Marger, 2012). The same is true of the largest corporations.

Some sociologists, such as Greeley (1974), argue that the degree of overall assimilation of white ethnic groups has been overestimated and that many Americans still identify themselves as Jews, Poles, Irish, and Italians and have distinctive attitudes, behaviors, and political interests. Research by Alba (1990) and Lieberson and Waters (1993) confirmed that most white Americans know their ethnic ancestry, but it also showed that white ethnicity is neither deep

Model Minorities—Does Class or Do Values Spell Success?

Why do some minorities suffer from poverty, unemployment, and discrimination while others do not? The nation's media have heralded Asian Americans as "the model minority" and "a superminority." Among white ethnic groups, Jewish immigrants and American-born Jews have long been recognized for their quick rise in U.S. society. And while Hispanic Americans as a whole are socio-economically disadvantaged, Cubans in particular have had quite rapid economic success. What accounts for the successes of these model minorities? Is it their values, or is it their class background?

One explanation for successful ethnic groups is that their values contribute to their upward mobility. This argument contends that thrift, strong family ties, and hard work are the keys to Asian American success and that their emphasis on education and excellence places them at an advantage in U.S. society. For example, a much higher proportion of Asian American adults than of whites have completed college. Asian American students are more likely than other students to enroll in college preparatory programs; they take more math and science courses and also spend more time on homework than other students (Zigli, 1984; Butterfield, 1986; O'Hare and Felt, 1991).

The "values" explanation for Jewish success is similar. Jews have encouraged independence and achievement more than other white ethnic groups, and their emphasis on education extends back for centuries (Marger, 2012). More than half of all Jewish adults have a college degree, compared with 21 percent of U.S. adults in general (Goldstein, 1992). As a result Jewish males are concentrated far more in the professional occupations (39 percent of Jewish males versus 16 percent of all white males) and far less in the working class (20 percent versus 52 percent of all U.S. white males).

But there's another explanation for the success of ethnic groups in the United States, and this explanation takes us back to the immigrants' roots, to their countries of origin. Sociologist Stephen Steinberg (1989) argued that Jewish immigrants had a significant advantage over other immigrants when they first came to the United States. Italians and other groups of European immigrants were primarily of peasant stock; Jews were frequently urban merchants or manufacturers, and they arrived in the United States at a time when its industrial economy was expanding rapidly and their skills could be put to immediate (and remunerative) use. In

nor stable. It tends to be what Gans (1979) called "symbolic ethnicity." This is an ethnicity that contributes to individual identity and family relationships but does not create or sustain strong ethnic group ties. Alba (1990) found that, among whites, the most common ethnic experiences are private and innocuous: eating ethnic foods, discussing one's ethnic background with others, feeling curious about others' ethnic experiences, and attending ethnic festivals.

Why has white ethnicity become symbolic? As Mary Waters (1990) pointed out, ethnicity does not have much effect on the everyday life of white Americans. It does not affect where they can live, what jobs they can get, who their friends are, whether they will be discriminated against, or, for the most part, whom they will marry. For these reasons, individual white ethnicities are increasingly a matter of choice that some Americans make, Waters maintained, because symbolic ethnicity provides individual identity and communalistic feelings with none of the costs that real ethnic affiliations require.

Sociological Perspectives on Inequalities of Race and Ethnicity

Functionalist, conflict, and interactionist theorists have different explanations for racial and ethnic stratification. In this section we will consider the contributions of each of these three major sociological perspectives to our understanding of the inequalities of race and ethnicity.

other words, class, not values, was the determining factor.

Likewise, some Asian immigrant groups have included a high proportion of doctors and engineers and others with advanced education, and their success in the United States reflects their upper-class, professional backgrounds in their home countries. Much of the potential for success was brought with these immigrants when they entered the United States. The income of lower-class Asian immigrants who come from rural areas and who possess few marketable skills is quite low (Dunn, 1994; Marger, 2012). Much of the success of Asians also may be due to other structural factors, such as the development of ethnic enclave economies that formed as a result of discrimination (Hirschman and Wong, 1986; Bonacich and Modell, 1980).

The experiences of Cuban immigrants also support the class explanation for the success of ethnic groups in the United States. While other Hispanic groups came to the United States in hopes of economic betterment, many Cuban immigrants in the early 1960s were middle-, upper-middle-, and upper-class citizens. These advantaged immigrants used their material, educational, and social resources (networks and relationships from pre-Castro Cuba) to create an ethnic enclave economy that benefited them and subsequent Cuban immigrants (Portes and Bach, 1985; Marger, 2012). Without a doubt strong family values and a willingness to sacrifice and work hard were critical factors in the success of Cuban Americans. However, the material and social advantages they brought with them assured success for a substantial number of Cuban Americans in considerably less than one generation.

Jewish, Asian, and Cuban Americans are good models of how some ethnic groups in the United States have achieved success. What their stories tell us, however, may be less about the importance of values, beliefs, and good habits, and more about the strong influence of material and social advantages in the success of immigrants in a new land.

Questions for Discussion

1. Pundits, radio talk show hosts, and other social commentators sometimes argue that disadvantaged minority groups in the United States such as Hispanics and African Americans would not be disadvantaged if they followed the examples set by "model minorities." How reasonable is this advice?

2. In your experience as a student, have you observed variability in academic success across various ethnic categories in either high school or college? If so, what factors do you think account for these differences? Do you think minority status or ethnicity is responsible for students' academic performances in the schools you have attended? Why or why not?

The Functionalist Perspective

Because functionalists conceive of society as resembling a living organism in which the various parts of a system contribute to its survival, they are interested in how racial and ethnic divisions affect the function of the whole social system. Functionalists argue that social consensus on core values and beliefs is an important foundation of social integration and stability and thus helps a society maintain its equilibrium. Ethnic differentiation may be *dysfunctional* because it reduces consensus, increases the chances of conflict, and threatens the equilibrium of a society, as is occurring in Iraq. Ethnic stratification may be particularly disruptive because it combines two societal cleavages, one based on culture and the other based on economic rewards and political power. Conflicts attributable to problems of ethnic stratification may reach a frequency and intensity that imperil the whole social system, as occurred in Lebanon in the 1970s and 1980s and in the former Yugoslavia in the 1990s.

But functionalists do not predict that ethnically differentiated societies will necessarily disintegrate or be perpetually unproductive and unjust. Instead, they suggest that because the tendency toward equilibrium and stability is very strong, ethnic stratification will gradually decline.

Functionalists also see ethnic conflict as serving some important *functions* in a society. First, conflict promotes group formation, and groups are the building blocks of a society. It facilitates a consciousness of kind—an awareness of shared or similar values. The distinction between "we," the in-group, and "they," the out-group, is established in and through conflict. Groups in turn bind people together within a set of social relationships and define the statuses people occupy in the social structure, particularly positions that are ascribed.

Second, not only is a group defined and its boundaries established through conflict, but conflict also promotes group cohesion. It makes group members more conscious of their group bonds and may increase their social participation, providing them with a means of identification in an uncertain, alienating world.

Third, ethnic and racial conflict may function as a safety valve for the society as a whole (Hepworth and West, 1988; Berkowitz, 1989). Prejudice provides for the release of hostile and aggressive impulses that are culturally taboo within other social contexts. By channeling hostilities from within family, occupational, and other crucial settings onto permissible targets, the stability of existing social structures may be promoted. This is known as the *scapegoating* mechanism.

Fourth, functionalists point out that a multiplicity of conflicts between large numbers of differing groups within a society may be conducive to a democratic as opposed to a totalitarian order. The multiple group affiliations of individuals contribute to a variety of conflicts crisscrossing society. If people are opponents in one conflict but allies in another, deep cleavages along one axis can be prevented. The different groups thus created operate as a check against one another and ensure input to the government from diverse points of view. In contrast, totalitarian societies have a maximum concentration of power in one institution—the monolithic state.

The Conflict Perspective

Conflict theorists contend that prejudice and discrimination can best be understood in terms of tension or conflict among competing groups.

They point out that three ingredients commonly come into play in the emergence and initial stabilization of racism (Noel, 1972; Vander Zanden, 1983): ethnocentrism, competition, and unequal power.

Ethnocentrism involves the tendency to judge the behavior of other groups by the standards of one's own (see Chapter 2, pp. 50–51). When individuals are strongly ethnocentric, they find it easy to perceive the out-group as an object of loathing. Competition intensifies ethnocentric sentiments and may lead to intergroup strife (Olzak, 1992). When people perceive that their own group can realize its goals only at the expense of another group, intergroup tensions mount, each group sees the other as a threat, and prejudicial attitudes are generated toward the out-group (Beck and Tolnay, 1990; Olzak, 1990; Fossett and Kiecolt, 1989; Quillian, 1995, 1996). The boys' camp experiment undertaken by Muzafer Sherif and his associates (1961) and described in Chapter 4 documents this process (pp. 100–101).

Competition provides the motivation for systems of social inequality, and ethnocentrism channels competition along racial and ethnic lines, but power determines which group will subordinate the other (Noel, 1972). Without power, prejudices cannot be translated into discrimination, and groups cannot turn their claims on scarce resources into institutional discrimination. In brief, power is the mechanism by which domination and subjugation are achieved.

Marxist-oriented theorists take the conflict thesis even further. They say that racial prejudice and exploitation arose in the Western world with the rise of capitalism (Cox, 1948; Szymanski, 1976; Geschwender, 1978) and benefit capitalists in four ways. First, ideologies of racial superiority make colonialism and racist practices palatable and acceptable to the white masses. Second, racism is profitable because capitalists can pay minority workers less. Third, racist ideologies divide the working class by pitting white workers and minority workers against one another. Fourth, capitalists require minority workers as an industrial reserve army that can be fired during times of economic stagnation and rehired during times of prosperity.

Marxists blame capitalists for generating racism, but sociologist Edna Bonacich (1972, 1975; Cheng and Bonacich, 1984) said that economic competition within a split labor market underlies the development of tensions among ethnic groups. A **split labor market** is an economic arena in which large differences exist in the price of labor at the same occupational level. Bonacich noted that when a group sells its labor at rates substantially lower than the prevailing ones, higher-paid labor faces severe competition to maintain its advantage. When the cheaper labor is of a differing racial or ethnic group, the resulting class antagonism takes the form of racism.

Regardless of the precise form that conflict theories take, they nonetheless contrast sharply with functionalist theories that normal social processes contribute to stability rather than to division and social strife.

The Interactionist Perspective

Interactionists argue that the way we act is dependent on the meanings we attach to people, objects, and events. Because these meanings are produced in social interaction, interactionists say that the world we experience is *socially constructed*. In this view ethnic groups are rooted in neither physical characteristics of people nor their primordial attachments. According to Shibutani and Kwan (1965), "Ethnic groups . . . generally do not share a common genetic strain; they are products of social interaction."

Communication was the key variable in ethnicity to Shibutani and Kwan (1965). Ethnicity arises when communication channels between groups are limited and different groups develop different systems of meanings. Ethnic distinctions tend to diminish when people in different groups experience the world in similar ways, are treated alike by others, and are able to communicate freely and easily with members of other groups.

When ethnic groups are stratified and the advantages enjoyed by the dominant group are fixed by custom and law, the prejudices of dominant group members, developed in cultural isolation from minority groups, will reflect a "sense of group position" (Blumer, 1958)—that is, a belief that the dominant group is superior and has a proprietary claim to privileges and resources and that the minority groups are not only alien but also a threat to the dominant group's advantageous position.

Although interactionists such as Shibutani and Kwan see ethnic stratification and the discrimination that accompanies it as the end result of competition and conflict among groups over scarce resources (as do the proponents of the conflict perspective), it is important to remember that groups can be conflictual only if they see themselves as distinct and different; otherwise, people cooperate as part of the same group or society. Ultimately, the causes of ethnic conflict and ethnic stratification are to be found in the social definitions groups have of each other and in the norms and patterns of interaction that perpetuate these definitions.

The Future of Ethnic and Minority Group Relations

In the late 1800s and early 1900s, the United States was a diverse multicultural society. Germans, French, Scandinavians, Bohemians, Russians, Italians, Greeks, Armenians, Irish, Scots, Poles, and many other groups—each speaking its own language—populated the nation's cities and farms. The children and grandchildren of these people grew up living in houses next to each other, went to school together, spoke English with one another, married people from each other's families, went into business with one another, and thought of themselves and one another primarily as Americans.

The situation is different for the many minority groups that populate the United States today. The Americans with African, Hispanic, Asian, and Native American roots not only may be culturally and linguistically distinct but also have physical characteristics that distinguish them. Because of the meanings attached to race, language, and culture in contemporary U.S. society, ethnic status for these groups is not "symbolic," is not a matter of choice, but remains heavily ascriptive. Clearly, ethnicity is not the same experience in the United States for white ethnics as it is for other minority groups (Waters, 1990), a problem that is likely to make communication about ethnic matters difficult and to perpetuate misunderstanding. The ethnic and minority distinctions that define the structure of contemporary America are not likely to diminish as quickly or in quite the same way as those of the white ethnics 100 years ago.

What do the major sociological perspectives predict will happen with regard to minority group relations in the United States?

The functionalist and conflict perspectives both suggest that if ethnic stratification continues in a society, then conflict and strife are likely outcomes and will be particularly likely and severe if class and ethnic cleavages coincide.

Where the two perspectives differ is that functionalists believe that long-run social trends are eliminating ascription and other irrational features from modern, industrial, socially differentiated societies. Basically, the problem we face is to manage the change from ascriptive to achievement-based stratification systems. From this view the civil rights movement and other equality-oriented movements are as much a consequence as they are a cause of these changes.

The conflict perspective, on the other hand, predicts that ethnic stratification will remain as long as it is in the interests of powerful dominant groups to keep it in place. If we want to reduce

ethnic stratification, we will have to directly intervene through government policies that enhance the chances that minority groups can increase their share of power and resources. According to this view, the civil rights activism that promotes affirmative action and civil rights legislation is an important causal agent in such change.

For interactionists, ethnic stratification cannot exist unless people define each other as different. Interactionists predict that as long as segregation and isolation of minority groups persist, particularly for the poorest groups, ethnocentrism will continue and probably worsen. Racism will not disappear, but will only change; the emergence of symbolic racism and subtle new forms of discrimination may be examples of such a change. Only if we break down barriers to interaction and communication will people begin to experience their common humanity, see one another as part of the same world, and work together to solve common problems.

Most observers suggest that if ethnic stratification persists, then ethnicity will persist as well. Minority group members will turn to their ethnic group for support, strength, and political mobilization. We should observe the emergence of new ethnicities as various groups of immigrants, minority, and even majority group members having a coincidence of interests define themselves as members of the same group. Some have suggested this is happening now in the emergence of "Hispanic Americans" and "Asian Americans," groups that, as we have seen, contain many nationalities.

If ethnic stratification diminishes significantly, it is possible that ethnicity for all groups will become increasingly "symbolic." If ethnic status does not dictate one's chances to be successful in life or is not needed to provide one with the hope that unjust conditions will be changed, then it is possible that its significance will reduce to being a source of individual identity and familial communion. In this situation ethnic groups will remain a rich source of personal meaning, but they will no longer enter into political and societal dynamics as they have in the past.

At present, however, ethnic and racial stratification remain important structural features of American society. As William J. Wilson pointed out in his book *More Than Just Race,* there are significant barriers to eliminating racial inequality (2009:135–6):

Policy makers who are dedicated to combating the problems of race and poverty and who recognize the importance of structural inequities face two challenges. First is the problem of institutional entrenchment, which always reduces the chances of reform . . . The second . . . is how to generate political support from Americans, who tend to place far more emphasis on cultural factors and individual behavior than on structural inequities in explaining social and economic outcomes . . . [B]eliefs that attribute joblessness and poverty to individual shortcomings do not engender strong support for social programs to end inequality.

As difficult and controversial as these issues are, Wilson argues that the way to deal with them is to confront them head on (pp. 141–2):

. . . in framing public policy we should not shy away from an explicit discussion of the specific issues of race and poverty; on the contrary, we should highlight them in our attempt to convince the nation that these problems should be seriously confronted and that there is an urgent need to address them. The issues of race and poverty should be framed in such a way that not only is a sense of fairness and justice to combat inequality generated, but also people are made aware that our country would be better off if these problems were seriously addressed and eradicated.

What Can Sociology Do for You?

This chapter presented information about inequalities of race and ethnicity. Sociology majors often are attractive to employers because of their understanding of diversity, race relations, institutional and individual discrimination, and ethnicity in the United States. If you decide to become a teacher, you may have opportunities to influence children's ideas and stereotypes and to improve the quality of education of disadvantaged youths. If you think teaching might be in your future, check out **http://www.teachersagainstprejudice.org/** to see what one group is doing in this area.

Many employers today are acutely aware of the need to strive for diversity in the workforce. Two websites you may want to visit are **www.diversity.com,** which bills itself as listing the best diversity employers, and **www.careerbuilder.com/JobSeeker/Jobs/subdiversity.aspx?jdv=yes,** which advertises a dedication to "recruit, hire, and retain a diverse workforce."

Are you interested in learning more about the material introduced in Chapter 7? You may want to take upper-level classes in race, minorities, stratification, inequality, or social problems.

The Chapter in Brief: *Inequalities of Race and Ethnicity*

Some U.S. racial and ethnic groups continue to be the victims of prejudice and discrimination. Sociologists address these questions: Where do race and ethnicity come from? Why and how are they associated with the distribution of society's rewards? How and why do racial and ethnic stratification change?

Racial and Ethnic Stratification

Stratification represents institutionalized inequality in the distribution of social rewards and burdens.

■ **Races**   The use of the concept of race for sociologists is as a social construct; a **race** is a group of people who see themselves—and are seen by others—as having hereditary traits that set them apart. An important concept based on race is **racism,** the belief that some racial groups are naturally superior and others are inferior.

■ **Ethnic Groups**   Groups that we identify chiefly on cultural grounds—language, folk practices, dress, gestures, mannerisms, or religion—are called **ethnic groups.** Ethnic groups often have a sense of peoplehood and may deem themselves to be a nation.

■ **Minority Groups**   Racial and ethnic groups are often **minority groups.** Five properties characterize a minority; most critical is that they lack power.

Prejudice and Discrimination

■ **Prejudice**   **Prejudice** refers to attitudes of aversion and hostility toward the members of a group simply because they belong to it and hence are presumed to have the objectionable qualities ascribed to it. A new form of prejudice against African Americans has been labeled **symbolic racism** by sociologists.

■ **Discrimination**   **Discrimination** is action, what people actually do in their daily activities, and involves the arbitrary denial of privilege, prestige, and power to members of a minority group. Since World War II, whites have shifted from more blatant forms of discrimination to more subtle forms.

■ **Institutional Discrimination**   The institutions of society may function in such a way that they produce unequal outcomes for different groups. This is called **institutional**

discrimination. Gatekeeping and **environmental racism** are mechanisms by which institutional discrimination occurs.

Patterns of Intergroup Relations: Assimilation and Pluralism

In multiethnic societies, ethnic groups may either lose their distinctiveness through a process of assimilation or retain their identity and integrity through pluralism.

■ **Assimilation**   **Assimilation** refers to those processes whereby groups with distinctive identities become culturally and socially fused. Its final stage is **amalgamation.** Two views toward assimilation have dominated within the United States: the "melting pot" view and the Anglo-conformity view. Cultural assimilation is **acculturation.** Structural assimilation is commonly referred to as **integration.**

■ **Pluralism**   In U.S. society, many groups have retained their identities and distinctiveness for many years, an example of **pluralism,** a situation in which diverse groups coexist and boundaries between them are maintained. In *equalitarian pluralism,* ethnic group members participate freely and equally in political and economic institutions. In *inequalitarian pluralism,* economic and political participation of minority groups is severely limited by the dominant group and may even entail **genocide.**

Racial and Ethnic Groups in the United States

The United States is undergoing a transition from a predominately white society rooted in western European culture to a global society composed of diverse racial and ethnic groups. By the year 2050, today's minorities will make up nearly half of the U.S. population.

■ **Hispanics/Latinos**   The nation's Hispanic population is not a consolidated minority.

Latino groups have different histories, distinct concentrations in different areas of the United States, and substantially different demographic and socioeconomic characteristics. Hispanics on average earn less than non-Hispanics.

■ **African Americans**   African Americans have made tremendous progress but remain disadvantaged. The expected lifetime earnings of African American men are significantly lower than those of white men, and housing segregation remains substantial. The full integration of African Americans is unlikely in the foreseeable future, primarily because of continuing social and economic barriers and low rates of interracial marriage.

■ **American Indians and Alaskan Natives**   Native American peoples vary substantially in their history, lifestyles, kin systems, language, political arrangements, religion, economy, current circumstances, and identities. They are the most severely disadvantaged of any population within the United States. Poverty and unemployment rates are high.

■ **Asian Americans**   The average family income of Chinese, Japanese, and Korean Americans in the second and subsequent generations is almost one-and-a-half times higher than that of non-Hispanic whites. But Asian Americans are a varied group, with considerable contrasts and diversity. The earnings of Laotians, Cambodians, and Vietnamese are generally low.

■ **White Ethnics**   Most white Americans, including those of northwestern European background, know and identify with their ethnic ancestry, but white ethnicity is neither deep nor stable. "Symbolic ethnicity" is an ethnicity that contributes to individual identity and perhaps to family communion, but does not create or sustain strong ethnic group ties.

Sociological Perspectives on Inequalities of Race and Ethnicity

■ **The Functionalist Perspective**   Functionalists say that ethnic differentiation reduces consensus, increases the chances of conflict, and threatens the equilibrium of a society, but it also promotes group formation and cohesion, functions as a safety valve through *scapegoating,* and helps maintain a democratic order.

■ **The Conflict Perspective**   Conflict theorists contend that prejudice and discrimination can best be understood in terms of tension or conflict among competing groups. At least three different conflict theories exist, and they are related to ethnocentrism, Marxism, and the **split labor market.**

■ **The Interactionist Perspective**   Interactionists say that the world we experience is socially constructed. In this view, ethnic groups are seen as products of social interaction. Ethnicity arises when communication channels between groups are limited and the different groups develop different systems of meanings.

The Future of Ethnic and Minority Group Relations

Ethnic status for Americans with African, Hispanic, Asian, and Native American roots is not "symbolic," is not a matter of choice, and remains heavily ascriptive.

Functionalists believe there are long-run social trends that are eliminating ascription and other irrational features from modern, industrial, socially differentiated societies. The conflict perspective predicts that ethnic stratification will remain as long as it is in the interests of powerful dominant groups to keep it in place. Interactionists say that as long as segregation and isolation of minority groups persist, ethnocentrism will continue and probably worsen.

If ethnic stratification persists, then ethnicity will persist as well; if it diminishes significantly, perhaps ethnicity for all groups will become increasingly "symbolic." William J. Wilson urges that the problems of race and poverty in the United States be discussed explicitly. Eradicating racial inequality will require overcoming institutional entrenchment and shifting Americans' emphasis from cultural and individual factors to structural inequities.

Glossary

acculturation Cultural assimilation, or the process in which cultural elements of one group change in the direction of another group.

amalgamation The final stage of assimilation, in which it becomes impossible to distinguish formerly distinct ethnic groups in a society.

assimilation Those processes whereby groups with distinctive identities become culturally and socially fused.

discrimination The arbitrary denial of privilege, prestige, and power to members of a minority group whose qualifications are equal to those of members of the dominant group.

environmental racism The practice of deliberately locating incinerators and other types of hazardous waste facilities in or next to minority communities.

ethnic groups Groups identified chiefly on cultural grounds—language, religion, folk practices, dress, gestures, and mannerisms.

gatekeeping The decision-making process whereby people are admitted to offices and positions of privilege, prestige, and power within a society.

genocide The deliberate and systematic extermination of a racial or ethnic group.

institutional discrimination The functioning of the institutions of society in a way that produces unequal outcomes for different groups.

institutional racism The functioning of the institutions of society to the disadvantage of racial minority groups.

integration Structural assimilation, or the participation of members of different ethnic groups in major institutional structures.

minority group A racially or culturally self-conscious population, with hereditary membership and a high degree of in-group marriage, which suffers oppression at the hands of a dominant segment of a nation-state.

pluralism A situation where diverse groups coexist side by side and mutually accommodate themselves to their differences.

prejudice Attitudes of aversion and hostility toward the members of a group simply because they belong to it and hence are presumed to have the objectionable qualities ascribed to it.

race A population that differs from other populations in the incidence of various hereditary traits.

racism The belief that some racial groups are naturally superior and others are inferior.

split labor market An economic arena in which large differences exist in the price of labor at the same occupational level.

symbolic racism A form of racism in which whites feel that blacks are too aggressive, do not play by the rules, and have negative characteristics.

Review Questions

1. What is race? How do sociologists define it?

2. What is an ethnic group?

3. List the five characteristics of minority groups.

4. What is the difference between prejudice and discrimination?

5. How does institutional discrimination work?

6. Define and contrast assimilation and pluralism.

7. Briefly describe the major racial and ethnic groups in the United States.

8. How do the functionalist, conflict, and interactionist perspectives explain racial and ethnic stratification?

9. Read again the first two paragraphs of this chapter (p. 211). Based on what you've learned in the rest of the chapter, how would you explain why President Obama is considered to be black?

 Internet Connection   www.mhhe.com/hughes11e

Research discussed in this chapter indicates that subjective racism and prejudiced attitudes have moderated considerably in the United States over the past 50 years. However, extreme prejudice still exists in the United States. Go to the website of the Southern Poverty Law Center, **http://www.splcenter.org/.** Explore this website for evidence of the existence of ethnocentrism and prejudice in the United States today. On the basis of these investigations and your reading of the current chapter, write a short report on (1) the nature and extent of extreme prejudice in the United States, (2) the causes of such prejudice, and (3) what can be done to eliminate it or reduce its negative effects.

Gender Inequality

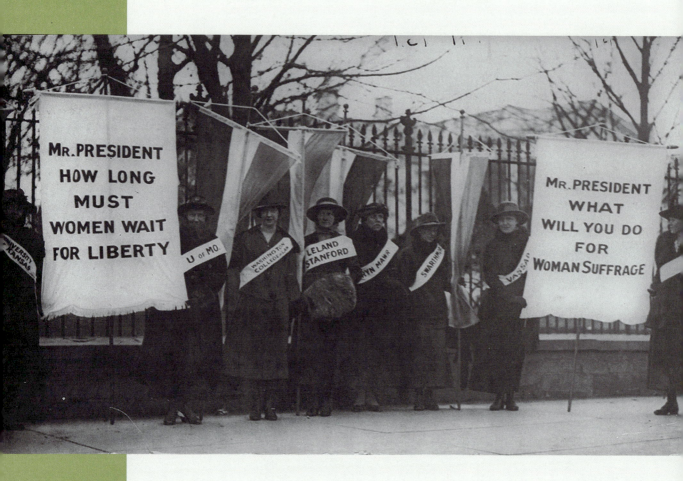

Gender Stratification

Sources of Gender Differences

Sociological Perspectives on Gender Stratification

W hat do *Black Beauty, Finding Nemo, Chicken Run, Babe, Toy Story, The Lion King, The Princess Diaries,* and *Monsters, Inc.* have in common?

(a) They are top box-office grossing films.

(b) They are rated G.

(c) They have mostly male characters.

(d) They are watched by kids, in theaters and on video, over and over again.

(e) All of the above.

Did you guess *e*? You're right. These and 94 other top box-office grossing, G-rated, live-action and animated films—all released between 1990 and 2005—were analyzed by University of Southern California researchers for gender balance (Kelly and Smith, 2006). Of a total of 4,249 speaking characters in the 101 films, 28 percent are female. Only a quarter of all the characters (speaking and nonspeaking) are female, and only 17 percent of the characters in crowd scenes are female. Even the narration is male dominated, with 83 percent of narrators being male.

Does it matter? Clearly, women have come a long way since the beginning of the 20th century, when many of them were farm wives slaving over hot stoves or were urban workers confined to low-paying occupations such as seamstress, laundry worker, or maid. Today, women in the United States can vote, run for office, control their own finances, and work outside the home in professional occupations. They now are more likely than men to earn bachelor's, master's, and doctoral degrees, and they are increasingly likely to do work previously thought of as "men's work."

At the same time, women still make up only a small proportion of our elected leaders, for the most part are passed over when top executives are being selected, are mostly excluded from a

247

wide variety of male-dominated occupations and careers, are portrayed and treated as sex objects in many ways, and are much more likely than men to be single parents, with full responsibility for housework and child care.

Patterns of gender representation in G-rated movies both reflect and help to perpetuate such gender disparities. These movies teach and reinforce the belief that activities of men are at the center of what is important, that men have the initiative and presence of mind to solve problems, and that men are the ones who have the authority, intelligence, and background to tell us what is worth knowing about the unfolding of events.

Of course, many factors go into producing gender inequality, and imagery that reinforces inequality in the media, including movies, is only one piece of the puzzle.

Just as our society structures inequalities based on race and ethnic membership, so it institutionalizes inequalities based on gender (Martin, 2004). Men and women differ in their access to privilege, prestige, and power. Despite advances in the United States and elsewhere, the distribution problem of who gets what, when, and how has nearly always been answered in favor of males.

In this chapter we examine inequalities based on gender. As we have seen, class, race, and ethnicity can result in segregation in residence, education, employment, and other areas of life. Gender stratification differs from other systems of stratification in that, for the most part, males and females work, live, go to school, and otherwise interact together on a daily basis. Nevertheless, inequalities exist. We begin our chapter by considering sex, gender, sexism, and patriarchy. We then take a closer look at the status of women in society, both in the United States and around the world. We will discuss the acquisition of gender identities, looking at the parts played by biology, culture, and socialization. Finally, we will examine the functionalist, conflict, interactionist, and feminist perspectives on gender stratification.

Gender Stratification

Throughout the world, human activities, practices, and institutional structures are organized with respect to the social distinction people make between men and women—in brief, by gender. For the most part the state, the law, politics, religion, higher education, and the economy are institutions that historically have been developed by men, are currently dominated by men, and are symbolically interpreted from the standpoint of men. As such they are "gendered institutions." The only major institution in which women have had a central, defining role, although a subordinate one, has been the family (Acker, 1992).

Before we continue our discussion of gender stratification, we need to define some basic terms. **Sex** refers to whether one is genetically male or female and determines the biological role that one will play in reproduction. **Gender,** on the other hand, is a form of social differentiation; it refers to the sociocultural distinction between males and females. While sex is given in nature, gender is a socially constructed framework that human beings have created to make sense of and deal with the sex difference.

Gender identities are the conceptions we have of ourselves as being male or female. One's gender identity is part of one's self-concept and consequently is a product of social interaction (see Chapter 3, p. 80). Our gender identities emerge as we enact gender roles and are reacted to by others as being either male or female.

Gender roles are sets of cultural expectations that define the ways in which the members of each sex should behave. Gender roles influence a wide range of human behaviors, including how people speak, dress, walk, engage in courtship, get angry, play sports, deal with distress, and choose a career.

The gender roles defined by a society have profound consequences for the lives of its men and women. They constitute master statuses that carry primary weight in people's interactions and relationships with others (see Chapter 2, p. 56). In doing so they place men and women in the social structure, establishing where and what they are in social terms. Thus, gender roles establish the framework within which men and women gain their identities, formulate their goals, and carry out their training. Gender roles are a major source of social inequality.

In this section we will consider sexism and patriarchy. We will then take a closer look at women's roles and gender inequality in society both around the world and in the United States.

Sexism and Patriarchy

Gender inequality is perpetuated by a set of complex processes referred to as **sexism.** Like racism, sexism operates at two levels. At the *individual level,* sexism is the belief that one sex is superior to the other. This form of sexism involves two basic ideas: (1) that because of inherent biological differences, men and women are naturally suited to different roles and (2) that this is the primary cause of the differential distribution of status, power, and income by gender. At the *institutional level,* sexism involves policies, procedures, and practices that produce unequal outcomes for men and women. In principle, sexism refers to disadvantages that may be experienced by either sex. In reality, the patterns of gender inequality in history and throughout the world today generally involve disadvantages for women and advantages for men. What we usually mean by sexism, then, is a set of cultural and social processes that justify and promote disadvantage for women.

Do Women Constitute a Minority Group?

Sexism operates against women the way racism operates against persons of minority racial backgrounds. However, although they are similar to a minority group, women are clearly not in the minority in most societies. Given higher mortality rates for men, as men and women age, there are increasingly more women than there are men. But as we noted in the previous chapter, being a minority group does not require relatively low numbers. The key characteristic of a minority group is that it *lacks power* relative to a dominant group. And this is true of the situation of women in virtually every society.

Let's look again at the five properties of a *minority group* we considered in Chapter 7 (pp. 214–215), this time with women in mind:

1. Historically, women have encountered *prejudice and discrimination* and have not had access to the institutionalized power needed to readily change this situation.

2. Women possess *physical and cultural traits* that distinguish them from men, the dominant group.

3. Through the efforts of the women's liberation movement and consciousness-raising groups, women have increasingly become a *self-conscious social group* characterized by an awareness of oneness.

4. *Membership is involuntary* since gender is an ascribed status that is assigned to a person at birth.

5. Only the fifth characteristic, endogamy, does not apply to women, because, of course, women are not required to marry women.

The existence of sexism not only disadvantages women but also has a wide-ranging impact on how we think about our lives and the places of women and men in them. As sociologist Jessie Bernard put it in a discussion of the impact of sexism on women:

[Sexism is] the unconscious, taken-for-granted, assumed, unquestioned, unexamined, unchallenged acceptance of the belief that the world as it looks to men is the only world, that the way of dealing with it which men have created

Gender inequality exists in every society around the world, but recent changes have moved many women who traditionally did only unpaid domestic labor into the paid labor force.

is the only way, that the values which men have evolved are the only ones, that the way sex looks to men is the only way it can look to anyone, that what men think about what women are like is the only way to think about what women are like. (Quoted in Gornick and Moran, 1971:xxv)

Patriarchy

The most pervasive form of institutional sexism is **patriarchy,** a system of social organization in which men have a disproportionate share of power. Patriarchy is rooted in cultural and legal systems that historically gave fathers authority in family and clan matters, made wives and children dependent on husbands and fathers, and organized descent and inheritance through the male line. Sociologist Judith Lorber (1994) believes that early societies may have been egalitarian for thousands of years, and Jeannine Davis-Kimball (1997) cites archaeological evidence of female military and social power. One possibility is that patriarchy emerged gradually as the economic arrangements of societies became more complicated (Barber, 1994; Ortner, 1996). Most sociologists believe that patriarchal systems serve the interests of men at the expense of women, and nearly all societies around the world today are patriarchal.

Although in some societies political change has undermined the legal basis of patriarchy, and attitudinal change has undermined its cultural power, modern societies include many patriarchal elements. An obvious one is the practice of women and children taking the last name of the husband and father; in the United States, only about 10 percent of all married women have not adopted their husbands' names (Golden and Shim, 2004). More importantly, men have more social, economic, and political power than women in societies around the world, the topic of our next section.

Gender Inequality around the World

In their book *Half the Sky,* Nicholas D. Kristof and Sheryl WuDunn describe the problems faced by women in countries in which men are valued more highly than women (2009:xvi–xvii):

In the wealthy countries of the West, discrimination is usually a matter of unequal pay or underfunded sports teams or unwanted touching from a boss. In contrast, in much of the world discrimination is lethal . . . The global statistics on the abuse of girls are numbing. It appears that more girls have been killed in the last fifty years, precisely because they were girls, than men were killed in all the battles of the twentieth century.

Sex-selective abortions, neglect of female infants, more food and better health care for boys and men, and other forms of discrimination have resulted in higher survival rates for males than for females in China, India, Pakistan, and other countries. How much higher? Researchers estimate that at least 2 million girls per year die and that between 60 million and 101 million women are missing from the world's population because of gender discrimination (Kristof and WuDunn, 2009).

The U.S. State Department's human rights report, which includes information from 194 countries, presents evidence of "continuing and escalating discrimination and persecution" of women around the world (Eisenbraun, 2010). In Ghana, Bangladesh, and many other countries, the trafficking of women and children for the sex trade and for forced labor remains a significant problem. Underage prostitution, sex tourism, and the sexual abuse of children also are listed in the human rights reports of many countries. Overall, one in three women has experienced violent victimization (Garcia-Moreno et al., 2005). The governments of many countries turn a blind eye to the abuse of women, and in many nations the state is a major institutional source of discrimination. In the Middle East and Northern Africa, for example, the legal system often excuses a man for killing his wife for alleged immoral acts—an "honor killing."

Maternal mortality is a major cause of death in many parts of the world. In 2008, an estimated 350,000 women died during pregnancy, childbirth, or the first six weeks after delivery (Hogan et al., 2010). Although women's ability to control their fertility has improved significantly, around the world, more than a quarter of the babies born are unwanted or unplanned. In less-developed countries, the percentage of women using contraception increased from 9 percent in 1960 to 59 percent in 2011 (Haub and Kaneda, 2011).

Women are sexually victimized throughout the world. One form of victimization is the traditional ethnic practice of female genital mutilation; another is the transmission of HIV to young women and girls by older men. Half of the world's HIV-infected population is now female, and in sub-Saharan Africa, 60 percent of the HIV-positive population is made up of women and girls (U.S. Department of Health and Human Services, 2012). Mass rape and sexual sadism in war are still common around the world, often accompanying the collapse of social order that occurs during war.

Two-thirds of the world's illiterate adults are female, and worldwide there are approximately 3.6 million girls not in primary school (UNESCO, 2011). The education gender gap is closing, however, with primary school gender parity improving in the regions of the world that have had the largest gender gaps in the past and increasing numbers of women participating in secondary and higher education. Women account for an increasing share of the labor force; however, in many places they still are concentrated in just a few occupations, have little or no authority on the job, and receive less pay than men. And women still do most of the housework, cooking, and child care all over the world, whether they work outside the home or not, although personal income, work arrangements, education, and the level of development in one's country affect this aspect of gender inequality (Craig and Mullan, 2012; Heisig, 2011).

Women around the world do considerably better than U.S. women in some areas. More than 160 countries provide paid maternity leave by law; the United States does not (Catalyst, 2011; Heymann et al., 2004; see Table 8.1). A number of nations have had a woman prime minister or president, including Great Britain, Canada, Ireland, Norway, Germany, Finland, Portugal, Iceland, the Philippines, Argentina, Bolivia, Chile, Nicaragua, Poland, Israel, Turkey, India, Pakistan, Bangladesh, Sri Lanka, Haiti, Netherlands Antilles, and Dominica (Reel, 2007; Lewis, 2006). For the first time, a country—Rwanda—has achieved equal representation of men and women in its legislature, and the world average for the percentage of women in the national parliaments has risen to

Table 8.1	Maternity Benefits, Selected Countries	
Country	Weeks of Leave Provided	Percentage of Pay
Belarus	18	100
Portugal	17	100
Austria	16	100
Netherlands	16	100
Poland	16	100
Spain	16	100
Congo	15	100
Gabon	14	100
Germany	14	100
China	13	100
Mexico	12	100
Zambia	12	100
Sweden*	68	80
Italy	20	80
Ireland	18	70
Czech Republic	28	69
Japan	14	60
Australia	52	0
Swaziland	12	0
United States	12	0

Sweden provides 390 days at 80 percent pay and 90 days at a flat rate.

Source: United Nations; data available at http://unstats .un.org/unsd/demographic/products/indwm/ww2005/ tab5c.htm.

18.9. Many countries have 30–40 percent of their legislatures composed of women, far ahead of the United States at 16.8 percent (see Figure 8.1). Changes for women also can be seen in other aspects of their lives, including concern about the barriers women face in scientific and engineering fields (Hill, Corbett, and Rose, 2010), increased attention to prostitute and sex slave trafficking, the disappearance of foot binding in China, and increases in education and employment opportunities for women in many countries. Research in Europe on affirmative action programs shows that they can increase women's willingness to compete without causing reverse discrimination or impeding postcompetition cooperation (Balafoutas and Sutter, 2012), and a "natural experiment" in India showed that female leadership raises the aspirations and educational attainments of girls (Beaman et al., 2012). Achievement gaps between boys and girls have been closing around the world, with no differences and even reversals of the gap in countries whose cultures are more gender-equal (Machin and Pekkarinen, 2008).

Gender Inequality in the United States

Social scientists have long noted many similarities between the status of African Americans and that of women within the United States (Myrdal, 1944; Hacker, 1951, 1974; Smith and Steward, 1983). Look, for example, at racist and sexist stereotypes. Both African Americans and women have been portrayed as intellectually inferior, emotional, irresponsible, dependent, and childlike. Both groups lack power, and the rationalization for their subordination has been similar—the myth of "contented African Americans who know their place" and the notion that "women's place is in the home." Recent generations of both African Americans and women have challenged those stereotypes by participating in social movements for equal rights.

How disadvantaged are women in U.S. society? That varies from state to state (see Box 8.1). In this section we look at the division of labor in the family, gender stratification in the workplace, the "glass ceiling," disparities in pay, career patterns, sexual harassment and rape, politics and government, and the women's movement.

Dividing Labor in the Family

Sexual inequality historically has been sustained by assigning the economic-provider role to men and the child-rearing role to women.

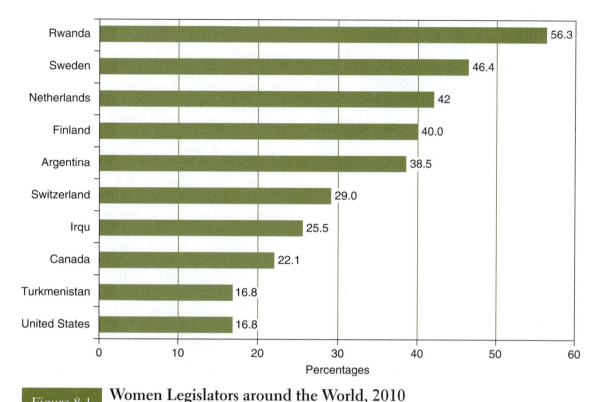

Figure 8.1 **Women Legislators around the World, 2010**
More than 50 percent of Rwanda's legislators are women, the highest proportion in the world. Seventy-three other countries are ahead of the United States, where 16.8 percent of legislators are female. A number of countries have no women legislators whatsoever, including Micronesia, Oman, the Solomon Islands, Saudi Arabia, and Belize.

Source: Figure generated by the authors using data for the lower, or single, House of each country; data from the Inter-Parliamentary Union's website, www.ipu.org.

Labor in the public sphere has been rewarded by money, prestige, and power, whereas labor in the domestic sphere typically has been isolated and undervalued (Crittenden, 2001; Daniels, 1987; Ferree, 1990; Kessler-Harris, 1990). Gender stereotypes arise in response to a gender division of labor and then serve to rationalize it by attributing to the sexes substantially different personality characteristics and traits (Hoffman and Hurst, 1990).

Historically, the gender division of labor has operated to bind women to their reproductive function. Women were viewed as providing men with sexual and domestic services in exchange for financial support. Within this arrangement a sexual double standard prevailed that permitted men, but not women, considerable sexual freedom. Until the 20th century, English and American common law viewed women as undergoing "civil death" upon marriage. Women lost their legal identity when they married and, in the eyes of the law, became "incorporated and consolidated" with their husbands. A wife could not own property in her own right or sign a contract. And a husband could require his wife to live wherever he chose and to submit to sexual intercourse against her will—a practice we now call rape.

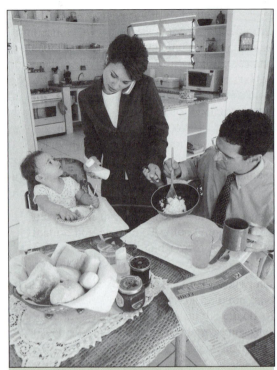

Since 1950 the number of American mothers who work outside the home has tripled, but most of them still do most of the household and child care work as well.

Today marriage and family have become less of an organizing force in the lives of contemporary American women. In 2010, more than half of American women were living without a spouse (U.S. Census Bureau, 2011a). Although they still place a high value on marriage and the family, younger women are now more likely to delay marriage and childbearing. The nearly half who are married, however, can expect a lot more help from their husbands than women received in the past. Over the last four decades, fathers have more than doubled the amount of time they spend doing housework and almost tripled the amount of time they spend caring for their children (Bianchi, Robinson, and Milkie, 2006). In time diary studies, in

which participants keep detailed accounts of their daily activities, researchers found that the total workloads of all married mothers and fathers were about the same. Paid work, child care, and housework added up to an average 65 hours per week for mothers and 64 hours per week for fathers, although mothers employed outside the home put in about 5 more hours of work per week than employed fathers (Bianchi, Robinson, and Milkie, 2006).

The 2010 American Time Use Survey (Bureau of Labor Statistics, 2011) confirms the time diary studies: Among working couples, the total amount of time spent working at home and in the workplace is very similar for men and women, though women work slightly more overall; the differences are in the distribution of that time to various tasks. Of full-time employees, men work longer in the workplace each day (8.2 hours on average versus 7.8 hours for women) but spend less time on household activities (2.1 hours a day compared to women's 2.6 hours). On an average workday, 20 percent of men but 49 percent of women do housework. In households with children under 6, women spend an average of 1.1 hours, compared to men's 26 minutes, on the physical care of children (bathing, changing diapers, feeding). The time diary research shows that the total workload of a mother employed fulltime is greater than a working father's by about a week and a half per year (Milkie, Raley, and Bianchi, 2009).

The Time Use Survey (Bureau of Labor Statistics, 2011) also tracked leisure time. Men reported an average of 5.8 hours per day (on an average workday) of leisure activity, while women reported an average of 5.1 hours. The presence of children in a household decreases by about an hour the amount of leisure time reported by adults, and much of what the survey labels "secondary child care" accompanies leisure time.

This combining of activities contributes to women's feelings of being overburdened and stressed. Sociologists Shira Offer and Barbara

8.1 Social Inequalities

For Gender Equality, It Matters Where You Live

The quality of people's lives has much to do with individual choices, abilities, and aspirations. But social institutions also affect quality of life. Women's vastly different experiences in different societies illustrate the importance of social institutions for gender equality and women's quality of life.

Women's experiences differ within the United States, too. In fact, women's political participation, employment and earnings, social and economic autonomy, reproductive rights, and health and well-being vary substantially from state to state. These factors have been assessed in an ongoing research project, *The Status of Women in the States,* conducted by the Institute for Women's Policy Research (Werschkul and Williams, 2004).

So—if you're a woman or a man interested in gender equality and better outcomes for women—where should you live? In 2004, the best states for women to live in were Vermont, Connecticut, Minnesota, and Washington. The worst state was Mississippi, followed by South Carolina, Kentucky, Arkansas and Oklahoma (tied), Tennessee, and Texas. How does the IWPR decide? The top states must rank in the top 10 of all the states in at least one of the factors listed above and must *not* appear in the bottom half of all states in any of the factors. In contrast, the worst states are identified as those that rank in the bottom 10 for at least one factor and in the bottom half for all factors.

How different are the differences? Let's look at political participation and representation as an example. In Hawaii only 51 percent of the state's women are registered to vote, while in North Dakota the comparable figure is 91 percent. In state legislatures, the proportion of women ranges from 9.4 percent (South Carolina) to 36.7 percent (Washington). Four states have had two female U.S. senators at the same time; five states have never had a woman elected to either the Senate or the House.

An IWPR assessment of state economies found favorable business climates for women in Maryland, New Mexico, and the District of Columbia, where more than 30 percent of businesses are owned by women (Hartmann et al., 2006). Women's wages have risen in all states over the past 25 years, with women earning the most in Maryland, the District of Columbia, and New Jersey.

While some of the states are "all good" or "all bad," others are strange mixes of benefits and problems for women. Women in the District of Columbia, for example, had the highest earnings in the nation in 2004, the least difference in pay between men and women, and the highest proportion of women in management and professional occupations (Werschkul and Williams, 2004). On the other hand, District women have the worst overall health status, high rates of poverty, and low rates of health insurance coverage.

Some general findings have emerged from the research. Racial and ethnic disparities in women's health status are wide in every state. The significantly higher probability that African American women will die of heart disease or breast cancer or will have AIDS is among the specific findings on health status. Another general finding is that a small wage gap, high earnings, and high representation in professional and managerial occupations co-occur in many states.

The IWPR research also identifies general patterns of progress and lack thereof for American women. Among the disappointing findings they list are an increase in women's poverty in 15 states and only a very small decrease in 15 others (Hartmann et al., 2006), a decrease in reproductive health services in a number of states, and only a very small increase in the proportion of women state legislators (Werschkul and Williams, 2004).

Questions for Discussion

1. How do you think your home state measures up in terms of women's rights? Go to www.iwpr.org and find the fact sheet for your state. What institutional factors (e.g., law, economy, politics, education, health care, religion) do you think determine the position of your state in the ranking?

2. One route to gender equality is to promote policies that lead to changes in social structure. How might the factors assessed by the IWPR be linked through this idea?

Schneider (2012) examined the activities that parents report as multitasking and found that women spend about 10 more hours per week than men multitasking, mostly in the areas of housework and child care, and that this is associated with stress, psychological distress, negative emotions, and work–family conflict for women.

Of course, these figures are meaningless for the 27 percent of children being raised by a single parent in the United States (U.S. Census Bureau, 2011). In these households, most of which are headed by women, one parent—the mother—earns a living, does all the household work, and takes care of the children.

Gender Stratification in the Workplace

In 2010, the labor-force participation rate for U.S. women 16 and older was 59 percent (U.S. Department of Labor, 2012); see Figure 8.2 for a comparison with other countries. Almost half—46 percent—of all U.S. workers are women. The labor-force participation of married women in the United States over the past 200 years is represented by a U-shaped curve, with relatively high participation rates in the 1790s, declining rates accompanying industrialization during the 19th century, and rising rates after the beginning of the 20th century—and mounting substantially after 1960. In recent decades, lower fertility and changing social attitudes contributed to the jump in the labor-force participation of women, while higher rates of divorce impelled more women to join the workforce. African American women have always worked for pay in larger proportions than white women (Herring and Wilson-Sadberry, 1993).

Since 1950, the number of American mothers employed outside the home has tripled. In 71 percent of the families with children under age 18, the mother is employed (U.S. Department of Labor, 2008). Mothers with older children are more likely to work than those with very young children. but young mothers also are very likely to work; two-thirds of women who had given birth in 2008 were in the workforce (Laughlin, 2011).

Women have gained ground by entering college in higher numbers than men (U.S. Census Bureau, 2009) and now earn more high school diplomas (Bergman, 2003) and more bachelor's, master's, and doctoral degrees than men and about the same number of medical and law degrees as men (Snyder, Dillow, and Hoffman, 2009). Women also have been moving into higher-paying fields traditionally dominated by men. For example, between 1980 and 2009, the percentage of women lawyers rose from 14 percent to 32 percent (U.S. Census Bureau, 2011). In the same time period, the proportion of female doctors increased from 13 percent to 32 percent.

Despite these changes many of the current figures on the employment of women bear a striking resemblance to those of previous decades. There was little substantial change in the gender segregation of occupations between 1900 and 1970. Levels of segregation did decline in the 1980s and 1990s, but 40 percent of women and 44 percent of men continue to work in what we might think of as sex-segregated occupations (Hegewisch and Liepmann, 2010). Women are especially underrepresented in science and technology fields (Economics and Statistics Administration, 2011). The stereotypes many of us hold are based on fact: 97 percent of all secretaries and administrative assistants are female, 92 percent of registered nurses are female, 90 percent of all hairdressers and cosmetologists are women, and 82 percent of elementary and middle-school teachers are female (U.S. Census Bureau, 2011a). One of the fastest-growing industries in the United States, the restaurant industry, provides some of the country's lowest-wage jobs, the lowest of which are disproportionately filled by women (Restaurant Opportunities Center United, 2012).

Men and women sort into occupational categories in some general ways: 59 percent of men work in precision production, craft, and repair jobs; executive, administrative, and managerial positions; professional specialty; and sales, while 73 percent of women work in administrative support, professional specialty, and service work, and hold executive, administrative, and

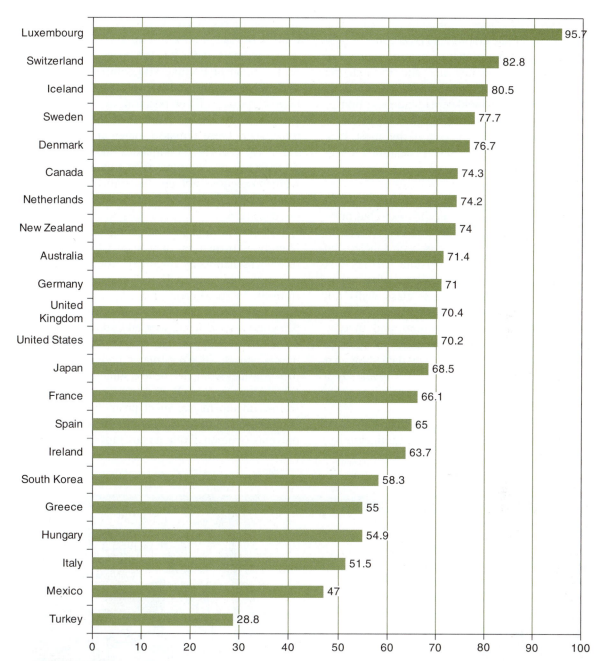

| Figure 8.2 | **Labor-Force Participation Rates for Women 15 to 64 years old for Selected Countries, 2009** |

The participation of women in the paid labor force in the United States is not the highest in the world, but neither is it the lowest.

Source: Figure generated by the authors using data from the U.S. Census Bureau, 2011a.

managerial positions (Spraggins, 2003). The increase in female employment has come largely through the displacement of men by women in some low-paying categories and through the rapid expansion of "pink-collar" occupations such as secretary, bookkeeper, and receptionist. The "sticky floor" is an apt metaphor for the occupational frustrations experienced by most U.S. working women in low-paying, dead-end jobs.

The Glass Ceiling

The number of women top executives and board directors has increased over the years, but positions at the top still elude women. Women in business crash into what has been labeled the "glass ceiling," a set of invisible barriers that prevent women from advancing. When glass ceilings do not stop women, glass walls do; these are barriers that prevent women from moving laterally in corporations and thereby gaining the experience they need to advance vertically (Lopez, 1992). Survey data show that both male CEOs and female executives say a major obstacle for women is insufficient work experience (Catalyst, 2003).

At the beginning of this century, 45 percent of the jobs classified as executive, administrative, and managerial were held by women (U.S. Census Bureau, 2003). But in 2011, very few of these women were at the very top: Only 16.1 percent of Fortune 500 companies' board seats were held by women, only 14.1 percent of their corporate officer positions were filled by women, and only 7.5 percent of the country's top earners were female (Soares et al., 2011). Ten percent of these companies had no women on their boards, and more than a quarter had no women executive officers; fewer than 20 percent had a quarter or more women directors or executive officers.

Women who make it to the top get there differently. One analysis of women CEOs showed that at least half were "imported" from outside the company, while male CEOs almost always come from the inside (Reed, 2005). A survey of both male and female corporate leaders showed that perceptions of men and women leaders are based on gender stereotypes, not on fact-based information (Catalyst, 2006). A major finding was that men consider women to be less skilled at problem solving than men are. With men far outnumbering women in top management positions, this idea "dominates current corporate thinking" and prevents women from advancing. The report

Although some women face a "glass ceiling" in their careers, most women are limited by a "sticky floor"—women are concentrated in low-paying service, support, and nurturance occupations.

SIX CHIX. Copyright © 2000 Margaret Shulock. King Features Syndicate.

recommends that companies educate managers and executives about stereotyping and ways to overcome it and that the achievements of women leaders be showcased. Companies that do manage do achieve gender diversity on their boards and among their executive officers attain better financial results than do companies with no women on their boards (Carter and Wagner, 2011).

Disparities in Pay

Women earn less than men. On average, women employed full-time in 2010 earned 81.2 cents for each dollar earned by males, up from 60.7 cents per dollar in 1960 (Dobuzinskis, 2011). The disparity is even greater when the analysis accounts for time taken off to perform family work, including bearing and raising children; a long-term study showed that over 15 years women earned only 38 cents for every dollar earned by men (Rose and Hartmann, 2004). More women than men have low incomes and live below the poverty level, and more men than women earn over $75,000 a year (DeNavas-Walt, Proctor, and Smith, 2011). Although the wage gap has closed over the past several decades, the rate of decrease has slowed (Dobuzinskis, 2011) and significant disparities remain overall (see Figure 8.3a)

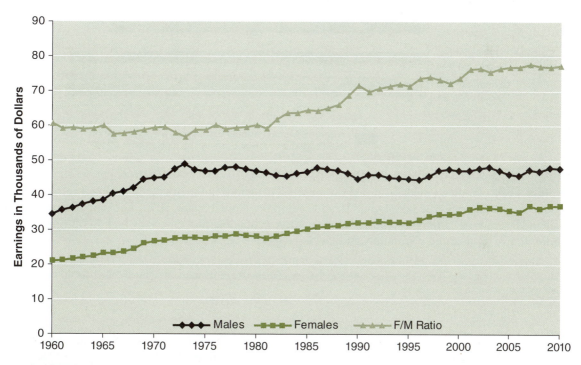

Figure 8.3a   **Disparities in Earnings Remain Significant**
Median yearly earnings in thousands of dollars of full-time, year-round workers in the United States by gender, in constant 2010 dollars, 1955–2010. The top line shows the ratio of median female earnings to median male earnings. Recent gains by women in terms of the ratio of their earnings to those of men are due both to a decrease in earnings of men and to an increase in earnings of women.

Source: Figure generated by the authors from data in DeNavas-Walt, Proctor, and Smith, 2011.

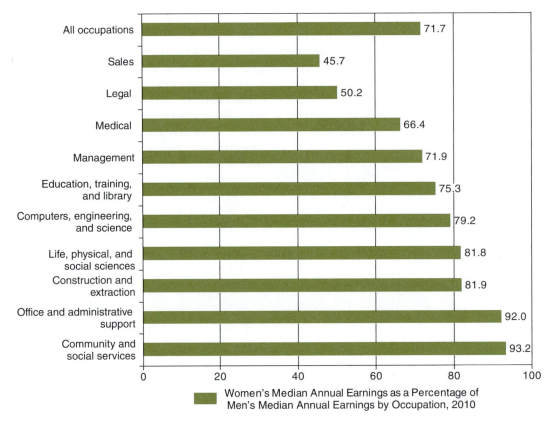

Women's Median Annual Earnings as a Percentage of
Men's Median Annual Earnings by Occupation, 2010

Figure 8.3b	**Disparities in Earnings Remain significant (*continued*)**

Women's median annual earnings as a percentage of men's median annual earnings by occupation for all employed persons age 16 and over in the United States, 2010. The ratio of female-to-male median annual earnings is especially low in sales occupations and especially high in office and administrative support and community and social services.

Source: Figure generated by the authors using data from the U.S. Census Bureau, 2010, American Community Survey, Table S2401: Occupation by sex and median earnings in the past 12 months (in 2010 inflation-adjusted dollars) for the civilian employed population 16 years and over.

as well as within occupational categories (see Figure 8.3b). Though the education gap between men and women has closed, there is a sharp disparity in earnings between men and women at all levels of education (see Figure 8.3c). In science and technology fields, where women hold only 24 percent of the jobs, the pay gap is less

but still present (Economics and Statistics Administration, 2011).

Paying a woman less to do the same job a man does is illegal. What, then, explains the pay gap? It is affected by many factors. Sociologist Paula England (1993b) suggested three major explanations. First, discrimination in

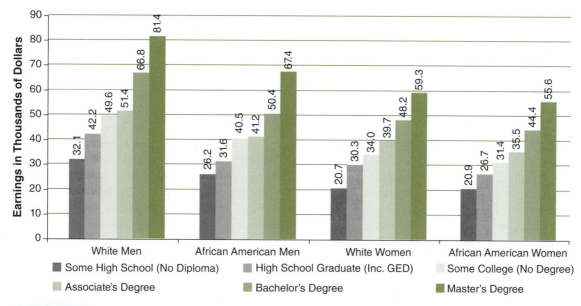

Figure 8.3c **Disparities in Earnings Remain Significant (*continued*)**
Yearly earnings in thousands of dollars of full-time, year-round workers 25 years and older, by gender, race, and education, 2010. Black and white women earn less in every educational category than black and white men.

Source: Figure generated by the authors using data from the U.S. Census Bureau, Current Population Survey, Annual Social and Economic Supplement, 2010.

hiring and placement reduces women's chances for high-paying jobs in occupations dominated by men, such as management, craft occupations, and some professions. Second, jobs that are occupied mostly by women provide lower wages than jobs that are dominated by men. In one analysis, it was found that nurses were paid less than fire truck mechanics, and librarians were paid less than custodians. Pay differentials for gendered occupations account for much, but not all, of the earnings gap (Boraas and Rodgers, 2003). Third, women often have less job experience than men because they interrupt their careers to care for children. This "motherhood penalty" has been found to be 5 percent per child even after the cost of lost

experience is accounted for, a penalty the researchers attributed to discrimination by employers against mothers and/or the effect of motherhood on productivity at work (Budig and England, 2001).

Other related factors also contribute to the pay gap. For example, on average, women work fewer hours than men and are less likely to work full-time, but this and related factors do not completely explain the gender gap in pay. A study of graduates of the University of Michigan law school found that men's salaries were 52 percent higher than women's salaries. The researchers looked at hours worked, law school grades, marital status, number of children, number of years practicing law, and type of legal practice and found that 23 percent of women's salary disadvantage remained unexplained by these factors (Noonan, Corcoran, and Courant, 2005). For all college graduates, the portion of the pay gap that remains unexplained after accounting for experience, training, education, personal characteristics, and college major is 5 percent one year after graduation and 12 percent 10 years after graduation, evidence of discrimination against women (Dey and Hill, 2007).

Differences in earnings vary by race and ethnicity, with Hispanic and African American women earning even less than white women compared to white men, and wage disparity continues to disadvantage women into retirement. In 2008, men receiving Social Security benefits were getting an average of $1,299 per month, while women were getting an average of $1,001 per month (Social Security Administration, 2010). Because benefits are based primarily on years worked and wages earned, women's lower wages and time out of the workforce for reproductive responsibilities result in smaller retirement benefits.

Career Patterns: Out of Sync with Family Life

The career patterns of women can be quite different from those of men. The economic advancement of women is complicated by the social organization of child care. Economist Sylvia Ann Hewlett observed (quoted in Castro, 1991:10):

[W]e have confused equal rights with identical treatment, ignoring the realities of family life. After all, only women can bear children. And in this country, women must still carry most of the burden of raising them. We think that we are being fair to everyone by stressing identical opportunities, but in fact we are punishing women and children.

The years between ages 25 and 35 are critical in the development of a career but also are when women are most likely to have children. If they leave the labor force to do so, they suffer in their ability to acquire critical skills and to achieve promotions. Very often they also suffer a complete loss of income for the time they are away from work, and they may also leave with no guarantee that they can return: The United States is one of only three industrialized nations that do not provide paid maternity leave by law (see Table 8.1), but more employers are providing it than in the past. Between 2006 and 2008, 51 percent of first-time mothers who were employed received paid leave of some sort (vacation, sick leave, or maternity leave), 42 percent received unpaid leave, and 80 percent of mothers who worked during their pregnancy returned to the same employer within a year of giving birth (Laughlin, 2011). Fathers are increasingly contributing to child care; 32 percent of fathers with working wives were a regular source of care for the family's children in 2010, and for 20 percent of families with preschoolers the father was the primary caregiver (Glasier, 2011).

Increased awareness of the problems women face in combining family and work responsibilities has resulted in efforts to retain female employees in some arenas. The National Science Foundation, for example, has established a set of "family-friendly policies" that allow the deferral of research grant awards for a year, the hiring of technicians to do laboratory work while the scientist is on family leave, and a reduction in travel requirements (Mervis, 2011). A survey of biochemists showed that women based their career decisions as much on family-related factors as on professional surroundings, but that men thought more about working conditions when making career decisions ("Making Choices," 2012).

Family issues continue to impede women's careers (Dey and Hill, 2007). Sociologist Mirra Komarovsky (1991:23) observed:

[I]n order to provide real options for men and women we shall have to reorganize economic and other institutions in a profound way, more profound in my opinion, than would be necessary,

for example, to solve the problems of the black minority in the United States. . . . Social investments in child care, maternity and paternity leaves, flexible work hours, job sharing, and other changes will be required to balance the private and public worlds for both men and women.

Sexual Harassment and Rape

The Equal Employment Opportunity Commission defines **sexual harassment** as unwelcome sexual attention, whether verbal or physical, that affects an employee's job conditions or creates a hostile working environment (Adler, 1991). Examples of sexual harassment include unsolicited and unwelcome flirtations, advances, or propositions; graphic or degrading comments about an employee's appearance, dress, or anatomy; the display of sexually suggestive objects or pictures; ill-received sexual jokes and offensive gestures; sexual or intrusive questions about an employee's personal life; explicit descriptions of a male's own sexual experiences; abuse of familiarities such as "honey," "baby," and "dear"; unnecessary, unwanted physical contact such as touching, hugging, pinching, patting, or kissing; whistling and catcalls; and leering.

Explanations of sexual harassment include societal-, organizational-, and individual-level approaches (Welsh, 1999). Researchers who have studied sexual harassment on the job find that women are much more likely to be harassed than men, and that important factors affecting sexual harassment in the workplace are power differences (financially vulnerable people are more likely to be harassed) and masculinity (Uggen and Blackstone, 2004).

Sexual harassment is not limited to the workplace. A 2011 report on sexual harassment at schools showed that 48 percent of students experience some type of sexual harassment, with verbal harassment being the most common; 30 percent of students reported being sexually harassed through texts, e-mail, Facebook, and other electronic means (Hill and Kearl, 2011). Nearly all the incidents were student-to-student. A nationwide study of college students showed that half of all college women have been subjected to sexist remarks, catcalls, or whistles; between 10 and 20 percent report having been stalked, getting obscene phone calls, being the subject of false rumors, or other forms of sexual victimization (Fisher, Cullen, and Turner, 2000).

Rape is the most violent form of sexual victimization. In 2011 the Federal Bureau of Investigation announced a new definition of rape: "The penetration, no matter how slight, of the vagina or anus with any body part or object, or oral penetration by a sex organ of another person, without the consent of the victim" (Federal Bureau of Investigation, 2012). Both males and females may be victim or perpetrator. The old definition, established in 1927, included the words "forcibly and against her will," but the revised definition protects anyone who does not give consent for any reason, and physical resistance is not required to demonstrate lack of consent. Although the legal definition of rape varies from state to state, the new FBI definition reflects most state rape statutes.

Because the rape of males has not until now been included in the definition of rape for the purposes of reporting data, we will not present comparative data. But rape of women by men is the much more common crime; rape of men by women is very rare. Estimates of the percentage of women in the United States who have been raped by men sometime in their lifetimes range from 10 to 25 percent (see Box 8.2).

Why do men rape women? Most rapists are *not* psychologically disturbed, sexually inadequate, or unable to relate to women in a normal way. Sociologists offer explanations that emphasize culture, socialization, and social structure.

Culture can create a context in which rapes are more likely to occur through the creation and dissemination of norms, values, and ways of thinking that encourage and justify rape. Examples are music videos, movies, television shows,

How Many People Get Raped?

Researcher Mary Koss made headlines—and drew heavy criticism—when she published her findings that more than a quarter of all college women have experienced an act that met the legal definition of rape (Koss, Gidycz, and Wisniewski, 1987). Her estimate was 10–15 times higher than comparable rates reported by the Bureau of Justice Statistics in their National Crime Victimization Survey (NCVS). Why are the numbers so different?

Rape may be the crime for which it is most difficult to get reliable numbers, and it seems that . how the data are gathered is critical. The Uniform Crime Reports (UCR) data, measured by the FBI Index of Crime, are based on police reports of crime. Based on the old definition of rape, before a rape appeared in the UCR, police had to be satisfied that "a man must have had (1) carnal knowledge of a woman, (2) forcibly, and (3) against her will" (Gove, Hughes, and Geerken, 1985).

While the NCVS typically uncovers higher rates of rape than appear in the UCR, the questions used to determine these rates do not actually ask a woman if she has ever been raped. A woman must tell the interviewer that she has been raped in response to general questions about whether she has ever been attacked or threatened. Rape itself is never mentioned; it is up to the person being questioned to volunteer the information (Gove, Hughes, and Geerken, 1985).

An obvious way to get more information is to ask people directly whether they have been raped. A national survey that asked this question of both men and women found that 9.2 percent of women and less than 1.0 percent of men had ever been raped (Kessler et al., 1995). Both numbers are significantly higher than those that appear in either the NCVS or the UCR.

Even higher rates are obtained when the question is phrased in a different way. When respondents were asked if anyone had ever forced them to do something sexual, 22 percent of women and 4 percent of men responded yes (Laumann et al., 1994; Michael et al., 1994). A study of nearly 5,000 women attending U.S. colleges and universities also found that what is asked makes a big difference (Fisher, Cullen, and Turner, 2000). This study included a comparison component that used methods similar to those in the NCVS. The main study, which included extremely detailed questions about "unwanted sexual experiences," found rates of rape and attempted rape that were 11 and 6 times higher, respectively, than the rates found by the comparison study.

The rates reported by Bonnie Fisher and her colleagues (2000) are in line with those reported by Mary Koss (1987) for college women and by others for the general population. Fisher's survey responses showed that 1.7 percent of the college women had experienced a rape and 1.1 percent an attempted rape during an average period of about seven months. What does such a rate mean? For a school with 10,000 female students, more than 350 of them experience rape or attempted rape in a single academic year. Projected over the five years that most students now spend getting an undergraduate degree, one-fifth to one-quarter of all college women would experience a rape or attempted rape.

magazine displays, and pornography that portray women as sex objects, always being ready for sex, and being coerced or forced into sexual activity. Masculine culture among young men often involves patterns of discussion, joking, and banter that treat women primarily as objects of sexual desire and as legitimate targets in sexual pursuits (Thio, 2010; Fields, 1993). This may not directly cause rape, but it creates a normative environment that makes the world safer for rape and rapists (Martin and Hummer, 1995). Studies show that campus athletes, perhaps the group most heavily influenced by the culture of masculinity, are more likely to exhibit sexual aggression than other college men (Koss and Gaines, 1993; Nelson, 1994; Crosset et al., 1996).

Cultural factors might not be such important factors in rape and sexual harassment if it were not for gender inequality. Because of gender inequality, women lack the power to respond forcefully and effectively to prevent harassment and rape and to deal with situations leading to them. Some social scientists argue that sexual harassment, sexual aggression, and rape are methods men use to intimidate women,

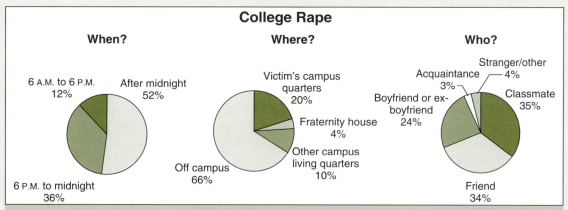

College Rape

When?

- 6 A.M. to 6 P.M. 12%
- After midnight 52%
- 6 P.M. to midnight 36%

Where?

- Victim's campus quarters 20%
- Fraternity house 4%
- Other campus living quarters 10%
- Off campus 66%

Who?

- Acquaintance 3%
- Stranger/other 4%
- Boyfriend or ex-boyfriend 24%
- Classmate 35%
- Friend 34%

It would appear that rape is not primarily a problem of public life. These data for college women apply to the general population. Rapists are not likely to be lurking in dark alleys; they are likely to be sitting in your living room or next to you in a car. Rape is primarily a problem of private life, and rapists are most likely to be people with whom the rape victim has a personal relationship.

Source: Figure generated by the authors using data from Fisher, Cullen, and Turner, 2000.

How many rapes we believe occur seems to depend primarily on how victims are asked about their experiences. Fisher and her colleagues concluded, "The use of graphically worded screen questions . . . likely prompted more women who had experienced a sexual victimization to report this fact to the interviewer" (Fisher, Cullen, and Turner, 2000:14).

Questions for Discussion

1. We have provided the new FBI definition of crime in the text. How do you think this definition will affect the rate of rape reported in the Uniform Crime Reports?

2. The data on college rape (above) show that rapists are most likely to be someone the victim knows, perhaps intimately. Why do rapes occur in such situations? What strategies would help prevent such rapes?

keeping them dependent, powerless, and out of male-dominated jobs (Graff, 2005; Peterson, 1992).

Culture and gender inequality combine to influence the prevalence of rape and sexual aggression. Sanday's (1981) study of small societies showed that societies with high rates of rape were those where males were heavily dominant and in which sexual aggression was a symbol of masculinity and of men's control and mastery of women, while those with little rape were those that discouraged sexual aggression. Sanday (1996) and other researchers (Schwartz and DeKeseredy, 1997; Martin and Hummer, 1995; Schwartz, 1995) have found that college campuses with low rates of rape are those in which the culture of masculinity is not strong and where sexual assault and rape are taken seriously and severely punished. Those with high rates of rape are those where the student culture values heavy drinking, male dominance, and traditional masculine values.

Politics and Government

The number of women in politics in the United States has increased in recent years, and Hillary

Clinton's bid for the Democratic Party presidential nomination drew the country's attention to a variety of gender issues. Although 27 states have never had a female governor, the others have, and six women were serving terms in 2010; in all, 35 women have governed a U.S. state. The U.S. Senate had 17 women serving in 2011, and 76 representatives were women (compared to 362 men). And women have turned out in greater numbers than men to vote in recent elections. Thousands of women have entered politics at the local and state levels over the last several decades, enlarging the pool of candidates for higher office.

But political success has not come easily to American women (Witt, Paget, and Matthews, 1993), and it is not proceeding at a steady pace. Although the number of women in the U.S. House and Senate has increased, the proportion—16 percent—has grown only slightly in recent years (Werschkul and Williams, 2004), and the proportion of women legislators is much smaller in the United States than in many other countries (see Figure 8.1). If the United States adds women to Congress at the rate it did during the past decade, we will have equal numbers of male and female senators and representatives in about 100 years (Werschkul and Williams, 2004).

Three sets of factors play a part in women's representation in politics (Paxton and Kunovich, 2003). Structural factors include the low "supply" of women candidates, as political candidates tend to come from the law and other professions in which women have been underrepresented. Political factors include the low "demand" for women candidates. Research has shown that ideology played a more important role than politics in predicting women's political representation in a country, affecting both supply and demand (Paxton and Kunovich, 2003).

Does having women in positions of leadership make a difference? A study of state supreme court judges found that female judges voted more liberally than males in the cases studied—death penalty and obscenity cases (Songer and

Crews-Meyer, 2000). The researchers also found that male judges were more likely to support liberal positions when there was a woman among their ranks. And researchers have found that in sex discrimination cases female judges are more likely than males to rule in favor of the victim, and male judges are more likely to rule in favor of the victim when female judges are serving with them (Boyd and Epstein, 2009).

Perhaps more important is the potential for women in positions of power to make real social structural changes. For example, it is unlikely to be mere coincidence that in Sweden, with one of the highest proportions of women legislators in the world, maternity benefits also are among the best in the world (see Table 8.1). And a study in India showed that in villages with women in positions of leadership, the gender gap in adolescent education disappeared, girls spent less time on household chores, and the gender gap

Increasing numbers of women are achieving positions of leadership and authority. Shown here is Ruth J. Simmons, president of Brown University. Harvard and MIT also have had female presidents.

in aspirations narrowed significantly for both parents and teens (Beaman et al., 2012).

The Women's Movement

Over the past 50 years, no social movement has had a more substantial impact on the way Americans think and act than the women's movement. In the 1960s the women's movement built upon earlier movements while gaining new impetus from the involvement of women in the civil rights movement (Taylor, 1989; Buechler, 1990; Simon and Danziger, 1991). Cross-national research suggests that the "first wave" (1800–1950) of women's movements focused primarily on legal equality, including the pursuit of suffrage, or the right to vote; the "second wave" (since the 1960s) has centered primarily on social equality, particularly in jobs and education (Chafetz and Dworkin, 1986; Schnittker, Freese, and Powell, 2003).

The revival of feminist activity in the 1960s was spearheaded by a variety of groups. Some, such as the National Organization for Women (NOW), were organized at the national level by well-known women. Others were grassroots groups that engaged in campaigns for abortion reform or welfare rights, consciousness-raising discussion sessions, or promotion of the interests of professional or lesbian women.

Significant progress has been made with regard to gender egalitarianism in U.S. society. Sociologist Fred Pampel contends that as structural changes have increased opportunities for women, egalitarian attitudes have been adopted; when people see women who are highly educated, providing effective business and political leadership, and performing competently in the workforce, they adopt values that support gender equality (Pampel, 2011). But an analysis of survey responses in the General Social Survey shows that gender role attitudes "stalled" in the mid-1990s and have changed little since then (Cotter, Hermsen, and Vanneman, 2011).

At about the same time that support for gender egalitarianism leveled off, so did the narrowing of the wage gap, the disappearance of gender differences in housework, women's entry into traditionally male occupations, married mothers' participation in the labor force, and women's success in state-level politics. The only area in which American women have made steady progress since the mid-1990s is education, where they now have surpassed men (Cotter, Hermsen, and Vanneman, 2011).

Cotter and his colleagues (2011) argue that this shift is not a return to the gender values of the 1950s; they see it as a reflection of societal support both for stay-at-home mothers and for women contributing to the labor force, with an emphasis on choice. Pampel's (2011) analysis of attitudes showed that men are less likely than women to hold egalitarian views and respond less than women do to social change, which may contribute to the stall reported by Cotter and colleagues.

Sources of Gender Differences

We have been focusing on gender inequality with respect to the macrostructural features of society. What about more micro- or individual-level explanations for gender differences? In this section we will look at gender differences and biology, culture, and identity.

Gender and Biology

The biological aspects of gender consist of the physical differences between men and women: Women have the capacity to ovulate, carry a fetus until delivery, and provide it with milk after birth; men have the ability to produce and transmit sperm. Women and men also differ in their responses to drugs and other medical interventions as well as in their susceptibilities to many illnesses (Greenberger, 2008; Simon, 2005).

The role biology plays in producing behavioral differences between men and women is far less clear than the role it plays in physical differences. A review of research published in the

1970s concluded that there were four fairly well established differences between girls and boys, including greater verbal ability among girls and greater visual-spatial and mathematical abilities and higher aggression among boys (Maccoby and Jacklin, 1974). However, recent research casts these findings in a new light. We now know that the vast majority of gender differences reported in studies have been small or essentially negligible. Janet Shibley Hyde (2005) reviewed 46 *meta-analyses,* in which researchers combine and summarize research findings from many studies of the same question. The 46 papers Hyde reviewed all were meta-analyses of gender difference studies, and they included a wide variety of specific topics: verbal skills, mathematical skills, physical strength, reading comprehension, spatial visualization, aggression, helping behaviors, sexuality, leadership abilities, self-esteem, depression, cheating, moral reasoning, and many more.

Hyde found that 78 percent of the gender differences in these meta-analyses were small or close to zero—in other words, hardly differences at all. Gender differences in most aspects of communication are small, as are gender differences in moral reasoning and moral orientation. Males and females differ very little in their life satisfaction, happiness, self-esteem, attitudes about work, approaches to leadership, reading and mathematics abilities, and many other variables.

Do men and women differ at all? Some gender differences were found to be large and reasonably stable, showing up in a variety of studies. Hyde's review of gender difference studies showed that the largest differences are in motor performance, especially after puberty, when male bone size and muscle mass begin to exceed that of females. Specifically, males are, on average, able to throw faster and farther than females. There also are moderate differences for other

"I broncobust *and* I Dust–Bust. You got a problem with that?"

measures of motor performance, with men having a stronger grip and being able to sprint faster.

Some of the measures of sexuality also showed large gender differences; males are more likely than females to masturbate frequently and to have a positive attitude about sex in casual and uncommitted relationships. A moderate gender difference was found for aggression, with men and boys more likely than women and girls to engage in physical aggression.

What about Maccoby and Jacklin's (1974) findings on verbal, mathematical, and visual-spatial abilities? Hyde's (2005) review found gender differences ranging in size from very small to moderate for cognitive variables. Two exceptions were moderate-to-large differences favoring males in mechanical reasoning and mental rotation. A study of public school children in grades 2 to 11 reported no gender differences in math skills (Hyde et al., 2008). Only very small differences have been found in language skills, and studies contradicted one another, with girls ahead of boys in vocabulary in one study but behind in another (Hyde, 2005).

Hyde's (2005) review of the information gathered in many studies also showed that some gender differences change with growth and development. Others depend on social context, with differences in aggression, smiling, interrupting, mathematical performance, and helping behaviors changing and even reversing under different circumstances.

In spite of arguments that deemphasize biology in gendered behavior, this issue is far from settled. Recently, some sociologists have proposed formally integrating social and biological factors in a single framework, and have argued that the effect of gender socialization depends on biological factors and vice versa. For example, Udry (2000) showed that prenatal exposure to testosterone (a male hormone that is found in both sexes) in females reduces the effects of gender socialization on adult gendered behavior. Udry concluded that biological and socialization factors work together in generating gendered behavior but that biology also sets individual limits on gender socialization

and additional limits to the macroconstruction of gender. Udry's findings and conclusions are controversial and have generated debate, making it clear that more research will be needed before we can arrive at firm conclusions in this area (Kennelly, Merz, and Lorber, 2001; Miller and Costello, 2001; Risman, 2001; Udry, 2001).

Gender and Culture

Despite the very few gender differences identified by researchers, all societies assign gender roles—the sets of cultural expectations that define the ways in which the members of each sex should behave. Anthropological evidence suggests that gender roles probably represent the earliest division of labor among human beings. Consequently, we are all born into societies with well-established cultural guidelines for the behavior of men and women (see Box 8.3).

That these cultural expectations are based on any "real" gender differences is cast into doubt by the results of a survey of 224 societies (Murdock, 1935). Anthropologist George P. Murdock found in his cross-cultural survey that vast differences exist in the social definitions of what constitutes appropriate masculine and feminine behavior. Indeed, as shown in Table 8.2, the allocation of duties often differs sharply from that of our own society. For example, for generations, U.S. communities have had laws restricting the weights that a working woman is permitted to lift. Yet the Arapesh of New Guinea assigned women the task of carrying heavy loads because their heads were believed to be harder and stronger than those of men. Among the Tasmanians of the South Pacific, the most dangerous type of hunting—swimming out to remote rocks in the sea to stalk and club sea otters—was assigned to women. Moreover, women formed the bodyguard of Dahomeyan kings because they were deemed to be particularly fierce fighters. And although most peoples believe that men should take the initiative in sexual matters, the Maori of New Zealand and the Trobriand Islanders (near New Guinea) give this prerogative to women (Ford and Beach, 1951).

Table 8.2	The Division of Labor by Sex in 224 Societies				
	Number of Societies and Sex of Person by Whom the Activity Is Performed				
Activity	Men Always	Men Usually	Either Sex	Women Usually	Women Always
Hunting	166	13	0	0	0
Trapping small animals	128	13	4	1	2
Herding	38	8	4	0	5
Fishing	98	34	19	3	4
Clearing agricultural land	73	22	17	5	13
Dairy operations	17	4	3	1	13
Preparing and planting soil	31	23	33	20	37
Erecting and dismantling shelter	14	2	5	6	22
Tending and harvesting crops	10	15	35	39	44
Bearing burdens	12	6	35	20	57
Cooking	5	1	9	28	158
Metalworking	78	0	0	0	0
Boat building	91	4	4	0	1
Working in stone	68	3	2	0	2
Basket making	25	3	10	6	82
Weaving	19	2	2	6	67
Manufacturing and repairing of clothing	12	3	8	9	95

Source: Reprinted by permission from Social Forces, May 15, 1937, "Comparative Data on the Division of Labor by Sex," by George P. Murdock. Copyright © The University of North Carolina Press.

The great variation in the gender roles of men and women from one society to another points to a social foundation for most of these differences (Bernard, 1987; South and Trent, 1988; Intons-Peterson, 1988). So do the changes observed from one time to another in sex-linked behavior patterns within the same society, such as hair length and style and clothing fashions. All this suggests that gender roles are largely a matter of social definition and socially constructed meanings.

Gender Identities

Gender identities are the conceptions we have of ourselves as being male or female. Most people have a good fit between their anatomy and their gender identity. Boys generally come to behave in ways their culture labels "masculine," and girls learn to be "feminine."

But there are some individuals for whom this is not the case. The most striking examples are *transsexuals*—individuals who have normal sexual organs but who psychologically feel like members of the opposite sex. Transsexuality should not be confused with homosexuality. Homosexuality is a sexual orientation, not a confused gender identity; lesbians have a strong sense of themselves as females, and they are sexually attracted to other females. In some

Gender Expectations: Cigars, Tupperware, and Condoms

Many—perhaps most—college students today believe that gender inequality is pretty much a thing of the past. Because they grew up in a time when women could vote, go to college, work outside the home, run for office, and the like, some students find feminist ideology to be extreme. So complacent are many students that they are quick to reject arguments of feminist sociologists that our culture promotes gender inequality through its "compulsory heterosexuality." But the results of more than 650 field observations recorded by sociology students over a 15-year period offer substantial evidence that compulsory heterosexuality is deeply embedded in American culture (Nielsen, Walden, and Kunkel, 2000).

Students were assigned to think up some way to violate a gender norm and to record what happened as a result of their violation. They were to choose and perform in public some act typically associated with the opposite sex and record both the reactions of others and their own feelings. Over the years, students came up with more than one hundred different "gender transgressions." Male students crocheted in public, bought sanitary napkins, wore women's clothes or shoes, cried, carried purses, tried out "women's occupations," painted their fingernails, and read romance novels. One even threw a Tupperware party. Female students opened doors for men, smoked cigars and pipes, chewed tobacco, sent men flowers, went shirtless while doing sports activities, bought condoms, and read *Playgirl*. Some displayed knowledge about "guy stuff," such as cars and sports.

And what were the reactions to these norm violations? Surprisingly, especially given the wide variety of projects, the reactions were easily categorized—and completely different depending on whether the norm violator was a woman or a man. Men were labeled homosexual or potentially homosexual, and women were considered either to be sexually aggressive and promiscuous or of dubious attractiveness to men. Comments heard by the male gender-norm violators included "We gotta sweet fella here," "What a fag!" and "Fairies aren't allowed in here." Comments recorded by female gender-norm violators included "It's a good thing she's married because she probably wouldn't get any dates," "Is this any way for two pretty young girls to behave?" and "There's a totally cute girl smoking a ——ing cigar!"

The experiences of the hundreds of students involved in this study clearly demonstrate the power of gender expectations. Gender-role norms function as a signal of the willingness of those adhering to them to be part of the heterosexual world, and they provide sanctions for those who would violate them. Feminist sociologists argue that compulsory heterosexuality is deeply embedded in our culture and in the demands it makes on us in our everyday lives. This study supports that argument.

Questions for Discussion

1. Have you ever knowingly or unknowingly violated a gender norm? What did you do? What was the reaction of those around you?

2. How do you feel when you see men dressed as women? Or women with men's haircuts, no makeup, and men's clothes? Explain your reaction.

---

cases of transsexuality, medical science has found a way to modify the person's anatomy to conform with the person's gender identity.

How do individuals develop gender identities? In this section we will examine three explanations.

Cultural Transmission Theory

Cultural transmission theorists contend that the acquisition of gender identities and behaviors is a gradual process of learning that begins in infancy (Bandura, 1971, 1973; Fagot, Leinbach, and O'Boyle, 1992). They suggest that parents, teachers, and other adults shape a child's behavior by reinforcing responses that are deemed appropriate to the child's gender role and discouraging inappropriate ones. Moreover, children are motivated to attend to, learn from, and imitate same-sex models because they think of same-sex models as more like themselves

(Mischel, 1970). Children are given cues to their gender roles in a great variety of ways, from how their rooms are decorated to what toys they are given to play with and clothes they are given to wear.

Cognitive Development Theory

Cultural transmission theory portrays children as passive individuals who are programmed for behavior by adults. *Cognitive development theory* calls our attention to the fact that children actively seek to acquire gender identities and roles.

According to cognitive development theory, as discussed in Chapter 3 (p. 71) (Kohlberg, 1966, 1969; Kohlberg and Ullian, 1974), children come to label themselves as "boys" or "girls" when they are between 18 months and three years of age. Once they have identified themselves as males or females, they want to adopt behaviors consistent with their newly discovered status. This process is called *self-socialization.* According to Kohlberg, children form a stereotyped conception of maleness and femaleness—an oversimplified, exaggerated, cartoonlike image. Then they use this stereotyped image to organize behavior and cultivate the attitudes and actions associated with being a boy or a girl. Neuroscientist Lise Eliot points out that very small cognitive gaps can grow because of positive feedback loops (Eliot, 2009).

Both the cultural transmission and cognitive development theories of gender-role learning have received research support (Maccoby and Jacklin, 1974; Bem, 1981; Serbin and Sprafkin, 1986; Martin and Little, 1990). Social and behavioral scientists increasingly see gender-role acquisition as being explained by elements from both theoretical approaches.

Self-Construals and Gender

In Chapter 3 (p. 80), we discussed self-conception and identity. Psychologists Susan Cross and Laura Madson used differences in self-construal, which is essentially synonymous with our term *self-conception,* to explain gender differences in the

United States (Cross and Madson, 1997). Individuals in some societies develop a sense of self that is highly interdependent; in East Asian cultures, for example, self-definition is based primarily on relationships and group memberships. Maintaining harmonious relationships with others is extremely important. Such a definition of self is referred to by psychologists as an *interdependent self-construal.* In contrast, many Western societies are individualistic, and self-definition is based on individualism: One's unique attributes and the importance of an individual distinguishing him- or herself from others are key to developing a sense of self. This definition of self has been called an *independent self-construal.*

Cross and Madson, with other researchers, pointed out that the independent self-construal model describes men better than it does women in the United States and that most U.S. women can probably be best described by the interdependent self-construal model. Many social influences in the United States promote independent ways of behaving, feeling, and thinking for men; for women, relational ways of behaving, feeling, and thinking are more likely to be promoted (e.g., Denny, 2011). This major difference in self-construal between men and women in the United States, Cross and Madson argued, has important consequences in terms of gender differences, including those in cognition, motivation, emotion, and social behavior. For example, they found that women are more willing to express most emotions, while men are more willing to express anger. Women are also more likely to be sensitive to the emotions of others and to base their own emotions on those.

Sociological Perspectives on Gender Stratification

As noted in Chapter 1 (p. 16), the roles, contributions, and experiences of women were not a major part of theory and social research for most of the history of sociology. Well into the

20th century, female social scientists, who were most likely to make contributions in this area, were marginalized and never able to establish themselves in academic sociology. As a result, traditional theories included little that was relevant to the issue of gender inequality. Perhaps the first work to attempt a systematic understanding of the differentiation of gender roles was Parsons and Bales' (1955) study of the family from the functionalist perspective. But as we will see, many sociologists view this work as both an attempt to explain gender roles *and* as a justification of prevailing gender inequalities.

Since the 1960s, however, sociologists have been heavily influenced by feminist thinking (see Chapter 1, p. 16). And while neither the conflict nor the interactionist perspective includes an organized theory of gender inequality, feminists and contemporary sociologists have drawn upon the insights of the conflict and interactionist perspectives to develop an understanding of the nature of gender inequality and the sociocultural forces that perpetuate it.

As you will see, the functionalist, conflict, and interactionist perspectives offer interpretations of gender stratification that resemble and parallel their positions on class and racial or ethnic stratification. We will look more closely at each in this section, as well as discuss the feminist perspective on gender inequality.

The Functionalist Perspective

Functionalists suggest that a division of labor originally arose between men and women because of the woman's role in reproduction. Because women were often pregnant or nursing, preindustrial societies assigned domestic and child-rearing tasks to them. In contrast, men were assigned hunting and defense tasks because of their larger size and greater muscular strength. Functionalists contend that a gender division of labor promoted the survival of the species and therefore was retained.

Sociologists Talcott Parsons and Robert Bales (1955) built upon principles derived from the study of the dynamics of small groups in refining their functionalist position. They argued that two types of leaders are essential if a small group is to function effectively (see Chapter 4, pp. 103–105). *Instrumental leaders* (task specialists) devote their attention to appraising the problem at hand and organizing people's activity to deal with it. *Expressive leaders* (social-emotional specialists) focus on overcoming interpersonal problems in the group, defusing tensions, and promoting solidarity. Parsons and Bales suggested that families are also organized along instrumental-expressive lines. Men specialize in instrumental tasks, particularly roles associated with having a job and making money, and women in expressive tasks, supporting their husbands, doing household labor, and caring for children.

Essentially, Parsons and Bales were arguing that it was functional and beneficial for the society, for families, and for individuals if males play instrumental, goal-oriented roles and females play expressive roles, supporting husbands and nurturing children. Through the 1960s, 1970s, and 1980s, many sociologists attacked this position as taking an idealized family form from the United States in the 1950s and claiming that it was the uniquely superior model for gender and family relations in industrial societies. Other patterns exist and meet the needs of individuals, families, and the society—for example, the household where both wife and husband work and the household headed by a single parent with resources that allow access to high-quality child care. Critics of the functionalist approach also pointed out that this idealized structure makes men the more powerful actors and women relatively powerless and dependent on men. By arguing that this arrangement is necessary, functionalism becomes a powerful justification for the existence of gender inequality.

The Conflict Perspective

Much of the critique of functionalism from the 1950s to the 1980s came from conflict theorists who rejected functionalist arguments as simply offering a rationale for male dominance. They contended that a sexual division of labor is a social vehicle devised by men to ensure for themselves privilege, prestige, and power in their relationships with women. Gender inequality exists because it benefits men, who use the power it gives them to ensure its perpetuation. By relegating women to the home, men have been able to deny women those resources they need to succeed in the larger world. More particularly, conflict theorists have advanced a number of explanations for gender stratification (Collins, 1975; Vogel, 1983; Collier, 1988; Bradley, 1989; Chafetz, 1990). Some argue that the motivation for gender stratification derives from the economic exploitation of women's labor. Others say that the fundamental motive is men's desire to have women readily available for sexual gratification. Still others emphasize that the appropriation of women is not for copulation but for procreation, especially to produce male heirs and daughters who can be used as exchanges in cementing political and economic alliances with other families.

Sociologist Joan Acker (1992) suggested that in industrial capitalist societies, production is valued over reproduction. Whereas business, commerce, and industry are viewed as an essential source of well-being and wealth, child rearing, child care, and elder care are seen as secondary and wealth-consuming. Although "the family" is enshrined and idealized, reproduction (the domain of women) is shrouded in societal shadows and devalued.

The Interactionist Perspective

Interactionism has had a very important impact on the thinking of sociologists about gender inequality. If meanings form the basis of social life, then as meanings change, patterns of social interaction can change, thus altering the nature of social structure. Sociologists also have made use of the interactionist idea that we experience the world as a constructed reality. They developed the idea that while sex is given in nature, gender is socially constructed; it is a product of sociocultural processes involving symbols and

meanings. Interactionists argue that cultural meanings, including those that give rise to gender inequality, are continuously emerging and changing through social interaction. If so, then people can intentionally change the structure of gender differentiation and inequality by changing the meanings that underlie them. For example, when men define themselves in traditional masculine terms, value male dominance, and view women primarily as objects of sexual pleasure, rape and sexual harassment are more likely to occur. When we replace these meanings with those that value gender equality and view women as complete human beings, the rates of rape and sexual harassment decline.

Another example of how interactionism has influenced specific ideas about gender inequality can be seen in the study of gender stereotyping in everyday language. Our use of language can imply that women are secondary to men, in less powerful positions than men, or less competent than men, all of which thus encourages us to think about women in ways that perpetuate inequality. This happens when we use words like "men" and "he" to refer to both men and women, when we refer to presidents and doctors as "he" but to secretaries and teachers as "she," and when we refer to adult women as "girls" but refrain from calling adult men "boys." Use of such a symbolic framework encourages people to think of women stereotypically as less suited for powerful instrumental roles, to behave toward them accordingly, and to limit the options available for women's self-definition (Richardson, 1987). Interactionist theorists argue that by influencing people's identities in this way, everyday sexist language helps to perpetuate gender inequality, and that changing our language patterns can help to eliminate it.

The Feminist Perspective

As we pointed out in Chapter 1 (p. 16), feminism is not a single theory but an evolving set of theoretical perspectives. Just as conditions for women may not change rapidly until some critical number of women attain positions of economic, social, and political power, so sociological research focused on women's experiences and activities has increased as a function of women becoming research sociologists. Feminist critique of or addition to other perspectives on gender inequality has emerged in recent decades. For example, Miriam Johnson (1993) argued that serving the expressive function in family and society need not lead to disadvantage for women but that it has led to disadvantage because it exists in the context of a patriarchal culture that values men's instrumentality over women's expressiveness. Changing the patriarchal normative order instead of changing patterns of role differentiation, then, is a more effective way to reduce gender inequality. However, this cultural change has so far eluded us, and we are left with the question of how patriarchal structures can be functional (Lengermann and Niebrugge, 2011). If they are, it would appear that they are primarily functional for men.

Myra Marx Ferree and Elaine J. Hall (2000) provide another critique of functionalism. While functionalists see group differences as beneficial, they explain, feminists "see this grouping process as a socially costly repression of individual variation and potential." Ferree and Hall argue that inequality does not arise from individual differences between people. Rather, their gender-relations model of inequality posits that social structures produce inequality and gender differences follow from them:

Gender is organized through micro-, meso-, and macro-level processes that apply gender labels to jobs, skills, institutions, and organizations as well as to people and that use these labels to produce, express, and legitimate inequality. . . . When gender itself operates in and through macro-social institutions, what it produces is not just differences . . . , but inequality. (2000:476)

Sociologists Cecilia Ridgeway and Lynn Smith-Lovin (1999) point out that gender is significantly different from other forms of social inequality. Unlike racial and ethnic inequality or class stratification, the key players in gender inequality—men and women—interact extensively at home, at work, at church, and in a variety of role relationships. These everyday interactions, they contend, re-create the gender system. Such interactions would act to undermine the gender system only in two cases: (1) if the interactions feature women with status or power advantages over men or (2) if they are peer interactions not driven by cultural beliefs about the competence of males and females.

Feminist research has added substantially to our knowledge of women's experiential, subjective, and emotional lives. Though a variety of perspectives make up the "feminist perspective," they are unified in the effort to develop understandings of gender inequality that can be used to transform society and women's lives.

What Can Sociology Do for You?

This chapter presented information about the challenges facing and opportunities available to women in contemporary U.S. society. Male or female, if you are concerned about gender equity in the United States, you may be interested in pursuing a career in policy, research, diversity training, employee retention, or the prevention of sexual harassment. The Business and Professional Women's Foundation promotes workplace equity for women and is a leading advocate for working women; check out its website at **http://www.bpwfoundation.org/index.php/resources/career_center.** Another website of interest might be **www.womensleadershipexchange.com.** For more information about how your choice of major affects your long-term earnings, see the American Association of University Women's 2007 study "Behind the Pay Gap" at **www.aauw.org/research/behindPayGap.cfm.**

If the issues raised in Chapter 8 were of interest to you, you may want to take upper-level sociology courses in gender or sexuality.

The Chapter in Brief: *Gender Inequality*

Gender Stratification

Men and women differ in their access to privilege, prestige, and power. The distribution problem of who gets what, when, and how has traditionally been answered in favor of males. **Sex** is a biologically determined characteristic; **gender** is a socially constructed characteristic. All societies use anatomical differences to assign **gender roles. Gender identities** are the conceptions we have of ourselves as being male or female.

■ **Sexism and Patriarchy**   **Sexism** operates at both an individual level and an institutional level. The most pervasive form of institutional sexism is **patriarchy.** Women exhibit four of the five properties associated with a *minority group.*

■ **Gender Inequality around the World**   No nation treats its women as well as its men. Women in many countries suffer discrimination and abuse, yet women around the world do considerably better than U.S. women in some areas.

■ **Gender Inequality in the United States**   U.S. women have made substantial gains over the past decades but continue to do most of the household work and child rearing. Despite increasing involvement in the paid workforce, women continue to be excluded from top jobs and to earn less than men. **Sexual harassment** remains a common workplace hazard for women, and somewhere between 10 and 25 percent of women have been raped. Men still dominate U.S. political life.

Sources of Gender Differences

Gender roles can be seen as arising from biological development or cultural contributions.

■ **Gender and Biology**   The biological aspects of gender consist of the physical differences between men and women, but the role biology plays in producing behavioral differences between men and women is shrouded in controversy.

■ **Gender and Culture**   Gender roles probably represent the earliest division of labor among humans. Various societies have specific social definitions of appropriate behavior for males and females.

■ **Gender Identities**   Gender identities are the concepts we have of ourselves as being male or female. Theories of the acquisition of gender identities include cultural transmission, cognitive development, and self-construals.

Sociological Perspectives on Gender Stratification

The major sociological perspectives offer interpretations of gender stratification that resemble and parallel their positions on class and racial or ethnic stratification.

■ **The Functionalist Perspective**   Functionalists suggest that families are organized along instrumental-expressive lines, with men specializing in instrumental tasks and women in expressive tasks.

■ **The Conflict Perspective**   Conflict theorists contend that a sexual division of labor is a social vehicle devised by men to ensure themselves of privilege, prestige, and power in their relationships with women.

■ **The Interactionist Perspective**   Interactionists argue that gender inequality persists because of the way we define men and women and their appropriate roles in society. Language helps perpetuate inequality.

■ **The Feminist Perspective** Feminism is not a single theory but an evolving set of theoretical perspectives. Feminists argue that women are disadvantaged because society is patriarchal; the assignment of group differences is socially costly and repressive. Everyday interactions between men and women re-create and support the gender system.

Glossary

gender The sociocultural distinction between males and females.

gender identities The conceptions we have of ourselves as being male or female.

gender roles Sets of cultural expectations that define the ways in which the members of each sex should behave.

patriarchy A system of social organization in which men have a disproportionate share of power.

sex A reference to whether one is genetically male or female; determines the biological role that one will play in reproduction.

sexism The set of cultural and social processes that justify and promote disadvantage for women.

sexual harassment Unwelcome sexual attention, whether verbal or physical, that affects an employee's job conditions or creates a hostile working environment.

Review Questions

1. Define sex and gender.
2. How do the terms *gender role* and *gender identity* differ?
3. What is patriarchy?
4. Briefly summarize the variability in quality of life experienced by women around the world.
5. How do U.S. women compare with U.S. men in terms of occupations, employment, earnings, and representation in politics?
6. Compare and contrast biological and cultural bases for gender differences.
7. Briefly describe the theories of gender identity acquisition.
8. How do the functionalist, conflict, interactionist, and feminist perspectives explain gender inequalities?

Internet Connection   www.mhhe.com/hughes11e

The most powerful political positions in most societies have almost always been held by men. Until recently, women's involvement in the formal operations of political institutions has been minimal. Go to the website of the Inter-Parliamentary Union, **http://www.ipu.org/.** Explore this site for information about women's involvement in political institutions in societies around the world. Using this information, and other information in the current chapter, write a short report about the nature of gender inequality in politics and the efforts of governments and political organizations and associations to promote change.

Political and Economic Power

C
ould you live for a year without products from China? It sounds easy, but
when Sarah Bongiorni and her family
tried for a year to buy absolutely nothing that
had been made in China, they were surprised at
how difficult it was (Bongiorni, 2007). They
expected to find that electronic devices and toys
came from China. But catch-and-release mouse-
traps? Clothespins, eating utensils, and bath-
mats? Apple juice, honey, canned goods,
freeze-dried strawberries, and pet food? Early
on in their experiment, Bongiorni spent two
weeks trying to find a non-China-produced pair
of sneakers for her son. As the year progressed,
she found that shirts, underwear, belts, and even
high-fashion items sold in specialty shops also
come to us from China. Holidays were especially challenging; plastic Halloween pumpkins,
Easter eggs, and Christmas tree lights are produced in China. Bongiorni's consumer research
led her to conclude that all of our holidays,
including the Fourth of July, are "Made in
China."

China's rapid expansion in the production
of goods has enabled Americans to obtain lots
of products much more cheaply than would
otherwise be the case. It also has meant a loss of
jobs for American workers in the textile industry, computer production, the steel industry, and
many other areas, including a myriad of small
manufacturing plants throughout the country.
For China, it has meant a rapidly growing economy, one that is projected to be the largest in the
world by 2041 (Jacques, 2009; Mahbubani,
2008; Wilson and Purushothaman, 2003), as
well as increasing geopolitical power.

China is not the only country whose economy is growing rapidly because it provides consumer goods and services that are marketed
worldwide. India, Brazil, Malaysia, Indonesia,
Mexico, and South Korea are also growing very
quickly. Of the six largest economies in the
world today (the G6—the United States, the

279

United Kingdom, France, Germany, Italy, and Japan), only the United States and Japan are predicted to be in the top six in 2025, and by 2050 the United States will no longer be number one (Jacques, 2009). The western European economies will be replaced by China, Brazil, India, Mexico, and Russia.

Important effects of this projected economic growth will be a huge increase in quality of life and a decline in poverty in many developing countries, effects we are already beginning to see (Mahbubani, 2008). China, for example, has increased its science and technology spending by 20 percent every year for more than a decade (Mervis, 2010). But what else is likely to happen? Because economic power is intimately connected with political power, we will probably experience dramatic shifts in the global balance of power, including a decline in U.S. power. In addition, the structure of power within societies is likely to change. We cannot predict exactly how these changes will affect our lives, but the concepts and ideas presented in this chapter provide a basis for thinking about what to expect. We can get started by discussing briefly why power and economic relations are so important and how they are connected.

Individuals and groups who control critical resources—rewards, punishments, and persuasive communications—are able to dictate the way social life is ordered. To command key organizations is to command people and to influence the direction and the outcomes in their lives. Thus, power is the bedrock of social organization (Bierstedt, 1950). Changes in how power is organized and distributed in a society lead to changes in how institutions and groups are created and perpetuated, and thus to fundamental changes in a society's way of life.

As we noted in Chapter 6, *power* is the ability of individuals and groups to realize their will in human affairs even if it involves the resistance of others. But when we say that some people have more power and other people have less, we are doing more than describing people's characteristics. We are describing their social relations with others.

As sociologist Richard Emerson (1962) argued, power is an attribute of a social relationship. If we have two people, A and B, the power of person A over B is determined by B's dependence on A. Thus, if A is in control of resources needed or desired by B, A will have some degree of power over B. A's power will be at its maximum when B has no alternative sources of the resource outside the A-B relationship. A and B need not be people. They can be groups, organizations, ethnic groups, or nations—any person or social unit that can be in a social relationship with another.

Viewed from this power-dependence framework, power is closely linked to economics. An *economy* is a social institution that organizes the production, distribution, and consumption of goods and services. Goods and services are the resources that individuals, groups, organizations, and nations need to survive. Control of resources, particularly control of production and distribution, leads directly to power. Alexander Hamilton expressed this nicely in *The Federalist* in 1788: "In the general course of human nature, a power over a man's subsistence amounts to a power over his will."

Power is not distributed randomly or arbitrarily; it is institutionalized in a patterned, recurrent manner and hence is embedded in stable social arrangements. It gives direction to human affairs, channeling people's actions along one course rather than another, often in very complex and even hidden ways (Lukes, 2007). The power that makes a real difference in the way social life works is the power that flows from the dominant organizations and institutions. In this chapter we will examine power that makes a real difference— that which is vested in economic and political institutions.

Power, Authority, and the State

The State

The **state**—the political institution—is an arrangement that consists of people who exercise an effective monopoly in the use of physical coercion within a given territory. The state rests on **force**—power whose basis is the threat or application of punishment. Clearly, the ability to take life and inflict suffering affords a critical advantage in human affairs. In effect, force constitutes a final court of appeals; there is usually no appeal to force other than the exercise of superior force. Sovereign nations restrict, and even prohibit, the independent exercise of force by their subjects; otherwise, governments could not suppress forceful challenges to their authority (Lenski, 1966; Lehman, 1988). But even though force is ultimately the basis of the state, it is only in unusual situations that societal power actually takes this form.

The state is a relatively recent institution in human history. The existence of a state, which requires that some people be able to devote time and energy to organizing power resources, was not possible as long as people could only produce enough to keep everybody alive. Changes in subsistence patterns that permitted the production of a *social surplus*—goods and services over and above those necessary for survival—provided the foundations for the state (see Chapter 2, p. 61).

External factors such as threats and trading partners also played a part. A state typically arose as part of a larger social arrangement or system of states called *nation-states*. The nation-state arrangement legitimates sovereignty, state purposes, a military, and territorial jurisdiction (Giddens, 1985).

The domain of the state in Western nations has expanded over time. A growing number of activities in education, medicine, the family, religion, working conditions, and technology have become incorporated within its general welfare function (Skocpol and Amenta, 1986). The public welfare expenditures of Western capitalist democracies rapidly increased after World War II, but the pace has slackened since the late 1970s. In some nations, especially those like Sweden with social democratic governments, social programs were transformed into comprehensive systems of universal benefits that guaranteed the citizenry a basic standard of living—what has been called the *welfare state*. During the New Deal years and through the 1960s, the United States also followed the conventional

Police officers help citizens with many everyday problems, but the firearms they carry are a constant reminder that they are agents of the state, which has a monopoly on the legitimate use of deadly force.

welfare-state path with the state directly financing and providing a variety of social services. Beginning in the 1970s, however, the nation shifted the focus of its public activity increasingly toward the managing and financing of various medical and elderly benefits through the private market. As the state has taken on more activities, it has become increasingly bureaucratic, guiding itself by explicit rules and procedures based on a division of function and authority as described by Max Weber's model of *bureaucracy* (Bourdieu, 1994), as discussed in Chapter 4 (pp. 112–114).

Sociological Perspectives on the State

Functionalists depict the state as an essential social institution that evolved as societies moved from traditional to modern ways. This image of the state predates contemporary sociological theory; it was articulated by 17th- and 18th-century social philosophers such as Thomas Hobbes (1588–1679), who said human beings were "naturally" a perverse and destructive lot. He conjectured that early in history human beings had voluntarily entered into a social agreement providing for central authority and collective defense as a measure to rid themselves of rampant brutality, violence, and chaos. But other philosophers such as Jean-Jacques Rousseau (1712–1778) disagreed. According to Rousseau, private property was the root of human social evils. Once private property was established, the state followed as an institution to define and defend property rights. In their original "state of nature," Rousseau said, human beings were "noble savages"—spontaneous, outgoing, loving, kind, and peaceful. The advent of private property ended this idyllic existence, bringing with it corruption, oppression, and obedience to a privileged class. Rousseau's approach foreshadowed the modern conflict perspective on the state. Let us examine the functionalist and conflict views more carefully.

The Functionalist Perspective on the State

Functionalists contend that there is a good reason the state arose and has assumed a dominant position in contemporary life: Society must maintain order and provide for the common good. More particularly, they point to four primary functions performed by the state.

Planning and Direction The complexity and scope of many activities in contemporary society require overall coordination and integration; personal and informal arrangements no longer suffice, and new norms are needed. Such norms—*laws*—result from conscious thought, deliberate planning, and formal declaration. In addition, in times of war, financial panic, or natural disaster, "central direction" is required, performed by only one or at most a few individuals who have the power and authority to implement their plans (Davis, 1949).

Enforcement of Norms In modern, complex societies characterized by a preponderance of secondary relationships, informal means of social control such as ridicule and shaming are relatively ineffective. Once laws are created, a special body or organization—the state—is required to ensure law and order by enforcing legal norms.

Arbitration of Conflicting Interests Because many resources are scarce and divisible— particularly privilege, prestige, and power— people find themselves in conflict as they pursue their goals. If no bonds other than the pursuit of immediate self-interest were to unite people, society would quickly degenerate into a Hobbesian nightmare in which "war against all" prevailed. Some agency is required that is sufficiently strong to contain conflict within tolerable limits—and that agency is the state (Goode, 1972).

Protection against Other Societies Both war and diplomacy call for centralized control and mobilization if a people are to maximize their position relative to their adversaries. The state meets this requirement. Indeed, sociologist Charles Tilly (1990) surveyed European history and concluded that states are shaped primarily by the need to prepare for and wage war.

The Conflict Perspective on the State

Functionalists see the state as a rather benign institution. Not so conflict theorists! They contend that the state is a vehicle by which one or more groups impose their values and stratification system upon other groups. As they view the matter, the state has its origin in the desire of ruling elites to give permanence to social arrangements that benefit themselves. More fundamentally, they depict the state as an instrument of violence and oppression.

Conflict theorists see the state arising in history along with the production of a social surplus, which we defined earlier as the goods and services over and above what is necessary for survival. In hunting and gathering societies, land is communally owned, and the members of the community share the food derived from it. The intensive agriculture technologies in agricultural societies produce food surpluses, so it is no longer essential that every human be employed in subsistence activities. Some members of society, those who can engineer more power for themselves, can live off the surplus produced by others. A new institution, the state with its police power, is required to enforce the unequal distribution of social and material rewards in order to preserve the position of this privileged elite.

Some conflict theorists (*instrumental theorists*) have taken literally the *Communist Manifesto*'s dictum that "the executive of the modern state is but a committee for managing the common affairs of the whole bourgeoisie." Seen in this manner, the state is an instrument of the capitalist class.

Other conflict theorists (*structural theorists*) contend that the state apparatus exercises "relative autonomy" in its relationship with the capitalist class. They say that the state is not simply the instrument of the capitalist class, but is an entity with its own interests and capacities that affect society (Skocpol, 1980; Quadagno, 1984). The state's actions, therefore, are not always in the interests of any particular class or of the society at large (Barkey and Parikh, 1991). According to this view, relentless *class conflict* between capitalists and workers, boom and bust economic cycles, and conflict among corporations place limits on the ability of the capitalist class to manipulate political institutions at will. Although the state may promote a climate favorable to capitalism, it must also legitimate the sanctity of the social order and maintain internal peace (O'Connor, 1973).

In time, a powerful state can reach outside itself and dominate people in other regions and societies. The empires of Britain, Spain, Austro-Hungary, Russia, and its successor, the Soviet Union, are historical examples of ruling elites who mobilized the power of the state in pursuit of resources that would result in even more power. This process creates subject peoples and establishes dominant-majority relationships. The 20th century witnessed the dismantling of these empires and the emergence of a host of formerly subjugated peoples pursuing long-repressed yearnings for nationhood. Many, including Indians, Pakistanis, South Africans, Czechs, Hungarians, and Ukrainians, have succeeded, while others such as the Kosovars and Chechens are still working on it.

Legitimacy and Authority

Force may be an effective means for seizing power, and it remains the ultimate foundation for the state, but it is not the most effective means for political rule (Lenski, 1966). Force is both inefficient and costly. Moreover, honor is denied to those who rule by force alone. The

English leader and orator Edmund Burke (1729–1797) captured the essence of these matters when he noted that power that is based on the use of force alone is temporary. A person who hijacks an airliner by threatening to shoot passengers has considerable power, but it is unstable and temporary.

All this highlights the importance of the distinction that sociologists make between power that is legitimate and power that is illegitimate. Legitimate power is **authority.** When individuals possess authority, they have a recognized and established right to give orders, determine policies, pronounce judgments, settle controversies, and, more broadly, act as leaders. Legitimacy—the social justification of power—takes a number of forms. Sociologist Max Weber (1921/1968) suggested a threefold classification of authority based on the manner in which the power is socially legitimated: legal-rational, traditional, and charismatic.

Traditional Authority

In **traditional authority,** power is legitimated by the sanctity of age-old customs. Often the claim to such authority rests on birthright, and it is perceived as eternal, inviolable, and sacred. For example, medieval kings and queens in Europe ruled in the name of a "divine right" ordained by God. A good deal of moral force stands behind traditional authority.

Legal-Rational Authority

In **legal-rational authority,** power is legitimated by explicit rules and rational procedures that define the rights and duties of the occupants of given positions. Weber depicted this type of authority as prevailing in his ideal-type bureaucracy (see Chapter 4, pp. 112–114). Under this arrangement, officials claim obedience on the grounds that their commands fall within the impersonal, formally defined scope of their office. Obedience is owed not to the person but to a set of impersonal principles that have been devised in a rational manner. Presumably, these principles are derived from a set of abstract goals with which people agree. For example, we obey the police officer directing traffic because we agree that traffic must flow smoothly and that for this to occur people must conform to a set of rational principles and rules devised to ensure it.

The authority of government leaders is accepted in the United States because Americans accept the premise that the law is supreme. Americans accept the exercise of power because they have come to believe that policies and orders are formulated in accordance with rules to which they subscribe. The system would crumble were a large number of Americans to reject these "rules of the game." However, a political system does not generate optimal outcomes simply because it is legitimate. As Johnson, Dowd, and Ridgeway (2006) argue, when people believe that the practices of an organization are legitimate and are strongly endorsed by others, they may comply with them even if they do not agree with and do not benefit from them. As a result, legitimization of status quo arrangements can promote the stability of inefficiency and inequality.

Charismatic Authority

In **charismatic authority,** power is legitimated by the extraordinary superhuman or supernatural qualities people attribute to a leader. Founders of world religions, prophets, military victors, and political heroes commonly derive their authority from charisma (meaning "gift of grace"). Followers are devoted to the person of the leader, not to tradition or to abstract rational rules and principles. Jesus, Napoléon Bonaparte, Fidel Castro, Julius Caesar, Adolf Hitler, Joan of Arc, and Ayatollah Ruhollah Khomeini all are examples.

The term *charisma* has passed from Weber's writings into our everyday language, and we often speak of "charismatic" leaders such as John F. Kennedy or "charismatic" pop stars such as Elvis Presley. But Weber did not have such examples in mind when he developed the concept of charisma. To Weber a charismatic leader has an impact on history, transforming social structure by mobilizing followers to pursue the leader's goals.

Weber viewed each of these three bases of authority as *ideal types,* concepts sociologists construct to portray the principal characteristics of a phenomenon. Hence, in practice any specific form of authority may involve various combinations and aspects of all three. For example, Franklin Delano Roosevelt gained the presidency through legal-rational principles. By the time he was elected president for the fourth time, his leadership had a good many traditional elements to it, while his great popularity meant that his leadership had some charismatic properties.

Political Power

Politics refers to the processes by which people and groups acquire and exercise power. We commonly think of politics as a feature of governments. But there is also politics in religious groups, educational groups, and scientific groups—even in friendship groups and families. When power is organized and wielded by the state, we speak of it as **political power.** In the modern state, power is wielded through democratic, authoritarian, or totalitarian means, depending on how much participation states allow from citizens and how much control is exercised over the everyday lives of citizens. Though democratic governments appear to be organized in the interests of average citizens, social scientists are not in agreement about how "democratic" such states are. In this section we will discuss forms of government, political power in the United States, and models of political power.

Types of Government

Government entails those political processes that have to do with the authoritative formulating of rules and policies that are binding and pervasive throughout a society. Three quite different types of government have competed in recent generations for people's allegiance: totalitarianism, authoritarianism, and democracy. Each can be considered an ideal type because in practice many nations have regimes with mixtures of totalitarian, authoritarian, and democratic elements. Totalitarian and authoritarian regimes are often referred to in the media and in political discussion as "dictatorships."

Totalitarianism

Totalitarianism is a "total state," one in which the government undertakes to control all parts of the society and all aspects of social life, such as occurs in contemporary North Korea. Those individuals and groups (elites) who dominate the state apparatus seek to control all subordinate governmental units, all institutions, and even individual families and cliques. The two major historical prototypes of totalitarianism—Nazi Germany under Hitler and communist Russia under Stalin—remind us that this form of government can incorporate either a capitalistic or a socialistic economy.

A totalitarian society typically has three characteristics: a monolithic political party, a compelling ideology, and pervasive social control. Only one political party is permitted, and it brooks no opposition. And only a small proportion of the population are party members, although party membership is a requisite for all important social positions. A totalitarian ideology is utopian in nature. It stipulates grandiose schemes for social reconstruction and societal betterment. To enforce its power and propagate its ideologies, a totalitarian regime employs every available means of social control. It uses educational and communications networks, as well as exercising terror by a secret police.

Authoritarianism

Authoritarianism is a political system in which the government tolerates little or no opposition to its rule but permits nongovernmental centers of influence and allows debate on some issues of public policy. Sometimes authoritarian governments evolve out of totalitarian governments, as occurred over the 1970s and 1980s in the People's Republic of China and the Soviet Union. In the ensuing years, the Soviet Union disintegrated and China replaced many of the socialist elements of its economy with capitalist features. However, in neither case did a democratic government emerge. Even though authoritarian and totalitarian governments are often unpopular, when they fail, they are not automatically replaced by democratic regimes.

Democracy

Democracy is a political system in which the powers of government derive from the consent of the governed and in which regular constitutional avenues exist for changing government officials. It is an arrangement that (1) permits the population a significant voice in decision making through the people's right to choose among contenders for political office, (2) allows for a broad, relatively equal citizenship among the populace, and (3) affords the citizenry protection from arbitrary state action. However, democratic governments are not distinguished from totalitarian or authoritarian regimes by the absence of powerful officials, and for the most part democracy is not characterized by the rule of the people themselves. Only in relatively rare instances, such as the New England town meeting, do we encounter *direct democracy*—face-to-face participation and decision making by the citizens. Rather, most democratic nations are characterized by *representative democracy*—officials are held accountable to the public through periodic elections that confirm them in power or replace them with new officials.

What Factors Promote Democracy? A number of sociologists have undertaken a search for those factors that promote a social climate favorable to a stable democracy (Lindblom, 1990; Patterson, 1991; Lipset, 1994). One factor they identify is the existence of a structure permitting competition for positions of power, challenges to incumbents, and shifts in the parties holding office. Many well-organized but countervailing interest groups serve as a check against one another. **Interest groups** are organizations of people who share common concerns or points of view. Each group is limited in influence because, in the process of governing, officials must also take into account the **interests,** or points of view, of other groups.

A second factor is a strong **civil society**—a social realm of mediating groups, networks, and institutions that sustains the public life outside the worlds of the state and the economy (Cohen and Arato, 1992). For example, in the United States today we have a broad array of public-interest and political organizations across the ideological spectrum that address a variety of issues and concerns of the populace. You are probably familiar with a number of these, including the Christian Coalition, the National Rifle Association, Planned Parenthood, and the American Civil Liberties Union. Citizens of all political and moral persuasions can join organizations that are pursuing their goals. Having a large number of such competing groups provides many links to government and ensures that no single group or institution can attain a monopoly of power.

A third factor is relative stability in economic and social conditions (Neuhouser, 1992). Significant institutional failure confronts people with stressful circumstances that can make them vulnerable to extremist social movements. For example, Germany experienced ruinous inflation and economic dislocation in the 1920s that made the middle classes susceptible to Nazism.

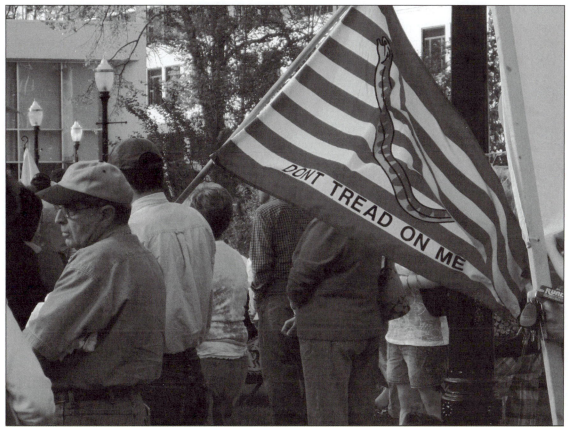

Democracies allow individuals, organizations, and social movements to pursue their perceived interests by pressuring elected officials, policy makers, and other voters through a variety of means, including public demonstrations. In 2009 and 2010, the Tea Party movement attracted people who opposed policy initiatives of President Obama's administration.

Fourth and finally, a stable democracy benefits from an underlying consensus among the populace that a democratic government is desirable and valid. Citizens believe they can realize their goals within the existing organizational framework because they enjoy "fair play" access to the seats of power. As we will see, voting is a key mechanism for achieving consensus. Although Americans wage their election campaigns with great fury and fervor, once the election returns are in, typically the candidates and parties accede to the results.

Political Power in the United States

Both totalitarian and democratic governments are marked by competition for political positions. But what distinguishes democracies and the American system is that the contest for positions of power is legitimized—norms define political competition and opposition as expected and appropriate. Free and competitive elections, the right to form opposition parties, freedom to criticize those in power, freedom to seek public office, and popular participation are among the commonly accepted hallmarks of democratic procedures. Central to the process are political parties, popular electoral participation, interest-group lobbying, and the mass media.

Political Parties

A **political party** is an organization designed to gain control of the government by putting its people in public office. It is not the same as an interest group, which seeks to control government policy decisions without assuming the direct responsibility of running the government. In contrast, political parties pursue the control of government as an end. Thus mass-based political parties tend to abandon or modify policy views that interfere with their gaining or maintaining political office.

Within American life, the major political parties function as brokers or intermediaries between the people and the government (Lipset, 1993). The relatively pragmatic nature of the parties and the structural peculiarities of the two-party system reflect this fact. To win control of the government, each party must shape itself to offer the widest possible appeal to the electorate. This requirement tends to pull each party toward a centrist position, leaving the more extreme elements at the fringes. In close elections both the Republican and Democratic parties strive for the support of the same uncommitted, often middle-of-the-road voters. In many respects, then, the two parties end up resembling one another. Critics of the U.S. political system say that centrist forces and pressures result in the lack of a real choice for voters. Proponents point out that what is really happening is that the parties are performing one of their chief functions: compromising different and conflicting points of view prior to the election (Olson and Meyer, 1975).

Electoral Participation and Voting Patterns

The U.S. political system is rooted in the participation of its citizenry in the governmental process through periodic elections. The principle

that each person has one vote is seen as a basic mechanism for offsetting the inequalities that otherwise abound in the society by virtue of class, gender, and racial inequalities. Still, many Americans do not vote. In 2008, 63.6 percent of voting-age U.S. citizens participated in the presidential election (File and Crissey, 2010). Mid-term elections, when congressional representatives and senators campaign for seats, have lower voter turnout, with between 40 and 50 percent voting in the last several elections. In contrast, in 1876, when memories of the Civil War were still fresh, 82 percent of eligible voters—mostly limited to white males—cast ballots. As indicated in Figure 9.1, nonvoters are more likely to be young, less educated, and Hispanic or Asian. Although in recent years women have been slightly more likely to vote than men, it has not always been so. Prior to 1920, women were not allowed to vote in most elections, and even after 1920, the voting rates of women were depressed (see Box 9.1).

The turnout rate in national elections is typically much lower in the United States than in other nations (see Figure 9.2). In western Europe, Canada, Australia, and New Zealand, the state is responsible for compiling and maintaining electoral registers. The United States is the only nation where the entire burden of registration falls on the individual rather than the government. Low voting rates may indicate that many Americans believe they cannot affect the political process on the national level. With more time, visibility, money, staff, and campaign experience than the typical challenger, incumbent U.S. senators and congressional representatives have very high reelection rates, which may contribute to the feeling among voters that they cannot effect change.

There are important differences in how various segments of the U.S. population vote. Generally, voters who are better off tend to support Republican candidates, and those who are less well off tend to support Democratic candidates. Prior to the 1930s, African American voters

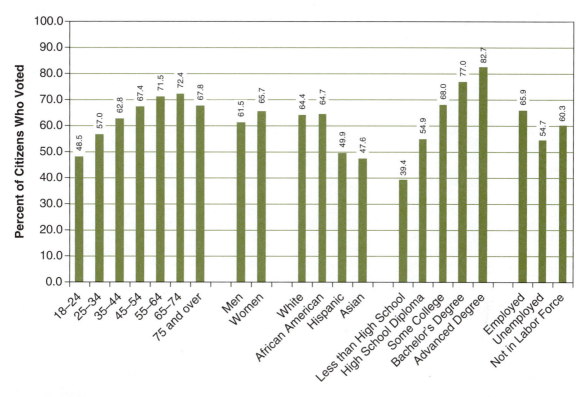

Figure 9.1	Who Votes? Percentage of Voting-Age Citizens Who Voted in the 2008 Presidential Election

Source: Figure generated by the authors from data presented in Thom File and Sarah Crissey, 2010, Voting and registration in the election of November 2008. U.S. Census Bureau, Current Population Reports, Series P20-562. Washington, DC.

tended to support the Republican Party, the party of Abraham Lincoln and African American emancipation, but since Franklin D. Roosevelt and the New Deal, they have voted overwhelmingly Democratic. Religion is often a good predictor of voting, but patterns can change. For many years Catholics were more likely to vote for Democratic than Republican candidates (Hamilton, 1972), but with the movement of many Catholics out of the working class, this is no longer true. However, the tendency of Jews to vote Democratic remains stable. There may be general patterns of voting among religions and denominations, but most people say that religion

does not affect their votes. Nearly half of white evangelical Christians, and 60 percent of highly committed evangelicals, report that their religion frequently guides their voting, compared to only 10 percent of mainline denomination Protestants and 12 percent of Catholics (Pew Research Center, 2003). Other factors affecting how people vote include the facial appearance of the candidate; voters infer characteristics such as intelligence, leadership ability, and competence from the face of the candidate and tend to stick with their first impressions (Antonakis and Dalgas, 2009).

Voter identification with a particular party is fairly strong. However, changes do occur,

What Oppression Teaches—The Long Reach of Disenfranchisement

Why don't people long oppressed by authoritarian regimes create effective democracies as soon as authoritarianism is lifted? Why, for example, has it not been easy to establish democracy in Afghanistan and Iraq after the demise of authoritarian regimes in the two countries in 2002 and 2003? Social structures teach people patterns of behavior that are not quickly and easily changed when the rules and laws governing political participation are changed. Though not as drastic as a change in regime, American women gaining the right to vote provides an example of this effect in action.

In 1920, the Nineteenth Amendment to the Constitution extended to women the right to vote: "The right of citizens of the United States to vote shall not be denied or abridged by the United States or by any State on account of sex." Women had worked long and hard to gain this right. Yet not nearly as many women as men voted in the first elections after the passage of the voting rights amendment. In fact, it was not until many years afterward that men and women voted at equal rates. Women born after 1925, who grew up after

the Nineteenth Amendment was passed and voting for women had become an "inalienable right," were the first group to go out and vote in equal numbers.

Sociologists Glenn Firebaugh and Kevin Chen (1995) showed that the oppression people experience during their early years can continue to affect their behavior long after the oppression itself is lifted. Using post-election survey data gathered from 1952 to 1988, Firebaugh and Chen found that the odds of women born in 1896 voting in any election were less than half as great as the odds of men voting. This disenfranchisement effect—women failing to vote despite having gained the right to do so—was only slightly less in a second group of women, those born between 1896 and 1905. The effect was again smaller for women born between 1906 and 1915, although women in this cohort still did not vote at the same rates as men, and women born between 1916 and 1925 also were somewhat less likely to vote than men.

This study illustrates the long-lasting effects of historical conditions experienced during one's

formative years. The data these researchers used were based on elections beginning *30 years* after women gained the right to vote in the United States, yet women born and socialized during and immediately after the period when women could *not* vote continued to vote at lower rates than men. Voting rates for men and women have now converged; women socialized in an era during which women have the right to vote are just as likely to vote as men are. As Firebaugh and Chen put it (1995:978), "After passage of the Nineteenth Amendment, historical conditions no longer 'taught' young women the impropriety of voting."

Questions for Discussion

1. Does the research presented here explain any of the voter data shown in Figure 9.1?

2. This box suggests that people learn not to be involved in voting if they are denied the right to vote. Can you think of other features of democracies in civil society that may be slow to develop after the demise of authoritarian regimes?

---

although not as precipitously as is commonly imagined (Alwin and Krosnick, 1991; Connelly, 2000). The rate of ticket splitting (casting votes for different party candidates) is between 20 and 28 percent (Forgette and Platt, 1999).

Interest-Group Lobbying

As we noted in the discussion of democracy, people's common concerns or points of view are called interests, and the groups that organize

those who share these concerns are called interest groups. A distinction is often made between special-interest groups and public-interest groups. **Special-interest groups** primarily seek benefits from which their members would derive more gains than the society as a whole. Examples include chambers of commerce, trade associations, labor unions, and farm organizations. **Public-interest groups** pursue policies that presumably would be of no greater benefit to their

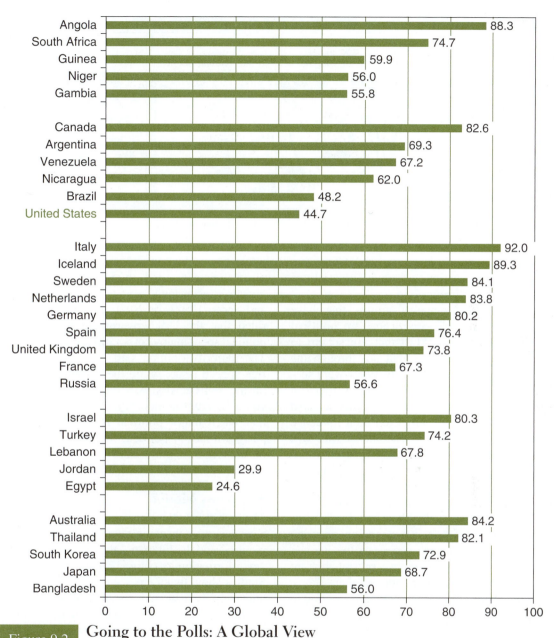

Figure 9.2	**Going to the Polls: A Global View**

Voter participation in U.S. national elections is traditionally low compared to other countries: 63.6 percent of those eligible to vote voted in the 2008 presidential election and 45.5 percent in the 2010 congressional elections (File and Crissey, 2010; U.S. Census Bureau, Voting and Registration in the Election of November 2010, Current Population Reports P20-562, 2010. See also http://www.census.gov/hhes/www/socdemo/voting/index.html).

Sources: Figure generated by the authors using data from Lopez Pintor and Gratschew, 2002, and U.S. Census Bureau, 2007. Bars represent the percent of the voting age population who voted in parliamentary or congressional elections, 1945–2001.

members than to the larger society. Consumer protection organizations are good illustrations of public-interest groups.

Among special-interest groups that have attracted considerable controversy are **political action committees (PACs)** that are set up to elect or defeat candidates, but not through the organization of a political party. PACs were specifically authorized by the Federal Election Campaign Act of 1971, but they had existed before then. PACs typically exert their influence by contributing money to candidates who will support their interests. They base their contributions less on ideological or geographical factors than on whether the recipient sits on a congressional committee that can help them (Berke, 1990). Many PACs hedge their bets by contributing to both candidates in a campaign, ensuring that they later will have access to the winner. Although members of Congress presumably are elected to represent the people in their states, more than half the senators seeking reelection to the Senate finance their campaigns primarily from contributions acquired outside their home states instead of from contributions made chiefly by their constituents (Berke, 1990). As Figure 9.3 shows, PACs run by business corporations contribute more money than other types of PACs, and they give much more of it to incumbents than to challengers. Contributions are the way

interest groups gain access to legislators to plead their cases and obtain special favors for given pieces of legislation (Clawson, Neustadtl, and Scott, 1992). In 2010, the Supreme Court ruled that the U.S. government may not ban political spending by corporations (Liptak, 2010). The majority opinion said that it was a basic free-speech issue, while the dissenting opinion on the 5–4 decision was that corporate money could "corrupt democracy." Research indicates that when major political issues are at stake, party affiliation, political ideology, and public opinion matter more than contributions from special interests (Burstein, 2003).

The Mass Media

The **mass media** consist of organizations—newspapers, magazines, television, radio, motion pictures, and the Internet—that undertake to convey information to a large segment of the public. Studies show that 71 percent of Americans cite television as their major source of national and international news, and recently the Internet surpassed newspapers as a major news source (Pew Research Center for the People and the Press, 2009b). The public secures information about candidates from television through news broadcasts and paid advertising.

Often the media's main role is that of "agenda setting": Media coverage places an issue

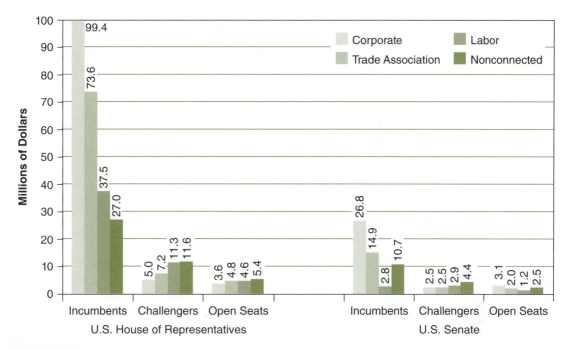

| Figure 9.3 | **Contributions by Political Action Committees (PACs) to U.S. House and Senate Candidates, in Millions of Dollars, 2007–2008, by Type of PAC** |

Source: Figure generated by the authors using data from the U.S. Census Bureau, 2011.

or problem foremost on the public's agenda, where it can become a central factor influencing the public's perception of the performance of an incumbent or challenger (Iyengar, 1991). Research findings contradict the commonly held idea that the media are biased against Republicans: Democratic and Republican gubernatorial candidates were not treated any differently over 20 years of newspaper coverage (Niven, 1999).

Increasingly, campaigns are being turned over to high-powered professionals who advise candidates on every detail, ranging from which issues they should tackle to the images they should project in their media appearances. Physical appearance and "good looks" have surfaced as paramount matters in an era when packaging candidates for the media is so critical. Moreover, TV advertising, on which candidates spend nearly half their campaign funds,

gives greater emphasis to style and personality than to substance. Computer technology is employed to target specific voter groups and then bombard them with TV advertising and direct-mail appeals specifically tailored to their interests. The 2008 Obama campaign used a high-tech grassroots strategy that included e-mail, Facebook, YouTube, text messages, online fundraising, ads on video games, concerts to appeal to young voters, and lots of television advertisements and "advertorials" (Lizza, 2008).

Models of Power in the United States

One of the longest-running debates in social sciences in the United States has to do with the nature of *power* in the United States. Is power concentrated in the hands of the few

According to the elitist perspective, it is the "power elite" that make fateful decisions such as the 2003 invasion of Iraq by the United States.

theorists), Whitt looked to the biases inherent in social institutions as shaping political outcomes. He portrayed society as structured in ways that place constraints on decision makers and render their formulation of policy largely a foregone conclusion. Given the capitalist orientation of institutions in Western nations, the ruling class usually need not take direct action to fashion outcomes favorable to its interests. The political outcomes are built within the capitalist ordering of affairs by the way agendas are set and alternatives are defined.

The Elitist Model

The elitist model found early expression in the ideas of several European sociologists of the late 19th and early 20th centuries, including Vilfredo Pareto, Gaetano Mosca, and Robert Michels. They undertook to show that the concentration of power in a small group of elites is inevitable within modern societies (Olsen, 1970). These theorists rejected Marx's idealistic vision of social change that would bring about a classless and stateless society. Instead, they depicted all societies past the bare subsistence level—be they totalitarian, monarchical, or democratic—as dominated by the few over the many. They held that the masses cannot and do not govern themselves. Even so, change occurs across time through the gradual replacement of one group of elites by another.

Within the United States, elitist theory has taken a somewhat different course, particularly as it was formulated in the work of sociologist C. Wright Mills (1956). Mills contended that the major decisions affecting Americans and others—especially those having to do with issues of war and peace—are made by a small number of individuals and groups whom he

or distributed widely among various groups within American society? What is the basis of power? Is the exercise of power in the United States unrestricted, or is it limited by the competing interests of numerous groups? Social scientists have supplied quite different answers to these questions, represented by three theoretical models. Two of these, the Marxist (or ruling-class) model and the elitist model, are part of the conflict perspective in sociology. The pluralist model is largely, though not completely, consistent with the functionalist perspective.

The Marxist Model

Marxist theory has had a profound impact on sociological thinking about power and social organization. Sociologists following in the Marxist tradition, such as J. Allen Whitt (1979, 1982), hold that political processes must be understood in terms of the ways in which the major social institutions (especially the economic institution) are organized. Rather than focusing primarily upon the individuals who control the seats of power (as do power elite termed the "power elite." The real rulers of the United States, said Mills, come from three groups: corporation executives, the military, and high-ranking politicians. According to Mills, it is these groups that formulate important policies such as the procurement of major weapons systems and make fateful decisions such as the 2003 invasion of Iraq by the United States.

The elitist model depicts elites as unified in purpose and outlook because of their similar social backgrounds, their dominant and overlapping positions in key social institutions, and the convergence of their economic interests (Domhoff, 1983, 1990; Akard, 1992). For instance, sociologist Michael Useem (1983) contended that an "inner circle" of interconnected corporate officers and directors assumes the stewardship of U.S. political and social affairs. He found that inner-group members are more likely to belong to exclusive social clubs, have upper-class parents, participate in major business associations, serve on government advisory boards, belong to the upper levels of nonprofit and charitable organizations, gain media coverage for themselves, maintain informal contacts with government leaders, and prefer one another's company. According to elitist theorists, elites invariably get their way whenever important public issues are at stake. Their power is pervasive; it leaves few areas of social life untouched and results in a relatively stable distribution of power.

The Pluralist Model

The pluralist model sharply contrasts with both the power elite and Marxist models. Pluralist theorists start with interest groups as the basic feature of organized political life. They say that no one group really runs the government, although many groups have the power to veto policies that run counter to their interests (Riesman, 1953; Dahl, 1961). Important decisions are made by different groups, depending on the institutional arena—business organizations, labor unions, farm blocs, racial and ethnic associations, and religious groups. When their interests

diverge, the various interest groups compete for allies among the unorganized public. But the same group or coalition of groups does not always set broad policies. Instead, group power varies with the issue (Burstein, 1991a).

Most groups remain inactive on most issues and mobilize their resources only when their interests are immediately at stake. The resulting distribution of power tends to be unstable because interests and alliances are typically short-lived, and new groups and coalitions are always being organized as old ones disintegrate. Government may retain a significant degree of autonomy from these powerful interest groups and operate as a balancing agent when they compete, reducing conflict and promoting societal stability. As noted previously, this is one of the important functions of the state. The result of such processes is not necessarily effectiveness in administration of government. Some pluralists argue that so many interest groups have sprung up in the United States, each demanding special attention to its own concerns, that government has become paralyzed (Shea, 1984).

Conclusions

What conclusions can we draw from the contending models of power? Each model has something of value to tell us, and a reasonable perspective on power would combine elements from each model (Burris, 1988). For example, elitist theorists such as Mills and even Marxian-oriented theorists do not argue that a power elite or governing class completely dominates U.S. society. When important decisions are made—especially on the critical issues of war and peace and on matters concerning the economy—many interest groups compete for influence, but some corporate, military, and political power centers clearly have greater input than other groups. Yet given the party divisions within the highest echelons of the U.S. government on welfare and defense spending and tax policies, it is exceedingly difficult to make a convincing case for a unified power elite.

Stealth Democracy

Are you registered to vote? Do you think your vote makes a difference in election outcomes? In large national elections, the probability that any one voter will cast the vote that decides the election is essentially zero (Kanazawa, 2000). Yet millions of Americans vote in every election. Why do they bother?

Sociologist Satoshi Kanazawa (2000) was intrigued by this question. Not only do individual votes not make a difference, but there also is no penalty for not voting. The outcomes of elections are enjoyed or suffered by everyone, whether you vote or not. "Why then," Kanazawa asks, "would rational actors invest their personal time and energy into going to the polls to cast their ballots?"

Kanazawa (2000) adapted a theory proposing that people change their behaviors according to their experiences. Using election data from six different presidential elections to test this model, he found that it helps explain voting behavior. Voters whose candidate is elected feel as if their vote has made a difference and are more likely to vote again, while those whose candidate loses feel as if their efforts were wasted and are less likely to vote in the next election. Similarly, nonvoters seem to be motivated to vote in the next election if the candidate they support loses—"If only I had voted for her, she might have won!"—while nonvoters whose favorite candidate gets elected apparently assume that their support wasn't needed and are less likely to vote in the future.

Voting behavior, then, seems to be influenced by whether election outcomes reward or punish voters and nonvoters according to their preferences. But what are their preferences? What are voters really looking for in candidates?

Campaign rhetoric seems to assume that Americans care about the issues, want to be informed about policies and decisions, and want to vote for a candidate to whom they can feel connected. But John R. Hibbing and Elizabeth Theiss-Morse (2002), who have been using survey data to study Americans' attitudes toward their government for a decade, disagree:

[People] do not want to make political decisions themselves; they do not want to provide much input to those who are assigned to make these decisions; and they would rather not know all the details of the decision-making process. Most people have strong feelings on few if any of the issues the government needs to address and would much prefer to spend their time in nonpolitical pursuits.

In fact, Hibbing and Theiss-Morse conclude that Americans prefer something they term *stealth democracy:*

[They] want democratic procedures to exist but not to be visible on a routine basis. . . . They want to know that the opportunity will be there for them even though they probably have no

current intention of getting involved in government or even of paying attention to it.

What sorts of issues get citizens riled up and ready to be more involved in politics? If you guess war, tax cuts, or gay marriage, you're wrong. What really riles Americans is thinking that government officials might be benefiting personally from their positions. "Citizens are usually less concerned with obtaining a policy outcome," Hibbing and Theiss-Morse report, "than with preventing others from using the process to feather their own nests."

Irritation with political leaders' self-interested behavior, then, might motivate citizens to vote in large numbers. The impact of each vote on the outcome, of course, decreases as the size of the turnout increases. But Kanazawa's findings suggest that the process of voting should lead to more political engagement in the future.

Questions for Discussion

1. Young people ages 18–25 have very low rates of voting. Is this fact explained by Kanazawa's theory? Why or why not?

2. What do you think explains the lack of interest in politics and government decision making that Hibbing and Theiss-Morse found among Americans? Do you think that the tendency they described varies in the population? If so, how?

And as structural Marxists remind us, political and economic institutions seem to gain an existence separate from the specific individuals who have ownership or positions of authority within them. Thus the question is not only, Who runs America? but also, What runs America? See Box 9.2 for another perspective.

Economic Power

Politics and economics are intimately related. Political systems not only create laws and exercise police power; they also facilitate the operation of the economy. In a **socialist economy** the government directly controls the economy, in many cases setting prices and wages and deciding what will be produced. In a **capitalist economy** the government oversees and sets parameters for the economy but in many ways leaves the economy alone, allowing the market to decide what the economy will do. In all cases economic organizations, whether they are government bureaucracies or large corporations, wield considerable power. One way we experience this power is as employees, doing the bidding of a company in order to get a paycheck and move up the ladder of success. But economic organizations also wield power in other ways, working to create a favorable environment for themselves by controlling the markets and political systems in which they operate. In this section we will discuss the different kinds of economic systems and how they fit into the global economy. In addition, we will focus on the power of national and multinational corporations.

Comparative Economic Systems

All societies confront three basic economic problems: *What* goods and services should they produce and in what quantities? *How* should they employ their limited resources—land, water, minerals, fuel, and labor—to produce the desired goods and services? And for *whom* should they produce the goods and services? The manner in which they answer these questions has profound consequences for the nature and the structure of societies. For instance, if they decide to produce guns and weaponry in large quantities, the standard of living of their citizens will be lower than if they emphasize the satisfaction of consumer needs. How they go about producing the desired goods and services shapes the world of work, the way it is organized, the satisfactions it provides, and the status it accords. And decisions regarding the "for whom" question influence the distribution of wealth, income, and prestige. The answers to these questions derive from the structuring of power within societies.

As we pointed out in Chapter 2 (pp. 60–61), people have responded differently over the course of human history to the dictates posed by economic survival. Hunting and gathering economies were followed by horticultural, agrarian, and industrial modes of production. Postindustrial social organization, focusing more on services than on manufacturing and integrating new information and communication technologies, will include profound changes in patterns of economic behavior and in market structure (International Labor Organization, 2001). Changes in the way people produce, distribute, and consume goods and services result in strong pressures for change in other institutional arrangements as well.

In the 20th century two fundamentally different types of economic systems competed for people's allegiance: the capitalist market economy and the socialist command economy. Each took a quite different approach to economic organization, and each has substantially different social and political implications.

Market and Command Economies

Modern economic systems differ from one another in two important aspects. First, they provide different answers to the question, How is economic activity organized—by the market or by the plan? Second, they provide different answers to the question, Who owns the means of production—individuals or the state? However, these questions do not demand an "either-or" answer. No contemporary nation falls totally at one or the other pole, although the United States and the pre-1991 Soviet Union typically gave opposite answers to both questions.

A *market economy* is one in which decisions about what will be produced, how much will be produced, and what products will cost are made in economic transactions between consumers and producers. Products that consumers do not want or that are overproduced fall in price. Items that are in short supply and that people want rise in price. Price movements act as signals to profit-making individuals and firms. They cut back on goods with falling prices and increase the production of goods with rising prices. Economists call this mechanism *consumer sovereignty.*

Underlying this approach is the belief that the interests of all will be best served if each economic unit is allowed to make free choices in pursuit of its own best interests, without government intrusion or involvement. However, markets have little in the way of traditional morality built into them. A truly free market can supply products that many people would prefer did not exist, including prostitution, child pornography, drugs of all kinds, and the services of hired killers, to name only a few.

A *command economy* is one in which the state or central planning authority determines the items that will be produced and their quantities. A command economy is often very good in moving a peasant society toward industrialization by mobilizing the masses to build miles of railroad and large dams. But a command economy finds it difficult to produce a complex array of consumer goods in the absence of market signals.

Free-market and command economies also differ in how they go about allocating resources to various productive activities. In free-market economies, competition among suppliers of goods and labor services is thought to ensure the most efficient and productive use of resources. Command economies, in contrast, are based on the assumption that rational decision making affords better results than the haphazard operation of market forces.

A major criticism of the market is that it is not a neutral mechanism and that the concept itself is ideologically driven (Swedberg, 2007). For example, critics have noted that the market fails to distribute income equitably. Market economies rely on the same price system that determines wages, interest rates, and profits for the distribution of income among people in the society. Income payments go in substantial amounts to private owners of physical capital—capitalists—or those who manage capitalist enterprises. Critics contend that some problems like the environmental crisis (see Chapter 12) and the absence of jobs for young inner-city African Americans (see Chapter 6) are not easily solved through the free market because such solutions do not produce a profit for capitalists. Accordingly, they say that different standards are called for in mature industrial societies like the United States, where free markets and social welfare must be balanced (Heilbroner, 1993).

Mixed Economies

When we look at the contemporary world, we are hard-pressed to find a pure form of a capitalist market economy. Even the United States in the early 19th century, which many economic historians deem to be as close to an example of pure capitalism as one can find, had government subsidies for railroads and canals. In the contemporary United States, although most people do not think of themselves as benefiting directly from a government social program, approximately 96 percent have done so at some time, including such federal programs as school breakfasts and lunches, college loans, home mortgage interest deductions, Medicare, Medicaid, and others (Mettler, 2011). Socialist countries had black markets and other "underground" market mechanisms. Most nations today are characterized by mixed economies that include elements of both command and market economies.

Liberal market economies, such as the United States and Great Britain, are closer to the capitalist ideal and allocate and coordinate resources primarily through markets. *Coordinated market economies,* such as Germany, Japan, and Sweden, use a variety of nonmarket mechanisms such as negotiation and traditional relationships to solve allocation and coordination problems (Berger, 2005).

In societies with coordinated market economies, most production is privately owned, but there may be a large public sector with publicly owned enterprises involved in public transportation, health care, air travel, mining, oil production, education, utilities, and more. Some of these societies, such as Sweden, Finland, and Denmark, have high taxes, particularly on the wealthy, and use the money to redistribute some of the wealth and to fund extensive social welfare and family support programs. In addition to having much lower economic inequality than the United States, societies with mixed economies usually score better than the United States

on important quality-of-life indicators such as rates of crime, divorce, and infant mortality and life expectancy.

The Power of Corporations

The government is an important participant in the U.S. economy, but the primary productive role is played by private business. Although most of the more than 20 million businesses in the United States are small, large corporations have a substantial impact on the economy. In this section we will discuss national corporations, multinational corporations, and various ways in which corporations are controlled.

The Power of National Corporations

When you drive a car, operate a computer, replace a lightbulb, purchase gasoline, or eat a breakfast cereal, you are using products manufactured by an oligopoly. An **oligopoly** is a market dominated by a few firms, the giants of U.S. business such as General Motors, IBM, and General Electric.

These firms exercise enormous power in American life. The decisions made by their executives have implications and ramifications that reach throughout the nation, including effects on transportation, the environment, and the products we consume and use. One of the barriers to reforming health care in the United States is the power of oligopolistic pharmaceutical and health care corporations. When the Supreme Court ruled against a bid to ban corporations from political spending in candidate elections, President Obama declared it "a major victory for big oil, Wall Street banks, health insurance companies and the other powerful interests that marshal their power every day in Washington to drown out the voices of everyday Americans" (Liptak, 2010).

Although corporations have power over people, people's behaviors and beliefs also exert

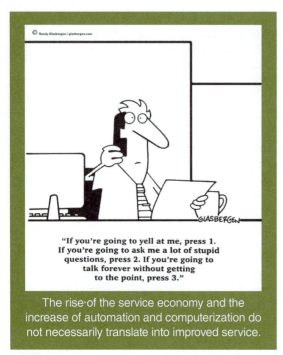

"If you're going to yell at me, press 1.
If you're going to ask me a lot of stupid
questions, press 2. If you're going to
talk forever without getting
to the point, press 3."

The rise·of the service economy and the increase of automation and computerization do not necessarily translate into improved service.

Copyright © Randy Glasbergen /glasbergen.com. Reprinted with permission.

strong influences on corporations and on the economy. Economists George A. Akerlof and Robert J. Shiller (2009) attribute the instability of the U.S. financial system to "social moods," including pessimism, overconfidence, euphoria, optimism, and panic, affected by news stories, sports events, crowd contagion, and other factors. They point out that corruption increases during boom periods and that it contributes to market collapses. The Great Depression followed the Roaring Twenties, the 1991 recession came right after the savings and loan crisis, the Enron scandal preceded the 2001 recession, and the 2008 recession was triggered by the subprime mortgage crisis.

Corporations also affect the lives of millions of U.S. workers. For example, restructuring and downsizing of large U.S. corporations meant the loss of 4 million jobs in America's 500 largest companies during the 1980s (Melloan, 1993), and these trends continue (Russakoff, 2006). Corporate executives contend that large-scale staff reductions are essential if their companies are to maintain competitiveness in a fast-changing global marketplace.

Yet considerable evidence suggests that companies slashing jobs often end up with more problems than profits. Sagging employee morale is a major roadblock that stands in the way of profit growth from downsizing. Workers begin to ask, "Am I going to have a job?" rather than, "This is a great place to work; how can I make it better?" (Snizek, 1994). Similarly, when wages fall, even when that reflects falling prices throughout the economy, worker morale falls, workers stop trusting their employers, and a drop in work effort translates into a drop in overall productivity (Akerlof and Shiller, 2009). Many companies offer their older employees early retirement, but most such companies find that they lose people they consider necessary and good performers. Firms also commonly make the mistake of eliminating workers but not the work, so that the surviving employees have to labor faster or longer. The consequences are employee burnout and work left undone (Snizek, 1994) or the ratcheting up again of costs by rehiring (Boroughs, 1992).

The Power of Multinational Corporations in the Global Economy

The rise of multinational corporations and the growing internationalization of the world economy have given a new dimension to economic power (Szymanski, 1981; Fennema, 1982; Biersteker, 1987; Barnet and Cavanagh, 1994). **Multinational corporations** are firms that have their central office in one country and subsidiaries in other countries. With the use of computer communications technology, companies no longer even need a geographical center. Managers and members of work teams can communicate as easily from country to country as they can from office to office. Today the annual income from sales of the largest multinational corporations exceeds the gross national product of most countries in which they do business. About half of the largest economic units in the world are not nations at all but multinational corporations.

Division of Labor

Multinational corporations are playing a growing role in the structuring of the division of labor within the world economy. The economic integration of less developed nations into the structures of a world economy can be traced to European exploration and colonization beginning in the 15th century. The arrangement has been characterized by the differentiation of core and periphery regions (Wallerstein, 1974, 1980, 1989). **Core regions** consist of geographical areas that dominate the world economy and exploit the rest of the system; **periphery regions** consist of areas that provide raw materials to the core and are exploited by it. At first, the peripheral areas exported spices, coffee, tea, and tobacco to Europe. Later, they became suppliers of agricultural and mineral raw materials, while their advantaged classes provided markets for industrial goods from Europe (Boswell, 1989; Chase-Dunn, 1989). Today companies go abroad in search of cheap raw materials and lower wages. This has caused huge losses in textile, clothing, shoe, auto, electronics, and other manufacturing jobs in industrialized countries and huge gains in developing countries in recent years.

Made in America?

U.S. multinationals now have a major stake in keeping much of their production overseas. They manufacture and sell nearly three times as much abroad as they make in and export from the United States. Likewise, multinational firms import to the United States parts they use in manufacturing that can be made more cheaply by foreign suppliers. Multinationals are not only the biggest exporters in the United States but also the nation's biggest importers, often bringing more into the United States than they ship out. The globalization of economic activity has fostered a trend toward a form of "stateless" corporation (Sklair, 1991). In the emerging global economy, it is becoming increasingly difficult to say what is an "American," a "Japanese," or a "Swedish" product. In some cases, for instance, vehicles sold in the United States are built in 12 countries, with parts coming from all over the globe. Nissan builds cars in Mississippi, and Toyota has manufacturing plants in Texas and Indiana.

There is considerable controversy about what impact multinational corporations in general have had on less developed or peripheral nations. One view, associated with mainstream Marxism, claims that international capitalism has made capitalist countries from precapitalist ones and established the foundation for worker-led socialist revolutions. The contrasting view argues that foreign investment in a country creates dependencies that have a less positive impact than domestic investment does (Dixon and Boswell, 1996; Firebaugh, 1996). The economies of developing nations often have become tied to a single industry, increasing dependence on foreign investors, distorting patterns of national economic development, and rendering the nations especially vulnerable to bust-and-boom economic cycles (Noble, 1989; Stokes and Anderson, 1990). But arrangements are increasingly complex. The passage of U.S. health care legislation generated business opportunities in India, where insurance claims processing, Medicare eligibility assessments, and other work is done, and employment opportunities in the United States, where Indian companies hire U.S. workers (Lakshmi, 2010).

Globalization and the Internet

The Internet has dramatically changed the way companies, including multinational corporations, do business. The addition of 47 million websites to the worldwide web in 2009 brought the total number of sites to 234 million (Royal Pingdom, 2010). The use of the Internet allows people in all countries to conduct business with others anywhere in the world. Analysts predict that the increase in location-independent work opportunities will change the quality of work, management practices, and the way work is contracted out (International Labor Organization, 2001). While use of the new information

"My parents sent back all my stuff that came from China."

and communication technologies results in job loss, new employment opportunities also are created, and the use of new information and communication technologies has the potential for increasing employment in developing countries (International Labor Organization, 2001). Some analysts estimate that up to 5 percent of the service-sector jobs in industrialized nations—approximately 12 million jobs—could be relocated to developing nations. But Internet use is still fairly limited in many parts of the world; only about a third of the world's population has Internet access. In 2011, more than about three-quarters of the population in the United States, Canada, Japan, South Korea, New Zealand, Australia, Singapore, and a number of European countries were using the Internet, but many people have no access. Countries with much lower percentages of their populations using the Internet include Brazil (37 percent), China (38 percent), Mexico (31 percent), and India (10 percent).

These countries are included in the top 20 countries in Internet use; in many countries the Internet is not available to most people (Internet World Stats, 2012). Politics plays a part in some countries. In Cuba, where what citizens hear and read is tightly controlled by the government, Internet technology also is under government control (Robinson, 2012). In 2011, only 14.5 percent of the Cuban population were Internet users, compared to 41 percent in the nearby Dominican Republic (Internet World Stats, 2012).

The Control of Corporations

We have seen that the decisions made by corporations have vast consequences not only for the citizens of one country but also for the global community. They have a substantial impact upon employment opportunities, economic conditions (depression and inflation), consumer choices, and political authority.

Who controls corporations—who are their decision makers? In 1932, Adolph Berle, Jr., and Gardiner C. Means published *The Modern Corporation and Private Property,* a book that has had a profound impact on scholarly thought on the matter. They wrote that corporate power resides with chief executives who themselves have little financial stake in the firms they manage. The logic of their argument rested on the assertion that the stock of most large corporations is widely dispersed. Consequently, no shareholders possess a sufficient block of stock to impose corporate policy on the managers who make the day-to-day decisions for their firms. This state of affairs has been labeled "the managerial revolution" (Burnham, 1941).

Emphasizing Short-Term Profits

Some critics see the managerial revolution as the source of many of America's current economic problems, with corporations rewarding executives who display impressive short-term results. U.S. executives keep research and technology on short rations and skimp on the investment needed to ensure competitiveness in the future; they are slow to innovate, and they avoid risk. Critics also charge that U.S. industries are managed by persons increasingly oriented toward realizing profits by financial stratagems, commodity speculation, and fast-return investments. Large investors and speculators—called corporate raiders—have found that they can make money by buying and selling companies.

Critics also say that executives adopt strategies that allow substantial expense accounts and high salaries for themselves. In 2001, for instance, the typical chief executive officer (CEO) in a modest-sized U.S. firm received nearly $2 million in total compensation—41 times the average U.S. worker's pay. In contrast, the average Japanese CEO made only 12 times the earnings of the average Japanese worker, and the average CEO in Germany made 13 times the pay of the average worker there (see Figure 9.4).

Economists Marianne Bertrand and Sendhil Mullainathan studied determinants of CEO pay from 1977 to 1994 and found that increases in the value of a company's stock led to increases in CEO pay, whether the increasing stock value was due to executive performance or fluctuations in economic conditions that were beyond the executive's control. In other words, increases in CEO pay are affected as much by luck as by performance (Bertrand and Mullainathan, 2001). In 2002, the third year of a sharp decline both in corporate performance and in stock prices in the United States, CEO pay nonetheless increased by 6 percent (McGeehan, 2003), which was significantly greater than the increase in the average worker's pay.

The disparity between workers' pay and CEOs' pay is much greater in very large corporations. Research on the total compensation (salary, bonuses, stock options, and other stock distributions) of CEOs in America's 800 largest corporations shows that the average compensation for the 100 highest-paid CEOs was $37.5 million in 1999 (see Piketty and Saez [2007] and updated tables at http://www.econ.berkeley.edu/~saez/). This was about $768 for every $1 made by the average worker in the United States in that year ($46,332). In 1970, the ratio of top CEO pay to the average worker's pay was only $39 to $1. This increase from $39 to $768 is much greater than the increase in the performance of these large corporations or of the economy over this period, suggesting that top CEOs' pay is not tightly connected to either CEO job performance or economic growth in general.

Although social scientists had long assumed that managers had wide discretion in leading their companies, research in the 1990s showed that important constraints operate on managers in discharging their responsibilities (Fligstein, 1990; Fligstein and Brantley, 1992). For one thing, because corporations are dependent on suppliers of raw materials, customers, employees, investors, and lenders, usually referred to as *stakeholders,* executives must act in ways that do not threaten these important relationships (Mintz and Schwartz, 1985; Loomis, 1988).

	CEO Compensation	Average Worker's Compensation	Ratio of CEO Pay to the Average Worker's Pay by Country
South Africa	$982,925	$12,035	82
Mexico	$1,002,357	$16,535	61
Brazil	$848,946	$14,068	60
India	$290,854	$5,737	51
Argentina	$431,300	$9,529	45
Venezuela	$467,868	$11,146	42
Singapore	$1,033,274	$26,274	39
United States	$2,164,952	$55,568	39
China (Shanghai)	$211,255	$5,885	36
Malaysia	$402,011	$12,612	32
United Kingdom	$1,184,936	$37,301	32
Italy	$1,137,326	$43,856	26
China (Hong Kong)	$651,339	$25,262	26
Poland	$396,466	$15,914	25
Canada	$1,068,964	$46,224	23
France	$1,202,145	$52,663	23
South Korea	$584,072	$25,778	23
Germany	$1,181,292	$58,702	20
Switzerland	$1,390,899	$72,194	19
Sweden	$948,990	$49,307	19
Belgium	$987,387	$54,935	18
Netherlands	$862,711	$48,393	18
Spain	$697,691	$40,534	17
Australia	$707,747	$45,349	16
Taiwan	$250,212	$18,322	14
Japan	$543,564	$50,379	11

Figure 9.4 **Ratio of CEO Pay to the Average Worker's Pay by Country**
Chief executive officers in large U.S. companies earn more than their counterparts in other industrialized and emerging nations, but the gap between a CEO and a skilled industrial worker is greater in some other countries (2005–2006 data).

Source: Figure generated by the authors using data from *Managing Global Pay and Benefits: Worldwide Total Remuneration 2005–2006*, available at http://www.towersperrin.com/tp/getwebcachedoc?webc=HRS/BRA/2006/200612/Brazil_11.pdf. These data are estimates of compensations for corporations with $500 million in annual worldwide sales. CEOs are the most senior executives in each corporation surveyed. Workers typically have five years of experience.

Corporate interlocks—networks of individuals who serve on the boards of directors of multiple corporations—are another set of constraints. Because members of the corporate board of one corporation may be board members or executives in other corporations, these corporate interlocks are mechanisms whereby corporate managers are constrained to some degree by interests of those outside the corporation (Kerbo, 2011). Interlocks also serve firms with the means to gather the strategic information their officials need to make corporate decisions and build favorable relationships with other firms (Bartol and Martin, 1998; Kerbo, 2011).

The beginning of the 21st century has seen some new business models, including open-source production such as the online encyclopedia Wikipedia, for which unpaid experts write entries and other unpaid "workers" read, comment on, and edit (Pink, 2009); anyone with Internet access can use the product for no charge. In addition, several states now allow "low-profit limited liability corporations" or L3Cs, corporations with the primary aim of benefiting society. For example, an L3C in North Carolina buys abandoned furniture factories, renovates the factories with environmentally sustainable principles in mind, and leases them at a low rate to struggling manufacturers, thereby benefiting the environment and local economies (Pink, 2009). There also are "social businesses" based on social-benefit principles and "B Corporations," companies with bylaws that reflect a higher commitment to long-term value and social impact than to short-term economic gain (Pink, 2009).

What Can Sociology Do for You?

One of the ways in which the world is changing rapidly is the massive shift in economic power. How will this affect the United States? What will your job opportunities look like in a world changed by rapid economic growth in China, India, Brazil, Russia, and other developing countries? How will the generation of U.S. citizens currently in college contribute to these changes and to our adaptations to them?

The jobs for sociology majors related to economics and politics are many. Do you hope to go to Washington, D.C.? Information about jobs on Capitol Hill is available at **http://thehill.com.** To learn about careers in international development, visit the U.S. Agency for International Development website at **http://www.usaid.gov/careers** or the World Bank site at **http://web.worldbank.org.** The USAID site includes information about volunteer student intern positions, including internships in the Office of Conflict Management and Mitigation and the Bureau for Legislative and Public Affairs, as well as paid jobs (click on "VACANCIES" on the menu on the right).

If you are interested in issues related to economic and political power, you might like to take courses in political science, government, economics, power, globalization, or international development.

The Chapter in Brief: *Political and Economic Power*

Power, Authority, and the State

Power determines which individuals and groups will be able to translate their preferences into the reality of day-to-day social organization.

■ **The State** The **state** rests on **force** and consists of people who exercise an effective monopoly in the use of physical coercion within a given territory.

■ **Sociological Perspectives on the State** Functionalists say the state performs four functions: enforcement of norms, overall social planning and direction, arbitration of conflicting interests, and protection of society's members and interests against outside groups. Conflict theorists say the state is a vehicle by which one or more groups impose their values and stratification system upon other groups, and they depict it as an instrument of violence and oppression.

■ **Legitimacy and Authority** Sociologists distinguish between power that is legitimate and power that is illegitimate. Legitimate power is **authority.** Sociologist Max Weber suggested that power may be legitimated by **traditional, legal-rational,** and/or **charismatic** means.

Political Power

Politics refers to the processes by which people and groups acquire and exercise power. **Political power** is power that is organized and wielded by the state.

■ **Types of Government** **Government** can take the form of **totalitarianism, authoritarianism,** or **democracy,** which is promoted by a strong **civil society.**

■ **Political Power in the United States** A constitutional system of government defines and prescribes the boundaries within which political power is pursued in the United States. Central to American political processes are **political parties,** popular electoral participation, **interest-group** lobbying (including **political action committees**), and the **mass media.**

■ **Models of Power in the United States** Marxist theory holds that political processes are affected by class interests and conflict. The elitist model depicts major decisions as being made by a power elite. The pluralist perspective says that no one group really runs the government.

Economic Power

■ **Comparative Economic Systems** Modern economic systems provide a different answer to the question of how economic activity is organized—by the market or by plan—and to the question of who owns the means of production, individuals or the state. **Capitalist economies** rely heavily on free markets and privately held property, and **socialist economies** rely primarily on state planning and publicly held property. Most nations are characterized by mixed economies that include elements of both.

The Power of Corporations

The government is an important participant in the U.S. economy, but the primary productive role is played by private business.

■ **The Power of National Corporations** Large corporations exercise enormous power in American life and constitute **oligopolies.** The decisions made by their executives have implications and ramifications that reach throughout the nation.

■ **The Power of Multinational Corporations in the Global Economy** The rise of **multinational corporations** and the growing internationalization of the world economy, including **core regions** and **periphery regions,** have given economic power a new dimension. Such firms rival nations in wealth and frequently operate as private governments pursuing their worldwide interests by well-developed foreign policies.

■ **The Control of Corporations** Some social scientists say that a managerial revolution has separated ownership and effective control in corporate life, but others point to the institutional constraints, such as **corporate interlocks,** that operate on corporate decision makers.

Glossary

authoritarianism A political system in which the government tolerates little or no opposition to its rules but permits non-governmental centers of influence and allows debate on issues of public policy.

authority Legitimate power.

capitalist economy An economic system relying primarily on free markets and privately held property.

charismatic authority Power that is legitimated by the extraordinary superhuman or supernatural qualities people attribute to a leader.

civil society A social realm of mediating groups, networks, and institutions that sustains public life outside the worlds of the state and the economy.

core regions Geographical areas that dominate the world economy and exploit the rest of the system.

corporate interlocks Networks of individuals who serve on the boards of directors of multiple corporations.

democracy A political system in which the powers of government derive from the consent of the governed and in which regular constitutional avenues exist for changing government officials.

force Power whose basis is the threat or application of punishment.

government Those political processes that have to do with the authoritative formulating of rules and policies that are binding and pervasive throughout a society.

interest groups Organizations of people who share common concerns or points of view.

interests Common concerns or points of view.

legal-rational authority Power that is legitimated by explicit rules and rational procedures that define the rights and duties of the occupants of given positions.

mass media Those organizations—newspapers, magazines, television, radio, motion pictures, and the Internet—that undertake to convey information to a large segment of the public.

multinational corporations Firms that have their central office in one country and subsidiaries in other countries.

oligopoly A market dominated by a few firms.

periphery regions Geographical areas that provide raw materials to the core and that are exploited by it.

political action committees (PACs) Interest groups set up to elect or defeat candidates, but not through the organization of a political party.

political party An organization designed to gain control of the government by putting its people in public office.

political power Power that is organized and wielded by the state.

politics The processes by which people and groups acquire and exercise power.

public-interest groups Interest groups that pursue policies that presumably would be of no greater benefit to their members than to the larger society.

socialist economy An economic system relying primarily on state planning and publicly held property.

special-interest groups Interest groups that primarily seek benefits from which their members would derive more gains than the society as a whole.

state An arrangement that consists of people who exercise an effective monopoly in the use of physical coercion within a given territory.

totalitarianism A "total state" in which the government undertakes to control all parts of the society and all aspects of social life.

traditional authority Power that is legitimated by the sanctity of age-old customs.

Review Questions

1. Define *the state* as sociologists use the term.

2. How do the functionalist and conflict perspectives on the state differ?

3. What do sociologists mean by legitimacy and authority? What are the three types of authority and how do they differ?

4. Define politics and political power.

5. How do totalitarianism, authoritarianism, and democracy differ?

6. What are the major elements of American political processes?

7. What is an oligopoly? What part do oligopolies play in the United States?

8. How do multinational corporations function?

9. Who controls corporations?

Internet Connection   www.mhhe.com/hughes11e

Are you registered to vote? Have you voted in a local, state, or national election? Use an Internet search engine such as yahoo.com or Google to find out what sorts of people are most likely to vote in national elections. Try using "voter characteristics" for searching. Are the percentages you find different from those presented in Figure 9.1? Are the data for a presidential election different from those for a midterm (Senate and House) election?

The Family

310

I n the 1950s, a television sitcom called *Leave It to Beaver* featured an all-American family, Ward and June Cleaver and their sons, Wally and Beaver. In 2012, a television sitcom called *Modern Family* featured three related all-American families: Claire, Phil, and their three children; Claire's father, Jay, his very-much-younger wife, Gloria, and her son, Manny, from a previous relationship; and Claire's brother, Mitchell, his gay partner, Cameron, and their adopted baby, Lily.

Families, and media depictions of them, have changed. At one time in American history, marriage was the primary defining social relationship for adults. As sociologist Paul Amato and his colleagues explain in their book *Alone Together: How Marriage in America Is Changing* (2007:1), getting married was associated with several life events:

- Leaving one's parents
- Creating one's own home
- Achieving economic independence
- Initiating regular sexual activity
- Having children

Today, half of all American women are living without a husband, about 64 percent of men and half of women ages 25–29 have not yet married, only 21 percent of all households in the United States are married couples with children (U.S. Census Bureau, 2011b), more than half the births among women under 30 occur outside wedlock (Martin et al., 2011), and between 60 and 70 percent of all married couples cohabit before they marry (Rhoades, Stanley, and Markman, 2009; Stanley, Whitton, and Markman, 2004). Clearly marriage and the family do not hold all of the same meanings they once did.

Americans now may have any of a number of **lifestyles**—the overall patterns of living people evolve to meet their biological, social, and emotional needs. Table 10.1 compares the circumstances of American children in 2011 with those in 1960; Figure 10.1 reveals the substantial shifts in American family arrangements. Whether American lifestyle changes are positive or not is a matter of opinion. Some observers argue that the changes to the family reveal its flexibility and resilience. They agree that the meaning of marriage has been changing, and with it the family institution, and they contend that earlier structures were flawed as conformity-ridden, male-dominated, and oppressive. Others cite gay marriage, easy divorce, the postponement of marriage, a rise in the proportion of the never-married, and the ready availability of contraception as forces that have eroded the family and compromised its "ultimate function"—the licensing of reproduction. No matter what we think family is, most of us think it's tremendously important: 76 percent of American adults say that family is the most important element in their lives, and about that

many also say they are "very satisfied" with their family life (Taylor, 2010).

The "family question" is not new. Concerns about the family have a long history (Coontz, 1992), and it is safe to assume that debate will continue. In this chapter we will look first at the structure of the family from a global perspective, including forms of marriage and family and patterns of courtship around the world. We will then focus on marriage and family in the United States, both the traditional nuclear family and other forms of family life. We will look at special challenges American families and American society face, including divorce, family violence and abuse, child care, and care for the elderly. Finally, we will see what the three major sociological perspectives have to offer to our understanding of the family.

Structure of the Family: A Global View

What is the family? Even experts on the family have trouble defining it; textbooks for courses on the family offer multiple definitions (e.g., Cherlin, 2010). Many of us still think of the family as a social unit consisting of Mom, Pop, and the kids, living in a comfortable home of their own. But as we will see in the course of the chapter, this definition is too restrictive. In the United States, this model of the family—a married couple, breadwinner husband and homemaker wife, raising children—now represents only one in five families. In many societies it is the kin group, and not a married couple and their children, that is the basic family unit.

Sociologists have traditionally viewed the **family** as a social group whose members are related by ancestry, marriage, or adoption and live together, cooperate economically, and care for the young (Murdock, 1949). Some argue that psychological bonds and intimacy are what families are all about; they see the family as a close-knit group of people who care about and

Table 10.1	A Comparison of the State of U.S. Children, 1960 and 2011	
	1960	2009–2011
Children born to unmarried mothers	5%	41%
Mothers returning to work within 1 year of a child's birth	17%	57%
Children under 18 living in a one-parent family	10%	27%
Infant mortality (deaths before first birthday)	28/1,000	6.1/1,000
Children under 18 living below the poverty line	27%	22%
Married women with children under 6 years old in labor force	18.6%	61.6%

Sources: U.S. Census Bureau, 2010; Haub and Kaneda, 2011; Centers for Disease Control, 2012.

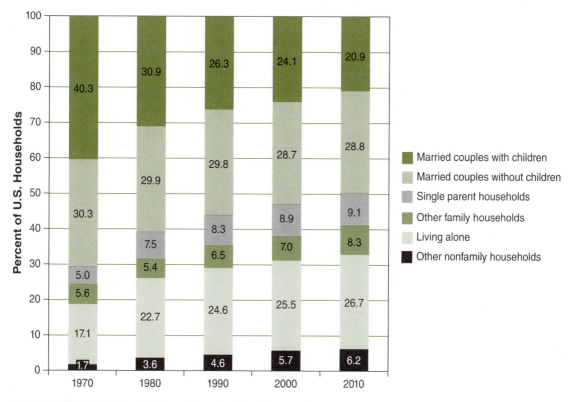

■	Married couples with children				
■	Married couples without children				
■	Single parent households				
■	Other family households				
■	Living alone				
■	Other nonfamily households				

Figure 10.1 **Today's Families Differ from Those of an Earlier Generation**

Source: Figure generated by the authors using data from the U.S. Census Bureau, 2011.

respect one another (e.g., Lauer and Lauer, 2000). The family, then, is a matter of social definition. Because the family is a social construct, family ties are often independent of legal or kin status (Gubrium and Holstein, 1990).

Defining the family is not simply an academic exercise. How we define it determines the kinds of families we will consider normal or deviant and what rights and obligations we will recognize as legally and socially binding. For example, a growing number of judges and legislators are extending to qualifying domestic partners some of the benefits traditionally accorded married heterosexuals, including health benefits, property and life insurance, bereavement leave, and annuity and pension rights. In 2010

President Obama mandated that hospitals allow patients to designate visitors and to choose who will make end-of-life decisions for them, regardless of traditional family ties (Shear, 2010).

In this section we will look at forms of the family, forms of marriage, and patterns of courtship in the United States and around the world.

Forms of the Family

Families are organized in many ways. Individuals differ in their thoughts about whether parents should be married, how many children make a perfect family, whether male or female offspring are preferable, and even whether having children at all is important (see Box 10.1).

A Wide Variety in Family Values

The family is among the most important institutions in every society, but exactly how people value the family varies from one society to the next. Data collected in 29 countries all over the world provide a picture of marriage and family (DeRose, 2011).

Let's look first at marriage. Crude marriage rates—the number of marriages that occur per year per 1,000 total population—allow us to see cultural differences among countries. Egypt, with a crude marriage rate of 9.9, the United States (7.3), China (7.2), and other countries in Asia and the Middle East all have marriage rates that are above average for the 29 countries assessed. Latin American countries, along with South Africa, are low, with marriage rates below 4 per 1,000. In the middle are most European and Oceanic countries.

Cohabitation—unmarried adults living together—is more common in countries with lower marriage rates, as one might expect. In Egypt, Saudi Arabia, South Korea, Taiwan, and Indonesia, fewer than 1 percent of adults live together outside wedlock, compared to France (16 percent), Sweden (18 percent), Peru (25 percent), and Colombia (31 percent).

Annual divorce rates range from 3.6 per 1,000 in the United States to no divorce at all in the Philippines, where it is illegal. An increase in divorce in countries where it was once uncommon and a decrease in the United States, Australia, New Zealand, and many European countries has resulted in a convergence of rates. Most developed countries have rates higher than 2 divorces per 1,000, though divorce in the Middle East remains rare.

Family size differs around the world (Haub and Kaneda, 2011), and we can get an idea of that through total fertility—the average number of children born to a woman during her lifetime. East Asia (1.5), Eastern Europe (1.5), and Southern Europe (1.4) currently have the lowest fertility rates in the world. Western African (5.5) and Middle African (5.7) countries have the highest fertility rates, along with high infant and child mortality rates that decrease family size.

Survey data provide a look at attitudes (DeRose, 2011). Support for the relevance of marriage in society, for example, is strong all over the world, although significant declines in this measure have been recorded in Chile, Mexico, Great Britain, and India. Most adults feel that a child should be raised in a home with both a mother and a father; this response is nearly unanimous in Middle Eastern and African countries and exceeds 90 percent in most Asian countries. Support is also strong in Latin American and most European countries; in fact, Sweden is the only country in the study in which fewer than 50 percent of adults supported the mother-father ideal.

Attitudes toward divorce, however, vary widely around the globe, with European, Oceanic, and both North and South American countries (with a few exceptions) showing a pattern of becoming increasingly permissive in their attitudes, and a number of other countries being quite restrictive. When asked whether family life deserves more emphasis, 80 percent and more of survey respondents reply affirmatively in almost every country included in the study.

Valuing the family may be universal, but family values are not. These findings strongly suggest that, like other cultural traits, family values vary because of differing social, economic, and other factors, such as religion. They also suggest that as our society, economy, and culture change, we are likely to observe more changes in our American family values.

Questions for Discussion

1. What explains the very low fertility rates in East Asia and Eastern and Southern Europe?

2. How do people reconcile their belief that children should be raised in a two-parent family with their desire to obtain a divorce?

More fundamentally, families vary in their composition and in their descent, residence, and authority patterns—characteristics we examine here.

Composition

Social relationships between adult males and females can be organized within families by emphasizing either spouse or kin relationships. In the **nuclear family** arrangement, spouses and their offspring constitute the core relationship; blood relatives are functionally marginal and peripheral. In contrast, in the **extended family** arrangement, kin—individuals related by common ancestry—provide the core relationship; spouses are functionally marginal and peripheral. Americans typically find themselves members of two nuclear families. First, an individual belongs to a nuclear family that consists of oneself and one's father, mother, and siblings, what sociologists call the **family of orientation**. Second, since over 90 percent of Americans marry at least once, most are or have been members of a nuclear family that consists of oneself and one's spouse and children—the **family of procreation.**

Extended families are found in numerous forms throughout the world. In the Nayara soldiering caste of southwestern India during the pre-British period, spouse ties were virtually absent (Fuller, 1976). The Mosuo people of Southwest China live in multigenerational households made up of a mother and her blood relatives (Stacey, 2009). Men stay with their maternal families when they reach adulthood and can visit a lover at night; the adults of each household raise all the children born to the women of that household.

For some time sociologists assumed that industrialization undercut extended family patterns while fostering nuclear family arrangements. A closer look shows a different pattern. By virtue of high mortality rates, the nuclear family had come to prevail in England before the Industrial Revolution got under way (Laslett, 1974, 1976; Stearns, 1977; Quadagno, 1982). When Tamara K. Hareven (1982) examined family life in a textile community in 19th-century New Hampshire, she discovered that industrialism promoted kin ties. Not only did different generations often reside together in the same household, but they provided a good deal of assistance to one another. Indeed, economic dislocations and the increased availability of non-nuclear kin may actually have encouraged the formation of extended family households in the early industrialization of England and the United States (Ruggles, 1987). Overall, a growing body of research suggests that a large number of factors—in addition to the nature of the political economy—interact with one another to produce a diversity of family life patterns (Cherlin, 2010; Taylor et al., 2010; Kertzer, 1991).

Descent

Societies trace descent and pass on property from one generation to the next in one of three ways. Under a **patrilineal** arrangement, a people reckon descent and transmit property through the line of the father. Under a **matrilineal** arrangement, descent and inheritance take place through the mother's side of the family. Under the **bilineal** arrangement, both sides of an individual's family are equally important. Americans are typically bilineal, reckoning descent through both the father and the mother; however, the surname typically is transmitted in a patrilineal manner.

Residence

Societies also differ in where couples take up residence after marriage. In the case of **patrilocal residence,** the bride and groom live in the household or community of the husband's family. The opposite pattern prevails in **matrilocal residence.** For example, among the Hopi of the Southwest, the husband moves upon marriage into the dwelling of his wife's family, where he eats and sleeps. In the United States, newlyweds tend to follow **neolocal residence** patterns, in which they set up a new place of residence independent of either of their parents or other relatives.

Authority

Although the authority a man or woman enjoys in family decision making is influenced by their personalities, societies nonetheless dictate who is expected to be the dominant figure. Under **patriarchal authority,** the eldest male or the husband fills this role. The ancient Hebrews, Greeks, and Romans and the 19th-century Chinese and Japanese provide a few examples. Logically, the construction of a **matriarchal authority** family type is very simple and would involve the vesting of power in women. Yet true matriarchies are rare (Hutter, 1998), and considerable controversy exists about whether the balance of power actually rests with the wife in any known society (Stephens, 1963). Matriarchies can arise through default upon the death of or desertion by the husband. In a third type of family, the **egalitarian authority** arrangement, power and authority are equally distributed between husband and wife. This pattern is on the increase in the United States.

Forms of Marriage

Marriage refers to a socially approved sexual union between two or more individuals that is undertaken with some idea of permanence. The parties to a marriage must be members of two different kin groups, which has crucial implications for the structuring of the family. Indeed, the continuity, and therefore the long-term welfare, of any kin group depends on obtaining spouses for the unmarried members of the group from other groups. A kin group has a stake in retaining some measure of control over at least a portion of its members after they marry (Lee, 1977). In this section we will define and discuss exogamy, endogamy, incest taboos, monogamy, polygyny, polyandry, and group marriage.

Exogamy and Endogamy

All societies regulate the pool of eligibles from which individuals are expected to select a mate. A child's kin generally have more in mind than simply getting the child married. They want the child married to the right spouse, especially where marriage has consequences for the larger kin group. Two types of marital regulations define the "right" spouse: endogamy and exogamy. **Endogamy** is the requirement that marriage occur within a group. Under these circumstances people must marry within their class, race, ethnic group, or religion. **Exogamy** is the requirement that marriage occur outside a group. Whether or not marriages should take place outside of specific groups can change rapidly, as in Iraq, where Sunni–Shiite marriages went from symbolizing a tolerant society to

being the source of conflict, hatred, and family breakdown (Raghavan, 2007).

Regulations relating to exogamy are based primarily on kinship and usually entail **incest taboos,** rules that prohibit sexual intercourse with close blood relatives and exist today in virtually every society (Olson and DeFrain, 1997). Such relationships not only are prohibited but also bring reactions of aversion and disgust. At one time social scientists singled out incest taboos as the only universal norm in a world of diverse moral codes. But sociologist Russell

Most couples in the United States and other western countries choose their partners, but this is not true of every society. It is likely that this Indian couple did not know each other until their parents arranged to have them wed.

Middleton (1962) found that brother–sister marriage was not only permitted but frequently practiced by the ancient Egyptians. He speculated that brother–sister marriage served to maintain the power and property of a family and prevented the splintering of an estate through inheritance. A similar arrangement apparently occurred among the royal families of Hawaii, the Inca of Peru, and the Dahomey of West Africa.

There have been numerous attempts to account for both the existence and the prevalence of incest taboos. Some have argued that incest taboos came about because of real or imagined negative effects of "inbreeding." However, the incest taboo has been found even in cultures where people were unaware of the father's role in reproduction (Hutter, 1998). Anthropologist Claude Lévi-Strauss (1956) suggested that incest taboos promote alliances between families and reinforce their social interdependence, as reflected by the Zulu saying: "They are our enemies, and so we marry them."

Types of Marriage

The relationships between a husband and wife may be structured in one of four ways: **monogamy,** one husband and one wife; **polygyny,** one husband and two or more wives; **polyandry,** two or more husbands and one wife; or **group marriage,** two or more husbands and two or more wives. Monogamy appears in all societies, although other forms may be not only permitted but preferred. Monogamy was the preferred or ideal type of marriage in fewer than 20 percent of 862 societies included in one cross-cultural sample (Murdock, 1967).

Polygyny has been widely practiced throughout the world. The Old Testament, for example, records polygynous practices among the Hebrews. In China, India, and the Islamic countries, polygyny has usually been the privilege of the wealthy few. In the United States, it is not legal, but it does exist. A man in Utah with five wives and 29 children was charged with bigamy and rape in 2000. An additional 30,000 polygynists are thought to be practicing "underground" (Arrillaga, 2000). The arrangement tends to be favored where large families are advantageous and women make substantial contributions to subsistence.

In contrast to polygyny, polyandry is exceedingly rare. Polyandry usually does not represent freedom of sexual choice for women; often, it involves the right or the opportunity of younger brothers to have sexual access to the wife of an older brother. If a family cannot afford wives or marriages for each of its sons, it may find a wife for the eldest son only.

Social scientists are far from agreement on whether group marriage has ever existed as a cultural norm. There is some evidence that it did occur among the Kaingang of Brazil, the Marquesans of the South Pacific, the Chukchee of Siberia, and the Todas of India. At times, polyandry appears to slip into group marriage, where a number of brothers share more than one wife (Stephens, 1963).

Patterns of Courtship

Marriage brings a new member into the inner circle of a family, and relatives have a stake in who is to be the spouse. Random mating might jeopardize these interests: If sons and daughters were permitted to "fall in love" with anybody, they might choose the wrong mate. Instead, courtship in many societies follows specific and traditional patterns, the topic of discussion of this section.

The Social Regulation of Love

Although love has many meanings, we usually think of the strong physical and emotional attraction between a man and a woman as **romantic love.** The ancient Greeks saw such love as a "diseased hysteria," an overwhelming force that irresistibly draws two people together and leads them to become passionately preoccupied with one another. Some societies view marriage without love as mildly shameful; others define strong romantic attachment as a laughable or tragic aberration.

Societies undertake to control love in a variety of ways. One approach is *child marriage,* which was employed at one time in India. A child bride went to live with her husband in a marriage that was not physically consummated until much later. In an *arranged marriage* the parents of the bride and groom make the arrangements for the marriage, sometimes when both are too young to marry but also when both are of marriageable ages.

Another approach involves the *social isolation* of young people from potential mates. For instance, the Manus of the Admiralty Islands secluded their young women in a lodge built on stilts over a lagoon. The *close supervision* of couples by chaperones was an arrangement found among 17th-century New England Puritans. Finally, *peer and parental pressures* may be brought to bear. For example, in the United States parents often threaten, cajole, wheedle, and bribe their children to limit their social contacts to youths with "suitable" ethnic, religious, and educational backgrounds. The net result of these approaches is the same—a person's range of choice is narrowed by social barriers.

Factors in Mate Selection

Given a field of eligible mates, why do we fall in love with and marry one person and not another? A variety of factors are at work. One is **homogamy**—the tendency of like to marry like. People of similar age, race, religion, nationality, education, intelligence, health, stature, attitudes, and countless other traits tend to marry one another to a degree greater than would be found by chance. Although homogamy seems to operate with respect to social characteristics, the evidence is less clear for psychological factors such as personality and temperament.

Physical attractiveness also plays a part in mate selection. We prefer the companionship and friendship of attractive people to that of unattractive people (Feingold, 1990). However, since the supply of unusually beautiful or handsome partners is limited, we tend in real life to select partners who have a degree of physical attractiveness similar to our own (Murstein, 1972, 1976; Feingold, 1988). According to the **matching hypothesis,** we typically experience the greatest payoff and the least cost when we follow this course; individuals of equal attractiveness are those most likely to reciprocate our advances.

The **complementary needs theory** (Winch, 1958) refers to two different personality traits that are the counterparts of each other and that provide a sense of completeness when they are joined. Dominant people find a complementary relationship with passive people, and talkative people find themselves attracted to good listeners. Interpersonal attraction depends on how well each partner fulfills the role expectations of the other and how mutually gratifying they find their "role fit" (Bluhm, Widiger, and Miele, 1990; Collins and Read, 1990).

Exchange theory links these three factors. It is based on the notion that we like those who reward us and dislike those who punish us (Molm, 1991; Lawler and Yoon, 1993). Many of our acts derive from our confidence that from them will flow some benefit—perhaps a desired expression of love, gratitude, recognition, security, or material reward. In the course of interacting, we reinforce the relationship by rewarding each other. Thus, people with similar social traits, attitudes, and values mutually reward one another. In selecting partners of comparable physical attractiveness, we minimize the risk of rejection while maximizing the profit from such a conquest. And the parties in complementary relationships offer each other high rewards at low cost to themselves. In sum, exchange theory proposes that people involved in a mutually satisfying relationship will exchange behaviors that have low cost and high reward.

Marriage and the Family in the United States

Let's take a brief look at the marriage and family statistics for the United States: In 2011, 52 percent of people 18 and over were married, and 65 percent of America's children were living with their own married parents, but married couples with children accounted for only 21 percent of all U.S. households (U.S. Census Bureau, 2011b). Children also were living with two unmarried parents (3.9 percent), a biological parent and a stepparent (5.2 percent), a single parent (27.2 percent), or no parent (3.9 percent). Same-sex couples accounted for 1 percent of all couple households, and 10 percent of children lived in a household that included a grandparent. In general, compared to 30 years ago, people are getting married later, they are less likely to divorce, and remarriage is less common (Isen and Stevenson, 2010). But interest in these age-old institutions has not disappeared: A 2011 survey of American singles showed that 33 percent of both sexes say they want to get married, and more men (51 percent) than women (46 percent) want to have children (Fisher, 2012).

In this section we will examine marriage, parenthood, and mothers in the labor force. We also will discuss singlehood, single parenthood, stepfamilies, cohabitation, and gay and lesbian couples.

Marriage

In the first comprehensive study on American marriage since the 1980s, Paul Amato, Alan Booth, David Johnson, and Stacy Rogers (2007) used two data sets to paint a portrait of marriage and the changes it has undergone. The Marital Instability over the Life Course Study was conducted in 1980, and the Survey of Marriage and Family Life in 2000. Similar research designs, target populations, and questionnaires allowed the researchers to use the data from the two studies to compare the quality of people's marriages—how happy they are with their marriages—in 1980 and in 2000. In this section we will look at important details from this study.

First, what defines a happy marriage? Amato and his co-authors found that happy couples were those who were committed to staying married. Happily married couples think that the division of labor in their marriage is fair, have nontraditional attitudes toward how labor should be divided, get married at older ages, share decision making, and have close friends in common. In addition, they are more likely to attend religious services together on a regular basis and to be affiliated with the same organizations. On the other hand, the researchers found that spouses who had grown up with divorced parents, had lived together before they got married, and were emotionally insecure had poorer-quality marriages.

What does a typical marriage look like? Amato and his co-authors categorized married couples into five groups. About 13 percent of the couples they surveyed were "disadvantaged, young, single-earner marriages." Another 13 percent of marriages were "upper-middle-class, prosperous, mostly dual-earner marriages." A larger group (18 percent) was the "working-class/middle-class, traditional, single-earner." Even more (26 percent) were in the "working-class, young, dual-earner" group. The largest category was the "middle-class, egalitarian, dual-earner" group, 30 percent of all marriages.

In general, the factors that were associated with a high-quality marriage were the same for men and women (Amato et al., 2007). Only one factor was consistently different for husbands and wives, and that was the husband's share of housework. To simplify results: When husbands did more housework, they were less happy with their marriages but wives were *more* happy with their marriages. The survey data showed that both husbands and wives had become less traditional in their views about the division of household labor, with women more so than men, and wives were more likely than husbands to feel that the division of labor was unfair to them. (See Chapter 8 for more about the division of labor by gender.)

Amato and his colleagues also found that age of first marriage had increased (see Figure 10.2) and that marrying at later ages is associated with greater marital happiness. The median age at first marriage for U.S. men rose to 28.2 in 2010 from a low of 22.6 in the mid-1950s (U.S. Census Bureau, 2011b). For U.S. women the figure rose to 26.1 years, up from a low of 20.2 years. Marrying at a young age, researchers have found, is a good predictor of divorce (Amato et al., 2007). Those who are young when they marry are less likely than older spouses to be financially secure, and they are less experienced and more naïve about relationships. In addition, those who marry young have spent less time looking for a spouse. Education plays a role: Women with college degrees are

more likely to marry in their 30s and 40s, while women without degrees are more likely to be married in their 20s (Isen and Stevenson, 2010).

The Amato et al. (2007) survey also found that the percentage of interracial marriages in the United States had doubled since 1980 (from 1.3 to 2.6). Married couples that included members of different religions also are more common, as are couples in which the wife is older than the husband. In a 2011 survey of singles in the United States, fewer men (20 percent) than women (29 percent) said that finding a partner of their own ethnic background was essential or very important, and fewer men (17 percent) than women (28 percent) said the same of religion (Fisher, 2012). These **heterogamous marriages,** in which spouses have different characteristics, have been found by some researchers to be associated with reports of less happiness, more quarreling, and less time engaged in positive interaction than for homogamous marriages (Amato et al., 2007).

The patriarchal family structure of 50 years ago is quickly disappearing. Paul Amato and his

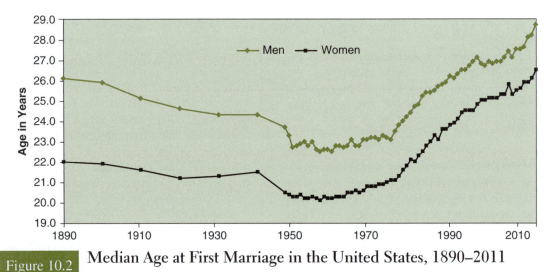

Figure 10.2   **Median Age at First Marriage in the United States, 1890–2011**

Source: U.S. Census Bureau, Current Population Survey, March and Annual Social and Economic Supplements, 2011, and earlier. (Available at www.census.gov/population/socdemo/hh-fam/ms2.xls.)

colleagues asked survey respondents whether there were any kinds of decisions made by married couples in which either the wife or the husband had the final word (Amato et al., 2007). Shared decision making, in which neither spouse has the final word, accounted for nearly 65 percent of both husbands' and wives' responses. Respondents indicated that they had the final word about some things while their spouses were in charge of other decisions; only a quarter of husbands and a fifth of wives reported that they were in charge of decision making in the household. Amato and his co-authors found that decision making was not affected by how much income the wife contributed to the household.

Family researchers Linda Waite and Maggie Gallagher (2000) say that marriage works best when wives and husbands need each other, but that these dependencies should be freely chosen. Whether both partners are paid for their work or not, marriage should be viewed as a "true partnership," not a shifting balance of domination and subordination.

Public opinion surveys indicate that Americans depend very heavily on marriage for their psychological well-being (Waite and Gallagher, 2000; Gove, Style, and Hughes, 1990; Glenn and Weaver, 1981). Although divorce rates increased dramatically earlier in the century, they have declined gradually since the early 1980s. And almost everyone tries marriage; only about 5 percent of Americans never marry.

Although Amato and his colleagues (2007) found a number of significant changes in U.S. marriages over the last 20 years of the 20th century, in general, married Americans seem to be fairly happy. Nearly half of all married people reported being "very happy" with the extent of agreement with their spouses, 56 percent describe their feelings of love for their spouse as "very strong," 53 percent were "very happy" with their sex lives, and 68 percent said that their marriage is "better than most."

Parenthood

Married couples who decide to have children find their lives transformed by parenthood. Among other changes, costs go up when children are added to a family: Total annual expenses per child range from $11,880 to $13,830 in a two-child, married-couple, middle income family (Lino, 2011).

Nuclear families that are not disrupted by divorce, desertion, or death typically pass through a series of changes and realignments across time, what sociologists call the **family life course.** These changes and realignments are related to the altered expectations and requirements imposed on a husband and wife as children are born and grow up.

In Chapter 4 you learned about group dynamics and the consequences of adding members to a group. A family typically begins with the husband–wife pair—a dyad—and becomes a triad with the addition of the first child. As the family grows, new roles are created and the number of relationships is multiplied. The family then stabilizes for a time, after which it begins shrinking as each of the adult children is launched. Finally, it returns once more to the husband–wife pair and eventually terminates with the death of a spouse. Decisive economic, social, political, or military events intervene to alter the normal course of events (Elder, 1983), and divorce, desertion, death, remarriage, and the blending of children from one marriage into another all complicate the family life course.

Each change in the role of one family member can affect all the other members. The arrival of the first child compels the reorganization of a couple's life. Parents have to juggle their work roles, alter their time schedules, change their communication patterns, and relinquish some privacy. Parenthood competes with the husband or wife role. After the birth of a first child, husbands and wives who could once focus unlimited attention on their spouses now have to split their attention between spouse and child. The

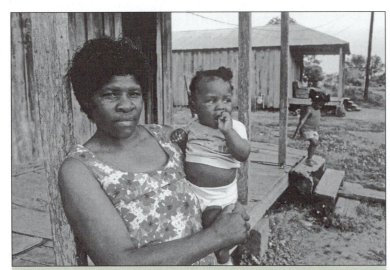

In 2011, 51.2 percent of African American children were living with a single parent. About 42 percent of all U.S. families headed by a single parent are living below the poverty threshold (U.S. Census Bureau, 2011b).

result is that new parents may feel that their spouses are not paying enough attention to them. Not surprisingly, marital adjustment ratings, an indicator of marital satisfaction, typically fall after the birth of a first child (Belsky and Rovine, 1990). The addition of a second child changes the family again, sometimes reducing the mother's participation in the paid labor force, increasing her responsibilities in housework, and making fathers feel more a part of the family (Boodman, 2000). A consistent finding is that the psychological well-being of parents is a little worse than that of childless couples, and it remains lower until children grow up and move out of the household (Evenson and Simon, 2005). Despite the challenges a child brings to their lives, most couples report enormous satisfaction with parenthood, ranking their families as more important than work, recreation, friendships, or status.

Most couples do not experience difficulty with the "empty nest" period when their children leave home; the majority view this stage as a

time of new freedoms. Indeed, national surveys show that middle-aged women whose children have left home experience greater general happiness and enjoyment of life, in addition to greater marital happiness, than middle-aged women with children still living at home (White and Edwards, 1990; Vander Zanden, 1993).

The "empty nest" has become an ill-defined stage. Young adults are establishing their own households later and often return to reside for varying lengths of time in their parents' home. We noted in Box 3.2 that one of the signs of adulthood is living on one's own. In a 2011 survey, 29 percent of parents of adult children (25–34) said that a child had moved back home in the past few years because of the economy (Parker, 2012). Nearly two-thirds of the young adults surveyed said that they had friends or family who had moved back home recently, again because of the economy. Structural features of society have prevented these young adults from gaining full adulthood, a key life goal. However, 78 percent of them reported being satisfied with their living arrangements and optimistic about the future. Their presence in the family home may have benefited their parents during the recession as well; 48 percent of the adult children paid rent, and 89 percent of them contributed to household expenses.

More than 60 percent of all mothers with children under six years of age are now in the workforce (U.S. Census Bureau, 2011a; see Figure 10.3). In 1950 only one in eight were working. In 1998 a record 59 percent of women with infants were employed, a proportion that has dropped a bit.

Dual-income couples evolve new patterns and traditions for family living and face

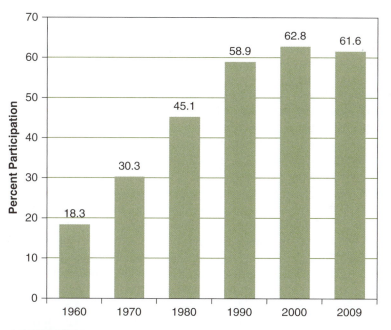

| Figure 10.3 | Labor-Force Participation Rates for Married Women in the U.S. with Children under Six Years Old, 1960–2009 |

Source: Figure generated by the authors using data from the U.S. Census Bureau, 2011a.

challenges and opportunities not experienced by families with two parents but only one breadwinner (Guelzow, Bird, and Koball, 1991; Vannoy and Philliber, 1992). But families seem to be adjusting to the change. In 1980, a wife employed outside the home was correlated with more marital conflict and other sorts of marital problems, while the 2000 data showed that an employed wife was associated with less conflict and fewer other marital problems (Amato et al., 2007). In both 1980 and 2000, however, when a wife spent long hours on the job marital quality suffered. Let's take a look at the effects of employment on women and children.

Mothers in the Labor Force

Both parents of many two-parent families now are employed, as are many single mothers. For single mothers, as for many married mothers, employment often is essential, as the United States lacks the support programs for families and children that other industrialized nations have. A study of working women experiencing their first births showed that only half received paid leave, and only some of that was maternity leave; others took paid vacation time or paid sick leave to give birth and spend time with their newborns (Laughlin, 2011). About 42 percent of women received unpaid maternity leave. Nearly 8 out of 10 women who worked during their pregnancy returned to the same employer within a year, and about 70 percent of these women returned to the same pay and hours.

Women who work outside the home still spend significantly more time on housework than do men (Milkie, Raley, and Bianchi, 2009; Bianchi, Robinson, and Milkie, 2006; Amato et al., 2007; Bittman et al., 2003). Time diary analyses showed that American fathers have nearly tripled the time they spend with their children over the past 40 years (Bianchi, Robinson, and Milkie, 2006). Despite this increase, when children enter the equation, the workload for women increases, and they are penalized in the labor force for their reproductive responsibilities, as we discussed in Chapter 8 (Dey and Hill, 2007; Budig and England, 2001; England, 2000). Time out of the labor force also carries career penalties (Aisenbrey, Evertsson, and Grunow, 2009).

Nevertheless, paid employment is typically beneficial to women's mental health and self-esteem, and juggling motherhood and paid employment also seems to be good for women's physical health (McMunn et al., 2006). Studies show that both married women working at a paid job who want to work and married women who are not in the paid labor force and do not want to be have good mental health (Ross, Mirowsky, and Huber, 1983). The problems arise for women who are either working or staying home when they don't want to. Husbands helping with housework and husbands having a positive attitude about their spouse's employment both reduce the psychological distress of working women (Ross, Mirowsky, and Huber, 1983). Over the past 30 years, home has been more likely to be a haven from work than vice versa for both men and women, and the trend for home to be a haven has increased for women and remained stable for men (Kiecolt, 2003).

Who Cares for the Children?

With increasing numbers of mothers in the labor force, two trends have emerged. One is the expansion of nonmaternal child care, with children being cared for by fathers, grandparents, or other relatives, babysitters, nannies, family day care, and child care centers (Glasier, 2011; see the section on child care later in this chapter). Anthropologist Sarah Blaffer Hrdy (2009) thinks that hunter-gatherer populations of humans depended on "child care" long ago, with infants and toddlers spending much of their time being cared for by nonparent individuals. Today, children under 6 whose mothers work spend an average of 37 hours per week in nonparent child care, which is often multiple forms of care patched together; in total, more than 12 million children are in day care (NACCRRA, 2009).

The other trend in care for children is that mothers have reprioritized their activities so that, despite the increase in time spent at work, the amount of time mothers spend with children now is not different from the norm decades ago (Bianchi, Robinson, and Milkie, 2006). An analysis of time diaries kept by parents showed that employed mothers have not given up sleep or leisure time to make time for their children;

they have made more of an effort to spend quality time with them by multi-tasking other responsibilities and by doing less housework. Other survey data have shown that wives' perceptions that they are doing an unfair amount of household labor increase when they become parents (Amato et al., 2007).

Effects on Children

Research findings are contradictory regarding the effects of maternal employment during a child's first year, with some studies reporting negative cognitive and social outcomes (Baydar and Brooks-Gunn, 1991; Nash, 1997), and others finding only minimal negative outcomes (Parcel and Menaghan, 1994). It is not maternal employment by itself that affects child development; rather, it is the quality of care the child receives in any situation. Studies show that parent and family characteristics are more important to the social behaviors, language, and cognitive development of children than are any aspects of child care (NICHD, 2007). High-quality day care and preschool programs have been shown to benefit children (Belsky et al., 2007; Field, 1991), and early educational intervention can offset some of the negative impacts of poverty on child development (Barnett, 2011). The problem is that many of the nation's children do not have access to high-quality child care (NICHD, 2007).

Working mothers provide a different role model for their children, one associated with less traditional gender-role concepts and a higher evaluation of female competence (Hoffman, 1989; Debold, Wilson, and Malave, 1993). Perhaps as a result, their children tend to be more unconventional (Amato and Booth, 1997). For children living with two employed parents, because socioeconomic status affects the ways that families link to the wider society, the benefits of growing up in a two-income family can be considerable (see Box 10.2).

10.2 Social Inequalities

Family Backgrounds and Unequal Childhoods

Sociologists have long known that social class has a powerful impact on children's life chances. In a classic study, sociologist James Coleman and his colleagues (Coleman et al., 1966) found that family background was the most important determinant of educational inequality. But what specific family processes are responsible for the link between parents' social class and children's outcomes?

This question was addressed in a study by Annette Lareau (2002). Lareau systematically observed the daily lives of poor, working-class, middle-class, and upper-middle-class families with 9- and 10-year-old children, spending hours at a time with each family. She found that organized activities dominate the lives of middle-class children; their parents engage in what she calls "concerted cultivation"—they manage their children's lives to optimize the cultivation of their talents and abilities. In poor and working-class families, leisure activities are left to the children themselves; their parents facilitate "the accomplishment of natural growth," and the provision of organized leisure activities is not seen as an essential part of good parenting.

Middle- and upper-middle-class children benefit directly from their parents' attempts to cultivate their talents; further, they gain a sense of entitlement and the skills for getting what they want or need from others, Lareau says. The poorer children she followed, on the other hand, learned to "keep their distance from people in positions of authority, to be distrustful of institutions, and . . . to resist officials' authority"

(2002:773). Another study showed that extracurricular activities help elementary school students develop abilities in task persistence, fitting in with peers, following instructions, dealing with authority figures, working in groups, and working independently (Covay and Carbonaro, 2010).

Data from the Census 2000's "A Child's Day" report (Lugaila, 2003) confirm Lareau's observations and bring into sharp focus the disadvantages faced by many American children. Five percent of all kids under 12, for example, had not been taken on an "outing" during the month before parents filled out their census surveys; an outing includes a trip to a park, a church, a playground, or a grocery store, or a visit with friends or relatives. That's 2.4 *million* children who apparently did nothing but go to school and come back home, for an entire month. Eight percent of the nation's 1- to 5-year-olds—1.6 million kids—had not been read to at all in the week before the survey, and only half were read to every day. As Lareau found in her observational study, many children engage in a variety of organized activities such as soccer, baseball, gymnastics, dance, Girl Scouts, Boy Scouts, music lessons, choir, and the like, but many children do not.

For many of the factors in the "Child's Day" report, family background, especially the income and education of the parents, is the critical element. For example, family characteristics that are associated with lower levels of reading to children include living in poverty, having parents with a high school

education or less, and having never-married parents. Children who live in poverty do not "go on outings," as the Census Bureau puts it, and they are much less likely to be involved in organized sports, clubs, or lessons. The level of education of the parents plays a major role in a child's participation in extracurricular activities, with about half of the children of parents with advanced degrees participating in sports, clubs, and lessons, compared to 20–30 percent of the children whose parents have a high school education or less. School opportunities are sorted by social class, too; half of the children whose parents have advanced degrees are enrolled in "gifted classes," compared to only 14 percent of the children whose parents have a high school education or less.

In other words, the children who might benefit greatly from extra attention, special activities, and more caring from adults in their lives—children from low-income families, children whose parents have little education, and children from broken homes—are the least likely to get it. As Lareau (2003) says in the book that elaborates her research, America is a land both of opportunity and of inequality.

Questions for Discussion

1. Based on the findings presented here, what sorts of enrichment programs would you recommend for children living in poverty?

2. Are there benefits to a childhood that is not dominated by organized activities?

Stepfamilies

Remarriage frequently results in stepfamilies, also termed "reconstituted" and "blended" families. Because more than half of remarried persons are parents, their new partners become stepparents. About 3.9 million American children live in a stepfamily. Eight out of ten stepchildren live with their biological mother and a stepfather.

Andrew Cherlin (1978, 2010) has called remarriage an "incomplete institution." A stepfamily functions differently than the traditional nuclear family (Pill, 1990; Larson, 1992); the stepparent role does not necessarily approximate that of a biological parent, particularly in authority, legitimacy, and respect. The family tree of a stepfamily can be very complex, populated not only by children of both spouses but by six sets of grandparents, relatives of former spouses, relatives of new spouses, and the people former spouses marry.

It appears, however, that these complicated family situations are becoming much more the norm in U.S. society, and data collected by Paul Amato and his colleagues (2007) support this. Most of the marriages they examined in their 2000 data set involved spouses who had been previously married, and more of the families included stepchildren than in 1980. And attitudes had changed: In 1980, having stepchildren in one's family was associated with lower levels of marital happiness, more conflict, and a higher level of a measure they called "divorce proneness"—a couple's propensity to divorce. In the 2000 survey, however, they found just the opposite—stepchildren were associated with more marital happiness, less marital conflict, and a lower level of divorce proneness.

Stepfathers can underrate their parenting skills and their contributions to the lives of their stepchildren (Bohannan and Erickson, 1978). Children living with stepfathers apparently do just as well, or just as poorly, in school and in their social lives as children living with natural fathers. And children with stepfathers on the whole do better than children from homes where the father is absent (Beer, 1988; Fine and Kurdek, 1992).

Singlehood

The number of Americans living alone more than doubled (increased 100 percent) between 1970 and 2000, a much greater increase than the 16 percent growth in married couples. In 2011, 28 percent of all U.S. households contained just one person (U.S. Census Bureau, 2011b). Because men marry later than women do, and because children of unmarried men are more likely to live with their mothers than with their fathers, until about age 45 men are more likely to live alone than women are. After age 45, women are increasingly more likely than men to live alone because men have higher mortality rates, and there are more widowed women than there are widowed men. The high incidence of divorce, the ability of the elderly to maintain their own homes alone, and the deferral of marriage among young adults have contributed to the high rate of increase in the number of nonfamily households.

Research strongly suggests that people live alone because they choose to (Michael, Fuchs, and Scott, 1980). People who live alone can avoid unwanted intrusions of others and have more latitude to construct their lives the way they wish to. This is probably why the mental health of persons who live alone is as good as or better than that of unmarried persons living with others (Hughes and Gove, 1981).

In 2011, 64 percent of men and 50.1 percent of women ages 25–29 had never been married. This is more than triple the 1970 rate for men and quadruple the rate for women (U.S. Census Bureau, 2011b; Saluter, 1996). More liberal sex standards, the high divorce rate, money woes, and the pursuit of education and careers have spurred young adults to marry later than at any time since the Census Bureau

Racial Diversity within Families

Nearly 40 percent of all U.S. adoptions involving children under the age of 2 and nearly 20 percent of all U.S. adoptions are now international adoptions (Tessler, Tuan, and Shiao, 2011). Often such adoptions result in multiracial families. Adoptions within the United States also may create a multiracial family. How do the children of multiracial families fare?

Rita J. Simon (1996) began studying transracial adoptees and their families in 1971 and followed the families until their children reached adulthood. Simon used the research method of intensive interviewing to conduct her study. Each family was visited by a team of one male and one female graduate student in 1971; often one interviewer was white and the other black. Simon and her associates interviewed 204 parents and 366 children during this first stage of her research. In 1979, 1983, and 1991, Simon was able to reinterview a sizable proportion of the parents and children.

What did Simon discover about the children's racial attitudes and racial identity? During 1971 and 1972, she and her associates found a complete absence of a racial preference for whites on the part of all the children. The children correctly identified themselves as black or white, and they showed no preference for white or negative reactions to black. In 1983, self-esteem scores were essentially the same for black adoptees, other transracial adoptees, white adoptees, and white birth children. A family integration scale similarly revealed no significant differences among the four groups of children; adopted children apparently felt as integrated into family life as birth children.

Perhaps the most compelling information about transracial adoption comes from the children themselves when they had reached adulthood. In 1991, Simon told the now-adult transracial adoptees and birth children that the National Association of Black Social Workers and several councils of Native Americans strongly opposed transracial adoption and asked them how they felt about that. Eighty percent of the transracial adoptees and 70 percent of the birth children said that they disagreed; 5 percent of the transracially adopted children said they agreed, and the others said they were not sure. When asked directly what effect being adopted and raised by white parents had on their self-image, a third said it had a positive effect, a third said it had no effect, and a third said they did not know. None of the transracially adopted children responded that it had a negative effect.

It would appear that in most racially diverse families, parents and children, both adopted and birth, do very well.

Questions for Discussion

1. Our society is increasingly characterized by racial diversity. What are some ways families can be racially diverse? Do you expect a decrease or increase in family racial diversity?

2. U.S. society has increased its acceptance of white parents adopting children of other races. What do you think societal reaction would be to parents of other races adopting white children?

started keeping track in 1890. Even so, the population remaining single today is smaller than it was in 1900, when fully 42 percent of all American adult men and 33 percent of adult women were never-marrieds (Kreider, 2008; Kain, 1984).

For many years research has shown that married people report greater happiness than unmarried, including the never-married. Over the period 1972 to 2008, both married men and women consistently reported higher levels of happiness than the never-married. The advantage for the married is even greater when we compare them to the widowed, separated, and divorced (data analyzed by the authors from the General Social Survey, Smith et al., 2010).

Single Parenthood

More than one American youngster in four lives with just one parent (Grall, 2011). Of all such children, 87 percent live with their mothers. However, men do raise children on their own; in 2011, 3.5 percent of the nation's children were living with their fathers only, or 13 percent of the children living in single-parent households.

Children in single-parent families may have parents who are divorced or widowed, or who were never married. In 2009, 13.7 million single parents had custody of 22 million children, with the other parent living elsewhere (Grall, 2011). In 2011, 55 percent of African American children under the age of 18 were living with a single parent. About 29 percent of Hispanic children, 22.3 percent of white children, and 10.3 percent of Asian American children also were in single-parent families (U.S. Census Bureau, 2011b).

As we pointed out in Chapter 6 (p. 191), female-headed households are likely to be low-income households. In 2011, 22 percent of all children lived below the poverty line, compared with 44.3 percent of children living only with their mothers and 21.3 percent of children living only with their fathers. Marital separation frequently produces a precipitous and sustained decline in household income for the mother and child. The overall financial situation of female-headed households in terms of their net worth is shown in Figure 10.4.

The single income associated with single parenthood can make childrearing difficult. In 2009 only 41 percent of custodial parents received the full amount of child support that was owed to them, and 29 percent of parents who were owed child support payments received none at all (Grall, 2011). The average amount of child support owed was about $300 per month.

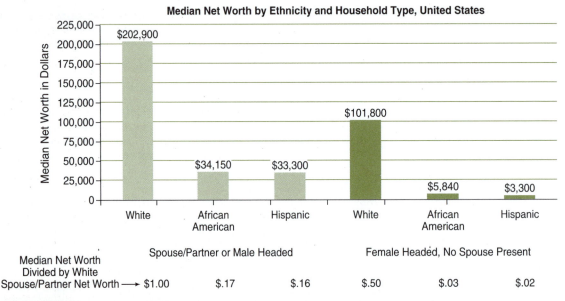

Median Net Worth by Ethnicity and Household Type, United States

	Spouse/Partner or Male Headed			Female Headed, No Spouse Present		
	White	African American	Hispanic	White	African American	Hispanic
Median Net Worth	$202,900	$34,150	$33,300	$101,800	$5,840	$3,300
Median Net Worth Divided by White Spouse/Partner Net Worth →	$1.00	$.17	$.16	$.50	$.03	$.02

Figure 10.4 **The Financial Status of Female-Headed Households**

Net worth, or wealth, of a household is all the assets of that household minus all debts. Female-headed households have far less net worth than other households. The situation of African American and Hispanic female-headed households is particularly grave; they have on average 3 and 2 cents, respectively, for every dollar of net worth owned by a white male-headed or spouse/partner household.

Source: Figure generated by the authors using data from the 2007 Survey of Consumer Finances, Board of Governors of the Federal Reserve System.

The proportion of births to unmarried women in the United States has risen steadily for many years, but total childbearing by unmarried women has fallen in all race and ethnicity categories (Martin et al., 2011). In 2009, 41 percent of all U.S. births occurred outside of marriage, up from 18 percent in 1980. Among teens, 87 percent of births are to unmarried mothers, and 62 percent of births to mothers 20 to 24 years old are nonmarital. Births outside of marriage are more common in some racial and ethnic groups than in others. In 2009, the percentage of births occurring to unmarried women was 17 percent among Asian Americans, 29 percent among non-Hispanic whites, 53 percent among Hispanic women, and 73 percent among African Americans.

Americans are not very accepting of unwed motherhood; in a nationwide attitudes survey, 69 percent identified single women having children as a bad thing, 24 percent said it made no difference, and only 4 percent said it was a good thing (Taylor, 2010).

Women heading a single-parent family typically experience greater stress than women in two-parent families (Fassinger, 1989; Simons et al., 1993). Lack of job training, loss of skills during the childbearing years, and discriminatory hiring and promotion patterns often mean that single mothers work for low wages. Female family heads report lower self-esteem, a lower sense of effectiveness, and less optimism about the future than their counterparts in two-parent settings. But research shows that women who head households on their own may choose not to marry depending on a variety of factors, including mistrust of men, fear of domestic violence, household decision making, respectability, and potential marriage partners who lack stable jobs with decent earnings (Edin, 2000).

Single fathers encounter many of the same problems as single mothers. Research shows that being single and having children to raise is worse on the mental health of men than on that of women (Simon, 1998; Hughes, 1989).

Juggling work and child care poses considerable difficulties, especially for fathers with preschool youngsters.

Some studies show that juvenile delinquency is twice as likely to occur in a single-parent home as in a two-parent home. Children of single parents are also more likely to drop out of school, be unemployed when they reach adulthood, have out-of-wedlock children, become sexually active at an earlier age, and cohabit (Musick and Bumpass, 1999).

Having children apparently is not a detriment to social life (Fisher, 2012): Single parents date more than singles without children, and more single parents (21 percent) than child-free singles (16 percent) were currently dating someone when surveyed in 2011.

Cohabitation

Marriage is differentiated from other types of intimate relationships by its institutionalized status. The number of unmarried adults who share living quarters with an unrelated adult of the opposite sex—a type of intimate relationship termed **cohabitation**—has increased in recent decades; 5.6 million American households were made up of unmarried couples in 2008, an increase of 16 percent since 2000 (www.census.gov/compendia/statab/2010/tables/10s0063.xls). More than 10 percent of all unmarried persons were cohabiting in 2008. Almost four percent of children live in a household that included either their mother's or their father's unmarried partner. Researchers estimate that about 40 percent of all out-of-wedlock births are to cohabiting parents (Bumpass and Lu, 2000). For white and Hispanic teens, living in cohabiting families is worse than living with single mothers; those living with cohabitors are more likely to have school troubles and emotional and behavioral problems (Nelson, Clark, and Acs, 2001). Cohabiting also seems to be less effective than remarriage at providing economic stability for the children of divorce (Morrison and Ritualo, 2000).

Only 2 percent of American women born between 1928 and 1932 cohabited before marrying or attaining age 30; 40 percent of those born between 1958 and 1962 did so (Schoen and Weinick, 1993). Cohabiting before marriage has become quite prevalent, with 41 percent of all married couples surveyed in 2000 having cohabited before they married (Amato et al., 2007), and researchers estimating that 60 to 70 percent of couples today will live together before they get married (Rhoades, Stanley, and Markman, 2009; Stanley, Whitton, and Markman, 2004). But not all unmarried people are cohabiting; a 2011 survey of singles showed that 24 percent of men and 23 percent of women aged 21–34 are virgins (Fisher, 2012).

The high proportion of married couples who live together prior to marriage suggests that premarital cohabitation may become institutionalized as a new step between dating and marriage. What are the effects of cohabitation on marriage? While some couples say that they are planning to live together before marriage to see what living together is like, studies show that more couples end up living together without making any real decision to do so or any serious commitment to one another. This "sliding into cohabitation" has been shown to be associated with lower levels of marital satisfaction, lower levels of male commitment to the spouse, greater likelihood of divorce, and more negative communication in marriage (Stanley and Rhoades, 2009). Amato and his colleagues (2007) also found that couples who had cohabited before marriage reported lower marital quality than those who had not. Stanley attributes this effect to the lack of commitment associated with cohabitation; he and other researchers suggest that marriage after cohabitation may occur more because the couple's financial, social, and emotional lives have become intertwined than because the couple makes a serious decision to get engaged and then married (Stanley and Rhoades, 2009). Couples who become engaged before cohabitation or who do not live together at all before they marry report higher marital satisfaction.

Gay and Lesbian Couples

Homosexuality also serves as the basis for family life, though with some differences from heterosexual couples. In terms of love and relationship satisfaction, heterosexual couples, gay couples, and lesbian couples do not differ (Savin-Williams and Esterberg, 2000). Gay and lesbian couples are more likely than heterosexual couples to be well educated. Their average incomes are similar, but homosexual couples are less likely to own their own homes (Associated Press, 2003).

Until 2004, when the first state legalized same-sex marriage, cohabitation was the only option for homosexual "family life" in the United States. Unlike Belgium, Denmark, and the Netherlands, where same-sex marriage is legal, the United States has only a handful of states in which marriage is legal for homosexual couples. Adding in states in which same-sex couples can register as domestic partners or have their relationships recognized as civil unions, there are 19 states that offer legal recognition to same-sex couples (Badgett and Herman, 2011). Between 2004, when same-sex marriage was legalized in Massachusetts, and 2010, fewer than 50,000 same-sex marriages have been performed (Lofquist, 2011). The 2010 census counted 594,000 same-sex households in the United States, or 1 percent of all "couple households"; 115,000 same-sex couple households include children, and a quarter of all same-sex households reported being spouses.

Population Size of Homosexuals Most estimates of the homosexual population range from 1 to 3 percent (Gates, 2011; Barringer, 1993; Crispell, 1993). One study found that 1.4 percent of women and 2.8 percent of men identified themselves as gay, lesbian, or bisexual (Laumann et al., 1994), and an assessment of population-based surveys showed that about 3.5 percent of U.S. adults identify as lesbian or gay (1.7 percent) or bisexual (1.8 percent), with women in that group more likely to identify as bisexual than as lesbian and men more likely to identify as gay than as bisexual (Gates, 2011).

The percentage of people who have engaged at some time in homosexual activity is substantially higher. Survey responses provide an estimate of 8.2 percent of U.S. adults who have engaged in same-sex sexual activity and 11 percent who report at least some amount of same-sex sexual attraction (Gates, 2011). A Kinsey Institute study (Fay et al., 1989) put the figure much higher, estimating that at least 20 percent of males have engaged in same-sex sexual activity. The problem with all these estimates is that they rely on self-reports and therefore almost certainly underestimate rates of homosexual involvement. Many people may be afraid to admit to homosexual activity out of fear of discrimination or ostracism.

What Is Homosexuality? Is homosexuality a condition or characteristic of people, or is it simply a way we have of describing an activity that some people engage in? Kinsey's study (Kinsey, Pomeroy, and Martin, 1948) revealed the interesting fact that homosexuality/heterosexuality was not a simple dichotomy. Kinsey found people all along the continuum from exclusively homosexual to exclusively heterosexual, combining homosexuality and heterosexuality in a variety of ways. Though he did find the majority to be exclusively heterosexual, he also found people who engaged in homosexual activity in certain periods of the life course and not in others. On the basis of findings like these, many sociologists and psychologists have concluded that it is more reasonable to think about heterosexual and homosexual *practices,* not homosexual *individuals* (Bell, Weinberg, and Hammersmith, 1981; Kirkpatrick, 2000). In this "constructionist" view, homosexuality and heterosexuality are social constructions that describe behaviors, roles that people may play, and identities, not inherent characteristics of persons.

The alternative "essentialist" view argues that homosexual orientation is either inborn or fixed very early in one's development and thus is an inherent part of what an individual is (LeVay, 1996, 1991). LeVay's 1991 study presented evidence that there are differences in the brain structures of homosexual and heterosexual men. Other studies show that identical twins, who share 100 percent of their genes, are more likely to have the same sexual orientation than are fraternal twins, who are as genetically alike as any siblings (Burr, 1996). However, it is still not clear whether findings such as these reflect

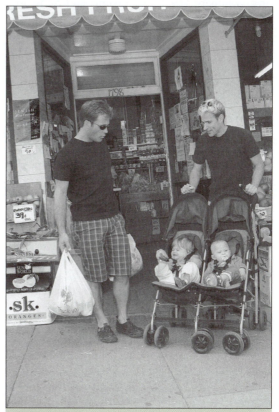

Except for their sexual preferences and practices, gays and lesbians differ little from their heterosexual counterparts. Some are or have been married, have children, and lead lives that in most respects are indistinguishable from those of the larger population.

the fact that homosexual preferences are caused or sustained by biological factors. In 1975 the American Psychological Association urged medical practitioners to stop thinking of homosexuality as a mental illness, and in 1997 it passed a resolution to limit therapy aimed at converting homosexuals to heterosexuals (Weiss, 1997).

What is not controversial is that, for the most part, gay and lesbian people, except for their sexual orientations and practices, represent a cross section of the U.S. population, differing little from their heterosexual counterparts (Bell and Weinberg, 1978; Blumstein and Schwartz, 1983). They are found in all occupational fields, political persuasions, religious faiths, and racial and ethnic groups. Some are married, have children, and lead lives that in most respects are indistinguishable from those of the larger population.

Attitudes Toward Gay Marriage Two years after the Netherlands legalized gay marriage, nearly 8 percent of weddings were same-sex couples, and the relationships were increasingly seen as commonplace and even "old-fashioned" (Richburg, 2003). What about in the United States? Americans' attitudes toward the morality of homosexuality have been increasingly liberal since 1990, and Americans have become steadily less willing to restrict the civil liberties of homosexuals. Most Americans think homosexuals should have equal rights in terms of job opportunities (Saad, 1996), and in 2011, 46 percent of Americans said that they thought same-sex should be legal (Pew Forum on Religion and Public Life, 2012). Despite the Catholic Church's rejection of homosexual activity, U.S. Catholic bishops have urged parents of homosexuals to accept and love them (Murphy, 1997).

When it comes to marriage and family, attitudes have changed quite rapidly in the past decade (see Box 13.2, p. 448). Support for same-sex unions increased more rapidly than did support for same-sex marriage, but in 2011 more Americans supported same-sex marriage (46 percent) than opposed it (42 percent) (Pew Forum on Religion and Public Life, 2012). This was up from 37 percent just two years previously, and the increase in support was found across generations.

Support also has increased for same-sex couples raising children. About 43 percent of the public thinks gay and lesbian couples raising children is a bad thing, while 12 percent say it is a good thing and 41 percent say it makes no difference (Taylor, 2010). Just over half of survey respondents said that the children of gay and lesbian couples would "face a lot more challenges" than the children of heterosexual couples.

There is a significant religious dimension to much of the opposition to same-sex marriage. When the Episcopal Church gave its bishops the option of allowing priests to bless committed homosexual relationships, polls showed that "a strong majority" of the public disapproved, especially frequent churchgoers (Morin and Cooperman, 2003). In the United States, American Baptist Churches USA, the U.S. Conference of Catholic Bishops, the Lutheran Church-Missouri Synod, Mormonism, the National Association of Evangelicals, Orthodox Judaism, the Southern Baptist Convention, the Presbyterian Church, the United Methodist Church, and Islam all define marriage as the union of a man and a woman (Pew Forum on Religion and Public Life, 2010).

Challenges for American Families and Society

Some family problems stay in the family; others spill over into society. For example, family violence, child abuse, and incest produce scarred members of society, many of whom go on to have families of their own in which the same terrible acts are repeated. In our society, people express considerable support for family values. But an assessment of parental leave policies in the United States, the availability and quality of child and elder care, the protection of children from abuse and neglect, and other issues suggests that people are less willing to support policies that would ensure the viability of the family. In this section, we will examine the challenges posed by abuse and neglect, child care, divorce, and an increasing population of the elderly.

Family Violence, Child Abuse, and Incest

Family violence, child abuse, and incest can tear families apart and have lasting effects. In this section we will present and discuss some of the data available about these problems.

Family Violence

Estimates of family violence vary widely. Nearly a quarter of women report having been physically assaulted by an intimate partner, and 8 percent report rape by an intimate partner (Cherlin, 2010). The World Health Organization (WHO) maintains a database on violence against women. In a study of 10 countries, it found that 35–76 percent of women over the age of 15 have been physically or sexually assaulted, most by a partner (Garcia-Moreno et al., 2005). In the United States, 22 percent of women have been assaulted by an intimate partner (WHO, 2000). Two sources of data suggest that domestic violence may be decreasing in the United States. A survey of married couples showed a decrease in the amount of violence ever occurring in the marriage from 21 percent in 1980 to only 12 percent in 2000, and rates of intimate partner violence (as reported in the National Crime Victimization Surveys) decreased by 41 percent between 1993 and 1999 (Amato et al., 2007).

Although both men and women engage in violence, men typically do more damage than their female partners and many more women than men report victimization (Cherlin, 2010). Women put up with battering for a variety of reasons (France, 2006). The fewer the resources a wife has in the way of education or job skills, the more vulnerable she is in the marriage. And violence is not faced only by young women—survey data suggest that 3–5 million Americans over 50 are in physically abusive relationships (France, 2006).

Child Abuse

One need spend only an hour or so in a supermarket or a shopping mall to observe instances of children being physically or verbally abused. Such public behavior is but the tip of the iceberg. A PBS survey found that 64 percent of American adults agree that "a good, hard spanking" is sometimes necessary in disciplining a child (PBS, 2005), despite evidence that children who get spanked regularly are more likely to cheat or lie, to be disobedient at school, to bully others, and to have less remorse for what they do wrong (Straus, Sugarman, and Giles-Sims, 1997). Child abuse goes far beyond unnecessary spanking; abuse cases may involve burning, scalding, beating, and smothering. Neglect of children is a closely related problem. In 2010, there were 754,000 confirmed cases of child maltreatment; 87,661 of these were infants in the first year of their lives (U.S. Department of Health and Human Services, 2012). Neglect has been shown to cause severe short- and long-term harm, including many mental and physical health problems, juvenile delinquency, and adult criminality (Dubowitz, 2007), and abuse also has long-term effects, including increased risk of suicide in adulthood (McGowan et al., 2009).

Approximately 1,537 children died in 2010 of abuse or neglect (U.S. Department of Health and Human Services, 2012). The age at which females are most at risk of homicide is from birth to age one, and the perpetrators are nearly always parents, family friends, or guardians (Tucker, 2000). Although the chances of males being murdered during infancy are even greater than for females, it is not the most dangerous time of life for them; the male homicide rate is more than four times higher at age 21 (Tucker,

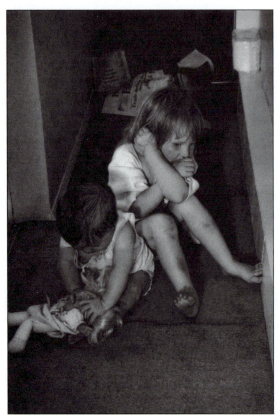

The functionalist perspective on the family stresses that an important function of the family is care and protection of family members, but evidence on child abuse demonstrates that families do not always serve this function.

Incest and Sexual Abuse

The status of incest as a taboo has not kept it from taking place but merely from being talked about. Probably the best available figures on sexual abuse come from a national survey of more than 2,000 adults undertaken in 1985 for the *Los Angeles Times* by psychologist David Finkelhor and his colleagues. They found that 27 percent of the women and 16 percent of the men disclosed a history of some sort of sexual abuse during their childhood (Darnton, 1991). A study of first intercourse experiences found that girls who had sex at age 11 or 12 were much more likely to have partners much older than themselves, and both older partners and early first intercourse were associated with a greater number of problem behaviors (Leitenberg and Saltzman, 2000).

The perpetrator in sexual abuse is commonly the father, uncle, or other male authority figure in the household, "family tyrants" who employ physical force and intimidation to control their families (Finkelhor, 1979; Herman and Hirschman, 1981). The mothers in incestuous families are commonly passive, have a poor self-image, and are overly dependent on their husbands, much the same traits found among battered wives. The victims of molestation are usually shamed or terrified into treating the experience as a dirty secret.

The sexual abuse of children often leads to behavior problems, learning difficulties, sexual promiscuity, runaway behavior, drug and alcohol abuse, gastrointestinal and genitourinary complaints, compulsive rituals, clinical depression, low self-esteem, and suicidal behavior. Victimized women tend to show lifetime patterns of psychological shame and stigmatization (Kendall-Tackett, Williams, and Finkelhor, 1993; Malinosky-Rummell and Hansen, 1993).

Looking to the Future

The problems of family violence, child abuse, and incest have emerged as major public issues. Some, but not all, researchers find that the arrest

2000). Child welfare workers say that risk to infants is related to whether parents and caregivers have any parenting skills and to situational factors including stress and social isolation.

Although exact numbers are hard to obtain, more than 1.5 million children, teenagers, and young adults are living on the streets in the United States (Stand Up for Kids, 2008), and more than 500,000 children are in foster care, living under the temporary care of nonrelated adults (AACAP, 2005).

of offenders is the most effective means for preventing new incidents of wife battery (Berk and Newton, 1985; Sherman et al., 1992). The adoption of no-fault divorce laws is associated with a drop in suicides among women, murder of women by their partners, and domestic violence against both men and women (Wolfers and Stevenson, 2006). A cultural revolution of attitudes and values is required to eradicate the abuse of women and children (Gelles, Straus, and Harrop, 1988; Buzawa and Buzawa, 1990). The drop in spousal violence between 1980 and 2000 (Amato et al., 2007) may suggest that such a cultural revolution is beginning.

Child Care

Research shows that 35 to 45 percent of America's children come to kindergarten with problems that interfere with success at school (Barnett, 2011), and a comprehensive study of child care in the United States showed that only 20 to 35 percent of centers meet guidelines set by the American Academy of Pediatrics and the American Public Health Association for group size and adult-to-child ratio for babies and toddlers (NICHD, 2006). One in 10 of America's children lives in extreme poverty, 22 percent live below the poverty line, and 44 percent are categorized as low income (Kids Count, 2010). How children are cared for should be a matter of concern to all Americans, whether they have children or not; children are, as politicians love to point out in speeches, "our future."

Over half of all mothers return to work within 6 months of birth, and 64 percent return to work within the first year after birth; a total of 14.5 million American children under age 6 (62 percent) are cared for by someone other than their parents for an average of 36 hours per week (NACCRRA, 2009). Nannies may get the most attention in books and movies, but child care centers and grandparents are the most commonly used form of child care in the United States. About one-fifth of children aged 5 to 14

are home alone after school; the others are in some type of after-school care. The quality and availability of child care resources play an essential role in the rearing of America's children.

High-quality day care and preschools can be good for children (Belsky et al., 2007; Field, 1991; MacKinnon and King, 1988; Kagan, Kearsley, and Zelazo, 1978). Such programs are characterized by small group size, high staff–child ratios, well-trained staffs, good equipment, and attractive and nurturing environments.

Unfortunately, high-quality care is often unavailable. Only 9.4 percent of child care centers (and less than 1 percent of family day cares) are accredited, meaning they meet high enough standards of quality to be accredited by a national organization. Teachers at child care centers are required to undergo training in early childhood education in only 13 states; all child care programs are required to meet licensing standards in only 11 states; and in 8 states, licensed programs are inspected less often than once a year (NACCRRA, 2009). Seventeen states allow family day care providers to have no training, and 43 percent of assistant child care center teachers and 44 percent of family day care teachers have only high school diplomas or less. Some centers hire caregivers without doing criminal background checks and do not require that caregivers be trained in CPR, first aid, or recognizing signs of child abuse. Child care workers rank among the lowest 10 percent of wage earners in the United States, earning less than parking lot attendants, and the high turnover rate of such workers creates low continuity of care for children (Clawson and Gerstel, 2002).

Quality of care is not the only problem. The number of children needing child care exceeds by nearly 4 million the number of available spaces in legally operating care programs (NACCRRA, 2009). About a third of children in child care are in multiple care arrangements, spending time each week with relatives, in a center, with a babysitter, or however parents are able to string together care. And cost is prohibitive for many families: The cost of having an infant in full-time child care exceeds the average annual cost of a public university education (NACCRRA, 2009). An increasing number of women find that they actually have to pay to work, which they may be willing to do in order to avoid losing work time that leads to promotions and retirement benefits (Dvorak, 2010).

No National Policy

Child care advocates warn that failure to develop a national policy toward child care will result in "a generation of neglected children." The United States is one of the few industrialized nations that does not have a comprehensive day care program. Access to early childhood education and care is a statutory right in Denmark, Finland, Sweden, France, Belgium, Italy, Germany, and Britain (Child Policy, 2004), and Japan has a "uniformly excellent" publicly supported day care system (Yamamoto and Struck, 2002). Further, while the United States provides no paid maternity or paternity leave by law, more than 140 countries, including most other industrialized nations, do. Recognizing the benefits of retaining experienced employees, some U.S. corporations are beginning to develop their own maternity leave programs (Catalyst, 2011).

National policy decisions about caring for the nation's children would need to incorporate standards to ensure that child care centers are not simply what consumer activist Ralph Nader describes as "children's warehouses." The book *The Irreducible Needs of Children* (Brazelton and Greenspan, 2000) describes the essential ingredients for the emotional and physical health and development of babies and children:

- An ongoing nurturing relationship
- Physical protection, safety, and regulation
- Experiences tailored to individual differences
- Developmentally appropriate experiences
- Limit setting, structure, and expectations
- Stable, supportive communities and cultural continuity
- A protected future

Most parents think public policy should focus on parental leave and other employment programs that would lessen the conflict between work and family (Williams and Boushey, 2010), instead of on child care. Three-quarters of survey respondents believe it is better for children to be at home with a parent, and 81 percent believe that children are more likely to get the affection and attention they need from a stay-at-home parent (Public Agenda, 2001).

Alternatives to Day Care

Among married-couple families with children under 15, 23 percent have a stay-at-home mother. One alternative to giving up work entirely or putting babies in day care is *sequencing*—arranging one's life to provide time to work, time to have children and stay home with them, and time to reenter the workforce again (Cardozo, 1996). But as we discussed in Chapter 8, women pay the price of interrupting their careers to care for children in the forms of loss of job experience, reduced wages, and discrimination from employers. While some people insist that two incomes are essential in the United States, a significant number find that it is possible to live—and even save for the future—on one middle-class income. Another alternative to full-time employment and full-time day care for children is part-time work or work from the home. Some child-friendly employers now allow babies and children to "come to the office"; one researcher found that 8.9 percent of employed mothers were caring for their children at work (Trost, 1990).

Clinical psychiatrist and pediatrician Stanley I. Greenspan (1997) recommended a "four-thirds solution": Each parent works two-thirds time and spends one-third of the time raising the children. Greenspan also called for government and industry support, including government incentives for employers to provide part-time work options, more flextime, and guaranteed parental leave.

Divorce

Although divorce rates increased sharply from the 1960s to the early 1980s, they have declined almost as dramatically since then (see Figure 10.5) but are still the highest in the world. It is unclear why divorce rates have declined since 1981. Two possible factors are the increased age of marriage and increasing education. Recent research shows that women with a college education marry later, have fewer children, are happier in their marriages and family life, and are both the least likely to divorce and have experienced the greatest declines in divorce since the 1970s compared to less educated women (Isen and Stevenson, 2010). People who marry later, have children later, and have personal resources are more likely to be able to arrange their lives in ways that promote their personal well-being, including the nature of their personal relationships.

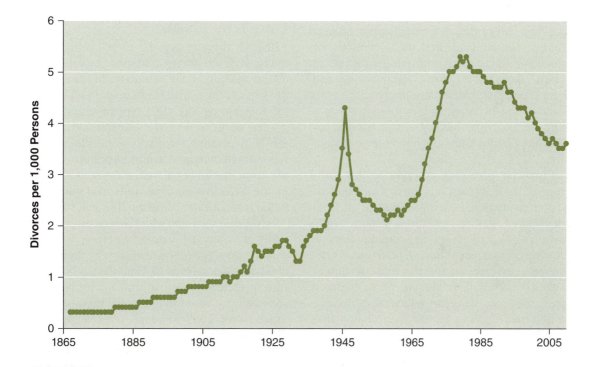

| Figure 10.5 | **Divorces per 1,000 Persons in the U.S. Population, 1867–2010** |

Divorce rates in the U.S. increased dramatically in the 20th century. The social disruptions caused by World War II produced a very sharp spike in the immediate postwar years. Rates have been declining since the early 1980s. Divorce rates in this chart from the 19th and very early 20th centuries are based on limited data.

Sources: Figure generated by the authors using data from the U.S. Department of Health, Education, and Welfare, 1973; U.S. Department of Health and Human Services, 1996; U.S. Census Bureau, 2009 and earlier, and the National Vital Statistics Reports. (Available at http://www.cdc.gov/nchs/products/nvsr.htm#vol58.)

Yet divorce rates still are high in comparison to historical trends, and divorce is a common part of contemporary society. When today's elderly were establishing families, divorce was relatively infrequent. With the number of divorced people increasing over the past 30 years and young people delaying the formation of new unions, the number of divorced people per 1,000 married people has nearly doubled in the past three decades. In 2011 there were 197 divorced people for every 1,000 married people (U.S. Census Bureau, 2011). Societal attitudes toward divorce have changed as well.

The Effects of Divorce on the Family

More than half of the couples who divorce have children. Researchers find that children of divorced or single parents have higher levels of anxiety, depression, stress, aggression, and school problems and are more likely to drop out of school and become parents themselves at a young age (Lugaila, 2003). Divorce has a negative effect on children's cognitive development (Kim, 2011).

Financial problems complicate the difficulties of both women and men. Only half of divorced mothers receive any money at all from their children's fathers, and this is seldom much. Most men also experience an economic decline following divorce (McManus and DiPrete, 2001). Moreover, divorce is not the end of family changes but often the beginning. Most divorced parents remarry, and because the rate of divorce among remarriages is greater than among first marriages, many children experience complex family lives (Furstenberg and Cherlin, 1991).

The notion that divorce has adverse consequences for children influences many couples to remain unhappily married until their youngsters reach adulthood. However, some evidence suggests that staying together for the sake of the children is not necessarily helpful if the marriage is marred by conflict, tension, and discord. Many of the emotional, behavioral, and academic problems children exhibit after their parents divorce are apparent before the time of the actual breakup of the family. Marital discord has a negative effect on children's emotional bonds with both parents (Amato and Sobolewski, 2001). On the other hand, clinical psychologist Mary Pipher argues that children may not be affected if their parents are unhappy but that divorce "shatters many children" (Pipher, 1994:133). Family sociologist Linda Waite says research supports that view: "As long as Mom and Dad don't fight too much, [children] thrive under the love, attention, and resources two married parents provide" (Waite and Gallagher, 2000:144).

Long-Term Effects

Although divorce may be more commonplace today, it is no more a routine experience for adults than it is for children. In many cases divorce exacts a greater emotional and physical toll than almost any other type of stress, including the death of a spouse (Kitson and Holmes, 1992). Separated and divorced people are overrepresented in mental institutions; more likely to die from cardiovascular disease, cancer, pneumonia, and cirrhosis of the liver; and more prone to die from accidents, homicides, and suicides.

Middle-aged and elderly women are especially devastated by divorce. These women—called *displaced homemakers*—often have dedicated themselves to managing a home and raising children, only to find themselves jettisoned after years of marriage. Within the United States, some 100,000 people over the age of 55 divorce each year.

Grown children of divorce have lower levels of psychological well-being (Amato and Sobolewski, 2001) and die, on average, four years sooner than adults who were raised by parents who did not divorce (Tucker et al., 1997). Children of divorce are more likely to marry as teens but less likely to marry at all once they get past age 20 (Wolfinger, 2003). On the other hand, adult children of divorced parents are now significantly less likely to divorce than children of a generation or two ago; between 1974 and 1993, the propensity to divorce if one's parents had divorced declined by about 50 percent (Wolfinger, 1999).

After Divorce

Most divorced people remarry. About five of every six divorced men and three of every four divorced women marry again. Divorced men are more likely to remarry than women. Because men usually marry younger women, divorced men have a larger pool of potential partners from which to choose. Divorced men also are more likely to marry someone not previously married. About 61 percent of men and 54 percent of women in their thirties who remarry will undergo a second divorce.

The Elderly

As life expectancy increases and the birth rate decreases, the proportion of elderly people in the United States also has increased, and a population structure in which those over 60 outnumber those under 15 will soon be a feature of U.S. society (Rowe et al., 2009). John Rowe and his colleagues in the MacArthur Foundation Research Network on an Aging Society have been working to identify changes needed to meet the challenges of this shift in age distribution in society. The elderly in the United States also will be characterized by better health and fewer disabilities than in the past, as improvements in medical care have resulted in a faster increase in "active life span" than even the increase in total life span. As asthma, obesity, and diabetes skyrocket among younger people, it's possible that our elderly population will find itself to be more healthy than middle-aged and younger Americans. Rowe and others contend that current approaches to the elderly were designed when being elderly was synonymous with being ill and cognitively or physically disabled and that they limit opportunities for the "new elderly" to be productive members of society.

At some point, of course, many of the elderly need help as they approach the ends of their lives, and this almost always involves the family. As our society ages, care facilities will need to be expanded and improved. Although some facilities for the care of the elderly are adequately staffed and provide adequate care, a government study in 2002 showed that more than half of the nursing homes in the United States are so understaffed that residents cannot be taken care of (Connolly, 2008). Thirty percent of seriously ill elderly survey respondents indicated that they would rather die than live in a nursing home, but seniors aren't always safe at home; elder abuse and neglect can be family problems and may include financial exploitation in addition to physical and psychological neglect and abuse (Connolly, 2008). Even our medical system is unprepared for the growing population of seniors in American society: Estimates for a future need for 30,000 geriatricians compare bleakly to the 9,000 currently in practice in the United States (Connolly, 2008).

Care for the elderly falls most often on daughters and daughters-in-law. These women have historically functioned as our society's "kin-keepers" (Brody, 1990; Brody et al., 1994). Although the average family caregiver is 45 years old, female, and married, 35 percent of caregivers to the elderly are themselves older than 65 years of age, and 10 percent are older than 75.

While some see an aging society as forcing policy makers to choose between investing in youth or investing in the elderly, Rowe and his colleagues point out that these are not mutually exclusive policies (2009:20):

[M]any programs that target the elderly have significant benefits for younger generations and should properly be seen as family programs. Social Security payments to older people relieve their middle-aged children of the economic burden of supporting their parents. But they also help the elderly support their children . . . Such

multigenerational win–win opportunities exist in many areas, including education, training and job flexibility, retirement, welfare, and health.

Sociological Perspectives on the Family

We have been following three major sociological perspectives—the functionalist, conflict, and interactionist—as we move through our introduction to sociology. What do these major theoretical frameworks have to tell us about the family?

The Functionalist Perspective

As we have noted in other chapters, functionalist theorists stress that if a society is to survive and operate with some measure of effectiveness, it must guarantee that certain essential tasks are performed. The performance of these tasks—or *functions*—cannot be left to chance (see Chapter 1, pp. 18–19). To do so would be to run the risk that some activities would not be carried out, and the society would disintegrate. Although acknowledging that families show a good deal of variation throughout the world, functionalists seek to identify a number of recurrent functions families typically perform (Davis, 1949).

Reproduction

If a society is to perpetuate itself, new members have to be created; families perform that function by providing social and cultural supports and motivations for having children.

Socialization

The family functions as an intermediary in the socialization process between the larger community and the individual. At birth, children are uninitiated in the ways of culture, and thus each new generation subjects society to a recurrent "barbarian invasion" (see Chapter 3). Through the process of socialization, children become inducted into their society's ways, and the family usually serves as the chief culture-transmitting agency.

Care, Protection, and Emotional Support

Human children must be fed, clothed, and provided with shelter well into puberty. Throughout the world, the family has been assigned the responsibility for shielding, protecting, sustaining, and otherwise maintaining not just children, but also the infirm and other dependent members of the community (Rossi and Rossi, 1990). The family also provides an important source for entering into intimate, constant, face-to-face contact with other people. Healthy family relationships afford companionship, love, security, a sense of worth, and a general feeling of well-being.

Assignment of Status

Infants must be placed within the social structure. The family confers ascribed statuses (see Chapter 2, p. 55) that (1) orient a person to a variety of interpersonal relationships, including those involving parents, siblings, and other kin and (2) orient a person to basic group memberships, including racial, ethnic, religious, class, national, and community relationships.

Regulation of Sexual Behavior

A society's norms regulate sexual behavior by specifying who may engage in sexual behavior with whom and under what circumstances. In no known society are people given total freedom for sexual expression. Although some 70 percent of the world's societies permit some form of sexual license, even those societies typically do not approve of childbirth out of wedlock—this is the **norm of legitimacy;** like other norms, this one is occasionally violated, and those who violate it are usually punished.

Critics of the functionalist perspective point out that these tasks can be performed in other ways. Indeed, by virtue of social change, many of the economic, child care, and educational functions once performed by the family have been taken over by other institutions. Even so, the family tends to be the social unit most commonly responsible for reproduction, socialization, and the other functions we considered.

The Conflict Perspective

Functionalists spotlight the tasks carried out by the family that serve the interests of society as a whole. Many conflict theorists, in contrast, have seen the family as a social arrangement benefiting some people more than others. Friedrich Engels (1884/1902), Karl Marx's close associate, viewed the family as a class society in miniature, with one class (men) oppressing another class (women). He contended that marriage was the first form of class antagonism in which the well-being of one group derived from the misery and repression of another. The motivation for sexual domination was the economic exploitation of a woman's labor.

Women as Sexual Property

Sociologist Randall Collins (1975, 1988a) has said that historically men have been the "sexual aggressors" and women the "sexual prizes for men." Women have been victimized by their smaller size and vulnerability as childbearers. Across an entire spectrum of societies women have been seen as sexual property, taken as booty in war, used by their fathers in economic bargaining, and considered as owned by their husbands.

According to Collins, marriage is a socially enforced contract of sexual property. Within Western tradition, a marriage was not legal until sexually consummated, sexual assault within marriage was not legally rape, and the principal ground for divorce was sexual infidelity. A woman's virginity was seen as the property of her father, and her sexuality as the property of her husband. Thus, rape has often traditionally been seen less as a crime perpetrated by a man against a woman than as a crime perpetrated by one man against another man.

In recent years, however, economic and political changes have improved women's bargaining position. The sexual bargains women strike can focus less on marriage and more on immediate pleasure, companionship, and sexual gratification.

Conflict as Natural and Necessary

Other social scientists have approached the issue of conflict somewhat differently. At the turn of the century psychoanalyst Sigmund Freud (1930/1961) and sociologist Georg Simmel (1908/1955, 1908/1959) also advanced a conflict approach to the family. They contended that intimate relationships inevitably involve antagonism as well as love. Sociologists like Jetse Sprey (1979) developed these ideas and suggested that conflict is a part of all systems and interactions, including the family and marital interactions. Viewed in this fashion, the family is a social arrangement that structures close interpersonal relationships through ongoing processes of negotiation, problem solving, and conflict management. This view is compatible with the interactionist perspective.

The Interactionist Perspective

As we saw in Chapters 2 and 3, symbolic interactionists emphasize that human beings create, use, and communicate with symbols. One way in which families reinforce and rejuvenate their bonds is through the symbolic mechanism of *rituals*. Social scientists find that household rituals such as gathering for meals are a hidden source of family strength. It seems that when families preserve their rituals, their children fare better emotionally, even when the family faces other disruptive problems (e.g., alcoholism). Some therapists help families establish rituals as a means to heal family stresses and tensions (Goleman, 1992; Pipher, 1997).

The symbolic interactionist perspective is a useful tool for examining the complexities of a relationship. When the roles of one family member change, there are consequences for other family members. For example, we have seen that parenthood alters the husband–wife relationship by creating new roles and increasing the complexity of the family unit. Likewise, family life is different in homes where a mother is in the paid labor force or where an economic provider is unemployed. And the loss of critical family roles caused by divorce has vast implications for family functioning (Gubrium and Holstein, 1990).

What Can Sociology Do for You?

This chapter has presented information about families in U.S. society and around the world. Issues related to families provide multiple career opportunities—in social work, in child or elder care, in policy and planning, or in family and marriage counseling, just to name a few. If you've ever thought you might like to be a counselor, you may want to go to **http://www .allpsychologyschools.com/faqs/become_ counselor.php** and read this site's information about counseling careers.

If you enjoyed Chapter 10 and are interested in family issues, you might want to take a family course, a marriage and courtship class, a course exploring the implications and challenges of our aging society, or other related classes.

The Chapter in Brief: *The Family*

Structure of the Family: A Global View

The way in which we define the family determines the kinds of **family** we will consider to be normal or deviant and what rights and obligations we will recognize as legally and socially binding. Americans adopt a variety of **lifestyles.**

■ **Forms of the Family** In the **nuclear family** arrangement, spouses and their offspring constitute the core relationship. In the **extended family** arrangement, kin provide the core relationship. Most Americans will belong to a **family of orientation** and a **family of procreation.** Descent and inheritance can be **patrilineal, matrilineal,** or **bilineal,** and couples may take a **patrilocal, matrilocal,** or **neolocal** residence. Most societies are **patriarchal,** with some industrialized nations becoming more **egalitarian;** none are known that are truly **matriarchal.**

■ **Forms of Marriage** **Marriage** refers to a socially approved sexual union undertaken with some idea of permanence. Two types of marital regulations define the "right" spouse: **endogamy** and **exogamy. Incest taboos** are rules that prohibit sexual intercourse with close blood relatives. Societies further structure marriage relationships in one of four ways: **monogamy, polygyny, polyandry,** and **group marriage.**

■ **Patterns of Courtship** Societies "control" love through child and arranged marriages, social isolation of young people, close supervision of couples, and peer and parental pressures. A variety of factors operate in the selection of a mate: **homogamy,** physical attractiveness (the **matching hypothesis**), and **complementary needs. Exchange theory** provides a unifying link among these factors.

Marriage and the Family in the United States

■ **Marriage** American couples with better marital quality are those who share decision making, have nontraditional views on the division of labor, and have close friendships and activities in common. Researchers have identified five common types of marriages.

■ **Parenthood** Nuclear families typically pass through a series of changes and realignments across time, what sociologists call the **family life course.** Altered expectations and requirements are imposed on a husband and wife as children are born and grow up.

■ **Mothers in the Labor Force** More than 60 percent of all mothers with children under age six are in the paid workforce. Such women also do more of the housework and child care than men. Research findings about the effect of working mothers on children are varied.

■ **Stepfamilies** "Blended" families, which occur when divorced or widowed parents remarry, are becoming the norm in American society, with stepchildren no longer likely to cause marital conflict or divorce.

■ **Singlehood** Twenty-eight percent of all American households are now made up of a single person, the result of the deferral of marriage, the rate of divorce, and the ability of the elderly to maintain their own homes.

■ **Single Parenthood** More than a quarter of America's children live with just one parent, the vast majority with their mothers. Single-parent families are more likely than two-parent families to be living in poverty.

■ **Cohabitation** Sociologists think that premarital **cohabitation** is becoming institutionalized as a step between dating and marriage, although it is not always associated with higher marital satisfaction.

■ **Gay and Lesbian Couples** Nineteen states now offer legal recognition of some kind to same-sex couples, and in 2010, 1 percent of

all "couple households" in the United States were same-sex households. About a fifth of those include children.

Challenges for American Families and Society

Some family problems stay in the family; others spill over into society.

■ **Family Violence, Child Abuse, and Incest** Family violence, child abuse, and incest can have lasting effects. The sexual abuse of children often leads to behavior problems, learning difficulties, sexual promiscuity, runaway behavior, drug and alcohol abuse, and suicidal behavior.

■ **Child Care** Most child psychologists agree that high-quality day care and preschools provide acceptable child care arrangements. The United States is one of the few industrialized nations that have no comprehensive day care program, and the quality of child care available is often poor.

■ **Divorce** Divorce exacts a considerable emotional and physical toll from all family members. Children raised by single parents are more likely to drop out of high school, to use drugs, to have teen births, to have illegitimate children, and to be poorer than children raised in two-parent homes. More than half the adults who remarry undergo a second divorce.

■ **The Elderly** The proportion of elderly people in the United States is increasing such that we will soon have a population structure with more over-60s than under-15s. These elderly will be characterized by better health and fewer disabilities than in the past and will continue to lead productive lives well past traditional retirement age. Resources, policies, and facilities for this increased population of elderly will be required.

Sociological Perspectives on the Family

■ **The Functionalist Perspective** Functionalists identify a number of functions families typically perform: reproduction; socialization; care, protection, and emotional support; assignment of status; and regulation of sexual behavior through the **norm of legitimacy.**

■ **The Conflict Perspective** Conflict theorists have seen the family as a social arrangement benefiting men more than women. Some conflict sociologists say that intimate relationships inevitably involve antagonism as well as love.

■ **The Interactionist Perspective** Symbolic interactionists emphasize that families reinforce and rejuvenate their bonds through the symbolic mechanism of rituals such as family meals and holidays.

Glossary

bilineal An arrangement based on reckoning descent and transmitting property through both the father and the mother.

cohabitation An intimate relationship that involves sharing living quarters with an unrelated adult of the opposite sex.

complementary needs Two different personality traits that are the counterparts of each other and that provide a sense of completeness when they are joined.

egalitarian authority An arrangement in which power and authority are equally distributed between husband and wife.

endogamy The requirement that marriage occur within a group.

exchange theory The view proposing that people involved in a mutually satisfying relationship will exchange behaviors that have low cost and high reward.

exogamy The requirement that marriage occur outside a group.

extended family A family arrangement in which kin— individuals related by common

ancestry—provide the core relationship; spouses are functionally marginal and peripheral.

family Traditionally defined as a social group whose members are related by ancestry, marriage, or adoption and who live together, cooperate economically, and care for the young.

family life course Changes and realignments related to the altered expectations and requirements imposed on a husband and a wife as children are born and grow up.

family of orientation A nuclear family that consists of oneself and one's father, mother, and siblings.

family of procreation A nuclear family that consists of oneself and one's spouse and children.

group marriage The marriage of two or more husbands and two or more wives.

heterogamous marriages Marriages in which spouses have different characteristics, including race or ethnicity, age, or religion.

homogamy The tendency of like to marry like.

homosexuality A preference for an individual of the same sex as a sexual partner.

incest taboos Rules that prohibit sexual intercourse with close blood relatives.

lifestyle The overall pattern of living that people evolve to meet their biological, social, and emotional needs.

marriage A socially approved sexual union between two or more individuals that is undertaken with some idea of permanence.

matching hypothesis The notion that we typically experience the greatest payoff and the least cost when we select partners who have a degree of physical attractiveness similar to our own.

matriarchal authority A family arrangement in which power is vested in women.

matrilineal An arrangement based on reckoning descent and inheritance through the mother's side of the family.

matrilocal residence   The residence pattern in which a bride and groom live in the household or community of the wife's family.

monogamy   The marriage of one husband and one wife.

neolocal residence   The residence pattern in which newlyweds set up a new place of residence independent of either of their parents or other relatives.

norm of legitimacy   The rule that children not be born out of wedlock.

nuclear family   A family arrangement in which the spouses and their offspring constitute the core relationship; blood relatives are functionally marginal and peripheral.

patriarchal authority   A family arrangement in which power is vested in men.

patrilineal   An arrangement based on reckoning descent and inheritance through the father's side of the family.

patrilocal residence   The residence pattern in which a bride and groom live in the household or community of the husband's family.

polyandry   The marriage of two or more husbands and one wife.

polygyny   The marriage of one husband and two or more wives.

romantic love   The strong physical and emotional attraction between a man and a woman.

Review Questions

1. Differentiate between nuclear and extended families and between family of orientation and family of procreation.

2. Describe the various forms of marriage found around the world.

3. How do courtship patterns control love?

4. What is the family life course?

5. What sorts of lifestyles do Americans adopt besides the traditional nuclear family?

6. Name and describe some of the challenges facing American families today.

7. How do the functionalist, conflict, and interactionist perspectives on the family differ?

Internet Connection   www.mhhe.com/hughes11e

Using a search engine such as **google.com,** do a search on "family values." Choose a number of the sites you find, and explore them further. Write a short report about the many ways "family values" are defined in our society. How is this term thought about differently by different interest and cultural groups, including political and religious groups?

Religion, Education, and Medicine

I n this chapter we turn our attention to three interconnected institutions: religion, medicine, and education. Each of these is focused on the solution to a set of problems encountered in social living. Depending on the time of history and culture under study, these institutions have interwoven their solutions to such problems. In the pages that follow, we will see how religious, educational, and medical institutions have evolved to meet basic needs for society.

Religion

Sociologists are interested in religious beliefs and commitments and in the effects religion has on health, education, the family, politics, and other matters. Throughout U.S. history the influence of religion on politics and government has been strong. In 2012, the U.S. health care debate was heavily influenced by religion. What role should religion play in public policy? This debate focuses not on the right of religious activists to lobby for laws consistent with their beliefs, but on determining the place a religiously defined morality has in a pluralist society (Olson and Carroll, 1992).

In this section we will review the varieties of religious behavior found among people around the world and take a look at religious organizations. We will consider secular change, religion in contemporary life, fundamentalism and evangelicalism, and issues of church and state. Finally, we will see what the sociological perspectives have to offer to our understanding of religion.

What Is Religion?

Religion has to do with those socially shared and organized ways of thinking, feeling, and acting that concern ultimate meanings about the existence of the supernatural or "beyond" (Stark and Bainbridge, 1987). As Émile Durkheim (1912/1965) pointed out, religion is centered in beliefs and practices that are related to sacred as opposed to profane things. Durkheim described the **sacred** as involving those aspects of social reality that are set apart and forbidden. In many religious systems, the sacred is seen as distinct from the **profane**—those aspects of social reality that are everyday and commonplace. The sacred, then, is extraordinary, mysterious, awe-inspiring, and even potentially dangerous—it is distinct from normal, routine life. The same object or behavior can be profane or sacred, depending on how people define it. A wafer made of flour when seen as bread is a profane object, but it becomes sacred to Catholics as the body of Christ when it is consecrated during Mass. Because the sacred is caught up with strong feelings of reverence and awe, it can usually be approached only through **rituals**—social acts prescribed by rules that dictate how human beings should behave in the presence of the sacred. In their religious behavior, human beings fashion a social world of meanings and rules that govern how and what they think, feel, and act.

A Global View: Varieties of Religious Behavior

Religious beliefs can be found in all cultures and all periods of history, and religion plays a role in most people's lives today, but its importance varies significantly across the globe. Where did religion come from? Did evolving humans develop a "moral compass" or derive that from religions once they arose? Research in the field of moral psychology supports the idea that religion evolved as a by-product of humans' ability to make moral judgments (Pyysiäinen and Hauser, 2009).

Religious behavior is so varied that we have difficulty thinking about it unless we devise some means for sorting it into relevant categories. Although no categories do justice to the diversity and richness of the human religious experience, sociologist Reece McGee (1975) provided us with a scheme that is both insightful and manageable: simple supernaturalism, animism, theism, and a system of abstract ideals.

Simple Supernaturalism

A belief in the supernatural entails the notion of **mana,** a diffuse, impersonal, supernatural force that exists in nature for good or evil. Mana is usually employed to reach relatively immediate goals—control of the weather, assurance of a good crop, cure of an illness, good performance on a test, success in love, or victory in battle. With mana, people do not entreat spirits or gods to intervene on their behalf; they use rituals to *compel* a superhuman power to behave as they wish. For instance, carrying a rabbit's foot is thought to bring good luck, while the bad luck associated with the number 13 is avoided by not labeling hotel and office building floors as "13."

Animism

Animism is a pattern of religious behavior that involves a belief in spirits or otherworldly beings. Animists might, for example, see spirits in animals, plants, rocks, stars, rivers, and at times other individuals. Love, punishment, reverence, and gifts have all been used to deal with superhuman spirits, as have cajolery, bribery, and false pretenses. Additionally, in animism, as with mana, supernatural power is often harnessed through rituals that compel a spirit to act in a desired way.

Theism

In **theism** religion is centered in a belief in gods who are thought to be powerful, to have an interest in human affairs, and to merit worship. Judaism, Christianity, and Islam are forms of **monotheism,** or belief in one god. They have established religious organizations, religious leaders or priests, traditional rituals, and sacred writings. Ancient Greek religion and

Hinduism (practiced primarily in India) are forms of **polytheism,** or belief in many gods with equal or relatively similar power. Hindu gods are often tribal, village, or caste deities associated with a particular place—a building, field, or mountain—or a certain object such as an animal or a tree. Hinduism can also be seen as monistic, with its many gods manifestations of one supreme being.

Abstract Ideals

Finally, some religions focus on a set of abstract ideals. Rather than centering on the worship of a god, they are dedicated to achieving moral and spiritual excellence. Many of the religions of Asia are of this type, including Taoism, Confucianism, and Buddhism. Buddhism is directed toward reaching an elevated state of consciousness, a method of purification that provides a release from suffering, ignorance, and selfishness. In the Western world, humanism is based on ethical principles. Its adherents discard all theological beliefs about God, heaven, hell, and immortality, and substitute for God the pursuit of good in the here and now.

Religious Organizations

Thousands of new religious groups have sprung to life all over the globe in recent years, and the Internet has made it easier for new groups to advertise themselves and to find adherents. Who are these groups? The world's population can be categorized by their adherence to various religions, including Hindus (14 percent), Muslims (19 percent), Buddhists (6 percent), Christians (33 percent), Sikhs (0.36 percent), Jews (0.22 percent), Chinese folk religionists (6 percent), primal indigenous (6 percent), and the nonreligious and nonaffiliated (16 percent). (These estimates are based on a wide variety of sources that can be found at www.adherents.com.) Christian groups worldwide include Roman Catholics, Protestants, and Anglican and Orthodox traditions. Atheists—those who

don't believe in God—may also call themselves humanists, secularists, free thinkers, rationalists, or brights (Jordan, 2007).

What defines religion? Norms, beliefs, and rituals provide the cultural fabric of religion, but there is more to the religious institution than its cultural heritage. As with other institutions, there is also the structural mosaic of social organization whereby people are bound together within networks of relatively stable relationships. In this section we will focus on four types of religious organization: churches, denominations, sects, and cults.

Church

In everyday language, "church" refers to a building, or it might refer to a specific religious organization such as the United Methodist Church or the Presbyterian Church in America. Sociologists use the familiar term "church" to refer to a form of religious organization that has never existed in the United States but has been common in history and still exists in parts of the world. The **church** is a religious organization that considers itself uniquely legitimate and typically enjoys a positive relationship with mainstream society. It usually operates with a bureaucratic structure and claims to include most members of a society. Religions organized along church lines either are integrated into a society's government or operate with explicit government sanction and support. Members are born into the church if their parents are affiliated with it; they do not have to join the church. The aim of the church is to be universal; in principle, all members of a society belong to it. Its response to competing groups is to suppress, ignore, or co-opt them (see Table 11.1).

The church attaches considerable importance to the means of grace that it administers, to the system of doctrine that it has formulated, and to the administration of rituals that it controls through an official clergy. It strives to dominate all aspects of social life—to teach and guide the members of society and dispense saving

Table 11.1 Types of Religious Organization

Characteristic	Church	Denomination	Sect	Cult
Size	Large	Moderate	Small	Small
Relationship with Secular World	Affirms prevailing culture and social arrangements	Supports current culture and social arrangements	Renounces or opposes prevailing culture and social arrangements	Although critical of society, focuses on evil within each person
Relationship with Other Religious Groups	Claims sole legitimacy	Accepts pluralistic legitimacy	Claims sole legitimacy	Accepts pluralistic legitimacy
Religious Services	Formal services with minimal congregational participation	Formal services with limited congregational participation	Informal services with high degree of congregational participation	Informal meetings that draw upon the participation of adherents
Clergy	Specialized, professional, full-time	Specialized, professional, full-time	Unspecialized, little formal training, part-time	Charismatic; founder or leader has little formal training
Doctrines	Literal interpretations of scriptures	Liberal interpretation of scriptures	Literal interpretation of scriptures	New and independent tradition with a rather secularized view of the divine
Social Class of Members	All social classes	Middle and upper	Primarily disadvantaged	Chiefly middle and educated
Sources of Members	Born into the faith; seeks universal membership	Often requires later validation of membership acquired from parents	Voluntary confessional membership	Often lacks formal membership
Emphasis	Religious education and transmission of religion to the children of members	Religious education and transmission of religious values to youth	Evangelism and adult membership	Living one's life in accordance with basic tenets
Church Property	Extensive	Depends on affluence of members	Little	None or limited

Source: Adapted from Glen M. Vernon, *Sociology of Religion*. Reprinted with the permission of McGraw-Hill, Inc.

grace. The church type is best exemplified by the Roman Catholic Church of 13th-century Europe and the Church of England.

The Denomination

The **denomination** accepts the legitimacy claims of other religions and enjoys a positive relationship with the dominant society. In many cases it is a sect (which we discuss next) in an advanced stage of development and adjustment to the secular world. The membership of the denomination comes largely from the middle class. The moral rigor and religious fervor of the sect are relaxed. It usually has an established clergy who have undergone specialized training at a theological seminary.

The denomination is content to be one organization among many, all of which are deemed acceptable in the sight of God. Examples of denominations include most of the major religious groups in the United States: Presbyterians, Baptists, Congregationalists, Methodists, Unitarians, Lutherans, Episcopalians, Roman Catholics, and Reform and Conservative Jews.

The Sect

The **sect** is a religious organization that stands apart from mainstream society but is rooted in established religious traditions. Christianity, for example, began as a sect of Judaism; Jesus was a Jew. The sect considers itself uniquely legitimate but is at odds with the dominant society. It usually consists of a small, voluntary fellowship of converts, most of whom are drawn from disadvantaged groups. The sect does not attempt to win the world over to its doctrines but instead practices exclusiveness. The sect is often founded by individuals who break away from another religious body and claim that they represent the true, cleansed version of the faith from which they split (Stark and Bainbridge, 1979; Wilson, 1990). Members who entertain heretical opinions or engage in immoral behavior are subject to expulsion.

The sect thinks of itself as a religious elite. Sect members believe that other religious interpretations are in error, and they portray the larger society as decadent and evil (see Table 11.1). It is often a form of social dissent, exemplified by the Anabaptists of the 16th- and 17th-century Reformation and the Mormons, Shakers, and Quakers of the 18th and 19th centuries. Most sects are small, and many of them fail to grow larger. Should they survive, gain adherents, and become dominant, they have a natural tendency to become churchlike. If they become widely popular in a religiously diverse and competitive environment like the United States, they become more like denominations.

The Cult

While a sect is formed out of an existing religion, a **cult** is a religious movement that represents a new and independent religious tradition (Stark and Bainbridge, 1979, 1987). The cult is alienated and viewed as deviant by the dominant society, but it tends to accept the legitimacy of other religious groups. Having no religious tradition, it is difficult for a cult to claim sole legitimacy. In addition, knowing that others view them with suspicion, cults have a sense of vulnerability and thus an interest in publicly supporting norms of tolerance.

Cults usually do not require their new members to pass strict doctrinal tests, but instead invite all to join their ranks. However, many cults are authoritarian and attempt to control the entire lives of their members. For example, in Abode of Dawn, a village in Siberia, Sergei Torop leads some 5,000 followers in a vegetarian lifestyle governed by his nine-volume Last Testament and 61 commandments, including no alcohol, smoking, or drugs (Sullivan, 2007).

Whereas churches and denominations typically exist in accommodation with the larger society, sects and cults often find themselves at odds with established social arrangements and practices. Cults differ from sects in that they are not rooted in existing religious traditions and tend to be more tolerant of other religious groups. In this respect, cults resemble denominations. In contrast, the sect, like the church, defines itself as being uniquely legitimate and possessing exclusive access to truth or salvation. This model is depicted in Figure 11.1.

Religion and Secular Change: The Protestant Ethic

People's religious beliefs and practices can promote socioeconomic change. Max Weber (1904/1958, 1916/1964, 1917/1958) studied several world religions in order to discern how a religious **ethic**—the perspective and values engendered by a religious way of thinking—can affect people's behavior. He suggested that there are periods in historical development when circumstances push a society toward a reaffirmation of old ways or toward new ways. At such critical junctures, religion—by supplying

	Positive Relationship with Society	Negative Relationship with Society
Claims Sole Legitimacy	CHURCH	SECT
Accepts Pluralistic Legitimacy	DENOMI-NATION	CULT

Figure 11.1 Types of Religious Organizations

Source: "Types of Religious Organizations" adapted from *Sectarianism: Analyses of Religious and Non-Religious Sects* by Roy Wallis, p, 41. New York: Wiley, 1975. Reprinted by permission of Peter Owen Ltd.

sources of individual motivation and defining the relationship of individuals to their society—can be a source of historical breakthrough. While a religious ethic does not necessarily lead to social action, it can give it impetus by shaping people's perceptions and definitions of their material and ideal interests.

Did Protestantism Lead to Capitalism?

In *The Protestant Ethic and the Spirit of Capitalism* (1904/1958), Weber sought a link between the rise of the Protestant view of life and the emergence of capitalist social arrangements in Western society. He maintained that the development of capitalism depended upon the creation of a pool of individuals who had the attitudes and values necessary to function as entrepreneurs. Once capitalism is established, it carries on in a self-perpetuating fashion.

The critical issue, Weber said, is to uncover the origin of the motivating spirit of capitalism in precapitalist society. He believed that Protestantism, particularly in the form of Calvinism, was crucial to, but not the only factor in, the rise of this spirit. Calvinism is based on the teachings of the French Protestant theologian and reformer John Calvin (1509–1564) and found expression in a variety of religious movements including Puritanism, Pietism, and Anabaptism.

Weber noted that Protestantism and modern capitalism appeared on the historical scene at roughly the same time, that capitalism initially attained its highest development in Protestant countries and regions, and that it was mostly Protestants, not Catholics, who became the early capitalist entrepreneurs. Based on these observations, Weber (1904/1958:64) concluded that the **Protestant ethic,** particularly as it was embodied in Calvinist doctrine, instilled an "attitude which seeks profit rationally and systematically."

The Doctrine of Predestination

The Calvinist ethos had other elements that fed capitalist motivation, particularly its *doctrine of predestination.* Calvin rejected the idea that a person's status in the afterlife is determined by the way he or she behaves here on earth. Instead, Calvin taught that at birth every soul is predestined for heaven or hell. This notion was especially disquieting because people did not know whether they were among the saved or the damned. According to Weber, Calvin's followers, in their search for reassurance, came to accept certain earthly signs of **asceticism** as proof of their salvation and genuine faith: hard work, sobriety, thrift, restraint, and the avoidance of fleshly pleasures. The Calvinists, preoccupied with their fate, subtly began to cultivate these very behaviors. Self-discipline and a willingness to delay gratification are qualities that lead people to amass capital and achieve economic success. Capitalist entrepreneurs could pursue profit and fulfill their Christian obligation; the Calvinist ethos took the spirit of capitalism out of the realm of individual ambition and translated it into an ethical duty.

Other Origins of Capitalism

Many scholars since Weber have raised serious questions regarding his hypothesis (Samuelsson, 1961; Cohen, 1980). They have looked to other factors in explaining the origins of capitalism, including a surge in commerce during the 15th and 16th centuries, technological innovations, the influx of capital resources from New World colonies, unrestrained markets, and the availability of a free labor force. Further, sociologist Randall G. Stokes (1975) showed that the beliefs comprised in the Protestant ethic do not necessarily lead people to engage in entrepreneurial activities. Even so, Weber's early work, although not necessarily accurate in all its particulars, remains a sociological landmark. It demonstrates the impact religion can have on human affairs in producing outcomes that are not necessarily intended or foreseen by its adherents.

Religion in Contemporary U.S. Life

Many of the first European immigrants to the North American continent made their journey to find religious freedom. As schoolchildren, we all are taught the stories of the strict Puritans of New England and the struggles of the pioneers to establish churches on the prairie frontier. The earliest days in the history of the American colonies seem steeped in religiosity.

The transformation of human societies from simple to complex forms is accompanied by industrialization, urbanization, bureaucratization, and rationalization. The **secularization thesis** adds the idea that as societies evolve, profane, or nonreligious, considerations will gain ascendancy over sacred, or religious, considerations (Herberg, 1955; Chaves, 1994). Is religion as important today as it apparently was in the early days of the colonies? Or is secularization occurring in the United States?

In fact, there is very little sociological evidence that secularization is occurring. On the contrary, the United States remains one of the world's most religious countries. The percentage of Americans who believe in God in some form is extremely high; the proportion of Americans professing belief in God or some higher power has not dipped below 90 percent over the past half-century (Princeton Religion Research Center, 1994; Smith et al., 2010). Only 1.6 percent are atheists (do not believe in God) and 2.4 percent are agnostics (do not know if God exists) (Pew Research Center, 2008). And according to historical and contemporary data (Finke and Starke, 1992; U.S. Census Bureau, 1999; Newport and Saad, 1997), the percentage of Americans who claim membership in a church or synagogue has risen dramatically over the past 200 years. When the Declaration of Independence was signed, only 17 percent of the population belonged to a church or synagogue. By 1860 that number had risen to 37 percent, and by 1926 it had increased again to 58 percent. At present, an estimated 61 percent of U.S. adults are members of a local church or other house of worship, and only 16.1 percent identify themselves as unaffiliated with any specific religious tradition (Pew Research Center, 2008). About a third of that 16.1 percent consider themselves to be religious; they simply don't see themselves as affiliated with any particular religious group. Table 11.2 provides a breakdown of religious affiliation in the United States.

Religion remains a powerful force in the United States, and survey respondents believe it has the potential to do even more. If more Americans were deeply religious, a strong majority of respondents said, crime would decrease, volunteer and charity work would increase, and parents would do a better job of raising children (Farkas et al., 2000).

In the 1990s, a new set of ideas in the sociology of religion, referred to by some as the "New Paradigm" (e.g., Warner, 1993), reformulated the idea of secularization to make sense of the continuing significance and vitality of religion in American life. According to the new paradigm, since religion is the only institution that can answer the ultimate questions of the meaning and purpose of life for most people, it is an inevitable feature of human society. Secularization in the new paradigm is a process in which religions become increasingly worldly

Table 11.2	Religious Affiliation in the United States
	Percentage of All Adults
Christian	**78.4**
Protestant	51.3
Evangelical churches	*26.3*
Mainline churches	*18.1*
Historically black churches	*6.9*
Catholic	23.9
Mormon	1.7
Jehovah's Witness	0.7
Orthodox	0.6
Greek Orthodox	*<0.3*
Russian Orthodox	*<0.3*
Other	*<0.3*
Other Christian	0.3
Other Religions	**4.7**
Jewish	1.7
Reform	*0.7*
Conservative	*0.5*
Orthodox	*<0.3*
Other	*0.3*
Buddhist	0.7
Zen Buddhist	*<0.3*
Theravada Buddhist	*<0.3*
Tibetan Buddhist	*<0.3*
Other	*0.3*
Muslim	0.6
Sunni	*0.3*
Shia	*<0.3*
Other	*<0.3*
Hindu	0.4
Other world religions	<0.3
Other faiths	1.2
Unitarians and other liberal faiths	*0.7*
New Age	*0.4*
Native American religions	*<0.3*
Unaffiliated	**16.1**
Atheist	1.6
Agnostic	2.4
Nothing in particular	12.1
Secular unaffiliated	*6.3*
Religious unaffiliated	*5.8*
Don't Know/Refused	**0.8**

Due to rounding, figures may not add to 100 and nested figures may not add to the subtotal indicated.

Source: Pew Research Center, 2008. Reprinted by permission.

and less focused on the supernatural (Stark, 1996). But instead of resulting in people turning to science for ultimate answers, secularization weakens old religious groups that are becoming less focused on the supernatural and creates opportunities for new ones.

Secularization in the United States has followed exactly this pattern, producing a decline in the old mainline Protestant denominations and an increase in strength among evangelical, fundamentalist, and sectlike groups. In this view, secularization is a "process that leads not to irreligion but to a shift in the sources of religion" (Stark, 1996:437). According to this perspective, as long as there is a free market in religion (see "The Religious Marketplace" on page 356) and people can change their religious attachments, secularization initiates a process that revitalizes religion rather than promoting its demise.

Fundamentalism and Evangelicalism

In the United States, *fundamentalism* is primarily a Protestant movement that opposes "modernist" theology and seeks to conserve the basic principles underlying traditional Christianity; it views the Bible as the literal and unerring word of God and reaffirms traditional authority. *Evangelicalism* is a "glad tidings" movement whose members profess a personal relationship with Jesus Christ; adherents believe that the Bible provides the only authoritative basis for faith, stress the importance of personal conversion, and emphasize the importance of intense zeal for Christian living. Although the public often lumps fundamentalists and evangelicals together, their differences are every bit as great as those dividing Catholics, Episcopalians, Methodists, and Baptists (Hadden and Shupe, 1988).

The increase in the number of fundamentalists and evangelicals (also referred to as conservative Christians) at least partially accounts for the high rate of church affiliation in the United States. Those denominations that sociologists of religion consider to be fundamentalist include Baptists, along with the Assemblies of God, the

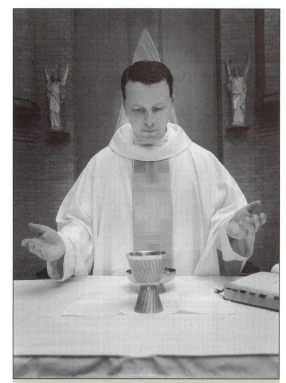

Active participation in religious organizations continues to be important for many Americans, and the United States remains one of the world's most religious countries.

Seventh-Day Adventists, the United Pentecostal Church, and the Church of God. Approximately a fifth of the total U.S. adult population, and a third of all Protestants, identify themselves as Baptists (Pew Research Center, 2008). In contrast, the more liberal Protestant denominations have quite small memberships: Lutherans account for only 7 percent of the population, Methodists 8 percent, Presbyterians 4 percent, and Episcopalians 3 percent. Memberships in these groups declined by 28–59 percent between 1960 and 1990, while memberships in fundamentalist churches increased by 12–900 percent (Stark, 1996).

The Religious Marketplace

The Pew Research Center (2008) study on religion found that religious affiliation in the United States is both "very diverse and extremely fluid": Many religious groups are represented in the United States, and many Americans change religious affiliation. More than a quarter of American adults have left the religion in which they were raised, while about 4 percent of American adults say that they were not raised in any religious tradition but have since become affiliated with one. About 10 percent of Americans are former Catholics.

Sociologists of religion portray religious groups as functioning much in the manner of firms competing for souls in a "religious marketplace" (Finke and Stark, 1992). Religions that gain members in this marketplace tend to be hard-line ones; historically, these have been "upstart sects," groups that today include Pentecostal, Holiness, and fundamentalist sects. In colonial times the established denominations went into decline when confronted with competition from Baptist and Methodist sects. In turn, Methodism went into decline when its circuit-rider clergy dismounted and became professionalized, its hellfire-and-brimstone theology cooled, and its rustic camp meetings became "respectable middle-class summer resorts" (Finke and Stark, 1992).

Survey data show major changes in the future for the American Catholic population. While a third of Americans are raised Catholic, fewer than a quarter are Catholic as adults, and the "drop-out rate" would appear even greater but for the 2.6 percent of Americans who switch from something else to Catholicism and the influx of foreign-born Catholics (Pew Research Center, 2008). Latinos currently account for about a third of adult Catholics in the United States and nearly half of all U.S. Catholics ages 18–29. Similarly, changes are in the offing for Protestant denominations. Currently, just over a quarter of American adults are members of evangelical Protestant churches, 18 percent are associated with mainline Protestant churches, and about 7 percent are members of historically black Protestant churches (Pew Research Center, 2008; see also Greeley and Hout, 2006). But there is a generational difference, with 62 percent of Americans age 70 or older being Protestant and only 43 percent of young adults (ages 18–29) being Protestant. Further, a quarter of Americans ages 18–29 claim no religious affiliation compared to only 8 percent of Americans age 70 or older. The Pew Research Center study found recent declines in Protestant affiliation and increases in the "unaffiliated" population; if generational differences persist, the report concludes, these trends may continue.

Many religious conservatives have entered the political arena. More than a quarter of Americans are white evangelical Protestants. Although there is not a single Christian right, the assortment of organizations, constituencies, and leaders who share traditional family values, favor school prayer, and oppose abortion, gay rights, and the teaching of evolution is large and powerful (Luo, 2006). More than half the Americans surveyed in 2000 said that it would be wrong to consider a candidate's religious affiliation when voting, although they would like political leaders to be more religious. But evangelicals were more likely than other groups to say that deeply religious politicians would make better leaders and that they should be less willing to compromise on key issues, instead voting as their religious beliefs dictate (Farkas et al., 2000).

High-cost faiths—those that impose sacrifices and even stigmas on their members—consistently outperform their more mainstream counterparts; hard-line religious groups also get rid of "free riders" who dilute the congregation's solidarity by using it for weddings, funerals, and an occasional spiritual boost without offering much in return (Iannaccone, 1994). In addition, denominations and individual churches that can extract more resources from members in terms of time and money grow faster than others (Iannaccone, Olson, and Stark, 1995). There seems to be an indissoluble link between how much a religion demands and how much its members feel it can offer in return. The "losers" in the marketplace are the mainline denominations, especially the Congregationalists, Presbyterians, and Episcopalians, who have evolved a well-educated, seminary-trained clergy.

Although the number of atheists in the United States is less than 2 percent (Pew Research Center, 2008), and has remained consistently low over the past 20 years (Smith et al., 2010), a "nonreligious movement" has been on the rise in this country as well as in Europe, with organized groups working against the imposition of religion on "an unwilling public" (Jordan, 2007). The Atheist Alliance International, for example, doubled its membership in 2006 and split into U.S. and global organizations in 2010. *The God Delusion* (Dawkins, 2006) and *God Is Not Great* (Hitchens, 2007) both hit the best-seller list in 2007 (Salmon, 2007), and *The Believing Brain* (Shermer, 2011) attempted to explain belief. What effect these atheistic and scientific efforts will have on the religious marketplace is not yet known.

Islamic Fundamentalism

Christianity is not the only religion with a fundamentalist movement; fundamentalism is a feature of all religious traditions that change and evolve over time. Islam is no exception. A pivotal event in Islamic fundamentalism in the 20th century was the Iranian Revolution of 1979, in which the Ayatollah Khomeini, an Islamic religious leader, overthrew the Shah Mohammed Riza Pahlavi, replacing his monarchy with a theocratic regime rooted in Islamic traditions and anti-Western fervor.

In creating this revolution, religious leaders drew on the Iranian people's intense resentment of persistent Western dominance and the imposition by the shah of Western ways that many Iranians viewed as incompatible with Islam. Through this revolution, Islamic fundamentalism went beyond religion and became a vehicle for political and nationalistic expression. Islamic fundamentalists also challenged several secular-oriented governments in North Africa and the Middle East in a pattern that can be seen as a defensive measure against the intrusions of Western society (Miller, 1992). Islamic fundamentalism has proven itself to be less reactionary than reactive: Its leaders typically have used traditional Islamic principles and ideas to power their resistance against outside forces, modernity, relativism, pluralism, and compromisers within their tradition (Marty and Appleby, 1992).

However, it is important to stress that Islam and Muslims are not monolithic. Throughout the world, Muslims are religiously, politically, and culturally pluralistic (Esposito, 1992). Episodes of terrorism, such as the September 11, 2001, attacks that were conducted by fundamentalist Islamic political extremists, are representative neither of Islamic fundamentalism nor of Islam in general. In fact, such terrorist acts signal not the growing power of fundamentalist political Islam, but rather its failure to mobilize and retain power in the Muslim world (Kepel, 2002; Roy, 1998).

State–Church Issues

The First Amendment, with its "Congress shall make no law respecting an establishment of religion," provided the foundation for the principle of the separation of church and state, by which organized religion and government have remained substantially independent of each other in the United States. Compared with many other nations, the United States has maintained a remarkably hands-off attitude toward religion. Some sociologists believe that the absence of a coerced monopoly has compelled American religious institutions to operate in a pluralistic environment comparable to a market economy (Warner, 1993). Even so, in a number of cases, laws have been enacted, and upheld by the Supreme Court, that have impinged upon religious practices, including those against polygamy among Mormons and against snake-handling by charismatic Christians.

Civil Religion

Although most Americans deem an individual's religious beliefs and practices to be a strictly private matter, there are nonetheless certain common elements of religious orientation that most Americans share. These religious dimensions are expressed in a set of beliefs, symbols, and rituals that sociologist Robert Bellah (1970; Bellah and Hammond, 1980) called **civil religion.** Its basic tenet is that the American nation is not an ultimate end in itself but a nation under God with a divine mission. Civil religion provides a supernatural legitimacy for nationalism. Although religious pluralism prevents any one denomination from supplying all Americans with a single source of meaning, civil religion compensates by providing an over-arching sacred canopy.

Civil religion finds expression in the statements and documents of the Founding Fathers, schoolchildren's Pledge of Allegiance, national holidays, historic shrines, mottos, and patriotic expressions in times of crisis and peril. There are four references to God in the Declaration of Independence. Every president but one has mentioned God in his inaugural address. And the government engages in many religious practices, from the phrase "In God We Trust" on its currency to the prayers said in Congress. Significantly, both liberal and conservative political actors employ civil religion to interpret and legitimate their places and agendas within national life (Williams and Demerath, 1991).

Religion and Morality

Determining the place a religiously defined morality should hold in a pluralist society continues to generate controversy in the United States. Abortion provides a good illustration. Some insist that abortion is a private moral choice and that the state has no right to make the practice illegal. Others contend that abortion is no more a matter of

private moral choice than slavery was and that the state has an obligation to stop it. In a nation-wide survey, only 35 percent (or fewer, depending on the issue) of respondents believe that elected officials should base their votes on their religious beliefs, even on such issues as abortion, the death penalty, and gay rights (Farkas et al., 2000). Survey respondents favored a moment of silence over spoken prayers in the public schools and expressed respect for religious diversity. Jewish and nonreligious respondents were particularly wary about mixing politics and religion.

The Functionalist Perspective

Functionalist theorists look to the contributions religion makes to society's survival. They reason that if every known society seems to have something called religion, its presence cannot be dismissed as a social accident (Davis, 1951). Data from the World Values Survey (Inglehart et al., 2000) show that the percentage of people reporting that religion is "very important" in their lives varies widely, from nearly 100 percent in Indonesia to fewer than 5 percent in China—but it is not zero in any society (see Figure 11.2). Accordingly, functionalists ask what functions are performed by religion in social life.

Durkheim: Social Cohesion and Social Control

In *The Elementary Forms of Religious Life* (1912/1965), the last of his major works, Émile Durkheim showed how religion serves the functions of social cohesion and social control in a study of the Arunta, an Australian aboriginal people. The Arunta practice **totemism,** a religious system in which a clan (a kin group) takes the name of, claims descent from, and attributes sacred properties to a plant or animal. Durkheim said that the totem plant or animal is not the source of totemism but a stand-in for the real source, society itself. He contended that religion—the

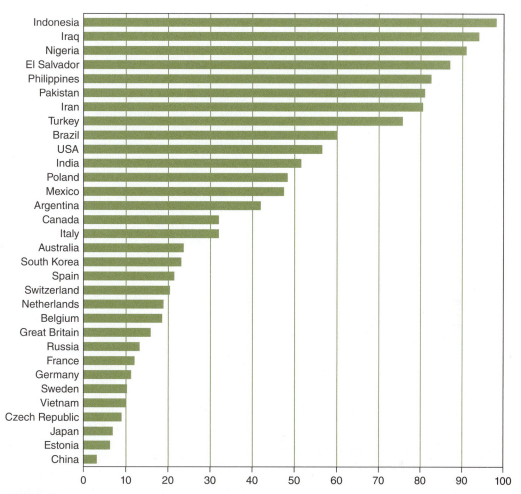

	Figure 11.2

Percentage Reporting That Religion Is "Very Important" in Their Lives

Source: Figure generated by the authors after analyzing data from selected countries surveyed in the World Values Surveys and the European Values Surveys, 1981–1984, 1990–1993, 1994–1997, and 1999–2004 (European Values Study Group and World Values Survey Association, 2006, *European and World Values Surveys Four-Wave Integrated Data File, 1981–2004, v. 20060423,* available at http://www.worldvaluessurvey.org/).

totem ancestor, God, or some other supernatural force—is the symbolization of society. By means of religious rituals, the group in effect worships itself. For functionalists the primary functions of religion are the creation, reinforcement, and maintenance of social solidarity and social control.

Religious rituals operate in two ways: (1) They provide vehicles by which we *reveal* to one another that we share a common mental state and (2) they *create* among us a shared consciousness that contributes to a social bonding.

Durkheim argued that the religious person is not the victim of an illusion. Behind the symbol—religion—lies a real force and reality: society, which, like religion, provides moral authority and inspires a sense of self-sacrifice, devotion, and even divinity (see the section "Civil Religion," on p. 358). Durkheim concluded that when religion is imperiled and not replaced by a satisfying substitute, society itself is jeopardized: Individuals pursue their private interests without regard to the dictates of the larger social enterprise.

Meaning and Uncertainty

Although science can tell us much about physical, chemical, and biological processes, it cannot inform us about the purpose of the universe and our place in it. It cannot tell us what the meaning of our lives is. While some people are satisfied with the notion that the universe and life have no ultimate purpose, and that our existence as beings ends with death, most people are not. One important function of religion is to provide answers to such questions. The answers that religion provides stress the supernatural and often link the individual to the supernatural through an intense emotional experience.

By focusing on questions of meaning and purpose, religion also helps people in dealing with life's uncertainties and tragedies: sudden deaths, disasters, epidemics, droughts, famines, wars, accidents, sickness, social disorder, guilt, personal defeat, humiliation, and injustice. Religion also often is involved in the transitional stages of life. Most religions celebrate and explain the major events of the life cycle—birth, puberty, marriage, and death—through *rites of passage* (ceremonies marking the transition from one status to another).

Functionalism and Social Change

Another function religion performs is as an impetus to social change (Warner, 1993). Social changes that are legitimated and justified in shared religious terms may be easier to accept and may proceed with less disruption than those that have a purely secular basis.

For example, African American churches historically have made a significant contribution to the mobilization of protest, as was evident in the civil rights movements of the 1950s and 1960s. African American churches provided the civil rights movement of the 1960s with an established mass base, a leadership structure that for the most part was economically independent of the white power structure, meeting places for the organization of protest activities, and a viable financial foundation. Currently, African American churches are a major force in the economic development and revitalization of inner-city neighborhoods. Similarly, the gay liberation movement has practiced the art of church-based mobilization. The Metropolitan Community Church in New York City was at the organizational center of the movement to legitimate gay culture in the United States.

The Conflict Perspective

From the writings of functionalist theorists, we gain a view of religion as a valuable and positive source promoting social integration and solidarity. We derive a quite different image from conflict theorists. Some of them depict religion as a weapon in the service of ruling elites who use it to hold in check the explosive tensions produced by social inequality and injustice. Others see religion as a source of social conflict and point to religious strife in the Middle East, India, and Northern Ireland. Still others, not so different from functionalists, see religion as a source of social change.

Marx: Religion as the Opium of the People

The stimulus for many of the contributions made by conflict theorists comes from the work of Karl Marx. Marx (1844/1960:43–44) portrayed religion as a painkiller for the frustration, deprivation, and subjugation experienced by oppressed peoples: "the opium of the people." He said that it soothes their distress but that any relief it may provide is illusory.

Marx saw religion as producing an otherworldly focus that diverts the oppressed from

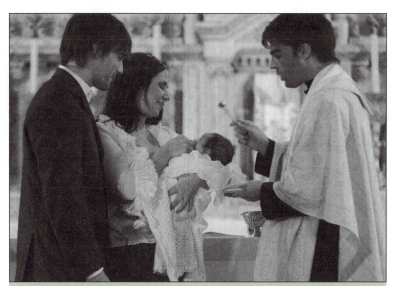

According to functionalism, religious rituals create among people a shared consciousness that contributes to a social bonding.

inequities, become defined as God-approved ways and highly resistant to change.

For example, American slavery was justified as part of God's "natural order." In 1863 the Presbyterian Church of the South met in General Synod and passed a resolution declaring slavery to be a divine institution ordained by God. In 1954 segregation was justified on similar grounds, when Louisiana State Senator W. M. Rainach said, "Segregation is a natural order— created by God, in His wisdom, who made black men black and white men white" (*Southern School News,* 1954:3). Likewise, the Hindu religion threatens believers who fail to obey caste rules with reincarnation (rebirth) at a lower caste level or as an animal. Imperialism has often been supported by religious or quasi-religious motivations and beliefs. In the 1890s, President William McKinley justified his decision to wage the expansionist war against Spain and seize Cuba and the Philippines as a way of "Christianizing" and civilizing these people (McGuire, 1981:188).

Religious organizations themselves are frequently motivated to legitimate the status quo because they also have vested interests to protect, including power, land, and wealth (Collins, 1981).

seeking social change in this world. More particularly, religion engenders a false consciousness among the working class that interferes with its attainment of true class consciousness. The focus on the supernatural and the afterlife also alienates people from themselves by directing their attention away from the material conditions of their own existence and their potential for controlling their own lives. This process of alienation is one of the primary mechanisms enabling the ruling class to dominate the working class and to exploit them for their labor power (Marx, 1844/1960:122).

Maintaining the Status Quo

Conflict theorists see an inherently conservative aspect to religion. The sense of the sacred links a person's present experience with meanings derived from the group's traditional past. Religious beliefs and practices provide taken-for-granted truths that are powerful forces militating against new ways of thinking and behaving. Practices handed down from previous generations, including institutional inequalities and

Conflict Theory and Social Change

Some conflict theorists see religion as an active force shaping the contours of social life. Thus, it can play a critical part in the birth and consolidation of new social structures and arrangements. While acknowledging that some aspects of religion inhibit change, like the functionalists, they point out that others challenge existing social arrangements and encourage change (Billings,

1990). Under some circumstances religion can be a profoundly revolutionary force that holds out a vision to people of how things might or ought to be. Religion is not invariably a functional or conservative factor in society, but often is one of the chief channels, and at times the only channel, for bringing about social revolution.

Throughout history religion has provided an unusually effective vehicle for change because of its ability to unite people and their social lives. American history has been no exception. The religious movements associated with the Great Awakening in the late 18th and early 19th centuries were an important impetus to the abolitionist movement and later to the temperance and prohibition movements. They also had an impact on the democratization of the U.S. political system, promoting popular participation in what was largely an oligarchy of the economically privileged.

Education

Social scientists view **learning** as a relatively permanent change in behavior or capability that results from experience. Because learning is so vital to social life, societies seldom leave it to chance. Most societies undertake to transmit particular attitudes, knowledge, and skills to their members through formal, systematic training—what sociologists call the institution of **education.**

Education is one aspect of the process of socialization by which people acquire behaviors essential for effective participation in society (see Chapter 3). It entails an explicit process in which some individuals assume the status of teacher and others the status of student and carry out their associated roles.

Schools initially came into existence several thousand years ago to prepare a select few for a limited number of leadership and professional positions. In the United States, as recently as 150 years ago, many children were not educated at a school; 90 percent of the population worked on farms, and about 1 in 10 children

attended school (Schneider and Keesler, 2007). As recently as the 1930s, fewer than half the students who attended school in fifth grade actually graduated from high school. Today the United States has a compulsory education system, with nearly all children ages 5–17 in school for much of every weekday. The curricula of schools—such "core" subjects as mathematics, natural science, and social science—are remarkably similar throughout the world. Exactly how government interacts with education, however, differs cross-culturally.

In this section we will examine the bureaucratic structure of schools, sociological perspectives on education, the effectiveness of schools in the United States and elsewhere around the world, alternatives to traditional public education, and the availability of higher education.

The Bureaucratic Structure of Schools

Like hospitals, factories, and businesses, schools have grown larger and more complex, very different from the one-room schoolhouses of 100 years ago. They have had to standardize and routinize many of their operations and establish formal operating and administrative procedures. In brief, they are bureaucracies—social structures made up of a hierarchy of statuses and roles prescribed by explicit rules and procedures and based on a division of function and authority (see Chapter 4, pp. 112–114).

At the very top of this organizational arrangement is the federal government, which profoundly influences educational life through the Department of Education, the federal court system, and other agencies. The No Child Left Behind (NCLB) Act of 2001 greatly expanded the role of the federal government in public education, holding states and schools accountable for math and reading standards (Schneider and Keesler, 2007). Under the Obama administration, many states proposed statewide educational reforms and plans to close achievement gaps in return for greater NCLB flexibility, transferring oversight of education from the federal government to state governments (U.S. Department of Education, 2012).

The formal organization of American schools and colleges typically consists of four levels: (1) the board of education or trustees, (2) administrators, (3) teachers or professors, and (4) students. The control of most schools and colleges is vested in an elected or appointed *board* of laypeople. The board generally appoints and assigns administrators and teachers, decides on the nature of educational programs, determines building construction, and approves operational budgets. The *administrators*—superintendents, principals, presidents, chancellors, and deans—are responsible for executing the policies of the board. Although in theory the board determines policy, in practice many policy questions are settled by administrators. *Teachers* are the immediate day-to-day link between the larger system and individual *students,* the latter occupying the lowest position in the school bureaucracy. In sum, the school system is characterized by a chain of command, a network of positions functionally interrelated for the purpose of accomplishing educational objectives.

By virtue of bureaucratic arrangements, most school environments are remarkably standardized in both their physical and social characteristics. Time is usually highly formalized, with the school day broken into discrete periods for various topics and activities. The physical layout of the school and the omnipresent symbols of adult authority emphasize and reinforce the subordinate status of the pupils.

The Functionalist Perspective

Why do we have schools? Viewed from the functionalist perspective, schools make a number of vital contributions to the survival and perpetuation of modern societies. Functionalists see schools as serving to complete socialization, socially integrate a diverse population, screen and select individuals, and develop new knowledge. In this section we will look at each of these functions in more detail.

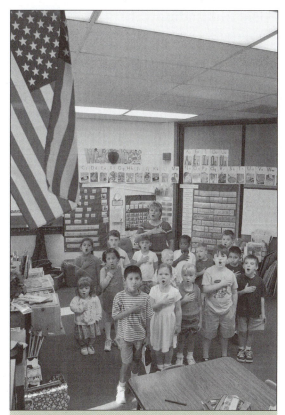

Functionalists say that one of the functions of public education is social integration. In performing this function, schools promote dominant values and try to shape a common national consciousness.

Completing Socialization

Many preliterate and peasant societies lack schools. They socialize their youngsters in the same "natural" way that parents teach their children to walk or talk. According to functionalists, the knowledge and skills required by contemporary living cannot be satisfied in a more or less automatic and "natural" way. Instead, a specialized educational agency is needed to transmit to young people the ways of thinking, feeling, and acting mandated by a rapidly changing urban and technologically based society.

Social Integration

Functionalists say that the education system functions to inculcate the dominant values of a society and shape a common national mind. Within the United States students learn what it means to be an American, become literate in the English language, gain a common heritage, and acquire mainstream standards and rules. Youngsters from diverse ethnic, religious, and racial backgrounds are immersed within the same Anglo-American culture and prepared for responsible citizenship (see Chapter 7). Historically, the nation's schools have played a prominent part in Americanizing the children of immigrants (Dunn, 1993); now, by including diversity as a part of the curriculum, many schools are also emphasizing the multicultural nature of the United States. Likewise, schools are geared to integrating the poor and disadvantaged into the fabric of dominant, mainstream institutions. How well the educational institution performs these functions will be discussed later in the chapter.

Screening and Selecting

We noted in Chapter 2 (p. 55) that all societies ascribe some statuses to individuals independent of their unique qualities or abilities. Other statuses are achieved through choice and competition. No society entirely ignores individual differences or overlooks individual accomplishment and failure. Modern societies in particular must select certain of their youths for positions that require special talents. The educational institution commonly performs this function, serving as an agency for screening and selecting individuals for different types of jobs. By conferring degrees, diplomas, and credentials that are prerequisites for many technical, managerial, and professional positions, it determines which young people will have access to scarce positions and offices of power, privilege, and status. For many members of modern society, the schools function as "mobility escalators," allowing able, gifted individuals to ascend the social ladder (Krymkowski, 1991).

Research and Development

For the most part, schools are designed to produce people who fit into society, not people who set out to change it. However, schools, particularly universities, may not only transmit culture but also add to the cultural heritage by developing new knowledge, especially in the physical and biological sciences, medicine, and engineering, and by producing literature, art, music, and theater. In recent decades the nation's leading universities have increasingly become research centers. This emphasis on research has led universities to judge professors not primarily in terms of their competence as teachers but as researchers with a primary function of the university being viewed as research.

A survey of tenure-track faculty members at four-year institutions revealed that the more hours an instructor spends in class per week, the lower the pay; faculty who teach only graduate students get paid the most; and the more time faculty members spend on research, the higher the compensation (Jacobson, 1992). Functionalism sees the university combining the functions of research and education. Even when students are not themselves involved in research projects, they benefit from the intellectual stimulation a research orientation brings to university life.

The Conflict Perspective

Conflict theorists see schools as agencies that reproduce and legitimate the current social order through the functions they perform. By reproducing and legitimating the existing social order, the educational institution is seen as benefiting some individuals and groups at the expense of others (Collins, 1977, 1979, 1988b). Let's take a closer look at how conflict theorists think this occurs.

Reproducing the Social Relations of Production

Some conflict theorists depict U.S. schools as reflecting the needs of capitalist production and as social instruments for convincing the population that private ownership and profit are just and in the best interests of the entire society (Apple, 1982). The **correspondence principle** states that the social relations of work find expression in the social relations of the school (Bowles and Gintis, 1976). Schools mirror the workplace and hence on a day-to-day basis prepare children for adult roles in the job market. The authoritarian structure of many schools reproduces the bureaucratic hierarchy of the corporation, rewarding diligence, submissiveness, and compliance. The system of grades employed to motivate students parallels the wage system for motivating workers. In short, the schools are seen as socializing a compliant labor force for the capitalist economy.

Control Devices

Conflict theorists agree with functionalist theorists that schools are agencies for drawing minorities and the disadvantaged into the dominant culture. But they do not see the function in benign terms. Sociologist Randall Collins (1976) contended that the educational system serves the interests of the dominant group by defusing the threat posed by minority ethnic groups. In large, multiethnic societies like the United States, the schools become instruments to "Americanize" minority people. Compulsory education erodes ethnic differences and loyalties and transmits to minorities and those at the bottom of the social hierarchy the values and lifeways of the dominant group. Schools, then, are viewed by conflict theorists as control devices employed by established elites.

Productive Capital

Conflict theorists see the research and development function of the universities quite differently than functionalist theorists do. For example,

Michael W. Apple (1982) provided a Marxist twist to the functionalist argument by contending that the educational institution produces the technical and administrative knowledge necessary for running a capitalist order. Viewed in this manner, education is part of the system of production. It not only reproduces existing social arrangements but also develops the know-how needed by capitalists to fuel the economy and gain competitive advantage in world markets (Barrow, 1990).

Credentialism

Collins (1979) also downplayed the functionalist argument that schools serve as mobility escalators. He cited evidence that students acquire little technical knowledge in school and that most technical skills are learned on the job. Although more education is needed to obtain most jobs, Collins said that this development is not explained by the technical requirements of the job. The level of skills required by receptionists, salesclerks, teachers, assembly-line workers, and many others is not much different than it was a generation or so ago. Collins called these tendencies **credentialism**—the requirement that a worker have a degree for its own sake, not because it certifies skills needed for the performance of a job.

Because education functions as a certification of class membership more than of technical skills, it functions as a means of class inheritance. For example, Scholastic Aptitude Test (SAT) scores play a particularly important role in determining acceptance or rejection by the nation's elite colleges and universities; approximately 84 percent of all U.S. four-year colleges use the SAT for admissions purposes. SAT scores also are highly correlated with family income and parents' education, and vary with race and ethnicity (see Figure 11.3). Students from advantaged backgrounds are the most likely to obtain college degrees and further education, thus reproducing class structure and inequalities.

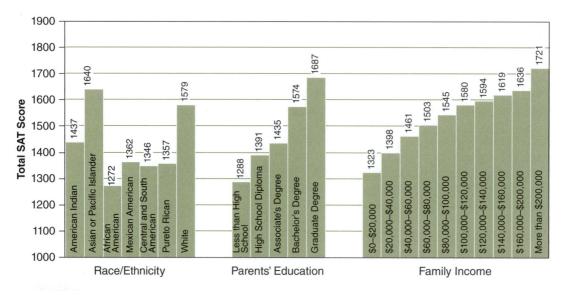

Figure 11.3 **Average Total SAT Scores of College-Bound Seniors by Race/ Ethnicity, Parents' Education, and Family Income, 2011**

Total SAT scores, the sum of scores for the critical reading, mathematical reasoning, and writing tests, vary considerably by socioeconomic status and race/ethnicity, both reflecting and perpetuating racial, ethnic, and class disadvantages. Scores for the individual tests range from 200 to 800 points and follow the same patterns across the categories in this figure, except that Asian/Pacific Islanders score slightly below whites on the critical reading test.

Source: Figure generated by the authors using data on the critical reading, mathematics reasoning, and writing tests taken by college bound seniors. The numbers in this figure are the total scores obtained by summing the average scores on the three tests. The data were provided by the College Entrance Examination Board and are available at http://professionals.collegeboard.com/ profdownload/cbs2011_total_group_report.pdf.

The Interactionist Perspective

Classrooms can be seen as self-contained worlds teeming with behavior. Symbolic interactionists undertake to capture these little worlds in their work. These sociologists do not view the school as a "black box" in which something goes in and something comes out. Instead, they are interested in the processes occurring in schools. We will look at some of those processes in this section.

Communication

Communication is the heart of classroom life. Philip W. Jackson (1968) estimated from his observations in several elementary classrooms that teachers average over 200 interpersonal exchanges every hour of the school day, much of it one-way. A more recent assessment of public school classrooms showed that fifth-grade children spend 91 percent of their time in the classroom either being addressed as a group or doing individual seatwork (Pianta et al., 2007). Fifth-grade teachers spend 17 percent of classroom time telling students how to manage materials or time and give students generic feedback rather than discussing alternative solutions to problems or encouraging students to go further in their thinking and work. The research, which included 2,500 classrooms in 1,000 elementary schools, concluded that "few opportunities were provided to learn in small groups, to improve analytical skills, or to interact extensively with teachers" (Pianta et al., 2007:1796).

Social Inequality

Classroom research also gives us insights into social inequality (Mehan, 1992). Many data suggest, for instance, that schools perform relatively well with upper- and middle-class youngsters. We would expect this to be the case, for the schools are staffed by middle-class teachers, the school's structure is modeled after middle-class life, and better school facilities are provided for these youngsters. In *Urban Schools, Public Will: Making Schools Work for All Children,* Norm Fruchter (2007) asserts that U.S. schools are more segregated today than they were in 1954 when the Supreme Court ruled against racial segregation. Fruchter claims that children of color in the United States have been doomed to "inadequate education and limited futures."

Because of historical patterns of racism, black children are currently more likely than white children to go to schools in high-poverty neighborhoods that are racially segregated. Research shows that the educational environment in such schools is poor, and that poverty worsens the educational environment more for black children than for white children (Logan, 2011).

Interactionists and conflict theorists are also interested in what they call the **hidden curriculum,** which consists of a complex of unarticulated values, attitudes, and behaviors that subtly mold children in the image preferred by the dominant institutions. Teachers model and reinforce traits that embody middle-class standards—industry, responsibility, conscientiousness, reliability, thoroughness, self-control, and efficiency. The hidden curriculum is at work when children learn to be quiet, to be on time, to line up, to wait their turn, to please their teachers, and to conform to group pressures. In addition, many students learn the unarticulated lesson that they are not capable of learning without school and teachers. Educator and writer John Holt (1969) described the effects of public education this way:

Almost every child, on the first day he sets foot in a school building, is smarter, more curious, less afraid of what he doesn't know, better at finding and figuring things out, more confident, resourceful, persistent and independent than he will ever be again in his schooling—or, unless he is very unusual and very lucky, for the rest of his life.

Holt pointed out that nearly all children, using only the feedback of the people around them and no formal schooling at all, accomplish a very complex task—learning to use language. He argued that children are equally up to the task of learning many other things, given appropriate resources, before schools "train them" differently.

Self-Fulfilling Prophecies

Educational self-fulfilling prophecies, or *teacher-expectation effects,* can victimize inner-city, minority, and immigrant children, as well as others. The children fail to learn because those who are charged with teaching them do not believe that they will learn, do not expect that they can learn, and do not act toward them in ways that help them to learn (Clark, 1965). Tracking students into groups can feed into teacher-expectation effects. If a group is labeled low achieving, teachers are likely to approach it differently. Among inner-city and minority children, negative teacher-expectation effects breed student alienation and school failure, encourage oppositional forms of behavior designed to undermine the school's control strategies, and foster attitudes that lead to the mocking, taunting, and ostracism of children who do their homework and strive toward academic excellence (Solomon, 1992).

The Effectiveness of Schools

Are U.S. schools effective? That depends on whom you ask and what you think schools ought to be doing; as you learned in the section on sociological perspectives, there is a wide variety of ideas about what schools do.

Let's start with academics. If you think that schools should be preparing citizens who will help our country compete globally in science and research, the answer is mixed. The National Academies of Science have reported that the United States is falling behind in scientific leadership, with "dwindling educational performance" contributing to fewer people completing Ph.D.s in science (Service, 2007). What about other sorts of leadership? A National Endowment for the Arts (NEA) study reported that 15- to 24-year-olds voluntarily read for an average of 7–10 minutes per day (Thompson, 2007). The report also noted that 38 percent of employers rate high school graduates as deficient in reading and 72 percent rate them as deficient in writing.

How does the United States compare academically with other countries? In a 48-country comparison, the standardized exam math scores for U.S. eighth-graders were higher than scores in 37 countries, about the same as those in 5 other countries, and lower than the scores in 5 countries, all of them in Asia (Gonzales et al., 2009). U.S. students in both fourth and eighth grade had higher math test scores in 2007 than students had had in 1995. In science, U.S. eighth-graders scored higher than students 35 countries, about the same as students in 3 countries, and lower than students in 9 countries. Science scores for fourth- and eighth-graders did not measurably improve between 1995 and 2007 in the United States. A closer look at the data shows that the countries that score ahead of the United States do not do so only because their brightest students outperform ours; their lower-achieving students also outperform our lower-achieving students. There are other measures of student growth and progress, and some educators and lawmakers want more attention paid to graduation rates and college attendance and to science, history, art, physical education, and problem solving (Betts and Atkinson, 2012; Glod, 2007).

What does the American public think about U.S. schools? More than half of U.S. survey respondents give public schools in general a grade of C, with only 22 percent awarding an A or B and 24 percent giving public schools a D or F grade (Howell, West, and Peterson, 2007). When you ask Americans about the public schools in their own communities, though, they are much more positive: 43 percent assign a grade of A or B, 38 percent a C, and 18 percent a D or F. Survey respondents say that the biggest problems facing public schools are lack of financial support (36 percent of respondents), lack of discipline (6 percent), overcrowding (6 percent), use of drugs (2 percent), and fighting or violence in schools (3 percent) (Maguire, 2010).

Functionalists see schools as performing the function of integrating those from disadvantaged backgrounds into mainstream institutions; conflict theorists cast schools as reproducing social inequalities. The reality of public education in the United States today tends to support conflict theory on this dimension. Many of the nation's schools are primarily black, primarily white, or primarily Hispanic, and nationwide testing shows that the achievement gap between advantaged whites and disadvantaged minority group students has not closed (Schneider and Keesler, 2007). High school graduation rates are currently highest for Asian Americans (88.7 percent), followed closely by whites (87.1 percent) and blacks (83 percent) but more distantly by Hispanics (62.3 percent). The disparities are much greater at the college level, with 52.4 percent of Asian Americans finishing college but only 33.3 percent of whites, 19.8 percent of blacks, and 13.9 percent of Hispanics (U.S. Census Bureau, 2011b). Gender inequalities have reversed, with women now earning more high school diplomas (Bergman, 2003), more bachelor's, master's, and doctoral degrees, and about the same number of medical and law degrees (Snyder, Dillow, and Hoffman, 2009). Researchers also have shown that as more girls began taking upper-level math classes the gender differences in math scores also have largely disappeared; a recent study of second- through eleventh-grade public school students found no gender differences in math skills (Hyde et al., 2008), but math SAT scores continue to show a gender difference (see Figure 11.4). Research shows that boys are leaving high school with worse reading skills than girls (Grimes, 2006). Judith Kleinfeld's study showed that 23 percent of high school seniors who are the sons of white, college-educated parents score "below basic" on national standardized reading tests (Grimes, 2006). Speaking at a White House conference, Kleinfeld said that boys are more likely than girls to be disengaged from school and that they are less likely to do homework or even come to school with the appropriate supplies.

Of course, the effectiveness of schools and academic achievement of students depends not only on what happens in schools but also on the structural inequities we discussed in Chapters 6, 7, and 8, and on the larger social and cultural environments of the students, including their families and communities, and the environment in which the school is located. Research shows that the effect of socioeconomic status (SES) on mental ability, for example, is already detectable by age 2, and the effect of low SES is so strong that it depresses any effect genetic variability might have (Tucker-Drob et al., 2011).

What would make schools more effective? Studies have shown that emotional and instructional support in elementary classrooms contributes to eliminating the racial/ethnic achievement gap and predicts both reading and math achievement growth and social functioning (Pianta et al., 2007). But in a measure of emotional atmosphere and instructional atmosphere in 2,500 classrooms, researchers found that only 17 percent of children were in classrooms with a consistently positive emotional climate and only

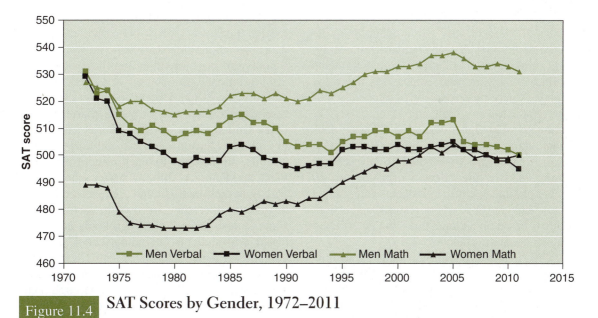

Figure 11.4 **SAT Scores by Gender, 1972–2011**

Source: Figure generated by the authors using data on the critical reading (verbal) and mathematics reasoning tests taken by college-bound seniors. The data were provided by the College Entrance Examination Board and are available at http://professionals.collegeboard.com/profdownload/cbs2011_total_group_report.pdf.

14 percent consistently experienced a positive instructional atmosphere. Pianta and his colleagues found that teachers with fewer years of experience, higher salaries, and more input into school policy and efficacy were more likely to have classrooms with high instructional quality. Most of the fifth-grade classrooms that they observed devoted most instructional time to basic reading and math skills and very little to problem solving or reasoning or to content areas besides math and reading.

A study of charter schools found that factors that often are measured—class size, expenditure per pupil, and whether teachers are certified or have advanced degrees—were not correlated with the effectiveness of schools (Dobbie and Fryer, 2011). What did seem to improve school success was a combination of high expectations, more instructional time, lots of tutoring and teacher feedback, and the use of data to guide instruction.

Finnish schools attracted attention in 2011 when they were found to have the world's smallest difference between their weakest and strongest students (Hancock, 2011). The country spends 30 percent less per student than the United States does, has no standardized testing, starts children in school at age 7, gives students minimal homework, and emphasizes the value of play. Ninety-three percent of Finland's students graduate from high school, and sixty-six percent go on to higher education. To what does Finland attribute its success? Among many factors, resources are distributed to all schools equally, teachers are selected from the top 10 percent of Finnish college graduates and granted doctor- and lawyer-levels of respect, and school policy is based on national goals but determined by town councils (Hancock, 2011).

The American public has ideas about how to improve U.S. education (Howell, West, and Peterson, 2007). Just over half of Americans think that government funding for the public schools in their districts should be increased or greatly increased. Nearly half don't think teacher certification is all that important. Almost

70 percent think teachers should receive a salary increase, and 53 percent think that teachers in challenging schools should receive a larger pay increase. There is strong support for stronger standards, with 85 percent somewhat or completely supporting a requirement that students pass an exam in order to receive a high school diploma. Americans also support more choice: 85 percent think that low-income students should be able to use vouchers to attend religious or nonreligious private schools.

Alternatives to Traditional Public Schools

In a movement some predict will transform education in the United States, parents are increasingly choosing to educate their children in ways other than enrolling them in traditional public schools. The number of students attending charter schools and private schools or being educated at home has increased significantly in recent years.

The number of charter schools, which receive taxpayer money but make their own decisions about how to teach, grew to 5,600 schools serving more than 2 million students in 2011 (National Association of Charter School Authorizers, 2012). Except for those on Indian reservations, there was only one charter school in the United States in 1992. Charter schools do not charge tuition and, as publicly funded schools, are not free to teach religion (Howell, West, and Peterson, 2007). Charter schools vary widely in their instructional approach and in the degree to which they are used in each state; in some states, "cyber" charter schools are being tested, with students "attending school" over the computer (Fletcher, 2002).

Private schools educate even more students: 11.4 percent of all kindergarten through 12th graders were enrolled in private schools in 2007 (National Center for Education Statistics, 2012). In Wisconsin, Ohio, and Washington, DC, publicly funded voucher programs enable low-income children to attend private schools (Howell, West, and Peterson, 2007). Other states have voucher programs for disabled children. Tax credit programs that help pay for a private school education are available in Pennsylvania, Arizona, Minnesota, Illinois, and Florida.

About 2.9 percent of the nation's children are taught at home (National Center for Education Statistics, 2012). Home schooling is legal in every state. Although it is difficult to compare achievement among home-schooled and other students, research indicates that home-schooled children do well on standardized tests (Byfield, 2001). Studies also show that home-schooled children do not suffer disadvantages in self-esteem, leadership, or other dimensions of personal development (Medlin, 2000).

Public, private, and home-schooled students may enroll in online distance education courses, taking high school advanced placement, foreign language, science, and many other classes unavailable at their schools (National Center for Education Statistics, 2012). Many college students also take classes online, and a number of universities have made many of their courses available online, to the public, for free. Massachusetts Institute of Technology's open courseware (http:/ocw.mit.edu) is an example, providing free lecture notes, exams, lecture videos, and more to anyone with Internet access.

The Availability of Higher Education

Despite our cherished picture of the United States as a place where education is available to all, college and university student populations are highly skewed in terms of race, ethnicity, and family income. Only 20 percent of the nation's undergraduates are young people ages 18–22 who are pursuing a parent-financed education. Two-fifths of all students are part-timers, and more than one-third of all undergraduates are over age 25.

The likelihood that African Americans and Hispanics receive a college education has increased over the past 40 years, but sharp disparities with whites and now Asian Americans remain (U.S. Census Bureau, 2011b). Many factors make it difficult for minority youths to gain entrance to and then remain in college. First, many of the students have weaker academic preparation in elementary and secondary schools than white students. Second, most campuses lack a "critical mass" of minority students and faculty who can serve as role models and make new students feel at home. Third, many minority students are first-generation collegians, and they do not secure the emotional or financial support from home that second- and third-generation collegians receive (Johnson, 1988).

An analysis of the admissions policies of America's top colleges and universities showed that the preference given to white students from wealthy families dwarfs any benefit minority students might get from affirmative action (Golden, 2006). *Wall Street Journal* reporter Daniel Golden found that elite private colleges give preference to the children of both alumni and faculty, wealthy applicants whose families have been identified by the college as potential donors, and participants in upper-class sports such as rowing and horseback riding. A 2006 study found that 3 percent of the freshmen at top colleges come from the bottom socioeconomic quartile, while 74 percent come from the top quartile (Karabel, 2006).

The cost of a college education plays an important role in selecting who will receive a degree. In recent years the cost of higher education has outpaced the growth in family income and available financial aid and is nearly triple the rate of inflation. Families with a child in a private college were found to spend a third of their income on college costs, up from a quarter in the early 1990s, and families with a child attending a public university spend about a fifth of their income on college (Whitson, 2006). Early-admissions programs are thought to work to the disadvantage of low-income applicants (Mathews, 2003). And although half of all students receive some kind of financial assistance,

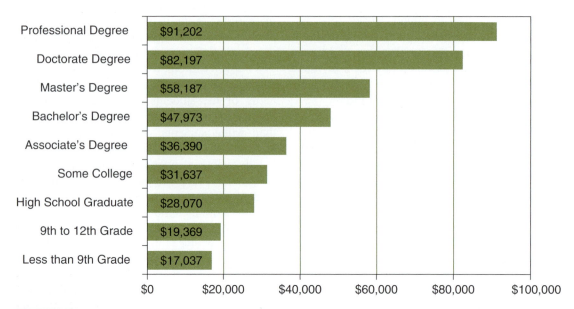

Professional Degree	$91,202
Doctorate Degree	$82,197
Master's Degree	$58,187
Bachelor's Degree	$47,973
Associate's Degree	$36,390
Some College	$31,637
High School Graduate	$28,070
9th to 12th Grade	$19,369
Less than 9th Grade	$17,037

$0 $20,000 $40,000 $60,000 $80,000 $100,000

Figure 11.5 **The Financial Value of a Postsecondary Education: Median Earnings by Education, 2010**

Average income increases with greater education.

Source: Figure generated by the authors with data from U.S. Census Bureau, Current Population Survey, 2011 Annual Social and Economic Supplement.

one study showed that white students received a larger dollar amount of aid per student (Bruno, 1996). At one time a college degree brought an elite occupational status with elite pay; today it brings a middle-class status with middle-class pay. Even so, a degree after high school affords financial benefits (see Figure 11.5).

Medicine

Like the educational institution, the functions now carried out by the medical institution were once embedded in the activities of the family and religious institutions. Only in relatively recent times has **medicine** emerged as a distinct institution, providing an enduring set of cultural patterns and social relationships responsible for problems of health and disease. The World Health Organization defines **health** as "a state of complete physical, mental, and social well-being and not merely the absence of disease or infirmity." We usually assess

people's health in terms of how well they are able to function in their daily lives and adapt to a changing environment. Health, then, has different meanings for different people. In contrast to health, most of us think of disease as an undesirable, serious, and limiting circumstance. **Disease** is a condition in which an organism does not function properly because of biological causes. The problems may result from microbial infection, dietary deficiency, heredity, or a harmful environmental agent.

In this section we will look at the American health care delivery system, consider health care costs and managed care, and compare the U.S. system with health care in other countries. Then we will see what the sociological perspectives contribute to our thinking about medicine.

Health Care in the United States

Many societies have evolved one or more "specialist" positions to deal with sickness (Weiss and Lonnquist, 2012). Curers, shamans, physicians, nurses, and other practitioners are relied upon to explain illness and to offer means for eliminating or controlling it. Drugs, poultices, surgery, bone-setting, confinement, acupuncture, electric shock, leeching, talking, ritual, magic, and appeal to the supernatural are techniques used by medical practitioners in one or more societies. Additionally, medical practitioners serve as gatekeepers who legitimately channel people into the sick role. And in modern societies physicians certify that people have been born, have died, are fit to work, are eligible for disability benefits, are entitled to accident claims, and are a danger to themselves or society.

How does the United States deal with sickness? In this section we will examine the health care system in the United States, including a discussion of hospitals, physicians, and nurses, and an overview of health care delivery.

A Disease-Cure System

Many health care analysts argue that the United States does not have a "health care system" but has a "disease-cure system" (Sommer, 2009; Weil, 2009; Konner, 1993). The public believes, and many physicians behave as if, most illnesses are curable. Americans typically view the body as if it were a machine with replaceable parts: Defects can be identified, removed, and replaced through medical treatment, be it by means of drugs, surgery, organ transplants, or gene therapy.

The expectation of cure in the U.S. health care system has generated an explosion of invasive, expensive, and often risky medical interventions. Analysts argue that many widely accepted treatments are unnecessary and ineffective, and many treatments are aimed at problems that patients could prevent (Sommer, 2009; Weil, 2009; Brownlee, 2007).

For example, most clinicians and researchers in the field of coronary artery disease concentrate on ways to clear out fatty plaque buildups in arteries or to replace clogged arteries surgically, techniques that do not cure the disease, work less often than we wish, are performed at great risk to patients, and cost a colossal amount of money.

Evidence suggests that heart disease can be prevented and reversed by changes in behavior: eating a diet low in saturated fat and cholesterol, avoiding smoking, and getting moderate exercise. Similarly, more than a third of cancer deaths worldwide could be prevented if people changed their behaviors (Danaei et al., 2005), and changes in tobacco use could prevent a billion deaths in the 21st century (Brandt, 2007). But behavior changes are not the focus of the disease-cure health care system in the United States.

Components of the System

Hospitals Separate facilities for the ill came into existence among the ancient Greeks. But not until the Middle Ages in western Europe did the hospital movement begin in earnest. By 1450 there were some 600 hospitals in England alone. Most hospitals were run by Catholic religious orders because healing and health care were deemed to be the province of religion. The hospitals also cared for the poor, the disabled, and the itinerant. The linking of medical and social functions had grave health consequences; travelers housed with sick people in one hospital would then carry germs to the next hospital. Toward the end of the 17th century and during the 18th century, financial abuses and the mismanagement of funds by some religious orders led local governments to take on greater responsibility for the management of hospitals. About the same time, care of the indigent was physically segregated in facilities separate from the ill (Rosen, 1963).

By the late 19th century, advances in medical research, especially bacteriology, provided a stronger scientific basis for the treatment and control of infection. New diagnostic tools and advances in surgery made diseases, injuries, and deformities more amenable to medical interventions. By the turn of the century, charity hospitals had begun to attract doctors who cared for well-to-do patients at home. Control was ceded to private physicians, who were more concerned with treating paying patients than administering charitable care. Hospitals became businesses governed by commercial incentives. As insurance developed first for hospital bills and later for physicians' bills, the hospital industry and the medical profession flourished. By 1965 Congress had established Medicare to pay some of the health care costs of the elderly and Medicaid for those of the "deserving" poor. By the mid-1960s, then, hospitals, physicians, private insurers, and the government had devised a system for financing health care that was ripe for big business and the emergence of for-profit hospital chains (Gray, 1991; Lindorff, 1992).

Physicians Sociologist Paul Starr (1982) traced the rise of the private medical practice and the transformation of health care from a household service to a market commodity. He showed that well into the 19th century most U.S. doctors eked out scant livings. Following the Civil War, however, a contracting household economy, a growing urban population, and more efficient transportation and communication expanded the market for medical services. By the turn of the 20th century, doctors were well on the road to endowing their profession with a "cultural authority" sufficient to justify claims to self-regulation, state protection, client deference, and control of the means of work. In turn, doctors capitalized on these gains to develop medical specialties and mutual networks that decreased competition and increased their economic and political power.

By the 1930s, private practitioners had acquired sufficient influence and prestige to establish themselves as virtually the sole arbiters of medicine in the United States. They dominated hospitals, medical technology, and other health practitioners, including nurses and pharmacists. Physicians have become highly specialized, with hospitalists managing and coordinating the team of specialists involved in a hospital patient's care (Baker, 2007). They have institutionalized their authority through a system of medical education and standardized educational licensing. (See Box 6.3 for more about how doctors took over medical care in the United States.)

Interaction between a physician and patient traditionally has been governed by inequality. Like other professionals, doctors derive their power from their command of an esoteric body of knowledge acquired through academic training and leavened by a service orientation toward the client. The "competence gap" justified both the physician's assumption of authority and the client's trust, confidence, and compliance.

More recently, a relationship based on consumerism has emerged between many physicians and their patients, and physicians' authority has been undermined by managed care (Cockerham, 2012). This relationship focuses on the purchaser's (the patient's) rights and the seller's (the physician's) obligations. But a study of encounters between patients and doctors found that it is doctors who manage the direction of the discussion, even though it is patients who have questions to be answered (Roberts, 2000).

Dissatisfaction with care provided by physicians, as well as other factors, has fostered the growth of alternative therapies, including chiropractic, acupuncture, biofeedback, homeopathic medicine, herbalism, and reflexology. Research indicates that more than 40 percent of the population consults alternative healers (Eisenberg et al., 1998).

Nurses The nursing profession grew out of the religious and charitable activities of early hospitals. Religious orders of nuns took on the care of the sick and the poor. By the latter half of the 19th century, however, increasing numbers of nonreligious personnel were being employed to perform various custodial functions in hospitals. Since the jobs required no formal training and were deemed to be menial labor, many poor and uneducated women entered the field. This heritage has contributed to the undeservedly low prestige that the profession of nursing has long endured (Baer, 1991). Wages in nursing, like those in other fields with a large concentration of women, remain low even today, despite the fact that most nurses now earn a bachelor of science degree in nursing in a four-year college degree program, and many go on to secure master's degrees in specialized areas.

Through the years the profession of nursing has remained almost exclusively female. About 60 percent of all registered nurses work in hospitals, where they serve simultaneously as managers of hospital wards and assistants to physicians. These dual functions often place nurses in situations of role conflict because they are responsible to both administrative and medical authorities (see Chapter 2, p. 58). Nurses have been steadily acquiring more autonomy in health care. At the same time, their workloads have increased so much that many say they cannot give patients the quality of care they need (Gordon, 1997; Trafford, 2001).

Organization of Health Care Delivery

From a virtual cottage industry dominated by individual physicians and not-for-profit hospitals, health care has evolved into a network of corporations running everything from hospitals and home health care services to retirement homes and health spas. The United States is the only Western industrialized nation that does not guarantee basic health care services to all its citizens (Sommer, 2009), yet its spending on health care is enormous. In 2009, health care expenditures accounted for 17.6 percent of the nation's gross domestic product (GDP) compared to about half that in Norway and Australia, nations that provide universal coverage. So formidable has the U.S. medical care industry become that some critics have labeled it "the medical-industrial complex."

A number of forces have pushed up the costs of medical care in the United States. First, the classical rules that govern marketplace exchanges have not been applied to the health care industry. The sellers—doctors and hospitals—have traditionally determined the price and product options; and the buyers—patients—have bought what the sellers have ordered instead of shopping around. Further, both labor and administrative costs have risen sharply. The continual upgrading in the scope and intensity of medical services also is costly. Technological advances include such accepted practices as hip replacement and coronary-bypass surgery, new therapies, and new diagnostic techniques—treatments and tests that not all agree are useful or beneficial. Physician fees account for only about 20 percent of total U.S. health care costs, which vary tremendously across the nation and even within states (Sommer, 2009).

Medical costs also are rising because the U.S. population is getting larger and older, because modern medicine increases costs by keeping sick people alive longer, and because we continue to expand our definition of health care. Health care costs now include infertility treatments, sexual dysfunction therapies, attention deficit drugs, drug and alcohol programs, and more.

Cost Control Soaring health care costs have led to new arrangements for financing health care. Their theme is competition—the notion that physicians, hospitals, and other health care providers should compete for patients in a price-sensitive market, not unlike the markets for other goods and services. Another approach to holding down costs is to keep people out of the hospital. Hospitals and independent medical companies set up satellite outpatient surgical centers, mobile diagnostic laboratories, hospices, and walk-in clinics for routine care. Government, in seeking to cut costs, has become progressively more involved in regulating the activities of both hospitals and physicians, yet the cost of government health care spending has mounted. In 1960 the federal government paid only 11 percent of the nation's health care costs; today it picks up nearly one-third of the tab (U.S. Census Bureau, 2011a). These attempts at cost control ignore the fact that more than half the illnesses treated and encounters with patients are the result of human behaviors—smoking, lack of exercise, and poor diet (Bortz, 2011).

Managed Care Many physicians have set up professional corporations to achieve the benefits of group practice and to take advantage of special tax-sheltering provisions. Private corporations such as Humana hire physicians for their health care clinics. And managed care arrangements, such as health maintenance organizations (HMOs) and preferred provider organizations (PPOs), are common.

Under health care network arrangements such as HMOs and PPOs, an employer or an insurer contracts with a network of physicians to provide its employees or members with health care for a fixed sum of money each year. Managed care controls the process of patient care through the incorporation of payment plans, regulations on how and where patients can be treated, and requirements for providers of all aspects of care, from prescription drug services to home health and hospice care (Mechanic, 2008).

Thirty years ago, nearly all insured employees in the United States were covered by conventional insurance without any managed care provisions. By 2009, 96 percent of insured employees were covered by conventional insurance that used managed care arrangements (Weiss and Lonnquist, 2012).

Does the System Work? Stanford School of Medicine physician Walter Bortz (2011) attacks U.S. medicine as unjust, corrupt, inefficient, irrelevant, too expensive, and too often harming people. Although the United States spends more money per capita on health care than any other industrialized nation, a ranking of health care quality by the World Health Organization placed the United States lower than 36 other countries (Reid, 2009). In a study of maternal mortality around the world, nearly all countries were found to have made progress in reducing the deaths of mothers in the period before, during, and after birth—except in the United States, where maternal mortality has been increasing (Hogan et al., 2010). Other countries are able to provide universal coverage, spend less, and have higher life expectancy and lower infant mortality rates than the United States (Figure 11.6).

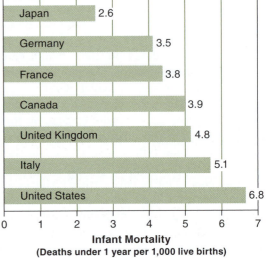

Figure 11.6 **Life Expectancy and Infant Mortality Rates for Major Industrialized Democracies, 2007**

Source: Figure generated by the authors using data from *OECD Health Data 2011*, November 2011. Available at http://www.oecd.org/document/60/0,3746,en_2649_33929_2085200_1_1_1_1,00.html.

In a 2006 comparison of the United States and England, for example, researchers found that although the United States spends more than twice as much money as England does on health care, U.S. residents are much less healthy than are citizens of England, which has a universal health care system that covers everyone (Banks et al., 2006) (see Figure 11.7). Among other problems, many people in the United States have not had any health insurance. But well-to-do Americans, who are very likely to have insurance, also are less healthy than British people of the same socioeconomic status (SES).

Why is health worse in the United States than it is in England at high incomes? This occurs because the U.S. health care system is a private, for-profit, disease-cure system designed to produce profits for insurance, managed care, and pharmaceutical companies. It is not specifically designed to promote the health of the U.S. population.

Every year tens of thousands of people die in the United States because they fail to receive the health care that the medical profession knows they need (McMillen, 2003). Health care not received may be less dangerous than health care received: Between 2006 and 2008, medical errors accounted for the deaths of nearly 100,000 Medicare patients (Gibson and Singh, 2010).

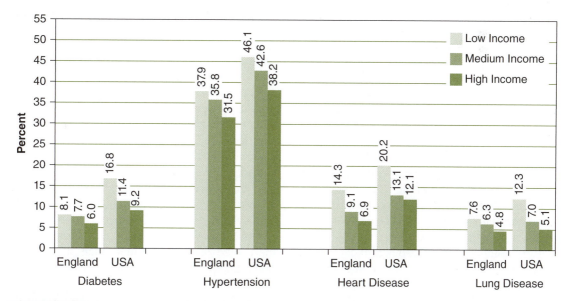

Figure 11.7 **Rates of Selected Chronic Physical Disorders by Income Level in England and the United States for Persons Ages 55–64 (Adjusted for Lifestyle Risk Factors)**

It is well known that socioeconomic status (SES) has a positive relationship with health. On average, health is worst at low SES, and it improves as SES rises. In this comparison of chronic physical disorders in the United States and England, we used income as an indicator of SES, and we found this positive association in both countries. But it also is clear that people are more likely to have physical disorders in the United States than in England *at every income level.*

Source: Figure generated by the authors with data from James Banks, Michael Marmot, Zoe Oldfield, and James P. Smith, "Disease and disadvantage in the United States and England," from *Journal of the American Medical Association* 295 (2006): 2037B2045.

Alternatives to U.S. Health Care: A Global Perspective

Four basic models of health care systems are in use around the world (Reid, 2009). The "out-of-pocket" model operates in most countries; those who can afford medical care get it, and those who cannot afford it do not. Canada, Taiwan, and South Korea use versions of a national health insurance model, in which health care providers are private but payment for health care is handled by a government-administered insurance program into which all citizens pay. Germany, Japan, France, Belgium, and Switzerland use a system termed the Bismarck model. Health care providers, payers, and insurance plans all are private entities operating under tight regulation of medical services and fees to cover all citizens. Variations of this model also are used in Latin America. The fourth model, the Beveridge model, features the provision and financing of health care by the government through tax payments. Most hospitals and clinics are owned by the government, and patients never see medical bills. Great Britain, Spain, Italy, most of Scandinavia, and Hong Kong operate under this model. Reid's comparison of health care systems around the world found that other industrialized nations outperform the United States not only in coverage and cost control, but also in quality and choice.

Reid points out that these health care models should sound familiar to people in the United States, because we have long operated under a combination of them. Medicare is a national health insurance program. All uninsured Americans have had access to health care on an "out-of-pocket" basis—if you can afford it, you can have it. People who are covered by insurance through employment share premiums for health insurance with their employers and then make co-payments or pay a percentage of medical fees, which is how the Bismarck model works. And the Beveridge model mirrors U.S. coverage of military personnel, veterans, and Native Americans: Doctors are government employees, clinics and hospitals are owned by the government, and patients receive no bills.

Perhaps because we share a border, U.S. citizens often point to Canada as an example of what's good or what's bad about another type of health care system. Let's take a closer look.

Canada's Health Care Plan

In 1971, the Canada Health Act mandated that the government pay for all medically necessary physician and hospital services. It allowed the 11 provinces and two territories to administer their own programs, negotiate doctors' fees, and set hospital budgets. The five basic principles of Canada's Health Act are that the system be not-for-profit and publicly administered; that the plan pay for all medically necessary services; that all citizens have the same access to treatments and drugs; that it pay for coverage anywhere; and that fees be fixed, without regard to age or illness (Reid, 2009).

The lower costs of health care in Canada are due to lower physician and hospital costs (physician fees are 2.4 times higher and hospital fees nearly 3 times higher in the United States than in Canada) and a slower rate in the introduction of new, expensive technology. Administrative costs are also lower in Canada. While the U.S. Medicare system spends 6 cents per dollar on administrative costs, private insurance companies in the United States spend more than 30 cents per dollar on approval and denial processes, marketing and advertising, and profits. Canada, in contrast, spends only 4 cents per dollar on administration (Reid, 2009). Despite Canada's lower spending, U.S. citizens receive, on a per capita basis, only about three-quarters of the doctors' services that Canadians do. It seems that by capping fees for procedures, Canadians have increased rather than limited access to care because the arrangement has induced doctors to do more procedures to maintain their incomes. And a look at Figure 11.6 shows the difference in health outcomes between the two countries.

But the Canadian-government-sponsored health care system is not without its critics, who point to long waits for some medical procedures and services and limitations in services and hospital beds (Farnsworth, 1991).

U.S. Health Care Reform

In 2010 the U.S. Congress passed health care reform legislation. Although the legislators failed to approve universal coverage, leaving the United States as the only wealthy nation that does not guarantee health coverage for every person, the legislation was aimed at solving some of the problems that have plagued the system. Only time will allow an analysis of its impact, but some of the provisions of the reform legislation include:

- A requirement that Americans who are uninsured purchase health insurance by 2014, with subsidies for moderate- and low-income people.

- Tax credits for small businesses to help them purchase insurance for employees.

- A prohibition on using preexisting medical conditions to deny coverage.

- A requirement that insurance plans cover adult children until age 26.

- The creation of state-run insurance exchanges for private plans to cover those who are self-employed, uninsured, or currently unemployed.

- A guarantee of basic benefits for everyone in Medicare and financial stabilization of the Medicare program for the next 10 years (Barry, 2010).

Some analysts have called the reform act the most significant piece of U.S. social policy legislation in almost 50 years (e.g., Gruber, 2010). Not only will it extend insurance coverage to 34 million currently uninsured Americans with only a slight short-term increase in national medical spending, MIT economist Jonathan Gruber (2010) says that many provisions in the new law have the potential to reduce the long-term growth of health care costs. Support for the reform act, however, was far from unanimous, and political opposition led to the almost immediate attempt by House Republican leaders to introduce a bill to repeal and replace it. While these changes should affect the availability of health care and health insurance for millions of Americans, many experts believe that more extensive change is required (Bortz, 2011). Simply allowing more people access to the current U.S. health care system, they argue, will not solve major problems (Sommer, 2009; Weil, 2009). These physicians and researchers identify the country's disease-intervention approach as the cause of runaway health costs and of our country's major causes of death and argue that a shift to disease prevention and health maintenance is required.

The Functionalist Perspective

Functionalists note that health is essential to the preservation of the human species and organized social life. If societies are to function smoothly and effectively, there must be a reasonable supply of productive members to carry out vital tasks. Where large numbers of people are ill or physically unfit (as in some developing nations where malaria is widespread), low vitality, low productivity, and poverty abound as major social problems. Moreover, community personnel, resources, facilities, and funds must be withdrawn from other essential activities to care for the nonproducing sick (Hertzler, 1961).

According to functionalists, the medical institution evolved across time to deal with problems of health and disease. More specifically, they see the medical institution performing a number of key functions in modern societies. First, it treats and seeks to cure disease. Second, the medical institution attempts to prevent disease through health maintenance programs (HMOs), including vaccinations, health education, periodic checkups, and public health and safety standards. Third, it undertakes research in the prevention, treatment, and cure of health problems. Fourth, it serves as an agency of social control by defining some behaviors as "normal" and "healthy" and others as "deviant" and "unhealthy."

Sociologist Talcott Parsons (1951) expanded upon the functionalist position in his analysis of the **sick role**—a set of cultural expectations that define what is appropriate and inappropriate behavior for people with a disease or health problem (see also Turner, 1987). He said that one way societies contain the negative effects of health problems is by institutionalizing illness in a special role, one having the following characteristics:

- Sick people are exempt from their usual social roles and responsibilities. They need not attend school or go to work, and other people will not censure them for doing so.

- Sick people are not thought to be at fault for their condition. Being sick is a physical matter, not a moral one.

- Sick people have the duty to get well and "not enjoy themselves too much." Because being sick is an undesirable state, sick people are obligated to seek competent help from medical practitioners.

- Sick people should cooperate with medical practitioners and follow their instructions.

Like other functionalists, Parsons assumed that illness must be socially controlled lest it impair societal functioning.

The Conflict Perspective

Implicit in the functionalist image of the sick role is the assumption that health care services are impartially and equally available to all members of a society. This image is challenged by conflict theorists (Waitzkin, 1983). They say that people of all societies prefer health to illness. Yet some people achieve better health than others because they have access to those resources that contribute to good health and to recovery should they become ill (see, for example, Figure 11.8).

Conflict theorists point out that the higher our social class, the more likely we are to enjoy good health, receive high-quality medical care, and live a long life. In practice, U.S. medical care has traditionally operated as a dual system in which the poor have utilized public sources— hospital outpatient departments, emergency rooms, and public clinics—while

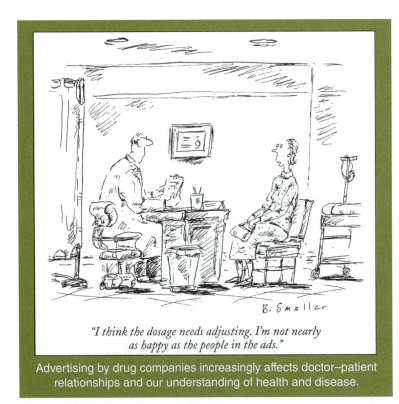

"I think the dosage needs adjusting. I'm not nearly as happy as the people in the ads."

Advertising by drug companies increasingly affects doctor–patient relationships and our understanding of health and disease.

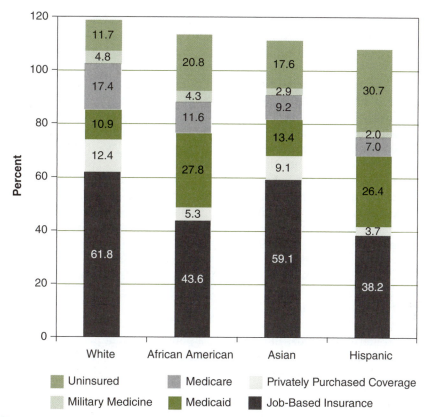

Figure 11.8 **Inequalities of Access to Health Care: Health Insurance Coverage in the United States by Race and Ethnicity, 2010**

Health care is unequally distributed in the United States, with African Americans and Hispanic Americans significantly less likely than white and Asian Americans to be insured or to receive high-quality care (Kaufman and Stein, 2006). Lack of insurance is related to the racial and ethnic differences in education, employment, and income that we have discussed in previous chapters. If the health reform legislation of 2010 results in providing insurance to the currently uninsured, we may see some change in these societal inequalities.

Source: Figure generated by the authors using data from DeNavas-Walt, Proctor, and Smith (2011), available at http://www.census.gov/prod/2011pubs/p60–239.pdf.

(Percentages do not add to 100 because people may be covered by more than one type of insurance.)

middle- and upper-income Americans use private sources such as physicians in private or group practice. Patients using public sources must often maneuver between multiple clinics to obtain their services, and the services are usually disease-oriented rather than preventive. In addition, the atmosphere in these institutions is often dehumanizing.

Even though access to health care among the poor has improved in recent years, low SES is still the strongest predictor of illness and death in the United States and the world (Williams, 1998), and there is growing recognition that social factors do not just contribute to but are causal agents in disease and mortality (Cockerham, 2012). Since African Americans,

Hispanics, and Native Americans are more likely than whites to be poor, these groups also experience higher rates of disease and shorter life expectancies.

Much research indicates that racial and ethnic minorities receive lower-quality health services than whites, even when their incomes and insurance coverage are the same (Smedley, Stith, and Nelson, 2003). Black men in Harlem, for example, have a lower life expectancy than any other group in the United States; it is lower, in fact, than the life expectancy of the citizens of Bangladesh. Black Americans as a group have a lower average life expectancy than the populations of 104 other countries (Sommer, 2009).

Conflict theorists point out that access to health care providers is not the only disadvantage faced by the poor. Lack of adequate nutrition leads to poor health; the current obesity and diabetes epidemic is related to diet, and diet is related to access to nutritious foods. Inner-city neighborhoods often lack nutritious grocery choices such as whole grains and fresh fruits and vegetables, and poverty often traps people in their own neighborhoods (Sommer, 2009). The U.S. Department of Agriculture (2012) estimates that at least 13.5 million Americans live in such "food deserts." The poor also are less likely to finish high school or go to college, and research suggests that educational differences are most responsible for the health disparities related to socioeconomic status (Mirowsky and Ross, 2003). As Johns Hopkins physician, researcher, and teacher Alfred Sommer summarizes (2009:112): "There is little doubt that poverty, ignorance, and discrimination combine in powerful and complex ways that adversely affect health."

Conflict theory provides a clear understanding of why reforming health care has been a persistent challenge in the United States. Between 1998 and 2004, drug companies topped the list of expenditures on lobbying for all industries (Petersen, 2008). As T. R. Reid expressed it (2009:22), "The vested interests that are doing well in the health business now—insurance companies, hospital chains, pharmaceutical companies—have blocked significant restructuring of our system."

The Interactionist Perspective

Symbolic interactionists view "sickness" as a condition to which we attach socially devised meanings. By way of analogy, consider the blight that attacks potatoes and corn. "Blight" is merely a human construct: If we wished to cultivate parasites instead of potatoes or corn, we would not view the condition as blight. In like manner, the invasion of an individual's body by cholera germs no more carries with it the stamp of sickness than the souring of milk by other forms of bacteria. For a condition to be interpreted as a sickness, the members of a society must define it as such.

Some conditions are so prevalent among a population that people typically do not consider them as unusual or symptomatic. Among many Hispanics in the Southwest, diarrhea, sweating, and coughing are taken-for-granted, everyday occurrences. Similarly, lower-back pain is a common condition experienced by many lower-class American women, who often view it not as a product of disease or disorder but as an integral part of their day-to-day lives.

Interactionists also are interested in how the medical profession and others define certain conditions as diseases. In *Selling Sickness,* authors Ray Moynihan and Alan Cassels (2005) explain how pharmaceutical corporations "sell" disease, convincing the public that menopause is an ailment that must be treated, for example, and marketing medical tests and treatments for conditions that a decade or two ago were not considered to be illnesses. Medical remedies also are subject to culturally and societally devised meanings (Goode, 1993).

In some cases a medical treatment is discovered *before* the condition is seen as a medical one. The discovery that the stimulant Ritalin has a calming effect on some youngsters led to the conclusion that their disruptive behavior, short attention span, temper tantrums, fidgeting, and difficulty in learning constitute a disorder—"attention-deficit hyperactivity disorder" (ADHD), the designation employed by the American Psychiatric Association (Conrad and Schneider, 1980). This new medical category was later expanded to adults (Conrad and Potter, 2000).

Today, an increasing number of behaviors that earlier generations defined as immoral or sinful are coming to be seen as forms of sickness, a process sociologists call the **medicalization of deviance.** Drug abuse, alcoholism, and child abuse are regarded in many quarters as psychological difficulties that are "medical" problems requiring treatment by physicians, especially psychiatrists. Whether incest, murder, and rape should be viewed as "crimes" that are best handled by jailers or as "sicknesses" best treated by medical practitioners is currently controversial.

What Can Sociology Do for You?

In this chapter we have presented baseline information about three major institutions: religion, education, and medicine. There are careers related to these institutions at many levels: teacher, principal, school psychologist, school social worker, professor of education, sociologist of education, educational researcher, test developer, nurse, doctor, hospital social worker, home health care worker or administrator, medical sociologist, minister, theologian, sociologist of religion, church youth leader, church musical director, and more. A good liberal arts background with a major in sociology could be the first step to many of these.

If you want to learn more about these institutions, check your school's course catalog for classes in medical sociology, sociology of religion, and sociology of education.

The Chapter in Brief: *Religion, Education, and Medicine*

Religion

■ **What Is Religion?** **Religion** has to do with those socially shared and organized ways of thinking, feeling, and acting that concern ultimate meanings and assume the existence of the supernatural or "beyond." Religion is centered in beliefs and practices that are related to **sacred** as opposed to **profane** things and often involves **rituals.**

■ **A Global View: Varieties of Religious Behavior** Religious behavior is so varied that sociologists attempt to categorize it. One scheme distinguishes between simple supernaturalism, **animism, theism** (including **monotheism** and **polytheism**), and a system of abstract ideals.

■ **Religious Organizations** Sociologists distinguish between four ideal types of religious organization: **churches, denominations, sects,** and **cults.** Whereas churches and denominations exist in a state of accommodation with the larger society, sects and cults find themselves at odds with established social arrangements and practices.

■ **Religion and Secular Change: The Protestant Ethic** Max Weber studied several world religions to see how a religious **ethic** can affect people's behavior and claimed that religion could be a source of social change. Specifically, he linked the rise of capitalism to the **Protestant ethic,** particularly Calvinism and **asceticism.**

■ **Religion in Contemporary U.S. Life**   The **secularization thesis** states that profane considerations gain ascendancy over sacred considerations in the course of social evolution, but little evidence supports the notion that secularization is occurring in the United States. Fundamentalist and evangelical groups are on the rise in the United States and elsewhere in the world. Fundamentalism opposes modernity and reaffirms traditional authority, accepting the Bible as the literal word of God. Evangelicals profess a personal relationship with Jesus Christ.

■ **State–Church Issues**   The First Amendment to the U.S. Constitution has provided the foundation for the principle of the separation of church and state. The basic tenet of **civil religion** is that the United States is a nation under God with a divine mission.

■ **The Functionalist Perspective**   Functionalist theorists look to the contributions religion makes to societal survival and are interested in **totemism.** According to Émile Durkheim, religion is the symbolization of society.

■ **The Conflict Perspective**   Some conflict theorists depict religion as a weapon in the service of ruling elites who use it to hold in check the explosive tensions produced by social inequality and injustice. Other conflict theorists see religion as an active force shaping the contours of social life.

Education

Social scientists view **learning** as a relatively permanent change in behavior or capability that results from experience. **Education** is one aspect of the many-sided process of socialization by which people acquire behaviors essential for effective participation in society.

■ **The Bureaucratic Structure of Schools**   As schools grew larger, they had to standardize and routinize many of their operations and establish formal operating and administrative procedures.

■ **The Functionalist Perspective**   Viewed from the functionalist perspective, a specialized educational agency is needed to transmit the ways of thinking, feeling, and acting mandated by a rapidly changing urban and technologically based society.

■ **The Conflict Perspective**   Conflict theorists see schools as agencies that reproduce and legitimate the current social order, citing **credentialism** as one factor and the **correspondence principle** as another. By reproducing and legitimating the existing social order, the educational institution benefits some individuals and groups at the expense of others.

■ **The Interactionist Perspective**   Symbolic interactionists see classrooms as little worlds teeming with behavior. They see U.S. schools primarily benefiting advantaged youngsters and alienating disadvantaged youngsters through the **hidden curriculum** and **educational self-fulfilling prophecies.**

■ **The Effectiveness of Schools**   Successful schools foster expectations that order will prevail and that learning is a serious matter. Cross-cultural research suggests that teachers in some other countries spend more time developing concepts, rather than simply stating them.

■ **Alternatives to Traditional Public Schools**   Parents are increasingly choosing to educate their children in ways other than in traditional public schools. Alternatives include charter schools, religious schools, nonreligious private schools, and home schooling.

■ **The Availability of Higher Education**   College and university student populations are highly skewed in terms of race, ethnicity, and family income. Only 20 percent of the nation's undergraduates are young people ages 18–22 who are pursuing a parent-financed education.

Medicine

The functions now carried out by the institution of **medicine** were once embedded in the activities of the family and religious institutions.

■ **Health Care in the United States**   In recent decades the medical care industry has grown appreciably larger, consuming about 16 percent of the nation's gross domestic product. Hospitals, physicians, and nurses assume central roles in the health care delivery system. Soaring health care costs have led to new arrangements for financing it. Managed care arrangements are part of many traditional insurance plans. They also form the basis for health maintenance and preferred provider organizations. Other countries provide universal health care coverage to their residents, spend less, and have higher life expectancy and lower infant mortality rates than the United States.

■ **Alternatives to U.S. Health Care: A Global Perspective**   Four basic models of health care systems are in use around the world: an "out-of-pocket" model, a national health insurance model, the Bismarck model (private health care providers, payers, and insurance plans operating under tight regulation), and the Beveridge model (the provision and financing of health care by the government through tax payments). Canada's system provides medically necessary physician and hospital services to all citizens.

■ **U.S. Health Care Reform**   In 2010 the U.S. Congress passed health care reform legislation, requiring uninsured Americans to purchase health insurance, providing tax credits for small business employee insurance plans, prohibiting the use of preexisting medical conditions to deny coverage, requiring insurance plans to cover adult children until age 26, creating state-run insurance exchanges, and guaranteeing basic benefits for everyone in Medicare. Many experts argue that more fundamental change of the country's disease-intervention approach is required.

■ **The Functionalist Perspective**   Functionalists note that **health** is essential to the preservation of the human species and organized social life. One way societies contain the negative effects of health problems and **disease** is through institutionalizing illness in a **sick role.**

■ **The Conflict Perspective**   Conflict theorists note that some people achieve better health than others because they have access to those resources that contribute to good health and recovery should they become ill.

■ **The Interactionist Perspective**   Interactionist theorists view sickness as a condition to which we attach socially devised meanings. For example, an increasing number of behaviors that earlier generations defined as immoral or sinful are coming to be seen as forms of sickness—the **medicalization of deviance.**

Glossary

animism   A belief in spirits or otherworldly beings.

asceticism   A way of life characterized by hard work, sobriety, thrift, restraint, and the avoidance of earthly pleasures.

church   A religious organization that considers itself uniquely legitimate and enjoys a positive relationship with the dominant society.

civil religion   Elements of nationalism and patriotism that take on the properties of a religion.

correspondence principle   The notion set forth by Samuel Bowles and Herbert Gintis that the social relations of work find expression in the social relations of the school.

credentialism The requirement that a worker have a degree that does not provide skills needed for the performance of a job.

cult A religious movement that represents a new and independent religious tradition.

denomination A religious organization that accepts the legitimacy of other religious groups and enjoys a positive relationship with the dominant society.

disease A condition in which an organism does not function properly because of biological causes.

education The transmission of particular attitudes, knowledge, and skills to the members of a society through formal, systematic training.

educational self-fulfilling prophecies (also called *teacher-expectation effects*) The fact that many children fail to learn, especially inner-city and minority youngsters, because those who are charged with teaching them do not believe that they will learn, do not expect that they can learn, and do not act toward them in ways that help them to learn.

ethic The perspective and values engendered by a religious way of thinking.

health As defined by the World Health Organization, "a state of complete physical, mental, and social well-being and not merely the absence of disease or infirmity."

hidden curriculum A complex of unarticulated values, attitudes, and behaviors that subtly mold children in the image preferred by the dominant institutions.

learning A relatively permanent change in behavior or capability that results from experience.

mana The notion that there is in nature a diffuse, impersonal, supernatural force operating for good or evil.

medicalization of deviance The process whereby an increasing number of behaviors that earlier generations defined as being immoral or sinful are coming to be seen as forms of sickness.

medicine An institution providing an enduring set of cultural patterns and social arrangements responsible for problems of health and disease.

monotheism The belief in one god.

polytheism The belief in many gods with equal or relatively similar power.

profane Those aspects of social reality that are everyday and commonplace.

Protestant ethic The Calvinist ethos that embodied the spirit of capitalism.

religion Those socially shared and organized ways of thinking, feeling, and acting that concern ultimate meanings and assume the existence of the supernatural or "beyond" and that are centered in beliefs and practices related to sacred things.

rituals Social acts prescribed by rules that dictate how human beings should comport themselves in the presence of the sacred.

sacred Those aspects of social reality that are set apart and forbidden.

sect A religious organization that stands apart from the dominant society but is rooted in established religious traditions.

secularization thesis The notion that profane (nonreligious) considerations gain ascendancy over sacred (religious) considerations in the course of social evolution.

sick role A set of cultural expectations that define what is appropriate and inappropriate behavior for people with a disease or health problem.

theism A religion centered in a belief in gods who are thought to be powerful, to have an interest in human affairs, and to merit worship.

totemism A religious system in which a clan (a kin group) takes the name of, claims descent from, and attributes sacred properties to a plant or animal.

Review Questions

1. What is religion? Discuss the differences among supernaturalism, animism, theism, and abstract ideals.

2. How do churches, denominations, sects, and cults differ?

3. What is the Protestant ethic?

4. Describe the secularization thesis.

5. How are fundamentalists and evangelicals different?

6. How do the church and the state interact in the United States?

7. Compare the functionalist and conflict perspectives on religion.

8. How does learning differ from education?

9. Describe school bureaucracy.

10. Are U.S. schools effective?

11. Describe higher education in the United States today.

12. Discuss the functionalist, conflict, and interactionist perspectives on education.

13. Define medicine and describe the U.S. health care system.

14. What is managed care? How does it work in the United States?

15. Compare the U.S. health care system with that from another country.

16. How do the functionalist, conflict, and interactionist perspectives on medicine differ?

Internet Connection   www.mhhe.com/hughes11e

Choose any one of the three institutions discussed in this chapter. Using a search engine such as **google.com,** enter the term "religion," "medicine," or "education" in the search window, and conduct a search. Follow the links you find. What do the resources you discover tell us about the nature of this institution in our society? Write a short report, describing the picture you form of the institution from the information available on the Internet and discussing whether it is possible to fully understand the institution using only the material and information you can find on the Internet.

CHAPTER 12

Population
and Environment

World population reached 7 billion in 2011 (Haub and Gribble, 2011). The effects of a world so populated with humans are evident everywhere: global warming, depleted and contaminated water supplies, species extinctions, fisheries collapses, air pollution, ocean acidification, the destruction of the world's rain forests, the spread of deserts, and famine. More than half the world's population is concentrated in cities (U.N. Population Division, 2006), where many of our most serious pollution problems already are to be found, but where many analysts see the greatest potential for environmentally sustainable lifestyles.

In the coming decades, population increases will occur almost entirely in developing countries, with the highest population growth projected for countries in Africa (Haub and Kaneda, 2011). Most industrialized countries will be affected more by migration than by internal population increases, with many countries actually experiencing population declines. The United States, Canada, New Zealand, and Australia will continue to grow both from immigration and from higher birth rates (Bremner et al., 2011).

Industrialized nations consume the vast majority of the world's resources, so even without substantial population increases they play a major role in climate change, resource consumption, pollution, and habitat destruction—and a major role in providing direction and assistance to developing countries.

In this chapter we will provide the basics about population, the environment, and life in cities. Understanding the problems humans face in these areas is not just important for your sociology grade, it is critical to your future.

Population

Demography is the science dealing with the size, distribution, composition, and changes in population. Demographic data show the world's

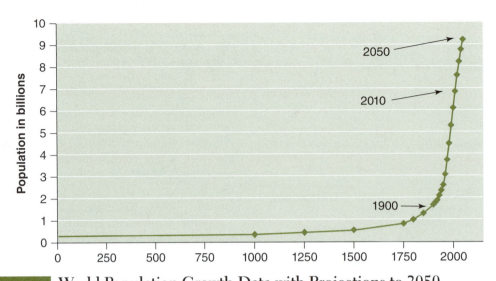

Figure 12.1 World Population Growth Data with Projections to 2050

For most of human history, population growth was very slow. During the 20th century, however, rates of growth were extraordinarily high. World population reached 6 billion in 1999, growing from 1 billion to 6 billion in less than 200 years. Demographers predict that rapid growth in world population will continue during most of the 21st century, with a total world population of between 8.1 billion and 10.6 billion in 2050 (Bloom, 2011).

Sources: Figure generated by the authors using population data and historical estimates reported by the U.S. Census Bureau. Available at http://www.census.gov/ipc/www/worldhis.html and http://www.census.gov/ipc/www/idb/worldpop.php.

population has passed 7 billion; during the last century, major improvements in nutrition, health care, and education resulted in people living longer lives and being more likely to live to reproduce. Both these contributed to very large increases in population growth rates: Many more humans were born than died. More than half the people in the world live in the seven most populous nations: China, India, the United States, Indonesia, Brazil, Pakistan, and Nigeria (Haub and Kaneda, 2011).

Humans are currently in the midst of their most rapid population expansion. It is estimated that some 40,000 years ago the world population stood at about 3 million. In 8000 B.C., the dawn of agriculture, it was 5 million. At the time of Christ, it was 200 million. By 1650 it had climbed to 500 million, and by 1830 to 1 billion. At the end of World War II and the advent of the nuclear age, world population

stood at 2.3 billion. It took nearly 200,000 years (White et al., 2003) for humankind to reach 1 billion in number, but within a century it had reached 2 billion, and within an additional quarter-century, 4 billion (see Figure 12.1).

Demographic studies help us to see that where population growth is occurring is critical to our understanding of the future. Most industrialized nations now have population declines, no population growth, or very slow population growth. The enormous increases in population expected to occur in the next decades will take place almost entirely in African, Asian, and South American countries. Although these developing nations currently use only about a quarter of the earth's resources, their rapid population growth and industrialization may combine to change that dramatically. In this section we will look at the basics of population change.

Elements in Population Change

All population change within a society can be reduced to three factors: the birth rate, the death rate, and the migration rate into or out of the society. In 2011 the population of the United States stood at 311.7 million, with a projected population of 351.4 million in 2025 and 422.6 million in 2050 (Haub and Kaneda, 2011).

Birth Rate

The **crude birth rate** is the number of live births per 1,000 members of a population in a given year. In 2011 the crude birth rate for the United States was 13 per 1,000, while in the countries where population growth is increasing rapidly it is much higher. In western Africa, Niger has a crude birth rate of 48 per 1,000, and Uganda in eastern Africa has a birthrate of 46 (Haub and Kaneda, 2011). The measure is called "crude" because it obscures important differences among races, ethnic groups, classes, age groups, and other categories within the population by lumping all births within a single figure.

The **general fertility rate** indicates the annual number of live births per 1,000 women ages 15–44. Demographers also calculate **age-specific fertility,** or the number of live births per 1,000 women in a specific age group. Fertility rates provide us with information regarding the actual reproductive patterns of a society. By contrast, the potential number of children that could be born if every woman of childbearing age bore all the children she possibly could is called **fecundity.**

It takes an average of 2.1 children per woman of childbearing age for a modern population to replace itself without immigration; this is the level of **zero population growth** (ZPG). For most of U.S. history, fertility rates exceeded the replacement level of 2.1. They dropped to 2.1 for the first time during the Great Depression of the 1930s. Following the Depression and World War II, fertility increased during the "baby boom" (1946–1965) but then declined again and dropped below replacement around 1970. Since then, fertility has slowly increased and has been hovering near replacement level since the late 1980s. In 2011, it was 2.0 (Haub and Kaneda, 2011).

Death Rate

The rapid world population growth we are currently experiencing is not caused by any dramatic increase in the birth rate; rather, it is caused by dramatic decreases in the death rate. The **crude death rate** is the number of deaths per 1,000 members of a population in a given year. In 2011 the crude death rate for Americans was 8 per 1,000. Death rates vary substantially around the world, from 1 per 1,000 in Qatar and the United Arab Emirates to 17 per 1,000 in the Democratic Republic of Congo in 2011 (Haub and Kaneda, 2011). Death rates primarily reflect the age distribution of a country's population, although war, disease, sanitation, and other factors play a part. In Swaziland, for example, more than a quarter of the population is infected with HIV, which directly affects the country's death rate and life expectancy (Haub and Kaneda, 2011).

As in the case of birth rates, demographers are interested in the **age-specific death rate,** or the number of deaths per 1,000 individuals in a specific age group. The disparity in death rates between some minority groups and non-Hispanic whites is highest in late adolescence and young adulthood. For example, the death rate for African Americans is 1.6 times higher at ages 25–34, and for American Indians and Alaskan Natives, it is 1.3 times higher at ages 15–24. For Asian Americans and Hispanic Americans, however, death rates in young adulthood are lower than for non-Hispanic whites (Murphy, Xu, and Kochanek, 2012). The major reason is that homicide and accidental death rates are substantially higher for these minorities than for whites.

The **infant mortality rate** is the number of deaths among infants under one year of age per 1,000 live births. In 2011 the infant mortality rate in the United States was 6.1 per 1,000 (Haub and Kaneda, 2011), with the rate for African Americans more than twice that for whites (Kids Count, 2011). Many industrialized nations report much lower infant mortality rates than the United States (see Figure 11.6): Hong Kong, 1.6; Iceland, 2.2; Sweden, 2.5; Finland and Japan, 2.6; Norway, 2.8; and others. We have mentioned that a decrease in the death rate results in population increases; likewise, as the infant mortality rate of developing nations drops, population growth increases rapidly. A high birth rate does not add a large number of people to the population if many of those born do not live past their first birthdays. When the number of surviving babies increases,

so does the number of children who grow up to have children themselves. The average infant mortality rate for more developed countries is 5 deaths per 1,000 live births, while for the least developed countries in the world it is 76 (Haub and Kaneda, 2011).

The life expectancy of Americans was 78 years in 2011 and varied by gender and race (see Figure 12.2). Overall, human life expectancy is nearly twice as long as it was in 1840, and research done in Sweden shows that the rate of increase in maximum life span has accelerated from 0.44 year per decade before 1969 to 1.11 years per decade since then (Wilmoth et al., 2000). A number of other developed nations have

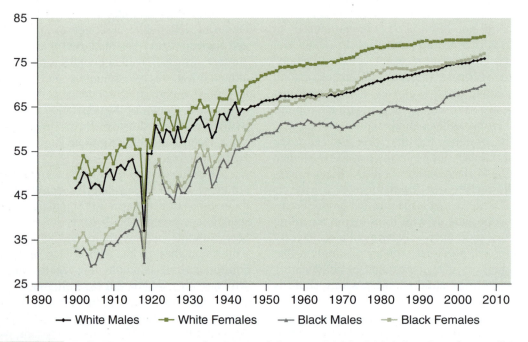

Figure 12.2 **Life Expectancy in the United States, 1900–2006, by Gender and Race**
Life expectancy has increased significantly over the past century, but significant gender and race differences remain. The dip in 1918 was due to the Great Flu Epidemic.

Sources: Figure generated by the authors using data from the National Center for Health Statistics, 2011, *Health, United States, 2010: With Special Feature on Death and Dying* (Hyattsville, MD, 2011), available at http://www.cdc.gov/nchs/data/hus/hus10.pdf#022; Arias, 2002, available at http://www.cdc.gov/nchs/data/hus/tables/2003/03hus027.pdf; Miniño, Heron, and Smith, 2006, available at http://www.cdc.gov/nchs/data/nvsr/nvsr54/nvsr54_19.pdf; and Hoyert, Kung, and Smith, 2005, available at http://www.cdc.gov/nchs/data/nvsr/nvsr53/nvsr53_15.pdf.

higher average life expectancies than the United States (see Figure 11.6). Japan, Hong Kong, and San Marino, with a life expectancy of 83 years, hold the lead among developed countries, closely followed by Australia, France, Macao, Spain, Sweden, and Switzerland (82 years); and Iceland, Italy, New Zealand, the Netherlands, and Canada (81 years) (Haub and Kaneda, 2011). In contrast, some of the lowest life expectancy figures are in the 40s, with the very lowest in African countries, for example, Zimbabwe, 46; Guinea-Bissau, 48; and Zambia, Lesotho, and the Democratic Republic of Congo, 49. The spread of AIDS has drastically reduced life expectancy in some countries. In general, life expectancy and population growth rates increase in developing nations along with improvements in education, nutrition, sanitation, income, and medicine (Oeppen and Vaupel, 2002).

Migration Rate

The **net migration rate** is the increase or decrease per 1,000 members of the population in a given year that results from people entering (immigrants) or leaving (emigrants) a society. Migration is the product of two factors. There are forces—*push* factors—that encourage people to leave a habitat they already occupy. And there are other forces—*pull* factors—that attract people to a new habitat. Before people actually migrate, they usually compare the relative opportunities offered by the current and the anticipated habitats. If the balance is on the side of the anticipated habitat, they typically migrate unless prevented from doing so by government action, immigration quotas, lack of financial resources, or some other compelling barrier.

In the 1840s the push of the potato famine in Ireland and the pull of employment opportunities in the United States made this country appear attractive to many Irish people. Both push and pull factors contribute to the entry into the United States of large numbers of illegal immigrants from Mexico. Low agricultural productivity and commodity prices in Mexican agriculture have served as a push factor, and comparatively high American wages have served as a pull factor, with illegalities an insufficient barrier to prevent migration.

Migrants may move to escape conflict and natural disaster, including floods, earthquakes, drought, and famine; Africa has one-quarter of the world's 10 million refugees (Bremner et al., 2009). Migration patterns also are influenced by other factors. For example, the U.S. military presence in Korea and the Philippines has meant that potential immigrants from these nations have been partially Americanized even before leaving their homeland; successful immigrants in turn pave the way for additional arrivals by supplying them with information, employment, and financial assistance (Suro, 1991).

Because migration is usually a burden of some kind involving costs of transportation, establishment of a new household, and loss of social networks in one's community, migrants are usually people who have the resources to bear such burdens. Consequently, migrants usually have better social, economic, and personal characteristics than those who are left behind (Chiswick, 1979). Migrants are younger, have more education, and are more ambitious than others.

Movement of people from one nation to another is called **international migration.** Only a small percentage of the world's population ever moves across national boundaries. About 62 million people have moved from less to more developed nations, but nearly as many (61 million) have moved from one developing country to another, usually in search of employment (Bremner et al., 2009). Some 38 million foreign-born people live in the United States, more than in any other single country in the world; this represents 20 percent of the world's immigrant population. Russia and Germany also host large numbers of immigrants (Bremner et al., 2009).

People also move about within a nation. **Internal migration** has resulted in a majority of the U.S. population residing in the South and West, with population increases continuing in those regions. In 2011, Texas, California, Florida, Georgia, and North Carolina were the fastest-growing states in terms of gaining the most total people (Bernstein, 2011). Boom states gain political clout nationally because congressional seats are allocated on the basis of population. And although rapid population growth often fuels economic growth, it simultaneously strains municipal and state services.

Growth Rate

The **growth rate** of a society is the difference between births and deaths, plus the difference between immigrants and emigrants, per 1,000 population. In recent years the growth rate of the United States has been roughly 1 percent. The **rate of natural increase** is simply the difference between the birth and death rates. For world population growth, we look only at the rate of natural increase, as immigration and emigration do not affect the total world population. It takes a population with an annual rate of increase of 1 percent 69 years to double its population; a 4 percent annual rate of increase leads to a doubling of the population in 17 years. In 2011 the rate of natural increase for the world was 1.2 percent (Haub and Kaneda, 2011). Although that rate is lower than it had been previously, world population will expand enormously in coming years and may reach 8 billion by 2023 (Haub and Gribble, 2011). This "momentum of population growth" is fueled by the huge population of children approaching their child-bearing years. About a fifth of the world's population, more than 1.2 billion people, is between the ages of 15 and 24, with 1.1 billion of these young people living in less developed countries (Bremner et al., 2009). For some countries the impact of this growth will be enormous. Niger, already one of the world's poorest countries, is projected to grow from its current population of 16.1 million to 55.4 million by 2050 (Haub and Kaneda, 2011).

The rate of natural increase is now negative for a number of countries, including Japan, Germany, Romania, Lithuania, Latvia, Russia, Hungary, Bulgaria, Monaco, and Ukraine. This means that the number of deaths in these countries exceeds the number of births. Without immigration the population of these countries will decrease.

Population Composition

Births, deaths, and migration affect population *size*. Sociologists are also interested in the *composition* or characteristics of a population. Among these characteristics are gender, age, rural or urban residence, race, religion, national origin, marital status, income, education, and occupation. The sex composition of a population is measured by the *sex ratio*—the number of males per 100 females. At birth there are roughly 105 males for every 100 females. However, males have higher mortality rates than females. During childhood and adolescence, this differential is primarily due to accidents, homicide, and suicide, which are more common among males. The result is that, at around age 21, women begin to outnumber men, and the trend accelerates as people grow older because men also have higher rates of illness for disorders that are the leading causes of death, such as cancer, heart disease, and stroke.

The greater longevity of women in the United States has resulted in a ratio of three women for every two men over the age of 65; in the over-85 bracket, the margin is higher than two to one. Why are sex ratios of interest to sociologists? Sex ratios affect the functioning of societies. For example, marriage is one of the main ways societies have of controlling the behavior of males. In countries where male offspring are valued over female, sex-selective abortions, infant abandonment, neglect, and preferential health care for boys have resulted in a higher population of males than females (Zhu, Lu, and Hesketh, 2009; Kristof and WuDunn, 2009). Finding a wife becomes more difficult; in Punjab (India), for example, where there are

SIX CHIX. Copyright © 2000 Ann Telnaes. King Features Syndicate. Reprinted with permission.

now 874 females for every 1,000 males, marriage brokers buy women from neighboring states and Bangladesh and sell them as brides (Naqvi, 2005). China, India, and other countries may face serious social problems in the future as a result of their many unattached males.

Another important population characteristic is age composition. A population heavily concentrated in the 20- to 65-year range has a large labor force relative to its nonproductive population. Its dependency burdens tend to be light. In contrast, a population concentrated at either extreme of the age distribution—either under 20, over 65, or both—has a heavy *dependency ratio* (a large number of nonproductive individuals relative to its productive population). We can gain an appreciation for the social significance of sex and age composition by examining population pyramids.

Population Pyramids

The age and sex composition of a population can be portrayed by a **population pyramid.** It is based either on absolute numbers or on proportions. Age groupings are placed in order on a vertical scale, with the youngest age group located at the bottom and the oldest age group at the top of the pyramid. The numbers or proportions that each specified age group represents of the total are plotted on the horizontal axis. The sum or portion corresponding to the male segment is placed to the left of the central dividing line and that composing the female segment is placed to the right of it. The pyramid itself represents the entire population. Demographers use population pyramids to visualize age and gender distributions. Sociologists use them to analyze trends in fertility, mortality, and migration. Businesses often use them to gain a better understanding of their markets.

The 2010 population pyramid for India shown in Figure 12.3 has the shape of a true pyramid. It is typical of a population that is growing by virtue of a high birth rate and a declining death rate. The U.S. pyramids shown in Figure 12.4 reveal a quite different picture. They illustrate the projected shape of the age structure of the United States from 1990 through 2050 as the baby-boom generation grows older; the size of future cohorts can only be estimated.

The population projections contained in Figure 12.4 presume fluctuating fertility patterns characterized by "booms" and "busts."

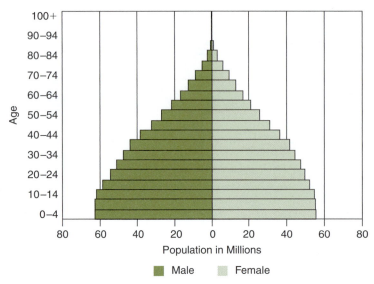

Figure 12.3 **Population Pyramid of India, 2010**
The pyramid reflects a young and growing population. Also note the sex ratio imbalance; there are many more males than females in the 30- to 34-year-old category and younger.

Source: Figure generated by the authors using projections made by the U.S. Census Bureau and presented in the Census Bureau's International Data Base. (Available at http://www.census.gov/ipc/www/idb/country.php.)

The complicating ramifications of migration are not considered here. Let's look at some specific aspects of these pyramids:

- The *baby-boom cohort* can be seen in all the pyramids. Demographers use the term "baby boom" to refer to the 19-year period (1946–1964) of high fertility following World War II. In 1990 the cohort extends across the middle section (ages 25–44), and by 2025 it constitutes the protruding bands of individuals ages 60–79.

  The baby-boom generation has had an enormous impact upon American life. In the 1950s the baby boomers made the United States a child-oriented society of new schools, suburbs, and station wagons. They watched *The Mickey Mouse Club,* listened to rock and

roll, went to Woodstock and Vietnam, and fueled the student, civil rights, and peace movements of the 1960s and early 1970s. By the year 2030 one out of every five Americans will be 65 years of age or older and dependent on a Social Security and Medicare system that must be supported by the smaller generations behind them. The Social Security dependency ratio—the number of workers compared with the number of recipients—was five to one in 1965, but it will drop to two to one by 2035.

- The *baby-bust cohort* stands in sharp relief to the baby boomers. The baby bust began in the early 1970s when fertility dropped rapidly, reaching its lowest level in 1976 and remaining very low until the mid-1980s. This cohort can be seen in the indentation just above the base of the 1990 pyramid.

- It in turn is succeeded by the *baby-boom echo,* sometimes called the "echo boom" or "baby boomlet." These are the children of the baby boomers. Not until 2025 when a rising mortality rate takes its toll of baby boomers will the echo cohort catch up to the baby-boom cohort in size.

- If we can use past fertility to predict future fertility, we might predict that a baby-bust echo will follow the baby-boom echo, but we won't know for sure about this until it occurs.

Smaller Cohort, Higher Fertility Rates

Much of the demographic theory dealing with U.S. fertility levels has been stimulated by the work of Richard A. Easterlin (1961, 1987), who has charted regular cycles that rise and fall every

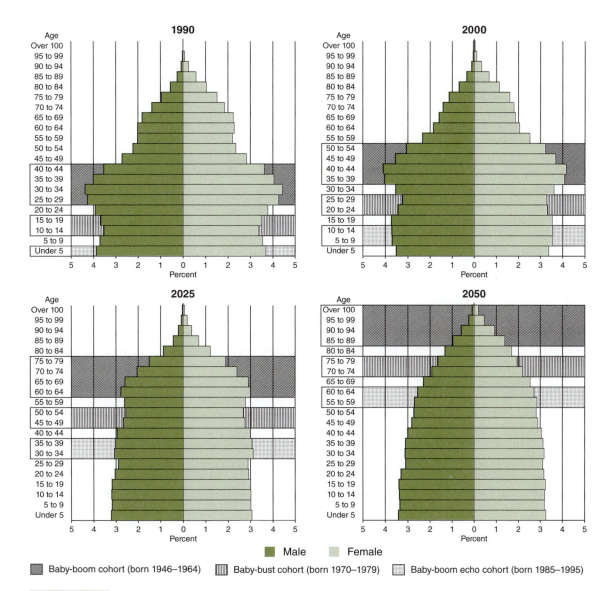

Figure 12.4 **Population Pyramids in the United States, 1990–2050**
The pyramids trace the demographic impact of the baby-boom cohort (born 1946–1964), the baby-bust cohort (born 1970–1979), and the baby-boom echo cohort (born 1985–1995).

Source: "Population Pyramids in the United States, 1990–2050" from National Estimates Program (1990), National Projection Program (2000, 2025, 2050). (Available at www.census.gov/population/www/projections/natchart.html.)

20 years or so. He suggested that small generations typically produce large ones and that large generations produce small ones. Easterlin conjectured that smaller cohorts have less competition for jobs as they enter the workforce, thereby encouraging early marriage and childbearing. This results in rising birth rates that produce a baby boom. Large generations confront the opposite situation when they reach adulthood. They delay marriage and have fewer children, contributing to a baby bust.

If Easterlin is correct, the total fertility rate in the United States should rise above the replacement level as members of the baby-bust cohort start their families. They should have a higher relative income and a more traditional family structure; as members of a small cohort they will have less difficulty finding jobs, allowing them to marry and start their families earlier (Pampel and Peters, 1995).

Malthus and Marx: Two Views of Population Growth

The relationship between population growth and the level of a nation's welfare has long been a central concern for those interested in population problems. In this section we will consider two classic arguments, those of Thomas Robert Malthus and Karl Marx.

Malthus

In 1798 the English economist and cleric Thomas Malthus (1766–1834) published *An Essay on the Principle of Population.* Many of the issues he raised are still debated today. Malthus asserted that human populations tend to increase at a more rapid rate than the food supply needed to sustain them. Human beings, Malthus said, confront two unchangeable and antagonistic natural laws: (1) the "need for food" and (2) the "passion between the sexes." He contended that, whereas agricultural production tends to increase in arithmetic fashion (1-2-3-4-5-6-7-8), population tends to increase

in geometric fashion (1-2-4-8-16-32-64-128). Population will invariably catch up with progress and literally "eat away" higher levels of living. Malthus considered famine, war, and pestilence to be the chief deterrents to excessive population growth. As an ordained minister, Malthus either did not consider that people might use birth control or viewed birth control as a sin and beneath human dignity. But he did believe that people could use what he called "moral restraint," postponing marriage and refraining from sexual relations when not married.

Was Malthus Right?

Malthus failed to appreciate the full possibilities of the Industrial Revolution and its ability to expand productive capacities to an extent unknown in his time. We now know that it is not true that food always and everywhere can increase only at an arithmetic rate. For example, within the United States the application of technology—farm machinery, irrigation, fertilizers, pesticides, and hybrid plants and animals—has resulted in the food supply growing faster than the population. And as previously noted, Malthus did not foresee the possibility of new birth control methods or their application within the context of a value system favoring small families.

Those who agree with many of Malthus's ideas but who disagree with his "moral restraint" approach to population control—they favor contraception instead—are termed neo-Malthusians. Like Malthus, they believe that ultimately population will be limited in one of two ways: decreasing births or increasing deaths. They recognize that economic growth has sustained larger populations in some parts of the world in recent times, but they predict that population growth will eventually wipe out these economic gains.

In the 1970s neo-Malthusian and biologist Paul Ehrlich made some central points in his book *The Population Bomb:* There are too many people in the world, there is too little food, and the environment is being degraded. Forty years later, global food security has become a major issue (Ash et al., 2010). Over the next 40 years, as population and consumption both continue to grow, agriculture will have to meet demands for increased efficiency in land, water, and energy use, reduce environmental impacts, and adapt to changes caused by global warming (Godfray et al., 2010).

Marx

Karl Marx (1867/1906) took issue with many Malthusian notions and formulations. He insisted that an excess of population, or more particularly of the working class, depends on the availability of employment opportunities, not a fixed supply of food. Marx believed that a deepening crisis of the capitalist system would inevitably force increasing numbers of workers into the ranks of the unemployed, leading some individuals to conclude that society is overpopulated. Indeed, Marx believed there was enough wealth to go around; it merely needed to be redistributed.

Under socialism, Marx argued, there would be no population problem because all workers would be integrated into the economy and there would be no unemployment. Through proper use of technology, a socialist economy would produce enough food for all. Thus, he traced the

problems associated with population growth to capitalist society and sought cures in a fundamental restructuring of the social and economic order. In sum, whereas Malthus looked primarily to the individual to restrain population growth through self-control, Marx looked to collective action to refashion institutional life.

Demographic Transition

A number of social scientists have employed the idea of demographic transition to map out the population growth characteristic of the modern era (Davis, 1945; Chesnais, 1992). Viewed as history, it seeks to explain what has happened in European nations over the past 200 years. Viewed as theory, it has been used to predict what will happen in developing nations in the future. **Demographic transition theory** holds that the process of modernization is associated with three stages in population change (see Figure 12.5).

Stage 1: High Potential Growth

Societies untouched by industrialization and urbanization are characterized by a high birth rate and a high death rate. As a result the population remains relatively stable. The stage is described as having "high potential growth"

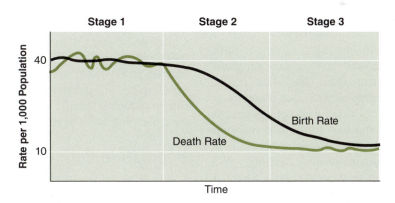

Figure 12.5   **Trends in Birth and Death Rates According to Demographic Transition Theory**

Source: James W. Vander Zanden.

because once the societies gain control over their death rates, their growth is likely to be rapid. No countries today are completely untouched by industrialization, but Uganda, Afghanistan, and Zambia have the high birth rates and fluctuating death rates characteristic of this stage (Haub and Gribble, 2011).

Stage 2: Transitional Growth

Modernization has its initial impact on mortality levels. Improved housing, better levels of nutrition, and improvements in health and sanitary measures bring about a steady decline in death rates, including the infant mortality rate. More babies survive and become parents. A drop in the death rate, while the birth rate of a population remains unchanged, results in a marked increase in the rate of population growth. As time passes, couples realize that with lower infant mortality rates, fewer births are required to produce the same number of surviving children, and they adjust their fertility accordingly. The costs and benefits associated with children change as modernization progresses, making small families economically advantageous. The second stage ends when the birth rate sinks toward the death rate. Ghana, Guatemala, and Iraq provide examples of this stage, with declining birth and death rates (Haub and Gribble, 2011).

Stage 3: Population Stability

Modernization both provides effective birth control techniques and undermines religious proscriptions against their use. The result, according to demographic transition theorists, is that modern societies come to be characterized by low mortality and low fertility, a situation approximating zero population growth. India is approaching replacement-level fertility, and Germany provides an example of a Stage 4 country, with very low birth and death rates (Haub and Gribble, 2011). Some demographic transition models also include Stage 5 for countries that are reproducing below replacement level, as many are in Europe.

Demographic Transition Theory Evaluated

Social scientists are not sure that the stages represent an accurate portrayal of European demographic history; the theory also may have limited usefulness in predicting population change in developing nations. Declines in infant mortality and increases in life expectancy can occur very rapidly in today's technologically advanced world and outpace a society's evolution of new attitudes about family size. When children have always been considered an economic asset, it may take a significant period of time to decrease a country's average family size. Although demographic transition theory has a number of underlying problems that are explored in Box 12.1, recent research provides some qualified support for the theory. Crenshaw, Christenson, and Oakey (2000) studied determinants of fertility in 64 developing countries from 1965 to 1990. Consistent with demographic transition theory, they found that reductions in child mortality were related to decreased fertility. They also found that growth of a service economy was related to fertility decline. Service sector dominance tends to reduce fertility because it employs many women and because complex service jobs are not appropriate for children, thus reducing the economic value of large families. Crenshaw, Christenson, and Oakey (2000) also found that independent of the effects of child mortality, service sector dominance, and other variables, family-planning programs played an important role in reducing fertility in developing countries over the 1965 to 1990 period.

Population Policies

For countries that want to control population growth, what are the alternatives? There are three basic schools of thought relating to fertility reduction policies. In this section we will discuss family planning, the developmentalist strategy, and the societalist perspective. We will

China's one-child policy was stipulated by law, enforced by the government, and encouraged by propaganda.

also consider the use of coercion to control fertility and the problems faced by countries whose population is decreasing instead of increasing.

Family Planning

Proponents of *family planning* contend that if contraceptives are made readily available and information regarding the value and need for birth planning is disseminated throughout a society, people will reduce their fertility. In turn, a reduction in fertility will allow investment in economic development. There are many countries in which the proportion of women using modern methods of contraception is less than 10 percent. The average for the world is 55 percent (Haub and Kaneda, 2011), and about 40 percent of the pregnancies that occur each year in developing countries are unintended (Bongaarts and Sinding, 2011). Contemporary Bangladesh provides a good illustration of a nation that is cutting its birth rate significantly

by promoting and supporting the adoption of modern contraceptive methods—without first waiting for the reduction that customarily comes with higher living standards. One of the world's most successful, Bangladesh's voluntary family-planning program includes outreach to husbands and village and religious leaders as well as female workers to distribute supplies and provide advice and information to women (Bongaarts and Sinding, 2011).

The Developmentalist Strategy

A second approach entails a *developmentalist* strategy, based on demographic transition theory. According to this school of thought, fertility is a pattern of behavior tied closely to the institutional and organizational structure of society. "Development is the best contraception" was a popular slogan of the 1970s. Although modernization has often been associated with a decline in fertility, as we discussed

Is Development the Best Contraceptive?

A basic principle in demographic transition theory is that there is a general inverse relationship between development and birth rate—that is, as development increases, the birth rate of an area decreases. This idea—that parents adjust their fertility when they see that large numbers of offspring are no longer needed to support their labor-intensive lifestyles—has been used to justify a hands-off policy toward population control in Third World countries. As development proceeds, family size will naturally decrease, without any programs to provide contraceptives or incentives to reduce the number of offspring per family.

Does any evidence support this notion? Demographers John Knodel and Etienne van de Walle (1979) undertook extensive archival research to determine the accuracy of the "general inverse relationship" in the historical record of European fertility. In general, Europe's change from an agricultural to an industrial society was accompanied by a drop in fertility. But two types of demographic studies, along with qualitative historical analysis, provided them with a better picture of changes in European fertility.

First, microlevel family studies based on church registers of baptisms, burials, and marriages allowed researchers to determine village populations during the pre-industrial period. The information gleaned from genealogies and church records can be used to look at changes in reproductive behavior over a long span of time.

Second, macrolevel studies based on data from published censuses and vital statistics can be used to analyze changes in fertility patterns over time for particular geopolitical units.

Knodel and van de Walle also found a third type of study useful: qualitative historical analysis, in which letters, novels, contemporary commentaries, and physicians' reports can be used to gain a sense of how much people knew about birth control and what their attitudes toward children and reproduction were at various times in history.

What did Knodel and van de Walle conclude from their assessment of so many sources of information?

First, sometimes birth rates declined as development increased, but just as often the two were *not* associated. Indeed, fertility declines took place under a wide variety of social, economic, and demographic conditions, not simply in inverse relationship to development.

Second, although a significant number of births may have been unwanted before fertility rates declined, taking action to limit one's family size was essentially unheard of among broad segments of the population.

Third, once people began to limit family size, increases in the practice of family limitation and the decline of marital fertility were basically irreversible.

Last, cultural setting influenced the onset and spread of fertility decline; the fertility rates of areas with similar socioeconomic conditions but dissimilar cultures began to decrease at different times, but the fertility rates of areas with different socioeconomic conditions and similar cultures began to fall at the same time.

In other words, the researchers found that *in addition to* a loose relationship between socioeconomic development and a decline in fertility, many other factors were linked to the decrease in family size in Europe. They proposed that introducing the concept of family planning (and providing means for controlling fertility), along with "the diffusion of tastes for modern consumer goods, higher material aspirations, and an awareness of alternative roles for women" (1979:239), could have a significant impact on modern populations in the developing world.

Knodel and van de Walle's findings suggest that population policies can be implemented in overpopulated countries *before* industrialization and modernization occur. They also suggest that simply waiting for industrialization and modernization to take care of fertility is foolish; development may in fact have no effect on the fertility rates of various countries or areas.

Questions for Discussion

1. Based on the findings presented here, what effect would you expect increased educational and employment opportunities for women to have on fertility rates in developing countries?

2. Which of the population policies discussed in the text are supported by the research findings of Knodel and van de Walle?

in the section on demographic transition theory, the relation is not clear-cut enough to justify a simple causal link between industrialization and smaller families (see Box 12.1).

The Societalist Perspective

A third approach involves a *societalist* perspective in which the government fashions policies designed to produce changes in demographic behavior. Demographer Kingsley Davis (1971: 403) suggested a number of social reforms that would reduce fertility by rewarding low fertility and penalizing high fertility, including tax, housing, and other advantages for single people; education and career opportunities for women; and free birth control and abortion services. Higher education for women and girls has been linked to reductions in fertility and to an improved quality of life for families (Bremner et al., 2009). In South Korea, concerns about severe population aging have led to social reforms aimed at population increases: tax and housing incentives, child care and education support, and assistance for infertile couples (Bremner et al., 2010).

Coercion

Another approach to population control is coercion. China adopted a one-child policy in 1980 and has reduced its total fertility rate to 1.5 percent and its rate of natural increase to 0.5 percent (Haub and Kaneda, 2011). China's Population and Family Planning law imposes fines on citizens who have more children than permitted by their area's regulations (Huiting, 2002), and compulsory abortions and sterilizations have been part of the program (Hvistendahl, 2009). The general goal is one child per family, but regulations vary, and couples can apply for permission to have a second child under certain circumstances (Huiting, 2002).

Because male children are valued more highly than female children in China, as in many other countries, the one-child policy has resulted in an imbalance in the sex ratio, with 120 males for every 100 females at birth (Hvistendahl, 2009)

and over 130 for some provinces (Zhu, Lu, and Hesketh, 2009). A new program aimed at bringing the sex ratio back into balance, the "care for girls" campaign, was started in 2000 (Zhu, Lu, and Hesketh, 2009).

Population Loss

In some nations population loss is of more concern than population growth. In Spain and Italy, traditionally nations of large families, the fertility rate has fallen to 1.4 children per woman, and population growth has dropped accordingly. The fertility rate for all of Europe is only 1.6, and its rate of natural increase is zero. In many European countries, without immigration, the population is decreasing. Although the pattern of low fertility is most extreme in European countries and in Japan, fertility rates have declined in many countries. In some countries fertility rates have been below replacement level for so long that the countries have negative growth momentum—even if fertility should rise to two children per woman, the population will continue to decline for decades.

The strong association that demographers have noted between high levels of economic development and low fertility (Bryant, 2007; Lee, 2003) suggests that it would be unlikely that trends in population decline can be slowed or turned around in either developed or developing countries. However, new research shows that fertility rates have recently increased in countries with very high levels of economic and social development (Myrskylä, Kohler, and Billari, 2009). Fertility has not increased above replacement level in these countries, but it has increased to the point that modest levels of immigration can prevent or significantly slow population loss.

Loss of population can create problems in the specific countries in which it occurs. For example, as the population ages, there may not be a sufficiently large cohort of workers to maintain the institutions of society and to support the retired and elderly cohort.

The Urban Environment

More than half the world's population now lives in cities, with 69 percent of the population projected to be city-dwellers by 2050 (Bloom, 2011). A **city** is defined by sociologists as a relatively dense and permanent concentration of people who secure their livelihoods chiefly through nonagricultural activities. The influence of the urban mode of life extends far beyond the immediate confines of a city's boundaries. Cities account for three-quarters of the energy consumption on earth and emit 80 percent of the greenhouse gases responsible for global warming (Ash et al., 2008). They also have been characterized as "essential crucibles for innovation, tolerance, diversity, novelty, surprise, and most of all, for economic prosperity" (Batty, 2008). In this section we will consider the origin and growth of cities, patterns of city growth, ecological processes at work in cities, urban crisis, and urban sprawl.

The Origin and Evolution of Cities

Cities constitute a relatively recent development in human history. The domestication of plants and the husbandry of animals were critical innovations that allowed human beings to live together in larger groups. When human beings could produce food instead of just finding it, population expanded in settled communities. Larger cities facilitate division of labor and economies of scale, and as cities grow they change shape, develop new energy needs, and experience increased congestion (Batty, 2008). The "optimal" size for a city is a matter of contention. Let's take a look at the history of cities in human civilization, from the earliest aggregates of humans to our contemporary metropolises.

Preindustrial Cities

Early Neolithic communities were more small villages than cities. A number of innovations were required for towns to evolve. Between 6000 and 4000 B.C., the invention of the ox-drawn plow, the wheeled cart, the sailboat, metallurgy, and irrigation and the cultivation of new plants allowed for new ways of living. These innovations resulted in an economy that could sustain the concentration of people in one place.

Among the early centers of urban development were Mesopotamia, the Nile River valley of Egypt, the Indus River valley of India, and the Yellow River basin of China (Davis, 1955, 1967). However, a productive economy was not by itself sufficient to bring about the growth of cities. New forms of social organization also were required. Bureaucratic structures and stratification systems arose that enabled government officials, religious personnel, merchants, and artisans to appropriate for themselves part of the produce grown by cultivators (see Chapters 4 and 6).

For the most part, preindustrial cities did not exceed 10 percent of the population of an area. Their sizes were limited by poor transportation, the difficulty of securing larger areas from outside threats, unsanitary conditions, and a feudal social structure that tied potential migrants to the land. Cities of 100,000 or more were rare, although under favorable social and economic conditions some cities surpassed this size.

Industrial-Urban Centers

Urbanization has proceeded quite rapidly during the past two centuries. In 1800, 3 percent of the world's population lived in urban areas; 100 years later, 14 percent of the world's population was urban, and 100 years beyond that brings us to the present, with more than half of the world's population living in urban areas. In 1950, just eight urban agglomerations had populations of 5 million or more (see Figure 12.6); this number had jumped to 41 by 2000 and was projected to be 59 by 2015. Most early urban communities were city-states, from which many modern nations have evolved.

Both social factors and technological innovations contributed to the acceleration of urban

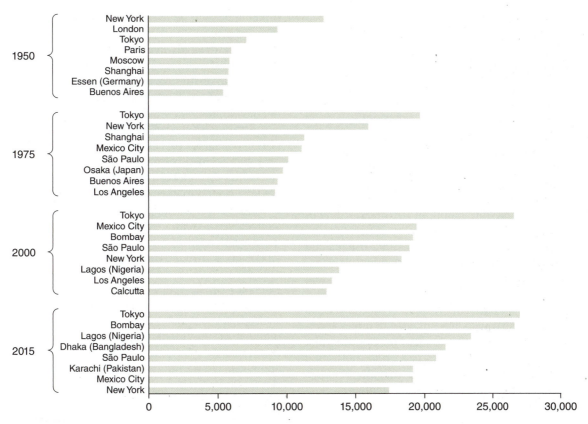

Figure 12.6

Population Size (in 1,000s) of the Eight Largest Urban Agglomerations in the World, in 1950, 1975, and 2000, with Projections to 2015

In the 1950s most of the largest urban agglomerations in the world were European and North American metropolitan cities that evolved out of industrial-urban centers of the 19th century. By 2000, more than half of the largest areas were in the developing world, a trend that urban demographers expect will continue into the 21st century. (The United Nations defines an *agglomeration* as "the population contained within the contours of a contiguous territory inhabited at urban density levels without regard to administrative boundaries" [United Nations, 2001]; that is, it is essentially equivalent to what we have defined as a metropolitan city.)

Source: Figure generated by the authors using data from United Nations, 2001. (Available at http://www.un.org/esa/population/publications/wup1999/wup99.htm.)

growth. Organizational changes permitted greater complexity in the division of labor. The use of steam as a source of energy promoted the use of machines. Widespread by the mid- to late-19th century, power-driven machines accelerated social trends that were moving manufacturing out of the home and into centralized factories. As the factory system expanded, increasing numbers of people moved to cities to find jobs. The Industrial Revolution is a part of American and European history and is now occurring elsewhere around the world.

Metropolitan Cities

Industrial-urban centers typically had only tenuous economic and social relations with the surrounding areas. More recently, metropolitan cities—central cities and suburbs—have emerged. This phase in urban development represents a widening and deepening of urban influences in every area of social life.

Electric power, rapid transit, the automobile, and the telephone made it possible for satellite and suburban areas to develop around city centers. In population, jobs, investment, construction, and shopping facilities, the suburbs rival the old inner cities. They are the sites of industrial plants, corporate offices and office towers, fine stores, independent newspapers, theaters, restaurants, superhotels, and big-league stadiums.

In many cases the rural interstices between metropolitan centers have filled with urban development, making a "strip city" or **megalopolis.** The northeastern seaboard is a good illustration of this process. A gigantic megalopolis lies along a 600-mile axis from southern New Hampshire to northern Virginia, encompassing 10 states, 117 counties, and 32 cities larger than 500,000 people, and embracing nearly a fifth of the U.S. population. Urban projections suggest that by the year 2050, if not sooner, another urbanized strip will extend from New York State through Pennsylvania, Ohio, northern Indiana and Illinois to Green Bay, Wisconsin, and Minneapolis–St. Paul.

The Global City

For most of the past 200 years, the largest cities in the world have been industrial urban centers in Europe and North America. By 1950 most of the largest urban agglomerations were still in Europe and America, but there had been significant urban growth in Asia and Latin America (United Nations, 2001). Urban demographers predict that by 2015 this situation will have completely changed, and most of the largest urban areas will be in the developing world (see Figure 12.6).

These changes have the potential to affect the rate of development in the now underdeveloped world as long as urbanization is accompanied by continued progress in education and in the development and diffusion of technology.

Sociologist and urban planner Saskia Sassen (1991) contended that changes in the world economy transformed major urban centers into what she called the "global city." Major urban centers are now central marketplaces for financial trading and investment banking and the kind of higher value-added activities (legal and accounting firms, advertising agencies, and management consultants) upon which contemporary corporations rely. New York, London, and Tokyo are prime examples of the global city; Amsterdam, Hong Kong, São Paulo, Sydney, and Toronto are others.

The critical processes fostering the development of the global city are dispersal and concentration. Advanced technology and telecommunications mean that manufacturing and production activities need not be concentrated in a few places, resulting in the transfer of routine jobs to low-wage areas of the world. At the same time, however, this worldwide dispersal of production and manufacturing requires the centralization of a variety of managerial and financial operations and services. These functions tend to cluster in big cities, and the cities in turn become centers for control and coordination of the global economy.

Clustered in big cities are "transnational spaces"—the locations of high-rolling finance and service corporations—that to one degree or another are outside the purview of any state or national government. They have evolved a kind of "global culture" so that the airports, hotels, restaurants, and high-price, high-prestige locations are more or less alike from one global city to another.

The benefits of development made possible by the global city may make little difference to the lives of the poor. According to Sassen, the

Concentric Zone Theory

Sector Theory

Multiple Nuclei Theory

1. Central Business District
2. Wholesale Light Manufacturing
3. Low-Class Residential

4. Medium-Class Residential
5. High-Class Residential
6. Heavy Manufacturing

7. Outlying Business District
8. Residential Suburb
9. Industrial Suburb
10. Commuters' Zone

Figure 12.7 **Theoretical Patterns of Urban Structure**
Urban areas (numbered 1–10) are indicated in each structure.

Source: The Nature of Cities Chauncy D. Harris and Edward L. Ullman Annals of the American Academy of Political and Social Science Vol. 242, Building the Future City (Nov., 1945), pp. 7-17 Published by: Sage Publications, Inc.

global economy and its cities have contributed to the emergence of a new urban class structure. The growth of transnational financial and service sectors has created a class of highly paid managers and professionals. But their success relies on a large, low-wage, insecure labor force—for example, the cleaning crew that comes in after hours and the truck drivers who deliver the office supplies. The global city becomes the terrain of the affluent and the poor, with the middle class all but disappearing (Sassen and Portes, 1993).

Patterns of City Growth

Human ecologists and urban sociologists are interested in understanding the spatial patterning of people's relationships and activities. They provide a number of models that attempt to capture the ecological patterns and structures of city growth. Here we present three classic models: the concentric circle model, the sector theory,

and the multiple nuclei theory (see Figure 12.7). Probably no city has grown in exactly the way any of these models suggest. However, each model emphasizes important processes that help us understand city growth.

Concentric Circle Model

In the period between the two world wars, sociologists at the University of Chicago viewed Chicago as a social laboratory and subjected it to intensive study. The **concentric circle model** enjoyed a prominent place in much of this work (Park, Burgess, and McKenzie, 1925). The Chicago group held that the modern city assumes a pattern of concentric circles, each with distinctive characteristics. At the center of the city—the *central business district*—are retail stores, financial institutions, hotels, theaters, and businesses. Next is an area of residential deterioration caused by the encroachment of business and industry— the *zone in transition*. The zone in transition shades into the *zone of workingmen's homes.* Beyond the zone occupied by the working class are *residential zones* housing small business proprietors, professional people, and managerial personnel. The outermost ring is small cities, towns, and hamlets, the *commuters' zone.*

The Sector Model

Homer Hoyt (1939) portrayed large cities as made up of a number of sectors rather than concentric circles—the **sector model** (see Figure 12.7). Low-rent districts often assume a wedge shape and extend from the center of the city to its periphery. In contrast, as a city grows, high-rent areas move outward, although remaining in the same sector. Districts within a sector that are abandoned by upper-income groups become obsolete and deteriorate. Industrial areas evolve along river valleys, watercourses, and railroad lines rather than forming a concentric circle around the central business district.

The Multiple Nuclei Model

Another model—the **multiple nuclei model**—depicts the city as having not one center but several (Harris and Ullman, 1945). Each center specializes in some activity and gives its distinctive cast to the surrounding area. A city might include a central business district, theater and recreation area, "automobile row," a government center, a wholesaling center, a heavy-manufacturing district, and a medical complex. Multiple centers evolve for a number of reasons. First, certain activities require specialized facilities; for example, the retail district needs to be accessible to all parts of the city. Second, similar activities often benefit from being clustered together; for example, a retail district profits by drawing customers for a variety of shops. Third, dissimilar activities are often antagonistic to one another; for example, affluent residential development tends to be incompatible with industrial development. Finally, some activities (e.g., bulk wholesaling and storage) cannot afford high-rent areas and hence locate in low-rent districts.

Contemporary Models

The models discussed above give us some insight into patterns of urban growth, but there is still much to learn about how cities evolve. Current thought includes the idea that cities are "complex systems that mainly grow from the bottom up," with their size and shape determined by the intense competition for space that occurs in cities (Batty, 2008:769). Urban economics and transportation behavior are essential ingredients. British researcher Michael Batty describes the state of the science of city planning this way (2008:771):

We have only just started in earnest to build theories of how cities function as complex systems. We do know, however, that idealized geometric plans produced without any regard to urban functioning are not likely to resolve any of our current urban ills, and this new physics makes us much more aware of the limits of planning. It is likely to lead to a view that as we learn more about the functioning of such complex systems, we will interfere less but in more appropriate ways.

Ecological Processes: Segregation and Gentrification

Some sociologists have applied the theories and vocabulary of **ecology** to human populations. "Human ecology" looks at the relationships between humans and their human environment and institutions. City development can be seen as the result of economic and social competition for urban space.

Segregation

One ecological process sociologists are interested in is **segregation**—a process of clustering wherein individuals and groups are sifted and sorted out in space based on their sharing of certain traits or activities in common. This clustering takes place voluntarily when people find that close spatial proximity is advantageous, and the resulting segregated areas have been termed **natural areas** because they do not result from any official planning by government units. For example, the multiple nuclei model of city growth suggests that certain similar activities profit from the cohesion provided by a segregated district.

Of course segregation may also be involuntary. Residential neighborhoods frequently attempt to exclude incompatible commercial and industrial activities through zoning ordinances. Ethnic and racial groups may systematically exclude other groups from their neighborhoods. These processes have produced an urban America that is highly segregated racially. African Americans are the most segregated minority group in the United States, followed in turn by Hispanics, Asians, and Native Americans. While racial and ethnic segregation is declining over time, the changes from 1980 to 2000 were very small (Iceland, Weinberg, and Steinmetz, 2002).

Class segregation—the separation of the rich from the poor—increased about 26 percent between 1970 and 1990 (Morin, 1998). The poor in the United States are increasingly concentrated in high-poverty inner-city neighborhoods. Between 1970 and 1990, the number of Americans living in poverty increased by 50 percent, but the number of poor neighborhoods has more than doubled (Jargowsky, 1997). At the same time, affluent people are increasingly living in affluent neighborhoods (Morin, 1998). Local politics are significantly affected by such segregation, with entire political jurisdictions increasingly becoming "poor" or "rich" and providing services accordingly.

Invasion and Succession

Invasion and succession are critical ecological processes and are concepts that have been borrowed by sociologists and applied to urban development. **Invasion** takes place when a new type of people, institution, or activity encroaches on an area occupied by a different type. Should the invasion continue until the encroaching type displaces the other, **succession** is said to have occurred. When people with very different backgrounds come to share or compete for urban neighborhoods, issues of race, class, and culture often become highlighted and lead to social conflict (Winnick, 1991; Wysocki, 1991).

Urban gentrification—the return of the middle class, usually young, white, childless professionals ("yuppies," for young urban professionals) to older neighborhoods—has happened in large cities throughout the United States: Haight-Ashbury in San Francisco, Queen Village in Philadelphia, Mount Adams in Cincinnati, New Town in Chicago, German Village in Columbus, Ohio, and the East Village and Soho in New York. Gentrification typically results in the displacement of the poor and minorities from these neighborhoods by upwardly mobile whites with financial resources and clout.

New Cities, Old Cities

More than 80 percent of Americans now live in urban areas (Bloom, 2011). Economist Edward Glaeser points out that the basics of city living are "clean water, safe neighborhoods, and fluid streets" (2011:594) and that urban density in the developing world and elsewhere may be associated instead with contagious disease, crime, and extreme traffic congestion. City governments around the world, he says, will have to invest in water and wastewater systems, public transportation, and crime control, which will present challenges in poor nations.

In industrialized countries such as the United States, where more than 80 percent of the population now lives in metropolitan areas, many urban problems are due to city decline. In many U.S. cities, metropolitan development since World War II has followed a pattern of extending rings of prosperous suburbs and new city growth, leaving behind a decaying central city. Some cities with this "doughnut structure" are seeing a revitalization of the doughnut "hole," as in New York City's Manhattan.

As populations increase and cities grow, urban infrastructures decay. Without proper repair and maintenance, disaster may ensue.

Urban decline can be descriptive or functional. *Descriptive decline* has to do with the loss of population or jobs. It occurs as people who have the resources to leave the city do, while those who are poor have little choice but to remain. The proportion of poor residents increases as their number is swelled by recent migrants who also are poor. Urban ills are thus aggravated and require an increasing share of a city's resources. Life in the city then becomes less agreeable and more costly for middle- and upper-income residents, who move out of the city. This cycle hurts the city and complicates its ability to be responsive to people's needs and results in increasing isolation of poor and immigrant populations.

Functional decline refers to a deterioration in city services and the social amenities of urban life. It is reflected in the decay of the urban infrastructure in older industrial cities—the network of roads, bridges, sewers, rails, and mass transit systems. According to the Environmental Protection Agency, many of the nation's water and wastewater facilities have water quality or public health problems; additionally, some cities lose as much as 30 percent of their daily water supply as a result of leaky pipes. Many roads and bridges are bearing far greater burdens than they were designed to accommodate, and many are deteriorating. Increases in population lead to increases in traffic, with heavier use of roads that are already in poor condition.

Both functional and descriptive decline provide opportunities for cities to solve a variety of problems. At a 2011 symposium on building sustainable cities, urban leaders said that cities are "turning green" both to solve financial problems and to improve quality of life for their residents (Ham, 2011). In Richmond, Virginia, bicycle paths, energy-efficient stoplights, and telework programs contribute to the city's sustainability efforts. Boston is installing electric car-charging stations and LED lighting in public places. In Dubuque, Iowa, overhaul of water, energy, and transportation systems reduced water use by 6 percent and improved the city's leak detection and repair system. Projects aimed at encouraging walking reduce traffic congestion and improve human health.

The Rise of "Edge" Cities

A new form of urban organization emerged in the United States over the past 50 years. Growing American metropolitan areas have sprouted multiple "outer cities," "mini-cities," or "edge cities" (Suro, 1990; Garreau, 1991). Whereas several decades ago a central city was relatively compact, now everything is spread over a much larger crescent of development. The transition has been facilitated by the development of a service-based economy in which telecommunications allow service sector firms to locate anywhere. Shopping malls or clusters of office buildings, warehouses, or factories are scattered around at interchanges along the broad, ballooning bands of inter-linked beltways. These centers of development generate other development. The typical dwelling units are the condominium, the large apartment complex, and the celebrated suburban home.

In many cases government structures and policies have trouble adapting to new patterns of growth. Regional approaches may be required to deal with issues such as taxation, highways, parks, water, and waste disposal. Not all urban planners view urban sprawl in a negative light. Robert Bruegmann (2005) argues that urban sprawl is a normal part of urban growth and has been going on for thousands of years. People and businesses move out of center cities because outer areas provide more space, privacy, and other benefits.

The Ecological Environment

Why discuss the environment in a sociology book? Scientists understand what problems the planet faces and, in many cases, what people ought to do to solve them. But implementing solutions is a human and social endeavor. The social sciences can help biologists, engineers, ecologists, and environmental managers to identify socially acceptable and politically feasible solutions to our problems (Reid et al., 2010; Hull and Robertson, 2000). As biologists have expressed it, "There is an urgent need to integrate biological and social disciplines in order to generate reliable recommendations for society" (Dirzo and Loreau, 2005).

How important are other species and the environment to humans? Beyond aesthetics, nature provides many irreplaceable services to humans: the raw materials for foods, medicines,

building materials, and energy; the production of oxygen, without which people cannot live; the filtering and detoxifying of pollutants; the provision of fresh water; and much more (Wilson, 2002). Humankind cannot afford *not* to take care of the environment.

Earlier in this chapter, we saw how rapidly the world's population has expanded. In this section we will look at the enormous effect that humans have on the **environment**—the surrounding conditions and influences that affect an organism or group of organisms. Most of earth's **ecosystems**—relatively stable communities of organisms that have interlocking relationships and exchanges with one another and their environment—are now dominated by humans. How has this domination affected our environment? We will explore the question in this section, beginning with an assessment of the health of the planet. We also will see what the sociological perspectives have to offer and close with a look at sustainability.

The Health of the Earth

How do we measure the health of the earth? For the purposes of our discussion, we will define it in terms of ourselves—humans. A team of 29 scientists from Europe, Australia, and the United States and led by Johan Rockström of Sweden (Rockström et al., 2009) has reviewed many studies of environmental processes and changes and identified nine processes they believe could disrupt earth's ability to support human life.

Before we discuss these processes, let's review some history. The earth has not always been as we see it today. But in a number of essential characteristics, it has been stable for most of the past 10,000 years, a period that geologists call the Holocene (Rockström et al., 2009). Many scientists refer to the period since the Industrial Revolution as the **Anthropocene;** the name reflects the belief that humans are now the major cause of global environmental change (Vince, 2011). During the Holocene, a number of factors that make life on earth possible to humans, including air, water, and land temperatures, all stayed within a narrow range.

Rockström and his colleagues (2009) found that our reliance on fossil fuels and industrialized agriculture now is threatening the systems that maintain earth's equilibrium and stability, with potentially irreversible environmental changes the predicted result. The nine environmental processes they identified are

- Climate change
- Biodiversity loss (terrestrial and marine species extinctions)
- Interference with nitrogen and phosphorus cycles
- Stratospheric ozone depletion
- Ocean acidification
- Global freshwater use
- Natural ecosystem conversion to cropland
- Chemical pollution
- Atmospheric aerosol loading

The scientists then determined "planetary boundaries" for each of these categories, the limits within which the earth will remain a place that supports human life and well-being. Their work represents the first time scientists have tried to quantify such limits. For three of the processes—climate change, species extinctions, and nitrogen and phosphorus pollution—we already have exceeded the boundaries. These three deserve a closer look.

Climate Change

The debate about global warming shifted several years ago from one about its existence to one about whether we have passed the "tipping point" beyond which it is too late to act to prevent catastrophic changes (Eilperin, 2006). Rockström and his colleagues (2009) present evidence that climate change already has caused changes from the stable Holocene state,

including the retreat of mountain glaciers, the retreat of summer sea ice in the Arctic, accelerating rates of sea-level rise, and the loss of mass from ice sheets in Greenland and West Antarctica. With immediate action to stabilize atmospheric carbon dioxide concentrations at 350 parts per million (ppm), they are hopeful that the large polar ice sheets can be preserved and that temperatures can be stabilized. The temperature increases associated with a doubling of atmospheric carbon dioxide "would severely challenge the viability of contemporary human societies" (Rockström et al., 2009:473).

Biodiversity Loss

Species became extinct before humans were around, but the rate at which extinctions occur has accelerated tremendously; it is now between a hundred and a thousand times faster than we would expect it to be without human interference. Rockström and his colleagues (2009) found that land use changes—from natural ecosystems to urban areas and croplands—are currently responsible, with climate change poised to take over as the most important driving force. They expect up to 30 percent of species of mammals, birds, and amphibians to be threatened with extinction this century.

In addition to the value of individual species for individual functions obvious to everyone (for example, swordfish will no longer appear on the restaurant menu when swordfish are extinct), a rich mix of species provides ecosystems with a greater degree of resilience against disturbances such as disease, natural disaster, and temperature fluctuations and other benefits we are just beginning to understand (Estes et al., 2011). Rockström and his colleagues acknowledge that there is much uncertainty about how many and what kinds of species can be lost without major impacts on humans, but they are certain that the earth "cannot sustain the current rate of loss without significant erosion of ecosystem resilience" (2009:474).

Nitrogen and Phosphorus Pollution

The use of fertilizers for agriculture around the globe has resulted in huge quantities of nitrogen and phosphorus polluting streams, rivers, and coastal waters, and nitrogen also can be found in an atmospheric gas form that, like carbon dioxide, is a greenhouse gas. Nitrogen and phosphorus can be found in soil, water, air, and rock under natural conditions and move through plants and animals and back to soil in processes called biogeochemical cycles. Humans have distorted these cycles dramatically, with current levels high enough to have created depositions in pristine, remote ecosystems (Holtgrieve et al., 2011) and to cause concern about mass extinctions in the oceans (Rockström et al., 2009).

What overall conclusions did Rockström and his colleagues reach? They recognize that there are many gaps in knowledge that prevent scientists from making more definite predictions. They also acknowledge that some of the interconnections between the processes for which they have identified boundaries are currently unknown (2009:475):

[B]ecause many of the boundaries are linked, exceeding one will have implications for others in ways that we do not as yet completely understand. There is also significant uncertainty over how long it takes to cause dangerous environmental change or to trigger other feedbacks that drastically reduce the ability of the Earth system, or important subsystems, to return to safe levels.

Sociological Perspectives on the Environment

How do sociologists think about environmental problems? If we have a fairly good scientific grasp of what our difficulties are, why are societies not taking action? Let's look at each of the three major sociological perspectives for some sociological insights.

The Functionalist Perspective

Functionalist theorists approach the ecological environment by examining the interconnections between the various parts composing the ecosystems (Faia, 1989). They see the ecosystem as exhibiting a tendency toward equilibrium, in which its components maintain a delicately balanced relationship with one another. The perspective is nicely captured by the notion of Spaceship Earth—the idea that our planet is a closed system with finite resources that, if destroyed or depleted, cannot be replaced. Life exists only in the biosphere, a thin skin of air, soil, and water on the surface of the planet. Functionalists stress that our survival depends on our ability to maintain the precarious balance among the living and nonliving components of the biosphere. They fear that our pollution of the environment and our depletion of the earth's natural resources are jeopardizing the very environment that is the basis for life.

Functionalists also argue that societies tend to react to challenges through adaptation and thus assume that environmental problems can be resolved through normal social and political processes. An example is the current discussion of how U.S. society might deal with the problem of harmful carbon emissions. If we believed that preventing a catastrophic rise in carbon and thus global temperatures depends upon eliminating fossil fuel use, we might give up in despair—our whole society is built on coal and oil.

But as economist Paul Krugman (2010) has noted, environmental economists agree that a market-based program could be the answer. The acid rain problem of the 20th century was mitigated through a cap-and-trade system in which individual companies managed their own emissions within regulatory limits; the emissions causing acid rain were cut in half, and electricity prices fell instead of rising. Action by one institution—government—resulted in reactions in the economic sector, and both the societal and atmospheric systems reached equilibrium again. Krugman (2010:38) argues that putting a price on greenhouse gas emissions will be required to achieve goals in emissions reduction. People will change consumer behaviors, he says, when produce that is shipped long distances costs more to reflect the environmental costs of such shipping and when insulating a home saves not just heating and air-conditioning costs but also taxes and fees for carbon emissions and electricity generation.

The Conflict Perspective

Conflict theorists point to power as the central element affecting macro social and political processes. The central question regarding climate change and other environmental problems is: Who benefits from lax regulation of environmental exploitation and pollution, including continued inaction on controlling greenhouse gas emissions? The beneficiaries are large corporate interests and the enterprises linked to them. Because economic power is strongly linked to national power, national governments often work to promote the economic interests of large corporations with little attention to their effects on the environment. In the United States, corporations spend huge amounts of money lobbying in Congress for legislative measures that benefit them and against measures that would limit their profits. In the early 1990s, when global warming had been established by scientists as a legitimate problem that needed to be addressed, the fossil fuels industry, its business allies, and conservative think tanks launched a major effort to discredit the scientific evidence (McCright and Dunlap, 2011). Global warming has become a major partisan issue in the United States (Antonio and Brulle, 2011).

Conflict theorists point out that interests tend to be separated into two camps on environmental issues. On one side are those who favor economic development and growth even if it results in environmental damage. On the other side are those who see environmental preservation as their primary goal and who believe that the environment must take precedence over economic goals. The two groups are at odds and contest each other in the political arena.

Some conflict theorists depict environmental problems as related more to the distribution of the world's resources than to a limited amount of resources available in the world. They say that the basic issue is not one of how much is available but one of which individuals and groups will secure a disproportionate share of what is available. Hence, the critical decisions that affect the environment are made not in the interests of present and future generations but in the interests of those groups that can impose their will on others. As long as there are resources left that can be exploited in a profitable manner, conflict theorists argue, there will be powerful humans and groups that profit.

The Interactionist Perspective

Symbolic interactionists give environmental issues a somewhat different twist, focusing their sociological eye upon "people behaviors." Interactionists have provided significant insight on the socially constructed understandings and myths people have about the environment.

For example, a considerable gap often exists between public and expert perceptions of risk. Global warming, which scientists see as a top concern because its long-term potential consequences are so damaging and its effects so widespread and difficult to reverse, was identified as a serious problem by only 35 percent of survey respondents in 2009 (Pew Research Center, 2009). Rather than being based in scientific

uncertainty, most disagreements about the consequences of such things as climate change, pesticides, deep-sea drilling, and nuclear waste disposal are associated with human beliefs and behaviors (Spiegelhalter, Pearson, and Short, 2011).

Another issue of interest to interactionists is generational changes in attitudes and actions. A comparison of high school seniors and entering college students from the Baby Boomer Generation (born between 1946 and 1961), the GenX'ers (born 1962–1981), and Millennials (born after 1982) revealed a steep decline in concern about the environment (Twenge, Campbell, and Freeman, 2012). Millennials were less likely than GenX'ers, and GenX'ers were less likely than Boomers, to make a personal effort to help the environment, to cut down on electricity use, to reduce heat usage during the winter, and to involve themselves in programs to clean up the environment.

Symbolic interactionists point out that environmental issues qualify for the adjective "social" because they involve human judgments, decisions, and choices. Environmental issues are also social issues because they entail the exercise of power. For example, the poor and minorities are much more exposed than other citizens to the dangers of natural and technological hazards, which is termed *environmental racism*. Similarly, the costs of global climate change will not be borne equally by the world's population and will have a greater impact on future generations than on those currently making decisions, factors that have served to complicate our response (Gardiner, 2011).

The head scientist for The Nature Conservancy, Peter Kareiva, argues that demonstrating to people the relevance and economic value of nature in their lives—that their survival depends on nature—is essential to the success of conservation efforts. "The key," he says, "is to take each of the major needs of people—water, food, livelihoods, security, and health—and find the future that meets these needs and protects nature" (Kareiva, 2011). Indeed, most risk is politically negotiated—a network of government agencies, corporations, and public-interest groups grapple daily with selected hazards.

A Critique

Environmental sociologists have criticized sociological theories, including those grounded in functionalism, conflict theory, and interactionism, for being too anthropocentric. They argue that the theories focus on human beings to the neglect of the natural and physical environment and that they interpret or understand the world primarily in terms of human experiences and values (Catton and Dunlap, 1978; Dunlap and Catton, 1979; Buttel, 1987; Goldman and Schurman, 2000). Instead, sociological theory should be formulated with four important principles in mind (Catton and Dunlap, 1980). First, human life is possible because human beings are interdependent with many species in a global ecosystem. Second, though we typically attempt to explain human activities with reference to social structural and cultural factors alone, these patterns of activity evolved in complex systems of cause and effect involving the nonhuman natural and physical world. Third, the biophysical world imposes significant restraints and limits on what humans may do and still maintain an environment capable of supporting human life. Fourth, although human beings may affect nature in positive ways that promote both human life and the environment, ecological laws cannot be ignored without threatening the system that supports the entirety of life.

Sustainability

Scientists have been warning for years that human beings are changing the climate, that people are overly dependent on fossil fuels, that they are endangering their own lives as they push more and more species of animals over the brink to extinction, and that human inhabitants must change their ways to survive. Now humankind stands poised to add an estimated 3 billion people to the world in the next 40 years—nearly half again as many as currently live on earth—and the race to organize a sustainable society is underway. **Sustainability** has been succinctly defined as "transforming our ways of living to maximize the chances that environmental and social conditions will indefinitely support human security, well-being, and health" (McMichael, Butler, and Folke, 2003).

Of special interest to sociologists are the effects of environmental problems on various institutions, social processes, and the organization of society. For example, if an area of the United States were to become significantly drier and warmer than it is now and agriculture collapsed in the area, what would be the effect on

Toxic Trash? Ship It to Another Country

What do you do with your old electronic equipment when you buy something new? E-waste, or electronic waste, is currently the most rapidly growing waste problem in the world, with amounts of E-waste increasing nearly three times more quickly than amounts of other municipal wastes. And E-waste is toxic waste: Computers and other electronic equipment contain lead, mercury, cadmium, barium, chromium, beryllium, PCBs, dioxins, and other pollutants. Consumers and business users have to pay recyclers to take E-waste off their hands.

Recycling materials from electronic equipment is time consuming and unprofitable—at least in industrialized nations. So Americans ship it to other countries. In *Exporting Harm: The High-Tech Trashing of Asia* (Puckett et al., 2002), investigators documented the toxic waste trade that makes Asian countries the recipients of as much as 80 percent of the E-waste collected by recyclers in the United States. Although the export of all hazardous wastes from rich to poor countries was banned through the Basel

Convention in 1994, the United States never ratified the treaty and continues to export E-waste, even to China, which passed its own ban on E-waste imports in 2002.

It is environmental, health, and safety regulations that make recycling E-waste unprofitable in the United States. It is the lack of such regulations in other countries that make recycling E-waste profitable—and dangerous. For example, in Guiyu, China, about 100,000 men, women, and children are employed in taking computers apart—mostly by hand—and extracting copper from wiring, gold from capacitors, and other valuable products. Employees work with no protection for their hands, eyes, skin, and respiratory systems. Plastics are burned in the open air, acids are poured into canals and rivers, and lead-laden monitor glass and other components are dumped where heavy metals can leach into groundwater.

Global inequality is at the root of E-waste exportation. In the wealthy, industrialized United States, protected by multiple layers of regulations, wastes are generated and exported.

In developing nations with few or no environmental and health regulations, people are willing and eager to work for $1.50 a day to handle toxic materials. As the *Exporting Harm* authors point out, people only do such dangerous work when they have no alternative:

> If left unchecked, the toxic effluent of the affluent will flood towards the world's poorest countries where labor is cheap and occupational and environmental protections are inadequate. A free trade in hazardous wastes leaves the poorer peoples of the world with an untenable choice between poverty and poison—a choice that nobody should have to make (Puckett et al., 2002:1).

Questions for Discussion

1. What policies or strategies might the United States adopt to reduce the export of toxic trash?

2. Does the United States protect itself from pollution by exporting toxic wastes?

---

farmers and farm families? What would happen to the businesses associated with agriculture and to the communities built up around the businesses? Let's widen the view: As resources become less available, how will competition for scarcer resources be managed? Should we expect more conflicts and even wars? Will we create new ways of dividing and using resources?

The United States bears a heavy share of the responsibility for the fix the world is in. For example, a quarter of the world's carbon dioxide emissions—the major cause of global warming—comes from the United States (Eilperin, 2005). Each U.S. citizen daily uses more than

five times the amount of energy calculated to be the worldwide average per capita. The U.S. population represents about 4 percent of the world population, yet its citizens are responsible for 25 percent of the total energy consumed worldwide. Likewise, the United States produces more waste and pollutants than other countries, some of which is shipped abroad (see Box 12.2).

The disparity between wealthy industrialized nations and poor developing nations whose populations are growing rapidly is a critical problem. Though population growth is stable or declining in industrialized nations, the American contribution to environmental problems stems from a wealthy and overconsuming lifestyle. Poor people in developing countries, on the other hand, contribute to environmental problems because they are struggling to survive, and that struggle includes cutting trees, growing crops, and grazing livestock in ecologically vulnerable and unstable environments. How development proceeds in emerging world powers such as India and China may play the dominant role in shaping the global environment in this century (Bawa et al., 2010).

The planet's environmental problems are global in nature. Climate change, radiation from nuclear reactor accidents, species extinction, depleted fisheries, ocean pollution, drifts of atmospheric particulate matter—all are problems with no political boundaries. It is thus increasingly clear that creating a sustainable world society will require a global effort.

What will that effort look like? A 2007 report by scientists representing dozens of the world's national science academies summed it up succinctly: Use energy more efficiently, put a price on carbon emissions, and develop green energy sources (Kintisch, 2007). Jonathan Foley (2010:57), one of Johan Rockström's colleagues on the planetary boundaries study, suggests these solutions: Make the transition to an efficient, low-carbon energy system; sharply curtail land clearing and degradation; and invest in revolutionary agricultural practices.

While some parts of the world have been denying the reality of global warming and others have been denying their part in the destruction of the environment, innovative researchers around the world have been quietly developing new methods for living sustainably, and out-of-the-box thinkers have been dreaming up new policies and guidelines. In China, urban planners are working on carbon-neutral cities, in which carbon emissions are offset by carbon absorption (Normile, 2008), and "reduce, reuse, and recycle" is being applied to industrial development, with the waste from one factory used as the input for another (Liu, 2010). In Israel, a network of

protected habitats coexists with one of the world's highest densities of humans (Kareiva, 2011).

New technology is definitely also part of the future. Solar power is a field that's set to explode, with advances far beyond the big solar grids we're used to seeing (Service, 2011). As global water resources are strained, the progress being made in converting salt water to drinking water (Elimelech and Phillip, 2011) becomes more important. And organizational approaches to environmental problems also are appearing. Fisheries management for balanced harvesting may help stabilize the protein source of much of the world's population (Garcia et al., 2012). A Commission on Sustainable Agriculture and Climate Change, set up in 2011, works to generate food security policy from scientific evidence (Beddington et al., 2012). Thin-film, nanotech, and biomimicry solar power technology all promise clean energy for the future (http://www.renewableenergyworld.com/rea/news/story?id=48187).

Humans have dealt with many problems in the past, and humans need to work hard now and into the future to avert disaster, protect our most vulnerable groups, and find a way to live sustainably on the earth. Questions of interest to sociologists include these: Do we need new global organizations to help meet our new global challenges? Which individuals and groups will translate their vision of reality into official public policy? How will individuals, groups, and societies cope with the changes ahead? Once policies are set, how will implementation proceed? How will organizations at all levels of society adapt and change? We can expect significant social change, the topic of our next chapter.

What Can Sociology Do for You?

This chapter has presented information about population, the environment, and cities. If you found the issues and information included here interesting, you may want to find out more about pursuing a career in demography. For information about salaries, the training required, and the sorts of jobs demographers get, try this website: **http://careers.stateuniversity.com/pages/395/Demographer.html.** Urban planners will be in constant demand over the next decades, as more and more of our population moves to cities and as cities grow and transform into more sustainable environments. Information about careers in urban planning is available at **http://www4.uwm.edu/SARUP/planning/About_career.htm,** and information about environmental sociology can be found at **http://envirosoc.org/gradprograms.php.**

Would you like to learn more now? Your school may offer classes in demography, urban sociology, urban planning, and statistics that would help satisfy your curiosity.

The Chapter in Brief: *Population and Environment*

Population

Demography is the science dealing with the size, distribution, composition, and changes in population.

■ **Elements in Population Change** All population change within a society can be reduced to three factors: the birth rate, the death rate, and the migration rate into or out of the society. Demographers look at **crude birth rate, general fertility rate, age-specific fertility, fecundity, zero population growth, crude death rate, age-specific death rates,** and **infant mortality rate.** Migration affects population, and demographers measure the **net migration rate.** Movement may take the form of **international migration** or **internal migration.** Births, deaths, and migration affect the **growth rate.**

■ **Population Composition** Sociologists are also interested in the composition of a population, particularly in the sex ratio and age composition. A **population pyramid** is a useful tool for analyzing population change and discerning population trends.

■ **Malthus and Marx: Two Views of Population Growth** Thomas Malthus held that population increases more quickly than the food supply. Karl Marx insisted that an excess of population is related to the availability of employment opportunities, not to a fixed supply of food. Neo-Malthusians are those who agree with many of Malthus's ideas but who favor contraception for population control.

■ **Demographic Transition** **Demographic transition theory** holds that the process of modernization is associated with three stages in population change: high potential growth, transitional growth, and population stability.

■ **Population Policies** Fertility reduction policies are based on family planning, a developmentalist strategy, or a societalist perspective. Decreasing populations have caused some governments to institute policies to raise fertility.

The Urban Environment

The **city** is one of the most striking features of the modern era, basic to many of the characteristics of modern society.

■ **The Origin and Evolution of Cities** Preindustrial cities were primarily small affairs. Urbanization has proceeded rapidly during the past 180 years, resulting in industrial-urban centers, metropolitan cities, **megalopolises,** and global cities.

■ **Patterns of City Growth**   Sociologists provide a number of models of city growth: the **concentric circle model,** the **sector model,** and the **multiple nuclei model.**

■ **Ecological Processes: Segregation and Gentrification**   The structural patterning of cities is described by sociologists using terms borrowed from **ecology.** One process by which **natural areas** are formed is **segregation. Invasion** and **succession** are also critical ecological processes. **Urban gentrification** is the return of middle-class professionals to older urban neighborhoods.

■ **New Cities, Old Cities**   Urban decline in many American cities has been both descriptive and functional. Increasing urbanization in developing countries demands attention to crime, sanitation, and traffic flow.

■ **The Rise of "Edge" Cities**   "Outer cities," "minicities," or "edge cities" have been made possible by beltways and expressways, and the development of a service-based economy in which telecommunications allow service-sector firms to locate anywhere.

The Ecological Environment

Sociology can help scientists and engineers identify socially acceptable and politically feasible ways to lessen human impact on the **environment** and to protect the earth's **ecosystems.**

■ **The Health of the Earth**   The health of the earth depends on nine environmental processes that could disrupt earth's ability to support human life, including climate change, biodiversity loss, interference with nitrogen and phosphorus cycles, stratospheric ozone depletion, ocean acidification, global freshwater use, natural ecosystem conversion to cropland, chemical pollution, and atmospheric aerosol loading. For climate change, species extinctions, and nitrogen and phosphorus pollution, we already have exceeded planetary boundaries, the limits within which the earth will remain a place that supports human life and well-being. Scientists refer to the period since the Industrial Revolution as the **Anthropocene.**

■ **Sociological Perspectives on the Environment**   Functionalist theorists see the ecosystem as exhibiting a tendency toward equilibrium in which its components maintain a delicately balanced relationship. They also assume that environmental problems can be resolved through normal social and political processes.

   Conflict theorists point to power as the central element affecting macro social and political processes. Some say that the basic issue is not one of how much is available but which individuals and groups will secure a disproportionate share of what is available.

   Symbolic interactionists focus on "people behaviors" related to environmental issues. Interests include the gap between people's attitudes and actions and the difference between public and expert perceptions of risk. Environmental sociologists criticize sociological theory for being too focused on human beings to the neglect of the natural and physical environment.

■ **Sustainability**   **Sustainability** has been defined as "transforming our ways of living to maximize the chances that environmental and social conditions will indefinitely support human security, well-being, and health." A worldwide team of scientists recommends making the transition to an efficient, low-carbon energy system, sharply curtailing land clearing and degradation, and investing in revolutionary agricultural practices.

Glossary

age-specific death rate The number of deaths per 1,000 individuals in a specific age group.

age-specific fertility The number of live births per 1,000 women in a specific age group.

Anthropocene The period since the Industrial Revolution, during which humans have become the major cause of global environmental change.

city A relatively dense and permanent concentration of people who secure their livelihood chiefly through nonagricultural activities.

concentric circle model The approach to city growth stating that the modern city assumes a pattern of concentric circles, each with distinctive characteristics.

crude birth rate The number of live births per 1,000 members of a population in a given year.

crude death rate The number of deaths per 1,000 members of a population in a given year.

demographic transition theory A view of population change holding that the process of modernization passes through three stages: high potential growth, transitional growth, and population stability.

demography The science dealing with the size, distribution, and composition of and changes in population.

ecology The study of the interrelations between the living and non-living components of an ecosystem.

ecosystem A relatively stable community of organisms that have established interlocking relationships and exchanges with one another and their natural habitat.

environment All the surrounding conditions and influences that affect an organism or group of organisms.

fecundity The potential number of children that could be born if every woman of childbearing age bore all the children she possibly could.

general fertility rate The annual number of live births per 1,000 women ages 15–44.

growth rate The difference between births and deaths, plus the difference between immigrants and emigrants per 1,000 population.

infant mortality rate The number of deaths among infants under one year of age per 1,000 live births.

internal migration Population movement within a nation.

international migration Population movement between nations.

invasion A new type of people, institution, or activity that encroaches on an area occupied by a different type.

megalopolis A strip city formed when the rural interstices between metropolitan centers fill with urban development.

multiple nuclei model The approach to city growth that assumes a city has several centers, each of which specializes in some activity and gives its distinctive cast to the surrounding area.

natural areas Geographic areas with distinctive characteristics.

net migration rate The increase or decrease per 1,000 members of the population in a given year that results from people entering (immigrants) or leaving (emigrants) a society.

population pyramid A chart that graphically displays the age and sex composition of a population.

rate of natural increase The difference between the birth rate and the death rate.

sector model The approach to city growth that assumes that large cities are made up of sectors—wedge-shaped areas—rather than concentric circles.

segregation A process of clustering wherein individuals and groups are sifted and sorted out in space based on their sharing certain traits or activities in common.

succession Invasion that continues until the encroaching type of people, institution, or activity displaces the previous type.

sustainability Living in a way that will indefinitely support human health, well-being, and security.

urban gentrification The return of the middle class—usually young, white, childless professionals—to older urban neighborhoods.

zero population growth The point at which a modern population replaces itself without immigration—2.1 children per woman.

Review Questions

1. What is demography?

2. What three factors account for all population change?

3. Describe the populations depicted in the population pyramids presented in this chapter.

4. Compare the views of Marx and Malthus on population growth.

5. What is demographic transition theory? Where would you place the United States in the figure showing the stages of demographic transition?

6. List and describe three population policies.

7. What is a city? How do cities grow?

8. Describe each of the following urban processes: segregation, gentrification, decline, and the growth of edge cities.

9. How does population growth relate to the natural environment?

10. What does sociology have to offer with regard to environmental problems?

11. How do functionalists, conflict theorists, and interactionists see environmental problems?

12. Describe global warming and U.S. policy on climate change.

Internet Connection   www.mhhe.com/hughes11e

Go to the website of the Population Reference Bureau (**www.prb.org**) and browse through several pages. Select a topic of interest related to the impact of population growth on the environment. Can you find an example of an environmental problem that affects population growth? Write a short report summarizing your findings.

As an interactive exercise, log into the Census Bureau International Data Base and investigate population distributions and change using population pyramids. Use your web browser to go to **http://www.census.gov/population/international/data/idb/informationGateway.php.**

Select a country and then select a year. Click on "Submit," and on the next page click on "Population Pyramids." Now select other countries or other years and compare. How different is the United States from other countries? Write a report describing the differences in population dynamics between the United States and other countries (both industrial and developing countries). Using what you have learned in this chapter, what accounts for these differences?

Social Change

When the World's Columbian Exposition opened in Chicago in 1893, 74 prominent Americans tried their hands at forecasting the future. What would the world be like 100 years later? One expressed the prevailing view that in 1993 the railroad would still be the fastest means of travel. Another was convinced that mail in 1993 would still travel by stagecoach and horseback rider. A few forecasters enthused about air travel—or, more precisely, "balloon travel." None of the 1893 forecasters apparently anticipated the automobile, let alone the cell phone, the Internet, a world of 7 billion people, the publication of a map of the human genome, the globalization of both our economy and our environmental problems, or a Library of Congress project to archive something called "Twitter" (Kang, 2010).

Then, as now, forecasters fell victim to two fundamental problems in attempting to predict the future. First, change is so much a part of our lives that we take it for granted, oblivious to or unimpressed by much of it; during the 1880s a number of Europeans had already produced experimental gasoline-powered cars, but the 1893 forecasters either did not know about the primitive "horseless carriages" or did not think they were important. Second, a rearview-mirror effect operates in which recent events color and dominate our thinking about the future; the railroads were developing rapidly in the 1880s and 1890s, so it took little imagination to predict that they would become faster and more widespread in the future (Cornish, 1993).

The study of social change is an attempt to understand and predict changes in the world. In this final chapter we will look at sources of social change and at social change in both the United States and developing countries. We will consider collective behavior, including explanations of crowd behavior. We will examine types and causes of social movements, and we will end with a look into the future.

425

A World of Change

Sociologists refer to fundamental alterations in the patterns of culture, structure, and social behavior over time as **social change.** It is a process by which society becomes something different while remaining in some respects the same. Consider the enormous transformations that have taken place across American life over the past 80 years. We have restyled many of our most basic values and norms: Racial upheaval, a sexual revolution, computer and communications breakthroughs, and a new national identity as a world power have remolded our national life. At a more personal level, research shows that college-aged GenX'ers (those born between 1962 and 1981) and Millennials (born after 1982) were more interested in money, image, and fame than were college-aged Baby Boomers (born 1946–1961) (Twenge, Campbell, and Freeman, 2012). Concern for others, interest in social problems, political participation, and willingness to take action to save energy and to help the environment all declined across these generations.

Social change has a tremendous impact on our lives. Let us begin our discussion of it by examining some of its sources. We will go on to consider perspectives on social change and to describe social change in the United States and in developing nations.

Sources of Social Change

Social change confronts people with new situations and compels them to fashion new forms of action. Many factors interact to generate changes in people's behavior and in the culture and structure of their society. Sociologists identify a number of particularly critical factors, the impact of which differs with the situation and the time and place. In this section we will consider the physical environment, population, conflict over resources and values, supporting norms and values, innovation, diffusion, and the mass media.

Physical Environment

If humans are to survive, they must achieve a working relationship with their environment. Among the chief adaptive mechanisms available to a population are social organization and technology. Hunting and gathering, horticultural, agricultural, and industrial societies all represent different types of adaptations. The expansion of desert land in Africa, the loss of glaciers in northern areas, and the increase in extreme weather events all are environmental changes requiring responses from human populations. Societies must make appropriate institutional changes, fashioning new forms of social organization and new technologies. Droughts, floods, epidemics, earthquakes, and other forces of nature are among the ever-present realities that alter people's lives. Added to them may be rising sea levels, massive loss of habitable shoreline, and a variety of other changes we are unable to foresee.

Population

Changes in the size, composition, and distribution of a population also affect culture and social structure. In Chapter 12 we discussed the implications of population growth. Nearly all such growth will occur in developing nations in the coming decades, with resource use in those parts of the world also increasing astronomically. The graying of the population is a principal factor in the United States, with Social Security, Medicaid, and health care costs soaring; those age 85 and over are the fastest-growing part of the population.

Clashes over Resources and Values

Conflict is a basic source of social change. The end result of conflict is not a simple quantitative mixing of the groups in conflict, but a completely new entity. Who can foretell today the ultimate form of the societies that arose in eastern Europe and the former Soviet empire following the collapse of communism? Old orders continually erode and new ones arise. The rapid increase in world population we now face will increase conflicts over drinking water, arable land, and other resources necessary to survival. How societies will evolve and adapt to meet these needs cannot be foretold. The resolution of ethnic and religious conflicts also will be accompanied by social change.

Supporting Values and Norms

A society's values and *norms* act as watchdogs or censors permitting, stimulating, or inhibiting certain innovations. It is interesting to compare our readiness to accept technological innovations with our resistance to changes in religion or the family. For example, we continuously debate changes in sexual behavior norms, while resistance to the lightbulb, the automobile, and the airplane disappeared almost immediately. Our use of the word *inventor* reflects this cultural bias. The inventor is one who innovates in material things, whereas the inventor of intangible ideas is often called a "revolutionary" or "radical," words with sometimes negative connotations.

Innovation

A **discovery** represents an addition to knowledge, whereas an **invention** uses existing knowledge in some novel form. Thus, a discovery constitutes the perception of a relationship or fact that had not previously been recognized or understood. Einstein's theory of relativity and Mendel's theory of heredity were discoveries. In contrast, the automobile—an invention—was composed of six old elements in a new combination: a liquid gas engine, a liquid gas receptacle, a running-gear mechanism, an intermediate clutch, a driving shaft, and a carriage body.

Innovations—both discoveries and inventions—are not single acts but combinations of existing elements plus new elements. The greater the number of cultural elements from which innovators may draw, the greater the frequency of discovery and invention. For example,

glass gave birth to lenses, costume jewelry, drinking goblets, windowpanes, and many other products. Lenses in turn gave birth to eyeglasses, magnifying glasses, telescopes, cameras, searchlights, and so on. Such developments reflect the *exponential principle*—as the cultural base increases, its possible uses tend to grow exponentially.

Diffusion

Diffusion is the process by which cultural traits spread from one social unit to another. Diffusion is a "people process" and hence is expedited or hindered by the social environment. Simply because a trait is functionally superior does not necessarily ensure that individuals will adopt it. Much depends on the network of relationships that tie people together in patterns of meaningful communication and influence (Strang and Tuma, 1993).

Diffusion is often overlooked. We point with pride to what other societies have acquired from us, but we often neglect to note what we have gained from them. Yet a global economy, combined with the fact that our society is composed almost entirely of immigrant groups, means that everything we use and do can be traced to other societies or cultures. As an illustration, consider the following now-classic account of the cultural content in the life of a "100 percent" American written as satire by anthropologist Ralph Linton (1937:427–429):

[D]awn finds the unsuspecting patriot garbed in pajamas, a garment of East Indian origin; and lying in a bed built on a pattern which originated in either Persia or Asia Minor. He is muffled to the ears in un-American materials: cotton, first domesticated in India; linen, domesticated in the Near East; wool from an animal native to Asia Minor; or silk whose uses were first discovered by the Chinese. . . .

If our patriot is old-fashioned enough to adhere to the so-called American breakfast, his coffee will be accompanied by an orange, domesticated in the Mediterranean region. He will follow this with a bowl of cereal made from grain domesticated in the Near East. . . . As a side dish he may have the egg of a bird domesticated in Southeastern Asia or strips of the flesh of an animal domesticated in the same region. . . .

The Mass Media

Diffusion is facilitated by the instant flooding of information across national, class, ethnic, and economic boundaries by means of the mass media. According to one view, the media function as a kind of giant hypodermic needle, discharging endless propaganda into the passive body of the population. Another view depicts the media as affording a "marketplace of ideas" in which an enlightened public carefully and rationally sifts and winnows a variety of attitudes and behaviors. Yet the media are not nearly as simple as the proponents of either view would have us believe. Most efforts at mass communication merely confirm the beliefs that people already hold. People typically expose themselves to mass communications that are congenial or favorable to their existing opinions and interests. Selective perception also operates so that people tend to misperceive and misinterpret persuasive communications in accordance with their existing opinions.

Nevertheless, the mass media have not-so-minimal effects. We typically think of news coverage as the media bringing to public attention the "important" happenings of the day by reporting on an objective reality "out there." But as symbolic interactionists point out, "news" is *constructed*—some selected occurrences come to be translated into "public events" for a mass constituency while others are ignored (Epstein, 1973). With round-the-clock news channels and Internet news sites, "news" has become an always-available commodity. Much of what is broadcast is repetitive, with little "new news" to flesh out the stories, yet the mere fact of their repetition lends them a significance beyond their actual importance. Sensational murders,

kidnappings, and celebrity news particularly fall into this category.

The media also perform other functions, including what social scientists call "agenda setting." The media set the agenda of issues and concerns we spend our time thinking about and discussing with others. Some communications experts argue that fictional media presentations have a "cultivation effect" in which images are provided that influence public attitudes and behavior about such social policies as crime, violence, and welfare

It didn't fit in your pocket, but in 1916 the player piano was the only way an average person could hear piano music without being in the presence of a pianist. The iPod is the most recent in a long line of exciting technological innovations in the world of popular music, including the player piano, the radio, the phonograph, the tape player, and the compact disc.

(Gerbner et al., 1978), though it is not always clear exactly what television and other media are cultivating in the minds of viewers (Hughes, 1980).

Perspectives on Social Change

The founders of sociology, particularly Auguste Comte and Herbert Spencer, looked to the grand sweep of history, searching for an understanding of how and why societies change. Many contemporary sociologists continue to be intrigued by these "big questions." The major sociological perspectives on social change, which we will consider in this section, fall within three broad categories: cyclical perspectives, functionalist perspectives, and conflict perspectives.

Cyclical Perspectives

Two influential historians argued that the course of civilization is cyclical, and they compared societies in a search for generalizations regarding their stages of growth and decline.

The German scholar Oswald Spengler (1880–1936) contended that culture passes through the same stages of growth and decline as individuals: a period of development, followed by maturity, eventual decline, and death. Based on his examination of eight cultures, Spengler said that each culture possesses a life span of approximately 1,000 years. Western culture, he held, emerged about A.D. 900, and therefore its end is close at hand.

English historian Arnold J. Toynbee (1934/1954) also sought to depict uniformities in the growth and decline of civilization and to identify the principles that underlie this development. Toynbee said that civilizations arise in response to some challenge, such as severe climate or warlike neighbors. A civilization grows and flourishes when the challenge is not too severe and when a creative minority (an intelligent elite) finds an adequate response to the challenge. When the creative minority fails to find a response adequate

to a challenge, the civilization breaks down and disintegrates.

Archaeologists have previously cited combinations of social, political, and economic factors as the root causes of societal collapse, but new research has allowed researchers to conclude that the primary agent in prehistoric and early-historic societal collapses was abrupt and highly disruptive climate change (Weiss and Bradley, 2001). Floods, droughts, and changes in the availability of the resources exploited by hunting and gathering societies have been identified with climate changes that led to societal collapses. Because human contributions of carbon to the atmosphere have been predicted to cause major climate changes in the future, our own societies may be forced to adapt and change rapidly.

Functionalist Perspectives

As we saw in Chapter 1 (p. 18), the concept of system is central to the structural-functional model of society. A system is a set of elements or components related in a more-or-less stable fashion over a period of time. One of the features of a system stressed by structural-functional theorists is its tendency toward *equilibrium.*

Structural-functional sociologists like Parsons (1966, 1977) have introduced the notion of evolution to the perspective to broaden the concept of equilibrium to include both developing and self-maintaining properties. The social group is portrayed as living in a state of dynamic or moving equilibrium. The equilibrated social system adjusts itself to disturbances that occur, accommodating them within the functioning structure and establishing a new level of equilibrium. Hence, even though society changes, it remains stable through new forms of social integration.

Sociologist William F. Ogburn (1922) drew upon evolutionary models to fashion a functionalist approach to social change. He distinguished between *material* and *nonmaterial* culture and located the source of change in material invention—tools, weapons, and technical processes. Nonmaterial culture—values, norms, beliefs, and institutions—must adapt or respond to changes in material culture, resulting in an adjustment gap Ogburn called **cultural lag.** Although the notion of cultural lag contains a valuable insight, it vastly oversimplifies matters. No single factor is capable of explaining social change; in real-life situations a vast array of forces converge in complex interaction with one another to give society its dynamic properties.

Social life abounds with examples of an uneven rate of change resulting in social dislocation. For instance, the automobile fostered a whole host of changes. It spurred tremendous growth in the oil, tire, glass, and accident insurance industries. It promoted suburban development, degradation of the natural environment, and an exodus of the central city's affluent population. Cultural lag is evident today in the many problems associated with the use of the Internet, including hacking, the spread of computer viruses, Internet pornography, Internet scams, and the Napster controversy. We can expect that our society also will require a significant amount of cultural adjustment as a result of the sequencing of the human genome (Jeffords and Daschle, 2001).

Closely related to the functionalist perspective on social change is the evolutionary theory developed by sociologist Gerhard Lenski (1966; Nolan and Lenski, 2010). Lenski held that evolution depends largely on changes in a society's level of technology and its mode of economic production. These changes in turn have consequences for other aspects of social life, including stratification systems, the organization of *power,* and family structures. According to Lenski, there is an underlying continuum in terms of which all societies can be ranked: hunting and gathering societies, simple horticultural societies, advanced horticultural societies, agrarian societies, and industrial societies. More specialized evolutionary bypaths include herding societies and hybrid societies such as fishing and maritime societies.

Conflict Perspectives

Conflict theorists hold that tensions between competing groups are the basic source of social change. Nowhere does one find a clearer exposition of the conflict perspective than that provided by Karl Marx, particularly as it finds expression in his notion of the *dialectic.* As we saw in Chapter 1 (p. 11), the dialectic depicts the world in dynamic terms as a world of *becoming* rather than *being.* According to Marxian *dialectical materialism,* every economic order grows to a state of maximum efficiency, at the same time developing internal contradictions or weaknesses that contribute to its decay. Class conflict is a particularly powerful source of change, and Marx saw it as the key to understanding human history.

Marx said that all change is the product of a constant conflict between opposites. All development—social, economic, or human—proceeds through the resolution of existing contradictions and the eventual emergence of new contradictions. The outcome of the clash between opposing forces is not a compromise (an averaging out of the differences among them), but an entirely new product, one born of struggle. In this manner both individuals and societies change. It is a dynamic process of complex interchanges among all facets of social life. As Marx (1867/1906) observed, "By acting on the external world and changing it, he [the individual] at the same time changes his own nature."

Not all conflict theorists agree with Marx that "all history is the history of class conflict." Other types of conflict may be equally important as or in some instances more important than class conflict, including conflict between nations, ethnic groups, religions, and economic interest groups (Coser, 1956, 1957; Dahrendorf, 1958).

Social Change in the United States

In this section we will examine one aspect of change, that associated with the rapid introduction of technology into American life. Sociological models depict technological innovations as a reweaving of the social fabric—a reshaping of the norms, roles, relationships, groups, and institutions that make up society. Today we hear a good deal about the construction of "information highways" and "information infrastructures." The building of another highway system—the interstate system—reminds us of the vast impact that changes can have. The system was inspired by a wish to improve commerce, foster physical and social mobility, and bolster national defense. But the interstate system also had many unanticipated consequences that permanently changed the nation's social landscape. It fostered the rapid growth of strip and edge cities and magnified the split between outlying communities and inner cities. Are "information highways" having both positive and negative effects?

The Information Revolution

The Industrial Revolution was a revolution because the steam engine, the cotton gin, the locomotive and rails, and the power loom were agents for great social change. They took people out of the fields and brought them into the factories. They gave rise to mass production and, through mass production, to a society in which wealth was not confined to the few.

In a similar fashion, computers are revolutionizing the structure of American life—what some have termed the *information revolution.* Growth in Internet use has been extremely rapid; in 1997 only 18 percent of U.S. households had Internet access, a number that more than quadrupled by 2011 (Internet World Stats, 2012). We can read the newspaper, access government data, order books and CDs and groceries, check on class assignments, read lectures, and exchange messages or talk directly with friends or strangers in virtually any part of the world—all on the Internet. Cell phone use also has dramatically changed the way we communicate

and get information. In 1990, only 2 percent of the U.S. population was using cell phones (U.S Census Bureau, 2011a). Twenty years later, more than 90 percent of Americans had cell phones, and many were using their phones to access the Internet.

A number of issues have been repeatedly raised about the social impact of computers. First, the computer automates workplace activities that traditionally have been performed by people. The Industrial Revolution centered on the supplementation and ultimate replacement of the muscles of humans and animals by introducing mechanical methods. The information revolution goes beyond this to supplement and replace some aspects of the minds of human beings by electronic methods. But it seems that job creation accompanies job destruction, with the highest rates of both occurring in the most technologically

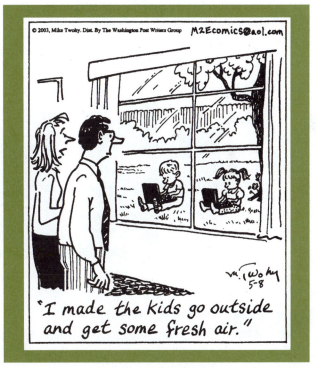

"I made the kids go outside and get some fresh air."

Copyright © 2003 Mike Twohy. Distributed by the Washington Post Writers Group. Reprinted with permission.

advanced sectors of the economy, where overall employment is increasing (International Labor Organization, 2001).

Second, information is a source of power, and computers mean information. The centralized accumulation of data permits the concentration of considerable power in those who have access to computers. These are most likely to be people who already have more power and advantages than others. While recent increases have occurred in all economic, racial, and ethnic groups, and the gender gap in Internet use has disappeared, some differences remain (see Figure 13.1). For example, African Americans are less likely than whites to use the Internet, and Internet use is correlated with family income and educational attainment (U.S. Census Bureau, 2011a). Research on households shows that African American (58 percent) and Hispanic (59 percent) households are less likely than non-Hispanic white (79 percent) households to have an Internet connection.

Asian American households (84 percent) are the most likely to be connected.

Internet use increases the advantages of those who have access to it. Dimaggio and Bonikowski (2008) show that, in the United States, Internet use either at home or at work boosts earnings. Results were not explained by occupation, education, or income level. The Internet may also be increasing the relative disadvantages of those in non-Western countries. Only 35 percent of the world's population has ever logged on (Internet World Stats, 2012).

Third, computers alter the way people relate to one another (see Box 13.1). On a telephone, we hear the other person's voice. In face-to-face contact, we see people smile, frown, and nod. But computer exchanges offer no such feedback. Thus, computers may have consequences for our sense of individuality. Computer exchanges differ in other ways as well. People are less likely to hold back strong feelings when communicating by computer. And as with any

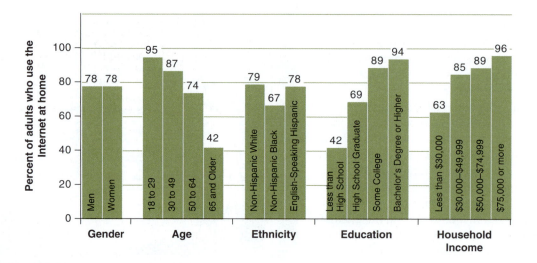

Figure 13.1   **The Digital Divide**

Although the gender gap in Internet use has disappeared, differences remain in age, racial, ethnic, education, and income groups. Age, race, and education in this figure are of the householder (i.e., "head of household").

Source: Figure generated by the authors using data from the U.S. Census Bureau, 2011a.

piece of writing, how clearly ideas are communicated depends on the writer's skill.

Fourth, computers have implications for individual privacy and the confidentiality of our communications and personal data. The growing use of computers to collect data and store information provides the technical capability for integrating several information files into networks of computerized data banks. With such networks, personal data that we provide for one purpose can potentially be accessed for other purposes. Thus, as people handle more and more of their activities through electronic instruments—mail, banking, shopping, entertainment, and travel plans—it becomes technically feasible to monitor these activities with unprecedented ease.

Finally, computers and the Internet provide new means and opportunity for crime and deviance. People have found innovative ways to use the Internet to commit extortion (Menn, 2010) and fraud and identity theft (O'Harrow, 2003), to solicit for prostitution, to prey upon the vulnerable, and to buy and sell illegal goods and pornography (e.g., Durkin and Bryant, 1995). We should expect more such innovation until means are developed to eliminate or reduce crime and deviance in this new medium of communication.

What the Information Revolution Cannot Do

While the changes to come in this still-very-young revolution will probably be dramatic, there also are clear limits to the impact the Internet will have on our lives. First, as we have mentioned, the "digital divide" effectively excludes much of the world and significant portions of the United States from participating in Internet-related activities. As the number of people who routinely use the Internet rises, those who have no access are at an increasing disadvantage. Second, how the Internet changes our lives depends entirely

on how we use it. In 2003, the biggest use of the Internet was for sending and receiving e-mail (88 percent of users); U.S. citizens also were using it to search for product and service information; to obtain news, weather, and sports information; to make online purchases; and to play games (Day, Janus, and Davis, 2005). In 2011, Americans also were increasingly using the Internet to entertain themselves; on any given day, survey research shows, 53 percent of young adults (18–29) go online "just to pass the time," and 58 percent of all U.S. adults say they sometimes use the Internet for entertainment (Rainie, 2011). To the extent that such activities reduce our use of paper, transportation, and other consumers of resources and energy, using the Internet can be seen as environmentally friendly. On the other hand, an assessment of energy consumption concluded that 8 percent of the electricity used in the United States can be attributed to computer use (*The Economist,* 2000). And when the end result of convenient

"On the Internet, nobody knows you're a dog."

Facebook Users: Socially Engaged, or Socially Isolated?

At any college or university student center, library, study lounge, dorm room, dining hall, bus stop, or lecture hall, students are checking their laptops or their cell phones for Facebook updates and new e-mails. Although sitting side by side, they often seem to be communicating not with one another but with a virtual someone off in cyberspace. Are they socially isolated, or socially engaged? How are young adults different in today's world of social media from young adults of 20 years ago, when only 2 percent of the U.S. population had cell phones and when Facebook didn't exist?

University of Pennsylvania sociologist Keith Hampton and his colleagues (Hampton et al., 2011) used a telephone survey of 2,255 adults (18 and older) to find out. In 2010, landline and cellular telephone numbers were randomly selected to represent all adults in the United States. Trained interviewers made at least seven attempts to reach someone at each number, placing their calls at different times of day and on different days of the week to increase the likelihood that they would reach someone. To make sure both women and men were represented in the survey, interviewers asked to speak to the youngest adult male in the home for half their calls; for the other half, they asked to speak to the youngest adult female in the home.

What did the researchers discover? First, and no surprise, many Americans use the Internet to communicate, and the use of social networking sites has grown rapidly: 79 percent of respondents reported using the Internet, and 47 percent (59 percent of Internet users) reported using at least one social networking site, almost twice as many as in a 2008 survey.

Among social networking site users, 92 percent use Facebook, 29 percent MySpace, 18 percent LinkedIn, and 13 percent Twitter. The researchers found big differences in frequency of use: About half of Facebook users and a third of Twitter users are on their accounts every day, but that is true for only 6 percent of LinkedIn and 7 percent of MySpace users.

Are all these people socially isolated? In 2000, Harvard political scientist Robert Putnam published *Bowling Alone*, in which he argued that Americans have become more disconnected from neighbors, local communities, friends, and family. Another study, published in 2006, found that people's support systems had shrunk to include pretty much just their families. What did Hampton and his colleagues find?

Far from being isolated, social networking site users in Hampton's study were more socially engaged with others both online and off. For example, Hampton and his colleagues found that Facebook users are more trusting than others—43 percent more likely than other Internet users to say that people can be trusted and more than three times more likely than non-Internet users. On other questions, the same pattern was found: Internet users were more socially engaged than non-Internet users, and Facebook users were more socially engaged than other Internet users. In "real life"—not just on the Internet—Facebook users had more close relationships and more social support and were more likely to be politically engaged.

As anyone with a Facebook account knows, using Facebook revives dormant relationships and supports distant ones; people you haven't seen for years or have met only a couple times find you and friend you, making it possible to keep in touch with a large number of people. But the researchers found that Facebook also facilitates close social ties. Two-fifths of social networking site users reported having friended all of their closest confidants, up from only 29 percent in the 2008 survey.

An earlier study (Hampton et al., 2009) found that, contrary to others' results, the extent of social isolation in the United States has changed little since 1985. It further found that cell phones and the Internet facilitate local contact as much as distant communication, and that use of both is associated with having more diverse social networks and with a greater likelihood of belonging to local voluntary organizations.

Questions for Discussion

1. How would the structure of their lives be different if young people did not have access to the Internet?

2. What do you think accounts for Internet users, and especially Facebook users, having higher levels of trust in others?

RHYMES WITH ORANGE (105945) © 2007 Hilary B. Price. King Features Syndicate.

order placing is increased consumption and delivery of goods, we are not helping the environment.

Neither, some analysts think, are we likely to significantly improve international relations and understanding via the Internet. In the mid-1850s, when the first transatlantic telegraph was sent, technology enthusiasts predicted that it would eradicate "old prejudices and hostilities" (*The Economist,* 2000). Likewise, the ease of communication offered by the Internet might be thought to have the potential to improve our understanding of those in other cultures. But some pin the blame for war and conflict on human nature, which remains unchanged by the information revolution: "Despite the claims of the techno-prophets, humanity cannot simply invent away its failings. The Internet is not the first technology to have been hailed as a panacea—and it will certainly not be the last" (*The Economist,* 2000:12). It may be that an intelligently structured and wisely applied computer technology will help a society to raise its standard of literacy, education, and general knowledgeability. But there is no automatic, positive link between knowledge and its enlightened use.

Is the Internet a new form of social integration that can challenge the power and dominance of governments around the world, as some utopian visionaries have argued? Goldsmith and Wu (2006) assert that it is not. Instead, our experiences of the Internet thus far demonstrate the importance of traditional institutions, not their obsolescence. When Internet forces have come into conflict with governments, international law, and business, these interests have won out. For example, when Yahoo! wanted to market Nazi paraphernalia in violation of French law, Yahoo! had to knuckle under or be banned in France.

Social Change in Developing Nations

Advances in communications and computer technology have made it possible for workers in developing nations to collaborate and compete in the global economy (Friedman, 2005). Employees in India prepare tax returns for U.S. citizens, American companies have software developers in Bangkok, and computer workers in China do data entry for Japanese medical and law firms. In 2010, world cell phone subscriptions surpassed 5 billion, meaning that more people in the world have access to a cell phone than to a flush toilet (Giridharadas, 2010). People in developing nations who have never had wired networks are using this wireless technology for receiving salaries, borrowing, and lending; job hunting; watching television; getting radio news; and connecting with friends and family. What effect will these and other changes have? Sociologists traditionally have approached social change in developing nations from two somewhat different perspectives: modernization and world system.

Modernization

Modernization describes the process by which a society moves from traditional or preindustrial social and economic arrangements to those characteristic of industrial societies. Implicit in the notion of modernization is the assumption that there is basically one predominant course of development—namely, that followed by advanced Western nations and Japan. Viewed in this manner, modernization entails patterns of convergence in which societies become increasingly urban, industry overshadows agriculture, the population increases in size and density, the division of labor becomes more specialized, and the knowledge base grows larger and more complex. East Asia, including Taiwan, South Korea, Hong Kong (now part of China), and Singapore, is the showcase of modernization theories.

The momentum for change derives from internal forces and processes. The chances that a developing country will evolve in the direction of liberal Western democracies are thought to be enhanced when a nation's economy provides for literacy, education, and communication; creates a pluralistic rather than a centrally dominated social order; and prevents extreme inequalities among the various social strata. Efficient systems of communication and a diversity of social groups and organizations are believed to distribute political resources and skills among multiple segments of the community and provide the foundation of effective opposition parties.

World System or Dependency

World system (and dependency) approaches view the social structures of developing nations as shaped by the historical experience of colonialism, the timing and manner of their incorporation into the global capitalist economy, and the perpetuation of their dependency through political domination, multinational corporations, and unfavorable exchange arrangements.

According to world system and dependency analysis, developing nations cannot recapitulate the developmental trajectory of Western nations and Japan. An unequal exchange takes place between core and periphery nations (see Chapter 9), with development in core nations occurring at the cost of underdevelopment in periphery nations (London and Williams, 1990; Walton and Ragin, 1990; Chase-Dunn and Hall, 1993). More particularly, specialization in the production and export of raw materials is said to be detrimental to the long-term growth prospects of developing nations. Such specialization distorts these nations' economies because they become responsive to the demands of the world market rather than to internal developmental needs; development is shaped primarily by external forces and processes. Further, investments in the production or mining of raw materials monopolize capital to the detriment of other types of investment. And class formation in the dependent nations results in a small elite whose economic interests are linked to foreign investors in the core countries (Berberoglu, 1987; Bradshaw, 1988). Dependency theorists see Latin America and Africa as offering stark evidence of the limits that dependency imposes on nations.

Rapid Change

Fast-moving world events have impacted the sociological study of change in developing nations. The social change field is in flux because it is confronting a host of new issues: Will an information age enable developing nations to leapfrog stages in economic development? How will rapid population growth, AIDS, and women's issues affect development policies? With India and China moving rapidly into high-technology areas and positions of economic power, what changes will occur in these densely populated countries? What effect will the outsourcing of labor and of knowledge work have on these and smaller countries? When the middle and upper classes of previously poor countries expand rapidly, how will societies adapt to changes in the consumption of products, services, and energy? These and other questions are of interest to sociologists.

Collective Behavior

Rapid social change and the upheavals that result from it also make it more likely that people will engage in **collective behaviors**—ways of thinking, feeling, and acting that develop among a large number of people and that are relatively spontaneous and unstructured. And collective behaviors can result in social change. From earliest recorded times, people have thrown themselves into a great many types of mass behavior, including social unrest, riots, manias, fads, panics, mass flights, lynchings, religious revivals, and rebellions. Accordingly, no discussion of social change can neglect collective behavior.

Varieties of Collective Behavior

Collective behavior comes in a great many forms. To gain a better appreciation for the impact such behavior has on our lives, let us consider a number of varieties of collective behavior at greater length.

Rumors

A **rumor** is a difficult-to-verify piece of information transmitted from person to person in relatively rapid fashion. We often think of rumors as providing false information, and in many cases this is true. But they also may be accurate or, at the very least, contain a kernel of truth. Rumors typically arise in situations in which people lack information or distrust the official sources of information. Rumors are both a form of collective behavior and an important element in most other forms of collective behavior.

Periods of anxiety and tension provide an environment in which rumors proliferate. After the September 11, 2001, terrorist attacks, rumors flew about a wide range of topics, including the sorts of biological and chemical weapons terrorists might unleash and the best antidotes to such weapons. Official information competed with rapidly circulating advice about sealing doors and windows with duct tape and laying in supplies of gas masks, food, water, and medicines.

Rumors tend to evolve and take on new details as people interact, and with the Internet they can spread around the world in the time it takes to walk to your neighbor's house to gossip. The Internet also can be used to try to control rumors. A high school student who is the subject of gossip may use Facebook to try to set the story straight or at least to provide readers with an alternate view of the story (Nussbaum, 2004).

One type of rumor that is particularly common involves alleged contamination. The Centers for Disease Control and Prevention (CDC) maintains a web page with information about recent and continuing rumors and hoaxes (http://www.cdc.gov/hoaxes_rumors.html). In early 2012 the page contained updates about a report that detergent packages were contaminated with the bacterium that causes anthrax; a CDC-lookalike website presenting false information about Lyme disease; and fraudulent e-mails requiring receivers to create a "swine flu vaccination profile." The CDC web page also suggests that persons wishing more information on hoaxes and rumors should consult the Snopes.com website (http://www.snopes.com/).

Fashions and Fads

The uniformity of dress on college campuses is sometimes so extreme as to make it appear that students are required to wear certain uniforms. Bell bottoms may have been in fashion once, but in 2012 skinny jeans and boots were required attire. Contemporary society is full of both fashions and fads. What is the difference?

A **fashion** is a folkway that lasts for a short time and enjoys widespread acceptance within society. Fashion finds expression in styles of clothing, automobile design, and home architecture.

A **fad** is a folkway that lasts for a short time and enjoys acceptance among only a segment of the population. Fads often appear in computer and video games, popular music, dance steps, health practices, movie idols, leisure-time activities, and slang. Adolescents are particularly prone to fads; the fads provide a sense of identity and belonging, with aspects of dress, gesture, and skill in activities serving as signs of an *in-group* or *out-group* status (Erikson, 1968).

Some fads become all-consuming passions. Such fads are called **crazes.** Financial speculation at times assumes craze proportions (Chatzky, 1992). In the famous Holland tulip mania in the 17th century, the value of tulip bulbs came to exceed their weight in gold; the bulbs were not planted, but bought and sold among speculators.

Mass Hysteria

Mass hysteria refers to the rapid dissemination of behaviors involving contagious anxiety, usually associated with some mysterious force. For instance, medieval witch hunts rested on the belief that many social ills were caused by witches. Likewise, some "epidemics" of illness— *mass psychogenic illness*—derive from hysterical contagion. Fears of terrorism have fueled a number of episodes of mass psychogenic illness in recent years (Bartholomew and Victor, 2004). Close on the heels of the September 11, 2001, terrorist attacks, commuters in both California and Maryland had to be treated for headache, nausea, and sore throats when strange odors— later determined to be harmless—were detected in the subway. Rumors of a bioterror attack in the Philippines resulted in 1,400 students seeking help from physicians. Some turned out to have a mild influenza, while most were suffering psychogenic reactions to the rumors. After the anthrax scare in 2001, mysterious skin rashes that came to be termed "the Bin Laden Itch"

were reported by thousands of students in dozens of U.S. schools. The rashes, suspected by students and parents to be anthrax-related, all were diagnosed as having been caused by allergens, insect bites, fungi, fiberglass, and other nonanthrax sources.

Panic

Panic involves irrational and uncoordinated but collective actions among people induced by the presence of an immediate, severe threat. For example, people commonly flee from a catastrophe such as a fire or flood. The behavior is collective because social interaction intensifies people's fright.

As with other forms of collective behavior, panics can be greatly amplified by modern information technologies. When the SARS epidemic spread from China to other countries in 2003, an "information epidemic" fueled a panic that affected the lives of millions of people (Rothkopf, 2003). Although the total number of people who died from SARS worldwide was smaller than the number of people who die from choking on small objects every year in the United States, the panic about the disease resulted in economic losses in Asia of an estimated $30 billion. Rothkopf traces the cause of an information epidemic to mainstream media, specialist media, and Internet sites combined with "informal" media, including pagers, e-mail, faxes, cell phones, and text messaging, all of which may be transmitting rumor, interpretation, propaganda, or fact.

Crowds

The **crowd** is one of the most familiar and at times spectacular forms of collective behavior. It is a temporary, relatively unorganized gathering of people in close physical proximity. Because a wide range of behavior is encompassed by the concept, sociologist Herbert Blumer (1946; see also McPhail, 1989) distinguished four basic types of crowd behavior. The first, a **casual crowd,** is a collection of people who have little in common except that they may be viewing a common event, such as looking through a department store window, visiting a museum, or attending a movie. The second, a **conventional crowd,** entails a number of people who have assembled for some specific purpose and who typically act in accordance with established norms, such as people attending a baseball game or a concert. The third, an **expressive crowd,** is an aggregation of people who have gotten together for self-stimulation and personal gratification, such as occurs at a religious revival or a rock festival. And fourth, an **acting crowd** is an excited, volatile collection of people who are engaged in rioting, looting, or other forms of aggressive behavior in which established norms carry little weight.

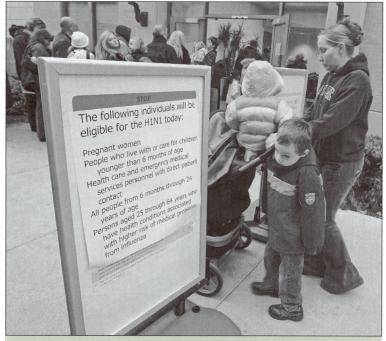

News reports and publicity about the H1N1 ("swine flu") virus initially generated panic and confusion. Long lines for the vaccine later gave way to public disinterest, and government programs were set up to get vulnerable groups vaccinated.

Although crowds differ from one another in many ways, they also share a number of characteristics:

- *Suggestibility.* The behavior of crowd members is not guided by conventional norms. Individuals are usually more susceptible to images, directions, and propositions emanating from others.

- *Deindividualization.* **Deindividualization** is a psychological state of diminished identity and self-awareness (Zimbardo, 1969). People feel less inhibited in committing disapproved acts in a group.

- *Invulnerability.* In crowd settings, individuals often acquire a sense that they are more powerful and invincible than they are in routine, everyday settings. Moreover, they feel that social control mechanisms are less likely to be applied to them as individuals, resulting in an increase in behavior not normally approved by society, such as aggression, risk taking, self-enhancement, theft, vandalism, and the uttering of obscenities (Dipboye, 1977; Mann, Newton, and Innes, 1982).

We will return to a discussion of crowds shortly, considering several theories of crowd behavior. But first, let us examine a number of preconditions for collective behavior.

Preconditions for Collective Behavior

Sociologist Neil J. Smelser (1963) provided a framework for examining collective behavior based on the value-added model popular among economists. **Value-added** is the idea that each step in the production process—from raw materials to the finished product—increases the economic value of manufactured goods.

As viewed by Smelser, episodes of collective behavior are products of a sequence of steps that constitute six determinants of collective behavior: (1) structural conduciveness, (2) structural strain, (3) growth and spread of a generalized belief, (4) precipitating factors, (5) mobilization of participants for action, and (6) the operation of social control. Each determinant is shaped by those that precede it, and each in turn shapes the ones that follow. Moreover, with the introduction of each successive determinant to the value-added sequence, the range of potential final outcomes becomes progressively narrowed. Smelser contended that each of the six factors in the scheme is a necessary condition for the production of collective behavior, while all six are believed to make collective behavior virtually inevitable. Let us take a closer look at each of the determinants in Smelser's model.

Structural Conduciveness

Structural conduciveness refers to social conditions that permit a particular variety of collective behavior to occur. Before a financial panic is possible, for example, such as the stock market crash of 1929, there must be a financial market where assets can be exchanged freely and rapidly. This basis does not exist in societies where property can be transferred only to the firstborn son on the father's death because the holders of property lack sufficient maneuverability to dispose of their assets on short notice.

Structural Strain

Structural strain is said to occur when important aspects of a social system are "out of joint." Wars, economic crises, natural disasters, and technological change disrupt the traditional rhythm of life and interfere with the way people normally carry out their activities. As stress accumulates across time, individuals experience *social malaise*—a feeling of underlying and pervasive discontent.

The Growth of a Generalized Belief

Structural strain and a sense of social malaise by themselves are not enough to produce collective behavior. People must define a situation as a problem in need of a solution. In the course of social interaction, they evolve a shared view of reality and common ideas about how they should respond to it. This type of belief regarding Martian invaders precipitated the panic associated with Orson Welles's famous 1938 Halloween broadcast of *War of the Worlds*.

Precipitating Factors

Some sort of event is needed to touch off or trigger collective action. A *precipitating event* creates, sharpens, or exaggerates conditions of conduciveness and strain. Additionally, it provides adherents of a belief with explicit evidence of the workings of evil forces or greater promise of success. Revolutions, for example, are often precipitated in this manner: The March 11, 1917, tsarist decrees against Petrograd strikers precipitated the Russian Revolution.

The Mobilization of Participants for Action

Collective behavior requires participants. Sociologists use the concept of "critical mass" to refer to the threshold or number of participants that must be reached before collective behavior erupts or explodes (Oliver and Marwell, 1988; Macy, 1991). Recruitment to religious *sects* and to *social movements* typically occurs through lines of preexisting social relationships—for example, among relatives, neighbors, friends, and work associates (McAdam and Paulsen, 1993).

Operation of Social Control

The sixth factor in Smelser's scheme is the operation of *social control,* a counterdeterminant that prevents, interrupts, deflects, or inhibits the accumulation of the other factors. Social control typically takes two forms. First, there are controls designed to prevent the occurrence of an episode of collective behavior by lessening conduciveness and strain (e.g., welfare programs that seek to pacify the underclasses). Second, there are controls that attempt to repress an episode of collective behavior after it has begun (e.g., police measures and curfews).

In some instances, however, the activities of the agents of social control precipitate collective behavior and even violence (Waddington, Jones, and Critcher, 1989). A good illustration of this occurred in the spring of 1963 when the Reverend Martin Luther King, Jr., took the civil rights fight to Birmingham, Alabama, alleged to be the most segregated large city in the South. The brutal social control brought to bear on Birmingham African Americans gave impetus to some 1,122 civil rights demonstrations in the following four months in cities throughout the nation.

Assessing the Value-Added Model

Smelser's value-added model provides a useful tool for grasping the complexity of collective behavior, but the approach does have serious limitations. In some cases of collective action, all six stages do not occur, or they do not take place in the sequence Smelser specified (Milgram, 1977). Additionally, some forms of crowd behavior are better explained by other perspectives, to which we turn next.

Explanations of Crowd Behavior

Although crowd members differ in a great many ways, their behavior seems to derive from a common impulse and to be dominated by a single spirit. What happens in the course of crowd behavior? What processes fashion people's behavior under crowd conditions? Three somewhat different answers have been supplied by sociologists to these questions.

Contagion Theory

Contagion theory emphasizes the part that rapidly communicated and uncritically accepted feelings, attitudes, and actions play in crowd settings. Its proponents assume that unanimity prevails within a crowd; crowd members often seem to act in identical ways and to be dominated by a similar impulse. Thus, a crowd is often spoken of in the singular, as if it were a real thing—"the crowd roars" and "the angry mob surges forward." This view of the crowd is embodied in the influential work of the 19th-century French writer Gustave Le Bon (1896: 23–24), who set forth the "law of the mental unity of crowds."

Le Bon's contagion theory depicted the crowd as characterized by a "mob mind" that overpowers and submerges the individual. A uniform mood and imagery evolve contagiously through three mechanisms: (1) *imitation*—the tendency for one person to do the same thing that others are doing; (2) *suggestibility*—a state in which individuals become susceptible to images, directions, and propositions emanating from others; and (3) *circular reaction*—a process whereby the emotions of others elicit the same emotions in oneself, in turn intensifying the emotions of others in a reciprocal manner. However, Le Bon's concept of the crowd mind as some sort of supraindividual entity—one that is endowed with thinking processes and a capacity for feeling and believing—is rejected by most social scientists (Milgram and Toch, 1969). Only individual human beings are capable of thought and emotion.

Convergence Theory

Whereas contagion theorists see normal, decent people being transformed under crowd influence, **convergence theory** proposes that a crowd consists of a highly unrepresentative body of people who assemble because they share the same predispositions. For instance, social psychologist Hadley Cantril (1941) studied a Leeville, Texas, lynching and contended that the active members came chiefly from the lowest economic bracket, and several had previous police records. As a class, poor whites were most likely to compete for jobs with African Americans and were most likely to find their own status threatened by the presence of successful African Americans. These individuals provided a reservoir of people who were ready for a lynching with a minimum of provocation.

Emergent-Norm Theory

The **emergent-norm theory** stresses the lack of unanimity in many crowd situations and the differences in motives, attitudes, and actions that characterize crowd members. They may be impulsive, suggestible, or opportunistic; they may be passive supporters, cautious activists, or passers-by. The approach denies that people find themselves spontaneously infected with the emotions of others to the extent that they want to behave as others do (Turner, 1964; Turner and Killian, 1972; Shibutani, 1986).

Instead, emergent-norm theory draws upon the work of psychologists Muzafer Sherif (1936) and Solomon Asch (1952) that deals with social conformity in ambiguous situations (see Chapter 4, pp. 108–109). Collective behavior entails an attempt by people to find meaning in an uncertain social setting (Turner and Killian, 1972). Individuals search for cues to appropriate and acceptable behavior. Like the subjects in Sherif's experiments, who developed group norms that were different from the standards they developed when they were alone, crowd members collectively evolve new standards for behavior. Crowd members then proceed to enforce the norm: They reward behavior consistent with it, inhibit behavior contrary to it, justify proselytizing, and institute actions that restrain dissenters. Since the new behavior differs from that in noncrowd situations, the norm must be specific to the situation—hence, an *emergent* norm.

Assessing the Perspectives

The three perspectives provide differing views of crowd behavior. Even so, they are not mutually exclusive. Consider what happens at a homecoming football game. Contagion contributes to the excitement through a process of circular reaction. Convergence operates; loyal alumni and football enthusiasts are selected out from the larger population and come together in the stadium. Finally, an emergent norm defines what constitutes an appropriate response to a particular event and suppresses incongruous behavior. Each perspective helps us understand crowd behavior.

Social Movements

Sociologists view a **social movement** as a more or less persistent and organized effort on the part of a relatively large number of people to bring about or resist change. The civil rights movement mobilized 200,000 people to march in Washington, DC, in 1963 and many more to demonstrate across the country, and it resulted in an end to segregated schools and other public facilities. The women's movement has transformed our society from one in which women are relegated to the kitchen to one in which women work alongside men in almost every type of career. Like collective behavior, social movements often appear in times of rapid social change. Both frequently provide an impetus to social change. Indeed, both occur outside the institutional framework that forms everyday life and break through the familiar web of ordered expectations. But while collective behavior is characterized by spontaneity and a lack of internal structure, social movements possess a considerable measure of internal order and purposeful orientation. This organizational potential allows social movements to challenge established institutions.

Central to the concept of social movement is the idea that people intervene in the process of social change. Rather than responding passively to the flow of life or to its troubling aspects, people seek to alter the course of history. Of equal significance, they undertake joint activity. Individuals consciously act together with a sense of engaging in a common enterprise. Christianity, the Crusades, the Reformation, the American Revolution, the antislavery movement, the labor movement, Zionism, and fascism—like other social movements—have profoundly affected the societies they have touched.

Causes of Social Movements

What social factors produce social movements, and what leads people to join and persist in social movements? Social movements may arise from social misery and, more particularly, from social and economic deprivation. They also require resources and organizations.

Deprivation Approaches

As noted in earlier chapters, Karl Marx held that capitalist exploitation leads to progressive impoverishment of the working class. He expected that over time conditions would become so abominable that workers would be compelled to recognize the social nature of their misery and overthrow their oppressors. However, Marx also recognized that the suffering of the underclasses can be so intense, and their resulting alienation so massive, that all social and revolutionary consciousness is deadened. Marx also recognized a type of **relative deprivation**—a discontent associated with the gap between what people actually have and what they have come to expect and feel to be their just due. He foresaw that the working class could become better off as capitalism advanced, but the gap between owners and workers would widen and produce among the latter deepening feelings of comparative disadvantage (Giddens, 1973; Harrington, 1976).

A number of sociologists have suggested that a major factor in the evolution of the civil rights movement in the 1960s was the emergence among African Americans of a growing sense of relative deprivation (Geschwender, 1964; Gurr, 1970). The prosperity of the 1950s and 1960s gave many African Americans a taste of the affluent society. They gained enough to arouse realistic hopes for more. Hence, grievances related to squalid housing, limited job opportunities, persistent unemployment, low pay, and police brutality were felt as severely frustrating. The civil rights movement arose not so much as a protest fed by despair as one fed by rising expectations.

Sociologist James Davies (1962, 1969, 1974) found that relative deprivation may also be fostered under another condition—that characterized by his "rise-and-drop," or "*J*-curve," hypothesis (see Figure 13.2). According to Davies, a revolution does not occur simply because there is a gap between what people want and what they get. Such dissatisfaction is fairly constant and does not cause social upheaval if it is not too severe. Even during a long period of social and economic improvement, people are not likely to get all that they desire. Their expectations for fulfillment increase as fast as actual improvements do, but because improvements are continuing, the gap is tolerable. Revolutions are most likely to occur when such a long period of improvement is followed by a sharp reversal in actual need satisfaction. People fear that the gains they achieved with great effort will be lost, and their mood becomes revolutionary.

Resource Mobilization Approaches

According to the resource mobilization school, social discontent is more or less constant and thus endemic within all modern societies (Tilly, 1978; Taylor, 1989; Walton and Ragin, 1990). Structural factors, such as the availability of resources for pursuing particular goals and the

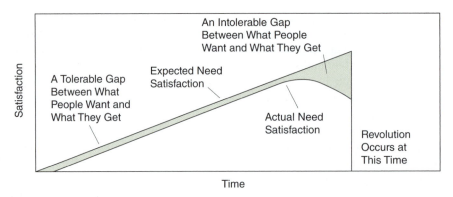

Figure 13.2

Davies's *J*-Curve Theory of Revolution

The figure illustrates Davies's theory that revolutions are often fostered when a period of social and economic betterment is succeeded by sharp reversals, fueling concern that the gains will be lost.

Source: From *American Sociological Review* 27 (February 1962): 6, figure 1. Courtesy of the American Sociological Association.

network of interpersonal relationships that serve as the focus for membership recruitment, are key. People are seen as participating in a social movement not as the result of deprivation but as a response to a rational decision-making process whereby they weigh the costs and benefits of participation. Consequently, conditions of political opportunity—for instance, support from established elites, contemporary models of successful political activism, and preexisting organizational networks and organizations—play a critical part in the development of social movements.

In many cases, resources and organizations outside the protest group are crucial in determining the scope and outcomes of collective action. External support is especially critical for movements of the poor. Sociologist J. Craig Jenkins (1985) contrasted the unsuccessful attempt to organize farmworkers by the National Farm Labor Union from 1946 to 1952 with the successful organization of Mexican farmworkers by the United Farm Workers from 1965 to 1972. Jenkins argued that the United Farm Workers succeeded because internal divisions in government neutralized opposition

elites, while the support of the liberal–labor coalition during the reform years of the 1960s and early 1970s turned the tide in favor of the farmworkers. Hence, the success or failure of a social movement derives from strategic factors and the political processes in which it becomes enmeshed (Burstein, 1991b; Morris, 1993).

What keeps people involved in social movements? The rational-choice model suggests that people get involved because of what they perceive the movements can do for them (Hechter, 1987). But once people are involved, how should leaders of the movements keep members actively participating and contributing and prevent them from engaging in "free ridership"—that is, being members in name but not actually contributing anything to the cause?

One answer is that leaders must get members and potential members to believe in the cause, to be committed to it out of personal, fervent belief. In addition, social mechanisms are required to control behavior and to maintain commitment to the movement for reasons beyond personal belief in its inherent worth.

Rosabeth Kanter (1968) showed that successful communal groups were more likely to have used mechanisms promoting commitment than unsuccessful groups. John Hall found that several factors were strongly associated with a group's long-term success (1988):

- A common ethnic background and/or a foreign language spoken by the group's members;

- A spiritual hierarchy, with those in authority being of higher moral status than other members;

- Obligatory confession, in which one's transgressions might be pointed out by other members or leaders;

- The wearing of uniforms, or special clothes that set group members apart from the rest of society.

An example might help make those characteristics more concrete: The Amish, a group that speaks German, has church leaders and elders, and dresses very differently than the "English," as Amish call non-Amish persons. Children are not taught to speak English until they attend school. If one transgresses in Amish society, the punishment can be shunning, in which the transgressor is cast out from Amish society and cut off from friends and family.

Hall found that in the groups that were the oldest and survived intact the longest, there were continuing high levels of control mechanisms. Hall's study shows that the mechanisms of social control are more important than other factors in maintaining group solidarity and promoting the longevity of social movements and groups.

Types of Social Movements

A set of ideas—an **ideology**—is critical to a social movement. An ideology provides individuals with conceptions of the movement's purposes, its rationale for existence, its indictment of existing conditions or arrangements, and its design for action (Moaddel, 1992). It functions as a kind of glue that joins people together in a fellowship of belief. But an ideology not only binds together otherwise isolated and separated individuals; it also unites them with a cause. In so doing it prepares them for self-sacrifice on behalf of the movement—at times even to lay down their lives for the "True God," "the New Nation," or "the Revolution."

Some movements pursue objectives that aim to change society through challenging fundamental values; others seek modifications within the framework of the existing value scheme. In the former case, **revolutionary movements** advocate replacement of the existing value scheme; in the latter, **reform movements** pursue changes that will implement the existing value scheme more adequately. The civil rights movement identified with the leadership of the Reverend Martin Luther King, Jr., had a reform emphasis. It sought to extend values already acknowledged as inherent in political democracy to the African American population of the United States. In contrast, a number of African American nationalist groups that arose in the late 1960s had a revolutionary emphasis. They sought to institute basic changes in the republican form of government in the United States, to rearrange the class structure, and to inaugurate a system of greater African American autonomy.

Organized efforts called **resistance movements** arise not only for the purpose of instituting change but also to block change or to eliminate a previously instituted change. Thus, the movement for civil rights in the South unleashed a white counterattack beginning in the 1950s that found expression in the organization of white citizens' councils and Ku Klux Klan groups (Vander Zanden, 1965, 1983).

Still other types of movements—**expressive movements**—are less concerned with institutional change than with a renovating or renewing of people from *within*, frequently with the promise of some future redemption. Pentecostal and holiness religious sects are the most common examples of expressive movements.

Less common are expressive movements that appeal primarily to the middle class, such as Zen Buddhism and *est* (Erhard Seminars Training), and that were popular in the United States in the 1970s and 1980s (Tipton, 1982). Although most expressive movements arise among the underprivileged, they do not seek comprehensive social change nor do they aim to save the world. Their goal is to save individuals from a world that is becoming progressively degenerate or oppressive.

Social Revolution

A **social revolution** involves the overthrow of a society's state and class structures and the creation of new social arrangements. Revolutions are most likely to occur under certain conditions.

First, a good deal of political power is concentrated in the state, so there is a centralized governing apparatus. Accordingly, the state can become the focus for collective anger and attack.

Second, the military's allegiance to the established regime is weakened so that the army is no longer a reliable tool for suppressing domestic disorder. Where army officers are drawn from elites in conflict with the central government, or when troops sympathize with their civilian counterparts, the unreliability of the army increases the vulnerability of the state.

Third, political crises—often associated with long-term international conflicts that result in military defeat—weaken the existing regime and contribute to the collapse of the state apparatus.

And fourth, a substantial segment of the population must mobilize in uprisings that bring a new elite to power. Peasant revolts usually stem from landlords' taking over peasant lands, substantial increases in taxation or rents, or famines. Urban uprisings commonly derive from sharp jumps in food prices and unusually high levels of unemployment (Skocpol, 1979; Goldstone, 1991).

Terrorism

The death of Osama bin Laden in May 2011 did not end terrorism. Although no one definition of **terrorism** is universally accepted, the U.S. Department of State offers this: "premeditated, politically motivated violence perpetrated against noncombatant targets by subnational groups or clandestine agents, usually intended to influence an audience" (Atran, 2003). The U.S. Congress defines acts of terror as acts that appear to be intended "(i) to intimidate or coerce a civilian population; (ii) to influence the policy of a government by intimidation or coercion; or (iii) to affect the conduct of a government by assassination or kidnapping." Familiar to all of us is *suicide terrorism*—the use of self-destructing humans to commit terrorist acts.

Political scientist Robert A. Pape (Pape, 2005; Pape and Feldman, 2010) has analyzed numerous acts of suicide terrorism that have occurred worldwide since 1980. He concluded that suicide terrorism is not grounded in fundamentalist religion, Islamic or otherwise, and that leaders of suicide terrorist groups are not irrational or fanatic. Rather, such attacks are part of campaigns to achieve specific political goals, typically to force concessions from democratic governments. The rate of suicide terrorism has increased in recent years because terrorists have learned that suicide attacks are effective in achieving their goals. Pape argues that the best strategy for dealing with suicide terrorism is to promote homeland security and to avoid military occupations in foreign countries.

In practice, what constitutes terrorism is a matter of social definition, with one side labeling people as "terrorists" while another side labels the same people as "freedom fighters." Similarly, whether an action is "aid to terrorists" as opposed to "covert support of friendly forces" is a matter of perspective, as illustrated by the Reagan administration's controversial support of the Nicaraguan contras, or counterrevolutionary fighters, in the mid-1980s. Research shows that public opinion provides a useful indicator of terrorist activity, with higher levels of terrorism when people disapprove of the leadership and policies of the target country (Krueger and Malečková, 2009).The researchers speculate that greater disapproval is linked to public support and encouragement for terrorist cells, an increase in public belief that terrorism is a legitimate tactic, and an increase in the number of people willing to join cells and carry out terrorist acts themselves.

A Media Event

Very often terrorism is aimed at a media audience, not the actual victims. The "theater of terror" becomes possible only when the media afford the stage and access to a worldwide audience. The act of media coverage also often enhances the importance of the issue that allegedly led to the terrorist activities. Newspaper readers and television viewers see the issue as of substantially greater importance and as justifying resolution by national or international action. As one analyst noted, "The primary target is not those actually killed or injured in the attack, but those made to witness it. The enemy's own information media amplify the attack's effects to the larger target population" (Atran, 2003).

Terrorists and Social Change

Although terrorists have sometimes been profiled as poor, uneducated, and politically powerless, research shows that suicide terrorists are as educated and economically well-to-do as

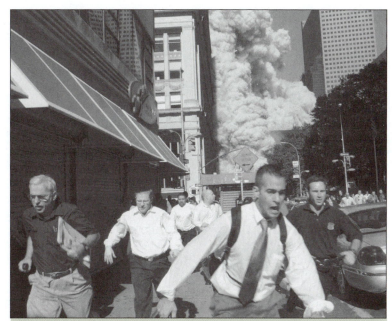

U.S. interest in and concern about terrorism accelerated rapidly with the September 11, 2001, attacks on Washington, DC, and New York City.

those in the surrounding populations (Pape and Feldman, 2010; Pape, 2005; Atran, 2003). And although political and social change may be what the terrorists' leaders are seeking, those who carry out the missions are motivated primarily by their group commitment. According to psychologists who studied the September 11 attacks, the 19 men who carried out the plans of Al-Qaeda were motivated less by religious zeal and hatred for the United States than by peer pressure—the commitment each had made to the others to go forward with the plan (Vedantam, 2001).

With terrorism a grim fact of contemporary life, some analysts are calling for incorporating the potential for terrorist acts into disaster planning. Although the causes of disaster differ, plans for relief, development of backup systems, and the incorporation of disaster resistance into

When Will Same-Sex Marriages Become "the Norm"?

Not long ago, most gay and lesbian people kept their sexual orientation a secret from most people, often even—or perhaps especially—from their families. As we launch a new century, there is increasing acceptance of people who are openly gay or lesbian and live together in same-sex couples. But different elements of society and culture often change at different rates, and in this case what people are willing to tolerate in the sexual behavior patterns of others has changed more rapidly than the societal institutions that have traditionally legitimated and controlled sexual behavior.

Marriage and family, two major American institutions, appear to be in the early stages of including same-sex unions in their definitions. Increased societal acceptance of homosexual lifestyles was one step. Legalization of same-sex unions is

another; since 2000, when Vermont passed the nation's first civil-union law, legal recognition of same-sex couples has been extended in one form or another in 19 states (Badgett and Herman, 2011), and in 2012 a California ban on same-sex marriage was found to be unconstitutional (Pew Forum on Religion and Public Life, 2012).

An obvious third step is religious sanction of same-sex unions. In 2003, when the Episcopal Church gave its bishops the option to allow priests to bless committed homosexual relationships, public outrage was immediate and loud. Polls showed that "a strong majority" of the public disapproved, especially frequent churchgoers (Morin and Cooperman, 2003). Some say that the reaction came from the extension of the word *marriage*—something Americans see as essentially a religious institution—

to same-sex unions. Sociologist Norval Glenn commented, "I know a lot of people who want to give all the rights and privileges to gay couples that married people have, but they don't want to change the traditional meaning of the term marriage" (Bumiller, 2003).

Why have Americans been able to accept gays and lesbians in their communities but less able to tolerate homosexual marriage? The answer is that social institutions change much more slowly than do patterns of behavior and tolerance. Simply put, many people have difficulty accepting homosexual unions as legitimate because neither religion nor traditional marriage provides a way to conceptualize homosexual behavior as morally correct.

How might this change? Various religious groups in the United States are extending their definitions

new communication, energy, water supply, and other systems are equally useful for dealing with natural disasters and large-scale acts of terrorism (D. Kennedy, 2002).

In an assessment of the root causes of and preventive measures for suicide terrorism, Scott Atran (2003) recommends sociological and psychological research on how terrorist institutions form and on recruitment and retention procedures. The first line of defense, he says, is to reduce the receptivity of potential recruits to recruiting organizations—but that cannot be done until planners understand more about the mix of community and institutional factors that make people eager to take part in terrorist groups. Atran also recommends that the

United States respond to terrorist acts by addressing the grievances of terrorist organizations: "Our society can ill afford to ignore either the consequences of its own actions or the causes behind the actions of others" (Atran, 2003).

Looking to the Future

We undertake many of our daily activities in anticipation of the future. We carry out our job responsibilities in the expectation that we will be paid at the end of the week or the month. We invest our money, energy, and time in an education based on the assumption that there will be a job payoff down the road. We involve ourselves of marriage to include same-sex relationships (Pew Forum on Religion and Public Life, 2010). Although many religions and denominations adhere to the "one man and one woman" definition of marriage (see p. 332), change is under way. Presbyterians, for example, define marriage as between a man and a woman but also allow ministers to bless same-sex unions. The Evangelical Lutheran Church in America voted in 2009 to allow congregations "to recognize, support and hold publicly accountable lifelong, monogamous, same-gender relationships." The United Church of Christ voted in 2005 not only to legally recognize but also to advocate in favor of same-sex marriage. Reform and Reconstructionist Jewish movements support same-sex marriage, and Conservative movement Judaism allows individual rabbis the option of recognizing same-sex unions.

It is not clear that same-sex marriage will ever be accepted by all Americans. Legally recognized domestic partnerships may increasingly be seen as the equivalent of civil marriage, as the line between the two kinds of unions slowly disappears. Legitimization of these unions by mainline denominations has already occurred. Acceptance in the remaining religious bodies will probably require more than a change of civil procedure. It will require changes in underlying religious beliefs and ideas.

Percent Americans who Favor Allowing Gays and Lesbians to Marry Legally

	2010	2011
Total	42	46
Protestant	31	34
White evangelical	20	19
White mainline	49	54
Black Protestant	28	30
Catholic	46	52
Non-Hispanic White Catholic	49	57
Hispanic Catholic	42	42
Unaffiliated	62	72

Source: Pew Forum on Religion and Public Life, 2012.

Questions for Discussion

1. How likely do you think it is that homosexual marriage will be legitimated in U.S. society? When and by what process do you think it will happen?

2. How do religious groups and organizations change their attitudes and policies about something like same-sex marriage? How might they reconcile such changes with their history and traditions?

in environmental, civil rights, antinuclear, or women's movements to have a voice in the shaping of tomorrow's world.

And yet we can only speculate on what the future will bring; see Box 13.2, for example, about the future of same-sex marriages in the United States. We will probably have little more success anticipating the century ahead than did our compatriots 100 years ago at the future-oriented World's Columbian Exposition in Chicago, which we discussed in the introduction to the chapter. For the most part the forecasts provided by 74 prominent Americans turned out to be almost entirely off the mark.

However, some social phenomena can be predicted fairly accurately. Selling insurance is based on mostly accurate estimates of the risk of loss the company will incur due to illness, death, accidents, crime, and other things. Economists can predict that if the price of a product is doubled, fewer people will buy it. Sociologists can predict the persistence of educational inequality. But social scientists do not do well in predicting major social changes (Hechter, 1995).

Many years ago philosopher Karl Popper distinguished between *scientific predictions,* which are conditional (e.g., a prediction that specific changes in a system will result in specific changes in outcomes), and *unconditional historical prophecies.* The characteristics re-quired to make accurate predictions for a system are that it be well isolated, stationary, and recurrent—characteristics that simply do not apply to societies. Societies can change, new social situations that we have never experienced before can arise, and the growth of technology and knowledge can shift things in directions we are unable now to anticipate (Hechter, 1995).

As a consequence, social scientists cannot predict with any accuracy major social phenomena such as revolution. But as Hechter pointed out, the utility of the physical and social sciences "may not rest in their ability to accurately forecast events"; rather, as Karl Popper said (Popper, 1963:343), the role of science in social life is "the modest one of helping us to understand even the more remote consequences of possible actions, and thus of helping us to choose our actions more wisely."

Futurists—individuals who specialize in the study of the future, seeking to understand, predict, and plan the future of society—have identified two broad trends that seem to be central to contemporary social life (Coates and Jarratt, 1990; Halal and Nikitin, 1990). First, the United States is being restructured from an industrial to an information society. Second, modern societies are increasingly shifting from a national to a global economy.

For 300 years technology has been cast in a mechanical model, one based on combustion processes. Now high-tech industries are becoming information-intensive rather than energy- or materials-intensive. This shift to an information economy may improve our ability to forecast the future using computer modeling and other techniques. Researchers are close to being able to track in a computer model all 7 billion people on earth, and very fast computers already are used to detect suspicious patterns in data that lead to identifying fraudulent tax returns and Medicare claims (Lane, 1998). Similar methods are being developed to use new information technologies to assess the future and develop long-term planning strategies to deal with the emerging challenges facing humankind (Lempert, Popper, and Bankes, 2003).

Global factors influencing our future are many. The rapid population growth that we cannot avoid in the next 50 years will test our abilities to adapt and change. We can expect increased conflicts over resources to be added to worldwide religious, ethnic, and nationalist conflicts. The AIDS epidemic has changed the demographics of a number of countries, and scientists predict that other diseases also will challenge our health care delivery systems. The shift in nations leading the world economically will have political repercussions as well. And the planet's environmental problems, particularly climate

These children, orphaned by AIDS and living in Chad, are growing up in a society that has a very different age distribution from the one in which their parents and grandparents grew up.

change, provide an unprecedented opportunity to work together: "We must . . . design strategies that minimize the impact of climate change on societies that are at greatest risk. This will require substantial international cooperation, without which the 21st century will likely witness unprecedented social disruptions" (Weiss and Bradley, 2001:610).

As we have noted throughout this textbook, sociology invites us to scrutinize the world and notice what we otherwise often ignore, neglect, or take for granted. It looks behind the outer reaches of the social experience and discerns its inner structure and processes—suspending the belief that things simply are as they seem. As such, sociology is uniquely suited to fostering the skills necessary for living in an ever-changing world filled with countless choices and seemingly endless uncertainty. The challenges we confront in the 21st century may well inspire you to pursue a sociological career.

 ### What Can Sociology Do for You?

This, our final chapter, presented information about social change, collective behavior, and social movements. Some of the earlier chapters

in this book introduced the possibilities of major social change in the future—the changes that will occur as China, Brazil, India, Mexico, and Russia become major economic forces, for example, and the changes that will be required to avert global warming or to adapt to it as it occurs. We hope that what you have learned in studying sociology will help you make sense of a rapidly changing world.

Sociologists study social interactions and social organization. Perhaps at this point in your course of study, you've discovered that you are interested enough in sociology to pursue an advanced degree—a master's or a Ph.D.—and a career doing academic research and teaching others about sociology. Or perhaps you would like to be actively involved in promoting social change in a particular direction as an activist, by working for a nongovernmental organization (NGO), or by getting involved in politics. What you learn as a sociology major will stand you in good stead for any of these.

If you found the material covered in Chapter 13 to be interesting, look for courses in social problems, collective behavior, social movements, globalization, and social change.

The Chapter in Brief: *Social Change*

A World of Change

Sociologists refer to fundamental alterations in the patterns of culture, structure, and social behavior over time as **social change.** It is a process by which society becomes something different while remaining in some respects the same.

■ **Sources of Social Change** Many factors interact to generate changes in people's behavior and in the culture and structure of their society, including the physical environment, population,

clashes over resources and values, supporting values and norms, innovation (**discoveries** and **inventions**), **diffusion,** and the mass media.

■ **Perspectives on Social Change** Cyclical theorists look to the course of a civilization or society, searching for generalizations regarding their stages of growth and decline. Functionalist theorists see society as a system that tends toward equilibrium, with **cultural lag** an important factor in social change. Conflict theorists hold that tensions between competing groups are the basic source of social change.

■ **Social Change in the United States**
Computers have consequences for the use and manipulation of social power. They alter the manner in which people relate to one another, and they have implications for individual privacy, the confidentiality of communications and personal data, and employment.

■ **Social Change in Developing Nations**
The **modernization** approach sees development as entailing a pattern of convergence as societies become increasingly urban, industry comes to overshadow agriculture, and other changes occur. According to **world system** and dependency analysis, an unequal exchange takes place between core and periphery nations, with development in core nations occurring at the cost of underdevelopment in periphery nations.

Collective Behavior

Collective behavior is not organized in terms of established norms and institutionalized lines of action.

■ **Varieties of Collective Behavior**   Collective behavior comes in many forms, including **rumors, fashions** and **fads** (which can turn into **crazes**), **mass hysteria, panic,** and **crowds.** Types of crowds include the **acting crowd,** the **casual crowd,** the **conventional crowd,** and the **expressive crowd.** These crowd types share three characteristics: suggestibility, **deindividualization,** and invulnerability.

■ **Preconditions for Collective Behavior**
One framework for examining collective behavior is based on the **value-added** model popular among economists and specifies six determinants of collective behavior, including **structural conduciveness** and **structural strain.**

■ **Explanations of Crowd Behavior**
Sociologists offer three approaches to crowd behavior: **contagion theory, convergence theory,** and **emergent-norm theory.**

Social Movements

Social movements are vehicles whereby people collectively seek to influence the course of human events through formal organizations.

■ **Causes of Social Movements**   Some sociologists seek the roots of social movements in social and economic deprivation; others look to the resources and organizations aggrieved persons can muster as providing the key to an understanding of social movements.

■ **Types of Social Movements**   An **ideology** is critical to a social movement. Common forms of social movements include **revolutionary, reform, resistance,** and **expressive movements.**

■ **Social Revolution**   **Social revolutions** are most likely to occur when (1) a good deal of political power is concentrated in the state, (2) the military is no longer a reliable tool for suppressing domestic disorders, (3) political crises weaken the existing regime, and (4) a substantial segment of the population mobilizes in uprisings.

■ **Terrorism**   Although what constitutes **terrorism** is a matter of social definition, sociologists have come to see terrorism as a new mode of warfare with far-reaching implications.

Looking to the Future

Futurists have identified two changes that seem to be central to contemporary social life: The United States is being restructured from an industrial to an information society, and modern societies are increasingly shifting from a national to a global economy.

Glossary

acting crowd An excited, volatile collection of people who are engaged in rioting, looting, or other forms of aggressive behavior in which established norms carry little weight.

casual crowd A collection of people who have little in common with one another except that they may be viewing a common event, such as looking through a department store window.

collective behavior Ways of thinking, feeling, and acting that develop among a large number of people and that are relatively spontaneous and unstructured.

contagion theory An approach to crowd behavior that emphasizes the part played in crowd settings by rapidly communicated and uncritically accepted feelings, attitudes, and actions.

conventional crowd A number of people who have assembled for some specific purpose and who typically act in accordance with established norms, such as people attending a baseball game or concert.

convergence theory An approach to crowd behavior stating that a crowd consists of a highly unrepresentative body of people who assemble because they share the same predispositions.

craze A fad that becomes an all-consuming passion.

crowd A temporary, relatively unorganized gathering of people who are in close physical proximity.

cultural lag The view that immaterial culture must constantly "catch up" with material culture, resulting in an adjustment gap between the two forms of culture.

deindividualization A psychological state of diminished identity and self-awareness.

diffusion The process by which culture traits spread from one social unit to another.

discovery An addition to knowledge.

emergent-norm theory An approach to crowd behavior stating that crowd members evolve new standards for behavior in a crowd setting and then enforce the expectations in the manner of norms.

expressive crowd An aggregation of people who have gotten together for self-stimulation and personal gratification, such as occurs at a religious revival or a rock concert.

expressive movement A movement that is less concerned with institutional change than with a renovating or renewing of people from within.

fad A folkway that lasts for a short time and enjoys acceptance among only a segment of the population.

fashion A folkway that lasts for a short time and enjoys widespread acceptance within society.

futurists Individuals specializing in the study of the future; they seek to understand, predict, and plan the future of society.

ideology A set of ideas that provides individuals with conceptions of the purposes of a social movement, a rationale for the movement's existence, an indictment of existing conditions, and a design for action.

invention The use of existing knowledge in a new form.

mass hysteria The rapid dissemination of behaviors involving contagious anxiety, usually associated with some mysterious force.

modernization The process by which a society moves from traditional or preindustrial social and economic arrangements to those characteristic of industrial societies.

panic Irrational and uncoordinated but collective action among people that is induced by the presence of an immediate, severe threat.

reform movement A social movement that pursues changes that will implement the existing value scheme of a society more adequately.

relative deprivation Discontent associated with the gap between what people actually have and what they believe they should have.

resistance movement A social movement that arises to block change or eliminate a previously instituted change.

revolutionary movement A social movement that advocates the replacement of a society's existing value scheme.

rumor A difficult-to-verify piece of information that is transmitted from person to person in relatively rapid fashion.

social change Fundamental alterations in the patterns of culture, structure, and social behavior over time.

social movement A more or less persistent and organized effort on the part of a relatively large number of people to bring about or resist change.

social revolution The overthrow of a society's state and class structures and the fashioning of new social arrangements.

structural conduciveness Social conditions that permit a particular variety of collective behavior to occur.

structural strain A condition in which important aspects of a social system are "out of joint."

terrorism The use of force or violence against persons or property to intimidate or coerce a government, a formal organization, or a civilian population in furtherance of political, religious, or social objectives.

value-added The idea that each step in the production process—from raw materials to the finished product—increases the economic value of manufactured goods.

world system An approach that views development as involving an unequal exchange between core and periphery nations, with development at the former end of the chain coming at the cost of underdevelopment at the other end.

Review Questions

1. What is social change? Give one example of a major social change that has taken place in the past 100 years. What were some of the factors responsible for that change?

2. Describe the major theories of social change.

3. How have computer use and Internet access affected life in the United States?

4. Compare the modernization and world system approaches to social change in developing nations.

5. What is collective behavior? List and define some of its forms.

6. What are the major explanations of crowd behavior?

7. What is a social movement? What causes a social movement?

8. What are the differences among revolutionary, reform, resistance, and expressive movements?

9. How does a social revolution occur?

10. What is terrorism?

Internet Connection www.mhhe.com/hughes11e

Select a social movement that you support or that is of interest to you—the women's movement, gun control, pro-life, pro-choice, rain forest preservation, and so on—and use a search engine such as **google.com** to find information about this movement. Write a short report about the movement. Is it a reform, resistance, or revolutionary movement? Which approach to social movements—deprivation or resource mobilization—best accounts for it?

References

A

AACAP. 2005. Foster care. No. 64, updated May 2005. American Academy of Child and Adolescent Psychiatry. http://www.aacap.org/os/root/facts_for_families/foster_care.

Abbott, Pamela, and **Claire Wallace.** 1997. *An Introduction to sociology: Feminist perspectives.* London: Routledge.

Acker, Joan. 1992. Gendered institutions. *Contemporary Sociology,* 21:565–69.

Acs, Gregory. 2011. *Downward mobility from the middle class: Waking up from the American dream.* The Pew Charitable Trusts: Economic Mobility Project (September):1–29.

Adam, Barbara, and **Stuart Allan,** eds. 1995. *Theorizing culture: An interdisciplinary critique after post-modernism.* New York: New York University Press.

Adler, Freda, Gerhard O. W. Mueller, and **William S. Laufer.** 2004. *Criminology and the criminal justice system.* New York: McGraw-Hill.

Adler, Patricia A., and **Peter Adler.** 1989. The gloried self: The aggrandizement and the constriction of self. *Social Psychological Quarterly,* 52:299, 310.

Adler, Stephen J. 1991. Suits over sexual harassment prove difficult due to issue of definition. *Wall Street Journal* (October 9):B1.

Aisenbrey, Silke, Marie Evertsson, and **Daniela Grunow**. 2009. Is there a career penalty for mothers' time out? A comparison of Germany, Sweden and the United States. *Social Forces*, 88(2):573–606.

Akard, Patrick J. 1992. Corporate mobilization and political power: The transformation of U.S. economic policy in the 1970s. *American Sociological Review,* 57:597–615.

Akerlof, George A., and **Robert J. Shiller.** 2009. *Animal spirits: How human psychology drives the economy, and why it matters for global capitalism.* Princeton, NJ: Princeton University Press.

Alba, Richard D. 1990. *Ethnic identity: The transformation of white America.* New Haven, CT: Yale University Press.

Alexander, Marcus, and **Fotini Christia.** 2011. Context modularity of human altruism. *Science,* 334: 1392–94.

Allport, Gordon W. 1954. *The nature of prejudice.* Boston: Beacon Press.

Altschiller, David. 1988. Selling the presidency: More dollars equal less message. *New York Times* (March 20):F3.

Alon, Sigal, Thurston Domina, and **Marta Tienda.** 2010. Stymied mobility or temporary lull? The puzzle of lagging Hispanic college degree attainment. *Social Forces,* 88(4):1807–32.

Alwin, Duane, F., and **Jon A. Krosnick.** 1991. Aging, cohorts, and the stability of sociopolitical orientations over the life span. *American Journal of Sociology,* 97:169–95.

Amato, Paul R., and **Alan Booth.** 1997. *A generation at risk: Growing up in an era of family upheaval.* Cambridge, MA: Harvard University Press.

Amato, Paul R., Alan Booth, David R. Johnson, and **Stacy J. Rogers.** 2007. *Alone together: How marriage in America is changing.* Cambridge, MA: Harvard University Press.

Amato, Paul R., and **Juliana M. Sobolewski.** 2001. The effects of divorce and marital discord on adult children's psychological well-being. *American Sociological Review,* 66:900–921.

American Academy of Pediatrics. 2001. Childhood, adolescents, and television. *Pediatrics,* 107(2): 423–26.

American Anthropological Association. 1997. *American Anthropological Association response to OMB Directive 15: Race and ethnic standards for federal statistics and administrative reporting.* Arlington, VA: American Anthropological Association.

American Sociological Association. 1989. Code of ethics. Washington, DC: American Sociological Association.

Andersen, Margaret, and **Patricia Hill Collins.** 2007. *Race, class, and gender: An anthology.* Belmont, CA: Wadsworth.

Anderson, Craig A., and **Brad J. Bushman.** 2002. The effects of media violence on society. *Science,* 295:2377–79.

Anderson, Elijah. 1990. *Streetwise: Race, class, and change in an urban community.* Chicago: University of Chicago Press.

Anderson, Elijah. 1999. *The code of the street: Decency, violence, and the moral life of the inner city.* New York: Norton.

Anderson, Elijah. 2001. Urban ethnography. *International encyclopedia of social sciences.* New York: Elsevier.

Anderson, Robert, and **Betty L. Smith.** 2005. Deaths: Leading Causes 2002. National Vital Statistics Reports, Vol. 53, No. 17. Hyattsville, MD: National Center for Health Statistics.

Anderson, Ron. 2009. The emerging class of the lucky-rich. *Contexts,* 8(1):72–73.

Anderson, Sarah E., Christina D. Economos, and **Aviva Must.** 2008. Active play and screen time in U.S. children aged 4 to 11 years in relation to sociodemographic and weight status characteristics: A nationally representative cross-sectional analysis. *BMC Public Health* 8:366doi: 10.1186/1471-2458-8-366.

Antonakis, John, and **Olaf Dalgas.** 2009. Predicting elections: Child's play! *Science,* 323:1183.

Antonio, Robert J., and **Robert J. Brulle.** 2011. The unbearable lightness of politics: Climate change denial and political polarization. *Sociological Quarterly,* 52:195–202.

Apple, Michael W. 1982. *Education and power.* London: Routledge & Kegan Paul.

Appy, Christian G. 1993. *Working-class war: American combat soldiers and Vietnam.* Chapel Hill: University of North Carolina Press.

Argetsinger, Amy. 2003. Legacy students pose challenge to affirmative action. *Washington Post* (March 12):A6.

Ariès, Philippe. 1962. *Centuries of childhood.* Trans. R. Baldick. New York: Random House.

Armas, Genaro C. 2003. Study: Rents up by one-third. Associated Press (September 9).

Arnold, Guy. 2011. *Migration: Changing the world.* London: Pluto Press.

Aronson, Elliot. 2008. *The social animal,* 10th ed. New York: Worth/ Freeman.

Arrillaga, Pauline. 2000. Putting polygamy on trial in Utah. *Washington Post* (December 8):A49.

Arrow, Kenneth, Samuel Bowles, and **Steven Durlauf,** eds. 2000. *Meritocracy and economic inequality.* Princeton, NJ: Princeton University Press.

Asch, Solomon. 1952. *Social psychology.* Englewood Cliffs, NJ: Prentice-Hall.

Ascher, Marcia. 2002. *Mathematics elsewhere: An exploration of ideas across cultures.* Princeton, NJ: Princeton University Press.

Ash, Caroline, Barbara R. Jasny, David A. Malakoff, and **Andrew M. Sugden.** 2010. Feeding the future. *Science,* 327:797.

Ash, Caroline, Barbara R. Jasny, Leslie Roberts, Richard Stone, and **Andrew M. Sugden.** 2008. Reimagining cities. *Science,* 319:739.

Associated Press. 2003. Gay-rights group compares gay couples to others. *Washington Post* (May 18):A7.

Association of American Medical Colleges. 2003. www.aamc.org/data/ facts/2003/2003school.htm.

Atkinson, Anthony B., Thomas Piketty, and **Emmanuel Saez.** 2011. Top incomes in the long run of history. *Journal of Economic Literature,* 49(1):3–71.

Atran, Scott. 2003. Genesis of suicide terrorism. *Science,* 299:1534–39.

Axelrod, Robert, 1984. *The evolution of cooperation.* New York: Basic Books.

B

Badgett, M. V. Lee, and **Jody L. Herman.** 2011. *Patterns of relationship recognition by same-sex couples in the United States.* The Williams Institute (November). Available at http://williamsinstitute.law.ucla.edu/ wp-content/uploads/Badgett-Herman-Marriage-Dissolution-Nov-2011.pdf.

Baer, Ellen D. 1991. The feminist disdain for nursing. *New York Times* (February 23):17.

Bakanic, Von. 2009. *Prejudice: Attitudes about race, class, and gender.* Upper Saddle River, NJ: Pearson Prentice-Hall.

Baker, Beth. 2003. Dead wrong: Most want to die at home. Here's why they don't succeed. *Washington Post* (May 13):F1.

Baker, Beth. 2007. The hospitalist is in . . . and taking over a role played by primary care physicians. *Washington Post* (September 11):F1.

Baker, Stephen. 1993. The owners vs. the boss at Weirton Steel. *Business Week* (November 15):38.

Balafoutas, Loukas, and **Matthias Sutter.** 2012. Affirmative action policies promote women and do not harm efficiency in the laboratory. *Science,* 335:579–81.

Bales, Robert F. 1970. *Personality and interpersonal behavior.* New York: Holt, Rinehart & Winston.

Bales, Robert F., and **Edgar F. Borgatta.** 1955. Size of group as a factor in the interaction profile. In A. P. Hare, E. F. Borgatta, and R. F. Bales, eds., *Small groups: Studies in social interaction.* New York: Knopf.

Bandura, Albert. 1965. Influence of models reinforcement contingencies on the acquisition of imitative responses. *Journal of Personality and Social Psychology,* 1:589–95.

Bandura, Albert. 1971. *Psychological modeling: Conflicting theories.* Chicago: Aldine-Atherton.

Bandura, Albert. 1973. *Aggression: A social learning analysis.* Englewood Cliffs, NJ: Prentice-Hall.

Bane, Mary Jo. 1997. Welfare as we might know it. *The American Prospect,* No. 30 (January– February):47–53.

Bane, Mary Jo, and **David T. Ellwood.** 1994. *Welfare realities: From rhetoric to reform.* Cambridge, MA: Harvard University Press.

Banks, James, Michael Marmot, Zoe Oldfield, and **James P. Smith.** 2006. Disease and disadvantage in the United States and England. *Journal of the American Medical Association,* 295:2037–45.

Barak, Gregg, ed. 1991. *Crimes by the capitalist state: An introduction to state criminality.* Albany: State University of New York Press.

Barber, Bonnie L., Jacquelynne S. Eccles, and **Margaret R. Stone.** 2001. Whatever happened to the Jock, the Brain, and the Princess? Young adult pathways linked to adolescent activity involvement and social identity. *Journal of Adolescent Research,* 16(5):429–55.

Barber, Elizabeth. 1994. *Women's work, the first 20,000 years.* New York: Norton.

Barenboim, Carl. 1981. The development of person perception in childhood and adolescence. *Child Development,* 52:129–44.

Barkey, Karen, and **Sunita Parikh.** 1991. Comparative perspectives on the state. *Annual Review of Sociology,* 11:523–49.

Barnes, Jessica S., and **Claudette Bennett.** 2002. The Asian Population 2000. U.S. Census Bureau C2KBR/01-16. Washington, DC: U.S. Government Printing Office.

Barnes, Robert. 2009. Justice will scrutinize life sentences for youths. *Washington Post* (October 29):1A.

Barnet, Richard J., and **John Cavanagh.** 1994. *Global dreams: Imperial corporations and the new world order.* New York: Simon & Schuster.

Barnett, W. S. 2011. Effectiveness of early educational intervention. *Science,* 333:975–78.

Barringer, Felicity. 1993. Sex survey of American men finds 1% are gay. *New York Times* (April 15): A1, A9.

Barrow, Clyde W. 1990. *Universities and the capitalist state: Corporate liberalism and the reconstruction of American higher education, 1894–1928.* Madison: University of Wisconsin Press.

Barry, Patricia. 2010. A user's guide to health care reform: Ten things you need to know about the new law. *AARP Bulletin,* 51(4):19.

Bartholomew, Robert E., and **Jeffrey S. Victor.** 2004. A social-psychological theory of collective anxiety attacks: The "Mad Gasser" reexamined. *The Sociological Quarterly,* 45(2):229–48.

Bartol, Kathryn M., and **David C. Martin.** 1998. *Management,* 3rd ed. New York: McGraw-Hill.

Bartollas, Clemens. 2003. *Juvenile delinquency.* Boston: Allyn and Bacon.

Bass, Bernard M. 1981. *Stogdill's handbook of leadership.* New York: Free Press.

Batty, Michael. 2008. The size, scale, and shape of cities. *Science,* 319:769–71.

Baudrillard, Jean. 1983. *Simulations.* New York: Semiotext(e).

Baudrillard, Jean. 1990. *Fatal Strategies.* New York: Semiotext(e).

Bawa, Kamaljit S., Lian Pin Koh, Tien Ming Lee, Jianguo Liu, P. S. Ramakrishnan, Douglas W. Yu, Ya-ping Zhang, and **Peter H. Raven.** 2010. China, India, and the environment. *Science,* 327:1457–59.

Baxter, Janeen. 1994. Is husband's class enough? Class location and class identity in the United States, Sweden, Norway, and Australia. *American Sociological Review,* 59:220–35.

Baydar, Nazli, and **Jeanne Brooks-Gunn.** 1991. Effects of maternal employment and child-care arrangements on preschoolers' cognitive and behavioral outcomes. Evidence from the children of the National Longitudinal Survey of Youth. *Developmental Psychology,* 27:932–45.

Beaman, Lori, Esther Duflo, Rohini Pande, and **Petia Topalova.** 2012. Female leadership raises aspirations and education attainment for girls: A policy experiment in India. *Science,* 335:582–86.

Bean, Frank D., and **Marta Tienda.** 1987. *The Hispanic population of the United States.* New York: Russell Sage Foundation.

Beck, Allen J., Paige M. Harrison, and **Paul Guerino.** 2010. Sexual victimization in juvenile facilities reported by youth, 2008–2009. Bureau of Justice Statistics Special Report (January): NCJ 228416. Washington, DC: U.S. Department of Justice.

Beck, E. M., Patrick Horan, and **Charles Tolbert.** 1980. Social stratification in industrial society: Further evidence for a structural alternative. *American Sociological Review,* 45:712–19.

Beck, E. M., and **Stewart E. Tolnay.** 1990. The killing fields of the Deep South: The market for cotton and the lynching of blacks, 1882–1930. *American Sociological Review,* 55:526–39.

Becker, Howard S. 1963. *Outsiders: Studies in the sociology of deviance.* New York: Free Press.

Beddington, J. R., M. Asaduzzaman, M. E. Clark, A. Fernández Bremauntz, et al. 2012. What next for agriculture after Durban? *Science,* 335:289–90.

Beeghley, Leonard. 2000. *The structure of social stratification in the United States.* Boston: Allyn & Bacon.

Begley, Sharon. 2003. Scientifically, race is only skin deep and not very useful. *Wall Street Journal* (August 1):B1.

Behrens, Timothy E. J., Laurence T. Hunt, and **Matthew F. S. Rushworth.** 2009. The computation of social behavior. *Science,* 1160–64.

Beisel, Nicola, and **Tamara Kay.** 2004. Abortion, race, and gender in nineteenth-century America. *American Sociological Review,* 69:498–518.

Bell, Alan P., and **Martin S. Weinberg.** 1978. *Homosexualities: A study of diversity among men and women.* New York: Simon & Schuster.

Bell, Alan P., Martin S. Weinberg, and **Sue K. Hammersmith.** 1981. *Sexual preference: Its development in men and women.* Bloomington: Indiana University Press.

Bell, Gordon, and **Jim Gemmell.** 2009. *Total recall: How the e-memory revolution will change everything.* New York: Dutton.

Bellah, Robert N. 1970. *Beyond belief.* New York: Harper & Row.

Bellah, Robert N., and **Phillip E. Hammond.** 1980. *Varieties of civil religions.* New York: Harper & Row.

Belsky, J., D. L. Vandell, M. Burchinal, K. A. Clarke-Stewart, K. McCartney, and **M. T. Owen.** 2007. Are there long-term effects of early child care? *Child Development,* 78(2):681–701.

Belsky, Jay, and **Michael Rovine.** 1990. Patterns of marital change across the transition to parenthood: Pregnancy to three years postpartum.

Journal of Marriage and the Family, 52:5–19.

Bem, Sandra. 1981. Gender schema theory: A cognitive account of sex typing. *Psychological Bulletin,* 88:354–64.

Bendix, Reinhard. 1977. Bureaucracy. *International encyclopedia of the social sciences.* New York: Free Press.

Bennett, Amanda. 1990. Quality programs may be shoddy stuff. *Wall Street Journal* (October 4):B1.

Benson, J. Kenneth. 1977. Organizations: A dialectical view. *Administrative Science Quarterly,* 22:121.

Berberoglu, Berch. 1987. *The internationalization of capital: Imperialism and capitalist development on a world scale.* New York: Praeger.

Berger, Peter L., and **Brigitte Berger.** 1972. *Sociology: A biographical approach.* New York: Basic Books.

Berger, Suzanne. 2005. *How we compete: What companies around the world are doing to make it in the global economy.* New York: Doubleday.

Bergesen, Albert J. 2004. Durkheim's theory of mental categories: A review of the evidence. *Annual Review of Sociology,* 30:395–408.

Bergman, Mike. 2003. Women edge men in high school diplomas, breaking 13-year deadlock. *U.S. Department of Commerce News* (March 21). Washington, DC: U.S. Census Bureau.

Berk, Richard A., and **Phyllis J. Newton.** 1985. Does arrest really deter wife battery? An effort to replicate the findings of the Minneapolis spouse abuse experiment. *American Sociological Review,* 50:253–62.

Berke, Richard L. 1990. Study confirms interest groups' pattern of giving. *New York Times* (September 16):18.

Berkman, Lisa F., Thomas Glass, Ian Brissette, and **Teresa E. Seeman.** 2000. From social integration to health: Durkheim in the new

millennium. *Social Science and Medicine,* 51:843–57.

Berkowitz, Leonard. 1989. Frustration-aggression hypothesis: Examination and reformulation. *Psychological Bulletin,* 106:59–73.

Berle, Adolph, Jr., and **Gardner C. Means.** 1932. *The modern corporation and private property.* New York: Harcourt, Brace & World.

Bernard, Jessie. 1987. *The female world from a global perspective.* Bloomington: Indiana University Press.

Bernstein, Aaron. 2003. Waking up from the American Dream: Dead-end jobs and the high cost of college could be choking off upward mobility. *Business Week Online,* December 1.

Bernstein, Ilene N., William R. Kelly, and **Patricia A. Doyle.** 1977. Social reactions to deviants: The case of criminal defendants. *American Sociological Review,* 42:743–55.

Bernstein, Nina. 2002. Side effect of welfare law: The no-parent family. *New York Times* (July 29).

Bernstein, Robert. 2011. Texas gains the most in population since the Census. (December 21) Available at http://www.census.gov/newsroom/releases/archives/population/cb11-215.html. Washington, DC: U.S. Census Bureau.

Bertrand, Marianne, and **Sendhil Mullainathan.** 2001. Are CEOs rewarded for luck? The ones without principles are. *Quarterly Journal of Economics,* 116:910–31.

Bertrand, Marianne, and **Sendhil Mullainathan.** 2003. Are Emily and Greg more employable than Lakisha and Jamal? A field experiment on labor market discrimination. *National Bureau of Economic Research.* Working Paper No. w9873.

Best, Steven, and **Douglas Kellner.** 1991. *Postmodern theory: Critical interrogations.* New York: Guilford Press.

Betts, Julian R., and **Richard C. Atkinson.** 2012. Better research needed on the impact of charter schools. *Science,* 335:171–72.

Beylotte, Frank. 2003. Genes and behavior take center stage. *Psychological Science Agenda,* 16(3):14.

Bhargava, Deepak, Timothy Casey, John Cavanagh, Karen Dolan, Peter Edelman, Barbara Ehrenreich, Sarita Gupta, Dedrick Muhammad, Diana Pearce, Steve Savner, and **Kevin Shih.** 2009. *Battered by the storm.* Institute for Policy Studies, the Center for Community Change, Jobs with Justice, and Legal Momentum.

Bianchi, Suzanne M., John P. Robinson, and **Melissa A. Milkie.** 2006. *Changing rhythms of American family life.* New York: Russell Sage Foundation.

Bickerton, Derek. 1995. *Language and human behavior.* Seattle: University of Washington Press.

Biderman, Albert D., and **James P. Lynch.** 1991. *Understanding crime incidence statistics: Why the UCR diverges from the NCS.* New York: Springer-Verlag.

Bierstedt, Robert. 1950. An analysis of social power. *American Sociological Review,* 15:730–38.

Biersteker, Thomas J. 1987. *Multinationals, the state and control of the Nigerian economy.* Princeton, NJ: Princeton University Press.

Billings, Dwight B. 1990. Religion as opposition: A Gramscian analysis. *American Journal of Sociology,* 96:131.

Birdwhistell, Raymond L. 1970. *Kinesics and context.* Philadelphia: University of Pennsylvania Press.

Birkett, Dea. 1997. *Serpent in paradise: Among the people of the Bounty.* New York: Doubleday.

Bittman, Michael, Paula England, Liana Sayer, Nancy Folbre, and **George Matheson.** 2003. When does gender trump money? Bargaining and time in household work. *American Journal of Sociology,* 109(1):186–214.

Blackwell, Brenda Sims. 2000. Perceived sanction threats, gender, and crime: A test and elaboration of power-control theory. *Criminology,* 38(2):439–88.

Blank, Robert H., and **Janna C. Merrick.** 2005. *End-of-life decision making: A cross-national study.* Cambridge, MA: MIT Press.

Blasi, Joseph R. 1988. *Employee ownership: Revolution or rip-off?* Cambridge, MA: Ballinger.

Blau, Judith R., and **Eric S. Brown.** 2001. Du Bois and diasporic identity: The *Veil* and the *Unveiling* project. *Sociological Theory,* 19:219–33.

Blau, Peter M., and **Richard A. Schoenherr.** 1971. *The structure of organizations.* New York: Basic Books.

Blau, Peter, and **Richard Scott.** 1962. *Formal organizations.* San Francisco: Chandler.

Blauner, Robert. 1964. *Alienation and freedom.* Chicago: University of Chicago Press.

Block, N. J., and **Gerald Dworkin,** eds. 1976. *The IQ controversy: Critical readings.* New York: Pantheon.

Bloom, David E. 2011. 7 billion and counting. *Science,* 333:562–69.

Bluhm, Carey, Thomas A. Widiger, and **Gloria M. Miele.** 1990. Interpersonal complementarity and individual differences. *Journal of Personality and Social Psychology,* 58:464–71.

Blum, Robert W., Trisha Beuhring, Marcia L. Shew, Linda H. Bearinger, Renee E. Sieving, and **Michael D. Resnick.** 2000. The effects of race/ethnicity, income, and family structure on adolescent risk behaviors. *American Journal of Public Health,* 90:1879–84.

Blumer, Herbert. 1946. Collective behavior. In A. M Lee, ed., *New outline of the principles of sociology.* New York: Barnes & Noble.

Blumer, Herbert. 1958. Race prejudice as a sense of group position. *Pacific Sociological Review,* 1:3–7.

Blumer, Herbert. 1969. *Symbolic interaction: Perspective and method.* Englewood Cliffs, NJ: Prentice-Hall.

Blumstein, Philip, and **Pepper Schwartz.** 1983. *American couples.* New York: Morrow.

Bobo, Lawrence. 1983. Whites' opposition to busing: Symbolic racism or realistic group conflict. *Journal of Personality and Social Psychology,* 45:1196–210.

Bobo, Lawrence, and **James R. Kluegel.** 1993. Opposition to race-targeting: Self-interest, stratification ideology, or racial attitudes? *American Sociological Review,* 58:443–64.

Boesch, Christophe. 2003. Is culture a golden barrier between human and chimpanzee? *Evolutionary Anthropology,* 12:82–91.

Bohannon, John. 2005. Disasters: Searching for lessons from a bad year. *Science,* 310 (December 23): 1883.

Bohannon, John. 2007. Hard data on hard drugs, grabbed from the environment. *Science,* 316:42–44.

Bohannon, John. 2011. Social science for pennies: Social scientists are turning to online retail giant Amazon.com to cheaply recruit people around the world for research studies. *Science,* 334:307.

Bok, Derek. 1993. *The cost of talent: How executives and professionals are paid and how it affects America.* New York: Free Press.

Bollen, Kenneth A., and **Stephen J. Appold.** 1993. National industrial structure and the global system. *American Sociological Review,* 58:283–301.

Bonacich, Edna. 1972. A theory of ethnic antagonism: A split-labor market. *American Sociological Review,* 37:547–59.

Bonacich, Edna. 1975. Abolition, the extension of slavery, and the position of free blacks: A study of split-labor markets in the United States, 1830–1863. *American Journal of Sociology,* 81:601–28.

Bonacich, Edna, and **John Modell.** 1980. *The economic basis of ethnic solidarity.* Berkeley: University of California Press.

Bonczar, Thomas P., and **Tracy L. Snell.** 2004. Capital Punishment, 2003. Washington, DC: U.S. Department of Justice (NCJ 206627; http://www.ojp.usdoj.gov/bjs/pub/pdf/cp03.pdf).

Bongaarts, John, and **Steven Sinding.** 2011. Population policy in transition in the developing world. *Science,* 333:574–76.

Bonger, William A. 1936. *An introduction to criminology.* London: Methuen.

Bongiorni, Sara. 2007. *A year without "Made in China": One family's true life adventure in the global economy.* New York: Wiley.

Boodman, Sandra G. 2000. Second thoughts: Think the arrival of your first child changed your life? Just wait until number two joins the family. *Washington Post Health Magazine* (November 28):6.

Boone-Heinonen, Janne, Ana V. Diez-Roux, Catarina I. Kiefe, Cora E. Lewis, David K. Guilkey, and **Penny Gordon-Larsen.** 2011. Neighborhood socioeconomic status predictors of physical activity through young to middle adulthood: The CARDIA study. *Social Science & Medicine,* 72(5):641–69.

Boraas, Stephanie, and **William M. Rodgers III.** 2003. How does gender play a role in the earnings gap? An update. *Monthly Labor Review* (March):9–15.

Boroughs, Don L. 1992. *U.S. News & World Report* (May 4):50–52.

Bortz, Walter M., II. 2011. *Next medicine: The science and civics of health.* Oxford: Oxford University Press.

Boswell, Terry. 1989. Colonial empires and the capitalist world-economy: A time series analysis of colonization, 1640–1960. *American Sociological Review,* 54:180–96.

Bouchard, Thomas J. 1994. Genes, environment, and personality. *Science,* 264:1700–1701.

Bouchard, Thomas J., David T. Lykken, Matthew McGue, Nancy L. Segal, and **Auke Tellegen.** 1990.

Sources of human psychological differences. The Minnesota study of twins reared apart. *Science,* 250:223–28.

Bourdieu, Pierre. 1994. Rethinking the state: Genesis and structure of the bureaucratic field. *Sociological Theory,* 12:118.

Boushey, Heather. 2005. Family-friendly policies: boosting mothers' wages. Center for Economic and Policy Research (April 6).

Bowles, Samuel, and **Herbert Gintis.** 1976. *Schooling and capitalist America.* New York: Basic Books.

Bowles, Samuel, and **Herbert Gintis.** 2000. Does schooling raise earnings by making people smarter? In Kenneth Arrow, Samuel Bowles, and Steven Durlauf, eds., *Meritocracy and economic inequality.* Princeton, NJ: Princeton University Press.

Bowman, Karlyn. 2009. *The state of the American worker: Attitudes about work in America.* AEI Studies in Public Opinion, American Enterprise Institute for Public Opinion Research, August 21. Available at http://www.aei.org/paper/14886.

Boyd, Christina L., and **Lee Epstein.** 2009. When women rule, it makes a difference. *Washington Post* (May 3):B5.

Bradley, Harriet. 1989. *Men's work, women's work: A sociological history of the sexual division of labour in employment.* Minneapolis: University of Minnesota Press.

Bradshaw, York W. 1988. Reassessing economic dependency and uneven development: The Kenyan experience. *American Sociological Review,* 53:693–708.

Brandt, Allan M. 2007. *The cigarette century.* New York: Basic Books.

Brand-Williams, Oralandar. 1997. Tiger's comments stir up racial-designation debate. *Detroit News* (April 25):Metro.

Braxton, John M., and **Alan E. Bayer.** 1999. *Faculty misconduct in collegiate teaching.* Baltimore: Johns Hopkins University Press.

Brazelton, T. Berry, and **Stanley I. Greenspan.** 2000. *The irreducible needs of children: What every child must have to grow, learn, and flourish.* Cambridge, MA: Perseus.

Breen, Richard, and **Jan O. Jonsson.** 2004. Inequality of opportunity in comparative perspective: Recent research on educational attainment and social mobility. *Annual Review of Sociology,* 31: 223–43.

Breines, Wini. 1980. Community and organization: The New Left and Michels' "iron law." *Social Problems,* 27:419–29.

Bremner, Jason, Ashley Frost, Carl Haub, Mark Mather, Karin Ringheim, and **Eric Zuehlke.** 2010. World population highlights: Key findings from PRB's 2010 World Population Data Sheet. *Population Bulletin,* 65(2):1–13.

Bremner, Jason, Carl Haub, Marlene Lee, Mark Mather, and **Eric Zuehlke.** 2009. World population highlights: Key findings from PRB's 2009 world population data sheet. *Population Bulletin,* 64, No. 3.

Bridges, George S., Robert D. Crutchfield, and **Edith E. Simpson.** 1987. Crime, social structure and criminal punishment: White and non-white rates of imprisonment. *Social Problems,* 34:345–61.

Briggs, Pam. 2002. Learning from *The Experiment. The Psychologist,* 15(7):344–45.

Brody, Elaine M. 1990. *Women in the middle: Their parent-care years.* New York: Springer.

Brody, Elaine M., Sandra J. Litvin, Steven M. Albert, and **Christine J. Hoffman.** 1994. Marital status of daughters and patterns of parent care. *Journal of Gerontology,* 49:S95–S103.

Brouillette, John R., and **Ronny E. Turner.** 1992. Creating the sociological imagination on the first day of class: The social construction of deviance. *Teaching Sociology,* 20:276–79.

Brown, Dee. 1971. *Bury my heart at Wounded Knee.* New York: Holt, Rinehart & Winston.

Brown, Kathryn. 2003. The medication merry-go-round. *Science,* 299: 1646–49.

Brown, Lester R., and **Christopher Flavin.** 1999. A new economy for a new century. In *State of the world 1999: A Worldwatch Institute report on progress toward a sustainable society.* New York: Norton.

Browne, Irene, and **Joya Misra.** 2003. The intersection of gender and race in the labor market. *Annual Review of Sociology,* 29:487–513.

Brownlee, Shannon. 2007. *Overtreated: Why too much medicine is making us sicker and poorer.* New York: Bloomsbury.

Bruegmann, Robert. 2005. *Sprawl: A compact history.* Chicago: University of Chicago Press.

Bruno, Rosalind R. 1996. *Postsecondary school financing.* Washington, DC: U.S. Bureau of the Census.

Bryant, John. 2007. Theories of fertility decline and the evidence from development indicators. *Population and Development Review,* 33:101–27.

Bryson, Bethany. 1996. Anything but heavy metal: Symbolic exclusion and musical dislikes. *American Sociological Review,* 61:884–99.

Buchmann, Marlis. 1989. *The script of life in modern society: Entry into adulthood in a changing world.* Chicago: University of Chicago Press.

Bucks, Brian K., Arthur B. Kennickell, Traci L. Mach, and **Kevin B. Moore.** 2009. Changes in U.S. family finances from 2004 to 2007: Evidence from the Survey of Consumer Finances. *Federal Reserve Bulletin,* 95:A1–A55.

Budig, Michelle J., and **Paula England.** 2001. The wage penalty for motherhood. *American Sociological Review,* 66:204–25.

Budros, Art. 2004. Social shocks and slave social mobility: Manumission in Brunswich County, Virginia, 1782–1862. *American Journal of Sociology,* 110:539–79.

Buechler, Steven M. 1990. *Women's movements in the United States:*

Woman suffrage, equal rights, and beyond. New Brunswick, NJ: Rutgers University Press.

Bumiller, Elisabeth. 2003. Why America has gay marriage jitters. *New York Times* (August 10): Week in Review.

Bumpass, L. L., and **H.-h. Lu.** 2000. Trends in cohabitation and implications for children's family contexts in the United States. *Population Studies,* 54:19–41.

Bumpass, Larry, and **Sara McLanahan.** 1989. Unmarried motherhood: Recent trends, composition, and black-white differences. *Demography,* 26:279–86.

Burawoy, Michael. 1979. *Manufacturing consent.* Chicago: University of Chicago Press.

Burbank, Victoria Katherine. 1988. *Aboriginal adolescence: Maidenhood in an aboriginal community.* New Brunswick, NJ: Rutgers University Press.

Bureau of Justice Statistics. 2003. U.S. Department of Justice Office of Justice Programs. Available at www .ojp.usdoj.gov/bjs/correct.htm.

Bureau of Labor Statistics. 2010. Labor force statistics from the current population survey. Seasonally adjusted unemployment rate for persons 16 years and over. Available at http://data.bls.gov/cgi-bin/surveymost.

Bureau of Labor Statistics. 2011. American Time Use Survey: 2010 results. U.S. Department of Labor USDL-11-0919 (June 22) (News Release).

Burke, Peter J. 2004. Identities and social structure: The 2003 Cooley-Meade Award address. *Social Psychology Quarterly,* 67:5–15.

Burke, Peter J. 2006. Identity change. *Social Psychology Quarterly,* 69:81–96.

Burkett, Steven R., and **Mervin White.** 1974. Hellfire and delinquency: Another look. *Journal for the Scientific Study of Religion,* 13:455–62.

Burnham, James. 1941. *The managerial revolution.* New York: John Day.

Burr, Chandler. 1996. *A separate creation: The search for the biological*

origins of sexual orientation. New York: Hyperion.

Burris, Val. 1988. The political partisanship of American business. *American Sociological Review,* 52:732–44.

Burstein, Paul. 1991a. Policy domains: Organization, culture, and policy outcomes. *Annual Review of Sociology,* 17:327–50.

Burstein, Paul. 1991b. Legal mobilization as a social movement tactic: The struggle for equal employment opportunity. *American Journal of Sociology,* 96:1201–25.

Burstein, Paul. 2003. Is Congress really for sale? *Contexts,* 2:19–25.

Buttel, Frederick H. 1987. New directions in environmental sociology. *Annual Review of Sociology,* 13:465–88.

Butterfield, Fox. 1986. Why Asians are going to the head of the class. *New York Times* (August 3): Educ. 18–23.

Butterfield, Fox. 1992. Studies find a family link to criminality. *New York Times* (January 31):A1, A8.

Buzawa, E. S., and **C. G. Buzawa.** 1990. *Domestic violence.* Newbury Park, CA: Sage.

Byfield, Joanne. 2001. Home is where the smarts are. *Report/ Newsmagazine,* 28(23):43–44.

C

Cacioppo, John T., Gary G. Bernston, John F. Sheridan, and **Martha K. McClintock.** 2000. Multilevel integrative analyses of human behavior: Social neuroscience and the complementing nature of social and biological approaches. *Psychological Bulletin,* 126:829–43.

Cahill, Kevin, with **Rob McMahon.** 2010. *Who owns the world: The surprising truth about every piece of land on the planet.* New York: Grand Central Publishing.

Calasanti, Toni, and **Anna M. Zajicek.** 1997. Gender, the state, and constructing the old as dependent: Lessons from the economic transition

in Poland. *The Gerontologist,* 37:452–61.

Calasanti, Toni M., and **Kathleen R. Slevin.** 2001. *Gender, social inequalities, and aging.* Walnut Creek, CA: AltaMira Press.

Calhoun, Craig. 2007. Sociology in America: An introduction. In Craig Calhoun, ed., *Sociology in America: A history.* Chicago: University of Chicago Press.

Campbell, Donald T. 1965. Ethnocentric and other altruistic motives. In Robert Levine, ed., *Nebraska Symposium on motivation.* Lincoln: University of Nebraska Press.

Cantril, Hadley. 1941. *The psychology of social movements.* New York: John Wiley.

Cardozo, Arlene Rossen. 1996. *Sequencing.* Minneapolis: Brownstone Books.

Carley, Kathleen. 1991. A theory of group stability. *American Sociological Review,* 56:331–54.

Carmichael, Stokely, and **Charles Hamilton.** 1967. *Black power.* New York: Random House.

Carter, Nancy M., and **Harvey M. Wagner.** 2011 *The bottom line: Corporate performance and women's representation on boards (2004–2008).* Catalyst. Available at http:// www.catalyst.org/publication/479/ the-bottom-line-corporate-performance-and-womens-representation-on-boards-20042008.

Caruso, Eugene M., Nicholas Epley, and **Max H. Bazerman.** 2006. The costs and benefits of undoing egocentric responsibility assessments in groups. *Journal of Personality and Social Psychology,* 91:857–71.

Case, J., and **R. C. R. Taylor.** 1979. *Co-ops, communes, and collectives: Experiments in social change in the 1960s and 1970s.* New York: Pantheon.

Caspi, Avshalom, Joseph McClay, Terrie E. Moffitt, Jonathan Mill, Judy Martin, Ian W. Craig, Alan Taylor, and **Richie Poulton.** 2002. Role of genotype in the cycle of violence in maltreated children. *Science,* 297:851–54.

Cast, A. D., and **P. J. Burke.** 2002. A theory of self-esteem. *Social Forces* 80(3):1041–68.

Castro, Janice. 1991. Watching a generation waste away. *Time* (August 26):10, 12.

Catalyst. 2003. *Women in U.S. Corporate Leadership: 2003.* www.catalystwomen.org.

Catalyst. 2005. *Women "take care," men "take charge": Stereotyping of U.S. business leaders exposed.* Available at www.catalyst.org.

Catalyst. 2006. 2005 Catalyst Census of Women Corporate Officers and Top Earners of the *Fortune* 500. Catalyst Publication Code D43. www.Catalyst.org.

Catalyst. 2011. *Family leave.* Available at http://www.catalyst.org/publication/240/family-leave-us-canada-and-global.

Catton, William R., and **Riley E. Dunlap.** 1978. Environmental sociology: A new paradigm. *The American Sociologist,* 13:41–49.

Catton, William R., and **Riley E. Dunlap.** 1980. A new ecological paradigm for post-exhuberant sociology. *American Behavioral Scientist,* 24:15–47.

Cave, Damien. 2012. Mexico updates death toll in drug war to 47,515, but critics dispute the data. The New York Times (January 11). Available at http://www.nytimes.com/2012/01/12/world/americas/mexico-updates-drug-war-death-toll-but-critics-dispute-data.html?_r=1.

CBS News. 2007. U. of Michigan to ban affirmative action. (January 10). http://www.cbsnews.com/stories/2007/01/10/national/main2349878.shtml.

Centers for Disease Control and Prevention. 2010. Youth Risk Behavior Surveillance: United States, 2009. Surveillance Summaries, June 4. *Morbidity and Mortality Weekly Report* 59 (No. SS-5). Available at http://www.cdc.gov/mmwr/pdf/ss/ss5905.pdf.

Centers for Disease Control and Prevention. 2012. Percent of live births to unmarried mothers. Available at http://www.cdc.gov/nchs/pressroom/states/UNMARRIED_STATE_2009.pdf.

Central Intelligence Agency. 2009. The World Factbook 2009. Available at https://www.cia.gov/library/publications/download/download-2009/index.html.

Central Intelligence Agency. 2009. *The World Factbook 2009.* Washington, DC: Central Intelligence Agency. Available at HYPERLINK "http://www.cia.gov/library/publications/the-world-factbook/index.html" \t "_blank" www.cia.gov/library/publications/the-world-factbook/index.html.

Cernkovich, Steven A., and **Peggy Giordano.** 1987. Family relationships and delinquency. *Criminology,* 25:295–319.

Cernkovich, Steven A., and **Peggy Giordano.** 1992. School bonding, race, and delinquency. *Criminology,* 30:261–91.

Chafetz, Janet Saltzman. 1990. *Gender equity: An integrated theory of stability and change.* Newbury Park, CA: Sage.

Chafetz, Janet Saltzman. 1997. Feminist theory and sociology: Underutilized contributions for mainstream theory. *Annual Review of Sociology,* 23:97–120.

Chafetz, Janet Saltzman, and **Anthony Gary Dworkin.** 1986. *Female revolt: Women's movements in world and historical perspective.* New York: Rowman & Allanheld.

Chambliss, William J. 1973. The Saints and the Roughnecks. *Society,* 2 (November):24–31.

Chambliss, William J., and **Robert B. Seidman.** 1971. *Law, order and power.* Reading, MA: Addison-Wesley.

Chan, Tak Wing, and **John H. Goldthorpe.** 2007. Class and status: The conceptual distinction and its empirical relevance. *American Sociological Review,* 72:512–32.

Chase, Susan E., and **Colleen S. Bell.** 1990. Ideology, discourse, and gender: How gatekeepers talk about women school superintendents. *Social Problems,* 37:163–86.

Chase-Dunn, Christopher. 1989. *Global formation: Structure of the world-economy.* Cambridge, MA: Blackwell.

Chase-Dunn, Christopher, and **Thomas D. Hall.** 1993. Comparing world-systems: Concepts and working hypotheses. *Social Forces,* 71:851–86.

Chatzky, Jean Sherman. 1992. A brief history of stock fads. *Forbes* (September 14):253–68.

Chaves, Mark. 1994. Secularization as declining religious authority. *Social Forces,* 72:749–74.

Chen, M. Keith, and **Jesse M. Shapiro.** 2007. Do harsher prison conditions reduce recidivism? A discontinuity-based approach. *American Journal of Law and Economics,* 9:10–29.

Chen, Li-Hui, Susan P. Baker, Elisa R. Braver, and **Guohua Li.** 2000. Carrying passengers as a risk factor for crashes fatal to 16- and 17-year-old drivers. *Journal of the American Medical Association,* 283:1578–82.

Cheng, Lucie, and **Edna Bonacich.** 1984. *Labor immigration under capitalism.* Berkeley: University of California Press.

Cherlin, Andrew. 1978. Remarriage as an incomplete institution. *American Journal of Sociology,* 84:634–50.

Cherlin, Andrew J. 2010. *Public and private families: An introduction.* New York: McGraw-Hill.

Chesnais, Jean-Claude. 1992. *The demographic transition: Stages, patterns and economic implications: A longitudinal study of sixty-seven countries.* Trans. Elizabeth and Philip Kreager. New York: Clarendon.

Child Policy. 2004. New 12-country study reveals substantial gaps in U.S. early childhood education and care policies. www.childpolicyintl. org/issuebrief1.

Childe, V. Gordon. 1941. *Man makes himself.* London: Watts.

Chiricos, Theodore, and **Gordon Waldo.** 1975. Socioeconomic status and criminal sentencing: An empirical assessment of a conflict proposition. *American Sociological Review,* 40:753–72.

Chiswick, Barry. 1979. The economic progress of immigrants: Some apparently universal patterns. In William Felner, ed., *Contemporary economic problems.* Washington, DC: American Enterprise Institute.

Chomsky, Noam. 1957. *Syntactic structures.* The Hague: Mouton.

Chomsky, Noam. 1980. *Rule and representations.* New York: Columbia University Press.

Clark, Kenneth B. 1965. *Dark ghetto.* New York: Harper & Row.

Clawson, Dan, and **Naomi Gerstel.** 2002. Caring for our young: Child care in Europe and the United States. *Contexts,* 1(Winter):42–51.

Clawson, Dan, Alan Neustadtl, and **Denise Scott.** 1992. *Money talks: Corporate PACs and political influence.* New York: Basic Books.

Clayton, Obie, ed. 1996. *An American dilemma revisited: Race relations in a changing world.* New York: Russell Sage Foundation.

Clinard, Marshall B. 1990. *Corporate corruption: The abuse of power.* New York: Praeger.

Clinard, Marshall B., and **Peter C. Yeager.** 1980. *Corporate crime.* New York: Free Press.

Clinard, Marshall B., and **Robert F. Meier.** 2011. *Sociology of deviant behavior,* 14th ed. Belmont, CA: Wadworth Centage Learning.

Coates, Joseph F., and **Jennifer Jarratt.** 1990. What futurists believe: Agreements and disagreements. *The Futurist* (November–December):22–28.

Cockerham, William C. 2011. *Sociology of mental disorder,* 8th ed. Upper Saddle River, NJ: Prentice-Hall.

Cockerham, William C. 2012. *Medical Sociology.* 12th ed. New York: Prentice-Hall.

Cohen, Albert K. 1955. *Delinquent boys.* New York: Free Press.

Cohen, Albert K. 1965. The sociology of the deviant act: Anomie theory and beyond. *American Sociological Review,* 30:5–14.

Cohen, Jean L., and **Andrew Arato.** 1992. *Civil society and political theory.* Cambridge, MA: MIT Press.

Cohen, Jere. 1980. Rational capitalism in Renaissance Italy. *American Journal of Sociology,* 85:1340–55.

Cohen, Jon. 2007. The world through a chimp's eyes. *Science,* 316:44–45.

Cohen, Jon. 2011. Large African TB study reveals powerful strategy to curb disease. *Science,* 334:581.

Cohen, Jordan J. 2003. The consequences of premature abandonment of affirmative action in medical school admissions. *Journal of the American Medical Association,* 289(9):1143–48.

Colasanto, Diane, and **Linda Williams.** 1987. The changing dynamics of race and class. *Public Opinion,* 9 (January–February): 50–53.

Coleman, James S., et al. 1966. *Equality of educational opportunity.* Washington, DC: U.S. Government Printing Office.

Coleman, James S. 1988. Social capital in the creation of human capital. *American Journal of Sociology,* 94:S95–S120.

Coleman, James S. 1990. *Foundations of social theory.* Cambridge, MA: Belknap Press.

Coleman, James W. 1987. Toward an integrated theory of white-collar crime. *American Journal of Sociology,* 93:406–39.

Coleman, Richard D., and **Lee Rainwater.** 1978. *Social standing in America.* New York: Basic Books.

Collier, Jane Fisburne. 1988. *Marriage and inequality in classless societies.* Stanford, CA: Stanford University Press.

Collins, Nancy L., and **Stephen J. Read.** 1990. Adult attachment, working models, and relationship quality in dating couples. *Journal of Personality and Social Psychology,* 58:644–63.

Collins, Patricia Hill. 2000. *Black feminist thought.* New York: Routledge.

Collins, Randall. 1975. *Conflict sociology.* New York: Academic Press.

Collins, Randall. 1976. Review of "Schooling in capitalist America." *Harvard Educational Review,* 46:246–51.

Collins, Randall. 1977. Some comparative principles of educational stratification. *Harvard Educational Review,* 47:1–27.

Collins, Randall. 1979. *Credential society.* New York: Academic Press.

Collins, Randall. 1981. *Sociology since midcentury: Essays in theory cumulation.* New York: Academic Press.

Collins, Randall. 1988a. *Sociology of marriage and the family,* 2nd ed. Chicago: Nelson Hall.

Collins, Randall. 1988b. *Theoretical sociology.* San Diego: Harcourt Brace Jovanovich.

Collins, Randall. 2000. Situational stratification: A micro-macro theory of inequality. *Sociological Theory,* 18:17–43.

Collins, W. Andrew, Eleanor E. Maccoby, Laurence Steinber, E. Mavis Hetherington, and **Marc H. Bornstein.** 2000. Contemporary research on parenting: The case for nature *and* nurture. *American Psychologist,* 55:218–32.

Conger, Rand D., Frederick O. Lorenz, Glen H. Elder, Jr., Ronald L. Simons, and **Xiaojia Ge.** 1993. Husband and wife differences in response to undesirable life events. *Journal of Health and Social Behavior,* 34:71–88.

Connelly, Marjorie. 2000. Who voted: A portrait of American politics, 1976–2000. *New York Times* (November 12):IV-4.

Connolly, Marie-Therese. 2008. A hidden crime: The hidden epidemic of elder abuse. *Washington Post* (January 27):B1.

Conrad, Peter. 2007. *The medicalization of society: On the transformation of human conditions into treatable disorders.* Baltimore, MD: Johns Hopkins University Press.

Conrad, Peter, and **Deborah Potter.** 2000. From hyperactive children to ADHD adults: Observations on the expansion of medical categories. *Social Problems,* 47(4):559–82.

Conrad, Peter, and **Joseph Schneider.** 1980. *Deviance and medicalization: From badness to sickness.* St. Louis: Mosby.

Cooley, Charles Horton. 1902/1964. *Human nature and the social order.* New York: Scribner.

Coontz, Stephanie. 1992. *The way we never were: American families and the nostalgia trap.* New York: Basic Books.

Copp, Terry, and **Bill McAndrew.** 1990. *Battle exhaustion: Soldiers and psychiatrists in the Canadian army, 1939–1945.* Montreal and Kingston: McGill-Queen's University Press.

Corcoran, Mary, Sandra K. Danziger, Ariel Kalil, and **Kristin S. Seefeldt.** 2000. *Annual Review of Sociology,* 26:241–69.

Cornish, Edward. 1993. 1993 as predicted in 1893: If they could see us now! *The Futurist* (May–June): 41–42.

Corsaro, William A., and **Donna Eder.** 1995. Development and socialization of children and adolescents. In Karen S. Cook. Gary Alan Fine, and James S. House, eds., *Sociological perspectives on social psychology.* Boston: Allyn & Bacon.

Coser, Lewis A. 1956. *The functions of social conflict.* New York: Free Press.

Coser, Lewis A. 1957. Social conflict and the theory of social change. *British Journal of Sociology,* 8: 170–83.

Cotter, David, Joan M. Hermsen, and **Reeve Vanneman.** 2011. The end of the gender revolution? Gender role attitudes from 1977 to 2008. *American Journal of Sociology,* 117(1):259–89.

Coughlin, Ellen K. 1988. Worsening plight of the "underclass" catches attention of researchers. *Chronicle of Higher Education* (March 30):A1.

Couzin, Jennifer. 2006. Breakdown of the year: Scientific fraud. *Science,* 314:1853.

Covay, Elizabeth, and **William Carbonaro.** 2010. After the bell: Participation in extracurricular activities, classroom behavior, and academic achievement. *Sociology of Education,* 83(1):20–45.

Cox, Oliver C. 1948. *Caste, class, and race.* Garden City, NY: Doubleday.

Craig, Lyn, and **Killian Mullan.** 2012. How mothers and fathers share childcare: A cross-national time-use comparison. *American Sociological Review,* 76(6):834–61.

Crane, Jonathan. 1991. The epidemic theory of ghettos and neighborhood effects on dropping out and teenage childbearing. *American Journal of Sociology,* 96:1226–59.

Crenshaw, E. M., M. Christenson, and **D. R. Oakey.** 2000. Demographic transition in ecological focus. *American Sociological Review,* 65(3):371–91.

Crispell, Diane. 1993. Sex surveys: Does anyone tell the truth? *American Demographics,* 15 (July):9–10.

Crittenden, Ann. 2001. *The price of motherhood. Why the most important job in the world is still the least valued.* New York: Henry Holt.

Crocker, Jennifer, and **Rila Luhtanen.** 1990. Collective self-esteem and ingroup bias. *Journal of Personality and Social Psychology,* 58:60–67.

Cross, Susan E., and **Laura Madson.** 1997. Models of the self: Self-construals and gender. *Psychological Bulletin,* 122:5–37.

Crosset, Todd W., J. Ptacek, M. A. McDonald, and **J. R. Benedict.** 1996. Male student-athletes and violence against women: A survey of campus judicial affairs offices. *Violence Against Women,* 2:163–79.

Crutchfield, Robert D., and **Susan R. Pitchford.** 1997. Work and crime: The effects of labor stratification. *Social Forces,* 76:93–118.

Cunningham, Sara. 2011. Manual High students' project raises issue of fair play in science. *Louisville Courier-Journal* (April 4).

D

Dahl, Robert. 1961. *Who governs? Democracy and power in an American city.* New Haven, CT: Yale University Press.

Dahrendorf, Ralf. 1958. Toward a theory of social conflict. *Journal of Conflict Resolution,* 2:170–83.

Dahrendorf, Ralf. 1959. *Class and class conflict in industrial society.* Stanford, CA: Stanford University Press.

D' Alessio, Stewart J., and **Lisa Stolzenberg.** 1995. Unemployment and the incarceration of pretrial defendants. *American Sociological Review,* 60:350–59.

Danaei, Goodarz, Stephen Vander Hoorn, Alan D. Lopez, Christopher J. L. Murray, Majid Ezzati, and the **Comparative Risk Assessment Collaborating Group** (Cancers). 2005. Causes of cancer in the world: Comparative risk assessment of nine behavioural and environmental risk factors. *Lancet,* 366:1784–93.

Dandeker, Christopher. 1990. *Surveillance, power and modernity: Bureaucracy and discipline from 1700 to the present day.* New York: St. Martin's Press.

Daniels, Arlene Kaplan. 1987. Invisible work. *Social Problems,* 34:403–15.

Daniels, Jessie. 2009. The Internet can't teach what the social world can. *Contexts,* 8(4):14–15.

Darnton, Nina. 1991. The pain of the last taboo. *Newsweek* (October 7):70–72.

Davidow, William H., and **Michael S. Malone.** 1993. *The virtual corporations: Structuring and revitalizing the corporation for the 21st century.* New York: Harper Business.

Davies, James. 1962. Toward a theory of revolution. *American Sociological Review,* 27:5–19.

Davies, James. 1969. The *J*-curve of rising and declining satisfactions as a cause of some great revolutions and a contained revolution. In H. D. Graham and T. R. Gurr, eds.,

The history of violence in America. New York: Bantam.

Davies, James. 1974. The *J*-curve and power struggle theories of collective violence. *American Sociological Review,* 39:607–10.

Davis, F. James. 1991. *Who is black? One nation's definition.* University Park: Pennsylvania State University Press.

Davis, Kingsley. 1945. The world demographic transition. *Annals of the American Academy of Political and Social Science,* 237:1–11.

Davis, Kingsley. 1949. *Human society.* New York: Macmillan.

Davis, Kingsley. 1951. Introduction. In William J. Goode, *Religion among the primitives.* New York: Free Press.

Davis, Kingsley. 1955. The origin and growth of urbanization in the world. *American Journal of Sociology,* 60:429–37.

Davis, Kingsley. 1959. The myth of functional analysis as a special method in sociology and anthropology. *American Sociological Review,* 24:757–72.

Davis, Kingsley. 1967. The urbanization of the human population. In *Cities.* New York: Knopf.

Davis, Kingsley. 1971. The world's population crisis. In Robert K. Merton and Robert A. Nisbet, eds., *Contemporary social problems,* 3rd ed. New York: Harcourt Brace Jovanovich.

Davis, Kingsley, and **Wilbert Moore.** 1945. Some principles of stratification. *American Sociological Review,* 10:242–49.

Davis-Kimball, Jeannine. 1997. Warrior women of the Eurasian steppes. *Archaeology* (January–February):44–48.

Dawidowicz, Lucy S. 1975. *The war against the Jews, 1933–1945.* New York: Holt, Rinehart, & Winston.

Dawkins, Richard. 2006. *The God delusion.* Boston: Houghton Mifflin.

Dawson, R. J. M. 1995. The "unusual episode" data revisited. *Journal of Statistics Education* [Online], 3(3), www.amstat.org/publications/jse/v3n3/datasets.dawson.html.

Day, Jennifer Cheeseman, Alex Janus, and **Jessica Davis.** 2005. *Computer and Internet use in the United States: 2003.* Washington, DC: U.S. Census Bureau, Current Population Reports, P23–208 (October 2005).

Death Penalty Information Center. 2012. Facts about the death penalty. (February 18). Available at http://www.deathpenaltyinfo.org.

Deaux, Kay, and **Lawrence S. Wrightsman.** 1984. *Social psychology in the 80s,* 4th ed. Monterey, CA: Brooks/Cole.

Debold, Elizabeth, Marie Wilson, and **Idelisse Malave.** 1993. *Mother-daughter revolution: From betrayal to power.* Reading, MA: Addison-Wesley.

DeBruine, Lisa. 2002. Facial resemblance enhances trust. *Proceedings of the Royal Society of London B,* 269:1307–12.

Decoo, Wilfried. 2002. *Crisis on campus: Confronting academic misconduct.* Cambridge, MA: MIT Press.

Deegan, Mary Jo. 1991. *Women in sociology: A bio-bibliographical sourcebook.* Westport, CT: Greenwood Press.

Deegan, Mary Jo. 2003. Textbooks, the history of sociology, and the sociological stock of knowledge. *Sociological Theory,* 21:298–305.

Deininger, Klaus, and **Lyn Squire.** 1996. A new data set measuring income inequality. *World Bank Economic Review,* 10(3):565–91.

Demos, Vasilikie. 1990. Black family studies in the *Journal of Marriage and the Family,* and the issue of distortion: A trend analysis. *Journal of Marriage and the Family,* 52:603–12.

DeNavas-Walt, Carmen, Bernadette D. Proctor, and **Jessica C. Smith.** 2011. U.S. Census Bureau, Current Population Reports, P60-239, *Income, poverty, and health insurance coverage in the United States: 2010.* Washington, DC: U.S. Government Printing Office. Available at http://www.census.gov/prod/2011pubs/p60-239.pdf.

Denny, Kathleen E. 2011. Gender in context, content, and approach: Comparing gender messages in Girl Scout and Boy Scout handbooks. *Gender & Society,* 25(1):27–47.

Denton, Nancy A., and **Douglas S. Massey.** 1989. Racial identity among Caribbean Hispanics: The effect of double minority status on residential segregation. *American Sociological Review,* 54:790–808.

DePalma, Anthony. 1991. How undergraduates can succeed: Study together, and in small classes. *New York Times* (November 6):B8.

DeParle, Jason. 2004. *American dream: Three women, ten kids, and a nation's drive to end welfare.* New York: Viking/Penguin.

DeRose, Laurie. 2011. International family indicators. In *The sustainable demographic dividend: What do marriage and fertility have to do with the economy?* Available at http://dl.dropbox.com/u/6464634/SDD-2011-Final.pdf.

DeVault, Marjorie L. 1996. Talking back to sociology: Distinctive contributions of feminist methodology. *Annual Review of Sociology,* 22: 29–50.

Devine, Patricia G. 1989. Stereotypes and prejudice: Their automatic and controlled components. *Journal of Personality and Social Psychology,* 56:518.

De Vries, Raymond G. 1981. Birth and death: Social construction of the poles of existence. *Social Forces,* 59:1074–93.

Dey, Judy Goldberg, and **Catherine Hill.** 2007. Behind the pay gap. AAUW Educational Foundation. www.aauw.org/research/behindPayGap.cfm.

Dickinson, David K. 2011. Teachers' language practices and academic outcomes of preschool children. *Science,* 333:964–67.

Dillman, Don A. 2009. *Internet, mail and mixed-mode surveys: The* *tailored design method,* 3rd ed. New York: Wiley.

Dillman, Don A., and **Lisa R. Carley-Baxter.** 2001. *Structural determinants of mail survey response rates over a 12-year period, 1988–1999.* 2000 Proceedings of American Statistical Association Survey Methods Section, Alexandria, VA.

DiMaggio, Paul, and **Bart Bonikowski.** 2008. Make money surfing the Web? The impact of Internet use on the earnings of U.S. workers. *American Sociological Review,* 73:227–50.

Dinkes, R., E. F. Cataldi, and **W. Lin-Kelly.** 2007. *Indicators of school crime and safety: 2007* (NCES 2008–021/NCJ 219553). National Center for Education Statistics, Institute of Education Sciences, U.S. Department of Education, and Bureau of Justice Statistics. Washington, DC: Office of Justice Programs, U.S. Department of Justice.

Dipboye, Robert L. 1977. Alternative approaches to deindividualization. *Psychological Bulletin,* 84:1057–75.

Dirzo, Rodolfo, and **Michel Loreau.** 2005. Biodiversity science evolves. *Science,* 310:943.

Dixon, William J., and **Terry Boswell.** 1996. Dependency, disarticulation, and denominator effects: Another look at foreign capital penetration. *American Journal of Sociology,* 102:543–62.

Djilas, Milovan. 1957. *The new class.* New York: Praeger.

Dobbie, Will, and **Roland G. Fryer.** 2011. *Getting beneath the veil of effective schools: Evidence from New York City.* National Bureau of Economic Research: NBER Working paper No. 17632. Available at http://nber.org/papers/w17632.

Dobuzinskis, Caroline. 2011. *Gender wage gap remains unchanged.* Institute for Women's Policy Research (September 16). Available at http://www.iwpr.org/press-room/press-releases/gender-wage-gap-remains-unchanged.

Domhoff, G. William. 1983. *Who rates America now? A view for the*

'80s. Englewood Cliffs, NJ: Prentice-Hall.

Domhoff, G. William. 1990. *The power elite and the state: How policy is made in America.* New York: Aldine de Gruyter.

Dubin, Robert. 1976. Work in modern society. In Robert Dubin, ed., *Handbook of work, organization, and society.* Chicago: Rand McNally.

Du Bois, W. E. B. 1903/1990. *The souls of black folk.* New York: Vintage.

Dubowitz, Howard. 2007. The tragedy of child neglect: Parents need society's help. *Washington Post* (April 1):B8.

Dugger, Celia W. 1992. U.S. study says Asian-Americans face widespread discrimination. *New York Times* (February 29):1, 5.

Duncan, Greg. 1984. *Years of poverty, years of plenty.* Ann Arbor: Institute for Social Research, University of Michigan.

Duncan, Greg J. 1987. On the slippery slope. *American Demographics,* 9 (May):30–35.

Duncan, Greg J., Martha S. Hill, and **Saul D. Hoffman.** 1988. Welfare dependence within and across generations. *Science,* 239:467–71.

Dunlap, Riley E. and **William R. Catton, Jr.** 1979. Environmental sociology. *Annual Review of Sociology,* 5:243–73.

Dunn, Ashley. 1994. Southeast Asians highly dependent on welfare in U.S. *New York Times* (May 19): A1, A13.

Dunn, J. R., and **M. V. Hayes.** 2000. Social inequality, population health, and housing: A study of two Vancouver neighborhoods. *Social Science and Medicine,* 51(4):563–87.

Dunn, William. 1993. Educating diversity. *American Demographics,* 15 (April):38–43.

Durkheim, Émile. 1893/1964. *The division of labor in society.* New York: Free Press.

Durkheim, Émile. 1895/1938. *The rules of sociological method.* Glencoe, IL: Free Press.

Durkheim, Émile. 1897/1951. *Suicide.* New York: Free Press.

Durkheim, Émile. 1912/1965. *The elementary forms of religious life.* New York: Free Press.

Durkin, Keith F., and **Clifton D. Bryant.** 1995. "Log on to sex": Some notes on the carnal computer and erotic cyberspace as an emerging research frontier. *Deviant Behavior,* 16:179–200.

Durr, Virginia Foster. 1985. *Outside the magic circle: The autobiography of Virginia Foster Durr.* Tuscaloosa: University of Alabama Press.

Dvorak, Petula. 2010. Costs of working rise for parents of young children. *Washington Post* (January 26):B1.

E

Eagly, A. H., M. C. Johannesen-Schmidt, and **M. L. van Engen.** 2003. Transformational, transactional, and laissez-faire leadership styles: A meta-analysis comparing women and men. *Psychological Bulletin,* 129(4):569–91.

Easterlin, Richard A. 1961. The American baby-boom in historical perspective. *American Economic Review,* 51:869–911.

Easterlin, Richard A. 1987. *Birth and fortune: The impact of numbers on personal welfare.* Chicago: University of Chicago Press.

Ebaugh, Helen Rose Fuchs. 1988. *Becoming an EX: The process of role exit.* Chicago: University of Chicago Press.

Eckholm, Eric. 2006. Plight deepens for black men, studies warn. *New York Times* (March 20).

Economics and Statistics Administration. 2011. *STEM: Where are the women?* U.S. Department of Commerce. Published in *Economics and Statistics Administration* (http://www.esa.doc.gov).

Economist, The. 2000. What the Internet cannot do. (August 19):11–12.

Edin, Kathryn. 2000. What do low-income single mothers say about marriage? *Social Problems,* 47(1):112–33.

Edwards, Richard. 1978. The social relations of production at the point of production. *Insurgent Sociologist,* 8:109–25.

Edwards, Richard. 1979. *Contested terrain.* New York: Basic Books.

Eibach, R. P., and **T. Keegan.** 2006. Free at last? Social dominance, loss aversion, and white and black Americans' differing assessments of progress towards racial equality. *Journal of Personality and Social Psychology,* 90:453–67.

Eichar, Douglas M. 1989. *Occupation and class consciousness in America.* New York: Greenwood Press.

Eilperin, Juliet. 2005. U.S. is dissenter on global warming; Kyoto parties near deal on new talks. *Washington Post* (December 10):A1.

Eilperin, Juliet. 2006. Scientists debate issue of climate's irreparable change; some experts on global warming foresee "tipping point" when it is too late to act. *Washington Post* (January 29):A1.

Eisenberg, David E., Roger B. Davis, Susan L. Ettner, Scott Appel, Sonja Wilkey, Maria Van Rompay, and **Ronald C. Kessler.** 1998. Trends in alternative medicine use in the United States, 1990–1997: Results of a follow-up national survey. *Journal of the American Medical Association,* 280:1569–75.

Eisenbraun, Stephen, ed. 2010. *2009 Country reports on human rights practices.* Washington, DC: U.S. Department of State, Bureau of Democracy, Human Rights, and Labor.

Ekman, Paul, Wallace V. Friesen, and **John Bear.** 1984. The international language of gesture. *Psychology Today,* 18 (May):64–67.

Ekman, Paul, Wallace V. Friesen, and **Maureen O'Sullivan.** 1988. Smiles when lying. *Journal of Personality and Social Psychology,* 54: 414–20.

Ekman, Paul, Walter V. Friesen, and **Maureen O'Sullivan.** 2005. Smiles when lying. In Paul Ekman and Erika L. Rosenberg, eds., *What the face reveals: Basic and applied studies of spontaneous expression using the facial action coding system*

(FACS). New York: Oxford University Press.

Elder, Glenn H., Jr. 1983. Families, kin, and the life course. In R. Parke, ed., *The family.* Chicago: University of Chicago Press.

Elder, Glenn H., Jr., and **Elizabeth C. Clipp.** 1988. Wartime losses and social bonding: Influences across 40 years in men's lives. *Psychiatry,* 51:177–97.

Elimelech, Menachem, and **William A. Phillip.** 2011. The future of seawater desalination: Energy, technology, and the environment. *Science,* 333:712–27.

Eliot, Lise. 2009. *Pink brain, blue brain: How small differences grow into troublesome gaps—and what we can do about it.* Boston: Houghton Mifflin Harcourt.

Ellyson, Steve I., John F. Dovidio, Randi L. Corson, and **Debbie L. Vinicur.** 1980. Visual dominance behavior in female dyads. *Social Psychology Quarterly,* 43:328–36.

Elman, Cheryl, and **Angela M. O'Rand.** 2004. The race is to the swift: Socioeconomic origins, adult education, and wage attainment. *American Journal of Sociology,* 110:123–60.

Emerson, Richard M. 1962. Power-dependence relations. *American Sociological Review,* 27:31–41.

Engels, Friedrich. 1884/1902. *The origin of the family, private property, and the state.* Chicago: Kerr.

England, Paula. 1993a. Sociological theories and the study of gender. In Paula England, ed., *Theory on gender/feminism on gender.* New York: Aldine de Gruyter.

England, Paula. 1993b. Work for pay and work at home: Women's double disadvantage. In Craig Calhoun and George Ritzer, eds., *Social Problems–Primis.* New York: McGraw-Hill. Revised version published 1997.

England, Paula. 2000. Marriage, the costs of children, and gender inequality. In Linda J. Waite, ed., *The ties that bind: Perspectives on marriage and cohabitation.* New York: Aldine de Gruyter.

Epstein, Edward J. 1973. *News from nowhere.* New York: Random House.

Erikson, Erik. 1963. *Childhood and society.* New York: Norton.

Erikson, Erik. 1968. *Identity: Youth and crisis.* New York: Norton.

Erikson, Kai T. 1962. Notes on the sociology of deviance. *Social Problems,* 9:307–14.

Erikson, Kai T. 1966. *Wayward Puritans: A study in the sociology of deviance.* New York: Wiley.

Ersche, Karen D., P. Simon Jones, Guy B. Williams, Abigail J. Turton, Trevor W. Robbins, and **Edward T. Bullmore.** 2012. Abnormal brain structure implicated in stimulant drug addiction. *Science,* 335:601–4.

ESOP Association. 2003. ESOP facts and figures. Available at www.esopassociation.org/pubs/stats.html.

Espiritu, Yen Le. 1992. *Asian American panethnicity: Bridging institutions and identities.* Philadelphia: Temple University Press.

Esposito, John L. 1992. *The Islamic threat: Myth or reality.* New York: Oxford University Press.

Estes, James A., John Terborgh, Justin S. Brashares, Mary E. Power, et al. 2011. Trophic downgrading of Planet Earth. *Science,* 333:301–6.

Etzioni, Amitai. 1975. *A comparative analysis of complex organizations.* New York: Free Press.

Evenson, Ranae J., and **Robin W. Simon.** 2005. Clarifying the relationship between parenthood and depression. *Journal of Health and Social Behavior,* 46(4):341–58.

F

Fagot, Beverly I., Mary D. Leinbach, and **Cherie O'Boyle.** 1992. Gender labeling, gender stereotyping, and parenting behaviors. *Developmental Psychology,* 28:225–30.

Faia, Michael A. 1989. Cultural materialism in the functionalist mode. *American Sociological Review,* 54:658–60.

Falk, Armin, and **James J. Heckman.** 2009. Lab experiments are a major source of knowledge in the social sciences. *Science,* 326:535–37.

Farkas, George, Robert P. Grobe, Daniel Sheehan, and **Yan Shuan.** 1990. Cultural resources and school success. Gender, ethnicity, and poverty groups within an urban school district. *American Sociological Review,* 55:127–42.

Farkas, Steve, Jean Johnson, Tony Foleno, Ann Duffett, and **Patrick Foley.** 2000. For goodness' sake. *Public Agenda.*

Farnsworth, Clyde H. 1991. Economic woes force Canada to reexamine medical system. *New York Times* (November 24):7.

Fassinger, Polly A. 1989. Becoming the breadwinner: Single mothers' reactions to changes in their paid work lives. *Family Relations,* 38:404–11.

Fay, R. E., Charles F. Turner, A. D. Klassen, and **John H. Gagnon.** 1989. Prevalence and patterns of same-gender contact among men. *Science,* 243:338–48.

Federal Bureau of Investigation. 2008. Crime in the United States, 2007. Washington, DC: U.S. Government Printing Office.

Federal Bureau of Investigation. 2010. http://www.fbi.gov/publications/strategicplan/stategicplantext.htm#whitecollar.

Federal Bureau of Investigation. 2011. *Crime in the United States, 2010.* Washington, DC: U.S. Government Printing Office.

Federal Bureau of Investigation. 2010a. Hate crime definition available at http://www.fbi.gov/about-us/investigate/civilrights/hate_crimes/overview.

Federal Bureau of Investigation. 2011a. http://www.fbi.gov/about-us/cjis/ucr/hate-crime/2010/narratives/hate-crime-2010-incidents-and-offenses.

Federal Bureau of Investigation. 2012. Attorney General Eric Holder announces revisions to the Uniform Crime Report's definition of rape. National press release (January 6) available at http://www.fbi.gov/news/pressrel/press-releases/attorney-general-eric-holder-announces-revisions-to-the-uniform-crime-reports-definition-of-rape.

Feingold, Alan. 1988. Matching for attractiveness in romantic partners and same-sex friends: A meta-analysis and theoretical critique. *Psychological Bulletin,* 104:226–35.

Feingold, Alan. 1990. Gender differences in effects of physical attractiveness on romantic attraction: A comparison across five research paradigms. *Journal of Personality and Social Psychology,* 59:981–93.

Feldman, Marcus W., Richard C. Lewontin, and **Mary-Clare King.** 2003. A genetic melting-pot. *Nature,* 424:374.

Feldman, Marcus W., Sarah P. Otto, and **Freddy B. Christiansen.** 2000. Genes, culture and inequality. In Kenneth Arrow, Samuel Bowles, and Steven Durlauf, eds., *Meritocracy and economic inequality.* Princeton, NJ: Princeton University Press.

Felson, Richard B., and **Mark D. Reed.** 1986. Reference groups and self-appraisals of academic ability and performance. *Social Psychology Quarterly,* 49:103–9.

Fennema, Meinhert. 1982. *International networks of banks and industry.* Boston: Martinius Nijhoff.

Ferree, Myra Marx. 1990. Beyond separate spheres: Feminism and family research. *Journal of Marriage and the Family,* 52:866–84.

Ferree, Myra Marx, and **Elaine J. Hall.** 2000. Gender stratification and paradigm change. *American Sociological Review,* 65(3):475–81.

Fiedler, Fred E., and **Joseph E. Garcia.** 1987. *New approaches to effective leadership: Cognitive resources and organizational performance.* New York: John Wiley.

Field, Tiffany. 1991. Quality infant day-care and grade school behavior and performance. *Child Development,* 62:863–70.

Fields, Suzanne. 1993. Rape as sport: The culture is at the root. *Insight on the News,* 9 (May 3):19–20.

File, Thom, and **Sarah Crissey.** 2010. *Voting and registration in the election of November 2008.* U.S. Census Bureau, Current Population Reports, Series P20-562. Washington, DC. Available at http://www.census.gov/prod/2010pubs/p20-562.pdf.

Fine, Gary Alan. 1993. The sad demise, mysterious disappearance, and glorious triumph of symbolic interactionism. *Annual Review of Sociology,* 19:61–87.

Fine, Mark A., and **Lawrence A. Kurdek.** 1992. The adjustment of adolescents in stepfather and step-mother families. *Journal of Marriage and the Family,* 54:725–36.

Finke, Roger, and **Rodney Stark.** 1992. *The churching of America, 1776–1990: Winners and losers in our religious economy.* New Brunswick, NJ: Rutgers University Press.

Finkelhor, David. 1979. *Sexually victimized children.* New York: Free Press.

Firebaugh, Glenn. 1992. Growth effects of foreign and domestic investment. *American Journal of Sociology,* 98:105–30.

Firebaugh, Glenn. 1996. Does foreign capital harm poor nations? New estimates based on Dixon and Boswell's measures of capital penetration. *American Journal of Sociology,* 102:563–75.

Firebaugh, Glenn. 2003. *The new geography of global income inequality.* Cambridge, MA: Harvard University Press.

Firebaugh, Glenn, and **Kevin Chen.** 1995. Vote turnout of nineteenth Amendment women: The enduring effect of disenfranchisement. *American Journal of Sociology,* 100(4):972–96.

Firebaugh, Glenn, and **Kenneth E. Davis.** 1988. Trends in anti-black prejudice, 1972–1984: Region and cohort effects. *American Journal of Sociology,* 94:251–72.

Fischer, Claude S., Michael Hout, Martin Sanchez Jankowski, Samuel R. Lucas, Ann Swidler, and **Kim Voss.** 1996. *Inequality by design: Cracking the bell curve myth.* Princeton, NJ: Princeton University Press.

Fisher, Bonnie S., Franels T. Cullen, and **Michael G. Turner.** 2000. *The sexual victimization of college women.* Washington, DC: National Institute of Justice, Bureau of Justice Statistics.

Fisher, Helen/Match.com. 2012. Personal communication.

Fiske, Susan T. 2011. *Envy up, scorn down: How status divides us.* New York: Russell Sage Foundation.

Fletcher, Michael A. 2002. Rocky start in "cyber" classrooms. *Washington Post* (February 26):A1.

Fligstein, Neil. 1990. *The transformation of corporate control.* Cambridge, MA: Harvard University Press.

Fligstein, Neil, and **Peter Brantley.** 1992. Bank control, owner control, or organization dynamics: Who controls the large modern corporation? *American Journal of Sociology,* 98:280–307.

Flynn, James R. 2000. IQ trends over time: Intelligence, race, and meritocracy. In Kenneth Arrow, Samuel Bowles, and Steven Durlauf, eds., *Meritocracy and economic inequality.* Princeton, NJ: Princeton University Press.

Foley, Jonathan. 2010. Boundaries for a healthy planet. *Scientific American* (April):54–7.

Folger, Tim. 2012. The calm before the wave. *National Geographic* (February):54–77.

Ford, C. S., and **F. A. Beach.** 1951. *Patterns of sexual behavior.* New York: Harper & Row.

Forgette, Richard, and **Glenn J. Platt.** 1999. Voting for the person, not the party: Party defection, issue voting, and process sophistication. *Social Science Quarterly,* 80(2):409–21.

Forster, Peter, and **Colin Renfrew.** 2011. Mother tongue and Y chromosomes. *Science,* 333:1390–91.

Fossett, Mark S., and **K. Jill Kiecolt.** 1989. The relative size of minority populations and white racial attitude. *Social Science Quarterly,* 70:820–35.

Foster, Terry. 1997. Woods correctly pays tribute to his heritage, but still has much to learn as a minority trailblazer. *Detroit News* (June 12): Sports.

Fowler, Floyd J., Jr. 2001. *Survey research methods.* Thousand Oaks, CA: Sage.

Fowler, James H, Laura A. Baker, and **Christopher T. Dawes.** 2008. Genetic variation in political participation. *American Political Science Review,* 102:233–48.

France, David. 2006. "And then he hit me": Too ashamed or too scared to speak up, tens of thousands of 50-plus victims of domestic violence suffer in silence. *AARP* (January–February):80–85/112.

Freud, Sigmund. 1930/1961. *Civilization and its discontents.* London: Hogarth.

Freud, Sigmund. 1938. *The basic writings of Sigmund Freud.* Trans. A. A. Brill. New York: Modern Library.

Friedman, Andrew. 1977. *Industry and labor: Class struggle at work and monopoly capitalism.* New York: Macmillan.

Friedman, Thomas L. 2005. *The world is flat: A brief history of the twenty-first century.* New York: Farrar, Straus & Giroux.

Fruchter, Norm. 2007. *Urban schools, public will: Making schools work for all children.* New York: Teachers College Press.

Fry, Richard, D'Vera Cohn, Gretchen Livingston, and **Paul Taylor.** 2011. The rising age gap in economic well-being. *Pew Research Center: Social & Demographic Trends* (November 7):1–36. Available at HYPERLINK "http://www.pewsocialtrends.org/" www.pewsocialtrends.org.

Fuhrman, Ellsworth R. 1980. *The sociology of knowledge in America, 1883–1915.* Charlottesville: University of Virginia Press.

Fuller, C. J. 1976. *The Nayars today.* Cambridge, MA: Cambridge University Press.

Furstenberg, Frank F., Jr., and **Andrew J. Cherlin.** 1991. *Divided families.* Cambridge, MA: Harvard University Press.

G

Gaertner, Lowell, and **Chester A. Insko.** 2000. Intergroup discrimination in the minimal group paradigm: Categorization, reciprocation, or fear? *Journal of Personality and Social Psychology,* 79:77–94.

Gaither, Avalaura L., and **Eric C. Newburger.** 2000. The emerging American voter: An examination of the increase in the black vote in November 1998. U.S. Census Bureau Population Division, Working Paper No. 44. Washington, DC: U.S. Government Printing Office.

Gans, Herbert J. 1972. The positive functions of poverty. *American Journal of Sociology,* 78:275–89.

Gans, Herbert J. 1979. Symbolic ethnicity: The future of ethnic groups and cultures in America. *Racial and Ethnic Studies,* 2:1–20.

Garcia, S. M., J. Kolding, J. Rice, M.-J. Rochet, et al. 2012. Reconsidering the consequences of selective fisheries. *Science,* 335: 1045–47.

Garcia-Moreno, Claudia, Lori Heise, Henrica A. F. M. Jansen, Mary Ellsberg, and **Charlotte Watts.** 2005. Violence against women. *Science,* 310:1282–83.

Gardiner, Stephen M. 2011. *A perfect moral storm: The ethical tragedy of climate change.* New York: Oxford University Press.

Gardner, LeGrande, and **Donald J. Shoemaker.** 1989. Social bonding and delinquency: A comparative analysis. *Sociological Quarterly,* 30:481–500.

Garfinkel, Harold. 1974. The origins of the term "ethnomethodology." In R. Turner, ed., *Ethno-methodology.* Harmondsworth, Eng.: Penguin Books.

Garland, David. 2003. *The culture of control: Crime and social order in contemporary society.* Chicago: University of Chicago Press.

Garrett, Brandon L. 2011. *Convicting the innocent: Where criminal prosecutions go wrong.* Cambridge, MA: Harvard University Press.

Gates, Gary J. 2011. How many people are lesbian, gay, bisexual, and transgender? The Williams Institute (April). Available at http://williams institute.law.ucla.edu/wp-content/uploads/Gates-How-Many-People-LGBT-Apr-2011.pdf.

Gecas, Viktor, and **Michael L. Schwalbe.** 1983. Beyond the looking-glass self: Social structure and efficacy-based self-esteem. *Social Psychology Quarterly,* 46:77–88.

Gecas, Viktor, and **Monica A. Seff.** 1990. Families and adolescents: A review of the 1980s. *Journal of Marriage and the Family,* 52:941–58.

Gelfand, Michele J., Jana L. Raver, Lisa Nishii, Lisa Leslie, et al. 2011. Differences between tight and loose cultures: A 33-nation study. *Science,* 332:1100–4.

Gelles, Richard J., Murray A. Straus, and **John W. Harrop.** 1988. Has family violence decreased? *Journal of Marriage and the Family,* 50:286–91.

Gerbner, George, Larry Gross, Michael F. Eleey, Marilyn Jackson-Beeck, Suzanne Jeffries-Fox, and **Nancy Signorielli.** 1978. Cultural indicators: Violence profile no. 9. *Journal of Communication,* 28:176–207.

Geschwender, James A. 1964. Social structure and the Negro revolt: An examination of some hypotheses. *Social Forces,* 43:248–56.

Geschwender, James A. 1978. *Racial stratification in America.* Dubuque, IA: William C. Brown.

Gibbons, Ann. 2008. The birth of childhood. *Science* 322:1040–43.

Gibbs, Jack P. 1989. *Control: Sociology's central notion.* Urbana: University of Illinois Press.

Gibson, Rosemary, and **Janardan Prasad Singh.** 2010. *The treatment trap: How the overuse of medical care is wrecking your health and what you can do to prevent it.* Lanham, MD: Ivan R. Dee.

Giddens, Anthony. 1973. *The class structure of the advanced societies.* New York: Harper & Row.

Giddens, Anthony. 1985. *A contemporary critique of historical materialism.* Vol. 2: *The nation-state and*

violence. Berkeley: University of California Press.

Gilligan, Carol. 1982. *In a different voice: Psychological theory and women's development.* Cambridge, MA: Harvard University Press.

Gilligan, Carol, J. V. Ward, and **J. M. Taylor,** eds. 1989. *Mapping the moral domain.* Cambridge, MA: Harvard University Press.

Ginther, Donna K., Walter T. Schaffer, Joshua Schnell, Beth Masimore, Faye Liu, Laurel L. Haak, and **Raynard Kington.** 2011. Race, ethnicity, and NIH research awards. *Science,* 333:1015–19.

Giridharadas, Anand. 2010. Where a cellphone is still cutting edge. *New York Times* (April 11):WK4.

Gittleman, Maury, and **Mary Joyce.** 1995. Earnings mobility in the United States, 1967–91. *Monthly Labor Review,* September 3–11.

Glaeser, Edward. 2011. Cities, productivity, and quality of life. *Science,* 333:592–94.

Glasier, Vicki. 2011. One-third of fathers with working wives regularly care for their children. Census Bureau reports. U.S. Census Bureau (December 5):CB11-198.

Glassman, Ronald M., William H. Swatos, Jr., and **Paul L. Rosen,** eds. 1987. *Bureaucracy against democracy and socialism.* Westport, CT: Greenwood Press.

Glenn, Norval D., and **C. N. Weaver.** 1981. The contribution of marital happiness to global happiness. *Journal of Marriage and the Family,* 43:161–68.

Glick, Clarence. 1980. *Sojourners and settlers: Chinese immigrants in Hawaii.* Honolulu: University of Hawaii Press.

Glod, Maria. 2007. Calls grow for a broader yardstick for schools. *Washington Post* (December 16):A11.

GMIS. 2007. Genome Management Information System. Minorities, race, and genomics. U.S. Department of Energy Genome Programs: Human Genome Project Information site. http://www.ornl.gov/sci/

techresources/Human_Genome/elsi/minorities.shtml.

Godfray, H. Charles J., John R. Beddington, Ian R. Crute, Lawrence Haddad, David Lawrence, James F. Muir, Jules Pretty, Sherman Robinson, Sandy M. Thomas, and **Camilla Toulmin.** 2010. Food security: The challenge of feeding 9 billion people. *Science,* 327:812–18.

Goffman, Erving. 1959. *The presentation of self in everyday life.* Garden City, NY: Doubleday.

Goffman, Erving. 1961a. *Encounters.* Indianapolis: Bobbs-Merrill.

Goffman, Erving. 1961b. *Asylums: Essays on the social situation of mental patients and other inmates.* Garden City, NY: Anchor Books.

Golden, Claudia, and **Maria Shim.** 2004. Making a name: Women's surnames at marriage and beyond. *Journal of Economic Perspectives,* 18:143–60.

Golden, Daniel. 2006. *The price of admission: How America's ruling class buys its way into elite colleges—and who gets left outside the gates.* New York: Crown.

Golder, Scott A., and **Michael W. Macy.** 2011. Diurnal and seasonal mood vary with work, sleep, and daylength across diverse cultures. *Science,* 333:1878–81.

Goldhagen, Daniel Jonah. 1996. *Hitler's willing executioners: Ordinary Germans and the Holocaust.* New York: Knopf.

Goldin-Meadow, Susan, and **Carolyn Mylander.** 1984. Gestural communication in deaf children. *Monographs of the Society for Research in Child Development,* 49, No. 207.

Goldman, Michael and **Rachel A. Schurman.** 2000. Closing the "Great Divide": New social theory on society and nature. *Annual Review of Sociology,* 26:563–84.

Goldsmith, Jack, and **Tim Wu.** 2006. *Who controls the Internet: Illusions of a borderless world.* New York: Oxford University Press.

Goldstein, Sidney. 1992. Profile of American Jewry: Insights from the 1990 National Jewish Population Survey. In *American Jewish Yearbook 1992.* New York: American Jewish Committee.

Goldstone, Jack A. 1991. *Revolution and rebellion in the early modern world.* Berkeley: University of California Press.

Goleman, Daniel. 1991. Doctors find comfort is a potent medicine. *New York Times* (November 26):B5.

Goleman, Daniel. 1992. Family rituals may promote better emotional adjustment. *New York Times* (March 11):B6.

Goleman, Daniel. 1994. Mental decline in aging need not be inevitable. *New York Times* (April 26): B5, B7.

Gonzales, P., Williams, T., Jocelyn, L., Roey, S., Kastberg, D., and **Brenwald, S.** 2009. *Highlights from TIMSS 2007: Mathematics and science achievement of U.S. fourth- and eighth-grade students in an international context* (NCES 2009–001 Revised). National Center for Education Statistics, Institute of Education Sciences. Washington, DC: U.S. Department of Education.

Goodall, Jane. 1990. *Through a window: My thirty years with the chimpanzees of Gombe.* Boston: Houghton Mifflin.

Goode, Erica E. 1993. The culture of illness. *U.S. News & World Report* (February 15):74–76.

Goode, William J. 1959. The theoretical importance of love. *American Sociological Review,* 24:38–47.

Goode, William J. 1972. The place of force in human society. *American Sociological Review,* 37:507–19.

Gordon, Milton M. 1964. *Assimilation in American life: The role of race, religion, and national origins.* New York: Oxford University Press.

Gordon, Suzanne. 1997. *Life support: Three nurses on the front lines.* Boston: Little, Brown.

Gornick, Vivian, and **B. K. Moran.** 1971. *Women in sexist society.* New York: New American Library.

Gove, Walter R. 1970. Societal reaction as an explanation of mental illness: An evaluation. *American Sociological Review,* 35:873–84.

Gove, Walter R. 1994. Why we do what we do: A biopsychosocial theory of human motivation. *Social Forces,* 73:363–94.

Gove, Walter R., Michael Hughes, and **Michael Geerken.** 1985. Are Uniform Crime Reports a valid indicator of the index crimes? An affirmative answer with minor qualifications. *Criminology,* 23:451–500.

Gove, Walter R., Carolyn Briggs Style, and **Michael Hughes.** 1990. The effect of marriage on the well-being of adults. *Journal of Family Issues,* 11(March):4–35.

Graff, E. J. 2005. Too pretty a picture. *Washington Post* (November 13):B1.

Grall, Timothy S. 2011. Custodial mothers and fathers and their child support: 2009. *Consumer Income,* Current Population Reports (December):P60–240.

Granados, Christine. 2000. "Hispanic" vs. "Latino": A new poll finds that the term "Hispanic" is preferred. *Hispanic Magazine* (December). Available at www .hispanicmagazine.com/2000/dec/ Features/latino.html.

Granberg, Ellen. 2006. "Is that all there is?" Possible selves, self-change, and weight loss. *Social Psychology Quarterly,* 69:109–26.

Granstrom, K., and **D. Stiwne.** 1998. A bipolar model of groupthink: An expansion of Janis's concept. *Small Group Research,* 29:32–56.

Grant, Don, Mary Nell Trautner, Liam Downey, and **Lisa Thiebaud.** 2010. Bringing the polluters back in: Environmental inequality and the organization of chemical production. *American Sociological Review,* 75(4):479–504.

Grant, Don Sherman, and **Ramiro Martinez.** 1997. Crime and the restructuring of the U.S. economy: A reconsideration of the class linkages. *Social Forces,* 75:769–99.

Grant, Jon E., Suck Won Kim, and **Brian L. Odlaug.** 2009. A double-blind, placebo-controlled study of the opiate antagonist, Naltrexone, in the treatment of kleptomania. *Biological Psychiatry,* 65(7):600–06.

Grattet, Ryken. 2009. The urban ecology of bias crime: A study of disorganized and defended neighborhoods. *Social Problems,* 56(1):132–50.

Gray, Bradford H. 1991. *The profit motive and patient care: The changing accountability of doctors and hospitals.* Cambridge, MA: Harvard University Press.

Gray, John. 2005. The world is round. *New York Review of Books,* 52(13):13–15.

Greeley, Andrew M. 1974. *Ethnicity in the United States: A preliminary reconnaissance.* New York: John Wiley.

Greeley, Andrew M. 1977. *The American Catholic: A social portrait.* New York: Harper & Row.

Greeley, Andrew M. 1989. *Religious change in America.* Cambridge, MA: Harvard University Press.

Greeley, Andrew, and **Michael Hout.** 2006. *The truth about conservative Christians: What they think and what they believe.* Chicago: University of Chicago Press.

Greenberger, Phyllis. 2008. Flaunting the feminine side of research studies. *Science,* 322: 1325–26.

Greenhouse, Linda. 2003. U. of Michigan ruling endorses the value of campus diversity. *New York Times* (June 24):A1.

Greenspan, Stanley J. 1997. The reason why we need to rely less on day care. *Washington Post* (October 19):C1.

Greenwald, A. G., and **A. R. Pratkanis.** 1984. The self. In R. S. Wyer and T. K. Srull, eds., *Handbook of social cognition.* Hillsdale, NJ: Erlbaum.

Greenwood, Peter W. 1982. *Selective incapacitation.* Santa Monica, CA: Rand Corporation.

Grieco, Elizabeth M. 2010. Race and Hispanic origin of the foreign-born population in the United States: 2007. American community survey reports ACS-11. Washington, DC: U.S. Census Bureau.

Grimes, Marmian. 2006. Study: Boys trail girls in literacy scores. University of Alaska Fairbanks Newsroom. http://www.uaf.edu/news/a_news/20060712142210.html.

Grimes, Michael D. 1991. *Class in twentieth-century American sociology: An analysis of theories and measurement strategies.* New York: Praeger.

Grimm, David. 2008. Staggering toward a global strategy on alcohol abuse. *Science,* 320:862–63.

Grimsley, Kirstin Downey. 1997. Avon calling . . . on a man: Board bypasses staff, names former Duracell chief next CEO. *Washington Post* (December 12):G1.

Grindstaff, Laura, and **Joseph Turow.** 2006. Video cultures: Television sociology in the "new TV" age. *Annual Review of Sociology,* 32:103–25.

Grob, Gerald N. 1983. *Mental illness and American society, 1875–1940.* Princeton, NJ: Princeton University Press.

Groves, Robert M., Don A. Dillman, John Eltinge, and **Roderick J. A. Little,** eds. 2002. *Survey nonresponse.* New York: Wiley-Interscience.

Gruber, Jonathan. 2010. The cost implications of health care reform. *New England Journal of Medicine,* 362(22):2050–51.

Gubrium, Jaber F., and **James A. Holstein.** 1990. *What is family?* Mountain View, CA: Mayfield.

Guelzow, Maureen, Gloria W. Bird, and **Elizabeth H. Koball.** 1991. An exploratory path analysis of the stress process for dual-career men and women. *Journal of Marriage and the Family,* 53: 151–64.

Guo, G. 1998. The timing of the influences of cumulative poverty on children's cognitive ability and achievement. *Social Forces,* 77(1):257–87.

Guo, Guang. 2005. Twin studies: What can they tell us about nature and nurture? *Contexts,* 4:43–47.

Gurr, Ted R. 1970. *Why men rebel.* Princeton, NJ: Princeton University Press.

Gusfield, Joseph R. 2006. Keyword: Culture. *Contexts,* 5(Winter):43–44.

H

Hacker, Helen Mayer. 1951. Women as a minority group. *Social Forces,* 30:60–69.

Hacker, Helen Mayer. 1974. Women as a minority group: Twenty years later. In Florence Denmark, ed., *Who discriminates against women?* Beverly Hills, CA: Sage.

Hadden, Jeffrey K., and **Anson Shupe.** 1988. *Televangelism, power, and politics in God's frontier.* New York: Henry Holt.

Hagan, John. 1980. The legislation of crime and delinquency: A review of theory, method, and research. *Law and Society Review,* 14:603–28.

Hagan, John. 1989. *Structural criminology.* New Brunswick, NJ: Rutgers University Press.

Hagan, John, Ilene N. Bernstein, and **Celesta Albonetti.** 1980. The differential sentencing of white-collar offenders. *American Sociological Review,* 42:587–98.

Hagan, John, and **Alberto Palloni.** 1999. Sociological criminology and the mythology of Hispanic immigration and crime. *Social Problems,* 46(4):617–32.

Halal, William E., and **Alexander I. Nikitin.** 1990. One world. *The Futurist* (November–December):8–14.

Hall, Edward T. 1966. *The hidden dimension.* Garden City, NY: Doubleday.

Hall, John R. 1988. Social organization and pathways of commitment: Types of communal groups, rational choice theory, and the Kanter Thesis.

American Sociological Review, 53:679–92.

Hall, Matthew, and **Barrett Lee.** 2010. How diverse are U.S. suburbs? *Urban Studies,* 47(1):3–28.

Ham, Becky. 2011. Cities find economic reasons to go green. *Science,* 334:470–71.

Hamburg, David A., and **Ruby Takanishi.** 1989. Preparing for life: The critical transition of adolescence. *American Psychologist,* 44:825–27.

Hamilton, Richard F. 1972. *Class and politics in the United States.* New York: John Wiley.

Hamper, Ben Rivethead. 1991. *Tales from the assembly line.* New York: Warner.

Hampton, Keith N., Lauren Sessions Goulet, Lee Rainie, and **Kristen Purcell.** 2011. *Social networking sites and our lives: How people's trust, personal relationships, and civic and political involvement are connected to their use of social networking sites and other technologies.* Pew Research Center's Internet and American Life Project (June 16).

Hampton, Keith N., Lauren F. Sessions, Eun Ja Her, and **Lee Rainie.** 2009. *Social Isolation and new technology: How the Internet and mobile phones impact Americans' social networks.* Pew Research Center's Internet and American Life Project (November).

Hancock, Lynnell. 2011. A+ for Finland. *Smithsonian* (September): 94–102.

Haney, C., C. Banks, and **Phillip Zimbardo.** 1973. Interpersonal dynamics in a simulated prison. *International Journal of Criminology and Penology,* 1:69–97.

Hardin, Garrett J. 1968. The tragedy of the commons. *Science,* 162:1243–48.

Hare, A. Paul. 1976. *Handbook of small group research,* 2nd ed. New York: Free Press.

Hareven, Tamara K. 1982. *Family time and industrial time.* New York: Cambridge University Press.

Harkins, Stephen G., and **Kate Szymanski.** 1989. Social loafing and group evaluation. *Journal of*

Personality and Social Psychology, 56:934–41.

Harper, Kristin N., Paolo S. Ocampo, Bret M. Steiner, Robert W. George, Michael S. Silverman, Shelly Bolotin, Allan Pillay, Nigel J. Saunders, and **George J. Armelagos.** 2008. On the origin of the Treponematoses: A phylogenetic approach. *PLoS Neglected Tropical Diseases,* 2(1):1–13.

Harper, Shannon, and **Barbara Reskin.** 2005. Affirmative action at school and on the job. *Annual Review of Sociology,* 31:357–79.

Harrington, Michael. 1976. *The twilight of capitalism.* New York: Simon & Schuster.

Harris, Alexes, Heather Evans, and **Katherine Beckett.** 2010. Drawing blood from stones: Legal debt and social inequality in the contemporary United States. *American Journal of Sociology,* 115(6):1753–99.

Harris, Chauncey D., and **Edward L. Ullman.** 1945. The nature of cities. *Annals of the American Academy of Political and Social Science,* 242:7–17.

Harris, Judith Rich. 1998. *The nurture assumption: Why children turn out the way they do.* New York: Free Press.

Hartjen, Clayton A., and **Sesbarajani Kethineini.** 1993. Culture, gender, delinquency: A study of youths in the United States and India. *Women and Criminal Justice,* 5:37–69.

Hartman, Curtis, and **Steven Pearlstein.** 1987. The job of working. *INC.* (November):61–71.

Hartmann, Heidi, Olga Sorokina, and **Erica Williams,** with **Vicky Lovell, Tori Finkle, Ashley English,** and **Amy Caiazza.** 2006. The best and worst state economies for women. Institute for Women's Policy research briefing paper No. R334. www.iwpr.org/pdf/R334_BWStateEconomies2006.pdf.

Haslam, S. Alexander, and **Stephen Reicher.** 2002. *A user's guide to The Experiment—Exploring the psychology of groups and power: Manual to accompany the BBC video.* London: BBC Worldwide.

Haslam, S. Alexander, and **Stephen Reicher.** 2007. Identity entrepreneurship and the consequences of identity failure: The dynamics of leadership in the BBC prison study. *Social Psychology Quarterly,* 2:125–47.

Haub, Carl, and **James Gribble.** 2011. The world at 7 billion. *Population Bulletin,* 66(2):1–13.

Haub, Carl, and **Toshiko Kaneda.** 2011. *2011 World Population Data Sheet: The world at 7 billion.* Washington, DC: Population Reference Bureau.

Hauser, Marc D., Noam Chomsky, and **W. Tecumseh Fitch.** 2002. The faculty of language: What is it, who has it, and how did it evolve? *Science,* 298:1569–79.

Hawkins, Darnell F. 1987. Beyond anomalies: Rethinking the conflict perspective on race and criminal punishment. *Social Forces,* 65:719–45.

Hawkley, Louise C., and **John T. Cacioppo.** 2010. Loneliness matters: A theoretical and empirical review of consequences and mechanisms. *Annals of Behavioral Medicine,* 40(2):218–27.

Haynie, Dana L. 2003. Context of risk? Explaining the link between girls' pubertal development and their delinquency involvement. *Social Forces,* 82(1):355–97.

Haynie, D. L. 2001. Delinquent peers revisited: Does network structure matter? *American Journal of Sociology,* 106(4):1013–57.

He, Wan, Manisha Sengupta, Victoria A. Velkoff, and **Kimberly A. DeBarros.** 2005. 65 + *in the United States: 2005.* U.S. Census Bureau, Current Population Reports, P23–209. Washington, DC: U.S. Government Printing Office. Available at http://www.census.gov/prod/2006pubs/p23-209.pdf.

Hechter, Michael. 1987. *Principles of group solidarity.* Los Angeles: University of California Press.

Hechter, Michael. 1995. Symposium on prediction in the social sciences: Introduction: Reflections on historical prophecy in the social sciences.

American Journal of Sociology, 100(6):1520–27.

Heckathorn, Douglas D. 1988. Collective sanctions and the emergence of prisoner's dilemma. *American Journal of Sociology,* 94:535–62.

Heckathorn, Douglas D. 1990. Collective sanctions and compliance norms: A formal theory of group-mediated social control. *American Sociological Review,* 55:366–84.

Hegewisch, Ariane, and **Hannah Liepmann.** 2010. *Fact sheet: The gender wage gap by occupation.* IWPR #C350a. Washington, DC: Institute for Women's Policy Research.

Heilbroner, Robert. 1993. *21st century capitalism.* New York: Norton.

Heisig, Jan Paul. 2011. Who does more housework: Rich or poor? A comparison of 33 countries. *American Sociological Review,* 76(1):74–99.

Helmuth, Laura. 2003. The wisdom of the wizened. *Science,* 299: 1300–1302.

Hendrix, Steve. 2009. Boomers see views relaxing on marijuana. *Washington Post* (November 16):1B.

Hepworth, Joseph T., and **Stephen G. West.** 1988. Lynchings and the economy: A time-series reanalysis of Hovland and Sears (1940). *Journal of Personality and Social Psychology,* 55:239–47.

Herberg, Will. 1955. *Protestant-Catholic-Jew.* Garden City, NY: Doubleday.

Herman, Judith, and **Lisa Hirschman.** 1981. Families at risk for father-daughter incest. *American Journal of Psychiatry.* 138:967–70.

Herring, Cedric, and **Karen Rose Wilson-Sadberry.** 1993. Preference or necessity? Changing work roles of black and white women, 1973–1990. *Journal of Marriage and the Family,* 55:314–25.

Herrnstein, Richard J., and **Charles Murray.** 1994. *The bell curve: Intelligence and class structure in American life.* New York: Free Press.

Hersey, Paul, and **Kenneth H. Blanchard.** 1988. *Management* *of organizational behavior: Utilizing human resources.* Englewood Cliffs, NJ: Prentice-Hall.

Hertzler, J. O. 1961. *American social institutions.* Boston: Allyn & Bacon.

Hewitt, James P., and **David Shulman.** 2011. *Self and society: A symbolic interactionist social psychology.* Upper Saddle River, NJ: Prentice-Hall.

Heymann, Jody, Alison Earle, Stephanie Simmons, Stephanie M. Breslow, and **April Kuehnhoff.** 2004. The work, family, and equity index: Where does the United States stand globally? The Project on Global Working Families, www.globalworkingfamilies.org.

Hibbing, John R., and **Elizabeth Theiss-Morse.** 2002. *Stealth democracy: Americans' beliefs about how government should work.* Cambridge: Cambridge University Press.

Hickman, Laura J., and **Marika J. Suttorp.** 2008. Are deportable aliens a unique threat to public safety? Comparing the recidivism of deportable and nondeportable aliens. *Criminology & Public Policy* 7:59–82.

Higginbotham, Elizabeth, and **Lynn Weber.** 1992. Moving up with kin and community: Upward social mobility for black and white women. *Gender & Society,* 6(3):416–40.

Hill, Catherine, Christianne Corbett, and **Andresse St. Rose.** 2010. *Why so few? Women in science, technology, engineering, and mathematics.* Washington, DC: AAUW. Available at http://www.aauw.org/learn/research/whysofew.cfm.

Hill, Catherine, and **Holly Kearl.** 2011. *Crossing the line: Sexual harassment at school.* Washington, DC: AAUW.

Hill, Kim R., Robert S. Walker, Miran Božičević, James Eder, et al. 2011. Co-residence patterns in hunter-gatherer societies show unique human social structure. *Science,* 331:1286–89.

Hirschi, Travis. 1969. *Causes of delinquency.* Berkeley: University of California Press.

Hirschi, Travis, and **Rodney Stark.** 1969. Hellfire and delinquency. *Social Problems,* 17:202–13.

Hirschman, Charles, and **Morrison G. Wong.** 1986. The extraordinary educational attainment of Asian Americans: A search for historical evidence and explanations. *Social Forces,* 65:1–27.

Hitchens, Christopher. 2007. *God is not great: How religion poisons everything.* New York: Hatchette Book Group USA.

Hitlin, Steven, and **Jane Allyn Piliavin.** 2004. Values: Reviving a dormant concept. *Annual Review of Sociology,* 30:359–93.

Hochschild, A. R. 1990. *The second shift.* New York: Avon Books.

Hodge, Robert, and **Donald Treiman.** 1968. Class identification in the United States. *American Journal of Sociology,* 73:535–47.

Hoebel, E. A. 1958. *Man in the primitive world,* 2nd ed. New York: McGraw-Hill.

Hoecker-Drysdale, Susan. 1994. *Harriet Martineau: First woman sociologist.* New York: Berg Press.

Hoffman, Curt, and **Nancy Hurst.** 1990. Gender stereotypes: Perception or rationalization? *Journal of Personality and Social Psychology,* 58, 197–208.

Hoffman, John P. 2003. A contextual analysis of differential association, social control, and strain theories of delinquency. *Social Forces,* 81(3):753–85.

Hoffman, Lois. 1989. Effects of maternal employment in the two-parent family. *American Psychologist,* 44:283–92.

Hogan, Margaret C., Kyle J. Foreman, Mohsen Naghavi, Stephanie Y. Ahn, Mengru Wang, Susanna M. Makela, Alan D. Lopez, Rafael Lozano, and **Christopher J. L. Murray.** 2010. Maternal mortality for 181 countries, 1980–2008: A systematic analysis of progress towards Millennium Development Goal 5. *The Lancet,* 375:1609–23.

Holden, Constance. 2009. Forensic science needs a major overhaul, panel says. *Science,* 323:1155.

Holder, Kelly. 2006. *Voting and registration in the election of November 2004.* U.S. Census Bureau, Current Population Reports, Series P20–556. Washington, DC.

Holdren, John P. 2008. Science and technology for sustainable well-being. *Science,* 319:424–34.

Holt, John. 1969. School is bad for children. *The Saturday Evening Post.* In Barbara Fine Clouse, *The student writer* (2008). New York: McGraw-Hill.

Holtgrieve, Gordon W., Daniel E. Schindler, William O. Hobbs, Peter R. Leavitt, et al. 2011. A coherent signature of anthropogenic nitrogen deposition to remote watersheds of the northern hemisphere. *Science,* 334:1545–48.

Horowitz, Carl. 1994. What's environmental racism? *Investor's Business Daily* (March 2):1–2.

Horowitz, Helen Lefkowitz. 1987. *Campus life: Undergraduate cultures from the end of the eighteenth century to the present.* New York: Knopf.

Hostetler, John A. 1980. *Amish society.* Baltimore: Johns Hopkins University Press.

House, James. 1995. Introduction: Social structure and personality: Past, present, and future. In Karen S. Cook, Gary Alan Fine, and James S. House, eds., *Sociological Perspectives on Social Psychology.* Boston: Allyn & Bacon.

House, James S., Karl R. Landis, and **Debra Umberson.** 1988. Social relationships and health. *Science,* 241:540–5.

Howell, William G., Martin R. West, and **Paul E. Peterson.** 2007. What Americans think about their schools. *Education Next* (Fall):12–26.

Hoyert, D. L., H. C. Kung, and **B. L. Smith.** 2005. Deaths: Preliminary data for 2003. *National Vital Statistics Report* 53(15):1–48. Available at http://www.cdc.gov/nchs/data/nvsr/nvsr53/nvsr53_15.pdf.

Hoyt, Homer. 1939. *The structure and growth of residential neighborhoods in American cities.* Washington, DC: Federal Housing Administration.

Hrdy, Sarah Blaffer. 2009. *Mothers and others: The evolutionary origins of mutual understanding.* Cambridge, MA: Harvard University Press.

Hsu, Frances L. K. 1943. Incentives to work in primitive communities. *American Sociological Review,* 8:638–42.

Hu, Yuanreng, and **Noreen Goldman.** 1990. Mortality differentials by marital status: An international comparison. *Demography,* 27:233–50.

Huesmann, L. Rowell, Jessica Moise-Titus, Cheryl-Lynn Podolski, and **Leonard D. Eron.** 2003. Longitudinal relations between children's exposure to TV violence and their aggressive and violent behavior in young adulthood: 1977–1992. *Developmental Psychology,* 39(2):201–21.

Huey, John. 1994. The new post-heroic leadership. *Fortune* (February 21):42–50.

Hughes, Charles C. 1968. Medical care: Ethnomedicine. In D. Sills, ed., *International Encyclopedia of Social Sciences,* Vol. 10. New York: Macmillan.

Hughes, Michael. 1980. The fruits of cultivation analysis: A reexamination of some effects of television watching. *Public Opinion Quarterly,* 44:289–302.

Hughes, Michael. 1989. Parenthood and psychological well-being among the formerly married: Are children the primary source of psychological distress? *Journal of Family Issues,* 10:163–81.

Hughes, Michael. 1997. Symbolic racism, old fashioned racism, and whites' opposition to affirmative action. In Steven A. Tuch and Jack K. Martin, eds., *Racial attitudes in the 1990s: Continuity and change.* Westport, CT: Praeger.

Hughes, Michael, and **David H. Demo.** 1989. Self-perceptions of black Americans: Self-esteem and personal efficacy. *American Journal of Sociology,* 95:139–59.

Hughes, Michael, and **Walter R. Gove.** 1981. Living alone, social integration, and mental health. *American Journal of Sociology,* 87:48–74.

Hughey, Matthew W. 2009. Cinethetic racism: White redemption and black stereotypes in "Magical Negro" films. *Social Problems,* 56(3):543–77.

Huiting, Hu. 2002. Family planning law and China's birth control situation. www.china.org.cn/english/2002/Oct/46138.htm.

Hull, R. Bruce, and **David P. Robertson.** 2000. Which nature? In Paul H. Gobster and R. Bruce Hull, eds., *Restoring nature: Perspectives from the social sciences and humanities.* Washington, DC: Island Press.

Humes, Karen R., Nicholas A. Jones, and **Roberto R. Ramirez.** 2011. *Overview of race and Hispanic origin: 2010.* U.S. Bureau of the Census, 2010 Census Brief (March), C2010BR-02. Available at http://www.census.gov/prod/cen2010/briefs/c2010br-02.pdf.

Humphrey, John A., and **Timothy J. Fogarty.** 1987. Race and plea-bargained outcomes: A research note. *Social Forces,* 66:176–82.

Hurst, Charles E. 1998. *Social inequality: Forms, causes, and consequences.* Boston: Allyn & Bacon.

Hutter, Mark. 1998. *The changing family,* 3rd ed. Boston: Allyn & Bacon.

Hvistendahl, Mara. 2009. Making every baby girl count. *Science,* 323:1164–66.

Hyde, Janet Shibley. 2005. The gender similarities hypothesis. *American Psychologist,* 60(6):581–92.

Hyde, Janet S., Sara M. Lindberg, Marcia C. Linn, Amy B. Ellis, and **Caroline C. Williams.** 2008. Gender similarities characterize math performance. *Science,* 321:494–95.

Hyman, Herbert H., and **Eleanor Singer.** 1968. Introduction. In H. H. Hyman and E. Singer, eds., *Readings in reference group theory and research.* New York: Free Press.

I

Iannaccone, Laurence R. 1994. Why strict churches are strong. *American Journal of Sociology,* 99:1180–11.

Iannaccone, Laurence R., Daniel V. A. Olson, and **Rodney Stark.** 1995. Religious resources and church growth. *Social Forces,* 74:705–31.

Iceland, John. 2003. *Dynamics of economic well-being: Poverty 1996–1999.* U.S. Census Bureau, Current Population Reports, P70–91. Washington, DC: U.S. Government Printing Office (available online at http://www.bls.census.gov/sipp/p70s/p70-91.pdf).

Iceland, John, Daniel H. Weinberg, and **Erika Steinmetz.** 2002. *Racial and ethnic residential segregation in the United States: 1980–2000.* U.S. Census Bureau, Series CENSR-3. Washington, DC: U.S. Government Printing Office.

Ingham, Alan G. 1974. The Ringelmann effect: Studies of group size and group performance. *Journal of Experimental Social Psychology,* 10:371–84.

Inglehart, Ronald, et al. 2000. *World values surveys and European values surveys, 1981–1984, 1990–1993, and 1995–1997* (computer file). ICPSR version. Ann Arbor, MI: Institute for Social Research.

Inkeles, Alex. 1968. Society, social structure, and child socialization. In John Clausen, ed., *Socialization and society.* Boston: Little, Brown.

International Labor Organization. 2001. *World Employment Report 2001: Life at work in the information economy.* International Labor Organization website, www.ilo.org.

Internet World Stats. 2012. http://www.internetworldstats.com/stats/htm.

Intons-Peterson, Margaret Jean. 1988. *Gender concepts of Swedish and American Youth.* Hillsdale, NJ: Erlbaum.

Isen, Adam, and **Betsey Stevenson.** 2010. Women's education and family behavior: Trends in marriage, divorce, and fertility. NBER Working Paper 15725, National Bureau of Economic Research. Available at http://www.nber.org/papers/w15725.

Iyengar, Shanto. 1991. *Is anyone responsible? How television frames political issues.* Chicago: University of Chicago Press.

J

Jackendoff, Ray. 2002. *Foundations of language: Brain, meaning, grammar, evolution.* New York: Oxford University Press.

Jackman, Mary R., and **Robert W. Jackman.** 1983. *Class awareness in the United States.* Berkeley: University of California Press.

Jackson, Philip W. 1968. *Life in classrooms.* New York: Holt, Rinehart & Winston.

Jackson, Walter A. 1990. *Gunnar Myrdal and America's conscience: Social engineering and racial liberalism, 1938–1987.* Chapel Hill: University of North Carolina Press.

Jacobs, David, and **Ronald E. Helms.** 1996. Toward a political model of incarceration: A time-series examination of multiple explanations for prison admission rates. *American Journal of Sociology,* 102:323–57.

Jacobs, David, and **Ronald E. Helms.** 1997. Testing coercive explanations for order: The determinants of law enforcement strength over time. *Social Forces,* 75:1361–92.

Jacobsen, Linda A., Mary Kent, Marlene Lee, and **Mark Mather.** 2011. America's aging population. *Population Bulletin,* 66(1):1–16.

Jacobson, Robert L. 1992. Professors who teach more are paid less, study finds. *Chronicle of Higher Education* (April 15):A17.

Jacques, Martin. 2009. *When China rules the world: The end of the Western world and the birth of a new global order.* New York: Penguin Press.

Jacquet, Jennifer, Christoph Hauert, Arne Traulsen, and **Manfred Milinski.** 2011. Shame and honour drive cooperation. *Biol. Lett.* Published online 1 June 2011 doi: 10.1098/rsbl.2011.0367.

Jaffee, David. 2001. *Organization theory: Tension and change.* New York: McGraw-Hill.

Janis, Irving L. 1982. *Groupthink,* 2nd ed. Boston: Houghton Mifflin.

Janis, Irving L. 1989. *Crucial decisions: Leadership in policy-making and crisis management.* New York: Free Press.

Janssen, Marco A., Robert Holahan, Allen Lee, and **Elinor Ostrom.** 2010. Lab experiments for the study of social-ecological systems. *Science,* 328:613–17.

Jargowsky, Paul A. 1997. *Poverty and place.* New York: Russell Sage Foundation.

Jaynes, Gerald D., and **Robin M. Williams,** eds. 1989. *A common destiny: Blacks and American society.* Washington, DC: National Academy Press.

Jeffords, James M., and **Tom Daschle.** 2001. Political issues in the genome era. *Science,* 291:1249–51.

Jencks, Christopher. 1992. *Rethinking social policy: Race, poverty, and the underclass.* Cambridge, MA: Harvard University Press.

Jencks, Christopher, and **Meredith Phillips.** 1998. *The black-white test score gap.* Washington, DC: Brookings Institution Press.

Jenkins, J. Craig. 1985. *The politics of insurgency: The farm worker movement in the 1960s.* New York: Columbia University Press.

Jenness, Valerie. 2004. Explaining criminalization: From demography and status politics to globalization and modernization. *Annual Review of Sociology,* 30:147–71.

Jensen, Gary F., and **Dean G. Rojek.** 1992. *Delinquency and youth crime.* Prospect Heights, IL: Waveland.

Johnson, Cathryn, Timothy J. Dowd, and **Cecilia L. Ridgeway.** 2006. Legitimacy as a social process. *Annual Review of Sociology,* 32:53–78.

Johnson, Hayes. 1988. Hispanics, blacks are dropping out. *USA Today* (March 23):D3.

Johnson, James Weldon. 1927/1989. *The autobiography of an ex-coloured man.* New York: Vintage Books.

Johnson, Jeffrey G., Patricia Cohen, Elizabeth M. Smailes, Stephanie Kasen, and **Judith S. Brook.** 2002. Television viewing and aggressive behavior during adolescence and adulthood. *Science,* 295:2468–71.

Johnson, Miriam. 1993. Functionalism and feminism: Is estrangement necessary? In Paula England, ed., *Theory on gender/feminism on gender.* New York: Aldine de Gruyter.

Johnson, W., Bouchard, T. J., Jr., McGue, M., Segal, N. L., Tellegen, A., Keyes, M., et al. 2007. Genetic and environmental influences on the Verbal-Perceptual-Image Rotation (VPR) model of the structure of mental abilities in the Minnesota Study of Twins Reared Apart. *Intelligence* 35:542–62.

Johnston, David Cay. 2003. Very richest's share of wealth grew even bigger, data show. *New York Times* (June 26):A1.

Jones, Jacqueline. 1992. *The dispossessed: America's underclasses from the Civil War to the present.* New York: Basic Books.

Jordan, Mary. 2007. In Europe and U.S., nonbelievers are increasingly vocal. *Washington Post* (September 15):A1.

Jordan, Winthrop D. 1969. *White over black: American attitudes toward the Negro, 1550–1812.* Baltimore: Penguin Books.

Josephy, Alvin M., Jr. 1991. *The Civil War in the American West.* New York: Knopf.

Joyce, Amy. 2007. Developing boomerang mothers: Some companies set up maternity-leave programs with an emphasis on the return. *Washington Post* (March 11):F1.

K

Kagan, Jerome, Richard B. Kearsley, and **Philip R. Zelazo.** 1978. *Infancy: Its place in human development.* Cambridge, MA: Harvard University Press.

Kain, Edward L. 1984. Surprising singles. *American Demographics,* 6 (August):16–19ff.

Kaiser, Jocelyn. 2011. Panel blasts ethics, science of 1940s Guatemala studies. *Science,* 333:1211.

Kalev, Alexandra, Frank Dobbin, and **Erin Kelly.** 2006. Best practices or best guesses? Assessing the efficacy of corporate affirmative action and diversity policies. *American Sociological Review,* 71:589–617.

Kalish, Susan. 1994. International migration: New findings on magnitude, importance. *Population Today,* 22:1–3.

Kanazawa, Satoshi. 2000. A new solution to the collective action problem: The paradox of voter turn-out. *American Sociological Review,* 65:433–42.

Kandel, William, Jamila Henderson, Heather Koball, and **Randy Capps.** 2011. Moving up in rural America: Economic attainment of nonmetro Latino immigrants. *Rural Sociology,* 76(1):1–28.

Kang, Cecilia. 2010. Big, permanent retweet by Library of Congress: Scholars will comb through messages to gain cultural insight. *Washington Post* (April 26):A21.

Kanter, Rosabeth M. 1968. Commitment and social organization: A study of commitment mechanisms in utopian communities. *American Sociological Review,* 46:141–58.

Kaplan, Howard B., Robert J. Johnson, and **Carol A. Bailey.** 1987. Deviant peers and deviant behavior: Further elaborations of a model. *Social Psychology Quarterly,* 50:277–84.

Karabel, Jerome. 2006. The best education money can buy. *Washington Post Book World* (September 10):8.

Karau, Steven J., and **Kipling D. Williams.** 1993. Social loafing: A meta-analytic review and theoretical integration. *Journal of Personality and Social Psychology,* 65:681–706.

Kareiva, Peter. 2011. The future of conservation: Balancing the needs of people and nature. *Nature Conservancy.* (Spring):38–39.

Karen, David. 1990. Toward a political-organizational model of gatekeeping. The case of elite colleges. *Sociology of Education,* 63:227–40.

Kawakami, Kerry, Elizabeth Dunn, Francine Karmali, and **John F. Dovidio.** 2009. Mispredicting affective and behavioral responses to racism. *Science,* 323:276–78.

Kaufman, Marc, and **Rob Stein.** 2006. Record share of economy spent on health care. *Washington Post* (January 10):A1.

Keister, Lisa A., and **Stephanie Moller.** 2000. Wealth inequality in the United States. *Annual Review of Sociology,* 26:63–81.

Keita, Gwendolyn Puryear, and **Steven L. Sauter,** eds. 1992. *Work and well-being: An agenda for the 1990s.* Washington, DC: American Psychological Association.

Keller, Helen. 1904. *The story of my life.* Garden City, NY: Doubleday.

Kelley, Raymond C. 1976. Witchcraft and sexual relations: An exploration in the social and semantic implications of the structure of belief. In Paula Brown and Georgeda Buchbinder, eds., *Man and woman in the New Guinea highlands,* a special publication of the American Anthropological Association, no. 8. Washington, DC: American Anthropological Association.

Kelly, Joe, and **Stacy L. Smith.** 2006. Where the girls aren't: Gender disparity saturates G-rated films. A research brief commissioned by the See Jane Program at Dads and Daughters. www.seejane.org.

Kendall-Tackett, Kathleen A., Linda Meyer Williams, and **David Finkelhor.** 1993. Impact of sexual abuse on children: A review and synthesis of recent empirical studies. *Psychological Bulletin,* 113:164–80.

Kennedy, Donald. 2002. Science, terrorism, and natural disasters. *Science,* 295:405.

Kennedy, Randall. 2011. *The persistence of the color line: Racial politics and the Obama presidency.* New York: Pantheon Books.

Kennelly, Ivy, Sabine N. Merz, and **Judith Lorber.** 2001. Comment: What is gender? *American Sociological Review,* 66:598–605.

Kennickell, Arthur B. 2003. A rolling tide: Changes in the distribution of wealth in the U.S., 1989–2001. Board of Governors of the Federal Reserve System (March 3). Available at www.federalreserve. gov/pubs/oss/ oss2/scfindex.html.

Kepel, Gilles. 2002. *Jihad: The trail of political Islam.* Cambridge, MA: Belknap.

Kerbo, Harold R. 2011. *Social stratification and inequality: Class conflict in historical, global, and comparative perspective,* 8th ed. New York: McGraw-Hill.

Kerr, Norman L. 1983. Motivation losses in small groups: A social dilemma analysis. *Journal of Personality and Social Psychology,* 45:819–28.

Kertzer, David. 1991. Household history and sociological theory. *Annual Review of Sociology,* 17:155–79.

Kessler, Ronald C., James S. House, A. Regula Herzog, and **Pamela Webster.** 1992. The relationship between age and depressive symptoms in two national surveys. *Psychology and Aging,* 7:119–26.

Kessler, Ronald C., Amanda Sonnega, Evelyn Bromet, Michael Hughes, and **Christopher B. Nelson.** 1995. Posttraumatic stress disorder in the National Comorbidity Survey. *Archives of General Psychiatry,* 52:1048–60.

Kessler-Harris, Alice. 1990. *A woman's wage: Historical meanings and social consequences.* Lexington: University Press of Kentucky.

Kett, J. F. 1977. *Rites of passage: Adolescence in America, 1870 to the present.* New York: Basic Books.

Kids Count. 2011. *America's children, America's challenge: Promoting opportunity for the next generation.* Baltimore, MD: The Annie E. Casey Foundation.

Kids Count. 2010. Children in single-parent families by race, 2008. Available at www.datacenter .kidscount.org/data/accrossstates/ Rankings.aspx?ind=107.

Kiecolt, K. Jill. 1994. Stress and the decision to change oneself: A theoretical model. *Social Psychology Quarterly,* 57:49–63.

Kiecolt, K. Jill. 2003. Satisfaction with work and family life: No evidence of a cultural reversal. *Journal of Marriage and Family,* 65:23–35.

Kim, Hyun Sik. 2011. Consequences of parental divorce for child development. *American Sociological Review,* 76(3):487–511.

Kim, Jae-On. 1987. Social mobility, status inheritance, and structural constraints: Conceptual and methodological considerations. *Social Forces,* 65:783–805.

Kinder, Donald R., and **Lynn M. Sanders.** 1996. *Divided by color: Racial politics and democratic ideals.* Chicago: University of Chicago Press.

Kinder, Donald R., and **David O. Sears.** 1981. Prejudice and politics. Symbolic racism versus racial threats to the good life. *Journal of Personality and Social Psychology,* 40:414–31.

King, Gary. 2011. Ensuring the data-rich future of the social sciences. *Science,* 331:719–21.

King, Ryan D., Robert D. Baller, and **Steven F. Messner.** 2009. Contemporary hate crimes, law enforcement, and the legacy of racial violence. *American Sociological Review,* 74(2):291–315.

Kinsey, Alfred C., Wardell B. Pomeroy, and **Clyde E. Martin.** 1948. *Sexual behavior in the human male.* Philadelphia: Saunders.

Kintisch, Eli. 2007. National academies make case for sustainable growth. *Science,* 318:547.

Kirkpatrick, R. C. 2000. The evolution of human homosexual behavior. *Current Anthropology,* 41(3):385–413.

Kitson, Gay C., and **William M. Holmes.** 1992. *Portrait of divorce: Adjustment to marital breakdown.* New York: Guilford.

Klass, Perri. 1987. When the doctor-patient relationship breaks down. *Discover,* 8(March):16.

Klein, Allison. 2010. As ID theft cases rise, "millennials" are most susceptible. *Washington Post* (March 17):B6.

Klein, Katherine J. 1987. Employee stock ownership and employee attitudes: A test of three models. *Journal of Applied Psychology,* 72:319–32.

Kluckhohn, Clyde. 1960. *Mirror for man.* Greenwich, CT: Fawcett.

Knodel, John, and **Etienne van de Walle.** 1979. Lessons from the past: Policy implications of historical fertility studies. *Population and Development Review,* 5:217–45.

Knottnerus, J. David. 1991. Status attainment's image of society: Individual factors, structural effect, and the transformation of the class structure. *Sociological Spectrum,* 11:147–76.

Kochhar, Rakesh, Richard Fry, and **Paul Taylor.** 2011. Wealth gaps rise to record highs between whites, blacks and Hispanics. *Pew Research Center: Social and Demographic Trends* (July 26):37. Available at HYPERLINK "http://www.pewresearch.org/" www.pewresearch.org.

Koenig, Barbara A., Sandra Soo-Jin Lee, and **Sarah S. Richardson,** eds. 2008. *Revisiting race in a genomic age.* New Brunswick, NJ: Rutgers University Press.

Kohlberg, Lawrence. 1966. A cognitive-developmental analysis of children's sex-role concepts and attitudes. In Eleanor F. Maccoby, ed., *The development of sex differences.* Stanford, CA: Stanford University Press.

Kohlberg, Lawrence. 1969. Stage and sequence: The cognitive-developmental approach to socialization. In D. A. Goslin, ed., *Handbook of socialization theory and research.* Chicago: Rand McNally.

Kohlberg, Lawrence. 1981. *The philosophy of moral development.* San Francisco: Harper & Row.

Kohlberg, Lawrence, and **D. Z. Ullian.** 1974. Stages in the development of psychosexual concepts and attitudes. In R. C. Friedman, R. N. Richart, and R. L. Van de Wiele, eds., *Sex differences in behavior.* New York: John Wiley.

Kohn, Melvin L., Atsushi Naoi, Carrie Schoenbach, Carmi Schooler, and **Kazimierz M. Slomczynski.** 1990. Position in the class structure and psychological functioning in the United States, Japan, and Poland. *American Journal of Sociology,* 95:964–1008.

Kohn, Melvin L., and **Carmi Schooler.** 1973. Occupational experience and psychological functioning: An assessment of reciprocal effects. *American Sociological Review,* 38:97–118.

Kohn, Melvin L., and **Carmi Schooler.** 1982. Job conditions and personality: A longitudinal assessment of their reciprocal effects. *American Journal of Sociology,* 87:1257–86.

Kohn, Melvin L., and **Carmi Schooler.** 1983. *Work and personality: An inquiry into the impact of social stratification.* Norwood, NJ: Ablex.

Kollock, Peter. 1993. "An eye for an eye leaves everyone blind": Cooperation and accounting systems. *American Sociological Review,* 58:768–86.

Kollock, Peter. 1998. Social dilemmas: The anatomy of cooperation. *Annual Review of Sociology,* 24: 183–214.

Komarovsky, Mirra. 1991. Reflections on feminist scholarship. *Annual Review of Sociology,* 17:1–25.

Konner, Melvin. 1993. *Medicine at the crossroads: The crisis in health care.* New York: Pantheon.

Kornhauser, William. 1959. *The politics of mass society.* New York: Free Press.

Koss, Mary P., and **J. A. Gaines.** 1993. The prediction of sexual aggression by alcohol use, athletic participation and fraternity affiliation. *Journal of Interpersonal Violence,* 8:94–108.

Koss, Mary, Christine A. Gidycz, and **Nadine Wisniewski.** 1987. The scope of rape: Incidence and prevalence of sexual aggression and victimization in a national sample of higher education students. *Journal of Consulting and Clinical Psychology,* 55:162–70.

Kreider, Rose M. 2008. *Living arrangements of children: 2004.* U.S. Census Bureau, Current Population Reports, pp. 70–114. Available at http://www.census.gov/prod/2008pubs/p70-114.pdf.

Kristal, Tali. 2010. Good times, bad times: Postwar labor's share of national income in capitalist democracies. *American Sociological Review,* 75:729–63.

Kristof, Nicholas D., and **Sheryl WuDunn.** 2009. *Half the sky: Turning oppression into opportunity for women worldwide.* New York: Knopf.

Krivo, Lauren J., Ruth D. Peterson, and **Danielle C. Kuhl.** 2009. Segregation, racial structure, and neighborhood violent crime. *American Journal of Sociology,* 114(6):1765–1802.

Krivo, Lauren J., and **Ruth D. Peterson.** 1996. Extremely disadvantaged neighborhoods and urban crime. *Social Forces,* 75:619–50.

Krivo, Lauren J., and **Ruth D. Peterson.** 2000. The structural context of homicide: Accounting for racial differences in process. *American Sociological Review,* 65:547–59.

Krueger, Alan B., and **Jitka Malečková.** 2009. Attitudes and action: Public opinion and the occurrence of international terrorism. *Science,* 325:1534–36.

Kruetzen, Michael, Janet Mann, Michael R. Heithaus, Richard C. Connor, Lars Bejder, and **William B. Sherwin.** 2005. Cultural transmission of tool use in bottlenose dolphins. *Proceedings of the National Academy of Sciences,* 102(25):8939–43.

Krugman, Paul. 2010. Green eonomics: How we can afford to tackle climate change. *New York Times Magazine* (April 11):34–41, 46, 49.

Kruttschnitt, Candace, Rosemary Gartner, and **Amy Miller.** 2000. Doing her own time? Women's responses to prison in the context of the old and the new penology. *Criminology,* 38(3):681–717.

Krymkowski, Daniel H. 1991. The process of status attainment among men in Poland, the U.S., and West Germany. *American Sociological Review,* 56:46–59.

Kübler-Ross, Elisabeth. 1969. *On death and dying.* New York: Macmillan.

Kübler-Ross, Elisabeth. 1981. *Living with death and dying.* New York: Macmillan.

Kubrin, Charis E., Tim Wadsworth, and **Stephanie DiPietro.** 2006. Deindustrialization, disadvantage, and suicide among young black males. *Social Forces,* 84:1559–79.

Kuhn, Manford. 1964. Major trends in symbolic interaction theory in the past twenty-five years. *Sociological Quarterly,* 5:61–84.

Kurdek, Lawrence A. 1993. The allocation of household labor in gay, lesbian, and heterosexual married couples. *Journal of Social Issues,* 49:127–39.

Kurlychek, Megan C., and **Brian D. Johnson.** 2010. Juvenility and punishment: Sentencing juveniles in adult criminal court. *Criminology,* 48(3):725–58.

L

Lakshmi, Rama. 2010. Expanded U.S. health care may mean big business for India. *Washington Post* (March 26):A13.

Lane, Charles. 2003. Ruling is landmark victory for gay rights. *Washington Post* (June 27):A1.

Lane, Charles. 2005. 5-4 Supreme Court abolishes juvenile executions. *Washington Post* (March 2):A2.

Lane, Earl. 1998. Crisis forcasting offers new ways to predict natural or human events. *Washington Post* (January 2):A16.

Lang, O. 1946. *Chinese family and society.* New Haven, CT: Yale University Press.

Langan, Patrick A., and **David J. Levin.** 2002. Recidivism of prisoners released in 1994. Washington, DC: U.S. Department of Justice. NCJ–193427.

Lareau, Annette. 2002. Invisible inequality: Social class and child-rearing in black families and white families. *American Sociological Review,* 67(5):747–76.

Lareau, Annette. 2003. *Unequal childhoods: Class, race, and family life.* Berkeley: University of California Press.

Larson, Jan. 1992. Understanding stepfamilies. *American Demographics,* 14 (July):36–40.

Laslett, Peter. 1974. *Household and family in past time.* New York: Cambridge University Press.

Laslett, Peter. 1976. Societal development and aging. In R. Binstock and E. Shanas, eds., *Handbook of aging and the social sciences.* New York: Van Nostrand/Reinhold.

Lasswell, Harold. 1936. *Politics: Who gets what, when and how.* New York: McGraw-Hill.

Lauer, Robert H., and **Jeanette C. Lauer.** 2000. *Marriage and family: The quest for intimacy.* New York: McGraw-Hill.

Laughlin, Laura. 2011. Maternity leave and employment patterns of first-time mothers: 1961–2008. *U.S. Census Bureau Household Economic Studies* (October):1–21. P70-128. Washington, DC: U.S. Census Bureau.

Laughlin, Patrick R., Erin C. Hatch, Jonathan S. Silver, and **Lee Boh.** 2006. Groups perform better than the best individuals on letters-to-numbers problems: Effects of group size. *Journal of Personality and Social Psychology,* 90(4):644–51.

Laumann, Edward O., John H. Gagnon, Robert T. Michael, and **Stuart Michaels.** 1994. *The social organization of sexuality: Sexual practices in the United States.* Chicago: University of Chicago Press.

Lawler, Edward J. 1992. Affective attachments to nested groups: A choice-process theory. *American Sociological Review,* 57:327–29.

Lawler, Edward J., Cecilia Ridgeway, and **Barry Markovsky.** 1993. Structural social psychology and the micro-macro problem. *Sociological Theory,* 11:269–90.

Lawler, Edward J., and **Jeongkoo Yoon.** 1993. Power and the emergence of commitment behavior in negotiated exchange. *American Sociological Review,* 58:465–81.

Leary, Mark R., and **Robin M. Kowalski.** 1990. Impression management: A literature review and two-component model. *Psychological Bulletin,* 107:34–47.

Le Bon, Gustav. 1896. *The crowd: A study of the popular mind.* London: Ernest Benn.

Lee, Felicia R. 1990. "Model minority" label adds to the burdens of Asian students. *New York Times* (March 20):A14.

Lee, Gary R. 1977. *Family structure and interaction: A comparative analysis.* Philadelphia: Lippincott.

Lee, Jennifer, and **Frank D. Bean.** 2004. America's changing color lines: Immigration, race/ethnicity, and multiracial identification. *Annual Review of Sociology,* 30:221–42.

Lee, Ronald. 2003. The demographic transition: Three centuries of fundamental change. *Journal of Economic Perspectives,* 17 (Fall):167–90.

Lehman, Edward W. 1988. The theory of the state versus the state of theory. *American Sociological Review,* 53:807–23.

Leitenberg, H., and **H. Saltzman.** 2000. A statewide survey of age at first intercourse for adolescent females and age of their male partners: Relation to other risk behaviors and statutory rape implications. *Archives of Sexual Behavior,* 29(3):203–15.

Lekuton, Joseph Lemasolai. 2003. *Facing the lion: Growing up Maasai on the African savanna.* Washington, DC: National Geographic.

Lemert, Charles. 2002. *Social things.* Lanham, MD: Rowman & Littlefield.

Lemert, Edwin M. 1951. *Social pathology: A systematic approach to the theory of sociopathic behavior.* New York: McGraw-Hill.

Lemert, Edwin M. 1972. *Human deviance, social problems and social control,* 2nd ed. Englewood Cliffs, NJ: Prentice-Hall.

Lempert, Robert J., Steven W. Popper, and **Steven C. Bankes.** 2003. *Shaping the next one hundred years: New methods for quantitative, long-term policy analysis.* Santa Monica, CA: RAND.

Lengerman, Patricia Madoo, and **Gillian Niebrugge.** 2011. Contemporary feminist theory. In George Ritzer, *Sociological theory.* New York: McGraw-Hill.

Lengermann, Patricia Madoo, and **Gillian Niebrugge-Brantley.** 2011. Early women sociologists and classical sociological theory: 1830–1930. In George Ritzer, *Classical sociological theory.* New York: McGraw-Hill.

Lenski, Gerhard E. 1966. *Power and privilege.* New York: McGraw-Hill.

Lessig, Lawrence. 2008. *Remix: Making art and commerce thrive in the hybrid economy.* New York: Penguin Press.

LeVay, Simon. 1991. A difference in hypothalamic structure between heterosexual and homosexual men. *Science,* 253:1034–37.

LeVay, Simon. 1996. *Queer science: The use and abuse of research into homosexuality.* Cambridge, MA: MIT Press.

Levin, Jack, and **Jim Nolan.** 2011. *The violence of hate: Confronting racism, anti-semitism, and other forms of bigotry.* Boston: Allyn & Bacon.

Levinson, Daniel J. 1986. A conception of adult development. *American Psychologist,* 41:3–13.

Levinson, Douglas F. 2006. The genetics of depression: A review. *Biological Psychiatry ,* 60:84–92.

Levinson, Harry. 1964. Money aside, why spend life working? *National Observer* (March 9):20.

Lévi-Strauss, Claude. 1956. The family. In Harry L. Shapiro, ed., *Man, culture and society.* New York: Oxford University Press.

Lewin, Kurt, Ronald Lippitt, and **Ralph K. White.** 1939. Patterns of aggressive behavior in experimentally created "social climates." *Journal of Social Psychology,* 10:271–99.

Lewis, Jone Johnson. 2006. Women's history. http://womenshistory .about.com/od/rulers20th/a/women _heads.htm.

Lewis, Michael, Margaret Wolan Sullivan, Catherine Stanger, and **Maya Weiss.** 1989. Self-development and self-conscious emotions. *Child Development,* 60:146–56.

Lewis, Oscar. 1966. *La vida: A Puerto Rican family in the culture of poverty, San Juan and New York.* New York: Random House.

Lewontin, R. C., Steven Rose, and **Leon J. Kamin.** 1984. *Not in our genes.* New York: Pantheon.

Lichter, Daniel T., and **Rukamalie Jayakody.** 2002. Welfare reform: How do we measure success? *Annual Review of Sociology,* 28:117–41.

Lichter, Daniel T., Deborah Roempke Graefe, and **J. Brian Brown.** 2003. Is marriage a panacea? Union formation among economically disadvantaged unwed mothers. *Social Problems,* 50(1):60–86.

Lieberman, Matthew D., and **Naomi I. Eisenberger.** 2009. Pains and pleasures of social life. *Science,* 323:890–91.

Lieberson, Stanley, and **Mary C. Waters.** 1988. *From many strands: Ethnic and racial groups in contemporary America.* New York: Russell Sage Foundation.

Lieberson, Stanley, and **Mary C. Waters.** 1993. The ethnic responses of whites: What causes their instability, simplification, and inconsistency? *Social Forces,* 72:421–50.

Liebow, Elliot. 1967/2003. *Tally's corner.* Lanham, MD: Rowman & Littlefield.

Liker, Jeffrey K., Carol J. Haddad, and **Jennifer Karlin.** 1999. Perspectives on technology and work organization. *Annual Review of Sociology,* 25:575–96.

Lim, May, Richard Metzler, and **Yaneer Bar-Yam.** 2007. Global pattern formation and ethnic/cultural violence. *Science,* 317:1540–44.

Lindblom, Charles E. 1990. *Inquiry and change: The troubled attempt to understand and shape society.* New Haven, CT: Yale University Press.

Lindorff, Dave. 1992. *Marketplace medicine: The rise of the for-profit hospital chains.* New York: Bantam Books.

Link, Bruce G., Francis T. Cullen, Elmer Struening, Patrick E. Shrout, and **Bruce P. Dohrenwend.** 1989. A modified labeling theory approach to mental disorders: An empirical assessment. *American Sociological Review,* 54:400–23.

Link, Bruce G., Jerrold Mirotznik, and **Francis T. Cullen.** 1991. The effectiveness of stigma coping orientations: Can negative consequences of mental labeling be avoided? *Journal of Health and Social Behavior,* 32:302–20.

Link, Bruce G., and **Jo C. Phelan.** 1995. Social conditions as fundamental causes of disease. *Journal of Health and Social Behavior* (extra issue):80–94.

Lino, Mark. 2011. *Expenditures on children by families, 2010.* Center for Nutrition Policy and Promotion. Miscellaneous Publication No. 1528-2010. Washington, DC: U.S. Department of Agriculture.

Linton, Ralph. 1937. One hundred per cent American. *American Mercury,* 40 (April):427–29.

Lipset, Seymour Martin. 1993. Reflections on capitalism, socialism and democracy. *Journal of Democracy,* 4:43–53.

Lipset, Seymour Martin. 1994. The social requisites of democracy revisited. *American Sociological Review,* 59:1–22.

Lipset, Seymour Martin, Martin A. Trow, and **James S. Coleman.** 1956. *Union democracy.* New York: Free Press.

Liptak, Adam. 2010. Justices, 5–4, reject corporate spending limit.

New York Times (January 22). Available at www.nytimes.com/2010/01/22/us/politics/22scotus.html.

Liska, Allen E. 1986. *Perspectives on deviance.* Englewood Cliffs, NJ: Prentice-Hall.

Liska, Allen E., and **Steven F. Messner.** 1999. *Perspectives on crime and deviance.* Upper Saddle River, NJ: Prentice-Hall.

Liu, Jianguo. 2010. China's road to sustainability. *Science,* 328:50.

Lizotte, Alan J. 1978. Extra-legal factors in Chicago's criminal courts: Testing the conflict model of criminal justice. *Social Problems,* 25:564–80.

Lizza, Ryan. 2008. Battle plans: How Obama won. *The New Yorker* (November 17).

Lofquist, Daphne. 2011. Same-sex couple households. American Community Survey Briefs (September):1–4. ACSBR/10-03. Washington, DC: U.S. Census Bureau.

Logan, John R. 2010. Separate and unequal: The neighborhood gap for blacks, Hispanics and Asians in metropolitan America. In *US2010: Discover America in a new century.* Brown University: U.S. 2010 Census Project. Available at www.s4.brown.edu/us2010/.

Logan, John R. 2011. *Whose schools are failing?* Report from the US2010 Project, Brown University. Available online at: http://www.s4.brown.edu/us2010/Data/Report/report5.pdf.

London, Bruce, and **Bruce A. Williams.** 1990. National political, international dependency, and basic needs provision: A cross-national analysis. *Social Forces,* 69:565–84.

Long, Tara C., Mounir Errami, Angela C. George, Zhaohui Sun, and **Harold R. Garner.** 2009. Responding to possible plagiarism. *Science,* 323:1293–94.

Loomis, Carol J. 1988. The new J. P. Morgans. *Fortune* (February 29): 44–52.

Lopez, Julie Amparano. 1992. Study says women face glass walls

as well as ceilings. *Wall Street Journal* (March 3):B1.

Lopez Pintor, Rafael, and **Maria Gratschew.** 2002. Voter turn-out since 1945: A global report. Stockholm, Sweden: International Institute for Democracy and Electoral Assistance (International IDEA). Available at http://www.idea/int.publications/voterturnout.html.

Lorber, Judith. 1994. *Paradoxes of gender.* New Haven, CT: Yale University Press.

Lucal, Betsy. 1994. Class stratification in introductory textbooks: Relational or distributional models? *Teaching Sociology,* 22:139–50.

Lugaila, Terry A. 2003. *A child's day: 2000 (Selected indicators of child well-being).* Current Population Reports P70–89. Washington, DC: U.S. Census Bureau.

Lukes, Steven. 1977. Alienation and anomie. In *Essays in social theory.* New York: Columbia University Press.

Lukes, Steven. 2007. Power. *Contexts,* 6:59–61.

Lundman, Richard J., and **Robert L. Kaufman.** 2003. Driving while black: Effects of race, ethnicity, and gender on citizen self-reports of traffic stops and police actions. *Criminology,* 41(1):195–220.

Luo, Michael. 2006. Evangelicals debate the meaning of "Evangelical." *New York Times* (April 16): Section 4:5.

Ly, Phuong. 2003. Girls teach teen cyber gab to FBI agents: MD students help catch pedophiles on the Internet. *Washington Post* (June 4):A1.

M

Maccoby, Eleanor E., and **Carol N. Jacklin.** 1974. *The psychology of sex differences.* Stanford, CA: Stanford University Press.

MacCoun, Robert J. 1993. Drugs and the law: A psychological analysis of drug prohibition. *Psychological Bulletin,* 113:497–512.

Machin, Stephen, and **Tuomas Pekkarinen.** 2008. Global sex differences in test score variability. *Science,* 322:1331–32.

MacKinnon, Carol E., and **Donna King.** 1988. Day care: A review of literature, implications for policy, and critique of resources. *Family Relations,* 37:229–36.

Macy, Michael W. 1991. Chains of cooperation: Threshold effects in collective action. *American Sociological Review,* 56:730–47.

Maguire, Kathleen, ed. 2012. *Sourcebook of criminal justice statistics* [online]. Bureau of Justice Statistics. Available http://www .albany.edu/sourcebook/.

Mahbubani, Kishore. 2008. *The new Asian hemisphere: The irresistible shift of global power to the east.* New York: Public Affairs.

Mahoney, James. 2004. Comparative-historical methodology. *Annual Review of Sociology,* 30:81–101. Making choices. 2012. *Science,* 335:510.

Malinosky-Rummell, Robin, and **David J. Hansen.** 1993. Long-term consequences of childhood physical abuse. *Psychological Bulletin,* 114:68–79.

Manis, Jerome G., and **Bernard N. Meltzer.** 1994. Chance in human affairs. *Sociological Theory,* 12:45–56.

Mann, Arnold. 2003. Relationships matter: Impact of parental, peer factors on teen, young adult substance abuse. *NIDA Notes,* 18(2):11–13.

Mann, Charles C. 2009. Chagnon critics overstepped bounds, historian says. *Science,* 326:1466.

Mann, Leon, James W. Newton, and **J. M. Innes.** 1982. A test between deindividuation and emergent norm theories of crowd aggression. *Journal of Personality and Social Psychology,* 12:260–72.

Marger, Martin N. 2012. *Race and ethnic relations: American and global perspectives,* 9th ed. Belmont, CA: Wadsworth/Thompson.

Marsh, Herbert W. 1986. Global self-esteem: Its relation to specific facets of self-concept and their importance. *Journal of Personality and Social Psychology,* 51:1224–36.

Martin, Carol Lynn, and **Jane K. Little.** 1990. The relation of gender understanding to children's sex-typed preferences and gender stereotypes. *Child Development,* 61:1427–39.

Martin, Joyce A., Brady E. Hamilton, Stephanie J. Ventura, Michelle J. K. Osterman, Sharon Kirmeyer, T. J. Mathews, and **Elizabeth C. Wilson.** 2011. Births: Final Data for 2009. *National Vital Statistics Reports,* 60(1). Hyattsville, MD: National Center for Health Statistics.

Martin, Laura. 1983. "Eskimo words for snow": A case study in the genesis and decay of an anthropological example. *American Anthropologist,* 88:418–23.

Martin, Patricia Yancey. 2004. Gender as a social institution. *Social Forces,* 82:1249–73.

Martin, Patricia Yancey, and **Robert A. Hummer.** 1995. Fraternities and rape on campus. In Alex Thio and Thomas C. Calhoun, eds., *Readings in deviant behavior.* New York: HarperCollins.

Marty, Martin E., and **R. Scott Appleby.** 1992. *The glory and the power: The fundamentalist challenge to the modern world.* Boston: Beacon Press.

Marx, Karl. 1844/1960. Estranged labour: Economic and philosophic manuscripts of 1844. In C. W. Mills, ed., *Images of man.* New York: Braziller.

Marx, Karl. 1867/1906. *Capital,* Vol. 1. New York: Modern Library.

Marx, Karl. 1970. *Critique of Hegel's "philosophy of right."* Trans. A. O'Malley and J. O'Malley. London: Cambridge University Press.

Marx, Karl, and **Friedrich Engels.** 1848/1955. *The communist manifesto.* Ed. S. H. Beer. New York: Appleton-Century-Crofts.

Massey, Douglas S. 1990. American apartheid: Segregation and the making of the underclass. *American Journal of Sociology,* 96:329–57.

Massey, Douglas S., and **Nancy A. Denton.** 1993. *American apart-heid: Segregation and the making of the underclass.* Cambridge, MA: Harvard University Press.

Maston, Cathy, and **Patsy Klaus.** 2010. Criminal victimization in the United States, 2007. Statistical tables. Available at http://bjs.ojp.usdoj.gov/ content/pub/pdf/cvus07.pdf.

Mathews, Jay. 2003. Colleges' admissions policies to be studied. *Washington Post* (September 7):A10.

Matsueda, Ross L. 1988. The current state of differential association theory. *Crime and Delinquency,* 34:277–306.

Matsueda, Ross L., and **Karen Heimer.** 1987. Race, family structure, and delinquency: A test of differential association and social control theories. *American Sociological Review,* 52:826–40.

Maxwell, Sheila Royo, and **Christopher D. Maxwell.** 2000. Examining the "criminal careers" of prostitutes within the nexus of drug use, drug selling, and other illicit activities. *Criminology,* 38(3):787–809.

Mayer, Karl Ulrich. 2009. New directions in life course research. *Annual Review of Sociology,* 35: 413–33.

Mazur, Allan. 1985. A biosocial model of status in face-to-face primate groups: Social groups. *Social Forces,* 64:377–402.

Mazus, Alexey. 2011. AIDS prevention plans must reflect local values. *Science,* 332:173.

McAdam, Doug, and **Ronnelle Paulsen.** 1993. Specifying the relationship between social ties and activism. *American Journal of Sociology,* 99:640–67.

McCabe, Donald L., Kenneth D. Butterfield, and **Linda Klebe Trevino.** 2006. Academic dishonesty in graduate business programs: Prevalence, causes and proposed action. *Academy of Management Learning and Education,* 5:294–305.

McCarthy, Bill. 2002. The new economics of sociological criminology. *Annual Review of Sociology,* 28: 417–42.

McCarthy, Ellen. 2009. What's going down on the "Marriage-Go-Round"? *Washington Post* (June 28):E5.

McCauley, Clark. 1989. The nature of social influence in groupthink: Compliance and internalization. *Journal of Personality and Social Psychology,* 57:250–60.

McClellan, Jon M., Ezra Susser, and **Mary-Claire King.** 2007. Schizophrenia: A common disease caused by multiple rare alleles. *British Journal of Psychiatry,* 190:194–99.

McConahay, John B. 1986. Modern racism, ambivalence, and the modern racism scale. In John F. Dovidio and Samuel Gaertner, eds., *Prejudice, discrimination, and racism.* Orlando, FL: Academic Press.

McCright, Aaron M., and **Riley E. Dunlap.** 2011. The politicization of climate change and polarization in the American public's views of global warming, 2001–2010. *Sociological Quarterly* 52:155–194.

McFalls, Joseph A., Jr. 2003. *Population: A lively introduction.* Washington, DC: Population Reference Bureau.

McGee, Reece. 1975. *Points of departure.* Hinsdale, IL: Dryden Press.

McGeehan, Patrick. 2003. Executive pay: A special report; again, money follows the pinstripes. *New York Times* (April 6):C1.

McGowan, Patrick O., Aya Sasaki, Ana C. D'Alessio, Sergiy Dymov, Benoit Labonté, Moshe Szyf, Gustavo Turecki, and **Michael J. Meaney.** 2009. Epigenetic regulation of the glucocorticoid receptor in human brain associates with childhood abuse. *Nature Neuroscience,* 12:342–48.

McGrew, William C. 2010. Chimpanzee technology. *Science,* 328:579–80.

McGuire, Meredith B. 1981. *Religion: The social context.* Belmont, CA: Wadsworth.

McKinnon, Jessie. 2003. *The black population in the United States: March 2002.* Current Population Reports P20–541. Washington, DC: U.S. Census Bureau.

McLaurin, Melton. 1992. Songs of the South: The changing image of the South in country music. In Melton McLaurin and Richard A. Peterson, eds., *You wrote my life: Lyrical themes in country music.* Philadelphia: Gordon & Breach.

McManus, Patricia A., and **Thomas A. DiPrete.** 2001. Losers and winners: The financial consequences of separation and divorce for men. *American Sociological Review,* 66:246–68.

McMichael, A. J., C. D. Butler, and **Carl Folke.** 2003. New visions for addressing sustainability. *Science,* 302:1919–20.

McMillen, Matt. 2003. Knowing, not doing: Study measures gap between medical knowledge, practice. *Washington Post* (September 30):F1.

McMunn, Anne, Mel Bartley, Rebecca Hardy, and **Diana Kuh.** 2006. Life course social roles and women's health in mid-life: causation or selection? *Journal of Epidemiology and Community Health,* 60: 484–89.

McPhail, Clark. 1989. Blumer's theory of collective behavior: The development of a non-symbolic interaction explanation. *Sociological Quarterly,* 30:401–23.

Mead, George Herbert. 1934/1962. *Mind, self, and other.* Chicago: University of Chicago Press.

Mechanic, David. 2008. *Mental health and social policy: Beyond managed care.* Boston: Allyn & Bacon.

Medlin, Richard G. 2000. Home schooling and the question of socialization. *Peabody Journal of Education,* 75:107–24.

Mehan, Hugh. 1992. Understanding inequality in schools: The contribution of interpretive studies. *Sociology of Education,* 65:1–20.

Mehrahian, Albert. 1968. Communication without words. *Psychology Today,* 2 (September):53–55.

Meier, Ann M. 2003. Adolescents' transition to first intercourse, religiosity, and attitudes about sex. *Social Forces,* 81(3):1031–52.

Melloan, George. 1993. Why America tops Europe in job creation. *Wall Street Journal* (December 13): A15.

Menaghan, Elizabeth G. 1991. Work experiences and family interaction processes: The long reach of the job? *Annual Review of Sociology,* 17:419–44.

Menn, Joseph. 2010. *Fatal system error: The hunt for the new crime lords who are bringing down the Internet.* New York: Public Affairs.

Merton, Robert. 1968. *Social theory and social structure,* rev. ed. New York: Free Press.

Merton, Robert K. 1995. The Thomas Theorem and the Matthew Effect. *Social Forces,* 74:379–422.

Mervis, Jeffrey. 2010. Trends document China's prowess. *Science,* 327:407.

Mervis, Jeffrey. 2011a. Weed-out courses hamper diversity. *Science,* 334:1333.

Mervis, Jeffrey. 2011b. NSF touts family-friendly policies as boon to women. *Science,* 333:1811.

Messner, Steven F., and **Marvin D. Krohn.** 1990. Class, compliance structures, and delinquency: Assessing integrated structural-Marxist theory. *American Journal of Sociology,* 96:300–28.

Messner, Steven F., and **Richard Rosenfeld.** 1997a. *Crime and the American dream,* 2nd ed. Belmont, CA: Wadsworth.

Messner, Steven F., and **Richard Rosenfeld.** 1997b. Political restraint of the market and levels of criminal homicide: A cross-national application of institutional-anomie theory. *Social Forces,* 75:1393–16.

Mettler, Suzanne. 2011. *The submerged state: How invisible government policies undermine American democracy.* Chicago: University of Chicago Press.

Michael, Robert T., John H. Gagnon, Edward O. Laumann, and **Gina Kolata.** 1994. *Sex in America.* Boston: Little, Brown.

Michael, Robert T., Victor R. Fuchs, and **Sharon R. Scott.** 1980. Changes in the propensity to live alone: 1950–1976. *Demography,* 17:39–56.

Michel, Jean-Baptiste, Yuan Kui Shen, Aviva Presser Aiden, Adrian Veres, et al. 2011. Quantitative analysis of culture using millions of digitized books. *Science,* 331:176–82.

Michels, Robert. 1911/1966. *Political parties.* New York: Free Press.

Middleton, Russell. 1962. A deviant case: Brother–sister and father–daughter marriage in ancient Egypt. *American Sociological Review,* 27:603–11.

Milgram, Stanley. 1963. Behavioral study of obedience. *Journal of Abnormal and Social Psychology,* 67(4):371–78.

Milgram, Stanley. 1964. Group pressure and action against a person. *Journal of Abnormal and Social Psychology,* 69(2):137–43.

Milgram, Stanley. 1977. *The individual in a social world.* Reading, MA: Addison-Wesley.

Milgram, Stanley, and **Hans Toch.** 1969. Collective behavior: Crowds and social movements. In G. Lindzey and E. Aronson, eds., *The handbook of social psychology,* 2nd ed., Vol. 2. Reading, MA: Addison-Wesley.

Milkie, Melissa A., Sara B. Raley, and **Suzanne M. Bianchi.** 2009. Taking on the second shift: Time allocations and time pressures of U.S. parents with preschoolers. *Social Forces,* 88(2):487–517.

Miller, Eleanor M., and **Carrie Yang Costello.** 2001. Comment: The limits of biological determinism. *American Sociological Review,* 66:592–98.

Miller, Greg. 2011a. The brain's social network. *Science,* 334:578–79.

Miller, Greg. 2011b. Using the psychology of evil to do good. *Science,* 332:530–32.

Miller, Judith. 1992. The Islamic wave. *New York Times Magazine* (May 31):23–42.

Mills, C. Wright. 1956. *The power elite.* New York: Oxford University Press.

Mills, C. Wright. 1959. *The sociological imagination.* New York: Oxford University Press.

Milner, Murray, Jr. 1987. Theories of inequality: An overview and a strategy for synthesis. *Social Forces,* 65:1053–89.

Miniño, A. M., M. P. Heron, and **B. L. Smith.** 2006. Deaths: preliminary data for 2004. *National Vital Statistics Report* 54(19): 1–50. Available at http://www .cdc.gov/nchs/data/nvsr/nvsr54/ nvsr54_19.pdf.

Mintz, Beth, and **Michael Schwartz.** 1985. *The power of American business.* Chicago: University of Chicago Press.

Mirowsky, John, and **Catherine E. Ross.** 2003. *Education, social status, and health.* New York: Aldine de Gruyter.

Mischel, Walter. 1970. Sex-typing and socialization. In P. H. Mussen, ed., *Carmichael's manual of child psychology,* 3rd ed., Vol. 2. New York: John Wiley.

Moaddel, Mansoor. 1992. Ideology as episodic discourse: The case of the Iranian revolution. *American Sociological Review,* 57:353–79.

Moaddel, Mansoor. 1994. Political conflict in the world economy: A cross-national analysis of modernization and world-system theories. *American Sociological Review,* 59:276–303.

Moffatt, Michael. 1989. *Coming of age in New Jersey.* New Brunswick, NJ: Rutgers University Press.

Moffitt, Terrie. 2005. The new look of behavioral genetics in developmental psychopathology: Gene-environment interplay in antisocial behaviors. *Psychological Bulletin,* 131:533–54.

Mohai, Paul, and **Robin Saha.** 2007. Racial inequality in the distribution of hazardous waste: A national-level reassessment. *Social Problems,* 54:343–70.

Moller, Stephanie, Arthur S. Alderson, and **Francois Nielsen.** 2009. Changing patterns of income inequality in U.S. counties, 1970–2000. *American Journal of Sociology,* 114(4):1037–101.

Moller, Stephanie, Evelyne Huber, John D. Stephens, David Bradley, and **Francois Nielsen.** 2003. Determinants of relative poverty in advanced capitalist democracies. *American Sociological Review,* 68:22–51.

Molm, Linda D. 1991. Affect and social exchange: Satisfaction in power-dependence relations. *American Sociological Review,* 56:475–93.

Molnar, Stephen. 1997. *Human variation.* Upper Saddle River, NJ: Prentice-Hall.

Moody, James, and **Douglas R. White.** 2003. Structural cohesion and embeddedness: A hierarchical concept of social groups. *American Sociological Review,* 68:103–27.

Morello, Carol. 2010. Results of polls on job satisfaction are at odds. *Washington Post* (January 6):A3.

Morin, Richard. 1998. The new great divide: More and more, where you live depends on what you're worth. *Washington Post Magazine* (January 18):14.

Morin, Richard, and **Alan Cooperman.** 2003. Majority against blessing gay unions. *Washington Post* (August 14):A1.

Morrill, Calvin, Mayer N. Zald, and **Hayagreeva Rao.** 2003. Covert political conflict in organizations: Challenges from below. *Annual Review of Sociology,* 29:391–415.

Morris, Aldon D. 1993. Birmingham confrontation reconsidered: An analysis of the dynamics and tactics of mobilization. *American Sociology Review,* 58:621–36.

Morrison, Donna Ruane, and **Amy Ritualo.** 2000. Routes to children's economic recovery after divorce: Are cohabitation and remarriage equivalent? *American Sociological Review,* 65:560–80.

Mortimer, Jeylan T., and **Roberta G. Simmons.** 1978. Adult socialization. *Annual Review of Sociology,* 4:421–54.

Moskos, Peter. 2009. If it's on the shelves, it's off the streets. *Washington Post* (October 25):4B.

Moskowitz, Breyne Arlene. 1978. The acquisition of language. *Scientific American, 239* (November):92–108.

Móuzelis, Nicos. 1992. The interaction order and the micro-macro distinction. *Sociological Theory,* 10:122–28.

Moynihan, Ray, and **Alan Cassels.** 2005. *Selling sickness: How the world's biggest pharmaceutical companies are turning us all into patients.* New York: Nation Books.

Mura, David. 1992. Bashed in the U.S.A. *New York Times* (April 2):A15.

Murdock, George P. 1934. *Our primitive contemporaries.* New York: Macmillan.

Murdock, George P. 1937. Comparative data on the division of labor by sex. *Social Forces,* 15:551–53.

Murdock, George P. 1949. *Social structure.* New York: Macmillan.

Murdock, George P. 1950. Feasibility and implementation of comparative community research. *American Sociological Review,* 15:713–20.

Murdock, George P. 1967. *Ethnographic atlas.* Pittsburgh: University of Pittsburgh Press.

Murphy, Caryle. 1997. U.S. Catholic bishops urge acceptance of gay orientation. *Washington Post* (October 1):A1.

Murphy, Sherry L., Jiaquan Xu, and **Kenneth D. Kochanek.** 2012. Deaths: Preliminary Data for 2010. *National Vital Statistics Reports* 60 (No. 4, January).

Murray, Charles. 1994. Does welfare bring more babies? *American Enterprise,* 5 (January–February): 52–59.

Murray, Sandra L., Dale W. Griffin, Paul Rose, and **Gina M. Bellavia.** 2003. Calibrating the sociometer: The relational contingencies of self-esteem. *Journal of Personality and Social Psychology,* 85(1):63–84.

Murstein, Bernard I. 1972. Physical attractiveness and marital choice. *Journal of Personality and Social Psychology,* 22:8–12.

Musick, Kelly, and **Larry Bumpass.** 1999. How do prior experiences in the family affect transitions to adulthood? In Alan Booth, Ann C. Crouter, and Michael J. Shanahan, eds., *Transitions to adulthood in a changing economy: No work, no family, no future?* Westport, CT: Praeger.

Musto, David F. 1987. *The American disease: Origins of narcotic control.* New York: Oxford University Press.

Myrdal, Gunnar. 1944. *An American dilemma.* New York: Harper.

Myrskylä, Mikko, Hans-Peter Kohler, and **Francesco C. Billari.** 2009. Advances in development reverse fertility declines. *Nature,* 460:741–43.

N

NACCRRA. 2009. Child care in America fact sheet. April 14. The Nation's Network of Child Care Resources and Referral.

Nagel, Joane. 1994. *American Indian ethnic renewal: Red power and the transformation of identity and culture.* New York: Oxford University Press.

Naimi, Timothy S., Robert D. Brewer, Ali Mokdad, Clark Denny, Mary K. Serdula, and **James S. Marks.** 2003. Binge drinking among U.S. adults. *Journal of the American Medical Association,* 289(1):70–75.

Nanda, Serena, and **Richard L. Warms.** 2011. *Cultural anthropology,* 10th ed. Belmont, CA: Wadsworth/Thomson Learning.

Naqvi, Muneeza. 2005. Short of brides, Indians turn to brokers: In rural Punjab province, preference for sons has led to population imbalance. *Washington Post* (December 5):A15.

Nash, J. Madeleine. 1997. Fertile minds: From birth a baby's brain cells proliferate wildly, making connections that may shape a lifetime of experience. The first three years are critical. *Time* (February 3):49–56.

National Association of Charter School Authorizers. 2012. *The state of charter school authorizing 2011: Fourth annual report on NACSA'S Authorizer Survey.* Available at http://www.qualitycharters.org/images/stories/pdfs/publications/nacsa2011_state_of_charter_school_authorizing.pdf.

National Center for Education Statistics. 2012. NCES Table 41. Available at http://nces.ed.gov/programs/digest/d10/tables/dt10_041.asp.

National Center for Health Statistics. 2010. *Health, United States, 2009.* Hyattsville, MD: Public Health Service.

National Low Income Housing Coalition. 2010. *Out of reach 2010.* Available at http://www.nlihc.org/oor/oor2010/.

Nazario, Sonia L. 1992. Medical science seeks a cure for doctors suffering from boorish bedside manner. *Wall Street Journal* (March 17):B1.

NCCIC. 2008. Statistical Information on Child Care in the United States. Available at http://nccic.acf.hhs.gov.

Needleman, Herbert L., and **David Bellinger,** eds. 1994. *Prenatal exposure to toxicants: Developmental consequences.* Baltimore, MD: Johns Hopkins University Press.

Neil, Cecily C., and **William E. Snizek.** 1988. Gender as a moderator of job satisfaction: A multivariate assessment. *Work and Occupations,* 15:201–19.

Nelson, Mariah Burton. 1994. *The stronger women get, the more men love football: Sexism and the*

American culture of sports. New York: Harcourt Brace.

Nelson, Sandi, Rebecca L. Clark, and **Gregory Acs.** 2001. *Beyond the two-parent family: How teenagers fare in cohabiting couple and blended families.* Washington, DC: The Urban Institute. New Federalism: National Survey of America's Families, No. B-31.

Nelson, Toben F., and **Henry Wechsler.** 2001. Alcohol and college athletes. *Medicine and Science in Sports and Exercise,* 33:43–47.

Nestler, Eric J. 2001. Total recall—the memory of addiction. *Science,* 292:2266–67.

Neugarten, Bernice L., and **Dail A. Neugarten.** 1987a. *Forum,* 62:25–27.

Neugarten, Bernice L., and **Dail A. Neugarten.** 1987b. The changing meanings of age. *Psychology Today,* 21 (May):29–33.

Neuhouser, Kevin. 1992. Democratic stability in Venezuela: Elite consensus or class compromise? *American Sociological Review,* 57:117–35.

Newcomb, Theodore M. 1950. *Social Psychology.* New York: Holt, Rinehart & Winston.

New long-term study of a generation announced. 2011. *Science,* 331:1246.

Newman, Katherine S. 2003. *A different shade of gray: Midlife and beyond in the inner city.* New York: New Press.

Newport, Frank, and **Lydia Saad.** 1997. Religious faith is widespread but many skip church. Gallup poll press release, March 29, 1997.

Newton, Michael. 2004. *Savage girls and wild boys: A history of feral children.* New York: Picador.

NICHD (Eunice Kennedy Shriver National Institute of Child Health and Human Development), NIH, DHHS. 2007. The NICHD study of early child care and youth development (SECCYD): Findings for children up to age 4 1/2 years (05–4318). Washington, DC: U.S. Government Printing Office.

Nielsen, Joyce McCarl, Glenda Walden, and **Charlotte A. Kunkel.**

2000. Gendered heteronormativity: Empirical illustrations in everyday life. *Sociological Quarterly,* 41(2):283–96.

Niemiec, Christopher P., Richard M. Ryan, and **Edward L. Deci.** 2009. The path taken: Consequences of attaining intrinsic and extrinsic aspirations in post-college life. *Journal of Research in Personality,* 43:291–306.

Nisbett, Richard E. 1998. Race, genetics, and IQ. In Christopher Jencks and Meredith Phillips, eds., *The black-white test score gap.* Washington, DC: Brookings Institution Press.

Niven, David. 1999. Partisan bias in the media? A new test. *Social Science Quarterly,* 80(4):847–57.

Noble, Kenneth B. 1989. Low commodity prices vex life in Ivory Coast. *New York Times* (November 19):6.

Noel, Donald L. 1968. A theory of the origin of ethnic stratification. *Social Problems,* 16:157–62.

Noel, Donald M. 1972. *The origins of American slavery and racism.* Columbus, OH: Charles E. Merrill.

Nolan, Martin F. 1997. Tiger's racial multiplicity. *Boston Globe* (April 26):A11.

Nolan, Patrick, and **Gerhard E. Lenski.** 2010. *Human societies: Introduction to macrosociology,* 11th ed. Boulder, CO: Paradigm.

Noonan, Mary C., Mary E. Corcoran, and **Paul N. Courant.** 2005. Pay differences among the highly trained: Cohort differences in the sex gap in lawyers' earnings. *Social Forces,* 84:853–72.

Normile, Dennis. 2008. China's living laboratory in urbanization. *Science,* 319:740–43.

Normile, Dennis, Gretchen Vogel, and **Jennifer Couzin.** 2006. South Korean team's remaining human stem cell claim demolished. *Science,* 311:156–57.

Norris, Tina, Paula L. Vines, and **Elizabeth M. Hoeffel.** 2012. The American Indian and Alaska Native population: 2010. 2010 Census Briefs

(January):1–21. C2010BR-10. Washington, DC: U.S. Census Bureau.

Nottelmann, Editha D. 1987. Competence and self-esteem during transition from childhood to adolescence. *Development Psychology,* 23:441–50.

Nuland, Sherwin B. 1994. *Reflections on life's final chapter.* New York: Knopf.

Nussbaum, Emily. 2004. My so-called blog. *The New York Times Magazine* (January 11):32–37.

O

O'Connor, Alice. 2000. Poverty research and policy for the post-welfare era. *Annual Review of Sociology,* 26:547–62.

O'Connor, James. 1973. *The fiscal crisis of the state.* New York: St. Martin's Press.

O'Dell, Jerry W. 1968. Group size and emotional interaction. *Journal of Personality and Social Psychology,* 8:75–78.

Oeppen, Jim, and **James W. Vaupel.** 2002. Broken limits to life expectancy. *Science,* 296:1029–31.

O'Fallon, Brendan D., and **Lars Fehren-Schmitz.** 2011. Native Americans experienced a strong population bottleneck coincident with European contact. *Proceedings of the National Academy of Sciences,* 108(51):20444–48.

Offer, Shira, and **Barbara Schneider.** 2012. Revisiting the gender gap in time-use patterns: Multitasking and well-being among mothers and fathers in dual-earner families. *American Sociological Review,* 76(6):809–33.

Ogburn, William F. 1922. *Social change.* New York: Hoebsch.

Ogunwole, Stella. 2006. *We the people: American Indians and Alaska Natives in the United States.* U.S. Census Bureau, Census 2000 Special Reports, CENSR-28. Washington D.C: U.S. Government Printing Office. Available at http://www.census.gov/prod/2006pubs/censr-28.pdf.

O'Hare, William P., and **Judy C. Felt.** 1991. Asian Americans: America's fastest growing minority group. *Population Trends and Public Policy.* Population Reference Bureau, No. 19.

O'Harrow, Robert, Jr. 2003. Identity crisis. *Washington Post Magazine* (August 10):14–18, 23–29.

Oliver, Pamela E., and Gerald Marwell. 1988. The paradox of group size in collective action: A theory of the critical mass. II. *American Sociological Review, 53:*1–8.

Olsen, Marvin E. 1970. *Power in societies.* New York: Macmillan.

Olson, Daniel V. A., and Jackson W. Carroll. 1992. Religiously based politics: Religious elites and the public. *Social Forces, 70:*765–86.

Olson, David H., and John DeFrain. 1997. *Marriage and the family: Diversity and strengths*, 2nd ed. Mountain View, CA: Mayfield.

Olson, David J., and Philip Meyer. 1975. *To keep the republic.* New York: McGraw-Hill.

Olzak, Susan. 1990. The political context of competition: Lynching and urban racial violence, 1882–1914. *Social Forces,* 69:395–421.

Olzak, Susan. 1992. *The dynamics of ethnic competition and conflict.* Stanford, CA: Stanford University Press.

Omi, Michael, and Howard Winant. 1994. *Racial formation in the United States from the 1960s to the 1990s,* 2nd ed. New York: Routledge.

Oppenheimer, Jerry. 2009. *Madoff with the money.* New York: John Wiley and Sons.

Orcutt, James D. 1987. Differential association and marijuana use: A closer look at Sutherland (with a little help from Becker). *Criminology,* 25:341–58.

Orfield, Gary, Daniel Losen, Johanna Wald, and Christopher B. Swanson. 2004. *Losing our future: How minority youth are being left behind by the graduation rate crisis.* The Urban Institute (http://www.urban.org/url.cfm?ID=410936).

Ortner, Sherry. 1996. *Making gender: The politics and erotics of culture.* Boston: Beacon Press.

Osgood, D. Wayne, Janet K. Wilson, Patrick M. O'Malley, Jerald G. Bachman, and Lloyd D. Johnston. 1996. Routine activities and individual deviant behavior. *American Sociological Review,* 61:635–55.

Ostrom, Elinor. 1990. *Governing the commons: The evolution of institutions for collective action.* New York: Cambridge University Press.

P

Packer, George. 2005. *The Assassins' Gate: America in Iraq.* New York: Farrar, Straus, & Giroux.

Page, Clarence. 1997. Grappling with the "one-drop" rule. *Chicago Tribune* (April 27):C19.

Page, Jake. 2003. *In the hands of the Great Spirit: The 20,000 year history of American Indians.* New York: Free Press.

Pager, Devah. 2003. The mark of a criminal record. *American Journal of Sociology,* 108(5):937–75.

Pager, Devah, and Lincoln Quillian. 2005. Walking the talk: What employers say versus what they do. *American Sociological Review,* 70:355–80.

Palermo, Tia. 2012. Counting sexual violence in Congo. *Contexts,* 11(1):10–11.

Pampel, Fred C. 2006. *Sociological lives and ideas: An introduction to the classical theorists*, 2nd ed. New York: Worth.

Pampel, Fred. 2011. Cohort changes in the socio-demographic determinants of gender egalitarianism. *Social Forces,* 89(3):961–82.

Pampel, Fred C., and H. Elizabeth Peters. 1995. The Easterlin effect. *Annual Review of Sociology,* 21:163–94.

Pape, Robert A. 2005. *Dying to win: The strategic logic of suicide terrorism.* New York: Random House.

Pape, Robert A., and James K. Feldman. 2010. *The explosion of global suicide terrorism and how to stop it.* Chicago: University of Chicago Press.

Parcel, Toby L., and Elizabeth G. Menaghan. 1994. Early parental work, family social capital, and early childhood outcomes. *American Journal of Sociology,* 99: 972–1009.

Park, Robert E., Ernest W. Burgess, and Roderick D. McKenzie. 1925. *The city.* Chicago: University of Chicago Press.

Park, Sangyoub. 2011. A 21st century gender revolution. *Contexts,* 10(1):58–59.

Parker, Kim. 2012. *The Boomerang Generation: Feeling OK about Living with Mom and Dad.* Pew Research Center. Available at http://www.pewsocialtrends.org/files/2012/03/PewSocialTrends-2012-Boomerang-Generation.pdf.

Parkinson, C. Northcote. 1962. *Parkinson's law.* Boston: Houghton Mifflin.

Parsons, Talcott. 1940. An analytical approach to the theory of social stratification. *American Journal of Sociology,* 45:841–62.

Parsons, Talcott. 1949. *The structure of social action,* 2nd ed. New York: McGraw-Hill.

Parsons, Talcott. 1951. *The social system.* New York: Free Press.

Parsons, Talcott. 1953. A revised analytical approach to the theory of social stratification. In Reinhard Bendix and Seymour M. Lipset, eds., *Class status and power: A reader in social stratification.* Glencoe, IL: Free Press.

Parsons, Talcott. 1966. *Societies: Evolutionary and comparative perspectives.* Englewood Cliffs, NJ: Prentice-Hall.

Parsons, Talcott. 1977. On building social system theory: A personal history. In Talcott Parsons, ed., *Social systems and evolution of action theory.* New York: Free Press.

Parsons, Talcott, and Robert F. Bales. 1955. *Family socialization and interaction process.* New York: Free Press.

Partlow, Joshua, and William Booth. 2009. Poverty, tendency to self-medicate help drive up flu deaths in Mexico. *Washington Post* (May 5):A1, A10.

Pastore, Ann L. and Kathleen Maguire, eds. 2010. *Sourcebook of criminal justice statistics,* Available at http://www.albany.edu/sourcebook/.

Paternoster, Raymond. 1989. Absolute and restrictive deterrence in a panel of youth: Explaining the onset, persistence/desistance, and frequency of delinquent offending. *Social Problems,* 36:289–309.

Patterson, Orlando. 1991. *Freedom.* Vol. 1: *Freedom in the making of Western culture.* New York: Basic Books.

Paulus, P. B. 1998. Developing consensus about groupthink after all these years. *Organizational Behavior and Human Decision Processes,* 73(2–3):362–74.

Pavcnik, Nina. 2011. Globalization and within-country income inequality, pp. 233–60, in *Making globalization socially sustainable,* ed. Marc Bacchetta and Marion Jansen. Geneva, Switzerland: World Trade Organization. Available at http://www.ilo.org/global/publications/books/WCMS_170985/lang—en/index.htm

Paxton, Pamela, and **Sheri Kunovich.** 2003. Women's political representation: The importance of ideology. *Social Forces,* 82(1): 87–114.

PBS. 2005. Poll: Americans idealize traditional family, even as nontraditional families are more accepted. *Faith and Family in America* (October 19):episode no. 908.

Peen, J., R. A. Scoevers, A. T. Beekman, and **J. Dekker.** 2010. The current status of urban-rural differences in psychiatric disorders. *Acta Psychiatr Scand,* 121:84–93.

Pennisi, Elizabeth. 2010. Conquering by copying. *Science,* 328:165–67.

Perkins, Kevin L., and **Anthony P. Placido.** 2010. Testimony. U.S. Senate Caucus on International Narcotics Control. Washington, DC: Drug Enforcement Agency. Available at http://www.fbi.gov/news/testimony/

drug-trafficking-violence-in-mexico-implications-for-the-united-states.

Perrow, Charles. 1982. Disintegrating social sciences. *Phi Delta Kappan,* 63:684–88.

Perrow, Charles. 1986. *Complex organizations.* New York: Random House.

Perry, Bruce D., Ronnie A. Pollard, Toi L. Blakley, William L. Baker, et al. 1995. Childhood trauma, the neurobiology of adaptation, and "use-dependent" development of the brain: How "states" become "traits." *Infant Mental Health Journal,* 16:271–91.

Perry, Susan, and **Joseph H. Manson.** 2003. Traditions in monkeys. *Evolutionary Anthropology,* 12:71–81.

Petersen, Melody. 2008. *Our daily meds: How the pharmaceutical companies transformed themselves into slick marketing machines and hooked the nation on prescription drugs.* New York: Farrar Straus Giroux.

Petersen, Trond. 1992. Individual, collective, and systems rationality in work groups: Dilemmas and market-type solutions. *American Journal of Sociology,* 98:469–510.

Peterson, Richard A. 1979. Revitalizing the culture concept. *Annual Review of Sociology,* 5:137–66.

Peterson, Richard A. 1982. Five constraints on the production of culture: Law, technology, market, organizational structure and occupational careers. *Journal of Popular Culture,* 16:143–53.

Peterson, Richard A. 2002. Roll over Beethoven, there's a new way to be cool. *Contexts,* 1 (Summer):34–39.

Peterson, Richard A., and **N. Anand.** 2004. The production of culture perspective. *Annual Review of Sociology,* 30:311–34.

Peterson, Ruth D. 1992. Rape and dimensions of gender socioeconomic inequality in U.S. metropolitan areas. *Journal of Research on Crime and Delinquency,* 29:162–77.

Peterson, Ruth D., and **Lauren J. Krivo.** 2005. Macrostructural analyses

of race, ethnicity, and violent crime: Recent lessons and new directions for research. *Annual Review of Sociology,* 31:331–56.

Petterson, Stephen M. 1997. Are young black men really less willing to work? *American Sociological Review,* 62:605–13.

Pettigrew, Thomas F., and **Joanne Martin.** 1987. Shaping the organizational context for black American inclusion. *Journal of Social Issues,* 43:41–78.

Pettigrew, Thomas J. 1967. Social evaluation theory: Convergences and applications. *Nebraska Symposium on Motivation,* 15, 241–311.

Pew Forum on Religion and Public Life. 2010. Religious groups' official positions on same-sex marriage (July 27). Pew Research Center. Available at http://www.pewforum.org/Gay-Marriage-and-Homosexuality/Religious-Groups-Official-Positions-on-Same-Sex-Marriage.aspx.

Pew Forum on Religion and Public Life. 2012. Religion and attitudes toward same-sex marriage (February 7). Pew Research Center. Available at http://www.pewforum.org/Gay-Marriage-and-Homosexuality/Religion-and-Attitudes-Toward-Same-Sex-Marriage.aspx.

Pew Research Center for the People and the Press. 2009a. Most still oppose same-sex marriage: Results from the 2009 Annual Religion and Public Life Survey. Available at http://people-press.org/reports/pdf/553.pdf.

Pew Research Center for the People and the Press. 2009b. Press accuracy rating hits two decade low: Public evaluations of the news media: 1985–2009. (September 13). Available at http://people-press.org/report/543/.

Pew Research Center. 2003. Religion and politics: Contention and consensus. Available at www.pewforum.org/PublicationPage.aspx?id=621.

Pew Research Center. 2008. *U.S. Religious Landscape Survey 2008.*

The Pew Forum on Religion and Public Life.

Pew Research Center. 2009. Modest support for "cap and trade" policy: Fewer Americans see solid evidence of global warming. *Survey Reports* (October 22). Available at http://www.people-press.org/files/legacy-pdf/556.pdf.

Pew Research Center. 2011. Wealth gaps rise to record highs between whites, blacks and Hispanics. *Social & Demographic Trends.*

Phelan, Jo C., Bruce G. Link, Ana Diez-Roux, Ichiro Kawachi, and **Bruce Levin.** 2004. "Fundamental causes" of social inequalities in mortality: A test of the theory. *Journal of Health and Social Behavior,* 45: 265–85.

Phillips, Scott. 2009. Status disparities in the capital of capital punishment. *Law & Society,* 43(4):807–38.

Piaget, Jean. 1926/1955. *The language and thought of the child.* New York: New American Library.

Pianta, Robert C., Jay Belsky, Renate Houts, Fred Morrison, and **The National Institute of Child Health and Human Development (NICHD) Early Child Care Research Network.** 2007. Opportunities to learn in America's elementary classrooms. *Science,* 315:1795–96.

Piketty, Thomas, and **Emmanuel Saez.** 2007. Income inequality in the United States, 1913–2002. In A. B. Atkinson and Thomas Piketty, eds., *Top incomes over the twentieth century: A contrast between continental European and English-speaking countries.* New York: Oxford University Press.

Pill, Cynthia J. 1990. Stepfamilies: Redefining the family. *Family Relations,* 39:186–93.

Pink, Daniel. 2009. *Drive: The surprising truth about what motivates us.* New York: Riverhead Books.

Pinker, Steven. 1994. *The language instinct.* New York: William Morrow.

Pinker, Steven. 2002. *The blank slate: The modern denial of human nature.* New York: Viking.

Pinker, Steven. 2007. *The stuff of thought: Language as a window into human nature.* New York: Viking.

Pipher, Mary. 1994. *Reviving Ophelia: Saving the selves of adolescent girls.* New York: Ballantine Books.

Pipher, Mary. 1997. *The shelter of each other.* New York: Ballantine Books.

Plumb, J. H. 1972. *Children.* London: Penguin Books.

Poe, Marshall T. 2011. *A history of communications: Media and society from the evolution of speech to the Internet.* Cambridge: Cambridge University Press.

Pope, Whitney. 1976. *Durkheim's suicide: A classic analyzed.* Chicago: University of Chicago Press.

Popper, Karl. 1963. *Conjectures and refutations: The growth of scientific knowledge.* London: Routledge & Kegan Paul.

Portes, Alejandro. 1987. The social origins of the Cuban enclave economy in Miami. *Sociological Perspectives,* 30:340–72.

Portes, Alejandro, and **Robert L. Bach.** 1985. *Latin journey: Cuban and Mexican immigrants in the United States.* Berkeley: University of California Press.

Portes, Alejandro, and **Leif Jensen.** 1989. The enclave and the entrants: Patterns of ethnic enterprise in Miami before and after Mariel. *American Sociological Review,* 54:929–49.

Portes, Alejandro, and **Kenneth L. Wilson.** 1976. Black-white differences in educational attainment. *American Sociological Review,* 41:414–31.

Poteete, Amy R., Marco A. Janssen, and **Elinor Ostrom.** 2010. *Working together: Collective action, the commons, and multiple methods in practice.* Princeton, NJ: Princeton University Press.

Potok, Mark. 2008. Hate rises. *Washington Post* (March 9):B2.

Pressler, Margaret. 2003. Cost and robbers: Shoplifting and employee thievery add dollars to price tags. *Washington Post* (February 16):H5.

Prewitt, Kenneth. 2011. Social science, spared again. *Science, 333:*673.

Princeton Religion Research Center. 1994. Religion index hits all-time low mark. *PRRC Emerging Trends,* 16 (March):1–2.

Pringle, Heather. 2011. For best ticket to the afterlife, pay up. *Science, 333:*403.

Pronin, Emily, Jonah Berger, and **Sarah Molouki.** 2007. Alone in a crowd of sheep: Asymmetric perceptions of conformity and their roots in an introspection illusion. *Journal of Personality and Social Psychology, 92:*585–95.

Public Agenda. 2001. *Child care issue guide.* www.publicagenda.com.

Puckett, Jim, Leslie Byster, Sarah Westervelt, Richard Gutierrez, Sheila Davis, Asma Hussain, and **Madhumitta Dutta.** 2002. *Exporting harm: The high-tech trashing of Asia.* The Basel Action Network and Silicon Valley Toxics Coalition (www.svtc.org).

Putterman, Louis. 2010. Cooperation and punishment. *Science, 328:*578–79.

Pyysiäinen, Ilkka, and **Marc Hauser.** 2009. The origins of religion: Evolved adaptation or by-product? *Trends in Cognitive Sciences,* 14(3):104–09.

Q

Quadagno, Jill S. 1982. *Aging in early industrial society.* New York: Academic Press.

Quadagno, Jill S. 1984. Welfare capitalism and the Social Security Act of 1935. *American Sociological Review,* 49:632–47.

Quillian, Lincoln. 1995. Prejudice as a response to perceived group threat: Population composition and anti-immigrant and racial prejudice in Europe. *American Sociological Review,* 60:586–611.

Quillian, Lincoln. 1996. Group threat and regional change in attitudes toward African Americans. *American Journal of Sociology,* 102:816–60.

Quillian, Lincoln. 2006. New approaches to understanding racial prejudice and discrimination. *Annual Review of Sociology,* 32:299–328.

Quinney, Richard. 1974. *Criminal justice in America.* Boston: Little, Brown.

Quinney, Richard. 1980. *Class, state, and crime.* New York: Longman.

R

Radelet, Michael L., and **Marian J. Borg.** 2000. The changing nature of death penalty debates. *Annual Review of Sociology,* 26:43–61.

Raghavan, Sudarsan. 2007. Marriages between sects come under siege in Iraq. *Washington Post* (March 4):A16.

Rahav, Giora. 1976. Family relations and delinquency in Israel. *Criminology,* 14:259–70.

Rainie, Lee. 2011. *The Internet as a diversion and destination: On a typical day, 53% of young adults go online just for fun and to pass the time* (December). Washington, DC: Pew Research Center's Internet & American Life Project. Available at http://pewinternet.org/Reports/2011/ Internet-as-diversion.aspx.

Ramirez, Roberto R., and **G. Patricia de la Cruz.** 2002. *The Hispanic population in the United States: March 2002.* Current Population Reports, P20–545. Washington, DC: U.S. Census Bureau.

Rand, Michael R. 2009. Criminal victimization, 2008. *Bureau of Justice Statistics Bulletin,* September 2009. NCJ 227777. Available at http://bjs.ojp.usdoj.gov/content/pub/ pdf/cv08.pdf.

Rank, M. R., and **T. A. Hirschi.** 2001. Rags or riches? Estimating the probabilities of poverty and affluence across the adult American life span. *Social Science Quarterly,* 82(4): 651–69.

Rank, Mark R. 2003. As American as apple pie: Poverty and welfare. *Contexts,* 2:41–49.

Rank, Mark R. 2011. Rethinking American poverty. *Contexts,* 10(2):16–21.

Rank, Mark Robert. 2004. *One nation, underprivileged: Why American poverty affects us all.* New York: Oxford University Press.

Raphael, Ray. 1988. *The men from the boys: Rites of passage in male America.* Lincoln: University of Nebraska Press.

Rastogi, Sonya, Tallese D. Johnson, Elizabeth M. Hoeffel, and **Malcolm P. Drewery, Jr.** 2011. The black population: 2010. 2010 Census Briefs (September):1–20. C2010BR-06. Washington, DC: U.S. Census Bureau.

Reckless, Walter C. 1961. A new theory of delinquency and crime. *Federal Probation,* 25:42–46.

Reckless, Walter C. 1967. *The crime problem,* 4th ed. New York: Appleton-Century-Crofts.

Rector, Robert. 1990. Poverty in U.S. is exaggerated by census. *Wall Street Journal* (September 25):A18.

Redman, Barbara K., and **Jon F. Merz.** 2008. Scientific misconduct: Do the punishments fit the crime? *Science* 321:775.

Reed, Susan E. 2005. Lawsuits won't break that glass ceiling. *Washington Post* (August 21):B3.

Reel, Monte. 2007. South America ushers in the era of La Presidenta: Women could soon lead a majority of continent's population. *Washington Post* (October 31):A12.

Reeves, Terrance J., and **Claudette E. Bennett.** 2004. *We the people: Asians in the United States.* U.S. Census Bureau, Census 2000 Special Reports, CENSR-17. Washington, DC: U.S. Government Printing Office. Available at http://www. census.gov/prod/2004pubs/censr-17 .pdf.

Regoli, Robert M., and **John D. Hewitt.** 2000. *Delinquency in society.* New York: McGraw-Hill.

Reicher, Stephen, and **Alex Haslam.** 2002. Ethics and "The Experiment." *The Psychologist,* 15(6):282.

Reicher, Stephen D., and **S. Alexander Haslam.** 2003a. Social psychology, science, and surveillance: Understanding The Experiment. *Social Psychology Review,* 5:7–17.

Reicher, Stephen D., and **S. Alexander Haslam.** 2003b. A new look at the psychology of tyranny: The BBC prison study. Unpublished paper.

Reid, T. R. 2009. *The healing of America: A global quest for better, cheaper, and fairer health care.* New York: Penguin Press.

Reid, W. V., D. Chen, L. Goldfarb, H. Hackmann, Y. T. Lee, K. Mokhele, E. Ostrom, K. Raivio, J. Rockström, H. J. Schellnhuber, and **A. Whyte.** 2010. Earth system science for global sustainability: Grand challenges. *Science,* 330:916–17.

Rennison, Callie. 2002. Criminal victimization 2001: Changes 2000–01 with trends 1993–2001. Washington, DC: U.S. Department of Justice. NCJ–194610.

Reno, Raymond R., Robert B. Cialdini, and **Carl A. Kallgren.** 1993. The transsituational influence of social norms. *Journal of Personality and Social Psychology,* 64:104–12.

Restaurant Opportunities Center United. 2012. *Tipped over the edge: Gender inequity in the restaurant industry.* Washington, DC: Institute for Women's Policy Research. http:// www.iwpr.org" www.iwpr.org.

Rheingold, Harriet L., Dale F. Hay, and **Meredith J. West.** 1976. Sharing in the second year of life. *Child Development,* 47:1148–58.

Rhoades, G. K., Stanley, S. M., and **Markman, H. J.** 2009. The pre-engagement cohabitation effect: A replication and extension of previous findings. *Journal of Family Psychology,* 23:233–58.

Richardson, Laurel. 1987. *The dynamics of sex and gender: A sociological perspective.* New York: Harper & Row.

Richardson, Laurel, Verta Taylor, and **Nancy Whittier.** 1997. *Feminist frontiers IV.* New York: McGraw-Hill.

Richburg, Keith. 2003. Gay marriage becomes routine for Dutch. *Washington Post* (September 23):A20.

Richtel, Matt. 2011. Egypt cuts off most Internet and cell service. *New York Times,* January 28. Available at http://www.nytimes.com/2011/01/29/techonlogy/internet/29cutoff.html. Accessed 1/24/12.

Ridgeway, C. L., and **L. Smith-Lovin.** 1999. The gender system and interaction. *Annual Review of Sociology,* 25:191–216.

Riesman, David. 1953. *The lonely crowd.* Garden City, NY: Doubleday.

Risman, Barbara J. 2001. Comment: Calling the bluff of value-free science. *American Sociological Review,* 66:605–11.

Risman, Barbara, and **Pepper Schwartz.** 2002. After the sexual revolution: Gender politics in teen dating. *Contexts,* 1 (Spring):16–24.

Ritch, Ellie. 2002. Prison experiment repeated for ratings. *Stanford Daily* (February 5). Available at www.stanforddaily.com.

Ritzer, George. 1995. *Expressing America: A critique of the increasingly global credit card society.* Thousand Oaks, CA: Sage.

Ritzer, George. 1997. *Postmodern social theory.* New York: McGraw-Hill.

Ritzer, George. 2011. *Sociological theory,* 8th ed. New York: McGraw-Hill.

Robbins, Alexandra. 2011. *The geeks shall inherit the earth: Popularity, quirk theory, and why outsiders thrive after high school.* New York: Hyperion.

Roberts, Brent W., Kate E. Walton, and **Wolfgang Viechtbauer.** 2006. Patterns of mean-level change in personality traits across the life course: A meta-analysis of longitudinal studies. *Psychological Bulletin,* 132:1–25.

Roberts, Felicia. 2000. The interactional construction of asymmetry: The medical agenda as a resource for delaying response to patient questions. *Sociological Quarterly,* 41(1):151–70.

Robinson, Circles. 2012. Cuba seeks Internet control with the help of Belarus. *Havana Times* (Business & Economy, Updates) (January 27) available at ttp://www.havanatimes.org/?p=60737.

Robinson, Dawn. 2007. Control theories in sociology. *Annual Review of Sociology,* 33:157–74.

Rockström, Johan, Will Steffen, Kevin Noone, Asa Persson, et al. 2009. A safe operating space for humanity. *Nature,* 461:472–75.

Roethlisberger, Fritz J., and **William J. Dickson.** 1939. *Management and the worker.* Cambridge, MA: Harvard University Press.

Rohan, Meg J. 2000. A rose by any name: The values construct. *Personality and Social Psychology Review,* 4:255–77.

Rokeach, Milton, and **Sandra J. Ball-Rokeach.** 1989. Stability and change in American value priorities, 1968–1981. *American Psychologist,* 44:775–84.

Romanelli, Elaine. 1991. The evolution of new organizational forms. *Annual Review of Sociology,* 17:79–103.

Rooney, James F. 1980. Organizational success through program failure: Skid Row rescue missions. *Social Forces,* 58:904–24.

Rose, Stephen P., and **Heidi Hartmann.** 2004. *Still a man's labor market: The long-term earnings gap.* Washington, DC: Institute for Women's Policy Research.

Rosecrance, Richard. 1990. Too many bosses, too few workers. *New York Times* (July 15):F11.

Rosen, George. 1963. The hospital: Historical sociology of a community institution. In E. Freidson, ed., *The hospital in modern society.* New York: Free Press.

Rosenberg, Morris. 1973. Which significant others? *American Behavioral Scientist,* 16:829–60.

Rosenberg, Morris. 1981. The self-concept: Social product and social force. In Morris Rosenberg and Ralph H. Turner, eds., *Social psychology:*

Sociological perspectives. New York: Basic Books.

Rosenberg, Morris. 1986. Self-concept from middle childhood through adolescence. In J. Suls and A. Greenwald, eds., *Psychological perspectives on the self,* Vol. 3. Hillsdale, NJ: Erlbaum.

Rosenberg, Morris. 1989. *Society and the adolescent self-image,* rev. ed. Middletown, CT: Wesleyan University Press.

Rosenberg, Noah A., Jonathan K. Prichard, James L. Weber, Howard M. Cann, Kenneth K. Kidd, Lev A. Zhivotovsky, and **Marcus W. Feldman.** 2002. Genetic structure of human populations. *Science,* 298:2381–85.

Rosenmerkel, Sean, Matthew Durose, and **Donald Farole, Jr.** 2009. *Felony sentences in state courts, 2006—Statistical tables.* Bureau of Justice Statistics Statistical Tables, December 2009, NCJ 226846. Available at http://bjs.ojp.usdoj.gov/index.cfm?ty=pbdetail&iid=2152.

Ross, Andrew. 2003. *No-collar: The humane workplace and its hidden costs.* New York: Basic Books.

Ross, Catherine E., John Mirowsky, and **Joan Huber.** 1983. Dividing work, sharing work, and in-between: Marriage patterns and depression. *American Sociological Review,* 48:809–23.

Rossi, Alice S., and **Peter H. Rossi.** 1990. *Of human bonding: Parent–child relations across the life course.* New York: Aldine de Gruyter.

Rothbart, Myron, and **Oliver P. John.** 1993. Intergroup relations and stereotype change: A social cognitive analysis and some longitudinal findings. In Paul M. Sniderman, Philip E. Tetlock, and Edward G. Carmines, eds., *Prejudice, politics, and the American dilemma.* Stanford, CA: Stanford University Press.

Rothchild, John. 1993. Sacred cows. *Worth* (December–January):55–58.

Rothkopf, David J. 2003. When the buzz bites back. *Washington Post* (May 11):B1.

Rothschild, Joyce, and **Raymond Russell.** 1986. Alternatives to bureaucracy: Democratic participation in the economy. *Annual Review of Sociology,* 12:307–28.

Rowe, John W., Lisa F. Berkman, Robert Binstock, Axel Boersch-Supan, John Cacioppo, Laura Carstensen, Dana Goldman, Linda Fried, James Jackson, Martin Kohli, Jay Olshansky, and **John Rother.** 2009. Facts and fictions about an aging America. *Contexts,* 8(4):16–21.

Roy, Oliver. 1998. *The failure of political Islam.* Cambridge, MA: Harvard University Press.

Royal Pingdom. 2010. Internet 2009 in numbers. Posted January 22, 2010. Available at http://royal.pingdom .com/2010/01/22/internet-2009-in -numbers/.

Ruef, Martin. 2004. The demise of an organizational form: Emancipation and plantation agriculture in the American South, 1960–1880. *American Journal of Sociology,* 109:1365–10.

Ruggles, Patricia. 1992. Measuring poverty. University of Wisconsin, Institute for Research on Poverty. *Focus,* 14:2.

Ruggles, Steven. 1987. *Prolonged connections: The rise of the extended family in nineteenth-century England and America.* Madison: University of Wisconsin Press.

Russakoff, Dale. 2006. In Motor City, anger yields to pragmatism. *Washington Post* (March 26):A1.

Ruth, Henry, and **Kevin R. Reitz.** 2003. *The challenge of crime: Rethinking our response.* Cambridge, MA: Harvard University Press.

Ryan, John. 1985. *The production of culture in the music industry: The ASCAP-BMI controversy.* Lanham, MD: University Press of America.

S

Saad, Lydia. 1996. Americans growing more tolerant of gays. Gallup poll.

Sagarin, Edward. 1975. *Deviants and deviance.* New York: Praeger.

Sakamoto, Arthur, and **Meichu D. Chen.** 1991. Inequality and attainment in a dual labor market. *American Sociological Review,* 56:295–308.

Salmon, Jacqueline L. 2007. In America, nonbelievers find strength in numbers. *Washington Post* (September 15):A14.

Sampson, Robert J. 2008. Rethinking immigration and crime. *Contexts: Understanding People in Their Social Worlds,* 7:28–33.

Sampson, Robert J., and **W. Byron Groves.** 1989. Community structure and crime: Testing social-disorganization theory. *American Journal of Sociology,* 94:774–802.

Samuelsson, Kurt. 1961. *Religion and economic action: A critique of Max Weber.* Trans. E. G. French. New York: Harper Torchbooks.

Sanday, Peggy Reeves. 1981. The socio-cultural context of rape: A cross-cultural study. *Journal of Social Issues,* 37:5–27.

Sanday, Peggy Reeves. 1996. Rape-prone versus rape-free campus cultures. *Violence Against Women,* 2:191–208.

Santos, Andreia, Andreas Meyer-Lindenberg, and **Christine Deruelle.** 2010. Absence of racial, but not gender stereotyping in Williams syndrome children. *Current Biology,* 20(7):307–8.

Saperstein, Aliya, and **Andrew M. Penner.** 2010. The race of a criminal record: How incarceration colors racial perceptions. *Social Problems,* 57(1):92–113.

Sapir, Edward. 1949. *Selected writings in language, culture, and personality.* Berkeley: University of California Press.

Saporito, Bill. 1986. The revolt against "working smarter." *Fortune* (July 21):58–65.

Sassen, Saskia. 1991. *The global city: New York, London, Tokyo.* Princeton, NJ: Princeton University Press.

Sassen, Saskia, and **Alejandro Portes.** 1993. Miami: A new global city? *Contemporary Sociology,* 22:471–77.

Satchell, Michael. 1993. Trashing the reservations? *U.S. News & World Report* (January 11):24–25.

Savage, Charlie. 2010. U.S. crime rates fell in '09 despite sour economy. *New York Times* (May 25):A15.

Savin-Williams, R. C., and **K. G. Esterberg.** 2000. Lesbian, gay, and bisexual families. In D. H. Demo, K. R. Allen, and M. A. Fine, eds., *Handbook of family diversity* (pp. 197–215). New York: Oxford University Press.

Savin-Williams, Ritch C., and **David H. Demo.** 1984. Developmental change and stability in adolescent self-concept. *Developmental Psychology,* 20:1100–10.

Sawa, Akira, and **Solomon H. Snyder.** 2005. Two genes link two distinct psychoses. *Science,* 310:1128–29.

Scales-Trent, Judy. 1995. *Notes of a white black woman: Race, color, and community.* University Park: Pennsylvania State University Press.

Schaeffer, Nora Cate, and **Stanley Presser.** 2003. The science of asking questions. *Annual Review of Sociology,* 29:65–88.

Schlenker, Barry R., Michael F. Weigold, and **John R. Hallam.** 1990. Self-serving attributions in social context: Effects of self-esteem and social pressure. *Journal of Personality and Social Psychology,* 58:855–63.

Schneider, Barbara L., and **Venessa A. Keesler.** 2007. School reform 2007: Transforming education into a scientific enterprise. *Annual Review of Sociology,* 33:197–217.

Schnittker, Jason, Jeremy Freese, and **Brian Powell.** 2003. Who are feminists and what do they believe? The role of generations. *American Sociological Review,* 68:1–17.

Schoen, Robert, and **Robin M. Weinick.** 1993. Partner choice in marriages and cohabitations. *Journal of Marriage and the Family,* 55:408–14.

Schorr, Alvin L. 1984. Redefining poverty levels. *New York Times* (May 9):27.

Schuldt, J. P., S. Konrath, and **N. Schwarz.** 2011. "Global warming" or "climate change"? Whether the planet is warming depends on question wording. *Public Opinion Quarterly,* 75:115–24.

Schuman, Howard, Charlotte Steeh, Lawrence Bobo, and **Maria Krysan.** 1997. *Racial attitudes in America.* Cambridge, MA: Harvard University Press.

Schur, Edwin. 1965. *Crimes without victims.* Englewood Cliffs, NJ: Prentice-Hall.

Schwartz, Jennifer, Darrell J. Steffensmeier, and **Ben Feldmeyer.** 2009. Assessing trends in women's violence via data triangulation: arrests, convictions, incarcerations, and victim reports. *Social Problems,* 56(3):494–525.

Schwartz, Martin D. 1995. Date rape on college campuses. In Alex Thio and Thomas C. Calhoun, eds., *Readings in deviant behavior.* New York: HarperCollins.

Schwartz, Martin D., and **Walter S. DeKeseredy.** 1997. *Sexual assault on the college campus: The role of male peer support.* Thousand Oaks, CA: Sage.

Scott, Janny. 2005. Life at the top in America isn't just better, it's longer. In *Class Matters.* New York: Henry Holt.

Scott, Janny, and **David Leonhardt.** 2005. Shadowy lines that still divide. In *Class Matters.* New York: Henry Holt.

Scott, W. Richard. 2004. Reflections on a half-century of organizational sociology. *Annual Review of Sociology,* 30:1–21.

Searle, John R. 1995. *The construction of social reality.* New York: Free Press.

Sears, David O., Jim Sidanius, and **Lawrence Bobo,** eds. 2000. *Racialized politics: The debate about racism in America.* Chicago: University of Chicago Press.

Seeman, Melvin. 1959. On the meaning of alienation. *American Sociological Review,* 24:783–91.

Selin, Helaine. 2002. An inclusive perspective. *Science,* 298:969–70.

Selltiz, Claire, Lawrence S. Wrightsman, and **Stuart W. Cook.** 1981. *Research methods in social relations.* New York: Holt, Rinehart & Winston.

Semler, Ricardo. 1993. *Maverick: The success story behind the world's most unusual workplace.* New York: Warner Books.

Serbin, Lisa A., and **Carol Sprafkin.** 1986. The salience of gender and the process of sex typing in three- to seven-year-old children. *Child Development,* 57:1188–99.

Service, Robert F. 2007. Chemistry reports warn of eroding American research lead. *Science,* 316:35.

Service, Robert F. 2011. Outlook brightens for plastic solar cells. *Science,* 332:293.

Sewell, William H., Jr. 1992. A theory of structure: Duality, agency, and transformation. *American Journal of Sociology,* 98:1–29.

Sewell, William H., Archibald O. Haller, and **George W. Ohlendorf.** 1970. The educational and early occupational status attainment process: Replication and revision. *American Sociological Review,* 35:1014–27.

Shattock, Robin J., Mitchell Warren, Sheena McCormack, and **Catherine A. Hankins.** 2011. Turning the tide against HIV. *Science,* 333:42–43.

Sewell, William H., and **Robert M. Hauser.** 1975. *Education, occupation, and earnings: Achievement in early career.* New York: Academic Press.

Shaw, Clifford R. 1930. *Natural history of a juvenile career.* Chicago: University of Chicago Press.

Shaw, Clifford R., and **Henry McKay.** 1942. *Juvenile delinquency in urban areas.* Chicago: University of Chicago Press.

Shea, John C. 1984. *American government: The great game of politics.* New York: St. Martin's Press.

Shear, Michael D. 2010. Obama extends hospital visitation rights to same-sex partners of gays. *Washington Post* (April 16):A1.

Sherif, Muzafer. 1936. *The psychology of social norms.* New York: Harper & Row.

Sherif, Muzafer, O. J. Harvey, B. Jack White, William R. Hood, and **Carolyn W. Sherif.** 1961. *Intergroup conflict and cooperation: The Robbers' Cave experiment.* Norman: University of Oklahoma Book Exchange.

Sherman, Lawrence W., Douglas A. Smith, Janell D. Schmidt, and **Dennis P. Rogan.** 1992. Crime, punishment, and stake in conformity: Legal and informal control of domestic violence. *American Sociological Review,* 57:680–90.

Shermer, Michael. 2011. *The believing brain: From ghosts and gods to politics and conspiracies—how we construct beliefs and reinforce them as truths.* New York: Times Books (Henry Holt).

Shibutani, Tamotsu. 1986. *Social processes: An introduction to sociology.* Berkeley: University of California Press.

Shibutani, Tamotsu, and **Kian M. Kwan.** 1965. *Ethnic Stratification.* New York: Macmillan.

Shils, Edward A., and **Morris Janowitz.** 1948. Cohesion and disintegration in the Wehrmacht in World War II. *Public Opinion Quarterly,* 12:280–315.

Shin, Hyon B., and **Robert A. Kominski.** 2010. Language use in the United States: 2007. *American Community Survey Reports* (April):1–16. ACS-12.

Shoemaker, Donald J. 2010. *Theories of delinquency: An examination of explanations of delinquent behavior.* New York: Oxford University Press.

Shonkoff, Jack P. 2011. Protecting brains, not simply stimulating minds. *Science,* 333:982–83.

Sica, Alan. 1996. Review essay: Sociology as worldview. *American Journal of Sociology,* 102:252–55.

Siebens, Julie, and **Tiffany Julian.** 2011. Native North American languages spoken at home in the United States and Puerto Rico: 2006–2010. *American Community Survey Briefs* (December):1–5. ACSBR/10-10.

Siegel, Larry J., and **Brandon C. Welch.** 2005. *Juvenile delinquency: The core,* 2nd ed. Belmont, CA: Thompson Wadsworth.

Sills, David. 1957. *The volunteers.* New York: Free Press.

Simmel, Georg. 1908/1955. *Conflict and the web of group affiliations.* New York: Free Press.

Simmel, Georg. 1908/1959. How is society possible? In Kurt Wolff, ed., *Essays in sociology, philosophy, and aesthetics.* New York: Harper & Row.

Simmel, Georg. 1950. *The sociology of Georg Simmel.* Ed. and trans. Kurt Wolff. New York: Free Press.

Simon, David R., and **D. Stanley Eitzen.** 1993. *Elite deviance.* Boston: Allyn & Bacon.

Simon, Rita J. 1996. Transracial adoptions: Experiences of a twenty-year study. *The American Sociologist,* 27:79–89.

Simon, Rita J., and **Gloria Danziger.** 1991. *Women's movements in America: Their successes, disappointments, and aspirations.* New York: Praeger.

Simon, Robin W. 1998. Assessing sex differences in vulnerability among employed parents: The importance of marital status. *Journal of Health and Social Behavior,* 39:38–54.

Simon, Viviana. 2005. Wanted: Women in clinical trials. *Science,* 308:1517.

Simons, Ronald L., Jay Beaman, Rand D. Conger, and **Wei Chao.** 1993. Stress, support, and antisocial behavior trait as determinants of emotional well-being and parenting practices among single mothers. *Journal of Marriage and the Family,* 55:385–98.

Simpson, Brent. 2004. Social values, subjective transformations, and cooperation in social dilemmas. *Social Psychology Quarterly,* 67:385–95.

Singer, Eleanor. 1981. Reference groups and social evaluations. In Morris Rosenberg and Ralph H. Turner, eds., *Social psychology: Sociological perspectives.* New York: Basic Books.

Skinner, B. F. 1953. *Science and human behavior.* New York: Macmillan.

Sklair, Leslie. 1991. *Sociology of the global system.* Baltimore: Johns Hopkins University Press.

Skocpol, Theda. 1979. *States and social revolution.* Cambridge: Cambridge University Press.

Skocpol, Theda. 1980. Political response to capital crisis: Neo-Marxist theories of the state and the case of the New Deal. *Politics and Society,* 10:155–201.

Skocpol, Theda, and **Edwin Amenta.** 1986. States and social politics. *Annual Review of Sociology,* 12:131–57.

Slotkin, James S. 1955. Culture and psychopathology. *Journal of Abnormal and Social Psychology,* 51:269–75.

Small, Stephen A., and **Dave Riley.** 1990. Toward a multidimensional assessment of work spillover into family life. *Journal of Marriage and the Family,* 52:51–61.

Smedley, Brian D., Adrienne Y. Stith, and **Alan R. Nelson,** eds. 2003. *Unequal treatment: Confronting racial and ethnic disparities in health care.* National Academies of Sciences.

Smelser, Neil J. 1963. *Theory of collective behavior.* New York: Free Press.

Smith, Althea, and **Abigail J. Steward.** 1983. Approaches to studying racism and sexism in black women's lives. *Journal of Social Issues,* 39:1–15.

Smith, Tom W., Peter V. Marsden, Michael Hout, and **Jibum Kim.** 2010. *General Social Surveys, 1972–2010: Cumulative codebook.* Chicago: National Opinion Research Center.

Snell, Tracy. 2011. *Capital punishment, 2010: Statistical tables.* U.S. Department of Justice, Bureau of Justice Statistics. Available at http://bjs.ojp.usdoj.gov/index.cfm?ty=pbdetail&iid=2236.

Snipp, C. Matthew. 1989. *American Indians: The first of this land.* New York: Russell Sage Foundation.

Snipp, C. Matthew. 2003. Racial measurement in the American census: Past practices and implications for the future. *Annual Review of Sociology,* 29:563–88.

Snizek, William E. 1994. Survivors as victims: Some little publicized consequences of corporate downsizing. Address delivered to cabinet members of the Dutch Ministry of Government, The Hague, July 1994.

Snizek, William E. 1995. Virtual offices: Some neglected considerations. *Communications of the ACM,* 38:15–17.

Snowden, Frank M., Jr. 1983. *Before color prejudice: The ancient view of blacks.* Cambridge, MA: Harvard University Press.

Snyder, Howard N., and **Melissa Sickmund.** 2006. Juvenile offenders and victims: 2006 national report. Washington, DC: Office of Justice Programs, National Center for Juvenile Justice.

Snyder, Thomas D., Sally A. Dillow, and **Charlene M. Hoffman.** 2009. *Digest of education statistics 2008* (NCES 2009–020). National Center for Education Statistics, Institute of Education Sciences. Washington, DC: U.S. Department of Education.

Soares, Rachel, Baye Cobb, Ellen Lebow, Allyson Regis, Hannah Winsten, and **Veronica Wojnas.** 2011. 2011 Catalyst census: Fortune 500 women board directors. *Catalyst Research Reports* (December). Catalyst. http://www.catalyst.org/file/533/2011_fortune_500_census_wbd.pdf.

Sobel, Richard. 1989. *The white-collar working class: From structure to politics.* New York: Praeger.

Social Security Administration. 2010. Annual statistical supplement to the Social Security Bulletin, 2009,

SSA Publication No. 13-11700, February 2010. Washington, DC: Social Security Administration Office of Retirement and Disability Policy, Office of Research Evaluation and Statistics. Available at http://www.ssa.gov/policy/docs/statcomps/supplement/2009/supplement09.pdf.

Solomon, Patrick. 1992. *Black resistance in high school: Forging a separatist culture.* Albany: State University of New York Press.

Sommer, Alfred. 2009. *Getting what we deserve: Health and medical care in America.* Baltimore: Johns Hopkins University Press.

Sommer, Robert. 1969. *Personal space.* Englewood Cliffs, NJ: Prentice-Hall.

Songer, Donald R., and **Kelley A. Crews-Meyer.** 2000. Does judge gender matter? Decision making in state supreme courts. *Social Science Quarterly,* 81(3):750–62.

Sørensen, Aage B. 2000. Toward a sounder basis for class analysis. *American Journal of Sociology,* 105:1523–58.

Sorokin, Pitirim. 1959. *Social and cultural mobility.* New York: Free Press.

Soupiset, Mark F. 2003. Striking back at fraud. *USAA Magazine* (August):14–18.

South, Scott J., and **Katherine Trent.** 1988. Sex ratios and women's roles: Cross-national analysis. *American Journal of Sociology,* 93:1096–1115.

Southern School News. 1954. Segregation. 1 (November):3.

Spates, James L. 1983. The sociology of values. *Annual Review of Sociology,* 9:27–49.

Spence, Michael. 2011. *The next convergence: The future of economic growth in a multispeed world.* New York: Farrar, Straus and Giroux.

Sperber, Murray. 2000. *Beer and circus: How big-time college sports is crippling undergraduate education.* New York: Henry Holt.

Spiegelhalter, David, Mike Pearson, and **Ian Short.** 2011. Visualizing uncertainty about the future. *Science,* 333:1393–1400.

Spohn, Cassia C. 2000. Thirty years of sentencing reform: The quest for a racially neutral sentencing process. *Criminal Justice 2000,* 3 (National Institute of Justice).

Spraggins, Renee E. 2003. Women and men in the United States: March 2002. U.S. Census Bureau. Washington, DC: Government Printing Office.

Sprague, Joey, and **Mary K. Zimmerman.** 1993. Overcoming dualisms: A feminist agenda for sociological methodology. In Paula England, ed., *Theory on gender/feminism on theory.* New York: Aldine de Gruyter.

Sprey, Jetse. 1979. Conflict theory and the study of marriage and the family. In Wesley R. Burr, Reuben Hill, F. Ivan Nye, and Ira L. Reiss, eds., *Contemporary theories about the family,* Vol. 2. New York: Free Press.

Stacey, Judith. 2009. Unhitching the horse from the carriage: Love and marriage among the Mosuo. *Journal of Law and Family Studies,* 11(2):239–74.

Stacey, Judith, and **Timothy J. Biblarz.** 2001. (How) does the sexual orientation of parents matter? *American Sociological Review,* 66:159–83.

Stand Up for Kids. 2008. http://www.standupforkids.org/FAQs.html.

Stanley, S. M., S. W. Whitton, and **H. J. Markman,** 2004. Maybe I do: Interpersonal commitment and premarital or nonmarital cohabitation. *Journal of Family Issues,* 25:496–519.

Stanley, Scott, and **Galena Rhoades.** 2009. "Sliding vs. deciding": Understanding a mystery. NCFR Report Summer 2009 Issue. National Council on Family Relations.

Stark, Rodney. 1996. *Sociology,* 6th ed. Belmont, CA: Wadsworth.

Stark, Rodney, and **William S. Bainbridge.** 1979. Of churches, sects, and cults: Preliminary concepts for a theory of religious movements. *Journal for the Scientific Study of Religion,* 18:117–33.

Stark, Rodney, and **William S. Bainbridge.** 1987. *A theory of religion.* New York: Peter Lang.

Starr, Paul. 1982. *The social transformation of American medicine.* New York: Basic Books.

Stearns, Peter N. 1977. *Old age in European society.* London: Croom Helm.

Steinberg, Stephen. 1989. *The ethnic myth: Race, ethnicity, and class in America.* Updated and expanded ed. New York: Atheneum.

Steinmetz, George, and **Erik Olin Wright.** 1989. The fall and rise of the petty bourgeoisie: Changing patterns of self-employment in the postwar United States. *American Journal of Sociology,* 94:973–1018.

Stephens, William N. 1963. *The family in cross-cultural perspective.* New York: Holt, Rinehart & Winston.

Stepp, Laura Sessions. 2000. New study questions teen risk factors: School woes, peers are stronger clues than race, income. *Washington Post* (November 30):A1.

Stepp, Laura Sessions. 2006. The kids are gone, and so are the friends. *Washington Post* (October 22):D1.

Sternheimer, Karen E. 2003. *It's not the media: The truth about pop culture's influence on children.* Boulder, CO: Westview Press.

Sternheimer, Karen E. 2007. Do video games kill? *Contexts,* 6:13–17.

Stevenson, David Lee. 1991. Deviant students as a collective resource in classroom control. *Sociology of Education,* 64:127–33.

Stiffler, Lisa. 2011. Orca culture: Researchers have found a variety of complex, learned behaviors that differ from pod to pod. *Smithsonian,* (July/August):87.

Stiles, Joan. 2008. The fundamentals of brain development: Integrating nature and nurture. Cambridge, MA: Harvard University Press.

Stinchcombe, Arthur L. 1983. *Economic sociology.* New York: Academic Press.

Stockard, Jean, and **Robert M. O'Brien.** 2002. Cohort effects on suicide rates: International variations. *American Sociological Review,* 67: 854–72.

Stokes, Randall G. 1975. Afrikaner Calvinism and economic action: The Weberian thesis in South Africa. *American Journal of Sociology,* 81:62–81.

Stokes, Randall G., and **Andy B. Anderson.** 1990. Disarticulation and human welfare in less developed countries. *American Sociological Review,* 55:63–74.

Stone, Richard, and **Richard A. Kerr.** 2005. Girding for the next killer wave. *Science,* 310:1602–05 (December 9).

Stowell, J. I., S. F. Messner, K. F. McGeever, and **L. E. Raffalovich.** 2009. Immigrants and the recent violent crime drop in the United States: A pooled, cross-sectional time-series analysis of metropolitan areas. *Criminology,* 47(3):889–928.

Strang, David, and **Nancy Brandon Tuma.** 1993. Spatial and temporal heterogeneity in diffusion. *American Journal of Sociology,* 99: 614–39.

Straus, Murray A., David B. Sugarman, and **Jean Giles-Sims.** 1997. Spanking by parents and subsequent antisocial behavior of children. *Archives of Pediatrics and Adolescent Medicine,* 151:761–67.

Strauss, Anselm, Leonard Schatzman, Rue Bucher, Danuta Ehrlich, and **Melvin Sabshin.** 1964. *Psychiatric ideologies and institutions.* New York: Free Press.

Stryker, Sheldon. 1980. *Symbolic interactionism: A social structural version.* Menlo Park, CA: Benjamin/Cummings.

Stuntz, William J. 2011. *The collapse of American criminal justice.* Cambridge, MA: Harvard University Press.

Substance Abuse and Mental Health Services Administration. 2005. *Results from the 2004 National Survey on Drug Use and Health:* *National Findings* (NSDUH Series H-28, DHHS Publication No. SMA 05-4062). Rockville, MD: Substance Abuse and Mental Health Services Administration, Office of Applied Studies.

Sudnow, David. 1967. *Passing on: The social organization of dying.* Englewood Cliffs, NJ: Prentice-Hall.

Sullivan, Kevin. 2007. Devotees of Siberian messiah "building heaven on earth." *Washington Post* (July 17):A1.

Sullivan, Kevin, and **Mary Jordan.** 2002. U.S. called the loser in war on drugs. *Washington Post* (October 31):A1.

Sumner, William Graham. 1906. *Folkways.* Boston: Ginn.

Sunstein, Cass R. 2003. Sober lemmings. *The New Republic* (April 14):34–37.

Super, David A., Sharon Parrott, Susan Steinmetz, and **Cindy Mann.** 1996. *The new welfare law— summary.* Washington, DC: Center on Budget and Policy Priorities.

Suro, Roberto. 1990. Where America is growing: The suburban cities. *New York Times* (February 23):1–10.

Suro, Roberto. 1991. Your tired, your poor, your masses yearning to be with relatives. *New York Times* (January 6):E4.

Sutherland, Edwin H. 1939. *Principles of criminology.* Philadelphia: Lippincott.

Sutherland, Edwin H. 1949. *White-collar crime.* New York: Dryden Press.

Sutton, John R. 1991. The political economy of madness: The expansion of the asylum in progressive America. *American Sociological Review,* 56:665–78.

Sutton, John R. 2000. Imprisonment and social classification in five common-law democracies, 1955–1985. *American Journal of Sociology,* 106:305–86.

Swedberg, Richard. 1991. *Joseph A. Schumpeter: His life and work.* Princeton, NJ: Princeton University Press.

Swedberg, Richard. 2003. The changing picture of Max Weber's sociology. *Annual Review of Sociology,* 29:283–306.

Swedberg, Richard. 2007. The market. *Contexts,* 6:64–67.

Swidler Ann. 1986. Culture in action: Symbols and strategies. *American Sociological Review,* 51:273–86

Syer, Cassidy A., and **Bruce M. Shore.** 2001. Science fairs: What are the sources of help for students and how prevalent is cheating? *School Science and Mathematics,* 10(4):206–20.

Szymanski, Albert. 1976. Racial discrimination and white gain. *American Sociological Review,* 41:403–14.

Szymanski, Albert. 1981. *The logic of imperialism.* New York: Praeger.

T

Tanioko, Ichiro, and **Daniel Glaser.** 1991. School uniforms, routine activities, and the social control of delinquency in Japan. *Youth and Society,* 23:50–75.

Taylor, Paul, ed. 2010. The decline of marriage and rise of new families. Pew Research Center. Available at http://www.pewsocialtrends.org/files/2010/11/pew-social-trends-2010-families.pdf.

Taylor, Paul, Jeffrey Passel, Richard Fry, Richard Morin, Wendy Wang, Gabriel Velasco, and **Daniel Dockterman.** 2010. *The return of the multi-generational family household.* Pew Research Center: A social and demographic trends report. Available at http://pewsocialtrends.org.

Taylor, Verta. 1989. Social movement continuity: The women's movement in abeyance. *American Sociological Review,* 54:761–75.

Tessler, Richard, Mia Tuan, and **Jannbin Lee Shiao.** 2011. The many faces of international adoption. *Contexts,* 10(4):34–39.

Tetlock, P. E., R. S. Peterson, C. McGuire, S. Chang, and **P. Feld.** 1992. Assessing political group dynamics: A test of the groupthink model. *Journal of Personality and Social Psychology,* 63:403–25.

Thio, Alex. 2010. *Deviant behavior,* 10th ed. Upper Saddle River, NJ: Pearson.

Thistle, Susan. 2000. The trouble with modernity: Gender and the remaking of social theory. *Sociological Theory,* 18:275–88.

Thoits, Peggy A. 1995. Identity-relevant events and psychological symptoms: A cautionary tale. *Social Forces,* 36:72–82.

Thomas, William I., and **Dorothy S. Thomas.** 1928. *The child in America: Behavior problems and programs.* New York: Knopf.

Thompson, Bob. 2007. A troubling case of readers' block: Citing decline among older kids, NEA report warns of dire effects. *Washington Post* (November 19):C1.

Thrasher, Frederic M. 1927. *The gang.* Chicago: University of Chicago Press.

Tilly, Charles. 1978. *From mobilization to revolution.* Reading, MA: Addison-Wesley.

Tilly, Charles. 1990. *Coercion, capital, and European states, AD 990–1990.* Cambridge, MA: Blackwell.

Tipton, Steven M. 1982. *Getting saved from the sixties.* Berkeley and Los Angeles: University of California Press.

Tittle, Charles R., and **Raymond Paternoster.** 2000. *Social deviance and crime: An organizational and theoretical approach.* Los Angeles, CA: Roxbury.

Tittle, Charles R., and **Alan R. Rowe.** 1974. Certainty of arrest and crime rates: A further test of the deterrence hypothesis. *Social Forces,* 52:455–62.

Tittle, Charles R., and **Michael R. Welch.** 1983. Religiosity and deviance: Toward a contingency theory of constraining effects. *Social Forces,* 61:653–82.

Tong, Rosemarie P. 1998. *Feminist thought: A more comprehensive introduction,* 2nd ed. Boulder, CO: Westview Press.

Toossi, Mitra. 2005. Labor force projections to 2014: Retiring boomers.

Monthly Labor Review (November):25–44. Available at http://www.bls.gov/opub/mlr/2005/11/art3full.pdf.

Tourangeau, Roger, Lance J. Rips, and **Kenneth Rasinski.** 2000. The psychology of survey response. New York: Cambridge University Press.

Toynbee, Arnold J. 1934/1954. *A study of history.* 10 vols. New York: Oxford University Press.

Trafford, Abigail. 2001. The hill tunes in to nurses' lament. *Washington Post* (February 27):8.

Trost, Cathy. 1990. Census survey on child care increases concern about how much poor can pay. *Wall Street Journal* (August 15): A10.

Truman, Jennifer L. 2011. *Criminal victimization, 2010.* Bureau of Justice Statistics, NCJ 235508, September 2011. Available at http://www.bjs.gov/content/pub/pdf/cv10.pdf.

Tuch, Steven A., and **Michael Hughes.** 1996. Whites' racial policy attitudes. *Social Science Quarterly,* 77:723–45.

Tuch, Steven A., and **Michael Hughes.** 2011. Whites' racial policy attitudes in the 21st century: The continuing significance of racial resentment. *The Annals of the American Academy of Political and Social Science* 634:134-152.

Tucker, Joan S., Joseph E. Schwartz, Carol Tomlinson-Keasey, Howard S. Friedman, Michael H. Criqui, Deborah L. Wingard, and **Leslie R. Martin.** 1997. Parental divorce: Effects on individual behavior and longevity. *Journal of Personality and Social Psychology,* 73(2):381–91.

Tucker, Neely. 2000. A matter of violent death and little girls. *Washington Post* (December 31):C1.

Tucker-Drob, Eliot M., Mijke Rhemtulla, K. Paige Harden, Eric Turkheimer, and **David Fask.** 2011. Emergence of a gene x socioeconomic status interaction on infant mental ability between 10 months and 2 years. *Psychological Science,* 22(1):125–33.

Tumin, Melvin M. 1953. Some principles of stratification: A critical analysis. *American Sociological Review,* 18:387–94.

Turkheimer, Eric, and **Mary Waldron.** 2000. Nonshared environment: A theoretical, methodological, and quantitative review. *Psychological Bulletin,* 126:78–108.

Turner, Bryan S. 1987. *Medical power and social knowledge.* Beverly Hills, CA: Sage.

Turner, Jonathan H. 1990. Émile Durkheim's theory of social organization. *Social Forces,* 68:1089–1103.

Turner, Ralph H. 1964. Collective behavior. In R. E. L. Faris, ed., *Handbook of modern sociology.* Chicago: Rand McNally.

Turner, Ralph H. 1968. The self-conception in social interaction. In C. Gordon and and K. J. Gergen, eds., *The self in social interaction.* New York: John Wiley.

Turner, Ralph H., and **Lewis M. Killian.** 1972. *Collective behavior,* 2nd ed. Englewood Cliffs, NJ: Prentice-Hall.

Twenge, Jean M., W. Keith Campbell, and **Elise C. Freeman.** 2012. Generational differences in young adults' life goals, concern for others, and civic orientation, 1966–2009. *Journal of Personality and Social Psychology,* DOI: 10.1037/a0027408.

U

Udry, J. Richard. 2000. Biological limits of gender construction. *American Sociological Review,* 65:443–57.

Udry, J. Richard. 2001. Reply: Feminist critics uncover determinism, positivism, and antiquated theory. *American Sociological Review,* 66:611–18.

Uggen, Christopher. 2000. Class, gender, and arrest: An intergenerational analysis of workplace power and control. *Criminology,* 38(3): 835–62.

Uggen, Christopher, and **Amy Blackstone.** 2004. Sexual harassment as a gendered expression of power. *American Sociological Review,* 69:64–92

Uggen, Christopher, and **Jeff Manza.** 2002. Democratic contraction? Political consequences of felon disenfranchisement in the United States. *American Sociological Review,* 67:777–803.

Ulrich, Laurel Thatcher. 1990. *A midwife's tale.* New York: Random House.

UNESCO. 2011. *Education for All Global Monitoring Report 2011. The Hidden Crisis: Armed Conflict and Education.* Available at http://unesdoc.unesco.org/images/0019/001911/191186e.pdf

United Nations. 2001. *World urbanization prospects: The 1999 revision.* New York: United Nations.

United Nations. 2003. *The world's women 2000: Trends and statistics.* Available at http://unstats.un.org/unsd/demographics/ww2000.

United Nations Population Division. 2006. *World urbanization prospects: The 2005 revision.* New York: United Nations.

U.S. Census Bureau. 1995. *Getting a helping hand: Long-term participants in assistance programs.* Bureau of the Census Statistical Brief, SB/95–27. Available at http://www.census.gov/apsd/www/statbrief/sb95_27.pdf.

U.S. Census Bureau. 1996. *Statistical abstract of the United States: 1997.* Washington, DC: U.S. Government Printing Office.

U.S. Census Bureau. 1997. *Statistical abstract of the United States: 1998.* Washington, DC: U.S. Government Printing Office.

U.S. Census Bureau. 1999. *Statistical abstract of the United States: 2000.* Washington, DC: U.S. Government Printing Office.

U.S. Census Bureau. 2004. U.S. interim projections by age, sex, race, and Hispanic origin. Available at http://www.census.gov/population/www/projections/usinterimproj/.

U.S. Census Bureau. 2007. *Statistical abstract of the United States: 2008.* Washington, DC: U.S. Government Printing Office. Available at http://www.census.gov/compendia/statab/2008edition.html.

U.S. Census Bureau. 2007a. Table MS-2: Estimated median age at first marriage, by sex: 1890 to the present. Current Population Survey, March, and Annual Social and Economic Supplements, 2006 and earlier. Available at http://www.census.gov/population/socdemo/hh-fam/ms2.xls

U.S. Census Bureau. 2009. *Statistical abstract of the United States: 2010* (129th edition). Washington, DC. Available at http://www.census.gov/statab/www/.

U.S. Census Bureau. 2010. Internet Use in the United States. Current Population Survey October 2009. Available at http://www.census.gov/population/www/socdemo/computer/2009.html.

U.S. Census Bureau. 2011a. *Statistical abstract of the United States: 2011–2012.* (130th edition). Washington, DC. Available at http://www.census.gov/statab/www/.

U.S. Census Bureau. 2011b. *Current Population Survey, 2010 Annual Social and Economic Supplement.* Washington, DC: U.S. Government Printing Office.

U.S. Department of Agriculture. 2012. Food deserts. Available at http://www.ers.usda.gov/data-products/food-desert-locator/documentation.aspx

U.S. Department of Education. 2010. Statistics about non-public education in the United States. Available at http://www2.ed.gov/about/offices/list/oii/nonpublic/statistics.html.

U.S. Department of Education. 2012. 26 more states and D.C. seek flexibility from NCLB to drive education reforms in second round of requests. (February 29). Available at http://www.ed.gov/news/press-releases/26-more-states-and-dc-seek-flexibility-nclb-drive-education-reforms-second-round.

U.S. Department of Health, Education, and Welfare. 1973. *100 years of marriage and divorce statistics: United States, 1867–1967.* Rockville, MD: Health Resources Administration, National Center for Health Statistics.

U.S. Department of Health and Human Services. 1996. *Vital statistics of the United States 1988: Volume III—marriage and divorce.* Hyattsville, MD: U.S. Department of Health and Human Services.

U.S. Department of Health and Human Services. 2000. *Healthy people 2010: Understanding and improving health,* 2nd ed. Washington, DC: U.S. Government Printing Office.

U.S. Department of Health and Human Services. 2009. *Temporary Assistance for Needy Families Program (TANF): Eighth annual report to Congress.* Available at http://www.acf.hhs.gov/programs/ofa/data-reports/annualreport8/ar8index.htm.

U.S. Department of Health and Human Services. 2012a. *Child Maltreatment 2010.* Available at http://www.acf.hhs.gov/programs/cb/pubs/cm10/cm10.pdf.

U.S. Department of Health and Human Services. 2012b. Available at http://www.acf.hhs.gov/programs/ofa/data-reports/caseload/caseload_current.htm.

U.S. Department of Health and Human Services. 2012c. Available at http://www.womenshealth.gov/hiv-aids/aids-worldwide/#a.

U.S. Department of the Interior. 2003. *American Indian population and labor force report 2003.* Washington, DC: Bureau of Indian Affairs, Office of Tribal Services.

U.S. Department of Labor. 2008. *Women in the labor force: A databook.* Available at www.bls.gov/cps/wlf-intro-2008.pdf.

U.S. Department of Labor. 2012. Household data annual averages. 3. Employment status of the civilian noninstitutional population by age, sex, and race. Available at ftp://ftp.bls .gov/pub/special.requests/lf/aat3.txt.

U.S. National Center for Educational Statistics. 1995. *Statistics in brief,* October 1995 (NCES 95–824). Washington, DC: U.S. National Center on Health Statistics.

Useem, Michael. 1983. *The inner circle.* New York: Oxford University Press.

V

Vago, Steven. 2012. *Law and society,* 10th ed. Upper Saddle River, NJ: Prentice-Hall.

Valentine, Charles. 1968. *Culture and poverty.* Chicago: University of Chicago Press.

Valentino, Nicholas A., and **David O. Sears.** 2005. Old times there are not forgotten: Race and partisan realignment in the contemporary South. *American Journal of Political Science,* 49:672–88.

Van Creveld, Martin. 1982. *Fighting power: German and U.S. Army performance, 1939–1945.* Westport, CT: Greenwood Press.

van den Berghe, Pierre. 1963. Dialectic and functionalism: Toward a theoretical synthesis. *American Sociological Review,* 28:695–705.

Vanderwert, R. E., P. J. Marshall, C. A. Nelson III, C. H. Zeanah, and **N. A. Fox.** 2010. Timing of intervention affects brain electrical activity in children exposed to severe psychosocial neglect. *PLoS ONE,* 5(7):e11415. doi:10.1371/journal.pone.0011415.

Vander Zanden, James W. 1965. *Race relations in transition.* New York: Random House.

Vander Zanden, James W. 1983. *American minority relations,* 4th ed. New York: Knopf.

Vander Zanden, James W. 1993. *Human development,* 5th ed. New York: McGraw-Hill.

Vannoy, Dana, and **William W. Philliber.** 1992. Wife's employment and quality of marriage. *Journal of Marriage and the Family,* 54:387–98.

Van Schaik, Carel P., Marc Ancrenaz, Gwendolyn Borgen, Birute Galdikas, Cheryl D. Knott, Ian Singleton, Akira Suzuki, Sri Suci Utami, and **Michelle Merrill.** 2003. Orangutan cultures and the evolution of material culture. *Science,* 299:102–5.

Veblen, Thorstein. 1899. *The theory of the leisure class.* New York: Viking.

Veblen, Thorstein. 1921. *Engineers and the price system.* New York: Viking.

Vedantam, Shankar. 2001. Peer pressure spurs terrorists, psychologists say. *Washington Post* (October 16):A16.

Vedantam, Shankar. 2008. Department of human behavior: Unequal perspectives on racial equality. *Washington Post* (March 24):A3.

Vince, Gaia. 2011. An epoch debate. *Science,* 334:32–37.

Visgaitis, Gary. 1994. A look at Native Americans across the USA. *USA Today* (April 28):A7.

Visher, Christy A., and **Jeremy Travis.** 2003. Transitions from prison to community: Understanding individual pathways. *Annual Review of Sociology,* 29:89–113.

Vogel, Gretchen. 2011. Psychologist accused of fraud on "astonishing scale." *Science,* 334:579.

Vogel, Lise. 1983. *Marxism and the oppression of women.* New Brunswick, NJ: Rutgers University Press.

Vroom, Victor H., and **Arthur G. Jago.** 1988. *The new leadership: Managing participation in organizations.* Englewood Cliffs, NJ: Prentice-Hall.

W

Waddington, David, Karen Jones, and **Chas Critcher.** 1989. *Flashpoints: Studies in disorder.* New York: Routledge.

Waddoups, Jeffrey, and **Djeto Assane.** 1993. Mobility and gender in a segmented labor market: A closer look. *American Journal of Economics and Sociology,* 52: 399–411.

Wade, Robert. 2004. Is globalization reducing poverty and inequality? *World Development,* 32:567–89.

Wagley, Charles, and **Marvin Harris.** 1964. *Minorities in the New World.* New York: Columbia University Press.

Wagmiller, Robert L., Jr., Mary Clare Lennon, Li Kuang, Philip M. Alberti, and **J. Lawrence Aber.** 2006. The dynamics of economic disadvantage and children's life chances. *American Sociological Review,* 71:847–66.

Waite, Linda J., and **Maggie Gallagher.** 2000. *The case for marriage: Why married people are happier, healthier, and better off financially.* New York: Doubleday.

Waitzkin, Howard. 1983. *The second sickness: Contradictions of capitalist health care.* New York: Free Press.

Waldo, Gordon P., and **Theodore G. Chiricos.** 1972. Perceived penal sanction and self-reported criminality: A neglected approach to deterrence research. *Social Problems,* 19:522–40.

Walker, Brian, Scott Barrett, Stephen Polasky, Victor Galaz, et al. 2009. Looming global-scale failures and missing institutions. *Science,* 325:1345–46.

Wallerstein, Immanuel. 1974. *The modern world-system: Capitalist agriculture and the origins of the European world economy in the 16th century.* New York: Academic Press.

Wallerstein, Immanuel. 1980. *The modern world-system II: Mercantilism and the consolidation of the European world-economy, 1600–1775.* New York: Academic Press.

Walmsley, Roy. 2009. *World prison population list,* 8th ed. London: International Centre for Prison Studies, King's College. Available at http://www.prisonstudies.org/info/ downloads/wppl-8th_41.pdf.

Walters, Nathan P., and **Edward N. Trevelyan.** 2011. The newly arrived foreign-born population of the United States: 2010. *American Community Survey Briefs* (November):1–7. ACSBR/10-16.

Walton, Gregory M., and **Geoffrey L. Cohen.** 2011. A brief social-belonging intervention improves academic and health outcomes of minority students. *Science,* 331:1447–51.

Walton, John, and **Charles Ragin,** 1990. Global and national sources of political protest: Third World responses to the debt crisis. *American Sociological Review,* 55:876–90.

Warner, R. Stephen. 1993. Work in progress toward a new paradigm for the sociological study of religion in the United States. *American Journal of Sociology,* 98:1044–93.

Warner, W. Lloyd, and **Paul S. Lunt.** 1941. *The social life of the modern community.* New Haven, CT: Yale University Press.

Warner, W. Lloyd, and **Paul S. Lunt.** 1942. *The status system of a modern community.* New Haven, CT: Yale University Press.

Warren, John Robert, Robert M. Hauser, and **Jennifer T. Sheridan.** 2002. Occupational stratification across the life course: Evidence from the Wisconsin Longitudinal Study. *American Sociological Review,* 67:432–55.

Waters, Mary C. 1990. *Ethnic options: Choosing identities in America.* Berkeley: University of California Press.

Waters, Mary C., and **Tomas R. Jimenez.** 2005. Assessing immigrant assimilation: New empirical and theoretical challenges. *Annual Review of Sociology,* 31:105–25.

Weber, Max. 1904/1958. *The Protestant ethic and the spirit of capitalism.* New York: Scribners.

Weber, Max. 1916/1964. *The religion of China: Confucianism and Taoism.* New York: Macmillan.

Weber, Max. 1917/1958. *The religion of India: The sociology of Hinduism and Buddhism.* New York: Free Press.

Weber, Max. 1921/1968. *Economy and society.* 3 vols. Totowa, NJ: Bedminster Press.

Weber, Max. 1946. *The theory of social and economic organization.* Ed. and trans. A. M. Henderson and Talcott Parsons. New York: Macmillan.

Weber, Max. 1947. *From Max Weber: Essays in sociology.* Ed. and trans. Hans H. Gerth and C. Wright Mills. New York: Oxford University Press.

Wechsler, Henry, Meichun Kuo, Hang Lee, and **George W. Dowdall.** 2000. Environmental correlates of underage alcohol use and related problems of college students. *American Journal of Preventative Medicine,* 19:24–29.

Wechsler, Henry, Jae Eun Lee, Meichun Kuo, and **Hang Lee.** 2000. College binge drinking in the 1990s: A continuing problem. Results of the Harvard School of Public Health 1999 College Alcohol Study. *Journal of American College Health,* 48: 199–210.

Weeden, Kim A. 2002. Why do some occupations pay more than others? Social closure and earnings inequality in the United States. *American Journal of Sociology,* 108(1):55–101.

Weeden, Kim A., and **David B. Grusky.** 2005. The case for a new class map. *American Journal of Sociology,* 111:141–212.

Weeks, Linton. 2006. The cheapest shot: The sociology of spitting. *Washington Post* (January 10):C1.

Weil, Andrew. 2009. *Why our health matters: A vision of medicine that can transform our future.* New York: Hudson Street Press.

Weiss, Gregory L., and **Lynne E. Lonnquist.** 2012. *The sociology of health, healing and illness.* Englewood Cliffs, NJ: Prentice-Hall.

Weiss, Harvey, and **Raymond S. Bradley.** 2001. What drives societal collapse? *Science,* 291:609–10.

Weiss, Rick. 1997. Psychologists' society adopts resolution seeking to limit gay "conversion" therapy. *Washington Post* (August 15):A14.

Welch, Kelly, and **Allison Ann Payne.** 2010. Racial threat and punitive school discipline. *Social Problems,* 57(1):25–48.

Welsh, Sandy. 1999. Gender and sexual harassment. *Annual Review of Sociology,* 25:169–90.

Werschkul, Misha, and **Erica Williams.** 2004. The 2004 national overview report: The status of women in the states. www.iwpr.org/states2004.

West, Heather C. 2010. *Prison inmates at midyear 2009: Statistical tables.* Bureau of Justice Statistics, NCJ 230113, June. Available at http://bjs.ojp.usdoj.gov/content/pub/pdf/pim09st.pdf.

Western, Bruce. 2002. The impact of incarceration on wage mobility and inequality. *American Sociological Review,* 67:526–46.

Wethington, Elaine, Hope Cooper, and **Carolyn S. Holmes.** 1997. Turning points in midlife. In Ian Gotlib and Blair Wheaton, eds., *Stress and adversity over the life course: Trajectories and turning points.* New York: Cambridge University Press.

White, Lynn, and **John N. Edwards.** 1990. Emptying the nest and parental well-being: An analysis of national panel data. *American Sociological Review,* 55:235–42.

White, Ralph K., and **Ronald O. Lippitt.** 1960. *Autocracy and democracy.* New York: Harper & Row.

Whitson, John. 2006. College costs hit where it hurts. *Union Leader* (May 1). www.unionleader.com.

Whitt, J. Allen. 1979. Toward a class-dialectical model of power: An empirical assessment of three competing models of political power. *American Sociological Review,* 44:81–100.

Whorf, Benjamin L. 1956. *Language, thought, and reality.* Cambridge, MA: MIT Press.

Wiggins, James A., Beverly B. Wiggins, and **James Vander Zanden.** 1994. *Social psychology.* New York: McGraw-Hill.

Wilke, John R. 1993. Computer links erode hierarchical nature of workplace culture. *Wall Street Journal* (December 9):A1, A7.

Williams, Gregory Howard. 1995. *Life on the color line: The true story of a white boy who discovered he was black.* New York: Dutton.

Williams, Joan C., and **Heather Boushey.** 2010. *The three faces of work-family conflict: The poor, the professionals, and the missing middle.* Washington, DC: Center for American Progress.

Williams, Kipling, Stephen Harkins, and **Bibb Latané.** 1981. Identifiability as a deterrent to social loafing: Two cheering experiments. *Journal of Personality and Social Psychology,* 40:303–11.

Williams, Redford B. 1998. Lower socioeconomic status and increased mortality. Early childhood roots and the potential for successful interventions. *Journal of the American Medical Association,* 279(21): 1745–46.

Williams, Rhys H., and **N. J. Demerath III.** 1991. Religion and political process in an American city. *American Sociological Review,* 56:417–31.

Williams, Robin M., Jr. 1964. *Strangers next door.* Englewood Cliffs, NJ: Prentice-Hall.

Williams, Robin M., Jr. 1970. *American society,* 3rd ed. New York: Knopf.

Wilmoth, J. R., L. J. Deegan, H. Lundstrom, and **S. Horiuchi.** 2000. Increase of maximum life-span in Sweden, 1861–1999. *Science,* 289:2366–68.

Wilson, Bryan R. 1990. *The social dimensions of sectarianism: Sects and new religious movements in con-temporary society.* New York: Oxford University Press.

Wilson, Dominic, and **Roopa Purushothaman.** 2003. Dreaming with BRICs: The path to 2050. Global Economics Paper No. 99, Goldman Sachs, 1 October 2003. Available at http://www2.goldmansachs.com/ ideas/brics/book/99-dreaming.pdf. www.adherents.com 2005.

Wilson, Edward O. 2002. *The future of life.* New York: Knopf.

Wilson, James Q. 1990. *What government agencies do and why they do it.* New York: Basic Books.

Wilson, James Q. 1993. Mr. Clinton, meet Mr. Gore. *Wall Street Journal* (October 28):A18.

Wilson, James Q. 1997. Hostility in America. *New Republic* (August 25):38–41.

Wilson, Peter J. 1988. *The domestication of the human species.* New Haven, CT: Yale University Press.

Wilson, William Julius. 1978. *The declining significance of race.* Chicago: University of Chicago Press.

Wilson, William Julius. 1987. *The truly disadvantaged: The inner city, the underclass, and public policy.* Chicago: University of Chicago Press.

Wilson, William Julius. 1991. Studying inner-city social dislocations: The challenge of public agenda research. *American Sociological Review,* 56:1–14.

Wilson, William Julius. 1996. *When work disappears.* New York: Knopf.

Wilson, William Julius. 2003. Introduction to the 2003 edition. In Elliot Liebow, *Tally's corner.* Lanham, MD: Rowman & Littlefield.

Wilson, William Julius. 2009. *More than just race: Being black and poor in the inner city.* New York: Norton.

Wilson, William Julius, and **Robert Aponte.** 1985. Urban poverty. *Annual Review of Sociology,* 11:213–58.

Winch, Robert F. 1958. *Mate selection: A study of complementary needs.* New York: Harper & Row.

Wingfield, Adia Harvey. 2010. Are some emotions marked "Whites Only"? Racialized feeling rules in professional workplaces. *Social Problems,* 57(2):251–68.

Winnick, Louis. 1991. *New people in old neighborhoods.* New York: Russell Sage Foundation.

Witt, Linda, Karen M. Paget, and **Glenna Matthews.** 1993. *Running as a woman: Gender and power in American politics.* New York: Free Press.

Wolfe, Tom. 1968. *The pump house gang.* New York: Farrar, Straus & Giroux.

Wolfers, Justin, and **Betsey Stevenson.** 2006. Bargaining in the shadow of the law: Divorce laws and family distress. *Quarterly Journal of Economics,* 121(1): 267–288.

Wolff, Edward N. 1995. *Top heavy: A study of the increasing inequality of wealth in America.* New York: Twentieth Century Fund Press.

Wolff, Edward N. 1996. International comparisons of wealth inequality. *Review of Income and Wealth.* Series 42, No. 4 (December):433–51.

Wolfgang, Marvin E., Robert M. Figlio, and **Thorsten Sellin.** 1972. *Delinquency in a birth cohort.* Chicago: University of Chicago Press.

Wolfinger, Nicholas H. 1999. Trends in the intergenerational transmission of divorce. *Demography,* 36:415–20.

Wolfinger, Nicholas H. 2003. Parental divorce and offspring marriage. Early or late? *Social Forces,* 82(1):337–53.

Woodard, Michael D. 1987. Voluntary association membership among black Americans: The post-civil-rights era. *Sociological Quarterly,* 28:285–301.

World Health Organization. 2000. Database on violence against women, 2000. In *The World's Women 2000: Trends and Statistics* (United Nations). Available at http://unstats .un.org/unsd/demographic/ww2000/ table6c.htm.

World Health Organization. 2003. Suicide rates (per 100,000), by country, year, and gender (data table). Geneva: World Health Organization. Available at http://www.who.int/mental_health/prevention/suicide/suiciderates/en/.

Wright, Emily M., and **Michael L. Benson.** 2010. Immigration and intimate partner violence: Exploring the immigrant paradox. *Social Problems,* 57(3):480–503.

Wright, Erik Olin. 1985. *Classes.* New York: Schocken.

Wright, Erik Olin. 1993. Typologies, scales, and class analysis: A comment on Halaby and Weakliem's "Ownership and authority in the earnings function." *American Sociological Review,* 58:31–34.

Wright, Erik Olin. 2000. Working-class power, capitalist-class interests, and class compromise. *American Journal of Sociology,* 105:957–1002.

Wright, Erik Olin. 2002. The shadow of exploitation in Weber's class analysis. *American Sociological Review,* 67:832–53.

Wright, John Paul, and **Francis T. Cullen.** 2000. Juvenile involvement in occupational delinquency. *Criminology,* 38(3):863–96.

Wrigley, Julia, and **Joanna Dreby.** 2005. Fatalities in child care in the United States, 1985–2003. *American Sociological Review,* 70:729–57.

www.adherents.com. 2007. For percentages of world religions, see http://www.adherents.com/Religions_By_Adherents.html.

Wysocki, Bernard, Jr. 1991. Influx of Asians brings prosperity to Flushing, a place for newcomers. *Wall Street Journal* (January 15):A1, A10.

Y

Yablonsky, Lewis, and **Martin R. Haskell.** 1988. *Juvenile delinquency,* 4th ed. New York: Harper & Row.

Yamagishi, Toshio. 1995. Social dilemmas. In Karen S. Cook, Gary Alan Fine, and James S. House, eds., *Sociological perspectives on social psychology.* Boston: Allyn & Bacon.

Yamaguchi, Kazuo, and **Yanatao Wang.** 2002. Class identification of married employed women and men in America. *American Journal of Sociology,* 108(2):440–75.

Yamamoto, Akiko, and **Doug Struck.** 2002. Pressured pregnancy in Japan: To get affordable day care, women must carefully plan due date. *Washington Post* (November 14):A20.

Yans-McLaughlin, Virginia. 1982. *Family and community: Italian immigrants in Buffalo, 1880–1930.* Urbana: University of Illinois Press.

Yinger, J. Milton. 1965. *Toward a field theory of behavior.* New York: Macmillan.

Young, Robert L. 2004. Guilty until proven innocent: Conviction orientation, racial attitudes, and support for capital punishment. *Deviant Behavior,* 25:151–67.

Z

Zhu, Wei Xing, Li Lu, and **Therese Hesketh.** 2009. China's excess males, sex selective abortion, and one child policy: Analysis of data from 2005 national intercensus survey. *BMJ* 338:b1211doi:10.1136/bmj.b1211.

Zigli, Barbara. 1984. Asian-Americans beat others in academic drive. *USA Today* (April 25):D1.

Zimbardo, Philip G. 1969. The human choice: Individuation, reason, and order versus deindividualization, impulse, and chaos. In W. Arnold and D. Levine, eds., *Nebraska Symposium on Motivation,* 17:237–307.

Zimbardo, Philip. 2007. *The Lucifer effect: Understanding how good people turn evil.* New York: Random House.

Zimmer, Carl. 2008. Isolated tribe gives clues to the origins of syphilis. *Science,* 319:272.

Zimmerman, Don H. 1971. The practicalities of rule use. In Jack Douglas, ed., *Understanding everyday life.* Chicago: Aldine.

Zimmerman, Frederick J., Dimitri A. Christakis, and **Andrew N. Meltzoff.** 2007. Television and DVD/video viewing in children younger than 2 years. *Archives of Pediatric and Adolescent Medicine,* 161:473–79.

Zimring, Franklin E. 2007. *The great american crime decline.* Oxford: Oxford University Press.

Zimring, Franklin E., and **Gordon Hawkins.** 1997. *Crime is not the problem: Lethal violence in America.* New York: Oxford University Press.

Zingraff, Matthew T., Jeffrey Leiter, Matthew C. Johnson, and **Kristen A. Myers.** 1994. The mediating effect of good school performance on the maltreatment-delinquency relationship. *Journal of Research in Crime and Delinquency,* 31:62–91.

Zuckerman, Miron, M. H. Kernis, S. M. Guarnera, J. F. Murphy, and **L. Rappoport.** 1983. The egocentric bias: Seeing oneself as cause and target of others' behavior. *Journal of Personality,* 51:621–30.

Zussman, Robert. 2005. The self. *Contexts,* 4:48–50.

Photo Credits

Chapter 1
Opener: Photo by Jason Hawkes/Getty Images; p.4: MCS 1st Class Matthew M. Bradley/US Navy/DoD; p.10: © Dave Moyer, McGraw-Hill Companies; p.15: © Corbis; p.17: © TongRo Image Stock/ Alamy RF; p.26: © U.S. Census Bureau, Public Information Office (PIO).

Chapter 2
Opener: © Sylvain Grandadam/The Image Bank/ Getty Images; p.43: Comstock Images/Jupiter Images/ Alamy RF; p.46: © Dr. Clive Bromhall/Oxford Scientific/Getty Images; p.49: © The McGraw-Hill Companies, Inc./Barry Barker, photographer.

Chapter 3
Opener: © Royalty Free/Corbis; p.72: © IT Stock/ Alamy RF; p.82: © The McGraw-Hill Companies, Inc./John Flournoy, photographer; p.89: Comstock Images/Corbis RF.

Chapter 4
Opener: © Banana Stock/JupiterImages RF; p.99: © Pascal Deloche/Godong/Corbis; p.104: © Radius Images/Alamy RF; p.112: © Fancy Photography/ Veer RF; p.115: © Ingram Publishing RF.

Chapter 5
Opener: © Andrew Lichtenstein/The Image Works; p.138: © Design Pics RF/ Kristy-Anne Glubish; p.145: © Lars A. Niki, McGraw-Hill Companies; p.150: Getty Images; p.159: © Brand X Pictures/ PunchStock RF.

Chapter 6
Opener: © Andrew Holbrooke/Corbis; p.191: © Ingram Publishing /Age Fotostock RF; p.196: © Adrian Dennis/ AFP/Getty Images; p.205: © Frank Trapper/Corbis.

Chapter 7
Opener: © Mark Peterson/Corbis; p.214: Courtesy of Gregory Howard Williams; p.223: Comstock/ Photolibrary RF; p.227: © The McGraw-Hill Companies, Inc./John Flournoy, photographer; p.232: © Dennis MacDonald/Alamy RF; p.234: Library of Congress, Prints & Photographs Division, LC-DIG-ppprs-00338.

Chapter 8
Opener: Library of Congress Prints and Photographs Division, LC-USZ62-31799; p.250: © Gideon Mendel/Corbis; p.254: © Rick Gomez/Masterfile; p.266: © Monica Almeida/The New York Times/ Redux Pictures.

Chapter 9
Opener: © Xinhua/Landov Images; p.281: © Masterfile RF; p.287: © Aaron Roeth Photography RF; p.294: © AP Photo/Samir Mizban.

Chapter 10
Opener: © Ariel Skelley/Blend Images/Alamy RF; p.316: © Plush Studios/Blend Images/Getty Images; p.322: © Robin Nelson/PhotoEdit; p.331: © Rachel Epstein/The Image Works; p.334: © Hannah Gal/ Corbis.

Chapter 11
Opener: © RF/Corbis; p.355: Design Pics/Con Tanasiuk; p.361: GoGo Images/age fotostock RF; p.363: © AP Photo/Steve Yeater.

Chapter 12
Opener: © Thierry Lauzun/Iconotec.com RF; p.401: © Owen Franken/Stock, Boston; p.410: © Marie Park Foss/epa/Corbis.

Chapter 13
Opener: © Robert Kohlhuber/Getty Images; p.428: © Library of Congress Prints & Photographs Division, LC-USZ62-80283; p.439: Photo by George Frey/Getty Images; p.447: © AP Photo/ Suzanne Plunkett; p.450: © Eric Travers/Sipa/AP Images.

Name Index

Subject Index